GENERAL GEORGE H. THOMAS

The Indomitable Warrior

"SUPREME IN DEFENSE AND IN COUNTERATTACK"

General George H. Thomas

THE INDOMITABLE WARRIOR

A BIOGRAPHY

by

Wilbur Thomas

ILLUSTRATED

An Exposition–Lochinvar Book

EXPOSITION PRESS   NEW YORK

Exposition Press Inc., 386 Park Avenue South, New York, N. Y.

FIRST EDITION

EP 42066

TO

MY WIFE

MOURN NOT THE DEAD

Mourn not the dead that in the cool earth lie—
 Dust unto dust—
The calm sweet earth that mothers all who die,
 As all men must;

Mourn not your captured comrades who must dwell—
 Too strong to strive—
Each in his steel-bound coffin of a cell,
 Buried alive;

But rather mourn the apathetic throng—
 The cowed and the meek—
Who see the world's great anguish and its wrong
 And dare not speak.

RALPH CHAPLIN

Preface

> The boast of heraldry, the pomp of power,
> And all that beauty, all that wealth e'er gave,
> Awaits alike th' inevitable hour:
> The paths of glory lead but to the grave.
>
> THOMAS GRAY

As British General James Wolfe sailed down the Saint Lawrence River in September, 1759, to attack and capture the French stronghold of Quebec, the reading of Thomas Gray's "Elegy Written in a Country Church-Yard" inspired him to comment, "I would rather have written those lines than take Quebec." In a similar spirit, and after many years of reflection, research, and study, the author would rather right the wrong of slander and neglect to General George H. Thomas, "the Rock of Chickamauga," than anything else.

If General Thomas's success in winning battles that broke the deadlock in the Civil War were fully known, his rightful place in the hearts of his countrymen would be secure, however belated it might be. Stated differently, if the approach to deserved recognition of General Thomas, and it was only an approach, had run its rightful course, he would now hold a place second to none in the esteem of the generations that have benefited from his victories. If such recognition had been accorded him, there would have been no need for the tremendous effort expended in producing this volume. There is not so much the need for a biography, as such, as there is a need to emphasize his remarkable achievements, to document them beyond argument, and thus to prove that he was wronged by self-seeking "name" generals.

Generals Grant and Sherman are the two commanders generally hailed as contributing most to the preservation of the Union, but this will be examined. These two generals were the authors and sponsors of the false charges of "sluggishness" and "slowness" leveled against General Thomas, although the record of neither of them nor of anyone else can favorably compare with his record. Grant in particular was impatient of Thomas during the several weeks needed to reorganize an army, while he stated his own objective in the promise,

"I will fight it out on this line if it takes all summer." His estimate was far under actual performance, but he was not threatened with removal and forever consigned to virtual anonymity because of it, as he consigned Thomas.

If to be cautious produced victory authored by Thomas—and it did —and if to be incautious produced useless bloodshed and defeat—and it did for other generals—all the criticism of Thomas's alleged slowness, which Grant and Sherman directed against him, should have become "as sounding brass, or a tinkling cymbal." It should have, but it did not, mainly because Grant's and Sherman's memoirs, and the writings of their backslapping and self-seeking eulogists, contain distortions and slanders so shockingly untrue, in the light of the *Official Records* that readily refute many of them, that the wonder is they were ever published or stated, much less accepted as reliable. What a paradox it is that these two men in particular, by a few well-chosen words spoken from the prestige of their powerful positions, were able to record their own version of battles and incidents on the printed page, despite overwhelming proof that they were often in error. Much of their unreliable material has been proved for what it is, but the amazing fact is that their erroneous versions still persist.

Many of the writings concerning the Civil War, including the memoirs, were set down during the 1870's and the 1880's. With Grant and Sherman in control of the military, it was dangerous for contemporary generals to attempt to correct misstatements of their superiors. This was demonstrated when General Sherman objected to General Fry's article in the *North American Review* (see Prologue), and tried to silence him by appealing to the War Department. In fairness to all, it should be stated that General Thomas died in 1870, and wrote no memoirs that might have enabled him to correct the misstatements made about him in particular and other matters in general.

Out of all the discussions, misstatements, claims, and counterclaims, it is a matter of never-ceasing wonder to this writer that after a century the opportunity has remained for him to seek a reversal of this, the greatest injustice to a man of unsurpassed achievements in the military history of the United States.

Equally surprising is the persistence of the "Grant legend," which credits him with being an able and indispensable general, when the very opposite was true. This is not to suggest that he won no victories, that he had no ability, and that he did not command the combined armies that brought the South to its knees. It is to state simply and unequivocally that by using the same methods employed by him against Lee, and with anywhere near the numbers commanded by Lee, the North would have lost the war. What further proof is needed than the fact that he outnumbered him by two to one and still did not defeat him in battle? He ground out the lives of his men by spending two for each one lost by Lee. At the end, Lee still held on, and he surrendered only when he had no more rations to give to his still willing soldiers. Grant was lucky, very lucky, as at Shiloh, which was the case in more instances than those in which he was victorious through any display of generalship.

To all of this should be added that Grant rewarded favorites, for example, Sheridan and Schofield; that he was jealous and vindictive, and at bitter cost to the Union cause deprived the Union of the full capabilities of its greatest general, Thomas; that he mistreated General Meade, the victor of Gettysburg and figurehead commander of the Army of the Potomac after he, Grant, came to power; and that he promoted Sheridan because he did not want the public to think Sheridan was being punished, which he should have been.

It is important also to look at Sherman's record, which shows no military achievements worth noting, other than the Atlanta campaign, largely the work of Thomas, or the glamorous but unopposed March to the Sea, with the flower of the Western armies, and through an area giving him little to do but take the remaining supplies of an already foredoomed enemy. There is no Gettysburg or Chickamauga, no Nashville or any other large-scale victory or defeat to add luster to his name or to label him great. His only victories are barely known; and any battlefield reputation he earned was for defeats rather than victories.

General Thomas, whose splendor was buried under the mighty weight of false-witnessing by Generals Grant and Sherman, unlocked the key to the Confederacy at Chattanooga, and paved the way thereto by saving, at Chickamauga, the glorious Army of the Cumberland, when everything, but for him, would have been lost.

The Union armies, viewed in proper perspective, were as one lengthy line, extending from the left flank in Virginia to the right flank on the Mississippi at the Gulf of Mexico. Grant captured Vicksburg, the final blow that permitted the river to flow "unvexed to the sea." The left flank, between Washington and Richmond, was a stalemate, which all the bloody battles between 1861 and 1864 did not resolve. The battles of First and Second Bull Run, Antietam, Fredericksburg, Chancellorsville, and Gettysburg left the two opposing armies about where they had begun when Grant was assigned to the chief command in 1864 and began to bleed white the Confederate Army and his own.

Things were happening at the center after Gettysburg, however; first came Chickamauga, followed by the battles around Chattanooga; then followed the campaign to Atlanta, in all of which General Thomas bore the dominant part. When Atlanta fell, Sherman's March to the Sea was undertaken; but again it was Thomas who destroyed at Nashville the forces under Hood, the army that Sherman in months of fighting could not bring to battle in his Atlanta campaign. After Nashville, all of the Union forces available closed in on General Lee, and less than four months later, on April 9, he surrendered at Appomattox.

All of the above is history, which the *Official Records* and collateral reference data substantiate, and is fully documented in this book. This documentation, the result of many years of work and a lifetime of devotion to the achievements and memory of one of the greatest men in history, is fully identified for whatever use desired.

Acknowledgments

ACKNOWLEDGMENT is made, first of all, to my wife, for the successful completion of this biography. Her forbearance during the more than seven years spent in acquiring and identifying reference material was indispensable. Not least in importance was her willingness to accompany me on trips, including several visits to the birthplace of General Thomas near Newsoms, Southampton County, Virginia; the United States Military Academy at West Point, New York; the battlefields on which Thomas left his mark, namely, Murfreesboro, Chickamauga, Orchard Knob, Lookout Mountain, Missionary Ridge, and Nashville; the high points of the Atlanta campaign; and his final resting place in Oakwood Cemetery, Troy, New York. Of importance also was her use as a sounding board for many of the viewpoints and reactions to important and controversial incidents in the life of General Thomas.

Grateful acknowledgment is also extended to the many friends and acquaintances who just listened as I talked on and on, almost invariably in an animated manner, about the deeds and character of the sublime soldier and gentleman whose fame was blighted by false accusations of Generals Grant and Sherman. Particular thanks are due Mr. Parke B. Jones, Manager of W. H. Lowdermilk & Company, famous booksellers in the nation's capital, and his capable and helpful assistant, Mr. N. Hill Dickson, for their invaluable aid in acquiring many important reference books. I am grateful to Mr. Jones, more especially for his beginning advice, when he emphasized above everything else that any book of this type, to be successful, should be thoroughly documented. His advice has been heeded to the full, and I am pleased to state that it is completely documented from recognized, reliable records. In the rare instances of doubt, such doubt has been expressed by a qualifying comment. There is nothing that can prevail against truth, however long suppressed; and such truth is identified in this work with appropriate notes.

It would be unjust not to mention two long-time friends, Mr. Arthur S. Bacon, an avid reader of the classics and things historical, who gave me many encouraging suggestions and opinions; and Mr. Leo J. Van Herpe, Sr., a certified public accountant and follower of the events and personalities of the Civil War, who gave me suggestions and material for use in the biography. Of some interest to me is the circumstance that Mr. Van Herpe formerly resided in Troy, New York, where General Thomas was buried, but now lives in Washington, as also does Mr. Bacon.

Not forgotten are those unnamed but helpful people at the Congressional Library, the National Archives, the Washington, D.C., public library, and the Library, United States Military Academy, West Point, New York, who went out of their way to aid me in obtaining needed reference matter.

Source material of inestimable value was obtained from the following sources, and full acknowledgment of their cooperativeness cannot be expressed in words:

Duke University Library, Durham, North Carolina, for providing copies of letters relating to General Thomas.

Mr. Norm Flayderman, dealer in antique firearms, who furnished pictures and details concerning the sword presented to General Thomas by the Fourth Kentucky Volunteer Infantry; also details of the medal given by the State of Tennessee to General Thomas in 1865.

Mr. Stanley F. Horn, for permission to use his valuable histories, *The Decisive Battle of Nashville,* and *The Army of Tennessee.*

The Huntington Library, San Marino, California, for furnishing film strips.

Mr. John N. Hough, who provided copies of the John N. Hough Papers and lent other material relating to the career of General Thomas. Mr. Hough is a grandson of Colonel Albert Lacey Hough, who was chief aide to General Thomas, in which capacity he was serving with the general at the time of the latter's death.

Mrs. Henry T. Miles, present resident-owner of the Thomas birthplace, Newsoms, Southampton County, Virginia, who described incidents in the family life of George and his sisters.

Rice University, Houston, Texas, for affording access to the newly discovered Buell Papers. Special thanks are extended to Dr. Frank E. Vandiver, noted historian and Civil War authority, for his kindness in permitting the use of these papers, and to Miss Turnbull, Curator of Rare Books and Manuscripts at the Rice University Library, for her guidance through the papers.

Miss Bessie T. Shands, deputy clerk of Southampton County, Courtland, Virginia, for her kindness in furnishing details from

the Mattie R. Tyler Papers on file in that office. Mattie R.
Tyler, a second cousin of General Thomas, was also a grand-
daughter of President John Tyler.

Tennessee State Library and Archives, Nashville, for valuable
information relating to the painting of General Thomas by
Dury, referred to in the biography, particularly in connection
with the restoration of the completed painting early in 1963,
and photographs of the restoration.

Virginia Historical Society, Richmond, Virginia, for information
and a picture of the sword given by the citizens of
Southampton County for the outstanding services of General
Thomas in the Mexican War.

Without exception, authorities, students, and just plain Civil
War buffs who have seen some of the underlying documentation herein, or have heard the basis on which the greatness of Thomas rests,
are agreed that he was the ablest soldier produced by the North.
All are equally agreed that his greatness has been clouded because
of Grant's and Sherman's slanderous and misleading statements and
writings, which were echoed and re-echoed by their publicists and
self-seekers; and that the nation needs to know the truth which this
book presents. For aiding so greatly in presenting this incontestable
truth, the author again acknowledges and thanks all who had a share in
it.

WILBUR D. THOMAS

Washington, D.C.

Contents

LIST OF MAPS

FIVE of these maps are reproduced from Thomas B. Van Horne's *The Life of Major General George H. Thomas*. Maps 3 and 4 are from the National Park Service Handbook Series, No. 10; map 9, from No. 25 of that series; maps 7 and 8, from the Department of the Interior; and maps 11 and 12, from John Fiske's *The Mississippi Valley in the Civil War*.

Prologue

"Time and History Will Do Me Justice."

IN HIS Preface to *The Life of Major General George H. Thomas*, Chaplain Van Horne ascribed to General Thomas the prediction, "Time and history will do me justice." This prediction may be interpreted as referring to the injustice that was his lot while living, as well as a promise that his major contribution to the preservation of the Union would be remembered and acknowledged after his death. In making this prohecy, he knew that the underlying facts were compelling, and that once they were known in the light of documentation, justice would follow. Time and history have not brought justice and recognition befitting his unmatched deeds; and nothing proves this more completely than the mass of Civil War literature currently flooding the country, which, almost without exception, barely mentions his name.

An example of neglect to General Thomas is found in *Great Battles of the Civil War*, a Centennial publication. It is surprising that so much prominence is given in this publication to defeated generals like, for example, General Ambrose E. Burnside, whose prominence was founded, not upon victories, but defeats. Burnside suffered one of the most disastrous and least justifiable defeats of the war at Fredericksburg, on December 13, 1862. In that battle his men were advanced repeatedly before concealed Confederate riflemen on Marye's Heights, with only a dim hope of success. The wonder is that he was made commander of that magnificent Army of the Potomac, a responsibility that, in fairness to him, he felt himself incapable of handling. This followed his poor work at Antietam, on September 17, 1862.

At Antietam, General George B. McClellan sent repeated orders to Burnside to attack the Confederates, but each time he elected to dislodge those on the bridge across Antietam Creek, although his men could have waded across, and each time was driven back. The resulting delay gave General Lee the time needed to bolster his hard-pressed left and center. But for this incident, Antietam might well have ended in greater Union success and an earlier end of the war.

General Joseph Hooker, successor to Burnside after Fredericksburg, outnumbered Lee at Chancellorsville by more than two to one. The result is known as Lee's greatest victory. Hooker was, nevertheless, a fine corps commander and performed brilliantly at Lookout Mountain and in the Atlanta campaign. Although he has a rightful place in this publication and in any history of the war, General Thomas, with the best record of all, is virtually ignored.

In this digest, *Great Battles of the Civil War*, General Thomas is barely mentioned for his part in saving the Union Army of the Cumberland at Chickamauga. It does tell us that General Thomas, "the Rock of Chickamauga," covered the retreat in a magnificent rear-guard fight and then fell back in good order. Nothing could be more misleading and in error than this description of Thomas's part in this battle. Not only did he conduct a rear-guard action and retire in good order; with twenty-five thousand men he held Snodgrass Hill or "Horseshoe Ridge" against the many charges of General Longstreet's fifty thousand seasoned veterans; and he not only saved his own force, but the entire army, Chattanooga, and the Union cause in the West, if not in the nation. His title, "the Rock of Chickamauga," was bestowed after fighting overwhelming odds against Longstreet, one of the best corps commanders in either army. He retreated, but under orders from his commander, and not before the success of his retreat was assured. General Thomas, master of the battlefield, was the noblest soldier of the Civil War. He was a man's man, a soldier's idol, fearless, reliable, self-reliant, and selfless to a fault, as proved by his complete ostracism by family and friends when he remained with the Union. He was invincible, incorruptible, and indispensable. Defeat never came to him, because within his being there was a compulsion to prepare for and confront, without yielding ground, every attack against him. He always salvaged something of value for future victory, if victory for the day was not forthcoming.

Thomas was distinctive by comparison with almost all other generals of the Civil War in that, whenever possible, he exploited the defeat of the enemy by immediate pursuit. The enemy never salvaged anything of value after clashing with him. The worst that ever befell him in this respect was his retreat to Rossville, by order of General Rosecrans, following his heroic stand at Chickamauga. His mastery of war was due in large part to his continuous service as a professional soldier from cadet days at West Point until his death. This unbroken career was in contrast to that of both Grant and Sherman. Grant left the army in 1854 and did not return until the outbreak of war in 1861,[1] and Sherman was out of military service from 1853 until 1861.[2]

General Thomas was the complete master of himself in any situation, but he demanded more of himself than of those who served under him. Not once during the war did he take military leave, which illustrates his supreme devotion to duty. The great esteem in which he was held by his men was enjoyed by no other Federal commander except McClellan.

The American people, both North and South, have the responsibility and the challenge to right the wrong of neglect and bitterness toward one of their greatest sons. No other leader so completely dominated the achievements of a Federal army as did Thomas the Army of the Cumberland. No other army on either side of the conflict so generally accomplished its objectives as did that army; and the life of General Thomas is so interwoven with the history of the Army of the Cumberland that it is impossible to chronicle his activities without summarizing the important exploits of that army.

General Thomas did more than any other commander to bring victory to the North and to preserve the Union. Paradoxically, American military history affords no other instance of neglect, mistreatment, and hatred toward one of unsurpassed integrity, courage, and performance in behalf of his country that even remotely compares with the mistreatment of this great man. The consequences to the Union cause, if Thomas had not made his indispensable contributions at Murfreesboro, Chickamauga, Chattanooga, Atlanta, and Nashville, prove the point. Certain defeat in either of the two first-named battles, but for Thomas, might well have resulted in permanent disunion growing out of the deadlocked Army of the Potomac and the Army of Northern Virginia.

These armies waged a tug of war, a stalemate, interrupted only by Lee's two invasions of Maryland and Pennsylvania, and by the occasional shifting to new battlefields on which Lee's victories were neutralized by the overwhelming manpower of the North. This stalemate was not broken until after the successes achieved by General Thomas with the Army of the Cumberland in the great battles of Chickamauga and in and around Chattanooga. Not only did these battles break the death struggle between armies protecting the capitals of Washington and Richmond; they also paved the way for the campaign to Atlanta, in which he bore the major part, and to the cutting in two of the Confederacy by Sherman's romp to the sea. Sherman's success was insured by Thomas's victory in the great and decisive

---

1. *Webster's Biographical Dictionary* (1953), p. 620; *Encyclopedia Americana* (New York: American Book—Stratford Press, Inc., 1954), Vol. XIII, p. 135.

2. B. H. Liddell Hart, *Sherman: Soldier, Realist, American* (New York: Frederick A. Praeger, 1958), p. 37.

Battle of Nashville, on December 15 and 16, 1864; this was the model battle that brought complete destruction to an army, the only instance of its kind in the war.

All of the participants of the Civil War are dead, and the basic facts of that war have been long since quite firmly established through documentation, but the numerous errors and distortions that were so much a part of the earlier writings, and that many times gave undeserved credit to some and denied merited credit to others, are all too often accepted as authoritative. It is vital to truth and justice that source material be checked heroically by writers on the Civil War, to insure accuracy and agreement with recognized reference material. It is no longer dangerous to dispute faulty narratives of men and events that cast luster on mediocrity and withheld deserved credit to heroes. Vengeance or reprisal toward those who state the facts, by military men with selfish ends to serve in suppressing the truth, is no longer to be feared. It is now possible for Northerners and Southerners alike to discuss "Our War" with mutual pride, in the knowledge that greater valor was never displayed in warfare than by those who fought in it. Now, also, as never before, men of good will throughout the Union have respect if not admiration for those who fought so valiantly for the cause in which they believed.

To illustrate the danger that once existed in the military service for one so bold as to dispute faulty narratives of men and events, as aforesaid, it is only necessary to cite the following example.

In *The North American Review* of December, 1885, appeared an article by General James B. Fry entitled "An Acquaintance With Grant." Correspondence growing out of the article appeared in the January, 1886, issue of the *Review*. In this article General Fry attributed to General William T. Sherman the statement, "General Sherman goes so far as to have said, since Grant's death [July 23, 1885], that had C. F. Smith lived, Grant would have disappeared to history after Donelson." When the article came to the attention of General Sherman, he wrote to the editor of *The North American Review*, December 1, 1885, "Will you be kind enough to inquire of General Fry from what paper he made the extract in his article in your December number (An Acquaintance with Grant), 'General Sherman goes so far as to have said, since Grant's death, that had C. F. Smith lived, Grant would have disappeared to history after Donelson'; but that is conjecture."

The next step in the correspondence occurred when the *North American Review* editor, as requested by General Sherman, on December 3, 1885, forwarded a copy of the Sherman letter to General

Fry. When General Fry received the copy of Sherman's letter, he wrote to the *North American Review* editor on December 5, 1885, as follows:

EDITOR, NORTH AMERICAN REVIEW, NEW YORK CITY.

DEAR SIR: In my article called, "An Acquaintance with Grant," published in your December issue, I assert that "General Sherman goes so far as to have said, since Grant's death, that had C. F. Smith lived, Grant would have disappeared to history after Donelson." I have just received your letter of the 3d instant, transmitting copy of a letter from General Sherman to you, dated Dec. 2, asking my authority for the foregoing statement. I do not understand that General Sherman denies the correctness of the statement attributed to him, or disavows the sentiment embodied in it. It, therefore, seems to me best to let the matter rest as it is.

If the correctness of my assertion should be denied, you would have a right to expect me to substantiate it, and I should feel bound to do so.

The next step was the sending to General Sherman, December 7, 1885, by the editor of *The North American Review,* of a copy of General Fry's letter, as above, and a letter to General Fry informing him of that action. This was soon followed by a letter from the editor of *The North American Review,* dated December 12, 1885, to General Fry, enclosing a copy of a letter from General Sherman, dated December 10, 1885, only the last paragraph of which is pertinent to the controversy:

EDITOR, NORTH AMERICAN REVIEW, NEW YORK CITY.

DEAR SIR:

The matter cannot rest where it is, as he suggests, nor do I admit his right to call on me to affirm or deny the "sentiment" till I choose to do so in my own way.

In his article he quotes specific words from me. I therefore renew my demand for his authority.

The next significant step was reflected in the December 13, 1885, reply of General Fry to the editor of *The North American Review:*

DEAR SIR: I have yours of yesterday, transmitting copy of a letter from Gen. Sherman, dated Dec. 10.

Without intending the slightest discourtesy to Gen. Sherman, I must say that I have no modification to make in my note to yours of the 5th instant.

General Sherman's action, following General Fry's refusal to modify his position, was to write a letter to the Adjutant General of the Army, General R. C. Drum.

GENERAL: In the North American Review, edited by Allen Thorndike Rice, for December, 1885, is printed an article entitled, "An Acquaintance with Grant," by General James B. Fry, in which occurs this paragraph:

"The time has not come for final judgment of Grant. He had great ability and great opportunities. Chance is undoubtedly an important factor in the race of glory, and perhaps it favored Grant in the war of rebellion. General Sherman goes so far as to have said, since Grant's death, that had 'C. F. Smith lived, Grant would have disappeared to history after Donelson,' but this is a conjecture. Grant was one of the 'singular few' who possessed qualities which probably would have gained for him a high place in history, no matter who had lived to compete with him in our great war."

When my attention was called to it I wrote the following letter. [See Sherman's letter of December 1, above, to the editor of *The North American Review*.]

To this I received by due course of mail a letter from Mr. Rice, of December 7, inclosing a copy of Gen. Fry's answer, as follows [see Fry's letter of Dec. 7, in the foregoing]:

I have never authorized General Fry to speak for me in matters requiring the use of precise language, and I surely take direct issue with him in the modern monstrous doctrine that a reporter may publish any falsehood or guess, leaving the victim to follow it up with a denial or qualification. I assert moreover that General Fry is an officer of the army, subject to discipline and bound in honor to answer such an inquiry as was addressed to him.

I therefore, with all due respect, lay the matter before the honorable Secretary of War, and invoke his authority to compel General Fry to disclose the source of his information or to qualify his positive assertion that "General Sherman goes so far as to have said since Grant's death that had C. F. Smith lived Grant would have disappeared to history after Donelson."

W. T. SHERMAN

On December 23, 1885, the Adjutant General replied to General Sherman's request to suppress General Fry's right to freedom of speech while a member of the armed forces in the following:

Sir: I have the honor to acknowledge the receipt of your communication of the 17th instant, embodying certain letters from you to Mr. Rice, editor of the North American Review, and General James B. Fry's letters in answer thereto, on the subject of certain statements made by General Fry in an article in the North American Review.

The question how far the unauthorized use, as an officer, of the expressions of another may render the former amenable to discipline, is a difficult one to answer, especially when the language imputed is not offensive or calculated to cast odium on the speaker or writer. If the quotations used by General Fry in his article were false and scandalous, or so garbled as to give a false impression of your utterances, he has laid himself open to grave accusations, but as there is nothing to indicate that the statement is of that character or that his intent was to do you injustice or injury, the Secretary of War instructs me to say he cannot see that it is in his power, under the law, to take in this case the action suggested in your letter. At the same time he is of the opinion that the question raised is one of good manners and proper courtesy, rather than of conduct subjecting General Fry to military discipline.

I am, General, very respectfully, your obedient servant,

R. C. Drum,
Adjutant-General.

Aside from the proof reflected in the foregoing somewhat lengthy correspondence that Sherman sought to silence a member of the armed services, it should be noted that at no time did he (Sherman) deny the truth of General Fry's article. All that he asked of General Fry was a statement regarding the source of his (Fry's) statement in the December article. If General Sherman had succeeded in suppressing General Fry, which would have resulted in public repudiation of General Fry and the article, the War Department and General Sherman would have been in the unenviable position of having muzzled a man who, from all appearances, spoke the truth. If this correspondence has no other result, it proves, as emphasized in this book, that the military hierarchy of Grant, Sherman, Sheridan, and Schofield exerted tremendous influence in giving their versions of events relating to the Civil War, particularly those in which they had a personal interest. This fact underlies the distorted, often false, accounts of the Civil War that succeeding generations are still seeking to correct. Thus we have the reason for the relative obscurity to which the words and deeds of Grant, Sherman, and Schofield consigned the greatest Northern general, George H. Thomas.

It is not surprising that writers who came after the memoirs were written accepted them at face value, although their reliability has been a matter of controversy ever since their publication. Related or contemporary writers often sought to magnify the deeds of Grant and Sherman out of proportion to the true facts. The most notable example is Adam Badeau, author of the three-volume *Military History of U. S. Grant,* a recognized masterpiece of distortion and unreliability. On the other hand, the work by Henry V. Boynton entitled *Sherman's Historical Raid—The Memoirs in the Light of the Record* cites proof of misstatements in Sherman's *Memoirs* that, unfortunately, were naturally accepted as fact by many who were glamorized by such over-credit to himself. This glamor was never earned on any battefield; and Sherman's chief claim to fame—the campaign from Chattanooga to Atlanta, in short, the Atlanta campaign—was largely the work of General Thomas and his Army of the Cumberland, which comprised two thirds of Sherman's army. Furthermore, although Sherman performed magnificently during that campaign in compelling Confederate Generals Johnston and Hood to retreat steadily before him, he outnumbered them by something like two to one and committed several serious blunders, notably at Kenesaw Mountain. General Johnston has been accorded, and rightfully so, the greater credit for generalship by his masterly retreats than has Sherman for his advance.

Reliable records of the achievements of General Thomas are available in the many books and articles published since the war. Despite this abundance of information, few if any writers have made a complete comparison of his record with that of other leading generals. It follows naturally that due almost solely to the groundless charges of Generals Grant and Sherman, his deserved place in history has not been fully recognized. Much of our knowledge concerning him is contained in the seven biographies.[3] Of these, the one by Van Horne is, in this writer's judgment, the most complete and authoritative, since it is based largely upon records and documents furnished by

3. Thomas B. Van Horne, *The Life of Major General George H. Thomas* (New York: Charles Scribner's Sons, 1882); Donn Piatt, *General George H. Thomas* (Cincinnati, 1891); Richard W. Johnson, *Memoir of Major General George H. Thomas* (Philadelphia: J. B. Lippincott Co., 1881); Henry Coppee, *General Thomas* (New York, 1893); Freeman Cleaves, *Rock of Chickamauga: The Life of General George H. Thomas* (Norman, Okla.: University of Oklahoma Press, 1949); Richard O'Connor, *Thomas, Rock of Chickamauga* (New York: Prentice-Hall, Inc., 1948); Frank F. McKinney, *Education in Violence: The Life of General George H. Thomas and the History of the Army of the Cumberland* (Detroit: Wayne State University Press, 1961).

Thomas, in addition to a personal acquaintanceship of long standing. Francis F. McKinney's *Education in Violence* (1961), although the most completely detailed of the seven biographies, is not fairly comparable with the other six, since it is also represented to be a history of the Army of the Cumberland.

The annual yearbooks of the activities of the Society of the Army of the Cumberland contain much material on the life of General Thomas. They consist principally of talks by contemporary officers covering his character and military accomplishments. Other important material is available in the 129-volume *Official Records,* including a one-volume index. These books were published from 1881 to 1901 and are regarded as the ultimate authority on the Civil War. Their contents are the result of exhaustive research and analysis of data submitted by participants and others, both North and South, and were prepared under the rigid direction of the United States Government.[4]

Every American should be familiar with the life of General Thomas. It was a life devoted at all times to the nobler virtues of morality and patriotism. His deeds are worthy of inspiration by every American of whatever degree, but more especially by those who may have forgotten the historic events of their country and the men who were at their destined places in the unfolding of those events. No one of proper maturity can fail to experience a rebirth of patriotism at the story of General Thomas at Chickamauga's Horseshoe Ridge on the fateful afternoon of September 20, 1863. This and Mission Ridge were two of the greatest moments in our history, and Thomas was the hero in both. It is disappointing that many otherwise well-informed Americans are not aware that on the field of Chickamauga he earned the nickname "the Rock of Chickamauga" by saving the Union Army from destruction after more than half the army had fled the field. Although a technical defeat for the Federals, the stand of Thomas saved the Union Army and prevented the recapture of the strategic city of Chattanooga. Confederate success there would have opened up Kentucky, Indiana, and other Midwestern states to invasion and might well have led to recognition of the Confederacy by European powers. Confederate General Daniel H. Hill said of Chickamauga that General Braxton Bragg, the Confederate commander, did not know of his victory until the morning of September 21, and with that knowledge was not disposed to pursue the Federals.[5]

At Murfreesboro or Stones River, Tennessee, where General

4. "Official Records," *Civil War Book Club Review* (July, 1959), Vol. IV, No. 10.

5. *The Century, Illustrated Monthly Magazine* (New York: The Century Co., November, 1886–April, 1887), Vol. XXXIII (New Series, Vol. XI).

Thomas commanded the center of the Union line, he masterfully held his ground, after the left and center were crushed, until both wings were established. This battle, fought on December 31, 1862 and January 1 and 2, 1863, demonstrated that his victory at Mill Springs, Kentucky, January 19, 1862, the first Union victory of the war, was the work of a gifted leader. It was during a council of war following the first day's battle at Murfreesboro that Thomas, when asked by Rosecrans what he had to say, replied, "Gentlemen, I know of no better place to die than right here."[6] His view prevailed, and within two days the Southern Army retreated. This trait in Thomas was so dominant that its continued display on other fields did much to bring final Union victory.

It is dismaying that, despite the preponderance of well-documented fact, which offers sturdy challenge to the claim, Generals Grant and Sherman are usually ranked above all other Union generals. The military record of General Thomas, which shows no defeats, no battle movements lost, and the rare genius of saving his army from disaster after the mistakes of other generals, gives him the unchallenged ranking.

"Names next to Lincoln's that will live longest in connection with the war are Grant, Thomas, Sherman and Sheridan . . . I think that is the way history will eventually write them."[7] If this is surprising to those who believe that Sherman should rank next to Grant, this authority also says, "Sherman was really great in almost every way, with the singular exception of not winning the battle in which he had personal command. He frequently commanded other officers who won battles."[8]

Another comment: "Sherman has given us several splendid illustrations of strategy and logistics, as witness his marches in Mississippi, Georgia, and the Carolinas, but his battles will never be quoted as brilliant examples of grand tactics."[9] Although Allan Nevins perhaps does not rate Thomas so highly, he nevertheless lists him as one of the half-dozen greatest military figures of the Union and Confederacy, namely, "Lee, Jackson, Grant, Sherman and Thomas after Farragut."[10]

6. Otto Eisenschiml and Ralph Newman, *The American Iliad* (Indianapolis: Bobbs-Merrill, 1947), p. 303; Henry A. Castle, "Some Glimpses of an Enlisted Man," in Military Order of the Loyal Legion of the United States, Minnesota Commandery (St. Paul, 1908).

7. Michael H. Fitch, *Echoes of the Civil War* (New York: Fenno and Co., 1905), pp. 296-98.

8. *Ibid.*, p. 309.

9. W. F. G. Shanks, *Personal Recollections of Distinguished Generals* (New York: Harper and Brothers, 1866), p. 92.

10. Allan Nevins, *The War for the Union: The Improvised War, 1861–1862* (New York: Charles Scribner's Sons, 1959), p. 94.

It is probable that he made no attempt to list these commanders in specific order. We read further: "Among Union generals . . . perhaps Thomas was the greatest of all, including Grant, McClellan, Meade and Sherman."[11] General Thomas was "one of the greatest soldiers produced by the Civil War, as well as one of the most attractive characters in American history since George Washington."[12]

When his countrymen have been made fully aware of the facts, General Thomas will be given due recognition, much belated, as the greatest Union general of the Civil War and as one of the foremost generals of the world. Numerous of his contemporaries stated their estimate of his outstanding character and ability, but none more convincingly than Major General Joseph Hooker, the hero of Lookout Mountain, the Battle Above the Clouds, in Tennessee:

> I was with the Army of the Cumberland but a short time, but that time was very eventful to the Republic and for the Army itself. Its records have been repeated to you to-day, and if they were surpassed by any Army of the Republic, I did not know of that Army. It had at the head of it the ablest, the most just, and the most beloved man I ever knew. I never shall know his equal. I never supposed a man of his merit could live. There is on record the name of but one man who was his equal. I need not name him to you. His is a character that we all may aim at and aspire to, but never can reach. GENERAL GEORGE H. THOMAS was nearer to it privately, officially, and publicly than any man I ever knew."[13]

This appraisal of General Thomas is typical of almost all officers who knew him with the rare exception of Generals Grant, Sherman, Sheridan, and Schofield, all of whose interest in their own achievements rendered them seemingly incapable of acknowledging the achievements of Thomas.

Another tribute, by General Joseph S. Fullerton, to the remarkable Army of the Cumberland and its great commander, General Thomas, is the following:

> Next to the Army of the Potomac the Army of the Cumberland was the largest Union Army in the field. It was the most compact, the most complete in all its departments, the most thoroughly organized and disciplined of any of the armies. Its

11. Matthew Page, *Virginia, the Old Dominion,* p. 520.

12. John Fiske, *The Mississippi Valley in the Civil War* (Boston, 1900), p. 54.

13. Society of the Army of the Cumberland, *Yearbook, 1871,* speech by General Hooker, p. 71.

esprit de corps was equaled by none. It worked like a machine, it lived like a family, it had the soul of honor. From head to foot there were neither malice, jealousies, plottings and intrigues. Its commander was a faultless soldier, an irreproachable man. As a general his record was perfect. It can be said of him as of no general in our own or in any other army—of no other living or dead—that he never made a military mistake; that he was never defeated in battle."[14]

This estimate may appear to be exaggerated, but the record substantiates. it. Nevertheless, as the following excerpts from General Henry V. Boynton's speech illustrate, the Army of the Cumberland was hard put to project the true facts of its achievements before the country in rebutting the many misrepresentations made against it.

Through long years of controversy the Army of the Cumberland is coming to its own. It is doubtful whether, in military history, there can be found another army with its notably great and successful record which contemporary writers of military history—I should rather say of military fiction—have so persistently misrepresented. It is not necessary to inquire into their motives or to asperse them. The fact remains that the Army of the Cumberland, after winning its victories in the field, has had to fight ever since to save the true record of them for history. And it is only of recent years, when the full official record has been accessible, and as the further results of many prolonged and bitter controversies, that the myths of this distorted history are taking up their march into oblivion. . . .[15]

Next we come to a name that excites universal acclaim from every fair-minded student or writer of our military history, wherever its wide and still-spreading fame has reached. George H. Thomas, that great Virginian, and greater American, is rapidly coming to his own. . . . Of him, and of him alone, among all our great and honored captains, can it be truthfully said that he never lost a movement or a battle. Mill Springs was the first Union victory of the three years' campaign, and it was complete. We know how the center held and what it did at Stones River. The world knows the significance of his title, "the Rock of Chickamauga." Every successful feature of the three days' battle about Chattanooga was his and not another's. Every modification of the plan of battle was his and every portion of the plan which

---

14. *Ibid.,* 1893, speech by General Pullerton, p. 62.
15. *Ibid.,* 1892, speech by H. V. Boynton, p. 74.

succeeded was modified. Had his advice, based on full reconnaissance, been followed of making a feint before the gorges
of Rocky Face, and sending his army rapidly through undefended
Snake Creek Gap, the decisive battle of the Atlanta Campaign
would have been fought in the vicinity of Resaca. He protested
against Kenesaw [Mountain] and his hands were clean of the
blood of that needless and so wicked slaughter [the responsibility
was Sherman's]. He was turned back from Atlanta with the small,
but valiant Fourth and Twenty-third Corps, and the remnants
which were cast off when a selected army was organized for a
picnic to the sea, to do battle with these and whatever else he
might gather against the whole force which had confronted the
three combined Union armies from Dalton to Atlanta. Never was
greater though unintentional tribute paid to his ability. The commanders he was saving from the sneers of mankind [Grant and
Sherman], railed at him from Washington and Savannah, but
with an imperturbability without parallel under the circumstances, at the risk of removal, in the face of removal, and, as we
now know, after the order for removal, he prepared the blow
which, when it fell at Nashville, utterly destroyed the opposing
army and saved the march to the sea from everlasting ridicule.
And here it is pertinent to remark that this was the only great
Confederate army destroyed in battle, before the final surrender,
by any Union Commander.[16]

Thus in summary do we have the highlights of the most successful
commander of the Civil War. Yet, to illustrate the type of misrepresentation to which this great man and the Army of the Cumberland was
subjected, the following excerpt from the pen of General Sherman
to General Grant, dated June 18, 1864, is presented:

> My chief source of trouble is with the army of the Cumber-
> land, which is dreadfully slow. A fresh furrow in a ploughed field
> will stop the whole column, and all begin to intrench. I have
> again and again tried to impress on Thomas that we must assail
> and not defend; we are the offensive, and yet it seems the whole
> Army of the Cumberland is so habituated to be on the defensive
> that, from its commander down to the lowest private, I can not
> get it out of their heads.[17]

This is an example of the incredibly malicious and unwarranted

---

16. *Ibid.*, pp. 76-77.
17. *Official Records of the War of the Rebellion* (Washington, D.C., 1880–
1901), Series 1, Vol. XXXVIII, Part IV, p. 507.

attacks made on Thomas and the Army of the Cumberland. Both Thomas and his army were engaged heroically and successfully in their assigned task of attacking the Confederate General Hood, thus insuring the success of Sherman's march to Atlanta. No worse example of injustice against Thomas and his great Army of the Cumberland can be found than this false statement by Sherman that General Thomas and his army were addicted to the defensive and that a fresh furrow would stop the whole column. When it is remembered that Sherman never won a major battle and that Thomas never lost a movement or a battle; also that the Army of the Cumberland suffered but one defeat, and that a technical one at Chickamauga, the transparency of Sherman's comments is clear. Sherman, a classmate of Thomas at West Point, has been represented as one of his very close friends; but it is good to know they were not enemies. This revelation of Sherman's treacherous conduct was made possible by the publication of the *Official Records*. It is gratifying to know that their publication after his death spared him the knowledge of his "friend's" injustice.

Perhaps the very best appraisal of General Thomas, certainly on a par with General James A. Garfield's highly regarded oration on Thomas before the Society of the Army of the Cumberland in 1870, is in William Swinton's *The Twelve Decisive Battles of the Civil War*. This book, published in 1867, during the lifetime of Thomas, goes a long way in dispelling the claim, sometimes made by eulogists of other leaders, that Thomas's deeds were exaggerated. Certain it is that Thomas had many champions and friends who praised him to the skies; but equally certain it is that he was so outstanding in every way that it is not possible to magnify his known accomplishments and character:

> The figure of Thomas looms up in many respects without a superior, in most instances without a rival even, among the Union Generals created by the war.
> When the Rebellion opened Major Thomas was a soldier of twenty years' experience, during which he had not only not turned aside to the attractions of civil life, but had accepted only two furloughs. . . .
> From this time the fame of General Thomas became national. His complete and admirable victory at Mill Springs was the first triumph of magnitude for the North since the disaster at Bull Run, and brought back a needed prestige to the Union arms. As commander of the Fourteenth Army Corps, under Rosecrans, he was conspicuous in the marching and fighting which preceded

Murfreesboro', and all-glorious in that decisive battle. . . . It was he who alone and unaided saved the Army of the Cumberland at Chickamauga, when the example of all around him might have excused him from flying from a lost field. And again, accordingly, the enthusiastic tribute of praise comes up in the report of Rosecrans: "To Major General Thomas, the true soldier, the prudent and undaunted commander, the modest and incorruptible patriot, the thanks and gratitude of the country are due for his conduct at the battle of Chickamauga." It was Thomas, whose troops "forming on the plain below with the precision of parade," made the wonderful charge on Missionary Ridge which threw Bragg back into Georgia. It was he who, in the grand Atlanta campaign, commanded under Sherman more than three-fifths of that Army, and who delivered the opening battle at Buzzard's Roost and the closing battle at Lovejoy's. It was Thomas, in fine, who set the seal of success on the Georgia campaign, 300 miles away at Nashville.[18]

The war showed that his gifts, like his qualities, were in the main of that more solid and substantial sort which gain less immediate applause than what is specious and glittering, but which lead on to enduring fame. . . . Cautious in undertaking, yet, once resolved, he was bold in execution; deliberate in forming his plan, and patiently waiting for events to mature, yet when the hour struck, he leaped into great activity. Discretion in him was obviously spurred on by earnestness, and earnestness tempered by discretion. Prudent by nature, not boastful, reticent, he was not the less free from the weakness of will and tameness of spirit which are as fatal to success as rashness. . . .

Of his complete mastery of his profession in all its details, of his consummate skill as a general, the best monument is the story of his battles; for he never lost a campaign or a field; he never met the enemy without giving him cause to grieve for the rencontre; and he culled laurels from fields on which brother officers were covered with disgrace and more than once plucked up drowning honor by the locks, as at Chickamauga. As he did not himself fail, so he did not suffer himself to be ruined by incompetency in superiors, much less in subordinates, for he was accustomed to consider beforehand such possibilities and to guard against them. . . .

He was a soldier who conned his maps before he marched

18. William Swinton, *The Twelve Decisive Battles of the Civil War* (New York: Dick and Fitzgerald, 1867), pp. 472-73.

his army, who planned his campaign before he fought it, who would not hurry, who would not learn by thoughtless experiments what study could teach, who believed in the duty of a general to organize victory at each step. . . . He was not a slave to method, but naturally distrusted what was unmethodical; and that he invariably won battles by virtue of time-honored principles, and in accordance with the rules of the art of war, was, besides its value to the country, a truth invaluable to military science in the land, whose teachings had been somewhat unjustly cast into contempt by the conduct of other successful soldiers.

His Nashville campaign gave more than one instance of the trait just noted. Superiors were vexed . . . behind the parapets of Nashville, at his delay to attack the investing force; but neither this vexation nor the danger of removal which threatened him could avail with Thomas, for that soldier would not be badgered into premature battle. Soon after, the wisdom of Thomas in delaying attack in order to mount his cavalry, approved itself, for never before in the war had grand victory been so energetically followed by pursuit. In the battle itself, too, spectators fancied that he was pausing too long before engaging his right flank, but he held that wing poised as it were in the air, till the fit moment, when he swung it like a mighty sledge upon the Confederate, and smote him to the dust.[19]

These common words describe a most uncommon man, in point of fact, a very great man.

Not to be forgotten is that General Thomas, by his splendid achievements throughout the war, in particular during the campaign of Chattanooga, earned the promotion that Sherman, his junior in rank and experience, received when Grant was made commander in chief. Nevertheless, he gave the best he had and served willingly under Sherman, seemingly unmindful that he himself should have been given the promotion; in fact, his achievements under Sherman only confirmed that the promotion should have been given to him.

General Thomas was no parade-ground soldier. He was a disciplinarian who stressed the importance of such apparently unimportant items as a buckle or a horseshoe nail for want of which a kingdom is said to have been lost. His concern for detail played its part in the unordered charge of his men up Missionary Ridge, and thus reflected the confident and determined spirit of their great commander. Assistant Secretary of War Charles A. Dana, who witnessed the charge, discussed later, proclaimed it "one of the greatest miracles in

19. *Ibid.*, pp. 473-75.

military history."[20] This charge was one of the only two instances during the entire war, with Thomas commanding both times, when a Confederate army was driven from an intrenched position in utter confusion. The other was in the great Battle of Nashville, on December 15 and 16, 1864, where Confederate General Hood was attacked and his army virtually destroyed.

It is surprising that General Thomas has for so long reposed in the shadow of lesser men, and that most of them were inferior to him both in performance and ability. One of the contributing reasons therefor was the glossing over of his deeds by the so-called name generals who, when writing their memoirs, appropriated maximum credit, as aforesaid, to themselves. Generals Grant, Sherman, Sheridan, and Schofield wrote their memoirs from the vantage point of mutual friendship and helpfulness, and Grant was the only one of this group whose deeds approached real comparison with those of Thomas. Sherman had access to available records in his capacity of commander of the United States Army after the election of Grant to the White House; however, his memory was not equal to the confidence he placed in it, nor was his word adequate to earn him the exalted place history has given him, as shown by some of his critics.[21] Both Grant and Sherman, by their eulogists, were made into false heroes, and all were equally guilty in underrating General Thomas, their superior in almost every aspect of military achievement.

The military clique of Generals Ulysses S. Grant, William T. Sherman, Phillip H. Sheridan, and John M. Schofield formed a dynasty of command that lasted for more than twenty years. His friendship with Grant, not his generalship, formed the basis for Sherman's selection to command the March to the Sea. Sherman had not won an important battle before that assignment, although his subordinates did, nor did he at any time thereafter. During this period of unprecedented military control, Sherman succeeded Grant as commander of the army in 1869; Sheridan succeeded Sherman as commander in 1884; and Schofield succeeded Sheridan as commander in 1888.[22]

General George Gordon Meade, the victor of Gettysburg, although commander of the Army of the Potomac, went into near eclipse following the accession of Grant as commander of all the armies. Crushed by the promotion of Sherman, Hancock, and Sheridan to the rank of major-general in the Regular Army, Meade complained

---

20. James H. Wilson, *The Life of Charles A. Dana* (New York, 1907), p. 293.

21. H. V. Boynton, *Sherman's Historical Raid: The Memoirs in the Light of the Record* (Cincinnati, 1875), p. 10.

22. *Webster's Biographical Dictionary* (1953), p. 1356.

to Grant that promoting these men over his head was an insult to the Army of the Potomac and to himself personally, and that he would resign when it occurred. Grant promised him that he would be made a major-general when assigned to the Middle Division operating in Western Virginia; also that he, Grant, would have put Meade in charge sooner if Sheridan had not fallen back at an earlier time, but he did not want the public to assume that Sheridan was meeting with disapproval for it. What an alibi that was! In fact, however, Grant was not honest with Meade, since he did not fulfill his promise, and we have Meade's appraisal of it: "The whole substance of the explanation was that he desired to advance his favorites, Sherman and Sheridan. . . . It is the same old story of inability to appreciate the sensitiveness of a man of character and honor."[23]

Another example of the earthiness of the "name" generals of the Civil War in the good graces of Grant relates to the Battle of Five Forks, Virginia, April 1, 1865, a scant eight days before Lee's surrender at Appomattox. General Sheridan was annoyed by the "slowness" of General G. K. Warren in bringing up troops for the battle and removed him from command. It was General Warren who, as chief engineer of the Army of the Potomac, sent troops to occupy Little Round Top on July 2, 1863, the second day of the Battle of Gettysburg, which did much to save the contest for the Federal Army. Although exonerated during President Hayes' administration of slowness at Five Forks and Sheridan's unjust charge, Warren died before the court's decision in exoneration was rendered. Warren's bitterness at Sheridan's injustice was so deep that he requested burial without a military uniform and other evidence of rank. A statue of General Warren stands on the site of Little Round Top at Gettysburg to commemorate his great contribution to the Union victory.[24]

Although Grant was the only member of the group of Grant, Sherman, Sheridan, and Schofield whose deeds compare somewhat with the record of General Thomas, Grant's record included 54,900 casualties incurred in slightly more than a month's operations in the battles of the Wilderness, Spottsylvania, and Cold Harbor. This bloodletting exceeded the total number of men in General Lee's Army. Such a shocking cost in human lives is without parallel in American history, and, at the end, the objective of Richmond still remained in Confederate hands. Winston Churchill tells of Cold Harbor, where after 7,000 of the Boys in Blue fell within an hour, the troops refused to continue furnishing the slaughter. Churchill calls this "unflinching

23. Clarence E. Macartney, *Grant and His Generals* (New York: McBride and Co., 1953), p. 48.

24. *Ibid.*, p. 126.

butchery."[25] Grant's determination "to fight it out on this line if it takes all summer" was a declaration to wage a war of attrition, the effect of which was to lose two men for each man lost by Lee.[26] No one can dispute that this kind of warfare is the very opposite of generalship.

The fourth member of the military dynasty was Major General John M. Schofield, who attempted to appropriate credit to himself for planning the Battle of Nashville. This was exclusively a General Thomas achievement, and the most cursory examination substantiates it. Testimony of contemporary and subordinate generals in full possession of the facts, *Official Records,* and other reliable sources, refute Schofield's claim in its entirety. Schofield and his impact on the career of Thomas is discussed in the last chapter in connection with the latter's death.

The tendency of most writers to err, as aforesaid, when writing about the Civil War, had its effect in denying deserved credit and in awarding undue credit to participants. In his speech before the 1893 meeting of the Society of the Army of the Cumberland, General J. S. Fullerton discussed the serious problems of errors and misrepresentations that had crept into the records of the war. Pertinent excerpts from his address are as follows:

> It is time we were using our endeavors to correct some of the many false statements concerning the Army of the Cumberland that have crept into history, and time that we filled up many serious omissions. . . . During the war newspaper reports of campaigns and battles, necessarily were imperfect, were accepted as history; and their errors and misrepresentations became fixed in the minds of the readers of those days. The men who fought were strong partisans. Often they were blind to the mistakes of their own commanders; often were unjust in their opinion of others. The bloody hand of war reached out to nearly every home in the land. The resulting distress and hatred warped men's judgments and unsettled their reason. The excited and inflamed minds of men were in no fit condition to arrive at correct conclusions concerning the operations of their own armies, and still less concerning the military acts of the enemy. It was impossible to justly determine the merit of commanders. Little men were exalted to high commands, and able men were hastily and unjustly cast down. Many errors of that day have been accepted as truth, are now

---

25. Winston Churchill, *A History of the English Speaking Peoples: The Great Democracies* (New York: Dodd, Mead and Co., 1958), p. 252.

26. *Ibid.,* p. 253.

recorded as historical facts. But the conditions are now favorable and the time has come to erase such errors from the pages of history. . . .

There are soldiers whose records shine brilliantly on the pages of our recent war history, because their military mistakes and errors were not made known to the world—their history was suppressed. In the heated and unsettled time of war, and during the days of surging passions that followed, one who would live in peace would not dare even to hint at the mistakes or shortcomings of a popular hero unless he wished to meet the fate of a martyr, and be stoned to political and social death. But what is far more melancholy is the fact that the names of some of our greatest soldiers and heroes are lusterless, and almost unkown to the generation that has come on since the war, because credit for the deeds of those great but modest men was unjustly assumed by or awarded to some hero of the hour.

You, men of the Army of the Cumberland, know of such a soldier; you have seen him; you remember him well. Now is the time, while your memories are yet fresh, your minds active, your spirits strong, to see that his star be properly set in the galaxy of great generals of the world.[27]

The soldier referred to, of course, was none other than General Thomas; and it is important to note well that this was an appeal to give him deserved although belated justice.

General Thomas has the confidence of the Army and the people, and will discharge his duty as he has from the commencement of the Rebellion. He will, in my opinion, if permitted, be one of the greatest generals of the war, if not the greatest. . . .[28]

Never before has such ample and excellent material been in reach of the historian. We have the facts; it is not necessary to conjecture, to guess, to depend on circumstantial evidence. Never before have the complete and official records of campaigns and battles, down to the minutest details, made by both sides, been gathered together, placed in safe keeping, and published in detail for the public use. One could not now write false or incorrect history of the war of the rebellion without detection. I wish that some of our generals had waited to examine the rebellion records before giving to the world their war memories; or that military

---

27. Society of the Army of the Cumberland, *Yearbook, 1893*, speech by General Pullerton, pp. 60-70.

28. *Ibid.*, p. 68.

historians had done the same. Then their works might have been correct. No man who depends on his memory for facts can write exact accounts, after a lapse of years, of the great and multifarious transactions in which he was an actor. The mind that dwells long on some wish or hope often regards it at last as a fact. An oft-repeated fiction comes to be held as truth; statements made by others and often repeated by one are sometimes counted as his own experience. One can not well account otherwise for the errors published as history in some of our soldiers' memoirs. Not long before his death, General Sherman told me that General Grant said to him that his memory of "acts and incidents of the war was so perfect that it was not necessary for him to refer to reports in preparing his memoirs." This explains how some mistakes were made; and General Sherman himself, though he wrote in the best of good faith, might need to account for some statements in his own memoirs by the fact of his writing often without having referred to reports.[29]

The remarks of General Fullerton show that much of the earlier history of the Civil War, written under varying conditions not susceptible to complete verification, was unreliable.

In considering the neglect of General Thomas by historians generally it is noteworthy that his native Virginia, against which he drew his sword in defense of the United States, has exceeded all bounds in its hatred of him. His old birthplace, where he spent his early years before attending West Point, is still standing, but no marker of any kind, not even his name, identifies it as the home of this great American soldier and gentleman. His only "sin" was in remaining loyal to his country as, in taking his oath to defend it, he was expected to do. His oath as a professional soldier outweighed his maiden sisters' objections to his remaining with the Union. So intense was their feeling against their brother that they turned his picture to the wall and, even unto death, would have nothing to do with him.[30] It was the attitude of these sisters that expanded to the immediate neighborhood, to Southampton County, to the state of Virginia, and to the Confederate South. Time has done little to soften the bitterness of Virginians toward one of her greatest sons, as evidenced by the absence of any monument to or reminder of his greatness.

Nothing better illustrates this strong feeling than the statement, "Many people remember the Misses Thomas well, but the author,

---

29. *Ibid.*, p. 61.

30. *Virginia* ("American Guide Series" [New York: Oxford University Press, 1941]), p. 473.

[Squires] although he asked constantly, could not find anyone even in 1915," forty-five years after his death, "who remembered General Thomas."[31] This writer met with better success in October, 1959, eighty-nine years after his death, but only after many inquiries of people in Courtland (formerly Jerusalem), the county seat, and in Newsoms near the Thomas home. A number of replies to questions, some erroneous, seeking the location of the home proved unproductive; in fact, some gave only a negative shake of the head. It remained for a storekeeper in Newsoms, who showed no reluctance, to give the desired information.

The intense animosity held by Southerners for Thomas is in sharp contrast to the esteem and reverence in which the name of General Robert E. Lee is held by both North and South. Lee was also a Virginian, but remained with his state when it seceded and eventually became the famous commander of the Army of Northern Virginia. It is doubtful whether any other generals of the Civil War compared as favorably as these two leaders. Each was educated at Government expense at the United States Military Academy for the very reason that defense of their native land, against all enemies both foreign and domestic, might be assured. Each served at the Military Academy after graduation, Lee as superintendent and Thomas as instructor in the artillery and the cavalry. It is worth noting that many officers, both North and South, spoke pridefully after the conflict of having had Thomas as their instructor at West Point.[32]

The degree of respect and admiration for the memory of General Lee is indicated by the exchange of letters between President Dwight D. Eisenhower and Dr. Leon W. Scott, Jr., of New Rochelle, New York. Dr. Scott questioned the propriety of having a picture of General Lee in the White House office, in view of his determined effort to divide the Union. President Eisenhower, in his reply of August 9, 1960, said in part:

> I would say, first, that we need to understand that at the time of the War Between the States the issue of secession had remained unresolved for more than seventy years. Men of probity, character, public standing and unquestioned loyalty, both North and South, had disagreed over the issue as a matter of principle from the day our Constitution was adopted. General Lee was, in my opinion, one of the supremely gifted men produced by our nation. He believed unswervingly in the constitutional validity of his

---

31. W. H. T. Squires, *The Days of Yester-year in Colony and Commonwealth* (Portsmouth, Va.: The Printcraft Press, 1928), p. 195.
32. *Ibid.*

cause which until 1865 was still an arguable question in America; he was a poised and inspiring leader, true to the high trust reposed in him by millions of his fellow citizens. . . . Through all his many trials, he remained selfless almost to a fault and unfailing in his faith in God. Taken altogether, he was noble as a leader and as a man, and unsullied as I read the pages of history. . . .[33]

Comrades and admirers of General Thomas generally have contributed much proof of his noble character. It was this trait that, above all others, motivated him always in avoiding any opportunity to benefit personally at the expense of anyone. His natural reserve also helped him in submerging any thought of advancing his personal interests. Nothing better emphasizes this than his appointment to succeed General Don Carlos Buell as commander of the Army of the Ohio. Thomas, second in command, notified Buell that he would decline the promotion, since to accept it would perpetrate an injustice on Buell; also, he did not consider himself ready for the assignment. Thomas wired General Halleck, the commander at Washington, giving his views and recommending that Buell be retained in command. This appeal, with that of others, was successful, and Buell was retained.[34] It is no less deserving of comment that Thomas refused at first to succeed General Rosecrans after the Battle of Chickamauga, but none other than Rosecrans himself influenced him to accept the appointment.[35]

As to where the path of duty lay for Generals Lee and Thomas, it would be only rank presumption now for anyone so far removed from the scenes, incidents, and influences that impelled men to "take their stand" to judge. There is no reason for doubt, however, that uppermost in the mind of each was a consideration of the possible effect of his decision upon relatives and friends and, of course, the United States. For his part Lee said in a letter to his sister, dated April 30, 1861, that "With all my devotion to the Union and the feeling of loyalty and duty of an American citizen, I have not been able to make up my mind to raise my hand against my relatives, my children, my home."[36] In this letter Lee also noted, "The whole South is in a state of revolution, into which Virginia, after a long struggle, has been drawn; and though I recognize no necessity for this state of things,

---

33. *Civil War Times,* October, 1960, p. 11.

34. Robert S. Henry, *The Story of the Confederacy* (Indianapolis: Bobbs-Merrill, 1936), p. 198.

35. Society of the Army of the Cumberland, *1879,* speech by General Rosecrans, p. 176.

36. Robert E. Lee, Jr., *Recollections and Letters of General Lee* (New York, 1926), p. 26.

and would have forborne and pleaded to the end for redress of grievances, real or supposed, yet in my own person I had to meet the question whether I should take part against my native state."[37]

We see that Lee's decision was based upon his devotion to his relatives and state; further, that in recognizing no necessity for the state of things then existing in Virginia he meant that he could see no reason for conflict. His oath to the United States, as his final decision proved, was second to the loyalty he gave to his immediate family and others he loved; however, no one can dispute that his oath foreclosed his leaving the Union. History has been very kind to General Lee in this, and no denial of honor and respect to his memory has been for long permitted by the Federal government. This benevolent attitude is expressed in the monuments, roads and other symbols of respect and honor that bear his name. Reference is made elsewhere in this work to the place of honor given his portrait at the U. S. Military Academy and to his election to the Hall of Fame.

One could say quite accurately that the similarities of Generals Lee and Thomas far exceeded their dissimilarities, even in the matter of death, which occurred for both in the year 1870. Said W. H. T. Squires:

> When all has been said, the character of Thomas was the finest of all leaders of the Federal cause. Unlike the cadets of West Point, we do not see resemblance to Washington, but there is a decided resemblance to Robert E. Lee. In the simple grandeur of his character, in the purity of his private life, in his transcendent genius as a military engineer, in the blind and unquestioning devotion of his followers, in his modesty, so pronounced that like Lee it becomes almost a weakness, in the splendid poise of temperament, in the immense reserve force one feels as he follows his career, in the comprehensiveness of his objectives once convinced he was right, he resembled the Southern chieftain.[38]

Said General Irvin McDowell:

> It is easy for some of us, born at the North, who have felt that the Union of these States was paramount to every consideration —paramount even to civil liberty for the time—to love the Union and take up arms against her enemies. General Thomas was born in a section of the country where such views were not universal; where those who held them faced political and social death, death without a resurrection. It was therefore, perhaps, some

---

37. *Ibid.*
38. Squires, *op. cit.*, p. 196.

struggle for him to turn his head in one direction when his affections, probably, called him in another. It is therefore the greater
credit to him that he was able to do with his intellect, what,
perhaps, his early education might not have helped him to do.[39]

In other words, General Thomas faced the same problems in reaching
his decision to remain with the Union that General Lee faced in
deciding to fight against the Union. The difference separating these
two great men should not, in any event, serve to bring respect and
honor to him who fought against the Union, and on the other hand
brand as a traitor to his state the one who remained true to his soldier's
oath and therefore the Union.

> Is it not, indeed, an immortal glory for Virginia to have pro-
> duced the noblest soldier of the Revolution and the noblest that
> fought for the North in the Civil War, as well as the noblest that
> fought for the South? I hope some day to see her erect a worthy
> monument to one of the greatest of her sons. But, as she grows
> every year richer, more prosperous, more fortunate, more loyal in
> the Union for which he helped to save her, she herself, whether
> she wills it or not, will more and more become his proudest
> monument.[40]

Regardless of the reasons for their following different paths, each
did his utmost to bring victory to his cause. Everything in their
careers, refutes the slightest doubt of their superior qualifications for
command; and the best available evidence we have, in addition to
their success on the battlefield, is in the stories telling of the blind
devotion both of the common soldier and subordinate officers in
following them without question. What is of all things least understood
is that General Thomas, who felt that there was no other choice to
make in staying in the Union, paid the price of complete ostracism
by his native Virginia. Indeed, the very Union for which he gave his
every energy, and without whose services its preservation might not
have been accomplished, has been almost equally remiss in honoring
him in accordance with his contribution.

Bruce Catton, the noted contemporary historian of the Civil War,
said of General Thomas, "What a general could do, Thomas did; no
more dependable soldier for a moment of crisis existed on the North
American continent, or ever did exist."[41] Again Catton tells us that

---

39. Society of the Army of the Cumberland, *Yearbook, 1879*, speech of
General Irvin McDowell, pp. 75-76.
40. Gamaliel Bradford, *Union Portraits* (Boston, New York, 1916), p. 129.
41. Bruce Catton, *This Hallowed Ground*, p. 283.

"Thomas comes down in history as The Rock of Chickamauga, the great defensive fighter, the man who could never be driven away but who was not much on the offensive. That may be a correct appraisal. Yet it may also be worth making note that just twice in all the war was a major Confederate army driven away from a prepared position in complete rout—at Chattanooga and at Nashville. Each time the blow that routed it was launched by Thomas."[42]

42. *Ibid.*, p. 369.

GENERAL GEORGE H. THOMAS

The Indomitable Warrior

of the educational and other influences in which he grew up. The
Thomas family did not curry favor or envy, as is so often done in

CHAPTER I

Early Life

GEORGE HENRY THOMAS was born on a farm about two miles north
of Newsoms, and about five miles north of the North Carolina border,
in Southampton County, Virginia, July 31, 1816.[1] The Thomas birthplace is still standing, and although only the first three-room part
was built before George was born, the present much-enlarged,
two-story white house is in a fairly good state of preservation. The
original house contained two rooms on the first floor and one room
on the second floor. George was born on the first floor.[2]

A remarkably large and beautiful old oak tree shades the front
of the home, and may well have been a "brave old oak" when George
was a boy. Something in the magnificence of this tree inspires comparison with the grand and enduring qualities for which Thomas was
known and respected, for there is in the tree, as there was in the
man, a quiet dignity, proportion, strength, reliability, and yet withal
a stately simplicity. One wonders whether the Creator, in His infinite
wisdom, may be appealing through this fine old tree for simple
justice from his countrymen to one of God's noblemen, who did his
whole duty unselfishly and with certainty of punishment from family
and friends. The wonder is all the greater, because those who have
chronicled histories of Virginia omit, almost without exception, any
mention of the one man from that state who can stand beside
George Washington and not lose stature.

Southampton County does not form a part of the rich farm area
of southern Virginia, so that the pattern of the great plantation, "flowing with milk and honey," and overrun with slaves, was not found
there in ante-bellum days. For that matter, Southampton County,
in many of its outward appearances, remains, both economically and

---

1. W. H. T. Squires, *The Days of Yester-year in Colony and Commonwealth*
(Portsmouth, Va., 1928), p. 185.

2. *Ibid.*, p. 186; interview with Mrs. H. T. Miles, resident owner, October,
1959; microfilmed tax lists of Southampton County for 1819 (in custody of
Virginia State Library, Richmond, Va.).

culturally, much as it was in the nineteenth century. The Thomas family lived in comfort, being neither rich nor poor, but definitely not wealthy as some writers have stated. It was in this atmosphere that George Thomas was born and grew to young manhood, although, as George wanted it, there is little information concerning his early boyhood. We know that he was one of nine children born of parents both cultivated and highly respected in the community.[3]

George was the natural product of his family, his environment, and of the educational and other influences in which he grew up. The Thomas family did not curry favor or envy, as is so often done in Virginia and elsewhere, by claiming ancestry from some particularly prominent branch or group. The parents were industrious and independent people who were satisfied to be judged and accepted on their own achievements.

His father, John C. Thomas, died on April 20, 1829,[4] at the age of 45,[5] as a result of a farm accident. The father's family came originally from Wales, but long residence and intermarriage in England produced a predominantly English blood strain before coming to America.[6] Some writers have stated that the family was wealthy or well-to-do before coming to Virginia,[7] but the history of population movements to other countries tends to disprove that comfortably endowed people are motivated to assume the hardships of a new and undeveloped country.

Exhaustive research has produced little information regarding the father, but we do know that he was a man of strong mind, body, and character.[8] He engaged in a number of activities, including services as guardian in appraising and settling estates, as overseer of elections, processor and surety, and finally as commissioner of highways.[9] Considering the times in which he lived and the limited means of transportation available, these activities reveal him to have been an unusually industrious and civic-minded citizen. The example set before

---

3. Mattie R. Tyler Papers, Southampton County Courthouse, Courtland, Va.; photograph of family gravestone, Newsoms, Va., listing all but George and Benjamin.

4. County Minute Book, Southampton County (in custody of Virginia State Library, Richmond, Va.) shows John C. Thomas, p. 263, but not found elsewhere.

5. Henry Coppee, *General Thomas* (New York, 1893), p. 3.

6. Mattie R. Tyler Papers, *op. cit.*

7. Coppee, *op. cit.*, pp. 2, 3; Thomas B. Van Horne, *The Life of Major General George H. Thomas* (New York: Charles Scribner's Sons, 1882), p. 1.

8. Coppee, *op. cit.*, pp. 2-3.

9. Southampton County Minute Books, 1810–1829 (in custody of the Virginia State Library, Richmond, Va.).

his family of industry and civic consciousness, which left him little time for social affairs, had its good effect, no doubt, in the development of George's character.

George's mother, Elizabeth Rochelle Thomas, was from French Huguenot stock. Her grandfather emigrated to America in 1690, following the Revocation of the Edict of Nantes in 1685 by Louis XIV of France.[10] The Edict of Nantes was proclaimed on April 13, 1598, by Henry IV of France, and granted tolerance to Protestant Huguenots in the free exercise of their religious beliefs and practices. This included freedom to worship in public and to build churches, except in Paris and at royal residences; the right to maintain the then existing four Protestant universities; the right to special chambers in the parliaments of Grenoble and Bordeaux; and the right to hold provincial and national synods.[11] As the years passed, the Huguenots became quite powerful because, in their political congress at La Rochelle, in 1620, they confiscated all Roman Catholic churches and set up a civil and military organization to help in attaining their objectives.[12]

Some time before the Edict of Nantes was revoked, certain restrictions were placed upon the liberties of Protestants, such as forbidding the holding of government office, membership in trade corporations, and marrying Roman Catholics. The Revocation ordered the destruction of churches, forbade religious meetings under penalty of confiscation of goods, exiled all Protestant ministers, and ordered Protestant children to be baptized and brought up as Roman Catholics.[13]

After the Revocation, more than four hundred thousand Protestant Huguenots left France,[14] and over one tenth of their number landed in England.[15] In the year 1690, a number left England for America,[16] and about three hundred of them sailed up the James River and established a settlement in Virginia that they named Monacantown, after a former Indian tribe.[17] In this New World environment, the

---

10. Captain Henry Rochelle, *Life of Rear Admiral John Randolph Tucker* (Washington, D.C.: Neale Publishing Co., 1903), p. 9; *Stanard's Genealogical and Biographical Register* (Richmond: Virginia Magazine of History and Biography), p. 112.

11. *Encyclopedia Americana* (New York: American Book—Stratford Press, Inc., 1954), Vol. IX, p. 584.

12. *Ibid.*

13. *Ibid.*

14. *Ibid.*, Vol. XIV, p. 582.

15. Rochelle, *op. cit.*, p. 9.

16. *Ibid.*

17. *Encyclopedia Americana, op. cit.*, Vol. XIV, p. 484.

need for defense against curtailment of their religious freedom was not required. In the settlement were three Rochelle brothers: William, who settled later in North Carolina; James, who settled in South Carolina; and John, who purchased 212 acres of land from William and Jonas Longbottom on the south side of the Nottoway River in Albemarle Parish, Southampton County, Virginia. John married Mary Gilliam, the beautiful daughter of Hinchia and Nathaniel Gilliam, who bore him four sons. John, the eldest son, married his cousin Judith Gilliam, who became the mother of six boys and three girls, including Elizabeth, the mother of the future Major General George H. Thomas. Another son, James, born in 1786,[18] became county clerk of Southampton County in 1815, and he it was who engaged his nephew George as his deputy, following completion of the latter's studies at Southampton Academy.[19]

Of the nine children born to George's parents, six were girls and three were boys, the exact reverse of George's mother's family of six boys and three girls. John William was the eldest child; Judith Elvira, the second; Benjamin, the third; and George Henry, the subject of this work, the fourth. Unfortunately, the remaining children cannot be placed in their order of birth.[20]

It was natural that George should inherit from his parents some of the traits of character that molded him into a great and good man. In the father's veins ran the blood of Welshmen and Englishmen noted for their fierce energy, devotion to duty, and independence. From his French mother he inherited the tenderness, sensitiveness, and warmth, coupled with the deep religious conviction and faith of the Huguenot strain, that endeared him to subordinates and equals alike.

The mother undoubtedly had a difficult struggle providing the means of livelihood for her family during her remaining twenty-seven years, following the death in 1829 of the husband and father. With a large family and farm to manage, including farmworkers and a number of slaves, the mother lived a full life of hard work.[21] Although the exact size of the farm during her widowhood is not known, Southampton County court records show that on February 22, 1904, 524½ acres were recorded in the transfer of title following the death of Francis Thomas, the last surviving member of the family.

---

18. Rochelle, *op. cit.*, pp. 9-10.
19. Van Horne, *op. cit.*, p. 2.
20. Mattie R. Tyler Papers, *op. cit.*
21. Southampton County Land and Personal Property Tax Lists, 1816 (microfilm, Virginia State Library, Richmond, Va.). Shows joint ownership with Edmond Spencer of 438 acres, 9 slaves, etc.

A number of writers on the subject have deplored the scarcity of details relating to the early life of George, principally because "it is not known under what inspiration and circumstances and at what time the ideals, of which his character was the realization, took definite shape in his own mind and consciousness."[22] This does not appear to be unusual when it is considered that the average biography is somewhat barren of incidents occurring before honor and fame are attained. His reserve in matters concerning his private life is to be blamed for this lack of knowledge, and it is unfortunate that too late it was his intention, stated a few days before his death, to unfold the story of his youth.[23]

The father's death occurred before George was thirteen years old and was certainly one of the more disturbing events of his early life. Perhaps the most shocking event was the Southampton Insurrection, sometimes known as the Slave Insurrection in Virginia, which occurred when he was about fifteen years old. This was the bloodiest uprising of slaves in all Southern history, and cost the lives of fifty-five men, women, and children[24] residing in the community surrounding the Thomas home. It can be assumed that some of the massacred children were his schoolmates, and that the memory of their death remained with him throughout his life. It is probable also that the incident made an abiding impression on his mind, this horrible example of man's age-old struggle for freedom, and that his later decision to remain with the Union had some part of its beginning in this revolt.

Nat Turner, leader of the Insurrection, was born of Negro parents on October 2, 1800, and was the property of Benjamin Davis.[25] His mother attempted to kill Nat when a baby, rather than raise him a slave, and his father was strong-willed and resentful of slavery to the full.[26] There is some evidence that Nat was strongly religious, if not somewhat fanatical. He was a Baptist preacher, presumably unordained, whose habits of truthfulness, honesty, and abstinence were strong points in his exemplary character.[27]

After his capture and conviction for his part in the killing of fifty-five whites, Nat told of a childhood incident that deeply affected him and was the beginning of the road that ended on the gallows.

22. Van Horne, *op. cit.*, p. 3.

23. *Ibid.*

24. *Encyclopedia Americana, op. cit.*, Vol. XXVII, p. 204.

25. William S. Drewry, *The Slave Insurrection in Virginia* (Washington, D.C.; Neale Publishing Co., 1900), p. 26; Arnold Whitridge, *No Compromise* (New York: Farrar, Straus and Cudahy, 1960), pp. 86-87.

26. *Virginia* ("American Guide Series" [New York: Oxford University Press, 1941]), p. 78.

27. Drewry, *op. cit.*, p. 26.

He said that while playing with a couple of other children about his own age he told them of an event that took place before he was born. This greatly surprised his mother, who overheard it, and impressed all those who knew it. It was felt that this showed the gift of prophecy and foretold that the Lord had great things in store for him.[28]

Nat recalled a voice speaking to him from heaven on May 12, 1828, and telling him that the serpent was loosed; that Christ had put down the yoke he had borne for men's sins; that he should take up the yoke and fight the serpent; and that the time was approaching when "the last should be first and the first last." He felt that now he should await a further sign from heaven telling him when to begin the fight. This sign appeared to him in the form of a solar eclipse in February, 1831, and he spoke at once of the plan to three companions. Another sign came to him on August 13, 1831, by way of the sun's disc changing from bright gold on rising to pale green, to blue, and then to a silvery white. In the afternoon the sun shone with a glowing light and the air was damp and heavy. After this sign the conspirators set August 21, 1831, as the time for action, and held a feast that morning, which Nat did not attend until about three o'clock, or after the men had time to eat and drink.[29]

The Misses Judith and Francis Thomas, among those witnesses interviewed personally in later years regarding the Insurrection, stated that when their family was warned of the approach of the slaves, their mother hitched up the horses for their flight to Jerusalem, now Courtland.[30] When the slaves came dangerously close, the family abandoned the team and fled through the near-by woods. When they reached the Thomas home, they forced the Thomas slaves to mount the available horses and follow them. Sam, the Negro overseer for the Thomas family, instructed his son Leonard to follow the insurgents at once, return to tell his mother at the Thomas home to get the keys hidden in the cider-press loft, and take care of the farm. Sam also escaped soon afterward, and rode promptly to Mrs. Thomas at Jerusalem, where all were lodged in jail for safety during the night.[31]

An interesting observation concerning the interview with the Thomas sisters is the absence of any reference to their brother George. It is also noteworthy that shortly after the Insurrection proposals were made to prevent future slave uprisings. Governor John Floyd

---

28. *Ibid.*, p. 29.
29. *Ibid.*, p. 33.
30. *Ibid.*, p. 21.
31. *Ibid.*, pp. 68-69.

of Virginia recommended that the legislature revise all laws to "preserve in due subordination the slave population." Thomas Jefferson Randolph, grandson of Thomas Jefferson, signer of the Declaration of Independence and third President of the United States, proposed that all slave children born after a designated year be purchased by the state and hired out until enough funds were accumulated to transport them from the United States. Unfortunately this proposal was defeated by a narrow margin, and laws were enacted prohibiting the teaching of reading and writing to the slaves, in addition to banning Negroes from all religious meetings unaccompanied by a licensed white minister.[32] Such attempts to solve the problems created by slavery were nothing more than attempts; but one can wish that enough sentiment might have been developed to solve the problems and thus avert the greatest of American tragedies, the Civil War.

The Abolitionist movement had been in progress for some years prior to the Southampton Insurrection, and some of the literature, urging the slaves to rise up and fight for emancipation, had been distributed to master and slave alike. It is conjectural whether the weekly *Liberator*, founded in Boston in 1831 by the famous Abolitionist William Lloyd Garrison, was ever read by Nat Turner. It was believed, however, that Garrison was at least indirectly responsible for the revolt, in that it had some of its roots in the agitation inspired by Abolitionists.

The Abolitionists were the militant wing of the antislavery movement, which was located principally in New England. Their advocacy of the immediate abolishment of slavery ignored the fact that slavery was debated by the delegates when the Articles of Confederation, underlying our Federal union, were in process of preparation. In the debates on the subject, including the matter of whether population should determine the basis of contributing Federal revenue by the states, it was decided that five slaves would be regarded as being equivalent to three recognized citizens or freemen. This was incorporated in the Constitution, Article 1, Section 2, as the basis for representation in the House of Representatives, and thus for the first time slavery was placed on a political foundation leading to sectional bitterness and eventual Civil War.[33]

Irrespective of legal and moral views on slavery, the South was legally within its rights in owning slaves. The efforts of Abolitionists, in petitioning for the abolishment of slavery, however morally right,

---

32. *Virginia, op. cit.*, p. 78.

33. Marion Mills Miller, *American Debate* (New York: Putnam, 1900), p. 96.

were opposed to such legal rights. Stated another way, the thirteen original colonies accepted union with slavery, under an agreement mutually binding on all the states. It is understandable, therefore, that when the question of the right to own slaves in one section of the Union was challenged by another section of the Union, and after the compact that formed the Union, the section challenged would resent the action as unwarranted interference with its rights. It was ever so simple for Abolitionists to petition for the abolishment of slavery in the South, where such labor was used, since the economy in the Northern states in general, and in the New England states in particular, had little need for slaves. The South had accepted slavery as its right, as aforesaid, as indispensable to its agricultural industry, and would not relinquish this chief factor in its economic life. One wonders why the Abolitionists were so oblivious to the mote of white-labor exploitation in the eye of the North and so intensely concerned with the beam of black bondage in the eye of the South. It would be absurd to contend that morally the mote of exploitation had the effect of offset against the beam of slavery; neither can it be denied that both are morally wrong.

When George Thomas was a boy, schools and academies were few and widely separated in Southampton County. This was due to the generally scattered population and to the limited means of transportation, which made it difficult to assemble students at reasonable cost. There was no system of public education in Virginia, and the private schools, on the average lacking uniform standards, did not rank very high. George attended a private school, conducted by James Parker, several miles from his home, and not far from Jerusalem, the county seat.[34] He completed his preliminary education at Southampton Academy, from which he was graduated with honor before his nineteenth birthday. This was the ultimate in education that the county afforded.[35]

Details are far from complete regarding his school days, but his teachers predicted a brilliant career for him based upon his unusual alertness, ability, and aptitude.[36] Upon graduation from Southampton Academy he was a year or so older than the average student, but this was due perhaps to the unhurried times in which he lived.

Mrs. Henry T. Miles, the present owner and occupant of the former Thomas home, told the author in October, 1959, that George

---

34. Drewry, *op. cit.*, p. 21; Squires, *op. cit.*, p. 186.
35. Van Horne, *op. cit.*, p. 2.
36. Richard W. Johnson, *Memoir of Major General George H. Thomas* (Philadelphia: J. B. Lippincott Co., 1881), p. 13.

attended school in the one-room brick building behind the Thomas home, although she was unable to state which subjects and grades were taught.[37] Some credibility may be given this story, since Mrs. Miles knew George's maiden sisters Francis (Fanny) and Judith Thomas as friends and neighbors and often talked with them before their death in 1902 and 1903, respectively. In view of the extreme bitterness of the sisters toward George, resulting from his loyalty to the Union and his corresponding "treason" against his native Virginia, it is not surprising that the use of the little brick building as a school-house attended by George is not generally known.

In addition to his formal education, George obtained valuable practical knowledge and experience in making equipment for the farm. Tools, nails, horseshoes, wagon and carriage tires, and other items were made from raw iron; lumber was produced from trees grown on the place and used in the making of useful articles; and hides from animals were utilized in making needed leather goods.[38] Long after he had grown to manhood, George told of observing, as a boy, a harness being made and of afterward making one himself. This is the only known instance in his boyhood that could be said to foretell the future resourcefulness and practicality of the man, both of which characteristics he possessed in an unusual degree.[39]

General Oliver Otis Howard once mentioned in a speech that a friend of his, about the age of Thomas, described him as "a boy of few words but of an excellent spirit."[40] He also told of an old Howard University student named Scott, a teacher in a colored school near Southampton, who spoke of some of the incidents an eighty-year-old colored man named Artise had described to him concerning George's boyhood. Artise knew George before he was old enough to attend school, at which time he explained he was quite playful and attractive to the young colored boys, to whom he would bring sugar from the house for use in catching coons and possums. Scott also said that Artise expressed hope that George would come back to Southampton County and relive the days when as boys they played church among other things under a big tree. This might well have been the big oak tree still standing in front of the old home. Artise also said that George taught the colored boys at night some of the things

---

37. See photograph of one-room, red-brick building elsewhere in this book.

38. Drewry, *op. cit.*, p. 104.

39. Van Horne, *op. cit.*, p. 3.

40. *Personal Recollections of the Rebellion* (New York: Military Order of the Loyal Legion, 1890), p. 287.

he knew or learned in the daytime; and finally that, upon his return from the Mexican War, George brought all of the colored boys new suits of clothes, and afterward taught them the Word of God.[41] If this tells anything, it is that Thomas had a deep feeling of sympathy and humanity towards the less fortunate Negroes. The 1850 Census shows that a Henry Artise was living with the Thomas family at that time;[42] therefore some basis for confidence exists in the details of George's boyhood furnished by Teacher Scott.

Shortly after graduating from Southampton Academy George began the study of law in the office of an uncle, James Rochelle, mentioned earlier, who was county clerk of Southampton County. As chief administrative officer of the county he levied, collected, and disbursed taxes, enforced the law, and had responsibility for all county court proceedings received by his office. After his uncle's death on August 17, 1835,[43] George was sworn in as deputy-clerk on November 18, 1835.[44]

Soon after taking the oath of office as deputy clerk, Congressman James Young Mason of the district offered him an appointment to the United States Military Academy at West Point. Mr. Mason knew the Thomas family well and had been a close friend of the deceased uncle, James Rochelle. Although George had not previously considered a military career, he accepted the appointment and in due time went to West Point, where he took and passed the entrance examination.[45] His acceptance of the appointment was in the Southern tradition at that time. Boys from the South had dominated the United States Army since the early days of the Republic. It was the natural and desirable thing for boys from the slave states, especially sons of well-to-do planters and others, to find glamor and satisfaction in a military career. It is not surprising, therefore, that the ratio of the population of the South to each cadet appointed therefrom was substantially lower than the ratio in the North. With this in mind it was almost inevitable that large numbers of West Point graduates would take up arms for their native state.

It is interesting to note that at the time of George's entrance to West Point the law forbade the inclusion in entrance examinations of subjects beyond the scope of work required in rural schools.

41. *Ibid.*

42. *Census of Southampton County, 1850* (Washington, D.C., National Archives).

43. *Stanard's Register, op. cit.*

44. Order Book, 1835-1839, Southampton County (microfilm), p. 37.

45. Coppee, *op. cit.,* p. 5; Henry Stone, *Some Federal and Confederate Commanders* (Boston: Houghton Mifflin Co., 1895), p. 167.

Ulysses S. Grant, of the Class of 1843, said that he never saw an algebra book until his appointment to the Academy.[46] Examination requirements during those days must have included little more than a good grounding in reading, writing, and arithmetic. A knowledge of geography, grammar, and Latin was desirable, but it was believed that stricter requirements would prove too discouraging to candidates with limited education.

---

46. Lloyd Lewis, *Sherman: Fighting Prophet* (New York: Harcourt, Brace and Co., 1932), p. 53.

CHAPTER II

Cadet Days at West Point

ONE could speculate whether the legal profession lost a promising barrister when George Thomas gave up his study of the law to accept an appointment to the Military Academy at West Point. There can be little doubt that almost all Virginians of the Civil War period would have preferred for him the role of attorney to that of the most successful Union commander of the Civil War. In the sure knowledge that the loss of his services to the Federal cause would have been irreparable, it is comforting, if not logical, to believe that Destiny influenced his choice of a career.

After discussing the appointment with George, Congressman Mason recommended him to Lewis Cass, the Secretary of War, in a letter dated March 1, 1836. He described him as about seventeen or eighteen years of age, of fine size, of fair complexion and with brown hair. He also stated that he was a young man of splendid habits and possessed a good preparatory education.[1] The young man was closer to being twenty years of age, or one or two years older than the average age of his classmates. This was due in part to the loss of a complete year following graduation from Southampton Academy, during which he began the study of law while working in his uncle's office.

About a month after Congressman Mason's recommendation of the appointment, his mother gave her consent in the following:

This is to certify that I give my consent for George H. Thomas to sign any articles by which he will bind himself to serve five years as a cadet in the United States Military Academy at West Point, unless sooner discharged.

Given under my hand this 26th day of March, 1836.

[Signed] ELIZABETH THOMAS—Guardian[2]

1. Adjutant General's Office, Old Records Division, National Archives, Washington, D.C.
2. Ibid.

While on his way to West Point he took time out to visit Congressman Mason in Washington, D. C., to thank him for his sponsorship of the appointment. In blunt language, Mr. Mason told him that no one appointed to the Military Academy from his district had ever graduated. He advised him further that "If you do not, I never want to see your face again."[3]

What Mr. Mason could not have known was that in George he was recommending an individual of heroic mold. The attributes of patience, determination, industry, and perseverance, as shown throughout his military career, were ingrained in him to a remarkable degree. He did not know that to Thomas the word "failure" could never be charged against him, that the word itself was repugnant to him.

Mr. Mason died in 1859, shortly before the outbreak of the Civil War; therefore he was spared the painful necessity of making a decision to either join the Secessionists or remain with the Union. It would be improper to venture the prediction that the Congressman, if he had lived, would have cast his lot with the South, as did the great majority of Virginians. It was generally believed that his strong feelings in matters affecting the South often influenced his judgment.[4] If he had been permitted to foresee the impact on the outcome of the war in this one appointment, his interest in George's success might have taken on a different character.

As if to emphasize his determination to be the first successful West Point graduate from Southampton County, George Thomas went to the Academy several weeks before opening day in order to brush up on some of his subjects.[5] This looking to the future, by doing today what was needed to insure it, was a principle that would pay rich dividends to his country on more than one battlefield. It meant stabilization of the center at Murfreesboro when the entire right was pushed back. At Chickamauga it was his foresight in felling logs and building defenses, the night before the fatal second day's fighting, that avoided disaster to the entire Union Army after most of the right and center had fled the field. He would not be goaded into fighting at Nashville by superiors unfamiliar with his problems, although subjected to their unprecedented abuse, until he knew he was prepared to win at a minimum cost in lives. The result was the most decisive victory in the open field, by either North or South, during the entire war.

---

3. Thomas B. Van Horne, *The Life of Major General George H. Thomas* (New York: Charles Scribner's Sons, 1882), p. 2.

4. Donn Piatt, *General George H. Thomas* (Cincinnati, 1891), p. 56.

5. Freeman Cleaves, *Rock of Chickamauga* (Norman, Okla.: University of Oklahoma Press, 1949), p. 9.

It is a mistake to define this quality of being prepared as stubbornness. Above all else it was the expression of his intensity concerning the righteousness of his cause. This spirit became a contagion that communicated to and emboldened those under him to seek to emulate his heroic deeds. Under the spell of such consuming fire it is no wonder that the enemy was almost invariably defeated.[6]

After becoming settled in his duties at the Military Academy, George sent the following letter to the Secretary of War, enclosing his mother's certificate of consent.

WEST POINT,
April 25, 1836

THE HONORABLE LEWIS CASS,
Secretary of War,
Washington, D.C.

SIR:

I had the honor a short time since of receiving my conditional appointment as Cadet in this institution which, with the consent and approbation of my Guardian, I take pleasure in accepting. The paper enclosed is the Certificate of my Guardian.

[*Signed*] GEORGE THOMAS[7]

The ideals of duty, honor, and country are inculcated at the Military Academy, and a new cadet soon learns that honor is his most prized possession. It is something he shares equally with all his fellow cadets. He prides himself in the knowledge that his word is always accepted at face value, and that he accepts the word of another cadet without asking or receiving proof.

Two of the more famous members of the Class of 1840 were assigned as roommates of Thomas during the first year. These were William Tecumseh Sherman, a lad of sixteen, from Ohio, and Stewart Van Vliet, about twenty-one years old, from Vermont.[8] William Stark Rosecrans, of the class of 1842, nicknamed Thomas "George Washington," after noting his striking resemblance to Stuart's portrait of Washington.[9] To others of his classmates he was known as "Tom" and "Slow Trot";[10] in later life he was to be known by his troops as "Old

---

6. Society of the Army of the Cumberland, *Yearbook, 1879,* pp. 136-37.

7. Adjutant General's Office, *op. cit.*

8. Lloyd Lewis, *Sherman: Fighting Prophet* (New York: Harcourt, Brace and Co., 1932), p. 57.

9. Society of the Army of the Cumberland. *op. cit.,* p. 173.

10. Gamaliel Bradford, *Union Portraits* (Boston: Houghton Mifflin Co., 1916), p. 181; Lewis, *op. cit.,* p. 57.

Pap," but as long as the battle is remembered he will be remembered as "the Rock of Chickamauga."

The dissimilarities between Sherman and Thomas probably had something to do with their congeniality, although Sherman's claim of being Thomas's best friend is hard to believe in the light of some of his biased and groundless pronouncements during the war years. Sherman was high-strung, nervous, wiry, and talkative. Thomas was dignified, silent, and grave. Both were conspicuously honest and sensitive, although in temperament they were distinctly different. Sherman has stated that when Thomas was a mere boy, and the family and neighbors were compelled to seek refuge in a blockhouse during a slave uprising, a messenger was needed to carry a communication; the one to deliver it was none other than the boy George, whom years later President Andrew Jackson rewarded by approving his appointment to the United States Military Academy.[11] Sherman's apparent reference here was to the Nat Turner Insurrection, which was discussed in some detail in the preceding chapter.

It is interesting, perhaps, more correctly, pleasing, to know that someone, somewhere, some time had the courage to stand up and confront hazing at West Point head-on, that custom which ofttimes subjects free Americans to indignities and injuries. Van Vliet described the close association of the three roommates, which had the good effect of discouraging annoyance by older cadets. One evening an upper classman came into their quarters and began giving orders, whereupon Thomas faced up to him and said, "Leave this room immediately or I will throw you through the window."[12] This, we are told, was sufficient to insure freedom from molestation during the remainder of their cadet days.

Although entrance requirements were not very high, judged by today's standards, a number of advantages accrued to the students that were valuable in later life. The training and discipline taught included neatness in dress and person and in the proper handling and treatment of personal effects and equipment. The benefit of association with students from other sections of the country neutralized some of the prejudices and misconceptions often entertained by members of different sections and groups. Some of this leavening effect carried over into the Civil War itself, as evidenced by the pride that officers of both North and South often expressed toward some former classmate who cast his lot with the other side.

It has been said that Sherman was a leader of the nighty forays that had as their purpose the replenishment of the cadet food supply.

---

11. Lewis, *ibid.*
12. Henry Coppee, *General Thomas* (New York, 1893), p. 323.

His 109 demerits as a plebe are explained as being due in large part to such excursions for food, and perhaps they afford a forecast of his genius for raiding, which was so well exemplified in the Atlanta and Carolinas campaigns. One wonders whether Sherman's reputation for being the best hashmaker at West Point was shared by and participated in by Thomas. Despite Thomas's grave demeanor, the fact that he and Sherman were roommates, and that he at no time bore the reputation or the appearance of being underfed, it is fair to conclude that he participated to some extent in these extracurricular activities.

William Dutton, of the Class of 1846, has left a realistic record of his experiences as a cadet.[13]

At 5 A.M. which is ½ an hour after the morning gun, the drums are beat by the barracks, & the cry grows—"fall in there," when we all have to be in the ranks or be reported. The roll is then called, we go to our rooms & have 15 minutes to roll up our blankets, put them up, wash, clean the room etc., when everything must be in order. We have no mattresses & only 2 blankets to lay on the floor . . . We then march to the mess hall, & if one speaks, raises his hand, looks to the right or left . . . we are reported, indeed we are reported for everything . . . When we arrive at the tables, the command is given "take seats" & then such a scrambling you never saw. For breakfast we have the remains of the meat of the former day's dinner, cut up with potato with considerable gravy—& not more than two-thirds of them can get a bit—bread cut in chunks, butter and coffee. We have to eat as fast as we can, & before we get enough the command is given "Squad rise," at dinner time we have "Roast Beef," and boiled potato & bread—no butter, at Tea, bread & butter & tea. We have to drill twice a day & a good many faint away . . . After we have marched from tea, we stay in our room till ½ hour past 9 when we can go to bed if we choose, & at taps at 10 every light must be out & after that the inspector in all times of night.

The summer uniform worn by the cadets during Thomas's period of study at the Academy consisted of a gray short-tailed coat, white vest and belt to match, tight trousers, a stand-up collar, and a dress cap of black felt. He took his turn performing guard duty, which consisted of walking post one hour and resting for two hours for the next turn of duty in each twenty-four hours.

---

13. Sidney Forman, "Cadet Life Before the Mexican War," U.S. Military Academy *Bulletin No. 1* (West Point Library No. 207642), pp. 12, 13.

Thomas was at first a cadet, then corporal, sergeant, and lieutenant, and his 87 demerits, averaging 22 yearly, attest to a fairly good behavior record. Of the recognized four leading Union generals of the Civil War, he enjoyed the highest rank at West Point, including Grant, Sherman, and Sheridan.[14] Somewhere along the line Sherman attained the rank of cadet sergeant, but his 380 demerits, 293 more than Thomas received, may have operated to bring about his reduction to private. Richard S. Ewell stood thirteenth, next behind Thomas, and became a lieutenant general and corps commander in the Confederate Army. It was Ewell who commanded one of the three corps under Lee at Gettysburg. Sherman, for all of his demerits, finished sixth in his class.[15]

The cadets who came and went during Thomas's attendance at the Academy included many who fought on opposite sides in the Civil War, then more than twenty years in the future. Among these were Don Carlos Buell, Class of 1841, and William S. Rosecrans, of the Class of 1842. Both had commanded the Army of the Cumberland before Thomas, who had been second in command to both of them, assumed command. Ulysses S. Grant, Class of 1843, would be superseded by Thomas early in the war only to become commander of all the armies in 1864. Braxton Bragg, fifth highest in the Class of 1837, would be Thomas's artillery captain and commander at Monterey in the Mexican War, but would oppose both Rosecrans and Thomas in the blood bath of Chickamauga, Georgia, on September 19 and 20, 1863. Daniel H. Hill, Class of 1842, would serve under Bragg both in the Mexican War and the Civil War, and would also oppose Rosecrans and Thomas at Chickamauga. William J. Hardee, Class of 1838, would be subjected to a murderous fire from Thomas's troops at Stones River. James Longstreet, Class of 1842, would graduate fifty-fourth in a class of fifty-six, but would become one of the great corps commanders of the Civil War, although a controversial figure for alleged procrastination at Gettysburg, and following the war for being a Republican. It would be the lot of Longstreet to effect the breakthrough at Chickamauga and put to rout more than half the Union Army, only to fail seven times in attempting to dislodge Thomas on Horseshoe Ridge and make the victory complete.

Surprise has been sometimes expressed that so few members of Thomas's class of 1840 became famous. Of the forty-two graduating,

---

14. Military Historical Society of Massachusetts; Henry Stone, *Some Federal and Confederate Commanders* (Boston: Houghton Mifflin Co., 1895), p. 167.

15. George W. Cullum, *Biographical Register of Officers and Cadets of the U. S. Military Academy)*, Vol. I.

six were killed, ten died, two resigned, and eight went with the South,[16] a total of twenty-six, or sixty-two per cent. Of the remaining sixteen, which included Sherman, Thomas, and Van Vliet, among others, the Class of 1840 did very well.

One of the popular ballads sung at the Military Academy during the period of George Thomas's attendance was entitled "Oh! Benny Havens, oh!" The first verse of this endless song, sung to the tune of "The Wearing of the Green," and written in 1838 by Lucius O'Brien, went like this:

> Come fill your glasses, fellows, and stand up in a row,
> To singing sentimentally, we're going for to go;
> In the army there's sobriety, promotion's very slow,
> So we'll sing our reminiscences of Benny Havens, oh!
> Oh! Benny Havens, oh! Oh! Benny Havens, oh!

Benny Havens was famed as a seller of contraband liquor and viands to cadets at the Military Academy, and his face was well known to those attending between the years 1816 and 1859. In the latter year he closed his business.[17] We may fairly conclude from the spirit of the song that life for the cadets was not entirely dull and empty.

Nothing better suggests an underlying reason for the attributes of sterling manhood, so well exemplified by the aggregate of West Point graduates, than the Cadet Prayer, which is part of the devotional service at the Cadet Chapel.

> O God, Our Father, Thou Searcher of men's hearts: help us to draw near to Thee in sincerity and truth. May our religion be filled with gladness, and may our worship of Thee be natural.
> Strengthen and increase our admiration for honest dealing and clean thinking, and suffer not our hatred of hypocrisy and pretense ever to diminish. Encourage us in our endeavor to live above the common level of life. Make us to choose the harder right instead of the easier wrong, and never to be content with half a truth when the whole can be won. Endow us with courage that is born of loyalty to all that is noble and worthy; that scorns to compromise with vice and injustice; and knows no fear when Truth and right are in jeopardy. Guard us against flippancy and irreverence in the sacred things of life. Grant us new ties of friendship and new opportunities of service. Kindle our hearts in fellowship with those of a cheerful countenance, and soften our hearts with sympathy for those who sorrow and

16. *Ibid.*
17. Forman, *op. cit.*, pp. 1, 2.

suffer. May we find genuine pleasure in clean and wholesome mirth, and feel inherent disgust for all coarse-minded humor.

Help us in our work and in our play, to keep ourselves physically strong, mentally awake and morally straight, that we may the better maintain the honor of the Corps untarnished and unsullied, and acquit ourselves like men in our effort to realize the ideals of West Point in doing our duty to Thee and to our Country. All of which we ask in the name of the Great Friend and Master of Men.

Of all earthly figures native to American soil whom it has been the privilege of the writer to have knowledge of, either in person or through the printed word, this beautiful prayer suggests that General George H. Thomas was more nearly the fulfillment of it than anyone else who comes to mind.

Not much has been written concerning the possible effect of John Rawle's book *A View of the Constitution* on shaping the minds of West Point students for the acceptance of secession as justifiable. Published in 1825, it was used as a text at the Academy during the 1825-1826 term in a course on American constitutional law.[18] Rawle theorized that the Union is dissoluble; this meant that in the event of dissolution the allegiance of the individual would revert to the state.[19] In other words, if national sovereignty were destroyed as a result of the withdrawal of states from the Federal Union, nothing would be left to which allegiance could be given by the individual but the state.

Many years after the Civil War the question whether secession was taught at West Point was still being debated with considerable feeling. A number of Confederate officers maintained that Rawle's textbook justified their joining the Confederacy and fighting against the Government under which they were born. The Government's determination to force the seceding states to return to the Union fold proved at least that there was another point of view.

Robert E. Lee, the great Southern military leader, is quoted as having stated to Bishop Wilmer of Alabama that "If it had not been for the instruction I got from Rawle's textbook at West Point, I would not have left the Old Army and joined the South at the breaking out of the late War Between the States."[20] This statement does not appear to be in character with General Lee's independence of mind.

---

18. Douglas Southall Freeman, *Robert E. Lee* (New York: Charles Scribner's Sons, 1935), Vol. I, p. 78.

19. *Ibid.*

20. Richard O'Connor, *Thomas, Rock of Chickamauga* (New York: Prentice-Hall, Inc., 1948), p. 66.

Surely General Lee had greater reason than what is set forth in this one book for leaving the Government and its Army, to which he had dedicated his life. Coming from Lee, this reason seems incredible for a number of other reasons. First, it implies that during his cadet days, and more especially during his term as Superintendent, the seriousness of his oath had been lost on him. It would thus follow that a mere book, encouraging dissolution of the country, his country, which he had been trained to defend and in the defense of which he had supervised the training of others, made a deeper impression upon him than did his obligation.

Second, in the event of dissolution, Lee was under strict moral and legal responsibility not to become an instrument for the perpetuation of disunion. If this were not so, one wonders when, if ever, one's country might be sure of the loyalty of those in whose hands its security lies.

Third, Lee stated in a letter to his son, William Henry Fitzhugh Lee, before the war that secession was nothing but revolution, and that anarchy, not government, would have been established by the founding fathers.[21] This statement would appear to have foreclosed Lee's subsequent withdrawal from the Union; however, it is important to state that when he withdrew he gave as the compelling reason the ties of family and friends. This would indicate that Rawle's textbook had little or nothing to do with his decision.

Some have held to the belief that Confederate President Jefferson Davis, if he had been brought to trial for his part in the war, would have used Rawle's textbook as vindication; but Davis himself is authority for the statement that although the book was used in prior classes, he had been taught Kant's *Commentaries*.[22] Again, as in the case of Lee, it is difficult to believe that Davis, even assuming that he had been taught from Rawle's book, would have been influenced by it alone to join the forces of secession. The same viewpoint toward the 296 West Point graduates who joined the Confederacy, representing 27 per cent of 1,096 graduates,[23] might also with logic be expressed.

One of the most thought-provoking analyses available, concerning West Point Military Academy as an institution for the training of officers to command our troops, is to be found in the first volume of *Military Reminiscences of the Civil War,* by Major General Jacob D.

21. Robert W. Winston, *Robert E. Lee* (New York: Grosset and Dunlap, 1934), p. 73.

22. Freeman, *op. cit.*, pp. 78, 79; *Southern Historical Society Papers,* Vol. XXII, p. 83.

23. Cullum, *op. cit.*, Vols. I and II.

Cox. This analysis is important in evaluating the reasons for the wide differences in results, as evidenced by the records of commanders in the field during the Civil War. Some of the important observations in this analysis, given below, are deserving of consideration and understanding. From this analysis it is possible to learn the factors that were important in developing successful officers of the caliber of Grant, Lee, Sheridan, Longstreet, Hancock, and Thomas, and why Hooker, Burnside, Pope, and Hood, among others, were generally not successful. All of these officers studied at West Point, but that alone did not insure military success. One must look to the more practical considerations of experience, temperament, and other factors in assessing reasons for the difference in results.

The fallacy is often entertained that by being a professional, success is insured, as, for example, attendance at West Point. In 1861 the only professional soldiers were officers who had graduated at the United States Military Academy, but their military experience was confined to the Mexican War of 1846-1848 and minor engagements with Indians on the frontier. Inevitably, therefore, no officer had ever commanded large numbers of troops on a scale comparable to that of the Civil War. In the Mexican War neither General Taylor nor General Scott, the American commanders, had more than 15,000 men in their separate armies at any time. General Gordon Granger, who came to the relief of General Thomas in the closing hours at Chickamauga, when surprise was expressed to him at the little additional knowledge acquired by line officers since Academy days, replied, "What could you expect of men who have had to spend their lives at a two-company post, when there was nothing to do when off duty but play draw-poker and drink whiskey at the sutler's shop?"[24]

It is a revelation to learn that the course of study at the Military Academy prior to the Civil War was far from complex. Although four years of study were required, preliminary entrance requirements were based upon work done in common schools. Grant, Sherman, and Sheridan, three recognized generals, stated in their biographies that a common-school education was the extent of their preparation for West Point.[25] The corps of teachers and professors at the Academy always ranked high as instructors, but it cannot be claimed that several years' attendance there was superior in general education to a similar period spent at any other good school. A few graduates expanded their knowledge by becoming instructors at the Academy, but the majority left their books to engage in duty on remote posts, far

24. Jacob D. Cox, *Military Reminiscences of the Civil War* (New York: Charles Scribner's Sons, 1900), Vol. I, pp. 174, 175.

25. *Ibid.*, p. 176.

removed from any opportunity to supplement their academic pursuits.[26]

In his first year at the Military Academy, Thomas stood twenty-sixth in a class of 76; fifteenth among 58 in his second year; seventeenth among 46 in his third year, and twelfth among 42 in his fourth and final year. Class standings in each subject were not published until his final year, but his standing of seventh in artillery undoubtedly influenced his assignment to the artillery upon graduation.[27] His performance in the Mexican War battles of Resaca de la Palma, Monterey, and Buena Vista, and in the Civil War battles of Stones River, Chickamauga, Peachtree Creek, and Nashville, confirmed his grades and the wisdom applied in his selection for the artillery.

In addition to standing seventh in artillery during his final year, Thomas stood eleventh in engineering and infantry tactics, tenth in ethics, and ninth in mineralogy and geology. First-year subjects taught were French, algebra, trigonometry, application of trigonometry to geometry, mensuration of planes and solids, and school of the soldier. Second-year subjects were French, rhetoric, geography, history, and part one of the course in artillery. Third-year courses were drawing, natural philosophy and chemistry, school of the battalion, part two of the course in artillery, and practice in duties of the sergeant. Fourth-year courses were engineering, science of war, mineralogy and geology, moral philosophy, political science, rhetoric, and the final part of the prescribed course in artillery. Each cadet's rank in each study was derived on the basis of his proficiency as evidenced by weekly class reports and semiannual examinations. The courses in mathematics, physics and chemistry, and also in fortification construction, may be said to have comprised the most difficult part of the curriculum. Surprisingly, there was no formal instruction in strategy, grand tactics, and military history so essential to a thorough grounding in the art of war. Mahan's text on outpost duty was the only book on theory, aside from the study of engineering. Jomini's *Introduction* to *Grandes Operations Militaires* was studied at one time at the Academy but had been dropped. As to its adequacy in fitting men to command armies in the field, it is important to note that aside from engineering the course of study did not include the military art in its true sense or as commonly understood.[28]

The education offered at West Point before 1861 was basically the same, as far as it went, as any other polytechnic school; the military part of the study desirable for West Point students was, as stated,

---

26. *Ibid.*, pp. 176-77.
27. Official Register of West Point, 1836–1840.
28. *Ibid; Cox, op. cit.*, Vol. I, pp. 177-78.

only in the engineering field. In actual war the building of forts and the undertaking of a siege were entrusted to professional engineers. For army field duty, therefore, the mental equipment of the West Pointer was not superior to that of any other liberally educated man.[29]

As to actual experience in command of troops, the plebe at West Point might advance to corporal, sergeant, lieutenant, or captain in the corps if he displayed the required aptitude. This advancement might never come to a cadet, which it did not in the cases of Grant and Sherman,[30] due in part to the practical consideration that there were just not enough places to be filled. It may be presumed that such experience is not all-important; however, any experience is surely better than none at all, and regardless of the wide difference between them, limited command is of more value in heading toward a general's rank than no command whatever.

Reverting to the factors that had a bearing in developing successful commanders in the Civil War, it is clear that West Point alone offered little beyond the education obtainable at first-class educational institutions. It is probable that the major reason for the difference between so-called successful and unsuccessful generals was experience in command. It is a fact that the most successful generals, both North and South, were experienced in the Mexican War of 1846-1848, among whom were Sherman, Thomas, Grant, Lee, Jackson, and Joseph E. Johnston. Additional effort in the pursuit of knowledge following graduation, relating to the profession of arms, undoubtedly had a place in the success of some commanders. All things being equal, this would give an advantage over those content with formal knowledge acquired only to the time of graduation.

In Piatt's biography of General Thomas it is stated that in the popular mind West Point on the Hudson was expected not only to give instruction in the art of war, but in the natural course to supply any lack of brains in the minds of graduates.[31]

Upon graduation in June, 1840, Thomas received his diploma and was granted the customary leave of absence to visit his home. On July 1, 1840, he was assigned to the Third Regiment of Artillery as a second lieutenant and given orders to report to the commanding officer at Fort Columbus, Governor's Island, New York, upon expiration of his leave of absence. Fort Columbus was at that time a recruiting and training area for active army replacements.

29. *Ibid.*, p. 179.
30. *Ibid.*, pp. 179-80.
31. Piatt, *op. cit.*, pp. 56-57.

CHAPTER III

The Seminole War

SHORTLY after reporting to his regiment Lieutenant Thomas was given orders, in October, 1840, to join that part of the Third Artillery serving in the Florida Everglades against the Seminole Indians.[1] The Everglades covers about 4,000 square miles and extends about 100 miles from Lake Okeechobee to the tip of the Florida peninsula.[2] This large swampy land is infested with alligators, moccasins, and other reptiles in addition to disease-bearing mosquitoes and other types of insects. One of the worst characteristics of the Everglades from a military standpoint was its tracklessness and inaccessibility, which made the seeking out of Indians both hazardous and almost wholly unrewarding.[3]

The Seminole War may be said to have consisted of two phases, of which the first was in 1817-1818, and ended when Andrew Jackson destroyed their villages and completely subdued them. The second phase, from 1835-1842, was the most severe of all Indian wars waged with the United States, and resulted from the refusal of the Seminoles to give up land and remove to Indian Territory pursuant to a treaty ratified in 1834.[4] These Indians fought first under their great leader, Osceola, who was captured under a flag of truce, imprisoned, and died at Fort Moultrie on January 30, 1838.[5]

An interesting account of Lieutenant Thomas's earlier experiences is given in the following letter written to Charles P. Kingsbury, who graduated second in the class of 1840:

1. Henry Coppee, *General Thomas* (New York, 1893), p. 6.
2. *Encyclopedia Americana* (New York: American Book—Stratford Press, Inc., 1954), Vol. X, p. 599.
3. Coppee, *op. cit.*, p. 7.
4. *Encyclopedia Americana, op. cit.*, Vol. XXIV, p. 547.
5. *Ibid.*, Vol. XXI, p. 18.

FORT LAUDERDALE, E.F., July 25, 1841

DEAR KINGSBURY: Owing to the quantity of business on my hands at this time, I have not been able to answer yours of the 22d May before.

What do you ordnance officers do for quartermasters and commissaries? Do you do the duty yourselves, or have you staff officers at your arsenals to perform those duties?

My duties at this post are so many that my whole time is taken up. I have to do the duty of commissary, quartermaster, ordnance officer, and adjutant; and if I find time to eat my meals, I think myself most infernal fortunate.

So the Democrat was not dismissed after all; you have, however, got him away from Watervliet, which must be some consolation at least. Old Van has become so much pleased with line duty that I hardly think he could be bribed to accept an appointment in a staff corps. I saw him yesterday; he came down in the boat with Major Childs, who has gone to Fort Dallas, below this place, with sixty men from his post and sixty from here, for the purpose of making an expedition into the Everglades to oust Sam Jones from his cornfields. I think it highly probable that they may do something if they will go to work properly, for the Indians are there, I know, as we have frequently seen their fires at night, and they do not expect to see any of our men there at this season of the year; therefore, if the major will only manage the affair well, he may add fresh laurels to those he has already won. I have been left behind to take care of this infernal place in consequence of being commissary, etc.

This will be the only opportunity I shall have of distinguishing myself, and not to be able to avail myself of it is too bad. They say at St. Augustine that the Third will be ordered to Old Point this fall, but there have been so many sayings of the kind this summer that I begin to have no faith in them.

Colonel Worth has been on a grand scout, but did not succeed in discovering any fields or Indians. Major Childs thinks that some regiment of infantry will come to these lower posts this fall, and we will be concentrated at Fort Pierce preparatory to a grand expedition to the Okechobee, where they think the whole Indian force has retired as the last point of safety.

I am glad you exposed the doings of those people of the Academic Board; they deserve something worse than exposition of the Engineer Department.

I have not heard from Gardiner or Martin yet; what they are doing I can not learn. Herbert has written only once since my arrival in Florida; he had just then returned from furlough. From his accounts I should say that he had been enjoying himself in fine style.

I have just heard that poor Job Lancaster has been killed by lightning. I have heard no news lately which has distressed me more, for he was one of the very best of men. Wardwell is also dead; he had the fever which has been prevailing in the western part of the territory. You must write again soon.

Yours truly,

[*signed*]   GEORGE H. THOMAS[6]

The four men mentioned in his letter were members of the Class of 1840 and at graduation stood as follows: Lancaster, seventh; Martin, fourteenth; Gardiner, twenty-sixth; and Wardwell, twenty-ninth. Of the four, Martin joined the Confederacy and fought for the South.[7]

The prolonged Seminole War was due to apathy and indifference on the part of Government officials who failed to appreciate its magnitude and to devise effective measures to cope with it. Defeat followed defeat, while the ever-mounting casualties were out of all proportion to the numbers of the enemy. The cost of the war was also extremely high in relation to the numbers engaged. The natural defenses of the fighting area enabled the Indians to withdraw when outnumbered, and to assume the offensive when smaller units opposed them and there was a good chance of slaughtering every member of it. This type of warfare continued with its toll of numerous officers and men to match the relatively insignificant losses by the Seminoles. Tragically, a well-planned campaign comprising full quotas of men and equipment would have ended the war in a minimum of time, cost, and human lives.[8]

Lieutenant Thomas spent almost a year in Florida before participating personally in an assignment of a strictly warlike nature. Early in November, 1841, the commander at Fort Lauderdale, Captain Richard D. A. Wade, was instructed to make an excursion into some of the Indian villages for the purpose of subjugating the inhabitants. Thomas was placed in charge of sixty men and named second in command to Captain Wade, under whom he had served since the beginning of his period of service against the Indians. Complete details of the expedition are described in the following report:

6. Coppee, *op. cit.*, pp. 7-9.

7. George W. Cullum, *Biographical Register of Officers and Cadets of the U. S. Military Academy* (Boston, 1891), Vol. I, p. 603.

8. Richard W. Johnson, *A Soldier's Reminiscences* (Philadelphia: J. B. Lippincott Co., 1886), p. 16.

FORT LAUDERDALE, E.F., November 13, 1841.

SIR,—In pursuance to the instructions contained in your communication of the 24th September, I set out on the morning of the 5th inst., accompanied by Lieutenant Thomas, Third Artillery, Assistant Surgeon Emerson and sixty non-commissioned officers and privates, embarked in twelve canoes and provisioned for fifteen days. We proceeded by the inland passage to the northward, coming out in the bay at the Hillsborough Inlet, and in such manner that our canoes were concealed from the view of an Indian whom I there discovered fishing on the northern point of the inlet. I made the requisite dispositions immediately to land, and succeeded in surprising him. By operating on his hopes and fears, I induced him to lead us to his Indian village, fifteen miles distant in a westerly direction. This we reached on the morning of the 6th; surprised and captured twenty Indians, men, women, and children; took six rifles, destroyed fourteen canoes and much provisions of the usual variety. Of those who attempted to escape eight were killed by our troops. We returned to our boats the same forenoon with our prisoners, and proceeded up a small stream towards the Orange Grove haul-over, where we encamped for the night. On the morning of the 7th, after proceeding three miles farther north, the stream became too shallow for canoe navigation, and we made here a camp, leaving the prisoners, the boats, and a sufficient guard in charge of Dr. Emerson. Under the guidance of an old Indian found among our prisoners, who is called Chia-chee, I took up the line of march through nearly a mile of deep bog and saw-grass, then through the pine barren and some hummocks to a cypress swamp a distance of some thirty miles northward. Here (on the 8th inst.) we were conducted to another village, which we also surrounded, and surprised and captured twenty-seven Indians, took six rifles and one shot-gun, and destroyed a large quantity of provisions and four canoes. The next morning (November 9) we set out on our return to the boats, on a more easterly route than the former, which led us to the shores of Lake Worth, where we found and destroyed a canoe, a field of pumpkins, and an old hut. In the afternoon of this day one man came in and surrendered himself, thus making the whole number of our Indian prisoners forty-nine. At 11 A.M. of the 10th we arrived at our boats and proceeded to the little Hillsborough bar by evening, and in the afternoon of the next day (November 11) we returned to Fort Lauderdale without any loss on our part, after an absence of six days. Having seen much in the old man Chia-chee to inspire my confidence in his integrity, I permitted him to go out from our camp (on the 10th November) to bring in other Indians, which he promised to do in three or four days. This promise he subsequently redeemed, having on the 14th inst. brought in six (four men and two boys) at Fort Lauderdale.

My warmest thanks are due to Dr. Emerson and Lieutenant Thomas for their valuable and efficient aid in carrying out my orders; and of the conduct of the troops likewise, without any exception, I can speak only in terms of the highest praise.

I have the honor to be, very respectfully,

> Your obedient servant,
> [*Signed*] R. D. A. WADE,
> *Captain Third Artillery,*
> *Commanding Expedition.*[9]

The report of Captain Wade was then forwarded to the adjutant-general by the commanding officer, Colonel W. J. Worth, with the following endorsement:

I have the satisfaction to forward the accompanying report of the successful operations of Captain Wade, Third Artillery, acting under the orders of his immediate commander, Major Childs. This very creditable affair will operate the most favorable influence upon the closing scenes of this protracted contest, and I but do equal justice to the distinguished merit and conduct of Captain Wade, and the expectations of the service, in respectfully asking that the special notice of the Department of War may be extended to him and his gallant assistant, Second Lieutenant G. H. Thomas, of the same regiment.

> Respectfully, etc.,
> [*Signed*] W. J. WORTH,
> *Colonel Commanding.*[10]

Pursuant to Colonel Worth's recommendation, Lieutenant Thomas was given the brevet rank of first lieutenant retroactive to November 8, 1841, "for gallantry and good conduct in the war against the Florida Indians."[11]

Second Lieutenant George H. Thomas, 3d artillery, was the second of Captain Wade in the important service rendered by that officer,

---

9. *Ibid.*, pp. 18-20; John T. Sprague, *The Florida War* (New York, 1848), pp. 392-93.

10. Johnson, *op. cit.*, pp. 20-21.

11. *Ibid.*, p. 21; Cullum, *op. cit.*, Vol. I, p. 600.

and his strenuous coadjutor; this officer has rendered very efficient service, and is highly meritorious, and deserving the brevet of first-lieutenant, for which he is recommended. [Sprague, *Florida War*, p. 556.]

It is true that the type of operations in the Seminole War cannot compare with open warfare between contending forces: nevertheless, a passing acquaintance with the events in which Thomas participated is important in showing that from the very start of his career he established a pattern of outstanding performance that enlarged as the difficulties expanded.

When the November 8 expedition returned, they found that a replacement, Captain Erasmus Darwin Keyes of the West Point Class of 1832, had been appointed to succeed Captain Wade in command of Fort Lauderdale. Captain Keyes discovered early that the bill of fare and living conditions generally were far below the standards enjoyed in a staff position in Washington, as told by none other than Keyes himself.[12]

> I went into another thatched hut, and sat down on a block of wood at a table composed of two unpainted planks which rested upon stakes driven into the sand. A complement of tin plates, pewter spoons, rusty knives, and two-pronged forks, constituted the table setting. The breakfast was brought in, and it consisted in muddy coffee without milk, brown sugar, hard bread, tough buckwheat cakes, and semi-fluid rancid butter, held in a cracked teacup.[13]

> My first dinner at Fort Lauderdale differed from my first breakfast by substitution of bean soup and salt pork for buckwheat cakes and commissary whiskey for muddy coffee which recalled the sumptuous fare in Washington.[14]

Captain Keyes and Lieutenant Thomas became well acquainted and entertained for each other a mutually high regard. Keyes observed that in Florida Lieutenant Thomas was about twenty-six years of age, six feet tall, his form symmetrical, inclining to plumpness, complexion blond and his eyes large and deep blue. In addition, "the shape and carriage of his head and facial expression corresponded with my idea of a patrician of ancient Rome."[15]

---

12. Erasmus D. Keyes, *Fifty Years' Observation of Men and Events* (New York, 1884), p. 166.

13. *Ibid.*, p. 164.

14. *Ibid.*, p. 165.

15. *Ibid.*, p. 166.

Keyes relieved Thomas of his duties as quartermaster, which he had held since his assignment to Florida, and told of the many evenings spent together discussing experiences and incidents of mutual interest. One of these concerned a Lieutenant Shrover, the new quartermaster, whom Keyes had tried three times unsuccessfully to locate in his tent. Thomas told him that Shrover would pass within twenty minutes. Keyes followed the suggestion and, sure enough, within ten minutes along came Shrover.[16] Another story related by Thomas described the method used to locate a certain officer who was addicted to the tobacco-chewing habit. This officer habitually sat in a position from which he could expectorate in any direction, either right, left, or straight ahead. "Now," said Thomas, "you may come in at the window and follow up the line of tobacco juice on the floor, or you may descend the chimney and trace from that, and at the intersection of the two lines you discover 'B'." These yarns illustrate that Thomas was not without a sense of humor. In summing up his experiences with Thomas, it is not surprising that Keyes reported, "The happiest illusion of my youth and the most joyous encounters of my life have left me no more benignant traces in my memory than my associations with George H. Thomas."[17]

The Seminoles moved far into the interior of the Everglades following the final fall campaign and, as a result, a new or inactive phase of the military occupation began. It was clear that warfare was either about over or that it was pushed somewhat into the future. Under the circumstances, Lieutenant Thomas embarked by boat with his company in December, 1841, and sailed around the Florida peninsula to Army Headquarters at the top of Tampa Bay.[18] The stay at Headquarters was short, however, and in February, 1842, the organization left for New Orleans in order mainly to replenish supplies and equipment.[19]

Keyes commented that Thomas was of an even temperament, was never violently demonstrative, and was calm when entering and leaving a battle. He observed also that although Thomas was seldom very early in filling an appointment, he never knew him to be late, impatient, or in a hurry. His movements were deliberate; he was supremely self-possessed but not arrogant; and he issued and followed orders with serenity. His deportment was dignified before friends and reserved before strangers and casual acquaintances. He was sociable and had a subtle humor that became evident through

---

16. *Ibid.*, p. 171.
17. *Ibid.*, pp. 166-69, 179.
18. *Ibid.*, p. 170.
19. *Ibid.*, p. 171.

his use of illustrations and similes. He was a most accomplished and capable officer whose turn of mind, although scientifically inclined, was directed toward good reading and other worthy interests. The qualities in which he outshone all of his contemporaries were judgment, impartiality, and integrity, in all of which he had no superiors. After the Civil War, Keyes and Thomas met in San Francisco where, as Major General, Thomas was commander of the Division of the Pacific.[20]

Keyes recalled that General Thomas attended the wedding of his daughter, Caroline, and that in conversation with him he said, "Thomas, I notice no change in our social relations now and when in Florida, New Orleans and Charleston I ordered you to go and drill the company." Thomas replied, "There is none, and why should there be?" "Three days after that conversation I saw him in his coffin, and such was the noble repose of his face that I might have supposed he was asleep.[21]

"There is a moral in the life and services of Thomas. He was strictly conscientious, he loved Virginia, and his affections for the South were strong. He was warm also to the Union."[22]

New Orleans, Fort Moultrie and Fort McHenry

Few details are available concerning the short period of service of Thomas in New Orleans, but it is probable that the fortifications and landmarks from the war of 1812 were of more than passing interest to him. This was the base of operations of the famous pirate Jean Lafitte, who gave vital aid to General Andrew Jackson in repelling the British invaders under General Sir Edward Pakenham at the Battle of New Orleans, January 8, 1815. This famous battle was fought after the treaty of peace was signed between Great Britain and the United States. The British troops, fresh from successes in the Peninsular War against Napoleon Bonaparte, numbered 10,000, and were opposed by slightly more than 5,000 Americans under General Jackson. Flushed with victory, nevertheless the British lost 2,036 men compared with only 71 lost by the Americans,[23] and suffered an overwhelming defeat. Thus Lieutenant Thomas could review firsthand the result of unerring marksmanship as exemplified by the American defenders behind a stout defensive position. The lesson

20. *Ibid.*, pp. 166-70.
21. *Ibid.*, p. 167.
22. *Ibid.*
23. *Encyclopedia Americana, op. cit.*, Vol. XX, p. 160.

was evidently not lost upon him, for at Chickamauga it was this type of barricade, in combination with splendid fire power and discipline, that successfully resisted the onslaughts of General Longstreet against Horseshoe Ridge commanded by Thomas. Certain it is that the soldiers and officers found New Orleans friendly and gay, and its dimly lighted streets beckoned them on nightly rounds of amusement.[24]

For a man whose life was devoted uninterruptedly to the military service, the few months of duty in New Orleans were unlike any other in the career of Thomas, with the possible exception of his tenure as an instructor at West Point. It was in these two assignments that he was either not under severe hardship comparable with actual warfare or on some remote and isolated tour of duty. Despite the comparative advantages of living adjacent to a city like New Orleans, no great disappointment was felt when the Third Regiment of Artillery was ordered to sail for Charleston, South Carolina, on July 1, 1842. The weather in New Orleans and other Gulf cities and towns was extremely hot and humid, and it was hoped that Charleston would be more enjoyable, if for no other reason. The heat through the Gulf was so intense that officers and men remained below deck during the day and walked above deck at nights. The trip lasted sixteen days, but they finally landed at Charleston on July 26, 1842.[25] The location of their quarters was Fort Moultrie, on Sullivan's Island in Charleston Harbor.[26] These troops, comprising companies D, E, G, and K of the Third Artillery, included a number of officers thereafter known to fame. William T. Sherman, of Company G, was to attain enduring fame by his March to the Sea in the Civil War; Braxton Bragg, Captain of Company E and commander of the Confederate Army in the battles before, in, and around Chattanooga, was to be thwarted from his quest for full victory by George H. Thomas, then a subaltern, not only at Chickamauga but also at Chattanooga; and John F. Reynolds, another subaltern of Bragg's at Fort Moultrie, was to be killed on the opening day of the Battle of Gettysburg, on July 1, 1863.[27]

Charleston society was delightful and something to look forward to by the young officers of the Army, who found it generally easy of access. Young well-to-do sons of the South had been fond of military life for a great number of years, and the life in no wise proved

24. Keyes, *op. cit.*, p. 173.

25. *Ibid.*

26. *Ibid.*

27. Don C. Seitz, *Braxton Bragg* (Columbia, S.C.: The State Co., 1924), pp. 3, 4.

a deterrent to their success in courting the young ladies.[28] It was not uncommon for officers at Fort Moultrie to invite prominent Charleston families to dinner at the fort.[29] Across the water from Fort Moultrie observers noted that ships from the North were unloading material for the construction of a foundation for Fort Sumter,[30] but they could not know that in April, 1861, Sumter would be fired on by the new nation of South Carolina from siege guns at Charleston. Indeed Federal Captain Robert Anderson at Fort Moultrie would surrender the fort on April 14, 1861, after thirty-two hours of bombardment from the shore batteries.

Fort Moultrie was constructed during the Revolutionary War by Colonel William Moultrie of the Second South Carolina Regiment. Material in its construction consisted primarily of palmetto logs, which were believed unable to withstand a siege, but the fort successfully withstood bombardment from the British Fleet commanded by Sir Peter Parker. On a miserably hot day, June 28, 1776, the palmetto logs absorbed the cannon balls as though they were being swallowed,[31] and the British Fleet withdrew in defeat.

During the early career of George H. Thomas it was the custom to grant a leave of absence to officers after two years of continuous duty. In November, 1843, he was granted leave so richly earned, and in company with Lieutenant John Pope began the trip northward, Thomas on his way to his home in Southampton County, Virginia, and Pope to Baltimore. They traveled by boat to Wilmington, North Carolina, where they boarded a train to Goldsboro, North Carolina. At Goldsboro they met another friend, Lieutenant John G. French, Class of 1843. The three decided to continue northward on the Weldon and Norfolk Railroad, which had a scheduled stop near the Thomas home. The night was extremely cold; snow covered the ground; and the rail accommodations were anything but comfortable. On the route to Norfolk the driving wheels of the locomotive could not make sufficient traction to move the train, due to heavy frost on the rails, and all were required to push the train over an elevation leading to a bridge.[32]

Pope had been graduated from West Point in 1842, seventeenth in a class of fifty-six,[33] and was destined to become the inglorious

28. *Ibid.*, p. 4.

29. Keyes, *op. cit.*, p. 173.

30. *Ibid.*, p. 176.

31. Howard H. Peckham, *The War for Independence* (Chicago: University of Chicago Press, 1959), p. 345.

32. Samuel G. French, *Two Wars* (Nashville, 1901), p. 24.

33. Cullum, *op. cit.*, Vol. II, p. 49.

commander of the defeated Union forces in the Second Battle of Manassas, August 29-30, 1862. French graduated fourteenth of thirty-nine in the Class of 1843, as stated, and although a native of New Jersey, he would fight for the South.[34]

Upon his return from leave, Lieutenant Thomas was assigned to Company C of the Third Artillery for duty at Fort McHenry, near Baltimore.[35] This was the site of the bombardment on September 13 and 14, 1814, by the British Fleet under Admiral Sir George Cockburn, and the defense of which, by the Americans under Major George Armistead, a Virginian, inspired the lines of "The Star-Spangled Banner" by Francis Scott Key.[36]

At the time Lieutenant Thomas served there, Fort McHenry was regarded as one of the most desirable Army posts in the service. The ladies of Baltimore, long famous for their beauty, undoubtedly had much to do with the attraction of the fort. It is reasonable to suppose that Lieutenant Thomas moved in these circles, and that such activities were appreciated all the more because of their contrast with the usual peacetime military service.[37] This tour of duty was not to be for long, however. In October, 1844, following his promotion to the permanent rank of first lieutenant, on April 30, 1844, he was reassigned to Company E of the Third Artillery at Fort Moultrie. In February, 1845, he was on a tour of recruiting duty in New York, but returned to Fort Moultrie in March, after a little more than a month of service.[38]

The limited size of the American Army in those early days was conducive to making the relatively few officers comprising it very much in demand for social occasions. The dignity, courtesy, manliness, and military bearing with which Lieutenant Thomas was endowed contributed to the highest regard of him as a gentleman. At both Fort Moultrie and Fort McHenry his excellent qualities, combined with his distinguished military service performed in the Florida Indian War, gave him unusual recognition.[39]

34. *Ibid.*, p. 9.

35. Donn Piatt, *General George H. Thomas* (Cincinnati, 1891), p. 63.

36. *Fort McHenry* (Washington, D.C.: National Park Service, 1950), pp. 10-15.

37. French, *op. cit.*, p. 4.

38. Thomas B. Van Horne, *The Life of Major General George H. Thomas* (New York: Charles Scribner's Sons, 1882), p. 4.

39. Coppee, *op. cit.*, p. 11.

CHAPTER IV

The Mexican War

ON JUNE 26, 1845, just a few months after his return from recruiting duty in New York, Lieutenant Thomas left with Company E under orders to report to General Zachary Taylor in Texas. They arrived at New Orleans on July 19 and left by boat on July 24 for Texas.[1] In August, Company E and the Third and Fourth Infantry Regiments established a position at Corpus Christi, Texas, and became the first United States troops to occupy the soil of Texas.[2] This was highly significant, since Texas declared her independence from Mexico following the victory at San Jacinto on April 12, 1836. The battle was fought about twenty miles from the present city of Houston between some 1,600 Mexicans under General Santa Anna and 783 Texans under General Sam Houston. The Mexican Army as a military organization was almost completely destroyed; 630 were killed, 200 wounded, and 730 taken prisoner. The Texans lost seven killed and two mortally wounded.[3]

After her declaration of independence from Mexico, Texas claimed that her western boundary was the Rio Grande to its source and thence due north to 42 degrees north latitude. In the wake of the victory at San Jacinto, the United States, France, and several other countries, excepting Mexico, recognized the independence of Texas. In December, 1845, the United States admitted Texas into the Union with the understanding that the dispute over the boundary would be settled by the United States. President Polk agreed with Texas on the claim, and on January 13, 1846, ordered the troops to occupy the east bank of the Rio Grande as the western boundary of the United States. Mexico contended that the true boundary was the Neuces

1. Thomas B. Van Horne, *The Life of Major General H. Thomas* (New York: Charles Scribner's Sons, 1882), p. 5.

2. *Ibid.*; Linus B. Brockett, *Our Great Captains* (New York, 1865), p. 164.

3. *Encyclopedia Americana* (New York: American Book—Stratford Press, Inc., 1954), Vol. XXIV, p. 241.

River, 100 miles to the west, and that therefore General Taylor was occupying Mexican territory.[4]

Before proceeding with the events in which Lieutenant Thomas participated, it is important to summarize the causes that led to the Mexican War.

The general belief prevails with the average knowledgeable American that the Mexican War was precipitated by a mighty nation, the United States, against a much weaker neighbor solely in order to increase her territory. Certainly this was the general impression sought to be created in the public mind by Whig politicians and by Abolitionist crusaders, who resisted fiercely any expansion of southwestern United States out of fear that it would also expand slavery.[5]

The direct cause of the break in diplomatic relations between the two countries was the annexation of Texas by the United States, and not the confused claims to territory between the Neuces River and the Rio Grande. Annexation did not come in a hurry; in fact, the United States delayed the act for nine years, or until it was certain that Texas was truly independent. Furthermore, there was strong evidence that Texas, recoiling from the apparent aloofness of the United States, was considering the formation of an alliance with Great Britain.[6]

Difficulties between the United States and Mexico, extending over a number of years prior to 1845, began to take definite outline. Texas, buoyed by the recognition given her by other countries, felt strong and independent enough to defy Mexico, from which she believed herself fully separated. No one familiar with the facts had any basis for believing that the former relationship, so much desired by Mexico, would be restored. The declaration of Mexico that she would not under any circumstances give recognition to Texas did not make her position popular. Daniel Webster was opposed to the annexation, although holding that recognition by the United States and other countries made Mexico's stand groundless. In any case grave national interests of the United States appeared to demand annexation.[7]

Another matter of interest at the time was the belief that all of northern Mexico was dissatisfied and therefore ready for secession from Mexico. This dissatisfaction was attributable to a lack of confidence in the government. There were those who feared that President

---

4. *Ibid.*, Vol. XVII, p. 737.

5. Robert S. Henry, *The Story of the Mexican War* (New York: Frederick Ungar Publishing Co., 1961), p. 32.

6. *Ibid.*

7. Justin H. Smith, *The War With Mexico* (New York, 1919), Vol. I, p. 82.

Sam Houston of Texas contemplated the establishing of a southwestern empire under European direction to include the present state of Oregon. It is obvious that this would have posed a serious threat to the security of the United States. In fact, the American Minister to Texas, Mr. A. J. Donelson, acknowledged that the creation of such an empire was possible, in which eventuality a bold and ambitious rival would have been at our back door. Another factor to be reckoned with was the antislavery movement in the United States, which, it was believed, impelled some Southerners to desire the withdrawal of their states from the Untied States and the merging with slave-holding Texas into a new union. This latter move not only would have made Texas a formidable rival both commercially and industrially; it also would have advanced the interests of Great Britain while simultaneously damaging the interests of the United States.[8]

Albert Gallatin, financier and statesman, opposed annexation in the beginning but wrote later that it was expedient, natural, and ultimately unavoidable. It was recognized that Mexico might resent and resist the actions of its former citizens, in rebelling against their government, taking a large slice of territory, defeating its army, capturing its president, and getting foreign recognition.[9]

On August 23, 1843, the Mexican ambassador warned the United States that his government would regard the annexation of Texas as a declaration of war. In November, further discussions were held, in which Secretary of State Calhoun reminded the Mexican representative that Texas was independent; therefore on this point it was felt that the annexation policy of the United States was at least in part approved. Perhaps in order to gain time to prove that his country's claim should be recognized, the Mexican ambassador was thought to have conveyed the impression to Calhoun that he believed his country considered Texas lost. He made it appear, however, that damages would be acceptable in settlement for the loss. At Calhoun's suggestion at this point further discussions were held, and Mexico was informed that, although no disrespect was intended, the United States had been compelled to conclude a treaty with Texas without consulting her. Assurances were given, however, that the United States was ready to settle all differences, including the boundary dispute. These proposals were rejected by the Mexican Cabinet, with the additional reminder that annexation meant war. In fact, proposals for settlement were construed as an admission of the validity of her claim, and instead of making a peaceful settlement of differences, all attempts

---

8. *Ibid.,* pp. 82-83.
9. *Ibid.,* p. 83.

at reaching a peaceful conclusion only increased the bitterness and danger of war.[10]

To further complicate matters, the treaty of annexation failed of passage in the United States Senate. Instead of finding a solution to her problems, Texas now found herself not only rejected by the United States but also in strained relations with England and France, which countries she had previously offended. Another danger to Texas rose when General Santa Anna, her long-time enemy, asked for 30,000 troops and a large sum of money to undertake another invasion of Texas. In an attempt to soften the bitterness between Mexico and Texas, Secretary of State Calhoun reminded Mexico that the United States was at fault, and that Texas should not be the object of her anger. He further reminded her that annexation was still pending, and for this reason, as well as that of humanity, the United States would not permit the matter to be resolved by threats and hostile actions.[11]

Following the signing of a joint resolution of Congress providing for annexation, Mexican Ambassador Almonte promptly broke diplomatic relations with the United States. Upon acceptance of annexation by Texas in mid-July, 1845, feeling once more rose to a high pitch, and Mexico prepared for war. A formal declaration was not made, inasmuch as she deemed sufficient her former warnings that annexation would be equivalent to a declaration. Actual war was to come, but it was still almost a year away.[12] The American Congress declared war on May 12, 1846, and President Polk signed it the next day.[13]

There can be little doubt that the long-standing troubles in the diplomatic area would have sooner or later led to war. Actual hostilities came about, however, in a very different manner. Diplomatic wrangles, claims, and counterclaims, aside from their ever-present danger of precipitating outright war, led to the presence of the Army of Occupation in Texas. The subsequent advance of the army under General Taylor increased still more the anger of Mexico and handed her an opportunity to strike back.[14]

It was inevitable that when Texas should approve annexation it would become the responsibility of the United States to defend her. For this reason the exact position of her southern boundary became a very important matter. In 1834, Mexico was not certain of the

10. *Ibid.*, pp. 84-86.
11. *Ibid.*, pp. 85-86.
12. *Ibid.*, pp. 86-87.
13. *Ibid.*, p. 183.
14. *Ibid.*, p. 138.

boundary and the American State Department was convinced that if an agreement over it had ever been reached it was now eliminated as a result of the war between Mexico and Texas. The claim of Texas extended as far as the Rio Grande, but she did not establish title through full occupation south of the Neuces River.[15]

The situation in respect of the United States was different. Before 1819, our government claimed that Louisiana's southwestern boundary ended at the Rio Grande. In other words, since the southern part of Louisiana was known as Texas, the latter state most certainly bordered on the Rio Grande. This contention was held by no less notable Americans than Jefferson, Madison, Monroe, John Quincy Adams, and Henry Clay, among many other prominent citizens. From this viewpoint it followed that when Texas was annexed to the United States the former official claim, maintained to the year 1819, became once more strengthened and confirmed. This viewpoint was supported as well by the knowledge that from 1819 to 1845 no other boundary line was established. Furthermore, since Texas had held her own against Mexico militarily while claiming the Rio Grande boundary, this viewpoint was strengthened still more. Belief in the old claim of the United States by President Polk, added to his promise to Texas that we would defend her claim if annexation should be accomplished, were factors that could not be ignored.[16]

Lieutenant Thomas participated in the engagements of Fort Brown, Resaca de la Palma, Monterey, and Buena Vista. He was brevetted three times for gallantry, two of which were to captain and major for his extraordinary conduct in the battles of Monterey and Buena Vista, respectively.[17] The other brevet, to first lieutenant, was for service in the Florida war against the Seminole Indians.

In March, 1846, Thomas and Company E of the Third Artillery, after service with the American Army at Corpus Christi, Texas, since July, 1845, were ordered to the Rio Grande. Together with Company I of the First Artillery and the Seventh Infantry Regiment under Major Jacob Brown, the fort, later named Fort Brown after the death of Major Brown, opposite Matamoras was occupied. General Taylor meanwhile dropped back to Point Isabel, where he established a base of supplies.[18]

At Fort Brown the troops were subjected to a continuous bombardment from May 3 to 8, and, although casualties were small, their gallant commander, Major Brown, was killed. He was succeeded by

15. *Ibid.*
16. *Ibid.*, pp. 138-39.
17. *Encyclopedia Americana, op. cit.*, Vol. XXII, p. 145.
18. Brockett, *op. cit.*, pp. 164-65; Van Horne, *op. cit.*, p. 5.

Captain Hawkins of the Seventh Infantry.[19] During the bombardment the officer in immediate command said to a young lieutenant who was sitting on a keg, with a calmness that contrasted with his associates and the general surroundings, "Well, Tom, what do you think of our service; good, eh?" Lieutenant Thomas replied, "Service excellent, but I am thinking you will need the ammunition you are throwing away." Thus was expressed a prophecy realized the very next day when the ammunition ran low.[20]

The Mexicans withdrew from their attack on May 8 in order to reinforce General Ampudia at Resaca de la Palma. Ampudia, on May 8, had been driven from Palo Alto, lying between Fort Brown and Point Isabel, in an indecisive battle, except for the retreat of the Mexicans. This engagement occurred while General Taylor was advancing to the relief of Fort Brown. On May 9 Ampudia was again defeated by Taylor at Resaca de la Palma and driven in headlong flight across the Rio Grande into Mexico at a point near Fort Brown. The troops in the fort played a major part in the victory, by pouring a steady rain of shot and shell into the disorganized columns of Mexicans seeking safety from the pursuing Taylor by crossing the Rio Grande.[21]

Lieutenant Thomas learned a valuable lesson at the siege of Fort Brown by reason of General Taylor's overextension of his lines of supply. It was therefore necessary for Taylor to obtain supplies before engaging the Mexicans. His success in the face of this inconvenience may be attributable to a lack of aggressiveness by the enemy; in short, if he had been of normal alertness the relieving force could have been stopped and the garrison defeated in due course. This experience must not have been lost upon Thomas, since the importance of being prepared for eventualities, come what may, was an outstanding characteristic throughout his career.[22] It is of more than passing interest that at Fort Brown and subsequently Thomas served under Captain Braxton Bragg, a future adversary on Tennessee and Georgia battlefields. Fort Brown, incidentally, was the forerunner of the present city of Brownsville, Texas.[23]

When Fort Brown was relieved, Matamoras was evacuated and occupied promptly by the Americans. General Taylor pitched his tent

19. Van Horne, *ibid.*

20. Donn Piatt, *General George H. Thomas* (Cincinnati, 1891), pp. 66-67.

21. Brockett, *op. cit.*, p. 165; Henry Coppee, *General Thomas* (New York, 1893), pp. 14-16.

22. W. S. Henry, *Campaign Sketches of the War With Mexico* (New York, 1847), p. 104.

23. Coppee, *op. cit.*, p. 15.

in the shade of a tree near the town. In his "attakapas pantaloons and a linen roundabout he sat enthroned in a box cushioned with an Arkansas blanket, and for dinner-table had a couple of rough blue chests. The pursuit of the Mexicans and a search for concealed weapons did not require his attention."[24]

On June 6, four companies of the First Infantry under Lieutenant Colonel Wilson, a company of Rangers, and two field pieces under command of Lieutenant Thomas were detailed to Reynosa, a town that had asked for American protection, some sixty miles distant.[25] Reynosa was on a high elevation and was dominated by a heavy church tower resembling an ancient castle. After spending a month there, Taylor ordered the force to Camargo, on the San Juan River near its confluence with the Rio Grande.[26]

Camargo was entered by the troops on July 14 and was found to be a town of some 5,000 inhabitants. A recent flood had severely damaged much of the town and left its surface covered with about a foot of mud. After clearing away much of the debris, an army of 15,000 men was accommodated over a distance of several miles along the river. To add to the discomfort, the place was very hot; drinking water was available only from the San Juan River; and sanitation was virtually nonexistent. Illness was suffered by the residents in epidemic proportions as a result of the intolerable conditions, and soon afterward contaminated the military; in fact, some regiments had as many as fifty per cent of their men incapacitated at one time The presence of ants, tarantulas, scorpions, mosquitos, frogs, and centipedes added to this made life for the troops a nightmare.[27] After about four months of such hardships, Lieutenant Thomas was ordered, in September, 1846, to return to his command.[28]

In a matter of just a few days Lieutenant Thomas and Company E under Captain Braxton Bragg, another artillery company under Captain Randolph Ridgeley, and two howitzers commanded by Captain Edward Webster, son of the great American orator Daniel Webster, advanced on the heavily defended adobe and stone stronghold of Monterey, about one hundred miles from Camargo.[29] The ground over which they marched was extremely dusty as far as Cerralvo, due to the soil deposits left by flood waters. The dust and

24. Smith, *op. cit.*, Vol. I, p. 204.
25. *Ibid.*
26. *Ibid.*, pp. 209-10.
27. *Ibid.*, pp. 211-12.
28. Brockett, *op. cit.*, p. 165.
29. Freeman Cleaves, *Rock of Chickamauga* (Norman, Okla.: University of Oklahoma Press, 1949), p. 30; Cadmus M. Wilcox, *History of the Mexican War* (Washington, D.C.: The Church News Publishing Co., 1892), p. 91.

the intense heat made day marching a severe hardship, and the shortage of good water was so acute that the men were almost crazed from thirst. When opportunity presented, they would brush the scum from stagnant water and drink, so thirsty were they. A gruesome sight along the route of march was the long line of wooden crosses marking the graves of deceased persons, not a few of which signified that a murder had been committed. The trip was not all bad, however. After the many discomforts experienced the awe-inspiring blue peaks of the Sierra Madre Mountains, which from day to day grew ever more distinct, came into fuller view.[30]

After leaving Cerralvo a far different picture of Mexico was observed, in addition to the beauty of the Sierra Madres. The country was fertile almost beyond description. Spanish dahlias and other flowers were in bloom. Fields of sugar cane and corn dotted the landscape, and groves of ebony and pecan were found in abundance. Cool sparkling water became plentiful every few miles during the remaining part of the march, so that thirst was no longer a problem.[31] In addition to all these gifts of nature, there were oranges, lemons, limes, pomegranates, bananas, and grapes.[32]

As the troops neared their destination of Monterey, they encamped near San Francisco, about ten miles therefrom, on September 19. General J. P. Henderson moved forward with the Texas troops and became engaged in a skirmish with the Mexican calvary, which promptly withdrew into the defenses of Monterey. Undaunted, the Texans followed as far as it was deemed expedient, or within full view of the Citadel, for perhaps a half hour or so, before retiring to the woods of San Domingo. Here General Taylor established headquarters about three miles from Monterey, in order to await the main army, and promptly ordered reconnaissances of the Mexican defenses both within and surrounding Monterey.[33]

The battle of Monterey began at six o'clock on the morning of September 21, 1846, when a Mexican cavalry force attacked the troops under General William Jenkins Worth at a point near the Topo and Saltillo roads. The deadly fire of the Texans was so destructive that the enemy retreated in confusion down the Saltillo road, after losing about a hundred men killed and wounded. The Americans hotly pursued them until the supply routes of the Mexicans were closed to them. In order to lend aid to General Worth's attack, General Taylor ordered infantry and artillery under General David E. Twiggs

30. Smith, *op. cit.,* Vol. I, p. 229.
31. *Ibid.,* pp. 236-37.
32. Samuel G. French, *Two Wars* (Nashville, 1901), p. 59.
33. Wilcox, *op. cit.,* pp. 90-91.

and General Pierce M. Butler, respectively, to advance toward Monterey. Part of this force was halted under the shelter of a slight ridge, and the remainder, including Bragg's battery of artillery, continued to the lower section of Monterey, to make a demonstration and take the enemy's works if possible without heavy losses.[34]

It was during the street fighting in Monterey that Thomas earned the brevet to captain "for gallant and meritorious conduct." General Henderson, commander of the Texas volunteers, wrote, "I beg leave also, under the authority of General Lamar, to compliment Lieutenant Thomas of the artillery and his brave men for the bold advance and efficient management of the force under his charge. When ordered to retire he reloaded his piece, fired a farewell shot at the foe and returned under a shower of bullets."[35] Additional praise came from General Twiggs, commander of the First Division, who said that Captains R. Ridgeley and B. Bragg and their subalterns, W. H. Shover, G. H. Thomas, J. F. Reynolds, C. L. Kilburn, and S. G. French deserve the highest praise for their skill and good conduct under the heaviest fire of the enemy, which, when an opportunity offered, was concentrated on them.[36]

On September 23, the third and last day of the Battle of Monterey, while Captain Bragg's battery centered its fire on the munitions stored in the Cathedral, Lieutenant S. G. French was ordered to clear a street leading to the plaza. After this mission was accomplished, General Taylor and staff marched through the street just cleared. Taylor immediately gained entrance to a corner store in the absence of the proprietor and was joined by General John A. Quitman with some troops and a gun under the command of Lieutenant Thomas. Quitman ordered French to fire his howitzer for the purpose of making a smoke screen through which Thomas might advance to a cross street. Upon gaining the objective, Thomas turned his gun into the barricaded street, which was defended by a piece of artillery. This was instrumental in gaining possession of the houses and driving the Mexicans toward the plaza.[37]

On November 14, General Quitman was chosen to proceed with his brigade to Tampico, and as artillery support he selected the units of Lieutenants Reynolds and French, both of whom were under the command of Thomas. The first objective was Victoria, the state capital of Tamaulipas, between Tampico and Monterey. The Sierra Madre Mountains were again enjoyed by the troops; this time they

34. *Ibid.,* pp. 92-93.
35. Van Horne, *op. cit.,* p. 5.
36. *Ibid.,* pp. 5-6.
37. French, *op. cit.,* pp. 66-67.

"looked thin enough for a man to sit astride of. In fact, at Santa Catarina, there is a vast hole through this ridge near 1,000 feet below the crest through which clouds, as if in another world, could be seen moving by day and stars by night."[38] The Christian holiday season had begun when the marchers stopped on a hilly road near the village of Villa Gran, on Christmas Day, 1846, in the midst of citrus groves and sugar estates. Lieutenants Reynolds and Thomas made the best of it by procuring eggs, but Lieutenant French failed in his search for a turkey.[39] General Quitman's force continued undisturbed until on December 29, 2,000 in number, they entered Victoria only a few hours after it had been abandoned by 1,500 enemy cavalry.[40] On January 4, 1847, General Taylor himself reached Victoria, his men no less tired and dirty than the detachment under General Quitman,[41] and was followed the same day by the troops under General Robert Patterson. This raised the total number of troops at Victoria to 6,000.[42]

The problem of supplies soon became acute, and General Taylor on January 12, 1847, ordered Generals Patterson and Twiggs to Tampico, with the assurance that he would follow if at all possible. The distance to be covered by the 4,733 men undertaking the trip to Tampico was roughly 168 miles by road, but the ten-day stay at Victoria gave them some rest in preparation for the arduous journey.[43] General Twiggs started with his force on January 14. He was followed by part of General Patterson's command on January 15 and the remainder on January 16.[44] These depletions left Taylor at Victoria with less than 1,000 Regulars, including Lieutenant Thomas with his two batteries, and a volunteer force made up in part of new recruits to confront 20,000 of the enemy.[45]

General Scott had been ordered on November 23, 1846, to take charge of all American troops in Mexico,[46] and when the news reached Taylor he is reported to have put mustard into his coffee instead of sugar.[47] It is only natural that General Taylor was disturbed and hurt by the elevation of Scott to over-all command; after all is said it was he who bore the brunt of the early campaigning and he was

38. *Ibid.*, p. 69; Wilcox, *op. cit.*, p. 187.

39. French, *op. cit.*, pp. 69-70.

40. Wilcox, *op. cit.*, p. 188; French, *op. cit.*, pp. 69-70.

41. Smith, *op. cit.*, Vol. I, p. 362.

42. George Gordon Meade, *The Life and Letters of General George Gordon Meade* (New York: Charles Scribner's Sons, 1913), pp. 172-73.

43. Smith, *op. cit.*, Vol. I, p. 365.

44. Wilcox, *op. cit.*, p. 194.

45. *Ibid.*, p. 195.

46. *Encyclopedia Americana*, *op. cit.*, Vol. XXIV, p. 546.

47. French, *op. cit.*, p. 71.

now expected to furnish seasoned troops developed under his command. It is not surprising that the lack of forethought on the part of the Government in failing to inform Taylor of his secondary role to Scott, and of the expropriation of his troops by Scott in the advance on Mexico City, was cause for misunderstanding.[48] This illustration of political bungling surely had its effect upon Lieutenant Thomas, who throughout his lifetime was noted for his distaste and contempt for the foibles of politics. Nothing better reflects this attitude of Thomas than his consistent refusal to benefit from other than well-earned promotion.

In order to familiarize Taylor with the objectives for prosecuting the war, General Scott dispatched a courier with his plans concerning, in particular, the movement of Taylor's troops to Tampico. It was contemplated that from the concentration point of Tampico the troops would sail by boat to Vera Cruz preparatory to the march on the Mexican capital. Unfortunately, the courier was intercepted by the Mexicans at Villa Gran and murdered, and, it is presumed, the plan intended for Taylor was delivered to the Mexican commander Santa Anna. Santa Anna was a former president of Mexico and commander of the Mexican forces in the struggle with Texas. Only recently he had returned from exile in Cuba.[49]

During the night of January 14, a copy of the message sent from Scott with the murdered courier was received by Taylor.[50] On January 16 Taylor started for Monterey with the remainder of his forces and arrived there on January 24.[51]

Early in February, Taylor moved south to strengthen the force at Saltillo and to aid in its defense. Here he established a camp, and by February 14 had 650 troops on the site with him. General Wool was left in command at La Angostura Pass, a little more than a mile distant, with 4,000 men. Taylor at once sent out reconnoitering parties from which he received the report that Santa Anna was advancing toward them in some force. Undaunted, he decided that if the enemy contemplated attack there was no better place than right here. He is reported to have said that if they do attack they will go back a good deal faster than they came.[52] Brave words indeed, but on February 21, following receipt of reliable reports that Santa Anna intended attacking Agua Nueva in full force, he withdrew in haste to Buena Vista. A number of versions of this action by Taylor

48. *Ibid.*
49. *Encyclopedia Americana, op. cit.,* Vol. XXIV, p. 276.
50. Smith, *op. cit.,* Vol. I, p. 365.
51. *Ibid.,* p. 368.
52. *Ibid.,* pp. 373-74; Wilcox, *op. cit.,* pp. 210-12.

are revealing in that they indicate a general awareness that he was not overendowed with military ability; and nothing better supports this conclusion than the statement attributed to him that he was leaving Agua Nueva because of being vulnerable from either side. This he should have known before the reported approach of Santa Anna.[53]

Smoke from burning wagons and supplies left at Agua Nueva in the wake of the retreating Americans convinced Santa Anna that his enemy had stampeded. Thus assured, he urged his command to an increased tempo hoping to intercept them before the Rio Grande could be reached. Taylor's advance forces, in the meantime, had reached the Hacienda of Buena Vista on the morning of February 22.[54]

The battlefield of Buena Vista is in a valley about two miles wide, on each side of which is a range of the Sierra Madre Mountains. A stream west of the road and cut deep into the earth flows northward, while to the east is an elevation joined to a still higher but narrow ridge, with a plateau extending to the base of the mountains. This opening between the high point of land and the stream is called La Angostura, or The Narrows, by the Mexicans.[55]

Near the front of The Narrows and east of the road are two short ravines, while beyond is a much larger one running southeastward toward the mountains. Next is a plateau through which runs a short ravine and another longer ravine. Beyond is a plateau, and farther on is a somewhat wider ravine running to the base of the mountains. Two columns of the Mexican army passed over a still higher ridge from the wide ravine, while under cover of the highest ridge General Santa Anna stopped and arranged his columns. All in all the topography of the area was such that both the cavalry and the artillery of the Mexicans were unable to exploit their advantage in numbers.[56]

The road at The Narrows was defended by eight guns of the Fourth Artillery under Major John M. Washington; two companies of the First Illinois, Lieutenant Colonel William Weatherford, held a short breastworks on the right of the road next to Washington's battery; the crest of the ridge on the left was held by the First and Second Illinois Regiments, Colonels Hardin and Bissell, with the latter a company of Texas Volunteers, Captain P. Edward Connor; the Second Kentucky, Colonel McKee, occupied the crest of the ridge on the left and rear; and the Arkansas and Kentucky cavalry

---

53. Smith, *op. cit.*, pp. 383, 554.
54. Wilcox, *op. cit.*, pp. 211-12; Smith, *op. cit.*, Vol. I, pp. 383, 554.
55. Wilcox, *ibid.*, p. 212.
56. *Ibid.*, 213.

regiments, Colonels Yell and Marshall, defended the extreme left near the base of the mountains.[57]

In reserve on the ridges just behind the front line were the Second and Third Indiana Regiments, Colonels Bowles and Lane; the Mississippi Rifles; the First and Second Dragoons; Captain Steen's and Brevet Lieutenant Colonel May's squadrons; and the Light Batteries of Captains Sherman and Bragg of the Third Artillery.[58]

As General Santa Anna approached The Narrows, after learning that General Taylor had evacuated Agua Nueva, General Wool in command there ordered the sounding of the long roll. The bands played "Hail, Columbia," the watchword "Honor of Washington" passed among the men, and before long they watched with keen delight the Mexicans approaching at a gallop in a cloud of dust. The Mexican commander saw at once that the Americans were in a strong position and decided to await the coming of his main army. He then transmitted a note through his chief medical officer, Dr. Vanderlinden, to General Taylor, at about 11 A.M., warning him that he was surrounded by 20,000 Mexicans and that he should surrender in order to avoid disaster. Further, aside from assurances that he wished to spare the certain cutting to pieces of Taylor's army, Santa Anna stipulated he would have an hour within which to make up his mind.[59] The reply from Taylor was immediate and to the point:

HEADQUARTERS ARMY OF OCCUPATION,
NEAR BUENA VISTA, February 22, 1847

SIR: In reply to your note of this date summoning me to surrender my forces at discretion, I beg leave to say that I decline acceding to your request.

With high respect, I am, sir, your obedient servant.

Z. TAYLOR,
Major-General United States Army.

SENOR GENERAL D. ANTONIO LOPEZ DE SANTA ANNA
Commander-in-Chief, Encantada.[60]

At about 3 P.M. Santa Anna deployed his forces and awaited the arrival of the remainder of his troops, which could be observed by

---

57. *Ibid.*
58. *Ibid.*
59. Smith, *op. cit.*, Vol. I, pp. 384-85; Wilcox, *op cit.*, pp. 214-15.
60. Wilcox, *ibid.*, pp. 214-15.

Taylor's spotters as they came up. General Ampudia then moved promptly toward the mountain base on the American left, as another force was dispatched to the American right and another detachment farther on. This latter force encountered Bragg's battery and the Second Kentucky, while on the left General Ampudia's troops exerted strong pressure against the Indiana, Kentucky, and Arkansas forces, which they outflanked but did not succeed in turning. Firing on both sides was lively, but a general engagement was not brought on until the following day.[61]

At about dawn on the morning of February 23, the Mexicans opened fire on the left and about sunrise the Mexicans advanced into a ravine separating the two opposing forces. This movement brought action from Lieutenant O'Brien's 12-pound howitzer and destruction to the enemy. In the meantime, the Mexicans attempted to escape musketry fire by scaling the ravine. On the right, Bragg's section of artillery remained in an advanced position. Washington continued in La Angostura Pass. To the left of the Second Illinois was a 12-pound howitzer under Lieutenant French and a 6-pounder under Lieutenant Thomas. The two remaining guns were in position as posted on the previous day under Captain Thomas W. Sherman and Lieutenant John F. Reynolds. All guns were supporting either infantry or other units defending the area against the enemy.[62]

Santa Anna's strategy was for General Blanco's division to create a diversion by moving against Major Washington's battery at La Angostura with cavalry and a twelve-pounder; but this move met with such withering fire from the defending guns that almost entire columns of Mexicans appeared to drop from view, while those still able to flee sped for cover. Next, the division of Manuel Lombardini, in position near an eight-pound battery, was ordered to advance, with cavalry support, across the ridges and ravines. F. Pacheco's division was directed to proceed up the main ravine and on to the plateau, there to join Lombardini in pushing back Taylor's left flank, which General Ampudia would turn. United, all of the divisions were to sweep everything before them, clear La Angostura Pass, and seal the victory.[63]

Pacheco's division, however, became engaged in a bitter struggle with the Second Indiana Regiment which was supported by the guns of Lieutenant O'Brien. After perhaps a half hour of desperate fighting, General Joe Lane ordered his Third Indiana to advance, hoping thus to drive Pacheco back into the ravine and also to move beyond range

61. *Ibid.*, pp. 215-217.
62. *Ibid.*, p. 219.
63. *Ibid.*, p. 220; Smith, *op. cit.*, Vol. I, p. 389.

of the Mexican guns then raking his left and rear. Lieutenant O'Brien moved forward with his battery and swept the enemy with grape and canister. At this time, unfortunately, Colonel Bowles ordered his Second Indiana to retreat, why, nobody seemed to know, but the retreat soon became a stampede in which four companies of Arkansas mounted riflemen joined. This left O'Brien alone and with no choice but to withdraw. This he did, leaving behind a four-pounder.[64]

Lombardini's division had been delayed but reached the line of Pacheco about this moment. Being wounded, however, he was replaced by F. Perez, who made a change of front that forced the Americans to retire. Bissel's regiment, the Second Illinois, Steen's dragoons, and the two guns of Thomas and French had remained in position. Thomas and French fired their guns at Pacheco's troops and inflicted upon them a terrible loss.[65] The Mexicans continued advancing, despite fierce opposition, and passed beyond the left of the Second Illinois and those supported by the guns of Lieutenants French and Thomas, who were holding their position. Captain Sherman was now sent to the plateau with his remaining force, and with Lieutenant Reynolds's aid maintained a continuous fire on the advancing Mexicans. The Second Kentucky Regiment and part of Bragg's battery also added strength to the guns of Sherman. Taken altogether, these units converged against the enemy at the foot of the mountains to the left, crossed the main plateau, came within range of the Mexicans, and wrought terrible destruction upon them, despite their standing firm for some time. The Mexican cavalry pursued the retreating Arkansas and Indiana troops and were united with Ampudia's force near the mountains, which latter had streamed down the mountain in considerable haste and gained higher ground, which reduced the Americans' former advantage of defense.[66]

General Taylor, who had gone to Saltillo the previous night with additional troops, returned to the battle in time to face the Mexican advance. To General Wool's remark to Taylor, "General, we are whipped," he replied, "That is for me to determine." Wool left at once in an attempt to restore order to the badly shattered American left, rallied the broken troops, and thereby rendered a most timely service.[67]

General Santa Anna was unable to push the Americans, including Sherman, McKee, Bragg, Hardee, and Bissell from the main plateau. However, he did succeed in bringing up a battery of sixteen-pounders

64. Wilcox, *op. cit.*, p. 220.
65. *Ibid.*, pp. 221-22.
66. *Ibid.*, pp. 222-23.
67. *Ibid.*, pp. 223-24.

to the point held by Lieutenant O'Brien, in the morning. These guns did much damage to the Americans, but the fire from Bragg's and Sherman's artillery did considerable damage also to the infantry supporting the sixteen-pounders and compelled them to retire. Lieutenant O'Brien once more made his appearance on the plateau, and with Lieutenants Thomas and Garnett, in conjunction with the First and Second Illinois and the Second Kentucky regiments, kept the Mexicans from advancing. To the rear of the plateau were long lines of Mexican cavalry and infantry. Confronting them on the right were Captains Sherman and Bragg with their subordinates Thomas and Kilburn and supporting infantry.[68]

Santa Anna at this stage could have more than likely defeated the Americans, but his delay permitted Taylor to shift troops where they were most needed. After desperate fighting, when it appeared that Taylor was beaten, some 1,500 Mexican cavalry moved forward to cut off his retreat at the Saltillo road; but much to the surprise of everyone, except perhaps themselves, they slowed down and finally stopped within range of the Mississippi Rifles, the Second and Third Indiana regiments and Sherman's twelve-pound howitzer, and were cut to pieces. From the plateau and The Pass, artillery opened on the Mexican right, and as they withdrew the guns inflicted further damage upon them. These actions turned the tide of battle, and shells and shrapnel were dumped into the intermingled infantry and cavalry. At this point something strange occurred, when Santa Anna asked Taylor, under a flag of truce, "what he wanted." The American batteries stopped firing, but the Mexican batteries continued and General Wool ended the truce. This intermission permitted the Mexicans to continue their withdrawal, although fired on by the guns of O'Brien and Thomas.[69]

The final Mexican attack by General Perez was made with the reserves toward the plateau. General Taylor, unaware of this move, ordered Colonel Hardin with his six companies of the First Illinois to charge the enemy, and he did so promptly. Soon other units, realizing the Mexican reserves were advancing, joined Hardin and moved along with him. Suddenly the enemy emerged from the ravine only to be confronted by a withering fire from Hardin's First Illinois, Bissell's Second Illinois, and McKee's Second Kentucky. Then O'Brien's two six-pounders and Thomas's single gun poured a hot fire into their ranks; but the Mexican fire was also damaging, killing many Americans, including Colonels Hardin and McKee, and wounding among others Lieutenant Colonel Henry Clay, Jr. This was the

68. *Ibid.*, pp. 225-26.
69. Smith, *op. cit.*, pp. 393-94; Wilcox, *op. cit.*, pp. 232-33.

period in the battle when victory for the Mexicans seemed certain. Fortunately General Taylor returned to the plateau after a short absence, although only Lieutenant O'Brien with his two guns and Lieutenant Thomas with his one gun were there. Troops ordered from the left were striving to reach the plateau, as were the artillery, cavalry and infantry from other points, as it became painfully evident that victory rested with the ability of O'Brien and Thomas to hold the enemy at bay until their arrival.

O'Brien was about a hundred yards from Thomas, but they loaded and reloaded their guns so rapidly that, although the enemy continued advancing, the ground was strewn with their dead and wounded. O'Brien and Thomas also suffered severe losses in both men and horses, but they had put a severe dent in the enemy's plans. Captain Bragg was first to reach the plateau and went immediately into action with his guns. It was not long before he received from General Taylor the famous message, "A little more grape, Captain Bragg; a great deal of grape, Captain Bragg." This must have produced the desired result, for in his report Taylor stated that Captain Bragg's first three discharges of canister routed the enemy and saved the day. Captain T. W. Sherman also reported that Lieutenant Thomas, his subordinate, "had been constantly engaged during the forenoon in the preservation of that important position; that he behaved nobly throughout the action as his coolness and firmness contributed not a little to the success of the day; and that he more than sustained the reputation he has long enjoyed in his regiment as an accurate and scientific artillerist."[70] It was therefore not surprising that Lieutenant Thomas was again promoted, this time to brevet major, making his third brevet, an almost unprecedented number up to that time. The promotion was dated February 23, 1847, "for gallant and meritorious conduct in the battle of Buena Vista."[71]

Buena Vista, one of the most extraordinary of battles, ended the war in the northern theater. The Americans had lost 267 killed, 456 wounded, and 23 missing, a total of 746 out of 4,757 engaged, whereas the enemy lost, according to best estimates, between 1,500 and 2,000 of an estimated total of 18,000 participating. This comparison looms all the more incredible in view of the fact that the bulk of experienced men had been sent to Scott, and that most of the men replacing them had never before seen action of any kind. The magnificent courage

70. Smith, *ibid.;* Wilcox, *op. cit.,* pp. 232-34; Van Horne, *op. cit.,* p. 6; Henry Stone, *Some Federal and Confederate Commanders* (Boston: Houghton Mifflin Co., 1895), pp. 168-69.

71. George W. Cullum, *Biographical Register of Officers and Cadets of the U. S. Military Academy* (Boston, 1891), Vol. I, p. 600.

displayed against immensely superior forces had seldom been surpassed in warfare. It was a battle in which Americans familiar with its difficulties and outstanding results have ever been justifiably proud. Not the least of its results was its endowment of the nickname "Old Rough and Ready" on General Taylor, and its help in installing him in the White House. Despite the reluctance of some critics to concede to him more than ordinary ability, it cannot be forgotten that his raw courage and energy, plus his ability to inspire confidence in his men, did much to bring the victory. Taylor acknowledged that the help of his professional officers, in particular General Wool, and the artillery were indispensable. General Wool reported that "I also desire to express my high admiration and to offer my warmest thanks to Captains Washington, Sherman and Bragg, and Lieutenants O'Brien and Thomas with their batteries, to whose services at this point and on every part of the field, I think it but justice to say we are mainly indebted for the great victory so successfully achieved by our arms over the great force opposed to us—more than twenty thousand men and seventeen pieces of artillery. Without our artillery we would not have maintained our position a single hour."[72]

72. Smith, *op. cit.*, pp. 395-96; Wilcox, *op. cit.*, pp. 236-38; Van Horne, *op. cit.*, pp. 6-7

George H. Thomas, exhibited in the campaign of Florida, at

CHAPTER V

From the Mexican War
to the Civil War

ONE OF the by-products of the Mexican War was the development
of officer material for the forthcoming Civil War. Among those who
later attained fame as Union officers were Ulysses S. Grant, Henry
W. Halleck, George G. Meade, George B. McClellan, John F.
Reynolds, William T. Sherman, John Sedgwick, and George H.
Thomas. Among the leading Confederate officers were Lewis A.
Armistead, Pierre Gustave T. Beauregard, Braxton Bragg, Daniel H.
Hill, Robert E. Lee, Thomas J. (Stonewall) Jackson, Albert Sidney
Johnston, and Joseph E. Johnston.

Lieutenant Thomas exhibited in the Mexican War those traits that
afforded a preview of still greater achievements to come in the Civil
War. His steadfastness and reliability at Monterey and Buena Vista
against great odds extended throughout his career to place him
above all others in American history in the mastery of the art of
defense.

Upon hearing of the exploits of Lieutenant Thomas, his native
Southampton County neighbors and friends were naturally most proud
and anxious to do him honor. Leading members of the community
called a meeting at Jerusalem, the county seat, on July 19, 1847,
selected Captain James Maget to preside, and named Mr. L. R.
Edwards as secretary. After delivering an appropriate address, in
which he recounted the character and gallant conduct of Captain
William Kello of the Eighth Infantry, another soldier from Southampton County, on leave due to illness, and Brevet-Major George H.
Thomas of the Third Artillery, on duty with General Zachary Taylor
in Mexico, Colonel William C. Parker proposed the following resolutions, which were approved unanimously:

Resolved, That whilst we glory in the unfailing fame which our heroic army in Mexico has acquired for herself and country, our attention has been especially drawn to the military skill, bravery and noble deportment of our fellow-countryman, George H. Thomas, exhibited in the campaign of Florida, at Fort Brown, Monterey and Buena Vista, in which he has given ample proof of the best requisites of a soldier—patience, fortitude, firmness and daring intrepedity.

Resolved, That as a testimonial of our high appreciation of his character as a citizen and a soldier, we will present to him a sword, with suitable emblems and devices and that [there] be appointed a committee to collect by subscription a sum sufficient for the purpose and cause to be fabricated a sword to be presented to the said George H. Thomas, through the hands of his noble and heroic commander, Major General Z. Taylor.

The committee appointed to collect funds to defray the cost of the sword and to order its fabrication and delivery consisted of Colonel W. C. Parker, Robert Ridley, Benjamin C. Pope, John Barham, Dr. Massenbury, Charles F. Urquhart, Jacob Barrett, Colonel Carr Barnes, William G. Thands, Robert G. Griffin and Dr. George W. Peete. The latter introduced a resolution, which was passed, that a copy of the proceedings be published, and that a copy be given to the mother and brothers of Lieutenant Thomas in addition to the copy accompanying the presentation of the sword.[1]

The sword, made by Horstman & Sons, of Philadelphia, may be described as follows:

"The pattern of the sabre is that used by the United States Dragoons. The blade is of the truest and prettiest steel, finished in a manner that would defy superiority of workmanship. The scabbard is of solid silver, standard value, beautifully enriched with engraved scroll work encircling military trophies, with the words: Florida, Ft. Brown, Monterey, Buena Vista, and an engraved vignette of the Battle of Monterey. The hilt is of basket form, most elaborately chased. The grip is solid silver, also enriched with engraved scrolls. The pommel is of gold, grasping an amethyst, and the rings and hands in bas-relief, and upon its grip is engraved an elephant."[2]

The underlying spirit of the citizens of Southampton County responsible for awarding the sword was in striking contrast to the

---

1. Thomas B. Van Horne, *The Life of Major General George H. Thomas* (New York: Charles Scribner's Sons, 1882), pp. 7-8; Donn Piatt, *General George H. Thomas* (Cincinnati, 1891), pp. 68-69.
2. Van Horne, *ibid.*, p. 9; Piatt, *ibid.*, p. 69.

bitterness directed toward him when he remained with the Union. The sword was kept in the family and finally turned over to the Virginia Historical Society shortly before the death of his sisters Judith and Fanny.[3] Judith is said to have refused to give the sword to George after the Civil War, and to have asserted that when the people who gave it to him demanded it she would surrender it.[4] The people who gave it were almost all long since deceased; furthermore, the sisters assumed an authority they did not have, since the sword was the property of George, none other. The sword was for services past, not subsequently, and their attitude was but an expression of the ridiculous and unwarranted hatred toward a great and loyal Southerner, an attitude that, thank God, has not been returned by the North against those who followed the South. It should be noted that the sword is still in the custody of the Virginia Historical Society; but unfortunately it is in a neglected condition, which still more reflects the attitude of Southerners toward one of their two greatest soldiers. There is little doubt that George cherished the sword above all other possessions, since he deemed it too precious to be worn except at his marriage.[5] His admiration for it is shown by the following letter acknowledging receipt of it:

BUENA VISTA, MEXICO
March 31, 1848

CAPTAIN JAMES MAGET,
Newsoms Depot,
Southampton, Va.

DEAR SIR:

Your letter of the 8th February transmitting the Resolutions of the citizens of Southampton County at a meeting in their Court House on the 19th July, 1847, was received by the last mail.

In accepting the Sword presented me by my fellow countrymen, and in acknowledging the very high compliment paid me in these resolutions, I beg you will present to the committee, and through my old friends of Southampton my sincere and heartfelt thanks—Aware that the little service I have been able to render my country, although performed with cheerfulness, and to the utmost of my ability, does not in the least entitle me to

3. Now in possession of the Virginia Historical Society, Richmond, Va.

4. *Virginia Magazine of History and Biography* (Richmond, 1932), Vol. XL, p. 331.

5. William S. Drewry, *The Southampton Insurrection* (Washington, D.C., 1900), p. 20.

this very high compliment from my old friends and fellow citizens. I shall always regard it as the result of kindness of heart and a friendliness of feeling on their part, which renders the obligation doubly grateful, and as such will ever be a proud collection to the last hour of my life. "Next to the consciousness of having done his duty the sympathy of friends is the highest reward of a soldier."

In conclusion, I beg you will accept my hearty acknowledgments for the very flattering and friendly manner in which you have communicated, to me, these resolutions, and with every wish for long continued health and happiness to yourself and family, I remain

Your friend and obedient servant,

GEORGE H. THOMAS[6]

The sentiment expressed by Thomas that "I shall always regard it [the sword] as the result of kindness of heart and a friendliness of feeling on their part," however confidently felt at the time, could not survive the bitterness toward him as a result of his enduring loyalty to the United States. Many must have been his hours of grief as he reflected upon the loss of family, and the bitterness toward him of these once friends and neighbors for doing his whole duty as he saw it. When this is considered in relation to the very great number of citizens in the seceded states who had no choice in secession, and the very large number who went north to fight for the Union, the bitterness toward Thomas does not make sense. Lincoln said, "It may well be questioned whether there is, to-day, a majority of the legally qualified voters of any State, except perhaps South Carolina, in favor of disunion."[7]

On August 20, 1847, Company E of the Third Artillery was ordered to return to Texas, where it established quarters at Brazos de Santiago, near the mouth of the Brazos River. Lieutenant Thomas was in charge of the commissary depot until February 1, 1849, on which date he was granted a six months' leave of absence. This was only the second such leave taken by him since his graduation from West Point in 1840, and speaks much for his devotion to duty. Upon his return on August 1, 1849, he rejoined Company E at Fort Adams, Rhode Island, to which it had been ordered from Texas in December, 1848, and on August 6, 1849, was transferred to Company B of the same regiment, the Third Artillery.[8]

---

6. Copy furnished by the Virginia Historical Society, Richmond, Va.

7. Paul M. Angle, *Lincoln's Speeches and Letters* (New York: E. P. Dutton and Co., 1957), p. 177.

8. Van Horne, *op. cit.*, pp. 7, 9.

Following the renewal of hostilities between the whites and Indians in Florida, Company B of the Third Artillery was ordered there on September 12, 1849. Soon after arriving, Thomas was instructed by his commanding officer to organize and lead an expedition against the Seminoles. Undoubtedly his prior military experience in Florida and Mexico was a factor in his selection for this important task, indicating once more, as throughout his career, that he was trusted and that he was worthy of such trust.[9]

While in Florida he was under the over-all command of Brigadier General David E. Twiggs, with whom he had had an unpleasant experience during the Mexican War. Twiggs was one of Thomas's very few personal enemies during his lifetime, and their trouble began over one of the most trivial and avoidable of incidents. Following the Battle of Monterey, Twiggs became incensed because Lieutenant Thomas refused him a battery team of mules for his personal convenience at headquarters. Thomas was able to make his decision stand up by appealing through higher authority, but Twiggs never forgave him for it, as is shown by has later attempts to take revenge.[10] General Twiggs bore the reputation of being pompous, vindictive, and somewhat of a ladies' man, despite his advancing years. This was a combination of traits that made it difficult for him to forget that a mere lieutenant had thwarted him. It is reported that during the Mexican War an officer named Tree, who had several weaknesses, was brought before Twiggs for disciplining. To the general's inquiries regarding his conduct, Tree replied, "You cannot blame me; just as the Twigg is bent, so is the Tree inclined," and thus he earned his freedom.[11]

After serving for a period of about fourteen months in Florida, Thomas was ordered to proceed to Texas for duty, but while at New Orleans *en route* thereto he was instructed to report for duty at Fort Independence in Boston Harbor. Perhaps it was on this voyage that he encountered an emergency in which the ship and all on board were saved, due to his efforts, during a severe storm off Cape Hatteras. The captain was too intoxicated to handle the ship, although persisting in giving orders that increased rather than lessened the danger. When the first officer informed Thomas that their lives were in danger, but that he personally could not assume command without incurring a charge of mutiny, it was clear to him what should be done. He instructed the captain to remain in his stateroom while he handled the

---

9. *Ibid.*, p. 10.

10. Richard W. Johnson, *Memoir of Major General George H. Thomas* (Philadelphia: J. B. Lippincott and Co., 1881), pp. 32-33.

11. Samuel G. French, *Two Wars* (Nashville, 1901), p. 102.

ship, and with the help of the first officer brought her through the storm without further incident. Such willingness to meet danger head-on was one of the factors that made Thomas a truly great man. In any event, he remained at Fort Independence from January to March, 1851, whence he was assigned as instructor of artillery and cavalry at West Point.[12]

It was during this period of service, from April 2, 1851, to May 1, 1854, that Thomas served perhaps the most enjoyable and serene period of his military life. It was here that he was dubbed "Old Slow Trot" by the young cadets who derived some amusement from his command to slow trot. The students were inclined to push their mounts at a faster gait, in anticipation of a command to do so. Being full of energy, they would go faster than their commander desired, whereupon Thomas would sonorously give the command, "Slow trot!" Naturally the cadets found some delight in this kind of thing, which, after all, was at worst a diversion, but which gave rise to the nickname for Thomas. It is quite likely that the command had some relation to his deference for the horse that was carrying his more than average weight.[13]

On September 1, 1852, Robert E. Lee became superintendent and remained in this position until March 31, 1855. During this tour of duty, Lee met for the first time that other great Virginian, George H. Thomas, and thus were together the two men who, more than any other two men of the Civil War, exemplified supreme military ability. Their natures were similar in many respects, although the Thomas family did not rate so high socially as that of Lee. There was always in Thomas, however, the stamp of nobility and character that, to borrow a line from Kipling, impressed those who knew him intimately as one who could "walk with kings nor lose the common touch."[14]

It is appropriate to note at this time that General Erasmus D. Keyes stated of both Lee and Thomas that of the hundreds of Southern men he knew intimately these were the fairest in their judgment of Northern men.[15] Keyes also gave another interesting observation, this concerning Lee, in which he stated, "I will not deny that the presence of Lee, and the multiform graces that clustered

---

12. Van Horne, *op. cit.*, pp. 10-11.

13. George W. Cullum, *Biographical Register of Officers and Cadets of the U.S. Military Academy* (Boston, 1901); Henry Coppee, *General Thomas* (New York, 1893), pp. 182-83.

14. Rudyard Kipling, "If" (framed poem in my home).

15. Erasmus D. Keyes, *Fifty Years Observation of Men and Events* (New York, 1884), p. 166.

around him, oftentimes oppressed me, though I never envied him, and I doubt if he ever excited envy in any man. All his accomplishments and alluring virtues appeared natural in him, and he was free from the anxiety, distrust and awkwardness that attend a sense of inferiority, unfriendly discipline and censure."[16] Interesting also is the testimonial to Thomas, in one of the greatest orations in tribute to a human being in the English language, delivered by James A. Garfield before the 1870 meeting of the Society of the Army of the Cumberland, which reads in part as follows:

> . . . Who shall collect and unite into one worthy picture, the bold outlines, the innumerable lights and shadows which make up the life and character of our great leader? Who shall condense into a single hour the record of a life which forms so large a chapter of the nation's history, and whose fame fills and overfills a hemisphere? No line can be omitted . . . which you, his soldiers, will not detect and deplore. I know that each of you here present, sees him in memory at this moment, as we often saw in life; erect and strong like a tower of solid masonry; his broad, square shoulders and massive head; his abundant hair and full beard of light brown, sprinkled with silver; his broad forehead, full face, and features that would appear colossal, but for their perfect harmony of proportion; his clear complexion, with just enough color to assure you of robust health and a well regulated life; his face lighted up by an eye which was cold gray to his enemies, but deep blue to his friends; not a man of iron, but of live oak; his attitude, form and features all assure you of inflexible firmness, of inexpugnable strength; while his welcoming smile set every feature aglow with a kindness that won your manliest affection. . . .[17]

What an example of character and devotion to duty these two great men have left to their countrymen! What a record of military ability and achievement to add luster and glow to the pages of their country's history! How shameful of us that, in great measure, we pay honor to Lee as though giving credit to him for saving the Union, although he did his utmost to destroy it; yet we at once withhold from Thomas due honor and recognition as though in punishment for seeking to destroy the Union, although he gave up everything in this earthly existence to save it. Thomas gave up family and friends, well

---

16. *Ibid.*, p. 205.
17. Society of the Army of the Cumberland, *Yearbook, 1870* (Cincinnati: Robert Clarke and Co., 1871), pp. 55-56.

knowing that exultation by them, from nothing less than Southern victory, might some day reunite them.

Although Lee has been said to have paid a fearful price for following Virginia out of the Union, it was as nothing compared with Thomas's stand for the Union, since Lee retained his friends and family. Indeed, Lee gave up the Union at a time when, in his own words, "I know no necessity for this state of things."[18] Conceding that Lee had a painful decision to make, Thomas knew that most of those nearest and dearest to him would bear the deepest animosity toward him for doing his duty. Both men were honorable, sincere, not given to hypocrisy, and endowed with intelligence to realize the full consequences that would result from their actions; no doubt can be entertained that each did what he deemed best in relation to all factors concerned. To add further to the problems of Thomas, however, his Southern birth rendered him subject to continued and unfounded suspicion, or so it has been said. What is more likely the truth of the matter, his troubles came more from the jealousy of Grant and Sherman than from all other reasons combined. He had no senator or congressman to intercede in his behalf in staying the hand of malice or in advancing the dates of his long-overdue promotions. With so many outstretched hands reaching for rewards from the politically motivated, the Civil War, in this one particular alone, was as no other in its shameful disregard of minimum standards of justice to the deserving and rewards to the incompetent. It has been clearly proved that both Grant and Sherman were chief beneficiaries of this disgraceful policy of advancement through self-seeking politicians, namely Senator John Sherman of Ohio, General Sherman's brother, and Congressman Israel Washburn of Maine; in short, political, not military, considerations governed their interest in both men. The modest, truthful, ever-faithful, and always successful Thomas was rewarded only after his deeds cried out for recognition and delay was no longer prudent.[19]

Lieutenant Thomas was approaching thirty-five years of age when assigned as an instructor at West Point in April, 1851. Nothing has come to light indicating that up to this time in his life he had ever paid court to a lady or that he had even thought of marriage. It would be rather unusual, however, if he had not kept company to some extent with any of the young women he met during his peace-time assignments to Baltimore, Charleston, and New Orleans. Of

---

18. Robert E. Lee, Jr., *Recollections and Letters of General Lee* (New York, 1926), p. 26.

19. Piatt, *op. cit.*, pp. 232-37; B. H. Liddell Hart, *Sherman: Soldier, Realist, American* (New York: Frederick A. Praeger, 1958), p. 67.

course we have seen elsewhere that he entered into the social life of these cities. He was twenty-four years of age when he was graduated from the Military Academy, and during the intervening years had spent considerable time in active service. One can only surmise that he had not previously met the required conditions needful in the development of a romance.

Just as young women from Maryland and the surrounding area have first opportunity to meet the young Naval Academy students, so New York has priority in this respect at the Military Academy. Mrs. Abigail Kellogg, of Troy, New York, a city situated some one hundred miles north of West Point, was the widow of Warren Kellogg, a retired hardware merchant, who died on February 23, 1835. Each year she visited the West Point Hotel with two of her daughters, Frances and Julia, and on one of these visits they were introduced to Lieutenant Thomas. It did not take much time for Thomas to note the attractive elder daughter Frances, who was also of excellent manners and gifted in conversation. Her tall, stately figure was a fitting match for him, and before too long, November 17, 1852, they were married. Miss Kellogg was born on January 25, 1821, and was therefore five years younger than her husband. Unfortunately they were destined to spend little time together, due to his Civil War career and to the requirements of military life. Although separated for long periods of time, Mrs. Thomas followed her husband's career with much interest. She was greatly admired and respected by members of the military service, just as was her husband throughout his life. She died childless on December 26, 1889, in Washington, D.C., of an affliction quite similar to that which resulted in the death of her husband.[20]

One of the pleasant events experienced by Thomas at West Point was his promotion to captain on December 24, 1853. This was probably about as fine a Christmas present as he ever received, and was most welcome after holding the rank of first lieutenant since April 30, 1844, a span of almost ten years. With promotions so rare in those years, the limited size of the Regular Army had much if not everything to do with it. We can sympathize with William T. Sherman and Ulysses S. Grant, who left the military service some years before the Civil War in order to improve their income, although both returned after hostilities commenced. One wonders how Thomas could have the fortitude and patience to remain in the army under such prohibitively limited opportunities for advancement. It is clear that there was something of fidelity and loyalty in the man in pursuit of

20. Timothy Hopkins, *The Kelloggs in the Old World and the New* (San Francisco, 1902), p. 23.

an action or of a cause that would not countenance turning back, both of which traits held him and his country in good stead on future battlefields.

An interesting sidelight on Thomas's character is shown in an incident that occurred while he was instructing at West Point. One of his students, Cadet Michael R. Morgan, as is true of most boys full of life and energy, was prankish and mirthsome to such a degree that he neglected his studies. Thomas was required to report him, in consequence of which he was penalized. Years afterward, during a meeting between the two, Thomas, thinking that Morgan still held it against him, expressed the hope that the younger man would forgive and forget the incident.[21] This is one more illustration of the solicitude and concern that were so rooted in Thomas that all who came within his sphere of activity felt the influence of his sterling sense of justice, and were thus bound to him "with hoops of steel."

In an address before the New York Commandery of the Loyal Legion, General Oliver Otis Howard stated that during the incumbency of Thomas as an instructor the cadets regarded him as an outstanding figure. His three brevets had stamped him as a man of valor, which, with his commanding presence, gave him a natural respect and devotion shared by few men. His mandatory voice rang through the hills during the rattle of guns and the clamor of section officers; and his posture on a large horse when he led a cavalry charge or jumped the hurdles was watched with keen interest. His easy, kind manner, and the good grades received for indifferent recitations in class, warmed the hearts of the cadets, many of whom would exclaim, "God bless Major Thomas!"[22]

Captain Thomas was relieved from duty as an instructor at the Military Academy on May 1, 1854, and returned to the Third Artillery Regiment in charge of a battalion. He was ordered to proceed with his command to Benicia Barracks, not far from San Francisco, which he did by boat to the Isthmus of Panama. They marched across the isthmus to the Pacific Ocean, and from thence by boat to San Francisco, where they arrived on June 1, 1854[23] The trip lasted about a month, during which considerable discomfort due to illness was suffered by a large number of his command. An added aggravation was experienced due to inadequate hospital facilities. Thomas spent two weeks at San Francisco awaiting his baggage before marching with his command to Fort Yuma Reservation in Lower California. He reported to his Pacific Division Headquarters that "The excessive

---

21. Van Horne. *op. cit.*, p. 4.
22. Johnson, *op. cit.*, p. 21.
23. Van Horne, *op. cit.*, p. 11.

heat and scarcity of water on the Desert caused the most intensive suffering, and it was only by the utmost precaution that I have succeeded in reaching the post with the command in an exhausted condition. For the six days we were on the Desert the Thermometer ranged from 115° to 130° in the sun, rendering it necessary to make our march at night and lay by during the day. This naturally broke in upon the rest of men and animals, and if I had not finally determined to make a depot of all the heavier stores . . . I doubt if I should have succeeded in getting half the command there."[24] The letter is sufficiently clear to convince the most casual reader that Captain Thomas was a sterling commander.

It is understandable that Fort Yuma was considered to be one of the most undesirable military assignments in the service for a number of reasons, but especially due to the intense heat in summer. Nights were so stifling that sleep was almost out of the question until far into the night. It is recorded that Thomas was fond of describing these conditions in a story told by old soldiers to impress new recruits. It seems that an extremely sinful man of the command died and was given the usual interment. His character and habits were so bad that all who knew him, particularly those whose faith decreed the awful fate awaiting the unrepentant, believed he had met his just reward. Shortly after his funeral he was observed in the squad room looking very much as he did in life. His former bunkmate began making inquiries of him, including the question, "What do you want?" In reply, Bill said, "Boys, I have been to h—l and came near freezing to death, so I just asked the 'boss' for a pass for an hour to enable me to come here for my blankets. Boys, h—l is only about a half-mile from Fort Yuma." After obtaining the blankets, Bill left permanently for his new abode. Thus the good illustration, fully enjoyed by Thomas, showing that Fort Yuma was hotter than h—l. Despite his serious bearing Thomas could appreciate a joke as well as anyone, and would often sit with friends and exchange light and serious conversation.[25]

While at Fort Yuma Thomas spent some time learning the language of the Indian tribes inhabiting the area. On May 12, 1855, he was promoted to the rank of major, although he was the youngest ranking captain of artillery, and transferred to the Second Cavalry Regiment, a different branch of the service. This appointment was offered to Captain Braxton Bragg of the same regiment, but he declined it due to his resignation, which had been accepted at the time, al-

24. Letters from Thomas to Major Townsend, dated June 1 and July 14, 1854, in the National Archives, Washington, D.C.

25. Johnson, *op. cit.*, pp. 28-29.

though not effective until about a year later. Captain Bragg was said to have recommended Thomas for the place; if so, he must have felt some confirmation of his judgment in after years when at Murfreesboro, Missionary Ridge, Chickamauga, and elsewhere he was opposed by the formidable Thomas. At any rate, Thomas left Fort Yuma on July 21, 1855, under orders to proceed to Jefferson Barracks, Missouri, where he arrived in September.[26]

The Second Cavalry was a new regiment, one of two cavalry regiments organized pursuant to Congressional action of March 3, 1855. Headquarters of the regiment was at Louisville, Kentucky, where the colonel and his staff were located, and field offices were established at Jefferson Barracks in the vicinity of Saint Louis, Missouri. No finer organization than the Second Cavalry at this time existed in the entire history of the United States military service for the quality of its officer material. With these associations, extending over a period of six years before the Civil War, it is small wonder that so many officers were mutually benefited, and that their skills would be displayed on numerous battlefields. Its commander was Colonel Albert Sidney Johnston of Kentucky; Lieutenant-Colonel Robert E. Lee of Virginia; Senior-Major William J. Hardee of Georgia and Junior-Major George H. Thomas of Virginia; Captains Earl Van Dorn of Mississippi and E. Kirby Smith of Florida; and Lieutenants John Bell Hood of Kentucky and James E. B. Stuart of Virginia.[27] Twenty-five officers of the regiment serving in the Civil War were graduates of West Point, of whom seventeen, or sixty-eight per cent, were from the South. This overwhelming proportion of Southern officers in comparison with the population has often been attributed to the carefully laid plan of Secretary of War Jefferson Davis, who was believed to have estimated the war as inevitable. Four of these officers commanded large armies and four others held independent commands.[28]

It is not illogical to assume that Major Thomas was assigned to the Second Cavalry for at least two reasons: one was his Southern birth and the other his excellent record in the Mexican War. When he was asked the question "Did not Mr. Davis depend upon you, as upon Generals Johnston, Lee, Hardee and other Southern officers, to fight for the South in the event of war?" he replied, "Certainly he did." Indeed there were but four officers of the regiment from states that left the Union, and only three from states that bordered on the

---

26. Coppee, *op. cit.*, p. 24; Johnson, *op. cit.*, p. 29.
27. Van Horne, *op. cit.*, p. 12; Cullum, *op. cit.*, Vol. I, *passim*; Johnson, *op. cit.*, p. 29.
28. Van Horne, *op. cit.*, pp. 12-13.

Confederacy, who remained loyal.[29] In the absence of direct evidence, one can only make assumptions, but the weight of circumstances indicates that the Second Cavalry was staffed intentionally by Secretary of War Davis to insure the regiment's adherence to the South in the event of war.

Upon reporting at Jefferson Barracks in September, 1855, the recruitment of men for the Second Cavalry was pursued with vigor. The officers were required not only to drill the men, but to participate personally in the drilling. The training both of officers and men was under the supervision of Major Thomas, and ample proof of his ability in this particular is shown by the distinguished officers, both North and South, who later gained fame after having pursued this course of instruction. On October 17, 1855, a surprisingly short time after the recruitment of the Second Cavalry was begun, the regiment was ordered to Fort Belknap, Texas, and ten days later, October 27, the journey began with a full complement of men and horses.[30] The experience gained in this operation may be considered in the nature of a dress rehearsal for the more serious preparation required before the Battle of Nashville, particularly in relation to the acquisition of animals. The rapidity with which men were drilled and cavalry horses were rounded up brought victory to the Union there, and actually decided the war in the West and ultimately Appomattox.

Almost a month after leaving Jefferson Barracks the Second Cavalry reached Fort Washita, Texas, at which place Thomas was under instructions to report for court-martial duty. Flood waters in Missouri delayed the movement of the regiment, in consequence of which the court was already sitting when Thomas reported. Thomas was therefore denied a seat. After remaining at Fort Washita until December, 1856, he obtained permission to join his regiment by way of New York City. This gave him an opportunity to see his wife, a fairly rare occurrence during his military career. While in New York he was assigned to the recruitment of musicians for the Second Cavalry. His acknowledgment of receipt of this instruction was dated one day prior to the death of his mother, on January 27, 1856. Little information has been provided concerning the circumstances of her death. We do not even know whether George attended the funeral, although probably not, and nothing is available from the personal letters and papers of Thomas, who was very reticent concerning family matters. We do know that she died at the family home near Newsoms, that her children were heirs at law of the

29. *Ibid.*
30. Johnson, *op. cit.*, p. 30.

estate, since she left no will, and that her death was probably
due to a farm accident as was that of her husband. Coppee stated
her age as sixty at the time of death, but this is highly improbable
in view of her marriage in 1808, at which time she would have been
but twelve years of age.[31]

Thomas was next appointed a member of the court-martial hearing
the case of Major Giles Porter at Camp Cooper, Texas, in 1856.
Here he met once more his former superintendent at West Point,
Robert E. Lee, a member of the court. Lee, in a letter to his wife
bearing the date of April 26, 1857, expressed concern for the table
fare available for Mrs. George Thomas, due in part to the awkwardness and lack of skill of his servant Kremer. It appears that Lee was
not so much concerned for a sufficiency of food, since he stated that
there was plenty of bread, beef, preserved fruits, and vegetables,
as for the lack of skill in its preparation. Lee mentioned also that he
had tried to obtain eggs and an old hen, which he could not reflect
upon. It is apparent that Colonel Lee and Major Thomas improved
their warm friendship begun at West Point during their recent tours
of duty. In his letter of March 28, 1857, Lee reported to his wife that
Major Thomas had brought his wife to Camp Cooper, and that she
had informed him (Lee) of her troubles as they related to her two
servants, both sisters, whom she had hired in New Orleans. One of
them had become engaged to a soldier at Fort Mason, and Colonel
Lee's thought was that we cannot escape troubles wherever we go. [32]
In an earlier letter, dated August 25, 1856, from Camp Cooper, Lee
told of leaving for the Rio Grande for a period of two and a half
months, and of his plan to join Major Thomas at Fort Mason. He
expressed belief that Thomas would be a great comfort to him as a
traveling companion.[33] In still another letter to his wife, dated
December 27, 1856, from Fort Brown, Texas, describing church
attendance on Christmas, Lee told of dining with Major Thomas
and his wife on roast turkey and plum pudding.[34] After this unusually
long period of court-martial duty, extending over a period of more
than six months, Thomas returned to Fort Mason, where he remained until 1858.[35]

Another reference to Lee, this time by Thomas to his sister
Fanny, was dated December 22, 1858, from Fort Belknap. This

---

31. Mattie R. Tyler Papers: Minute Book 21 (Feb. 18, 1856), p. 75. In
County Courthouse, Southampton County, Va.; Coppee, *op. cit.*, p. 3; Letters
on file in National Archives, Washington, D.C.

32. Fitzhugh Lee, *General Lee* (1894), pp. 72-74.

33. *Ibid.*, pp. 65-66.

34. *Ibid.*, pp. 69-70.

35. Johnson, *op. cit.*, pp. 31-32; Cullum, *op. cit.*, Vol. I, p. 600.

letter is in the possession of Miss Bessie T. Shands, Deputy Clerk, Southampton County, Virginia, and reads as follows:

MY DEAR FANNY,

Yours of the 7th ult. has been in my possession for some time. I have been waiting to learn if Col. Lee will join the Regiment before answering it, as I had previously written that we would go on leave when he joined. A few days ago, I learned that his leave had been extended until the 1st of May, next. So we shall have to wait until that time unless some other Field Officer joins the Regiment. It does not make a great deal of difference now as Mrs. Kellogg's health has improved so much that Fanny [his wife Frances] is no longer anxious about her. However I must manage somehow to get out next May as she is not only almost out of clothes but I promised her mother to take her north this last Spring and should not like to delay it any longer than the next.

You must have had a bustling and noisy time of it during the visit of Ben's family. I hope they all enjoyed themselves. I should have liked very much to have been with you too.

I do not know when we can ever visit Ben or have him and his family with us.

He wrote me that he would have come with his family to Fort Leavenworth to see us had we been so fortunate as to get there, and I am in hopes still that we may be able to invite them some day.

This place continues as wretchedly dull as ever, and we have had one or two as cold spells as I ever experienced in New York even at this season of the year.

The high winds during the whole winter here are as bleak and disagreeable as the March winds in Va. and it frequently and very unexpectedly turns excessively cold. So we are constantly uneasy about the weather all winter. Please tell Judy that I will send her the $100 for the church as soon as a Pay Master comes up from San Antonio. If she cannot get the neighbours to join in building one, I wish her to expend it in charitable purposes among the needy of the neighbourhood.

I hope she has made a good crop this year.

Fanny joins me in wishing you all a happy Christmas & sends much love.

Yours truly,
GEO. H. THOMAS

MISS FANNY C. THOMAS
Newsoms Depot—Southampton, Va.

Several matters in the letter are revealing. First, perhaps, is the closing, which appears extremely distant for a brother to his sister. This can be somewhat reconciled, however, when it is remembered that George had been away from home almost constantly since 1836, a lapse of twenty-two years, in which conditions were not conducive to the maintenance of close relationships. It is easier to understand, in view of these many years of separation, that it was much easier for these same two sisters, Fanny and Judy, to show such intense bitterness toward their brother George when he adhered to the Union. It is reasonable to believe that if George had remained at home, and in that case not having taken the oath of allegiance, he might have served in the Confederate Army. This is not in any sense an attempt to predict that he would have made a different decision; it seems natural that by remaining at home his family ties would have had a greater influence upon him than they otherwise did.

Another matter of interest is in George's donating one hundred dollars for the church. This was a not inconsiderable amount in 1858 and suggests that George, who throughout his military life had little opportunity to ally himself with a religious organization, was concerned for the welfare of his fellow man.

Colonel Albert Sidney Johnston, commander of the Second Cavalry, was assigned to lead all troops ordered to Salt Lake for the purpose of subduing the Mormons who were reported to be causing "trouble." After surveying the situation and estimating the anticipated resistance of this religious sect under the leadership of Brigham Young, Johnston asked the War Department for an entire regiment to cope with them. General David E. Twiggs, commander of the Department of Texas, was ordered to assemble the Second Cavalry at Fort Belknap, Texas, from which point the long trek to Utah was scheduled to commence. After all preparations were completed, including the sending of women and children to safety, the order was countermanded, much to the disappointment and disgust of all concerned. Some doubt has been raised as to the actual existence of "trouble," in view of the statement that the proposed expedition was "authorized by President James Buchanan and sent ostensibly to suppress a Mormon rebellion that had no existence except as a popular opinion based on false reports."[36] Cancellation of the order for the expedition gives support to the contention that the "trouble" did not justify such extreme measures.

Although the trip was abandoned, General Twiggs, true to

36. *Encyclopedia Americana* (New York: American Book–Stratford Press, 1954), Vol. XIX, p. 464; Johnson, *op. cit.*, p. 32.

character, availed himself of his opportunity as commander to settle scores that he had authored with Thomas. He split up the Second Cavalry by ordering two companies to Camp Cooper, Texas, on the Clear Fork of the Brazos River, and eight companies to the Wichita Mountains under command of Captain and Brevet-Major Earl Van Dorn. Thomas was left at Fort Belknap with the sick, the band personnel, and noncommissioned officers. Thomas, it should be noted, was acting commander of the Second Cavalry at Fort Mason, San Antonio, Fort Belknap, and Camp Cooper during about three years from 1856 to 1860. This arbitrary action by Twiggs in ignoring Thomas so outraged him that he protested it to the commander in chief, and Twiggs was directed to give Thomas command of the Wichita Mountains expedition. Not to be outdone in his deep-seated compulsion to humiliate Thomas, Twiggs canceled the Wichita Mountains trip and assigned the eight companies to various posts in the department. To Thomas he gave the command of Camp Cooper, a most undesirable assignment, who promptly organized an expedition to the Red River country that lasted from the end of the year 1859 until the spring of 1860. This was a most fruitful exploration, covering the area lying at the head waters of the Canadian and Red rivers, on which valuable geological and geographical data were obtained.[37]

After returning from the Red River expedition he was ordered to explore the sources both of the Concho and Colorado rivers, and again valuable information was obtained regarding the geology and topography of the country. This was known as the Kiowa expedition and was not without serious incident. On August 26, 1860, the command engaged in a sharp fight with a band of plundering Indians from whom were recaptured a number of animals stolen from the white population. In this encounter Thomas was painfully wounded by an arrow that he removed from his chest after it had first entered his chin. This was the only time in his career that he was wounded, although exposed to danger many times. When it was certain that all of the Indians would be either killed or captured, one old badly wounded Indian heroically sacrificed himself, although wounded many more times, and permitted his companions, including women and children, to escape. Thomas told his interpreter to inform the Indian that his life would be spared if he would but surrender. However, the brave man replied, "Surrender? Never! Come on, Long-knives!" and went to his death.[38]

---

37. Johnson, *ibid.*, pp. 33-34; Cullum, *op. cit.*, pp. 13-14.

38. Johnson, *op. cit.*, pp. 33-34; Coppee, *op. cit.*, p. 25; Van Horne, *op. cit.*, p. 14.

In his August 31, 1860, report of the engagement with the Indians, Major Thomas reported in part as follows:

I have the honor to submit for the information of the department commander, the following report of the operations of the expedition under my command, to the head waters of the Concho and Colorado rivers, during the months of July and August . . . On the morning of the 25th inst. about fourteen miles east of the mountain pass, one of the Indian guides (Dloss) discovered a fresh horse trail crossing the road. As soon as the packs could be arranged and our wagons despatched with the remains of our baggage to the post, with the teams (two sick—the hospital steward and a private of the band—too sick to ride) I followed the trail with all the remainder of the department and three guides, in a west northwest direction for about forty miles, that day, traveling as long as we could see the trail after night-fall. On the 26th, about 7 A.M., the Delaware guide (Dloss) discovered the Indians, eleven in number, at camp. He and their spy discovered each other about the same time, and giving me the signal agreed upon, the party moved at once in a gallop for a mile and a half before coming in sight of their camp, which was located on the opposite side of a deep ravine, (running North, and I presume, into the Clear Fork), impassable except at a few points. Here we lost considerable time searching for a crossing, and only succeeded, finally, in getting over by dismounting and leading our animals. In the meantime the Indians being already mounted and having their animals collected together, had increased their distance from us by at least half a mile. As soon as the crossing was effected and the men re-mounted, we pursued them at full speed for about three miles and a half further, pushing them so closely that they abandoned their loose animals, and continued their flight, effecting their escape solely from the fact that our animals had been completely exhausted by the fatiguing pace at which the pursuit had been kept up. As we were gradually over-hauling them, one fellow, more persevering than the rest, suddenly dismounted and prepared to fight, and our men, in their eagerness to despatch him, hurried upon him so quickly that several of his arrows took effect, wounding myself in the chin and chest, also Private William Murphy, of Company "D", in the left shoulder, and Privates John Tile and Casper Siddle, of the band, each in the leg, before he fell, by twenty or more shots. . . . By this time the main body of the Indians, who were mounted on their best animals, were at least two miles from us, retiring at a rapid pace, and it being impossible to overtake them, on account of the exhausted condition of our animals, the pursuit was discontinued. . . .

The foregoing report is interesting in demonstrating that the same care and attention to detail thus early employed was characteristic of the man throughout his career.[39]

An interesting episode from the tour of duty at Fort Belknap, Texas, concerned the regimental band. Major Thomas asked the captain of each company to detail a man for instruction in music with eventual assignment to the band. The only requirement was, if they could not play an instrument, that they could whistle a tune. One of the captains detailed a man named Hannah, whose knowledge of music was so negligible that he could not distinguish "Hail, Columbia!" from "taps" on the drum. After giving Hannah a trial the bandmaster reported his lack of musical ability to Major Thomas, who remarked, "Well, I will order him back to his company. Poor fellow! he was mistaken; possibly he had a sister by that name who could play on some instrument."[40]

It is of more than passing interest that when the expedition to Utah was being fitted out Major Thomas wrote to the adjutant general under date of July 7, 1857, to report valuable information obtained while serving as an artillery officer at Fort Yuma, several years earlier. This concerned the possibility of navigating the Colorado River, the basis for which resulted from the questioning of Navajo and Pay-Ute Indians, to within one or two hundred miles of Salt Lake City. If his estimate was correct, he reported, "It will be not only the most direct, but the most convenient and safest route to convey supplies to the troops stationed in Utah territory."[41]

Thomas was interested in everything that could be productive of success in his profession.

---

39. Van Horne, *ibid.*, pp. 14-15.

40. Johnson, *op. cit.*, p. 35.

41. Henry Stone, *Some Federal and Confederate Commanders* (Boston: Houghton Mifflin Co., 1895), p. 171.

CHAPTER VI

To "Nobly Save...the Last Best Hope of Earth" [1]

FOR THE third time in his army career, extending over a period of twenty years, Major Thomas asked for and obtained a year's leave of absence, in October, 1860. On November 1, before the election that placed Abraham Lincoln in the White House, which further stimulated the eleven Southern states to consider seceding from the Union, however mistaken they may have been in thus interpreting it, Thomas left Camp Cooper, Texas, for a reunion with his wife in New York. His departure from Texas presented the personal problem of disposing of a slave woman he had acquired there under the necessity of obtaining help that was most difficult to get in any other way. With his deep sympathy for the slave children he knew on the farm during his boyhood, it is not surprising that he "could not sell a human being." Buying a slave was one thing, selling one was another, since ownership passed and gave no assurance that his own kind treatment would be continued. He had no legal reason for withholding her from sale, an action that would have proved the easiest solution, except for one thing: the thought of selling her was so revolting to him that he decided to keep her. He arranged with his family in Southampton County, Virginia, to take care of her, thus assuring him that she would not be an object of abuse, as often occurred in the American slavery system. [2]

One can ascribe to Thomas in this incident the reaction that anyone endowed with normal human feelings would experience in a similar circumstance between employer and employe, or between master and servant. It would be only natural that in such a relationship mutual trust and perhaps affection would develop. To one of his

---

1. Lincoln's Annual Message to Congress, December 1, 1862, last paragraph.

2. Thomas B. Van Horne, *The Life of Major General George H. Thomas* (New York: Charles Scribner's Sons, 1882), pp. 16-17.

mold it would be difficult to abandon an association in which the emotions of joy and sorrow were known and shared or in which attachments born of souls laid bare to hardships endured and successes achieved were experienced. To repudiate a relationship of such long standing would be an impossibility for a man whose heart was filled to overflowing with all that is true and noble. Whether he was abolitionist or perchance some modification of the term did not matter. He liked people; he was kind and just to them always; and he could not summarily dismiss this woman who, slave or not, was entitled to kind treatment. He did not see her again until after the Civil War had ended, when, free, he paid for her removal, with her husband and children, from Virginia to Nashville, Tennessee, where he was commander of the Military Department of the Tennessee. Naturally this was a source of considerable expense and inconvenience to him, but he did his best to help her family become self-supporting and independent. It is understandable that former slaves would be fearful, under their new and untried freedom, of leaving the only home they knew for the uncertainties of life, after four long years of devastating warfare. They remained with him until he was shifted to the command of the Military Division of the Pacific, in 1869, when he found it no longer possible to be responsible for them. After obtaining their consent, however, he arranged with his brother Benjamin, then living in Mississippi, to provide them with employment after first paying their transportation. In passing, it is worthy of note that Benjamin was the only member of his family with whom George had contact after the war. If any bitterness ever existed between them because of George's loyalty to the Union, and no such evidence has come to light, their former good relationship was renewed afterward.[3]

It should be remembered that when Major Thomas began his extended period of leave, secession and war were still in the future. He was under no compunction to furnish an alibi in justification of this, his third vacation in twenty years of faithful and arduous service to his country; but he would have been a most unusual person and soldier if the events unfolding before him did not compel his serious thought and concern. Long association with the profession of arms alone would reject any thought that he was indifferent to the challenging times. He had heard for many years the bitterness expressed in legislative halls, in the press, and by personal experience over the question of slavery; and he knew only too well the dreadful possibility if not probability of civil strife. It would be absurd to

3. *Ibid.*, p. 17.

assert later, when others were professedly writhing in anguish while groping for the decision that would lead them out of the Union, that the idealistic and noble Thomas reacted to the challenge with supreme unemotional objectivity while deciding to fight for the preservation of the Union. No man of Thomas's character could conceivably abandon the ties of blood and friendship without weighing their loss to him against the still greater loss of his convictions and of course his country. An appropriate word picture by historian Robert Selph Henry describing the struggle faced by Robert E. Lee applied with equal force to men of sincerity on both sides of the conflict. In this we see the distraught figure of Lee pacing the floor of his Arlington home in search of the answer his previous declarations had foretold with considerable accuracy. His decision to join the Confederacy was consistent with the action of a large majority of Southern men of standing; but Virginia-born George H. Thomas, perhaps the ablest Union soldier the war produced, and Admiral David Glasgow Farragut of Tennessee,[4] the greatest sea captain in American history up to that time, were rare exceptions. These two men, or perhaps either of them, by sitting out the war or by changing sides, might well have decided the war against the Union, just as their fighting for the Union helped bring victory.

Ironically, most of the officers who recognized through long acquaintance the superior military qualifications of Thomas went with the South. This served the purpose of a two-edged sword; if Thomas had gone with his native Virginia, his rise to military renown would surely have been more rapid, and conceivably, as aforesaid, his decision might well have meant the difference between Southern defeat and Southern independence. If this suggests fantasy, it can be soon dispelled by assuming that General Thomas was in command of the Confederate forces in the Chattanooga campaign instead of General Braxton Bragg; or, contrariwise, with General Bragg in command of the Confederate forces, by assuming that for some reason General Thomas was unavailable to oppose him on that fateful afternoon of September 20, 1863, the day he earned the nickname of "The Rock of Chickamauga." In either assumption there would have been no Thomas to save the Union, the entire Federal army would have been ripe for destruction, and the Confederates would have been in a tremendously improved position to bargain for a separate peace. The Army of the Cumberland, it will be remembered, was the largest Federal army next to the Army of the Potomac, and a Confederate success of such dimensions would have brought discouragement to an already

---

4. Robert S. Henry, *The Story of the Confederacy* (Indianapolis: Bobbs-Merrill Co., 1936), p. 36.

bleeding and war-weary North. The role of Thomas in this campaign thus takes on an importance unapproached by any other Union commander. By contrast, the North received him with coldness, if not hostility; and whatever grudging recognition he obtained was always belated and doubly proved by his achievements on the battlefield. In addition to this he was an object of suspicion and distrust, because he had been a friend, through performance of his military requirements, of a large number of officers from the South who aligned themselves with the Confederacy.

Not only were long friendships ended by the conflict. Many instances occurred in which families were divided, and in some cases opposed each other on the field of battle. Perhaps no other state affords a better example of such divisions as the border state of Kentucky. John C. Breckinridge, Vice President of the United States under President Buchanan, went with the Confederacy. His brother, Jefferson Breckinridge, a former lawyer turned clergyman, was a staunch supporter of the Union; but two of his sons went with the South and the other two remained with the Union.[5] Another notable example of family disunion was the John Jordan Crittenden family, also of Kentucky, one of whose sons fought for the North and the other for the South. Quite coincidentally, George Bibb Crittenden became a Confederate brigadier general and was part of the defeated Confederate Army at the Battle of Mill Springs, Kentucky, won by General George Thomas on January 19, 1862. His brother, Thomas Leonidas Crittenden, became a major general in the Union Army and fought at Chickamauga, after which he was court-martialed but cleared of any misconduct in the debacle. Their father was a United States senator, a United States attorney general, a governor of Kentucky, and a staunch Unionist who did much to hold his state in the Union.[6]

Just what would a soldier do in a situation in which his family brought pressure on him from one side while from the other was the tremendous pull arising out of his deeply rooted training, convictions, and habits? First of all, Major Thomas was not a politician; he was a soldier dedicated to his country; and he looked upon his flag as a symbol of that dedication. He instinctively regarded the President of the United States as his Commander in Chief, as the commander of all military personnel and the representative of his country before the world. As a Virginian he loved every foot of her soil, and every custom, every bit of her history, and the traditions that make one

5. *Encyclopedia Americana* (New York: American Book—Stratford Press, 1954), Vol. IV, pp. 457-58.

6. *Ibid.*, Vol. VII, pp. 213-14.

proud. George H. Thomas would not lightly turn his back upon his beloved Virginia without giving most serious thought to the consequences of his act to himself, to his state, and to his country; and being the nobleman and gentleman he was he would spend every moment in quest of victory, as history so indelibly records, once his decision was made. Few people would know the pangs of regret, the heartaches suffered, at the loss of dear friends and relatives, as did Thomas, as he made his decision and witnessed their departure from his life, perhaps forever. Many of them had been friends and relatives whose loyalty to God, to principles, and to country were beyond dispute. Friends he had been proud to claim, including women whose smiles fell upon one like a benediction, were weighed against the duty he felt he owed the Union; and there was no other choice for him within the range of his conscience but to place the Union first.[7]

An example of the suffering endured by those of Unionist leanings in the border states is shown by the Union officer who left his home in Paris, Kentucky, during the summer of 1861. He reported to General William Nelson, who was establishing a military camp in Lancaster, Kentucky. Having occasion to return to his Paris home, following a tour of recruiting duty for General Nelson, he found the attitude of his former friends and neighbors completely changed. People who knew him well passed him on the street with averted faces. Women of the church he had attended refused to recognize him. He would have been more favorably situated among strangers, despite his being in his own home town. Sadly, although perhaps inevitably, men were involved in political arguments; and murders were committed for no other reason than that the victims were Union men. Some men were called to their doors at midnight and killed in cold blood. All of this was bad enough but to a man like Thomas it was hardly worse than parting with those he had known for a quarter of a century.[8]

As he wandered northward on his leave of absence Major Thomas must have pondered the vexing problems facing his country and the possible role he would have in solving them. It would not have been surprising if he had decided to take no part in a war in which he would be fighting against his own countrymen, whether he chose the North or the South. Yet he never wavered in his sworn duty to defend the Federal Government, although men generally were carried away by the tremendous emotion generated on both sides and were swept into a decision. The country was split so completely that nothing

7. Gilbert C. Kniffen, *Life and Services of Major General George H. Thomas* (Washington, D.C.: Military Order of the Loyal Legion, D.C. Commandery, 1887), pp. 7-8.

8. *Ibid.*, pp. 8-9.

but war could ever unite it, if war ever unites anything so thoroughly disunited. It is not for anyone to say, more than one hundred years after the commencement of hostilities, who was right and who was wrong. Each citizen becomes more a creature of his immediate environment and far more moved by conditions within that environment than from forces or considerations far removed from the locale that nurtured him. It was a rare person who permitted his reason to dictate his actions, as did Thomas, instead of pursuing the easier course of going with his state. Many influences must be taken into account, like lifelong friendships in the locality of one's birth; the long-continued struggle between the several slave states and the free states, and the fact that even among the local population in every slave state there was strong Union sentiment, when trying to comprehend the terrible decision confronting many people in the Confederacy. To take a stand for the Union in an area in which the majority were for secession required great courage, if not actual departure from the scene; and this was often just as true in the border states, where the minority were for the Confederacy.

Whereas Robert E. Lee knew of no reason why any state should leave the Union, but followed Virginia out of it, George H. Thomas, who also saw no reason strong enough or compelling enough to cause disunion, remained in the Union. It is one thing to feel sympathy for Lee, who painfully, yet voluntarily, gave up his country, but in doing so retained his beloved Virginia and his relatives and friends. It is not only inconsistent, but terribly unjust, to feel sympathy for Lee while ignoring the infinitely greater sacrifice made by Thomas, who, in holding to his country, also gave up his beloved Virginia and his relatives and friends. What is worse, Thomas incurred the undying displeasure and hatred of his relatives and friends, who branded him a traitor to his state. Nothing in this earthly life is more manifestly unjust than for a man who is pleged by the deepest considerations surrounding the solemnity of his oath before Almighty God to be mistreated as was Thomas for remaining true to that oath. This is in no sense an indictment of Lee for his decision when faced with the same considerations; rather it is an appeal to the conscience of the American people for recognition of Thomas for his achievements as one of the great soldiers produced on this or any other continent, and to elevate him to the rightful place his deeds so richly earned for him. When everything is considered in appraising the contributions of participants in the Civil War, the factor that weighed most heavily in helping them to reach a decision was the natural inclination to follow leaders of local communities, and to believe that they were defending a way of life, the way, that is, as described by these leaders.

It was something like this that influenced Lee, who was well equipped to see the true issues through emotion and hysteria, to follow Virginia from the Union while proclaiming that he saw no reason for the state of things then existing.[9]

The interesting letter, referred to in Chapter II, that General Lee wrote to his son William Henry Fitzhugh "Roony" Lee, on January 29, 1861, was recently acquired by the Virginia Historical Society. This letter, in addition to discussing family problems, expressed great concern for the impending withdrawal of Virginia from the Union. The Reverend J. William Jones, who had access to the letter shortly after Lee's death, published excerpts from it in his *Personal Reminiscences* of General Lee, published in 1874, and also in his *Life and Letters of Robert Edward Lee*, published in 1906, but he omitted some of the most important parts of the letter, and, pardonably perhaps, committed some errors. The entire letter is now available for the first time, although, for the present purpose, only the part relating to secession is significant. That part is as follows:

The South in my opinion has been aggrieved by the acts of the North as you say. I feel the aggression, and I am willing to take every proper step for its redress. It is the principle I contend for, not individual or private benefit. As an American citizen I take great pride in my country, her prosperity and institutions, and would defend any State if her rights were invaded. But I can anticipate no greater calamity for the country than a dissolution of the Union. It would be an accumulation of all the evils we complain of and I am willing to sacrifice everything but honour for its preservation. I hope therefore that all Constitutional means will be exhausted, before there is a resort to force. Secession is nothing but revolution. The framers of our Constitution never exhausted so much labor, wisdom and forbearance in its formation and surrounded it with so may guards and securities, if it was intended to be broken by every member of the confederacy at will. It was intended for perpetual union, so expressed in the preamble [Lee was confused; he did not realize that the Constitution provides for a "more perfect union," to supersede the "perpetual union" of the Articles of Confederation.] and for the establishment of a government, not a compact, which can only be dissolved by revolution or the consent of all the people in convention assembled. It is idle to talk of secession. Anarchy would have been established and not a government, by Washington,

---

9. Robert E. Lee, Jr., *Recollections and Letters of General Lee* (New York, 1926), p. 26.

Hamilton, Jefferson, Madison and the other patriots of the Revolution. In 1808 when the New England States resisted Mr. Jefferson's Imbargo law and the Hartford Convention assembled, secession was termed treason by Virginia statesmen. What can it be now? Still a union that can only be maintained by swords and bayonets, and in which strife and civil war are to take the place of brotherly love and kindness, has no charm for me. If the Union is dissolved and the government disrupted, I shall return to my native State and share the miseries of my people and save in her defense will draw my sword on none. Give much love to Charlotte, to my dear little son, and believe me always your devoted father.[10]

This letter is notable for a number of reasons. First, Lee himself recognized that "secession was termed treason by Virginia statesmen," and he asked, "What can it be now?" Then he stated that "The South in my opinion has been aggrieved by the acts of the North," but almost three months later, in a letter to "My dear sister," dated April 20, 1861, he stated:

Now we are in a state of war which will yield to nothing. The whole South is in a state of revolution, into which Virginia, after a long struggle, has been drawn; and though I recognize no necessity for this state of things, and would have forborne and pleaded to the end for a redress of grievances, real or supposed, yet in my own person I had to meet the question whether I should take part against my native State. With all my devotion to the Union and the feeling of loyalty and duty of an American citizen, I have not been able to make up my mind to raise my hand against my relatives, my children, my home. I have therefore resigned my commission in the Army, and save in defense of my native State, with the sincere hope that my poor services may never be needed, I hope I may never be called on to draw my sword. I know you will blame me; but you must think as kindly of me as you can, and believe that I have endeavored to do what I thought right.[11]

This letter is of particular interest in that Lee stated that he recognized "no necessity for this state of things," meaning literally that he saw no need for secession three months after his January 29 letter, in which he thought the South was aggrieved, although he

10. *Virginia Magazine of History and Biography* (Richmond, Va.; January, 1961), Vol. LXIX, No. 1, pp. 5-6.

11. Lee, *op. cit.*, pp. 25-26.

recognized then that, although aggrieved, secession would constitute treason. With all due credit to General Lee for his sincerity, and his sincerity is not in question, he did not strike out boldly on the basis of his convictions. He followed his state out of the Union, an act in which his only part was to acquiesce in the acts of others, acts regarding which, in his own words, he did not believe.

Another point of significance, Lee stated that he would have pleaded to the end for redress of grievances, although there is nothing to indicate his pleadings were heard in the centers where they might have had influence in calming the agitation. He did plead with his sister to think kindly of him, although recognizing that she would blame him. It seems clear here that General Lee made his own decision. Arguments to the contrary notwithstanding, that he would not turn his back on friends and relatives, he must have turned his back on at least this one sister.

What we learn from these letters above everything else is that General Lee was human, not superhuman, and it is ridiculous to weep and wail over him for the difficulty of his decision, a decision that all Southern military men had to make, but a decision that was his own and was made for his own selfish interests. Are not all such decisions selfish, at least to the extent that they are made with the end in view of aspiring to what the one making the decision desires? The tragedy of it is that we are generally too prone to criticize those who made a decision contrary to the one we believe we would have made. In general, the most we can say is that we cannot with certainty be sure what that decision would have been.

One of the most beautiful gestures ever made toward a former foe was the unveiling, at the United States Military Academy on January 19, 1952, of a portrait of General Robert E. Lee in the uniform of a general of the Confederate Army. This date marked the one hundred and forty-fifty anniversary of General Lee's birth in 1807, and the year 1952 represented the one hundredth anniversary of his taking the superintendency at West Point. The ceremony was one of the events marking the sesquicentennial, or one hundred and fiftieth anniversary, of the founding of the Military Academy.

This portrait of Lee by Sidney E. Dickinson of Wallingford, Connecticut, in 1951, is more than a likeness. It reflects the character, the personality, and the quality of soul of the subject, and is truly a splendid work of art. The portrait hangs in the West Point Library, a building constructed in 1841 in the Tudor-Gothic style of architecture, and one of the few buildings now at West Point that were in existence when Lee served there as superintendent. The location of the portrait is at one side of the large window in the rotunda of the library, and the portrait of General Grant, which formerly hung in Cullum Hall, was placed on the other side, to the left of the window.[12]

Accompanying the portrait of General Lee is a legend in explanation of its presence; and seemingly this legend appeals to the reader for fairness and understanding toward a former son and superintendent of the Military Academy who, having left the fold for a time, was once more and in this manner brought back to it. It reads as follows:

> The people of the United States honor the heroes of the War of 1861-1865 without regard to the section from which they came. The joint exhibition of two great American military leaders, graduates of West Point, represents the present national unity of our country. In their devotion to principle and integrity of character both Grant and Lee exemplified the ideals of the Military Academy.
>
> Just as General Grant is depicted in the uniform he wore at the height of his fame as commander of the Union armies, so General Lee is portrayed in the uniform for which he is remembered, that of the head of the Confederate armies.

One cannot but be impressed before these paintings, and glory in the greatness of our common country. In simplest terms, the honor done to a former son and enemy by the people who might have been divided reflects the magnificent spirit that now prevails and makes that country more united than before. The conviction is inescapable that the minimum of justice is due another West Point graduate, General George H. Thomas, without whose victories and all-around contribution the union of Grant and Lee, so eloquently stated in the above legend, would not have been possible. In not one degree less than General Lee, General Thomas is entitled to fairness from the North, for which he fought, and from the South, which so consistently ignores him. It cannot be stated both ways; that is, we cannot with consistency and fairness honor Lee for his many qualities and fail to give even minimum credit to Thomas for his services, which were second to none in preserving the Union.

General Lee is doing all right in the hearts and minds of his countrymen, both North and South. Not only has his memory been honored by the beautiful painting, placed there by an admiring nation as a symbol that the past is forgotten; his bust, referred to in the Epilogue hereinafter, is in the New York University Hall of Fame,

---

12. *West Point Assembly* (Sesquicentennial Edition), January, 1952.

although he fought to divide his country; and he has been cited, without question, as a model of manhood and honor for the youth of both the North and the South. Paradoxically, the one man without whose services the American nation might well have become permanently divided has not been so honored; and the time is long since past for this united country to pay due honor and respect to General Thomas who, from any conceivable standpoint, was the equal of General Lee.

It is fervently hoped that the words of General Maxwell D. Taylor, Deputy Chief of Staff and former Military Academy superintendent, when making the dedicatory address, will be implemented to the utmost by every American: "To-day there is no North or South, no East or West, but one people. Let us hope that future generations of West Point men, gazing upon the noble features of Robert E. Lee, will be moved thereby to become better cadets, better officers, better citizens, and better Americans."

The United States Military Academy was founded by President Thomas Jefferson in 1802, on the recommendation of George Washington, John Adams, Alexander Hamilton, and Alexander Knox. In that year ten cadets reported for duty, but it is not clear how the two members of the graduating class completed the course in one year, unless given credit for prior military service in the armed forces.

Sylvanus Thayer, a graduate of the class of 1808, and a veteran of distinguished service in the War of 1812, became superintendent of the Academy in 1817. During his tenure, which ended in 1833, Superintendent Thayer proved to be an able administrator. Many of the policies, principles, and methods inaugurated by him have endured to this time.

Southern officers began leaving the service at a rapid rate, following notification that their various native states had seceded. They were confused, as might have been expected, following the dissolution of their country. Many vainly hoped that, even if their states left the Union, there would be no bloodshed, and correspondingly that they would not be compelled to fight against their former countrymen.

Thomas was a major at the time his native Virginia seceded, but his experience, extending over twenty years, combined with his capacity for study and observation on many subjects, made him better qualified than most of his contemporaries. The Mexican War was the only experience of consequence any of the participants had had, and to this might be added the minor brushes with frontier Indian tribes and the Seminole Indians of Florida. In the Mexican War hardly more than ten thousand troops were engaged on the American side in any battle. Moreover, there were barely more than that number under the over-all command of either General Scott or General Taylor during the entire Mexican War. Notwithstanding, Thomas had remained in the service and had taught cavalry and artillery at the Military Academy, where he associated with the best minds in studying the art of war. His extra activities included the study of botany, geology, and mineralogy, and at Fort Yuma he studied the language of the Yuma Indians and sought to put it into written form. In these endeavors he was becoming equipped for his later role as commander of a large army; and it is clear that his superiority over his contemporaries was due in great measure to their failure to keep pace with him. General Thomas had far more extensive preparation for command than either Grant or Sherman, both of whom were out of service for a number of years; in fact, General Thomas had greater experience than any other officer of the Army of the Cumberland.[13]

Not only did Thomas possess superior ability and experience; his appearance naturally inspired confidence in men, especially the rank and file. He gave every indication of power, an impression that escaped few men who saw him for the first time. His real power, of course, went far beyond mere visual impression, as evidenced by its translation into his outstandingly successful command of large armies.[14]

While proceeding northward from Richmond to Washington during his extended leave of absence, Major Thomas met with the most serious accident of his military life. He alighted from a railroad train in the dark near Lynchburg, Virginia, and instead of gaining solid footing, as he expected, he fell into a deep ravine, which resulted in permanent injury to his spine. A complete description of the accident is contained in a letter received by Henry Coppee, one of Thomas's biographers, from a lady who knew Thomas well:

> General Thomas came out of Texas with a year's leave of absence, in November, 1860, to join Mrs. Thomas in New York, having obtained the leave some months and only waiting for some one to relieve him at his post, without any thought of political troubles in the country, and with no reference to the arrow wound, from which he speedily recovered and never felt any effects afterward. He met with a serious accident on his journey, not from a railroad disaster, as commonly asserted, but

13. George W. Cullum, *Biographical Register of Officers and Cadets of the U.S. Military Academy* (Boston, 1891), Vols. I, II.

14. Van Horne, *op. cit.*, p. 19.

from a misstep in getting out of the car at night while the train was taking in water somewhere near Lynchburg. Deceived by the shadows of the moonlight, he stepped out on what he supposed was the road, but proved to be down a deep ravine, sustaining a fall of twenty feet or more. He continued his journey to Norfolk, where Mrs. Thomas joined him and remained there until he was able to go to his mother's home in Southampton County, Virginia, suffering severely. After a visit of several weeks he went with Mrs. Thomas to New York, stopping a few days at Washington en route. It was while in New York that he fully realized the extent of his injury, and fearing he would never be able to do duty again with his regiment, he began to think what he could do in the event of being obliged to give up his military life. Mrs. Thomas saw in the columns of the National Intelligencer an advertisement for commandant of cadets at the Virginia Military Institute, read it aloud to him, and asked if he could do that duty. He said he thought he could, and accordingly wrote to the superintendent, Major F. H. Smith, asking about the vacancy, and received word in reply that the vacancy had been filled. There the matter rested, and from these facts the story had grown that General Thomas applied for an appointment in the Confederate army. He was in New York when his regiment arrived from Texas, and could easily have obtained a surgeon's certificate for inability to do any duty, but preferred to make the effort, suffering and disabled as he was. He obeyed the order immediately to join his regiment at Carlisle and refit it for service. It was while on the train for Carlisle that he first heard of the attack on Fort Sumter, and wrote to Mrs. Thomas on his arrival: "Whichever way he turned the matter over in his mind, his oath of allegiance to his Government always came uppermost."[15]

This injury has been held responsible for his slower and deliberate movements during the war. His confinement for six weeks in the Norfolk hospital is some indication of its seriousness.[16] It is probably true that the startling change in his appearance, as reflected by pictures taken of him in the latter days of the war, in contrast to the much younger-appearing pictures of him taken in the earlier days of the war, was the result of this accident.

From this accident there developed a groundless if not scurrilous charge that Thomas was lukewarm in his loyalty to the Union. This

---

15. Henry Coppee, *General Thomas* (New York, 1893), pp. 28-29, 35-36.
16. Van Horne, *op. cit.*, pp. 19-20.

undoubtedly relates to his reply to the article in the *National Intelligencer* of January 18, 1861, referred to in the foregoing letter, advertising for a commandant of cadets at Virginia Military Institute. It has been charged that this letter indicated his intention to withdraw from the Army and to correspondingly remove himself from the sectional dispute. It was said also that he offered his sword to the governor of Virginia, a statement apparently arising from the letter of application submitted by Thomas, which is as follows:

NEW YORK HOTEL, NEW YORK CITY
January 18th, 1861

COLONEL FRANCIS H. SMITH,
  Sup't. Virginia Military Institute, Lexington, Va.

DEAR SIR: In looking over the files of the National Intelligencer, this morning, I met with your advertisement for a commandant of cadets and instructor on tactics at the Institute. If not already filled, I will be under obligations if you will inform me what salary and allowances pertain to the situation, as from present appearances I fear it will soon be necessary for me to be looking up some means of support.

Very respectfully, your obedient servant,
GEO. H. THOMAS,
Major, U. S. Army[17]

What there is in this letter to suggest that Thomas ever gave the remotest thought of leaving the Army is not evident. The fact that he was concerned about his spinal injury, and the possible effect it would have on his means of livelihood, was surely the immediate and compelling factor in applying for the position. It should be remembered that Virginia at that time was still in the Union, and that it was by no means certain that she would leave it. Leading figures in Virginia were doing their utmost to settle the vexing problems facing them without recourse to secession and armed conflict; and Robert E. Lee was still closely associated with General Winfield Scott, head of the United States Army, while General Joseph E. Johnston was still quartermaster general of that Army.[18]

In addition to these facts, his recent injury and his answering of the advertisement were so closely related in time that, even if he had felt concern regarding his own part in a possible war between North and South, the most literal construction possible from his comment, "from present appearances," was an intent not to take any

---

17. *Ibid.*, p. 22.
18. *Ibid.*, p. 23.

part in it. When all has been said, it should be remembered that it was nothing more than an inquiry regarding salary and allowances; there is nothing to signify that he would have accepted the position, since the income might not have been up to expectations.

Now let us examine the letter from Major Thomas to Governor Letcher, about which some Confederate officers and political leaders have attempted to convict him of secessionist leanings.

New York Hotel, March 12, 1861

To His Excellency, Gov. Letcher, Richmond, Va.

Dear Sir: I received yesterday a letter from Major Gilham, of the Virginia Military Institute, dated the 9th inst., in reference to the position of Chief of Ordnance of the State, in which he informed me that you had requested him to ask me if I would resign from the service, and if so, whether that post would be acceptable to me. As he requested me to make my reply to you direct, I have the honor to state, after expressing my most sincere thanks for your very kind offer, that it is not my wish to leave the service of the United States as long as it is honorable for me to remain in it, and, therefore, as long as my native state [Virginia] remains in the Union, it is my purpose to remain in the army, unless requested to perform duties alike repulsive to honor and humanity. I am very respectfully your obedient servant.

George H. Thomas
Major United States Army[19]

There are those who prefer to interpret this letter as meaning that Thomas intended to remain in the Army as long as Virginia remained in the Union; in fact, there could be no other way to interpret it, for that is precisely what he stated. Since Virginia was still in the Union, any statement by Thomas that he even thought of leaving the Army if Virginia seceded would have been regarded as not only premature but totally unwise. If he had stated that he would not leave the Union under any circumstances, he would have incurred the ill-will of his fellow Southerners. If he had stated that he intended going with Virginia and the South, he would have been forever under a cloud in the event Virginia did not secede. He mentioned the matter in the only way open to a prudent man not yet confronted with a decision.

If the letter to Governor Letcher proves anything, it is that nothing bordering on withdrawal from the Union was in his mind. This is equally proved by the letter he wrote to the Virginia Military Institute,

---

19. Donn Piatt, *General George H. Thomas* (Cincinnati, 1891), pp. 82-83.

about which so much controversy has revolved. Any possible doubt regarding the first letter was removed by the letter to Governor Letcher. Let the evidence afforded by both letters be construed in either of two ways: he intended to remain in the Union, or he intended to leave the Union. Either construction would make no difference, since he had not been faced with events that required him to state a position. It would be just as reasonable for the South to criticize Robert E. Lee and other Southern officers who joined the Confederacy for ever having entertained doubt whether they might leave the United States Army. The entire argument is ridiculous, not only because the letters contain nothing to condemn Thomas, but more especially because hardly anyone of responsibility believed that war would come, at the time the letter was written to Virginia Military Institute.

Following a period of convalescence from his injury at his old Southampton County home place, Major Thomas proceeded to his own home in New York City, in January, 1861. On the way north he stopped at Washington to report to General Winfield Scott his belief that General David E. Twiggs contemplated turning his command over to the authorities of Texas, if Texas decided to leave the Union. Thomas was aware that Twiggs was closely identified with the secessionist movement in Texas, and felt it important enough also to express this concern to Quartermaster General Joseph Eggleston Johnston. General Johnston would be heard from later as one of the great Southern military figures of the Confederacy. What is most important to note in this incident is its complete refutation that Thomas thus early entertained the slightest thought of disloyalty. South Carolina was the only state that had seceded, but the general exodus of Southern states from the Union was even then quite clearly indicated.

It is not known what effect the report of Major Thomas had upon the anticipated treachery of General Twiggs, but shortly thereafter he was relieved of his command of the Department of Texas and ordered to relinquish the reins to Colonel White. His removal was not made, however, before he had shown, through his plan of action, that he favored the South. He had granted leaves of absence to all officers desiring to seek preferred positions in the Confederate Army or in their respective states. Lieutenant Colonel Robert E. Lee of the Second Cavalry, commander of the Department of Texas since February, 1860, was granted a leave of absence in December, 1860. Lee had not reached the stage requiring a decision, but he did say, "I shall never bear arms against the United States, but it may be necessary for me to carry a musket in defense of my native state, Virginia, in which case I shall not prove recreant to my duty," a most ambiguous statement.[20]

Captain Earl Van Dorn of the Second Cavalry obtained a prospective commission as brigadier general, and returned to his regiment before the hoped-for disarming of all troops in the Southwest. Van Dorn served the Southern cause still more by offering promotions to all officers and noncommisioned officers in the United States Army if they would serve in the Confederate Army.[21]

General Twiggs disobeyed the order to turn over his command to Colonel White and surrendered to Texas authorities instead. Van Dorn, in a United States Army uniform, boarded the steamship *Star of the West* at Indianola, which was sent there to transport the disarmed troops to the North, and, posing as an officer of the United States Army, ordered the ship to New Orleans without the troops. It had been hoped that the troops could be induced to give up their pledge of allegiance to the United States. Colonel Albert Sidney Johnston, commander of the Second Cavalry, on leave in command of the Pacific Department, shared the same fate as all other regular soldiers stationed in Texas. Major Thomas was also on leave, as mentioned elsewhere, and Major William J. Hardee of the same regiment had been serving as commandant of cadets at West Point from July, 1856, to September, 1860.[22]

Major Thomas continued his convalescence in New York City while still on leave and showed gradual improvement from his spinal injury into the month of April, 1861.[23] It is surprising to learn that in this definitely northern city, even in the New York Hotel where he was residing, the flame of secession burned as fiercely as in South Carolina. Strife and discord were so bitter that great fear was entertained that there might not be left a nation for anyone to claim as his own. This seething ferment must have caused Thomas great anxiety, although it surely had a part in cementing his loyalty to the Union. His regiment, the Second Cavalry, or what was left of it after being traitorously surrendered to the Texas insurgents by General Twiggs, began arriving in New York in the early days of April.[24]

---

20. Richard W. Johnson, *A Soldier's Reminiscences* (Philadelphia: J. B. Lippincott Co., 1886), p. 133; Van Horne, *op. cit.*, pp. 20-21.

21. Van Horne, *ibid.*, p. 21.

22. Cullum, *op. cit.*, Vol. I, p. 561.

23. Van Horne, *op. cit.*, p. 23.

24. Henry Stone, *Some Federal and Confederate Commanders* (Boston: Houghton Mifflin Co., 1895), p. 172; Van Horne, *op. cit.*, pp. 27-28; Coppee, *op. cit.*, p. 31.

On April 10, the remaining leave of Major Thomas was canceled, and he was ordered to duty as commander of the Second Cavalry upon arrival of the remnants of the various companies in New York. His orders included the sending of two companies of the regiment to Army Headquarters in Washington, and the conducting of the other companies to Carlisle Barracks, Carlisle, Pennsylvania, for reorganization. While *en route* to Carlisle he learned of the firing on Fort Sumter, in Charleston Harbor, by the Confederate shore batteries commanded by General P. G. T. Beauregard. He promptly presented himself before a magistrate in Carlisle, before whom he renewed his pledge of allegiance to the United States.[25] This unequivocal act refuted for all time the false statement by some Southern officers that he wavered in his loyalty to the United States.

It would be inexcusable, if not unpardonable, to omit mention of the slander perpetrated against Thomas, as published in the Richmond, Virginia, *Dispatch* of April 23, 1870. This story referred to a letter from Fitzhugh Lee, a former Confederate general, and at one time a lieutenant in the Second Cavalry in which Thomas was a major. In this letter Lee is alleged to have stated "that just before the war Thomas's feelings were strongly Southern; that in 1861 he expressed his intention to resign; and about the same time, sent a letter to Governor Letcher, offering his services to Virginia." This article, it will be seen, was published within less than a month after General Thomas's death, on March 28, 1870, and is notable for two things: first, no such outright claim was made during his lifetime by Lee or anyone else; and second, failure to produce any such letter is sufficient proof of its nonexistence.

General James A. Garfield, subsequently President of the United States, in his famous oration before the Society of the Army of the Cumberland in April, 1870, had much to say in eulogy of General Thomas. He refuted the attempted efforts to cast doubt upon Thomas's loyalty, and in reference to Lee's letter, he stated:

> To this statement I invite the most searching scrutiny. That prior to the war the sentiments of Thomas were generally in accord with those which prevailed in Virginia, and that he strongly reprobated many of the opinions and much of the conduct of Northern politicians, were facts well known to his friends and always frankly avowed by himself. That in the winter of 1860-61, he contemplated the resignation of his commission, we have no proof except the declaration of Fitzhugh Lee. But it would not be in the least surprising or inconsistent, if, at that

25. Stone, *op. cit.*, p. 172.

time, it seemed to him more than probable that disunion would be accomplished, and the army dissolved by political action and without war. Should that happen, he must perforce abandon his profession and seek some other employment. If it should appear that at that time he made inquiries looking toward a prospective employment as professor in some college, the fact would only indicate his fear that the politicians would so ruin both his country and its army, that the commission of a soldier would be no longer an object of honorable desire.

When Fitzhugh Lee's letter was published, he was challenged on all sides to produce the letter which he alleged Thomas had written, tendering his services to the rebellion. His utter failure to produce any such letter, or any proof that such a letter was ever written, is a complete refutation of the charge.[26]

One can only conclude that Fitzhugh Lee either maliciously or thoughtlessly sought to create the impression that Thomas wavered in his loyalty, and that he was in accord with the many Southern officers of the United States Army who fought for the Confederacy.

General Garfield stated that testimony from all quarters completely disproved Lee's groundless charge against Thomas. One of these testimonials, from General George L. Hartsuff, who was on leave in New York near the close of 1860, and was therefore in the company of Major Thomas many times, is as follows:

General Thomas was strong and bitter in his denunciations against all parties North and South that seemed to him responsible for the condition of affairs. . . . But while he reprobated very strongly, certain men and parties North, in that respect going as far as any of those who afterward joined the rebels, he never, in my hearing, agreed with them respecting the necessity of going with their States; but he denounced the idea, and denied the necessity of dividing the country, or destroying the Government. This was before the actual secession of any of the States, when the prospect of war was not strong.

This is pretty conclusive proof that Thomas certainly had no intention ever of leaving the Union; but Garfield argued that the question was not what were the opinions of Thomas concerning political causes of the war. Rather it was, "Did he give any countenance, sympathy, or support to the idea of disunion, or of war against the Government?"[27]

---

26. Society of the Army of the Cumberland, *Yearbook, 1870* (Cincinnati: Robert Clarke and Co., 1871), pp. 65-66.

27. *Ibid.*, p. 67.

Further corroboration of Thomas's stand for the Union and a contradiction of Lee's allegation was given by Brigadier General Richard W. Johnson. It lends greater strength to the competent testimony received. General Johnson stated:

> After the surrender in Texas, my regiment [of which Thomas was major] concentrated at Carlisle Barracks. I was intimately associated with General Thomas from that time until the close of the war. During the Patterson campaign we messed together, and frequently conversed freely together in regard to the war. I remember to have asked him what he should do if Virginia seceded. His reply was characteristic of the man: "I will help to whip her back again." General Thomas never flinched nor faltered, nor wavered in his devotion to his country.[28]

Garfield furnished still further testimony, this from General Robert Patterson, under whom Thomas served during May and June, 1861. General Patterson said of him:

> General Thomas contemplated with horror the prospect of a war between the people of his own State and the Union; but he never for a moment hesitated, never wavered, never swerved, from his allegiance to the nation that had educated him and whose servant he was. From the beginning I would have pledged my hopes here and hereafter on the loyalty of Thomas. . . . He was the most unselfish man I ever knew; a perfectly honest man, who feared God and obeyed his commandments.[29]

Still more testimony is given by Garfield in a letter received from William T. Sherman, under whom Thomas served during the latter part of the war. It states:

> It was June 16, the very day Patterson's army crossed the Potomac. I had a long personal conversation with Thomas that day, and after discussing the events that then pressed so heavily on all who dreaded civil war, especially the course taken by our friends who had abandoned our service and gone South, I asked him how he felt. His answer was emphatic: "I have thought it all over," he said, "and I shall stand firm in the service of the Government."

If this is not enough to convince the most skeptical, then the word of long-time aide-de-camp, Colonel Alfred Lacey Hough, who, incidentally, was with Thomas in his last hours on earth, should dispel any remaining doubt:

---

28. *Ibid.*, p. 68.
29. *Ibid.*

A slander upon the general was often repeated in the Southern papers during and immediately subsequent to the rebellion. It was given upon the authority of prominent rebel officers, and not denied by them. It was to the effect that he was disappointed in not getting a high command in the rebel army he had sought for, hence his refusal to join the rebellion. In a conversation with him on the subject, the general said: this was an entire fabrication, not having an atom of foundation; not a line ever passed between him and the rebel authorities; they had no genuine letter of his, nor was a word spoken by him to any one that could even lead to such an inference. He defied any one to produce any testimony, written or oral, to sustain such allegations; he never entertained such an idea, for his duty was clear to him from the beginning.

The last sentence sums up the nobility of his character and the complete consistency and predictability of his life. Colonel Hough offered the further observation that these slanders against Thomas were authored by men who knew they had erred, but were seeking justification for themselves by making it appear that those who did not follow their course, as was of course the case with Thomas, Farragut, and others, had committed a great wrong. Hough believed these men were determined that no Southern-born man who had remained with the national Government should bear a good reputation.[30]

One of the most interesting conversations with Thomas, as related by Colonel Hough, concerned his opinion of the authors of such slanders and his views regarding their leaving the Union and joining the Confederacy. Colonel Hough reported:

In a discussion of the causes given for their action by some officers who deserted the Government at the beginning of the rebellion, I ventured the assertion that, perhaps, some of them at distinct posts had acted ignorantly; that I had been informed that some of them had been imposed upon by friends and relatives, and led to believe that there was to be a peaceable dissolution of the Union; that there would be no actual government for the whole country, and by resigning their commission they were only taking the necessary steps towards returning to the allegiance of their respective States, he replied that this was but a poor excuse, he could not believe officers of the army were so ignorant of their own form of government as to suppose such proceedings could occur, and as they had sworn allegiance to the government

---

30. Van Horne, *op. cit.*, p. 25.

they were bound to adhere to it, and would have done so if they had been so inclined. He said there was no excuse whatever in a United States officer claiming the right of secession, and the only excuse for their deserting the government was what none of them admitted having engaged in—a revolution against a tyranny, because the tyranny did not exist, and they well knew it. I then asked him, "Supposing such a state of affairs existed, that arrangements were being made for a peaceable dissolution of the Union by the Government, the North from the South, and that it was in progress, what would you have done?" He promptly replied, "That is not a supposable case; the government cannot dissolve itself; it is the creature of the people, and until they had agreed by their votes to dissolve it, and it was accomplished in accordance therewith, the government to which they had sworn allegiance remained, and as long as it did exist I should have adhered to it."[31]

Another most interesting comment relating to the withdrawal of Southern officers from the United States military service is given by Thomas's biographer Van Horne, in summation of the attitudes and influences that led to their decision. He stated that these officers claimed their oath of office was obligatory only during the period when they held office, and that any obligation terminated with their resignation, especially when their resignations were accepted.

This contention is based upon the assumption that prior allegiance is to the individual's state, and not to the aggregate or Union of states under the Federal Government. This process of rationalizing their decision to leave the Union was not shared by Thomas; rather, although he did not share the Northern view on slavery, he maintained his allegiance to the National Government because he believed it was the only choice for him. It is a strange viewpoint, indeed, that permitted these men to hold their states above the National Government; but strangest of all is that they could go beyond the surrendering of their commissions and take up arms against the very Government that educated them. Surely no one believed, upon taking the oath of allegiance, that some day he could take up arms against the very nation he was at this moment swearing to defend. Thomas felt that the National Government was in grave error when it accepted these resignations, particularly when everyone knew they intended to fight against it; but this viewpoint would not have restrained Robert E. Lee from leaving the army. Virginia passed the Ordnance of

31. *Ibid.*, pp. 25-26.

Secession on April 17, 1861; Lee resigned from the United States Army on April 20, 1861. The Virginia Convention confirmed his nomination as commander of the military and naval forces of Virginia on April 22, 1861, with the rank of major-general; and on April 23, 1861, two days before his resignation from the United States Army was accepted, and five days after Virginia militia had twice assaulted United States troops, this man . . . placed himself before the world as the enemy of the United States by accepting the position of commander-in-chief of the military and naval forces of his native State.[32]

Another fallacy, which probably had its origin in the disinclination of Southern sympathizers to realize that George H. Thomas could stand alone, if necessary, in doing what he believed right, concerned the alleged influence of his wife in holding him in the Union. This allegation is so out of character with his life and deeds that it is deserving of nothing but contempt; however, for the record, although he could have obtained a release from military service because of his spinal injury, he wrote to his wife upon arriving at Carlisle: "Whichever way I turn the matter over in my mind, my oath of allegiance always comes out uppermost."[33]

Before departing from New York, Major Thomas arranged with his wife to meet him at Carlisle in a few days, but after learning of the firing on the Federal garrison at Fort Sumter by the Confederates, he knew that the climactic event had occurred that would require the shedding of much blood before its fury would be spent. He sent her a telegram, and followed with a letter, telling her to remain in New York. He also wrote to his sisters in the old home at Southampton County, near Newsoms, Virginia, informing them of his decision.[34] Thus began that period in his life, filled with sadness, we may be sure, which meant estrangement from relatives and friends who branded him a traitor to his state for having dared to do his duty as he believed he should.

Regarding her husband's decision to remain in the United States Army, Mrs. Thomas said that "never a word passed between General Thomas and myself, or any one of the family, upon the subject of his remaining loyal to the Union."[35] There are those who refuse to concede that this statement of Mrs. Thomas is accurate, implying by their comments that she was not speaking the whole truth. This

---

32. *Ibid.*, pp. 26-29.
33. Coppee, *op. cit.*, pp. 35-36.
34. Van Horne, *op. cit.*, p. 28.
35. William Jeans, *Parliamentary Reminiscences* (London: Chapman and Hall, Ltd., 1912), p. 5.

skepticism is expressed by Gamaliel Bradford in his excellent book *Union Portraits*. Bradford noted that Thomas spent the greater part of the winter of 1860-61 with his wife in New York; also that everyone in New York was talking politics at that time and that therefore it was "almost incomprehensible" that no word on the subject was spoken to his wife by Thomas. Bradford illustrated his skepticism by citing that Lee was influenced by his wife, his friends, and his relatives; therefore, to make his argument complete, runs the implication, how could anyone believe that Thomas was not likewise influenced?[36] This kind of analysis and deduction is distressing, particularly the comparison of Lee with Thomas on the question of secession, on which they were far apart. Lee's opposition to secession was unequivocal, as expressed a number of times; in fact, as stated elsewhere herein, he called secession treason, and, in addition, stated his conviction that there was no necessity for the breaking up of the Union. By contrast, despite all attempts to prove otherwise based upon false reasoning and erroneous conclusions, there is nothing available to show what Thomas would do in the event of secession until he announced it; also no evidence has been produced to show the remotest instance when Thomas took a stand on principle and later turned his back on it. Nothing can take from Thomas the luster of his complete dependability, and the honor attaching to his incomparable character. The statement of Mrs. Thomas, in the absence of a reasonable basis for doubt as to its truth, should be accepted without question, because she was a truthful person. If General Thomas had the courage to remain in the Union despite all costs, which he did, he also had the courage, as did his wife, who knew him for the honest man he was, to tell the truth throughout.

---

36. Gamaliel Bradford, *Union Portraits* (Boston: Houghton Mifflin Co., 1916), p. 103.

CHAPTER VII

From Pennsylvania to
Camp Dick Robinson, Kentucky

BALTIMORE, Maryland, at the head of Chesapeake Bay, was the principal port of entry by road or railroad from the Northern states to the Capital at Washington, when the shadow of Civil War spread across the nation in 1861.

Washington, on the northern edge of the Confederacy, and about forty miles from Baltimore, was faced with two great dangers. One of these was the possibility of invasion from the South; the other was the Trojan horse of spies and saboteurs from within the city who sought to destroy the nation that gave them birth. Any interference with the movement of troops through Baltimore would pose a serious threat to Washington, since but one railroad entered the city, and the only other transportation was by way of the Potomac River. This latter, however, was extremely hazardous, as the river flowed through enemy-held territory at a number of points. It was inevitable, therefore, that the Federal authorities would be vitally interested in the attitude of the Maryland people, particularly Baltimoreans, many of whom were believed to have secessionist leanings. Since the neighboring state of Virginia had already left the Union, it was feared that Maryland might be encouraged to follow her lead.

President Lincoln's call for troops to quell the Southern uprising, and to compel the seceded states to return to the Union, but not least of all to protect the Capital, brought prompt response from the Northern states. Massachusetts was already in an advanced state of preparation for combat when the call for troops was made, and the Sixth Massachusetts Infantry Regiment rapidly filled its ranks and entrained for Washington. The journey through New England and New York was most receptive, and noisy demonstrations of good will were encountered everywhere. As expected, the greatest reception was from the residents of Philadelphia, the Cradle of Liberty, the home of the Liberty Bell, and the birthplace of the United States. Here they were warned that Maryland secessionists would not be so enthusiastic, but in obedience to orders, following a midnight bivouac, they left Philadelphia on the morning of April 19, *en route* to Washington by way of Baltimore. Having been forewarned, the Sixth Regiment commander, Colonel Edward F. Jones, issued the following order:

> The regiment will march through Baltimore in columns of sections, arms at will. You will undoubtedly be insulted, abused, and perhaps assaulted, to which you must pay no attention whatever, but march with your faces square to the front, and pay no attention to the mob; even if they throw stones, bricks, or other missiles; but if you are fired upon, and any one of you is hit, your officers will order you to fire. Do not fire into any promiscuous crowd; but select any man whom you may see aiming at you, and be sure you drop him.[1]

These instructions were based on the supposition that the troops would be transferred on foot from the Pennsylvania Railroad, which brought them from Philadelphia, to the Baltimore and Ohio Railroad, for movement to Washington. For some unknown reason the railroad people changed the plan, which was a stunning surprise to Colonel Jones; so instead of forming his regiment for a march to the Baltimore and Ohio, he was required to make the trip in horse-drawn cars. These cars succeeded in reaching the Baltimore and Ohio in safety, although a large crowd of hostile citizens disputed their way. The excited crowd used vile language and threatened the soldiers with knives and pistols, before they were enabled, with the help of police, to change cars. Not so fortunate were the soldiers who came later; these were opposed by a much larger mob, which followed them through the streets and, nearing Pratt Street, hurled paving stones and fired an occasional rifle or revolver. Fortunately, only a few of the soldiers were wounded; but as the crowd persisted, the soldiers were ordered to lie on the floor of the cars, load, and fire at will. Mayor George W. Brown, of Baltimore, intervened at this point to request that the remaining troops march through the city as originally planned, and to insure that the change should be made with the least amount of friction, he ordered additional police protection for the marchers. Not content with letting the matter end there, the rioters began

---

1. John G. Nicolay and John Hay, *Abraham Lincoln: A History* (New York: The Century Co., 1909), Vol. IV, pp. 104-11.

tearing up the tracks and piling loose stones and dirt all about to interfere with the further movement of the troops.[2]

The order to march through Baltimore did not reach the remaining four companies, although they likewise marched after learning of the trouble experienced by the advance companies in the horse-drawn cars. Almost at once they were met with shouts and epithets from the increasing mob, and eventually a struggle ensued for the secessionist banner borne by the rioters. The soldiers ran on the double-quick to avert trouble, but this only incited the mob to greater fury, the rioters interpreting it as a show of cowardice. The angry attackers took after the soldiers, but the soldiers were able to reach comparative safety on the opposite side of a damaged bridge. From this vantage point the soldiers returned the fire, which ended the rioting, but only after four soldiers were killed and eight wounded. Eight civilians were also killed and an unknown number were wounded.[3]

This was somewhat representative of the feeling in the border states when Major Thomas, with four companies of the Second Cavalry, moved, on April 21, 1861, to protect the Northern Central Railroad from another mob of Maryland secessionists.[4] From this incident a strong reaction resulted in both North and South, and, not surprisingly, a number of inspirational songs were thenceforth produced. The most famous, in the judgment of some, "Maryland, My Maryland," by James Ryder Randall, refers in the opening lines to the April 19 rioting in Baltimore:

The despot's heel is on thy shore, Maryland, my Maryland!
His torch is at thy temple door, Maryland, my Maryland!
Avenge the patriotic gore, that flecked the streets of Baltimore,
And be the battle queen of yore, Maryland, my Maryland!

Randall, a native of Maryland, was teaching in a small college near New Orleans, Louisiana, when the Sixth Massachusetts was stoned, which he alluded to in the last two lines above. The following lines appeal to his beloved Maryland to put on the armor of chivalry during his absence:

---

2. *Ibid.*, pp. 111-14.
3. *Ibid.*, pp. 115-17.
4. Thomas B. Van Horne, *The Life of Major General George H. Thomas* (New York: Charles Scribner's Sons, 1882), p. 30; The Fitz John Porter Papers (Washington, D.C.: Library of Congress), Vol. I, p. 49; *Encyclopedia Americana* (New York: American Book—Stratford Press, 1954), Vol. XXIII, pp. 207-8; Benson J. Lossing, *A Pictorial History of the Civil War in the United States* (Elgin, Pa., 1885), Vol. I, pp. 411, 413.

Hark to an absent son's appeal, Maryland, my Maryland!
My mother state, to thee I kneel, Maryland, my Maryland!
For life or death, for woe or weal, thy peerless chivalry reveal,
And gird thy beauteous limbs with steel, Maryland, my Maryland!

These inspired lines were set to the tune of the German Christmas carol, "O Tannenbaum," and next to the famous Southern battle cry of Dixie, it was the most popular song of the Confederacy. Doctor Oliver Wendell Holmes is said to have regarded it as the finest song produced by either side during the war.[5]

In view of the trouble in Baltimore, Major Thomas was directed by Secretary of War Cameron to return to Pennsylvania with his command. This action was the result of an appeal by Mayor Brown, who asked that no more troops be routed through Baltimore until conditions were improved.[6]

On April 25, 1861, Major Thomas was promoted to the rank of Lieutenant Colonel to fill the vacancy created by the resignation of Robert E. Lee. On May 3, just eight days later, he was again promoted, this time to a full colonelcy, to fill the place of Albert Sidney Johnston. Johnston had resigned while in California, and was *en route* to Texas to join the Confederacy, after learning that his native Kentucky was remaining in the Union.[7] Less than a year later General Johnston met his death at the controversial Battle of Shiloh. These promotions were due to the large number of vacancies created by resignations of Southern officers and were not in any sense gratuitous. Immediately following the commencement of hostilities, the Washington authorities required that all officers take an oath of allegiance, although they had taken such an oath when entering the service. It was thought by some officers that this was an unwarranted insult, but when Major Thomas was asked his opinion regarding it, he replied, "I do not care a snap of my finger about it. If they want me to take the oath before each meal I am ready to comply." This oath incorporated a promise to "bear true faith and allegiance to the United States of America against all enemies and opposers whomsoever."[8] Inevitably Thomas

5. Willard A. and Porter W. Heaps, *The Singing Sixties* (Norman, Okla.: University of Oklahoma Press, 1960), p. 28.

6. Porter Papers, *op. cit.*, Vol. I, pp. 34, 61, 68; Freeman Cleaves, *Rock of Chickamauga* (Norman, Okla.: University of Oklahoma Press, 1949), pp. 68-69.

7. Henry Stone, *Some Federal and Confederate Commanders* (Boston: Houghton Mifflin Co., 1885), p. 173; George W. Cullum, *Biographical Register of Officers and Cadets of the U. S. Military Academy* (Boston, 1891), Vol. I, p. 600.

8. Richard W. Johnson, *A Soldier's Reminiscences* (Philadelphia: J. B. Lippincott Co., 1886), p. 161.

took two additional oaths of allegiance upon receiving his two recent promotions, but these would not have been requested if there had been serious doubt of his loyalty.

General Robert Patterson, a veteran of the War of 1812 and also the Mexican War, was commissioned major-general and placed in command of a force at Chambersburg, Pennsylvania. In response to Patterson's request for cavalry to round out his force, Colonel Thomas was directed to report to him with Companies A, C, F, and K of the Second Cavalry. These companies were ready to move promptly, and on May 27, 1861, arrived at Chambersburg, where they encamped in a beautiful wooded area near the town. On May 29, Thomas was given command of the First Brigade, including the famous Philadelphia City Troop, which was organized during the American Revolution, and included the cream of Philadelphia society. This famous Troop escorted General George Washington from Philadelphia to Boston in 1775.[9]

During the final days at Chambersburg, when moving southward was under discussion, a difference of opinion arose between Commander in Chief General Winfield Scott and General Patterson regarding the point at which Patterson should cross the Potomac into Virginia. It was Patterson's idea to cross opposite Leesburg, Virginia, but Scott directed him to cross at Williamsport, Maryland. This directive became a subject of controversy later, since the reinforcing of Beauregard at the Battle of Bull Run, by the variously estimated force of from six to sixteen thousand men, under General Joseph E. Johnston, turned the tide in favor of the South and led to the dismissal of Patterson.[10] Much discussion has revolved around Patterson's responsibility for the debacle at Bull Run, it being felt that he should have held Johnston in check; but it is interesting enough that Thomas, in the following letter, supported Patterson, his former commander.

HEADQUARTERS, DEPARTMENT OF THE CUMBERLAND,
BEFORE ATLANTA, GA., Aug. 8th, 1864

MY DEAR GENERAL:

Your favor of the 16th July, was duly received a few days since, owing doubtless to the irregularities of the mails at the front. In the council of war at Martinsburg, I in substance advised an advance towards Winchester, at least as far as Bunker

9. Henry Coppee, *General Thomas* (New York, 1893), p. 31; Stone, *op. cit.*, p. 173; Cullum, *op. cit.*, Vol. I, p. 600; Richard W. Johnson, *Memoir of Major General George H. Thomas* (Philadelphia: J. B. Lippincott Co., 1881), p. 38.

10. Johnson, *ibid.*, pp. 42-43; Johnson, *Reminiscences*, p. 168; *Battles and Leaders of the Civil War* (New York, 1884), Vol. I, p. 182.

Hill, and if your information, after the army reached Bunker Hill, led you to believe that Johnston still occupied Winchester in force, then to shift our troops over to Charleston, as that would place our communications with our depot of supplies in safety, and still threaten and hold Johnston at Winchester, which I understand was all that you were expected to do. I should have advised a direct advance on Winchester, but for the character of the troops composing your army. They were all, with the exception of a couple of squadrons of Second U. S. Cavalry and two batteries of regular artillery, three-month's men, and their terms of service would expire in a few days. Judging of them as of other Volunteer troops, had I been commander, I should not have been willing to risk them in a heavy battle, coming off within a few days of the expiration of their service.

I have always believed, and have frequently so expressed myself, that your management of the three-month's campaign was able and judicious, and was in the best interest of the service, considering the means at your disposal, and the nature of the troops under your command.

With much respect and esteem, I remain, General,

Very sincerely and truly yours,

GEORGE H. THOMAS,
Major-General, U.S.V.

MAJOR-GENERAL ROBERT PATTERSON,
Philadelphia, Pa. [11]

This expression of Thomas's loyalty to his former commander is consistent with his conduct throughout his military career; and he did not, in this instance or at any future time, withhold his judgment when to do so might subject himself to reprisal from higher authorities. Whether or not we may have a contrary opinion as to the withdrawal of Johnston to join Beauregard, thereby seemingly, it appeared, eluding Patterson, Thomas knew the circumstances and believed that Patterson was blameless. It is plain that something could be said for Patterson's choice of Leesburg, rather than Scott's choice of Williamsport, at which to cross the Potomac. It is evident that Leesburg offered a greater opportunity for Patterson to join McDowell, regardless of what happened to Johnston, due to its much shorter distance to the battlefield of Bull Run. One shudders at the thought of Johnston's movement of troops to Bull Run, and of the possible effect on the outcome of the war, if Patterson's plan to cross at Leesburg had been

11. Robert Patterson, *A Narrative of the Campaign in the Valley of the Shenandoah in 1861* (Philadelphia, 1865), pp. 106-7.

approved. This plan had the agreement of Colonel Thomas; and the Battle of Bull Run was decided by Johnston's quick movement to the battlefield, while Patterson was handicapped by lack of specific instructions from the over-all command. It is surprising that Johnston, either before or after Bull Run, did not attempt to combine forces with Beauregard for an attack on Washington.[12]

The advance force of Patterson's army under Colonel J. J. Abercrombie marched to the Potomac, and at 4:00 A.M. on July 2, followed by Thomas, crossed into Virginia. After a march of approximately four miles, a Confederate force, estimated variously at between two thousand five hundred and three thousand men, under Thomas J. Jackson, later to become world famous as "Stonewall," was encountered at Falling Waters, near Martinsburg, Virginia, now West Virginia. Colonel Abercrombie deployed his men promptly, and Colonel Thomas also moved up at once and formed a line on Abercrombie's right. When the line moved forward the Confederates retreated under the steady fire directed at them, but the Federals pursued them several miles until darkness ended the engagement.[13] Federal losses were eight killed and fifteen wounded, and the Confederates lost thirteen killed and about fifty wounded.[14] These losses may be accepted with some reservation, as should also the numbers engaged on each side. Exhaustive research has failed to disclose reliable statistics concerning either the casualties or the number engaged. It seems clear, however, that, although Jackson withdrew, he was under orders from Johnston to avoid bringing on a general engagement; but perhaps the most compelling reason was that he was greatly outnumbered.

As a military action, Falling Waters was a mere skirmish, although it was regarded by the North as a moral victory. It was, perhaps, the principal clash of arms in that section before the Battle of Bull Run. One of the chief matters of interest was the presence on opposite sides, in their only meeting of the war, of two of the greatest military leaders produced on this continent. Although little is said by writers concerning Jackson's part in the skirmish, there is enough left to us to know that Thomas showed poise of the highest quality, as evidenced by the favorable comment in reports of the action.[15] These two men were giants in character and determination; and future generations, in search of an example of propriety on

12. Johnson, *Memoir*, pp. 43-44.

13. *Ibid.*, p. 44.

14. Edgar A. Werner, *Historical Sketches of the War of the Rebellion, 1861–1865* (Albany, N.Y.: West, Parsons and Co., 1890), p. 164.

15. Stone, *loc. cit.*

the field of battle and in the quietude of civilian pursuits, need not look further than to these two great men. Both were noted for their devotion to duty and to clean living. No Northern soldier was more dedicated to his cause than was George H. Thomas; and Thomas J. Jackson was equally devoted to his beloved South.

It was not easy for Thomas figuratively to "cross the Rubicon," and thus take his stand for the Union some months before crossing the Potomac; but his decision once arrived at after mature consideration of his duty to his country and his friends, his purpose in entering Virginia, if it should come to that, was not conquest but national unity. His duty having been clear from the beginning, there was nothing to do now but perform it. If he had any doubt of the wisdom of his earlier decision, here, with his face to the South and under orders to cross the Potomac, was the time to change his mind. The idea of turning back was definitely not entertained; he knew where he was going, having "thought it all out," and there was no turning back; now was the time, therefore, to unsheath his sword to bring his state back into the fold or, as he put it, "to help to whip her back again."

On July 3, following the flight of the Confederates from Falling Waters to Martinsburg, Colonel Thomas and his troops, comprising the advance of Patterson's army, skirmished occasionally with the retreating foe. In the march toward Winchester he again led the advance, and on July 15 succeeded in driving forward the rear guard of the enemy at Bunker Hill.[16]

The designation of the Second Cavalry was changed by Act of Congress to the Fifth Cavalry on August 3, 1861, which resulted in consolidation of the dragoons, mounted rifles, and cavalry into a single branch of the service. On August 17, Colonel Thomas was appointed a brigadier general of volunteers and directed to report to Brigadier General Robert Anderson at Louisville, Kentucky. General Anderson, the commander of Fort Sumter in the opening engagement of the Civil War, had accepted the command of troops in his native Kentucky on condition that he could appoint four brigadier generals to serve under him. He had thus far selected William T. Sherman, Don Carlos Buell, and Ormsby M. Mitchell, and was considering the appointment of Simon Bolivar Buckner as the fourth man. His nephew, Lieutenant Thomas M. Anderson of the Fifth Cavalry, visited him while in Washington, and when Anderson mentioned that he was planning to recommend Buckner, the nephew assured him that Buckner was going with the South, and that Colonel Thomas should be considered for the vacancy. Citing the fine performance of Thomas with

16. Van Horne, *op. cit.*, p. 32.

Patterson, in addition to his definite loyalty, young Anderson persuaded his uncle that Thomas was the man he needed.[17] Buckner subsequently became commander of the Confederates at Fort Donelson, and, as such, recipient of one of the most famous dispatches in American military history. This dispatch stated in part, "No terms except unconditional and immediate surrender can be accepted," and became the basis for General Grant's nickname of "Unconditional Surrender" Grant, as suggested by the initials U.S. Buckner's son, Simon Bolivar Buckner, Jr., born in 1886 when his father was sixty-three years old, became a lieutenant general in the United States Army in World War II, and was killed by shrapnel at Okinawa on June 18, 1945. His father was also a lieutenant general in the Confederate Army, and reached the ripe old age of ninety-one.[18]

A letter from General Thomas to General Anderson confirms the latter's selection of Thomas. Sherman's *Memoirs* refer to a conversation in Washington with General Anderson, in which the latter had difficulty convincing President Lincoln that Thomas was deserving a promotion to the rank of brigadier general, as so many other Southern officers had left the Union. Sherman stated that he stressed to the President his own endorsement of Thomas, based principally upon a conversation he had had with him at the time of Patterson's move across the Potomac, whereupon the promotion was made. There is little to support Sherman's contention; in fact, from whatever else we have available as emanating from Sherman concerning Thomas, we may correctly infer that Sherman was not really a friend to Thomas. We may read Sherman's protestations of friendship, but his actions spoke so loudly that his words were inaudible; in fact, if Sherman had given Thomas his due, the need for such a work as this, to set the record straight, would hardly be necessary. Sherman no doubt alluded to a meeting in his brother John's lodgings, in a tavern near Williamsport, when discussing Thomas's promotion with the President. The letter is as follows:

CAMP NEAR HYATTSTON, MD.
August 26, 1861

DEAR GENERAL:

Your letter of the 19th inst. enclosing my appointment as a Brigadier General of Volunteers was received on last Saturday. It will give me the greatest pleasure to be under your command and I will endeavor to report in person in Cincinnati on the 1st

---

17. Johnson, *Reminiscences*, *op. cit.*, pp. 170-71; Van Horne, *op. cit.*, pp. 32, 35.

18. *Encyclopedia Americana*, *op. cit.*, Vol. IV, p. 669.

of Sept. for further instructions from you. I was very much gratified to find from your letter that I was to be associated with
Generals Sherman and Burnside, both old and valued friends.

　　I am General,

Yours very truly,
GEORGE H. THOMAS
Brig. Gen. U.S. Vol.[19]

Referring again to the meeting between Sherman and Thomas at
Williamsport, the two former West Point classmates here met for the
first time in many years. The meeting was enlivened by a discussion
of the probable strategy necessary for victory in the forthcoming
North-South struggle. On their knees, animatedly looking at a large
map they had spread before them on the floor, they pointed out the
important strategic points for attack and defense. These were
Richmond, Vicksburg, Nashville, Knoxville, and Chattanooga, among
others. John Sherman said later that to him it was always strange
that they were able to predict confidently and correctly the lines of
operation and the strategic locations of a war not yet begun, and what
is not of small importance is that they would be leading figures
in battles at a number of the places listed by them.[20]

　　The endorsement of Thomas for promotion, by one of his men in
the ranks, is of more than usual interest, for it shows the confidence
others had in him even at that early date. This unique letter is
helpful in demonstrating the hold Thomas had upon the hearts and
minds of those serving under him, even before he had demonstrated
his unsurpassed ability on the battlefields of the South.

SANDY HOOK, MD., Aug. 3, 1861.

FRIEND SCOTT:

　　I hear you are the Assistant Secretary of War. Rest assured
that no man delights more in your high position than I do. I
notice that the Government is now considering the appointment of
proper persons to be brigadier generals. In the name of God, let
them be men fully competent to discharge the duties of the
positions to which they may be assigned. Inefficiency is the evil of
the hour. This opinion is based upon our observation of nearly
three months. Most of the time, in fact nearly all of the time,
we have been under the command of Colonel George H. Thomas,
now commanding one of the brigades here. He is thoroughly

---

19. Letter on file in the U.S. Military Academy Library, West Point, N.Y.
20. John Sherman, *Recollections of Forty Years in the U.S. Senate, House
and Cabinet* (New York, 1895), Vol. I, p. 250; William T. Sherman, *Personal
Memoirs* (New York, 1891), Vol. I, p. 192.

competent to be a brigadier-general, has the confidence of every man in his command for the reason that they recognize and appreciate capacity—which to them in every hour of the day is so essential to their safety. Now let me as a friend of this Administration, in so far as the war is concerned and the preservation of the Union is involved, urge upon General Cameron to select Colonel Thomas as one of the proposed brigadiers. I am, as perhaps you know, a private in the First City Cavalry of Philadelphia, and I never saw Colonel Thomas until I saw him on parade, and our intercourse has been such as exists between a colonel and one of his soldiers; hence you see my recommendation comes from pure motives, and entirely free from social and political considerations. I speak for and write in behalf of the brave men who, in this hour of our country's peril, are coming forward and endangering their own lives, and perhaps leaving those most dear to them without support. I write warmly, because I think I know the necessity of the case. You will do the country a service by giving my letter a serious consideration. I hope to be in Washington some time about the 1st of September, when I shall try to see you. Will you please present my regards to General Cameron, and if he has time to read this letter, hand it to him.

Yours truly,
SAMUEL J. RANDALL[21]

It is not difficult to perceive from this letter that much of the success of Thomas in the days to follow had its beginning in the instinctive confidence and loyalty he inspired in men. It is this virtue, call it *esprit de corps,* morale, or whatever, that carries leadership to heights not enjoyed by men not so endowed.

General Anderson must have regarded General Thomas's Southern birth as an important factor in his selection for promotion and assignment to Kentucky, just as it had been a factor in the selection of himself (Anderson), and also Richard W. Johnson and Thomas J. Wood, among others. Such men, it was believed, would have greater influence in the continuing effort to hold Kentucky in the Union.

Any confidence that Samuel Randall's letter might have exerted a material influence in the selection of Thomas for promotion should be tempered by a knowledge of political realities, and these were many. When the first list of promotions was issued, there were included thereon the names of Fitz John Porter, adjutant general to Patterson; Charles P. Stone, a brigade commander; George A. McCall of the

---

21. Van Horne, *op. cit.,* p. 37.

Pennsylvania militia; Charles S. Hamilton, a Wisconsin colonel; and other lesser political generals of the type of John A. McClernand, all of which promotions were to date from May 17, 1861; but the name of Colonel Thomas, who had done more than any of them to earn promotion, was not included in the list. Tragically, as it turned out, not only for Thomas but for the country, some of these appointees obtained seniority over Thomas for the first time; in fact, Thomas stood fifty-fifth on the new list, although on the old army list he outranked all of the officers who became his superiors in the volunteer service.[22]

For those who have maintained, both orally and through the printed word, that Thomas was advanced rapidly and that his eulogists bellowed Thomas's claims when there was no reason for it, this instance alone is sufficient to show that if merit had been considered he would not have become subordinate to inferiors. It is sad but undoubtedly true that Thomas, despite his unquestioned loyalty, paid the price of Southern ostracism for fighting with the Union, and of Northern indifference, in part due to the fact that he did not fight for the South. No basis existed for any distrust of him; in fact, the very opposite is true, since, with his uninterrupted successes, he earned every right to the fullest confidence. The factor of distrust, if true, is ridiculous, since, if this were so, how did Admiral Farragut, the great Union naval hero of the Civil War and a Southerner, succeed? Then there was Governor Andrew Johnson, later Vice President of the United States and eventually President, who was from Tennessee. The answer seems to be that neither Farragut nor Johnson had Grant and Sherman to damn them with faint praise through the accusation of "slowness," which meant writing off his every success. The tragedy is that the American people have not been able to see through the remarks of Grant and Sherman, but more especially to ask, "Where are the victories and achievements of Grant and Sherman to match those of Thomas?" Then the remark, in speaking of Thomas, "He was never brilliant but always cool, reliable and steady, maybe a little slow."[23] The fast generals were Grant at Shiloh, Cold Harbor, Petersburg; Sherman at Chickasaw Bayou, Missionary Ridge, Kenesaw; McDowell at First Bull Run; Pope at Second Bull Run; Burnside at Fredericksburg; Hooker at Chancellorsville. Thomas is not mentioned here, yet he had no defeats, made no mistakes, accomplished nothing but victories and salvages from disaster, all the latter of which were due to the mistakes of others.

---

22. Stone, *op. cit.*, pp. 174-75.
23. William T. Sherman, *The Sherman Letters* (New York: Charles Scribner's Sons, 1894), p. 123.

Following his appointment to the rank of brigadier general, Thomas was assigned to the Department of the Cumberland, which had been constituted on August 15, 1861, and comprised the states of Kentucky and Tennessee.[24] The assignment order by Headquarters of the Army, dated August 24, 1861, was as follows:

The following assignment is made of the general officers of the Volunteer Service, whose appointment was announced in General Orders No. 62, from the War Department.

To the Department of the Cumberland, Brigadier-General Robert Anderson commanding:
Brigadier-General W. T. Sherman
Brigadier-General George H. Thomas
By command of Lieutenant-General Scott.

E. D. TOWNSEND
Assistant Adjutant-General

On August 26, General Thomas was relieved from command of the First Brigade, then under the over-all command of Major General Nathaniel P. Banks, successor to General Patterson, and instructed to report to his new commander, General Robert Anderson, at Louisville, Kentucky. He arrived at Louisville on September 6, and was assigned by General Anderson to command Camp Dick Robinson on September 10. Thus began a career in the Army of the Cumberland that lasted virtually until the end of the Civil War. No individual on either side was more identified with an army than was General Thomas with that army. Particularly important in this tenure of command was the degree of skill with which he solved the many problems incident to training his men and aiding in holding Kentucky for the Union; and too much credit cannot be given General Anderson for the wisdom he showed in selecting the men to serve with him in accomplishing these objectives.[25]

The command of Camp Dick Robinson was the most important assignment in the Department at that time, and it undoubtedly reflected the confidence of General Anderson in the ability of Thomas to supervise the important task of preparing raw troops for combat service. The camp was situated in a beautiful blue-grass location in Garrard County, not far from where the pike for Lancaster and Crab Orchard leaves the Lexington and Danville pike, between Danville and Lexington and between the Dix and Kentucky rivers. It

24. *Legends of Operations of the Army of the Cumberland* (Washington, D.C.: Government Printing Office, 1869), p. 3.
25. Van Horne, *op. cit.*, p. 40; *Official Records of the War of the Rebellion* (Washington, D.C., 1880–1901), Series 1, Vol. IV, p. 257.

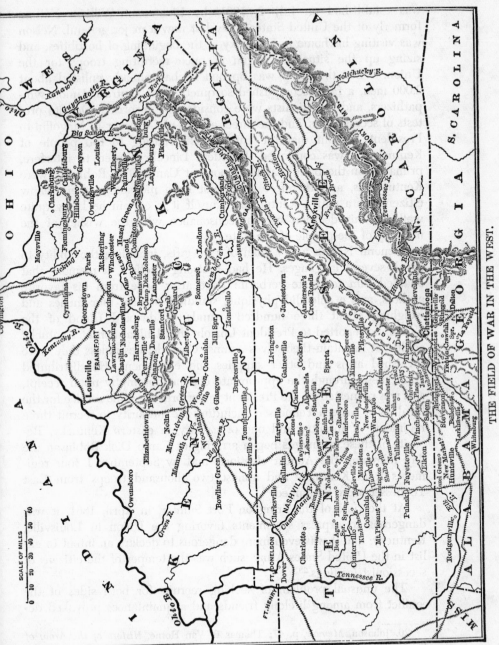

THE FIELD OF WAR IN THE WEST.

was established on July 2, 1861, by Lieutenant William Nelson, formerly of the United States Navy but now a major general. Nelson was visiting his home in Kentucky at the beginning of hostilities, and sizing up the situation, began at once recruiting troops for the Union. When the camp was opened he had already enlisted about 2,000 men, a fact accomplished so quietly that neutrals, Union sympathizers, and secessionists were considerably surprised. Despite protests of secessionists, and the direct appeal of Governor B. Magoffin to President Lincoln that the camp was irritating to the people of Kentucky, it was continued. President Lincoln refused to interfere, primarily on the basis that the troops at Camp Dick Robinson were Kentuckians, and therefore could not be a menace to their fellow citizens. As a native Kentuckian himself it is certain he knew quite well that his decision was in consonance with the wishes of the majority of the people of the state.[26]

General Nelson was a man of rare gifts, including the ability to speak several languages. He had a strong intellect, a memory that enabled him to recite verbatim page after page from his favorite authors, and a splendid physique, standing six feet four inches and weighing about three hundred pounds. A devoted friend of the Union, he reported to President Lincoln that Union men of Kentucky could not maintain themselves against Confederates unless they were furnished arms and other supplies and equipment. He distributed all of these through the appropriate channels promptly upon receipt, and was requested by the President to perform the same service for the loyalists of eastern Tennessee, including the authority to recruit three regiments of infantry and one of cavalry in eastern Kentucky. Recruits of these regiments began arriving at Camp Dick Robinson the day following the August elections, and by September 1 four regiments from Kentucky and almost two thousand troops from East Tennessee were encamped.[27]

At the time of the firing on Fort Sumter, in April, 1861, it was dangerous to express sentiments favoring the Union in Louisville, Kentucky; and it was even more dangerous to declare an intent to enlist in the United States Army, such was the temper of the citizens of secessionist leanings.[28]

The unusual problem of seeking recruits for both sides of the conflict from among lifelong friends and acquaintances provoked de-

26. Johnson, *Memoir*, p. 47; Thomas B. Van Horne, *History of the Army of the Cumberland* (Cincinnati: Robert Clarke and Co., 1875), Vol. I, pp. 16-17; *Battles and Leaders, op. cit.*, Vol. I, pp. 375-77.

27. *Battles and Leaders, ibid.*

28. Van Horne, *Army of the Cumberland*, Vol. I, p. 14.

nunciations and threats by Southerners who openly recruited troops for their cause. It was a common occurrence to see the Confederate flag flying in front of men marching away as enemies of their country; but toward those who enlisted in defense of the Union the Southern sympathizers felt loathing and contempt usually reserved for those guilty of traitorous actions.[29]

On July 22, the day following the Federal defeat at Bull Run, a menacing development occurred at Louisville, when secessionists led by one Tompkins, a notorious local chief of the Knights of the Golden Circle, gave strong evidence of an intent to take over the city. When Tompkins was killed by a loyal policeman named G. A. Green, the ensuing excitement disclosed the preponderance of loyalists in such convincing numbers that plans for controlling Louisville were abandoned.[30]

Kentucky had strong hopes of remaining neutral in the forthcoming struggle, but this was but an idle dream; and since all evidence pointed to its remaining in the Union, many secessionists joined the Confederate forces in northern Tennessee. These same men then looked ahead to the day when they might re-enter their native Kentucky as an invading force, despite the clear wishes of a majority of its people, and compel the state to leave the Union. One does not need to think much beyond this fact to realize that it was one thing to proclaim loudly for the rights of states, but quite a different matter when the exercise of such rights did not correspond with the desires of those who gave loudest voice to their belief in the exercise of those rights. To these men states' rights meant the right only to believe in what the secessionists believed, namely, withdrawal from the Federal Union.[31]

On September 5, General Leonidas Polk occupied Hickman and Chalk Bluffs, Kentucky, and on the seventh he also occupied Columbus, Kentucky. In order to meet this threat, Brigadier General U. S. Grant landed troops at Paducah, Kentucky, supported by two gunboats; reinforcements were also sent him on the seventh, and so for the first time the United States and Confederate forces occupied the state of Kentucky. General Felix K. Zollicoffer strengthened these forces a few days later, when he occupied Cumberland Gap and moved part of his troops into Kentucky. Any hope of neutrality by the people of the state was abandoned at this occurrence, and they were compelled to take sides; in fact, the only alternative to taking sides was armed resistance to both forces, which would have been an utterly

29. *Ibid.*, p. 15.
30. *Ibid.*, pp. 20-21.
31. *Ibid.*, p. 23.

impracticable if not ridiculous undertaking. "Neutrality, considered as a principle, or viewed in relation to the organic subordination of the individual state to the general government and the imperative requirements of patriotism, is wholly without justification." There may be some debate whether or not the delay in declaring for one side or the other was an over-all advantage to her people; but it is equally certain that as events unfolded and time lengthened the people were enabled to see through the maze of conflicting claims and counter-claims relating to the war, they were convinced that the Union was not a deterrent to their rights, their freedom, or their way of life. It is important to note that Kentucky gave fifty-six thousand men to the Federal service, most of them in the Western armies, and that many important leaders of the North were Kentuckians.[32]

Shortly before General Thomas left Louisville the State Guard, then under the control of Southerners, including Colonel Humphrey Marshall and Major John C. Breckinridge, Jr., among others, planned an encampment at Lexington, Kentucky, ostensibly with a view toward conducting drills, but actually for the purpose of capturing the Frankfort Arsenal and taking over the state. Appeals were made through a number of Kentucky newspapers and in posters placed in conspicuous places throughout the state urging States Rights and Peace Men to assemble on September 20 for drilling over a period of several days. Upon learning of this development General Thomas, on September 20, ordered Colonel Thomas E. Bramlette with his Third Kentucky Infantry to proceed to Lexington to defeat the move by the Confederates. The movement of Bramlette was so quietly con-ducted that he succeeded in occupying the Fair Grounds the night before the expected seizure of the Arsenal, and the plan had to be abandoned. It seems certain that this quick action by Thomas averted bloodshed, although its true importance was not fully realized until some time later. It is not surprising that Southern sympathizers planned to capture General Thomas while on his way to Kentucky, but for some unexplained reason the plot fell through, and he arrived on September 15 without serious incident.[33]

When General Thomas arrived at Camp Dick Robinson, he found only a small quantity of firearms, ammunition, supplies, and no quartermaster. These and other deficiencies made it totally inadequate for approximately six thousand troops. The troops, in a partly organ-ized condition, had been assembled by General Nelson, despite the opposition of both loyalists and secessionists. The troops anticipated

32. *Ibid.*, pp. 23-25.
33. *Ibid.*, p. 30.

the arrival of Thomas with some degree of enthusiasm, because they were dissatisfied with General Nelson's salty speech and manner,[34] although he had worked mightily to mold them into a competent fighting oranization. In addition to four partly organized regiments from Kentucky, there were men from Ohio, Indiana, Illinois, Tennessee, and other neighboring states. It would have occasioned no surprise if General Thomas had felt misgivings at the sight of some of these men of varying degrees of social and economic status; but he knew that they were men of a noble bent who needed but the discipline of military life to bring out the qualities that would make their presence felt on many battlefields. Most of the men had come from mountainous and rural areas, which are conducive to the rustic habits and accompanying independence that offer resistance to the enforcement of military control; yet they were to become what may be considered the beginning of the magnificent, the unsurpassed, Army of the Cumberland. What an achievement it was for Thomas to organize, train, instruct, and shape these men into the nucleus that expanded into that unyielding force at Mill Springs, Murfreesboro, Chickamauga, Missionary Ridge, Lookout Mountain, and in the hard-fought battles on the way to Atlanta; and what is more, they would sweep from Atlanta to the sea and from thence through the Carolinas and Virginia to the close of the war! Many in this army would learn that while in their country's service their homes were laid waste by marauding guerrillas, their families scattered to whatever shelter available, and similar harassments. Unmindful of the cost to themselves personally, they did their whole duty as they understood it.[35]

Not only did General Thomas personally direct the enlisted personnel in the minutest details of organization and equipment; he also had the responsibility of directing the Home Guard in central Kentucky. His nearness to the Kentucky capital naturally drew the attention of the authorities to his usefulness in connection with their interests, and they held discussions with him concerning the threat from General Zollicoffer and his force. Zollicoffer was hoping to prevent the movement of east Tennesseeans to the Federal armies; to prevent the advance of reinforcements to Federal troops in Kentucky; to hold at all hazards the vitally important East Tennessee and Virginia Railroad; and to help as much as possible Confederate forces seeking permanent occupancy of the state. In this atmosphere, the legislature

---

34. Johnson, *Memoir*, p. 47; Gilbert C. Kniffen, *Life and Services of Major General George H. Thomas* (Washington, D.C.; Military Order of the Loyal Legion, D.C. Commandery, 1887), p. 12.

35. *Ibid.*, pp. 13-14; Van Horne, *Army of the Cumberland*, Vol. I, p. 26.

of Kentucky, backed by loyal citizens of the state, requested him to protect Lexington with Federal troops, as stated previously.[36]

General Thomas was of the proper temperament to command men of whatever background and, from their admiration and respect of him, born of his commanding presence and personality, train them to become unconquerable soldiers. Thomas was the type who "used no stilts"; in other words, he was as restrained in his private conduct and demeanor as when on the parade ground or before groups in which restraint was the required or expected behavior pattern. He was as respectful, attentive, and patient with a subordinate as with an equal or a superior. No time was lost by him in complaints, finding fault, and wasteful and destructive criticism; but with an earnest and dedicated application to the task, he welded his men into a highly trained, supremely disciplined, confident and mighty army. He covered the fields for miles around with squads of troops performing the various types of drudgery relating to drill of the company; he was in attendance at each dress parade of each regiment under his command; he inspected the clothing and equipment of his men; he instructed the quartermaster, the commissary, the ordnance officer, and the provost marshal in their respective duties; and he gave to each of the latter an hour, by either day or night, at their request, when needed for improvement of their efficiency. With the excellent morale resulting from superb leadership in all ranks, it did not require many weeks for tangible results. This beneficial effect upon his command also had its counterpart in its effect upon their leader. The colonel of the Tenth Kentucky Infantry, John Marshall Harlan, subsequently an associate justice of the United States Supreme Court, stated that General Thomas was a greater man at the end of the war than at the beginning, due in some measure to his experience with volunteer troops. He bore himself with such kingly dignity that he won from those under him the involuntary homage due a sovereign.[37]

General Thomas organized the First Kentucky Brigade, the first in that state, and also the first full brigade of the Army of the Cumberland. The Third and Fourth Infantry Regiments and the First Kentucky Cavalry were the first regiments organized in Kentucky, although the Third and Fourth Infantry were originally named the First and Second Kentucky Infantry. However, when the state definitely adhered to the Union, the legislature recognized the two regiments that Colonels Guthrie and Woodruff organized in Ohio, and designated them the First and Second.[38]

---

36. Van Horne, *ibid.,* pp. 26-27.
37. *Ibid.,* pp. 14-15.
38. *Ibid.,* p. 27.

It has been stated that General Nelson, predecessor of General Thomas at Camp Dick Robinson, had a salty tongue and a temper; this does not necessarily imply that Thomas was not without strong feelings and convictions. The politicians surrounding his command were naturally addicted to speech-making and to offering advice on matters strictly within the realm of the military. Speech-making became a particular burden to Thomas, and before too long he had taken enough of it. On an occasion when General Sherman visited the command, former Senator J. J. Crittenden, Senator Andrew Johnson, and Horace Maynard were also there. When a band from camp began to serenade these visitors at the solicitation of the soldiers, who were not yet fully indoctrinated in the ways of military life, and to clamor for speeches from them, Thomas withdrew to the privacy of a small room adjacent to the forum from which they were speaking. One of his aides, writing in a corner of the room used as an office, was unobserved as Thomas began pacing restlessly across the room. After Sherman had finished his speech, the crowd began yelling for Thomas to come out and speak; but he blurted aloud, "I won't speak! What does a man want to make a speech for, anyhow!" When he realized that he had been overheard, he stalked from the room and remained in his quarters during the rest of the evening.[39]

---

39. *Battles and Leaders, op. cit.*, Vol. I, p. 382.

CHAPTER VIII

Girding for Battle: Mill Springs,
First Union Victory

ON OCTOBER 6, 1861, General Winfield Scott wired General Robert
Anderson as follows:

> To give you rest necessary to restoration of health, call
> Brigadier General Sherman to command the Department of the
> Cumberland. Turn over to him your instructions, and report here
> in person as soon as you may, without retarding your recovery.

WINFIELD SCOTT.[1]

The news of General Anderson's illness and replacement was
received by General Thomas with some degree of sadness, since he
felt a friend's normal anxiety; but more than that the change in command meant the loss of his chief sponsor. In General Anderson's
order of October 8, 1861, informing his command of the change, he
expressed the hope that with God's help General Sherman "may
be the means of delivering this department from the marauding
bands, who, under the guise of relieving and benefiting Kentucky,
are doing all the injury they can to those who will not join them in
their accursed warfare." General Sherman assumed command of the
department on October 8, in accordance with his instructions.[2]

Among the first matters of importance to engage the attention of
General Thomas following his arrival in Kentucky was the invasion
of East Tennessee through Cumberland Gap. He knew that in that
area there was a large reservoir of Union sympathizers who only
wanted some assurance that Federal authorities would support them
before they declared their loyalty outright. It is true that Tennessee

---

1. Thomas B. Van Horne, *History of the Army of the Cumberland* (Cincinnati: Robert Clarke and Co., 1875), Vol. I, p. 35.

2. *Official Records of the War of the Rebellion* (Washington, D.C., 1880–
1881), Ser. 1, Vol. IV, pp. 296-97.

had seceded from the Union; but this action, resulting from the vote of the legislature, did not by any means express the will of all the people. Those in the mountain areas, and others throughout East Tennessee who owned small tracts of land, felt little sympathy for or interest in the stand of wealthy planters intent upon perpetuating the inhuman system of involuntary servitude. East Tennesseeans had no illusions about the economic fact that the institution of slavery was no panacea, no boon, to those who did not own slaves; in fact, the system of slavery made the lot of poor white people extremely diffi-cult, since they could not possibly compete in the labor market for the necessities of life against the slave living under the most primitive conditions, with a fair return for his labor denied him. It was natural, therefore, that these poor people would join the Army of the Cumber-land; and the knowledge that so many men from that area had joined his command was sufficient evidence to General Thomas that many more would declare their loyalty if afforded a reasonable opportunity. The plight of these people during the early days of the war was sad indeed. In the cruel border warfare many lost their homes and farms, and were able to find shelter only by escaping into Kentucky or by hiding in the mountains.

Cumberland Gap is a deep break in the Cumberland Mountains near the junction of the states of Kentucky, Virginia, and Tennessee, and to a less extent it is also an avenue of approach to North Carolina. The Gap was made to order for an invasion from Kentucky to East Tennessee, and General Thomas had urged General Anderson that it be utilized as early as possible for an offensive movement in that direction. This would, it was also hoped, render difficult or impossible the further movement of Confederate troops from Virginia and other Southern states into Kentucky.[3] The proposed movement had another purpose, that of gaining possession of the East Tennessee and Virginia Railroad, the only rail line connecting northern sections of Mississippi, Alabama, and Georgia and the entire state of Tennessee, with Rich-mond, the Confederate capital. Control of this railroad, it was believed, would also aid in freeing East Tennessee from Confederate domina-tion; but from the beginning insurmountable difficulties were en-countered. Among these was an insufficiency of supplies and equip-ment for the army, and, when troops were furnished belatedly and after frequent requests, too often the necessary equipment and sup-plies for their use did not follow them. Then, too, many of the troops from East Tennessee were naturally anxious to visit their homes, for which they had some basis for concern. One thing and another served to retard the effort to raise an army ready for com-

---

3. Van Horne, *op. cit.*, p. 37.

bat. General Thomas's manpower was somewhat inadequate, and almost everything else essential to successful brigade and regimental organization was in low supply. In due course, nevertheless, General Thomas completed a few regiments sufficiently strong to earn credit, as stated elsewhere, for the first brigade organized in Kentucky. Poetic justice thus decreed that General Thomas would also command the entire Army of the Cumberland, consisting of almost two hundred thousand men, when it was mustered out of service.[4]

The plan of invasion through Cumberland Gap proposed by General Thomas was quite readily accepted by the Washington authorities, but unfortunately the many obstacles to its success prevented its prompt implementation. If it had been undertaken as promptly as possible after being made known to the authorities, the war might well have been materially altered and certainly its termination would have been brought nearer. There is not a trace of acknowledgment to Thomas for the plan, and, sadly enough, it was assigned to another for execution. This is shown by a letter from General Ormsby M. Mitchel to Assistant Secretary of War Scott, dated October 11, 1861, informing him that Secretary of War Simon Cameron had placed him, Mitchel, in charge of Camp Dick Robinson; also Mitchel reported that he had received instructions to prepare for an immediate advance toward Cumberland Gap.[5] General Thomas was busily engaged in making preparations for this very invasion when the first inkling that Mitchel was to replace him came from Mitchel himself, in the following telegram:

HEADQUARTERS, DEPARTMENT OF THE OHIO,
CINCINNATI, OHIO, October 10, 1861.

BRIGADIER-GENERAL GEORGE H. THOMAS, CAMP DICK ROBINSON:

GENERAL: Under orders from the Secretary of War of this date, I am directed to repair to Camp Dick Robinson, and there prepare the troops for an onward movement, the object being to take possession of Cumberland Ford and Cumberland Gap, and ultimately seize the East Tennessee and Virginia Railroad.

In compliance with these orders, I desire you to move the three Ohio regiments now in Camp Dick Robinson to some convenient point beyond your camp, in the hope that they may escape the epidemic now prevailing among your men. You will order the regiments at Nicholasville to remain there until their transportation shall arrive.

---

4. Thomas B. Van Horne, *The Life of Major General George H. Thomas* (New York: Charles Scribner's Sons, 1882), pp. 41-42.

5. *Official Records, op. cit.*, p. 303.

I beg you, general, to make every preparation in your power for this expedition in which we are about to be united.

O. M. MITCHEL,
Brigadier-General Commanding[6]

To a dedicated and conscientious man like Thomas this letter was shockingly cruel in its clear implication that his loyalty to the Union and his proved record of success had failed to give him well-deserved recognition. He was terribly hurt and shamed at what can be more accurately described as a colossal indignity. This was the opportunity to show how unjust were his Southern detractors, who, after his death, when he was unable to answer them, insisted that he was lukewarm and wavering in his fidelity to the Union. Any doubts regarding his loyalty should have been dispelled when he invaded his native Virginia with the First Brigade of Patterson's Army. This indignity offered him a clear opportunity, if he had desired it, to relinquish his command to General Mitchel and withdraw from the Army in disgust. That he did not do so should silence forever those who would still repeat the groundless yarn concerning his loyalty; and, what is more, his acceptance of this indignity without resigning his commission proves his greatness as an American patriot. He knew that, although General Mitchel was his senior in service by but a matter of days, he was ill prepared to undertake the assignment of invading East Tennessee. He also knew that since he himself had done everything possible to prepare for the invasion, the action of the Secretary of War was unjust; and the action could stem only from one of two possible reasons, namely, dissatisfaction with his preparations, which he regarded as above criticism, or, as was more likely the case, the desire of someone to put Mitchel in command for political reasons. Certain it is that no one gave General Thomas the opportunity to discuss personally the reason for the change in command. Although he did not resign his commission, he did state to Mitchel his desire to be relieved from his command:

HEADQUARTERS, CAMP DICK ROBINSON,
GARRARD COUNTY, KENTUCKY, October 11, 1861

BRIGADIER-GENERAL O. M. MITCHEL,
COMMANDING DEPARTMENT OF THE OHIO, CINCINNATI, OHIO:

GENERAL: Your communication of the 10th instant was received to-day at the hands of Governor Johnson of Tennessee.

I have been doing all in my power to prepare the troops for a move on Cumberland Ford and to seize the Tennessee and

---

6. *Ibid.*, pp. 301-2.

Virginia Railroad, and shall continue to do all I can to assist you until your arrival here; but justice to myself requires that I ask to be relieved from duty with these troops, since the Secretary has thought it necessary to supersede me in the command, without, as I conceive, any just cause for so doing.

I have already sent one regiment forward, and shall send the others as soon as I can get the transportation. It was my desire to have advanced two regiments and a battery about 6 miles beyond London, to secure the road to Barboursville, and to protect a large tract of country abounding in forage, but up to this time have not been able to get the transportation.

I have also been very much embarrassed in my operations from the want of funds, not having received any since my arrival here, nearly a month ago. I hope the Government will be more liberal with you.

I am, general, respectfully, etc., your obedient servant,

GEO. H. THOMAS,
Brigadier-General, U.S. Volunteers, Commanding.[7]

Many there are who believe that this unfortunate action of the Secretary of War indicated either distrust of Thomas as a commander, as stated, or a lack of confidence in his loyalty to the Government. It was natural, therefore, that he would request release from troops over whom he had been commander and was now expected to be subordinate to another commander. His objection is proof positive that he had a keen sense of justice, that he had the courage to stand up to anyone in protest when he deemed his rights were violated, and that he had the utmost confidence in his ability to exercise command independently, despite the arguments of some that he shrank from responsibility.[8]

Following his letter to General Mitchel declaring his intention to be relieved from his command and a consequent reduction in rank, General Thomas wrote the following letter to his commander, General William T. Sherman:

HEADQUARTERS CAMP DICK ROBINSON,
GARRARD COUNTY, KENTUCKY, October 11, 1861.

BRIGADIER-GENERAL W. T. SHERMAN.
COM'D'G. DEPT. OF THE CUMBERLAND, LOUISVILLE, KY.:

GENERAL: I received an official communication to-day from

---

7. *Ibid.*, p. 303; Donn Piatt, *General George H. Thomas* (Cincinnati, 1891), p. 110.

8. Van Horne, *Life of Thomas*, pp. 42-43.

Brigadier-General O. M. Mitchel, informing me that he had been ordered by the Secretary of War to repair to this Camp and prepare the troops for a forward movement, first to Cumberland Ford, and eventually to seize upon the Tennessee and Virginia Railroad. As I have been doing all in my power to effect this very thing, to have the execution of it taken from me when nearly prepared to take the field, is extremely mortifying. I have therefore respectfully to ask to be relieved from duty with the troops on the arrival of General Mitchel.

I am, General, very respectfully,
Your obedient servant,
GEO. H. THOMAS, *Brigadier-General, U.S.V. Com'd'g.*[9]

General Sherman's reply was prompt and apparently to the point in assuring the capable Thomas that he would do his utmost to insure that he could complete his plans for the penetration of East Tennessee. It is well to keep in mind that Sherman, although he avowed time and again his deep friendship for Thomas, often citing his effort to obtain for him a brigadier-generalship despite the proved credit for it to General Anderson, was Thomas's friend when being so helped Sherman. Certainly he recognized the ability of Thomas by supporting the move to leave him to face the Confederate Hood before and in the battle of Nashville; but Sherman was most prone to criticize and find fault with Thomas, helping in the process to perpetuate the falsehood that Thomas was "slow," yet proving his actual opinion of him by leaving him to fight the only formidable Confederate Army, which, if it had defeated Thomas, would have caused the removal of both Grant and Sherman from their important commands. Sherman's unjust criticism of Thomas had the beneficial effect, as did Grant's coldness and injustice to him, of eliminating a strong man from competition with both of them. In any case, here is the Sherman letter to Thomas seeking to assure him that he could go ahead with plans for invading East Tennessee:

LOUISVILLE, KY., October 13, 1861.

BRIG. GEN. GEORGE H. THOMAS, COMDG. CAMP DICK ROBINSON:

SIR: Your letters of the 11th and 12th of October,* were received last night.

*Not found in *Official Records*, but see Van Horne, *Life of Thomas*, p. 44, Note 45.

9. *Ibid.*, p. 44.

I would start for your camp at once, but am notified by the Secretary of War that he will be here to meet me.

The paymaster is here with funds. Colonel Swords, quartermaster, has just reported, and I am assured that ample funds will be provided for all necessaries. I myself was compelled to indorse a draft to get money in bank. The fact is, the arrangement for the supply of money promised us before leaving Washington has not been promptly kept, but I am certain that very soon we will be supplied, and your loan of the bank shall be paid, if my order will accomplish it. In like manner I authorize you to go on and prepare your command for active service.

General Mitchel is subject to my orders, and I will, if possible, give you the opportunity of completing what you have begun. Of course I would do anything in my power to carry out your wishes, but feel that the affairs of Kentucky call for the united action of all engaged in the cause of preserving our Government.

> I am, with great respect, your obedient servant,
> W. T. SHERMAN,
> *Brigadier-General Commanding.*[10]

The attempted removal of General Thomas without the slightest justification was only the first of a number of incidents to badger and harass him during the war. It is sobering to contemplate the possibility for irreparable damage, not only to a most outstanding patriot, gentleman, and leader, but to the Union cause for which he fought so valiantly and successfully, and without whose services, in a number of moments of great crisis it might have been lost. No one can estimate the pain to Thomas at this most extraordinary cruelty without assuming similar treatment to oneself. After he had taken a stand for the Union, with all the hazards and heartaches that stand entailed, he had every reason for just and dignified consideration from the leaders of the country. It has been asserted that Governor Andrew Johnson of Tennessee claimed some credit for the retention of Thomas in command at this time, but it is extremely possible that he did so after learning the political fact that the Tennesseeans under Thomas favored his retention, if indeed he did. Considerable doubt attaches to the governor's claim for credit, which is based upon a letter from General Thomas to Governor Johnson setting forth his reply to demands by the Governor to get on with the invasion of East Tennessee. It is not easy to believe that Johnson at that time would have recommended General Thomas for anything. Certain it is that the attempt to replace Thomas with Mitchel was dropped,

---

10. *Official Records, op. cit.,* p. 306.

and more than likely because of the public esteem in which Thomas was held. The Thomas reply to Governor Johnson is as follows:

HEADQUARTERS,
CRAB ORCHARD, November 7, 1861.

GOV. ANDREW JOHNSON, LONDON, KY.:

DEAR SIR: Your favor of the 6th instant is at hand. I have done all in my power to get troops and transportation and means to advance into Tennessee. I believe General Sherman has done the same. Up to this time we have been successful.

Have you heard by authority that the troops at London were to fall back? I have not, and shall not move any of them back unless ordered; because, if not interfered with, I can have them subsisted there as well as here. I am inclined to think that the rumor has grown out of the feverish excitement which seems to exist in the minds of some of the regiments that if we stop for a day that no further advance is contemplated. I can only say I am doing the best I can. Our commanding general is doing the same, and using all his influence to equip a force for the rescue of Tennesseeans.

If the Tennesseeans are not content and must go, then the risk of disaster will remain with them. Some of our troops are not yet clothed, and it seems impossible to get clothing.

For information respecting the organization of regiments, I inclose you General Orders, No. 70, from the War Department.

If the gentlemen you name can raise regiments agreeably to the conditions and instructions contained in said order, the Government will accept them, and I hope will have arms to place in their hands in the course of two or three months.

Very respectfully and truly, yours,
GEO. H. THOMAS,
Brigadier-General U. S. Volunteers.[11]

General Thomas explained earlier that the reason for establishing a depot at Crab Orchard was to render the provisioning of his troops easier and less costly; furthermore, this would make it possible for regiments to obtain supplies in their own vehicles while avoiding the payment of toll bills.[12]

Now that General Thomas was to remain at least temporarily with his command and in due course continue preparations for the East

11. *Ibid.*, pp. 342-43.
12. *Ibid.*, p. 322.

Tennessee invasion, obstacles to the plan developed as rapidly as preparations were made. Just as the Federals realized the importance of control of the routes through the Cumberland Mountains, so did the Confederates realize the great danger to their supply lines and troop movements if these vital arteries were lost to them. In order to circumvent any such moves, secessionists hoped to aid the Confederate cause in Kentucky by sending troops into the state by way of Cumberland Ford, Barboursville, and Tompkinsville. They were also alert to the danger of losing the East Tennessee and Virginia Railroad, the preservation of which to them assured the solid phalanx of Confederate states so vital to all their expectations for military success and an independent nation. This evidence of intent by the Confederates to invade Kentucky had its discouraging effect on the morale of the loyal residents of East Tennessee; and simultaneously a clamor came from Kentuckians for defensive measures to resist the expected invasion.[13]

Confronted by this new threat, General Thomas placed some of his best troops at Rockcastle Hills, about thirty miles south of Camp Dick Robinson and moved others forward to their support as rapidly as possible. The enemy at first advanced columns of troops as if determined to reach definite objectives, but before reaching such points they immediately withdrew. It soon became clear that these troops, commanded by General Felix K. Zollicoffer, were up to something more important than creating confusion in Colonel Kenner Garrard's Third Kentucky Infantry at Rockcastle Hills. Brigadier General Albin Schoepf was placed in command at Rockcastle Hills after his arrival with the three regiments of reinforcements commanded respectively by Colonels John Coburn, James B. Steedman, and Frank Wolford, and was supported by the battery of Captain William E Standart. These additional units increased the National forces to about five thousand troops, to confront the Confederates in their attack of October 21 with about six thousand infantry and some fifteen hundred cavalry. After a short but sharp engagement, the enemy withdrew with a loss of about thirty killed and an undetermined number wounded. The loss of the Federals was four killed and about twenty wounded. The Confederates retreated to Laurel Ridge, about nine miles south of London, Kentucky, and from thence proceeded to Cumberland Ford near the Cumberland Mountains.[14]

The Confederate retreat revived once more the subject of an advance into East Tennessee, and General Thomas ordered General

13. Van Horne, *Life of Thomas,* p. 45.
14. *Ibid.,* p. 46; *Official Records, op. cit.,* pp. 205-11.

Schoepf to move with his command to London, there to await reinforcements, supplies, and transportation. Thomas also moved his headquarters to Crab Orchard in order to improve his position preparatory to the expected advance into East Tennessee.[15] He suggested that a force be sent to the Big Sandy River, a tributary of the Ohio flowing northward through a rugged terrain and forming the northeastern boundary of Kentucky adjacent to what is now West Virginia, while he would advance by Barboursville to East Tennessee and attack Zollicoffer as soon as adequately strengthened. He awaited the fulfillment of conditions that would give strong hopes for success; this, of course, is not "slowness," as often charged against him[16] by those whose records were not comparable with his, but common-sense precautions against useless loss of life, and failure.

During this trying time of preparation, the loyal East Tennesseans became impatient of the delay, and apparently inspired Governor Johnson to press General Thomas for immediate action. Particulars of Governor Johnson's letter of November 6 and General Thomas's reply of the seventh were forwarded to General Schoepf in the following letter:

HEADQUARTERS CRAB ORCHARD,
November 7, 1861

BRIGADIER-GENERAL SCHOEPF,
COM'D'G. CAMP CALVERT, LONDON, KY.

GENERAL:

I find it necessary to reply to Governor Johnson's letter in the foregoing, which I send to you for your information. It is time that discontented persons should be silent, both in and out of the service. I sympathize with the East Tennesseans on account of their natural anxiety to relieve their friends and families from the terrible apprehension which they are now suffering. But to make the attempt to rescue them when not half prepared is culpable, especially when our enemies are perhaps as anxious that we should make the move as the Tennesseans themselves, for it is well known by our commanding general that Buckner has an overwhelming force within striking distance, whenever he can get us at a disadvantage.

I hope you will therefore see the necessity of dealing decidedly with such people, and you have my authority and orders for doing so.

15. John Fitch, *Annals of the Army of the Cumberland* (Philadelphia: J. B. Lippincott and Co., 1864), pp. 60-61.
16. Van Horne, *Life of Thomas*, p. 46.

We must learn to abide our time or we will never be successful.

Respectfully Your Obedient Servant,
GEORGE H. THOMAS,
Brigadier-General U.S.V.[17]

This letter demonstrates a dominant characteristic of Thomas, that of refusing to jeopardize his possibilities of success, no matter who the person or what the occasion, until his judgment was satisfied by adequate preparation. He would not be pressured to yield even to a governor, as in this instance, who wielded great political strength; on the contrary, he displayed courage of a high order in refusing to do what he did not believe right. This trait throughout his career underlay his uninterrupted success; and even when he commanded only part of an army, as at Murfreesboro and Chickamauga, he held his ground because he was prepared, although the rest of the army was broken. There is no doubt of his deep feeling for the Tennessee people, but he would not expose them and his army to the dire consequences of rash and precipitate action.

Information received from Governor Johnson stating his understanding of an order for the withdrawal of troops from London proved to be well founded. General Sherman did give such an order, as shown by the following dispatch:

LOUISVILLE, KY., NOVEMBER 11, 1861.

GENERAL THOMAS:

I am just in receipt of a telegraphic dispatch from McCook, at Camp Nevin, that the force in his front along Green River has disappeared, and that there is a rumor that Buckner is moving in force toward Lexington between us. If not engaged in front, at once withdraw your force back of Kentucky River, and act according to the state of facts then. If it be true that the force at the Gap has been increased, as represented, to twenty thousand, it would be madness to contend. My information is positive as to the state of affairs along Green River, but conjectured as to the other, and I send a special messenger to convey it to you.

Yours,
W. T. SHERMAN,
Brigadier-General[18]

Sherman's estimate of the situation was certainly not shared by

17. *Ibid.*, p. 47.
18. Van Horne, *Army of the Cumberland*, p. 43.

General Thomas. His reply of November 12 stated firmly that he would "give orders at once for a retrograde movement, but I am sure the enemy are not moving between us. All my information indicates that they are moving south." On November 13 he again wrote to Sherman as follows:

HEADQUARTERS, CRAB ORCHARD, November 13, 1861.

GENERAL W. T. SHERMAN, COMMANDING DEPARTMENT OF THE CUMBERLAND, LOUISVILLE, KY.

GENERAL: Colonel Bramlette writes me from Somerset, on the 11th, but does not think that the enemy have any intention of advancing.

From General Schoepf's camp the report is that Zollicoffer has retired beyond Cumberland Gap, leaving some cavalry pickets on the Tennessee side of Cumberland Ford. I will send you a copy of Colonel Bramlette's report to-night by mail.

Respectfully, your obedient servant,
GEO. H. THOMAS,
Brigadier-General U.S.V.[19]

The foregoing letter to Sherman was in reply to his dispatch of November 12, which stated in part, "I am convinced from many facts that Albert Sidney Johnston is making herculean efforts to strike a blow in Kentucky; that he designs to move from Bowling Green on Lexington, Louisville, and Cincinnati. I may be in error, but he has pressed into service some one thousand five hundred wagons at and near Bowling Green, and his force is not far short of forty-five thousand men, with a large portion of artillery."[20] In brief, Sherman believed that Johnston planned to move with forty-five thousand Confederates between Thomas at Crab Orchard and McCook at Nolensville on the Louisville and Nashville Railroad. He directed Thomas to be prepared to withdraw to a point back of Danville, Kentucky, with most of his command; the remainder was left at Rock Castle Hills for the time being. This backward movement resulted in considerable loss of equipment; and besides the great number of troops ill at the time were considerably inconvenienced and their condition aggravated by the hasty withdrawal. Correspondents and others reporting these conditions, which were not in the least offset by compensating benefits, blamed Thomas for them. No one could have been less to blame than he, but he bore stoically all

19. *Ibid.*, p. 44.
20. *Ibid.*

accusations as the price of obedience to orders in the certain knowledge that he was performing his duty and that the move was in the best interest of his country.[21]

On November 15, Brigadier General Don Carlos Buell was placed in command of the Department of the Cumberland, and on that day also this designation was changed to the Army of the Ohio. General Buell was a man of strong professional pride, a great organizer, and of capabilities expected of one possessing his lengthy military training and experience. He graduated thirty-second of fifty-two in the West Point class of 1841, and was a classmate of the gallant Major-General John F. Reynolds, who was killed on the opening day at Gettysburg; of Brigadier-General Nathaniel Lyon, killed at the Battle of Wilson's Creek, Missouri; and of Major-General John M. Brannan, who is perhaps best known in connection with the tragic order from Rosecrans's Headquarters, on the second day at Chickamauga, for Brigadier-General Thomas J. Wood to close up on Reynolds, Brannan occupying a position between Wood and Reynolds, thus creating a tremendous break through which Confederate General Longstreet poured his troops and routed the Federal forces. Buell was a disciplinarian bordering on severity and harshness, if in fact he did not overlap these areas, although the older men of his command recognized that his all-consuming desire was to train them to become superior in battle for their own and their country's good.[22]

One of the first, and certainly the most important, tasks to which Buell addressed himself soon after assuming command was the reorganization of his troops into brigades and divisions. He was scrupulous in seeing to it that his men were well cared for and that their camp sites were well chosen and properly drained. He issued an order dated December 2, 1861, announcing that six divisions would be formed from the troops comprising his command and supplemented by additional troops to be assigned later. The First Division, commanded by General Thomas, contained four brigades; the Second, commanded by Brigadier-General Alexander McDowell McCook, also contained four brigades; the Fourth commanded by Brigadier-General William Nelson contained three brigades; and the Fifth, under command of Brigadier-General Thomas L. Crittenden, contained three brigades. The sixth was organized in January, 1861, under command of General T. J. Wood, and consisted of three brigades. Attached to each brigade was a battery of artillery.[23]

21. Van Horne, *Life of Thomas*, p. 49.

22. Henry M. Cist, *The Army of the Cumberland* (New York, 1882), pp. 21-22; *Legends of Operations of the Army of the Cumberland* (Washington, D.C.: Government Printing Office, 1869), p. 4.

23. Cist, *ibid.*, pp. 22-23; *Legends of Operations, ibid.*, p. 4.

On November 17, General Buell directed General Thomas to with-draw his command from Crab Orchard, but to leave Acting Brigadier-General Carter's brigade in the withdrawal, but before the movement was under way a new order directed that Carter remain at London. The Department of the Ohio was expanded to include not only Kentucky and Tennessee, but also the states of Ohio, Indiana, and Michigan. For the first time Buell, as commander of this force, was given full authority to control the new troops organized in the states comprising the Army of the Ohio, an advantage not given to his predecessors. On November 20, General Thomas was ordered to move his force to Lebanon, although at first the instruction was to move to Columbia.[24]

General Albert Sidney Johnston had fifteen thousand Confederates at Bowling Green, a circumstance that makes ridiculous Sherman's fear that he had forty-five thousand; however, tragically enough, this miscalculation underlay Sherman's dispatch to Thomas to withdraw the greater portion of his command to the vicinity of Danville, with the consequent deterioration of affairs in eastern Kentucky and eastern Tennessee.[25] Nothing better illustrates the difference between Generals Sherman and Thomas than this circumstance relating to poor information concerning the strength of Johnston at Bowling Green, which of course inspired his directive to Thomas to move to Danville. This miscalculation, or misinformation, or both, led him to see three Confederates in Johnston's command for every soldier actually serving under him. Thomas, on the other hand, although not in over-all com-mand, and therefore not presumed to have access to such complete sources of information as would Sherman as commander in chief, was able to state positively and accurately to Sherman on November 12 that he was sure the Confederates were not seeking to come between his own and McCook's commands. Thomas's ability to appraise correctly the intentions and strength of the enemy was not a mere trusting to chance; it will be shown in subsequent pages the extent to which he availed himself of all possible sources of information regarding the enemy, and, additionally, of the plans of his colleagues, if not offered voluntarily when needed in connection with his own operations.

General Zollicoffer was encouraged by the shifting of General Thomas from Crab Orchard and London to advance against Somerset. Within a few days, Thomas was informed by Lieutenant Samuel P. Carter, United States Navy, in charge of a brigade in East Ten-

---

24. *Battles and Leaders of the Civil War* (New York, 1884), Vol. I, p. 385; Van Horne, *Army of the Cumberland*, p. 46.

25. Van Horne, *Life of Thomas*, p. 50.

nessee, of the Confederate advance, and of his inability to delay it
or prevent it. Thomas therefore ordered General Schoepf's brigade
at Lebanon, and Wolford's cavalry at Columbia, to proceed to
Somerset; but his order to bring up reinforcements was countermanded by General Buell, who deemed the force at Lebanon sufficient to meet the threat. Besides, he was entertaining other plans.
He forbade Thomas to exercise similar future discretion without his
personal approval; therefore Thomas was prevented from invading
East Tennessee and also from reinforcing Schoepf at Somerset.[26]

Belated but none the less definite confirmation of the reasons
underlying Thomas's desire to reinforce Schoepf at Somerset was not
long in coming. On December 29, General Buell ordered him to
advance toward the newly fortified Confederate position near
Somerset, on the north bank of the Cumberland River, and, with
General Schoepf in front, to place his force on the Confederate left
for the purpose of making a combined attack on the enemy position.
Buell's instructions were rather broad and necessarily limited in detail,
due to the impossibility of foreseeing in advance the conditions to
be met.[27]

The advance from Lebanon began on January 1, 1862, over roads
made almost impassable by heavy rainfall. There was fortunately a
good turnpike to Columbia, but from there to the end of the march
the roads were so muddy that artillery carriages and wagons sank
to their axles. During one period of eight days on the march, only
forty miles were accomplished, but finally, on January 17, they came
to Logan's Cross Roads or Fishing Creek, better known as Mill
Springs. At this point they were only about ten miles north of the
Confederate position and about the same distance west of Somerset.
Since he was directed not to attack the enemy before joining forces
with General Schoepf, General Thomas placed his troops in position
to afford maximum advantage in the event either of attack or defense.
One of his two advance regiments was designated to command the
road leading directly to the Confederate position; the other was
assigned to the road leading from the Confederate position.[28]

In order to guard against surprise attacks, Thomas stationed
cavalry and infantry close to the front and chose a site contiguous to
both roads for convenience in making a quick junction with the force
of General Schoepf. He also ordered the latter to send the Twelfth
Kentucky and the First and Second Tennessee regiments to his sup-

26. *Ibid.*, p. 51.

27. *Ibid.*

28. *Ibid.*; Charles C. Coffin, *The Drum Beat of the Nation* (New York:
Harper and Brothers, 1887), p. 133; *Battles and Leaders, op. cit.*, p. 382.

port promptly for maximum advantage in the event of delay, when a union of forces might be necessary. These regiments were needed because the Fourth and Tenth Kentucky, the Fourteenth Ohio, the Eighteenth Regular Infantry, and Wetmore's battery of artillery had not yet arrived, due to the bad roads. In the meantime, hearing of a large wagon train sent on a foraging expedition by General Zollicoffer, Thomas assigned Colonel James B. Steedman with his Fourteenth Ohio to capture or disperse it, since it was believed to be within about six miles of the latter's camp. On the evening of the eighteenth, the Fourth Kentucky, the battalion of Michigan Engineers, and Wetmore's artillery arrived and went into camp near the Tenth Indiana Infantry.[29]

A few days before the arrival of the advance forces under General Thomas, General George B. Crittenden had replaced General Zollicoffer in supreme command of the Confederates. Upon learning that Thomas had arrived, and realizing that Fishing Creek was unfordable at almost any other time, but more especially at that time, due to the heavy rains, Crittenden called a council of regimental and brigade commanders to determine a course of action. The principal decision to make was whether Thomas should be attacked at once, before he could unite with General Schoepf and the regiments to his rear. It was agreed that their camp could not be maintained against a spirited attack, and that the facilities for crossing the stream, should that be necessary, were not sufficient to avert great loss, such loss depending upon the vigor of the Union attack. The decision was made, therefore, to attack Thomas before he became too strong in his position; and accordingly, at midnight of January 18, the Confederate advance began.[30]

General Zollicoffer, under orders from General Crittenden, advanced with two companies of cavalry, one Mississippi regiment, three Tennessee regiments, and a battery of artillery. At the end of the column were an Alabama regiment and two reserve cavalry regiments. The march of nine miles through rain and mud ended at about 5:30 A.M. on January 19, when it came into contact with Federal cavalry pickets, which retired in good order after delivering a volley of rifle fire. Two companies of the Tenth Indiana joined the withdrawing cavalry and were soon supported by the remainder of the Tenth Indiana. It was not long before the Fourth Kentucky, the Second Minnesota, and a battery of artillery were engaged; and after eight regiments and two batteries arrived on the field, General Thomas made a furious charge against the enemy and threw him back. The Fourth Kentucky took position along a fence at the edge of the

29. *Battles and Leaders, ibid.,* p. 387; Van Horne, *Life of Thomas,* p. 52.
30. *Ibid.,* pp. 386-87; *ibid.,* pp. 52-53.

woods, with its right resting near the Mill Springs road; and it was but a short time before the enemy began leaving the woods and advancing into the open field. A ravine ran through the field, parallel to the Fourth Kentucky front, and leading toward the road on the right of that regiment it sloped steeply to the front, while on the left it sloped only gradually. Before the arrival of the Fourth Kentucky, General Zollicoffer deployed his brigade and forced Wolford's cavalry and the Tenth Indiana to drop back. In the fight he almost captured Wolford's horses while the men were fighting on foot. Wolford and part of his command, with a company of the Tenth Indiana, rallied on the Fourth Kentucky, during which time the remainder of the Tenth Indiana dropped back to its encampment to reform its lines. Soon the Fourth Kentucky was attacked vigorously in front by the enemy, after coming to within a short distance under cover of the ravine before opening fire. Their commander denounced this action of the Confederates and demanded that they stand up and fight like men.[31]

When a lull occurred in the fighting, Colonel Fry rode forward a short distance to reconnoiter at a time when the woods were filled with smoke. As he undertook to return to his former position, he noted an officer wearing a waterproof coat. They were close enough for their knees to touch when the officer addressed him thus: "We must not fire on our own men." Colonel Fry replied, "Of course not. I would not do so intentionally." As he turned to go back to his regiment, he saw another officer on horseback who fired and wounded his horse. Colonel Fry immediately returned the fire of the officer who had spoken to him, whereupon several men of his regiment also fired at the officer, who fell dead from a pistol shot in the breast and two musket balls. It was the Confederate General Zollicoffer.

Zollicoffer was an extremely venomous Southerner, who is quoted as having said to his troops, when undertaking the advance that it was hoped would carry the war into the Northern states, "I will take you to Indiana, or I will go to hell myself." General Zollicoffer was a former Congressman from the Nashville district of Tennessee, and, although he had no previous military experience, he did his utmost to take Tennessee out of the Federal Union.

In the interim, the enemy was exerting pressure against the front of the Fourth Kentucky and overlapping its right beyond the danger point. On the right of the Fourth, the combatants were separated by a fence, and in order to relieve the burden of the enemy on that flank, Colonel Fry moved thereto two companies from his unassailed

---

31. John S. C. Abbott, *History of the Civil War in America* (New York, 1867), Vol. II, p. 337; *Battles and Leaders, op. cit.*, p. 388.

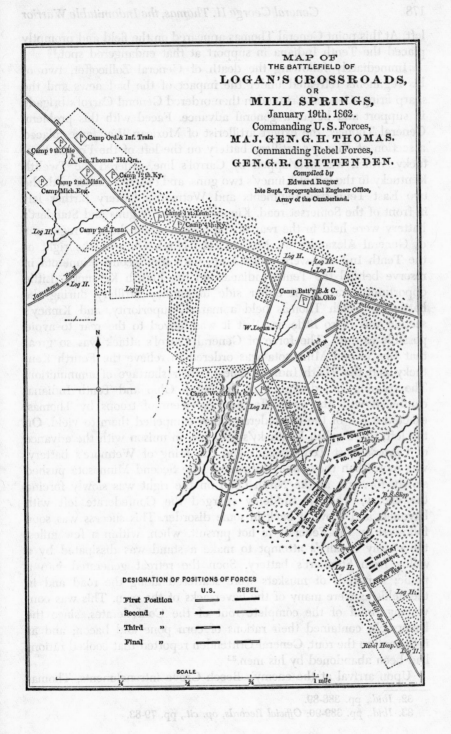

left. At this point General Thomas appeared on the field and promptly placed the Tenth Indiana in support at that endangered spot.[32]

Immediately following the death of General Zollicoffer, two of his regiments retreated under the impact of the bad news and the sharp firing. General Crittenden then ordered General Carrol's brigade in support and began a general advance. Faced with this problem, General Thomas, the expert artillerist of Mexican War fame, placed a section of Kinney's artillery battery on the left of the Fourth Kentucky, which was overlapped by Carrol's line, ordered the Twelfth Kentucky to the left of Kinney's two guns, and ordered Carter with the two East Tennessee regiments and Wetmore's battery farther left in front of the Somerset road. Kinney's remaining guns and Standart's battery were held in the rear of the center, while the two regiments of General Alexander M. McCook, the Ninth Ohio on the right of the Tenth Indiana, were ordered up, with the Second Minnesota in reserve behind the Tenth Indiana and the Fourth Kentucky. Little opportunity was given either side to employ artillery during the battle, of which Thomas held a marked superiority, and Kinney's section was of so little use that it was moved to the rear to avoid possible capture. The force of General Carrol's attack was so great that the Second Minnesota was ordered to relieve the Fourth Kentucky and the Tenth Indiana, due to their shortage of ammunition. The training and discipline of the Ninth Ohio and Tenth Indiana, combined with the very effective placement of troops by Thomas, exacted a toll of the Confederates that compelled them to yield. On the left, the Twelfth Kentucky's advance, in unison with the advance of Carter's East Tennesseeans and the firing of Wetmore's battery, was more than they could withstand. The Second Minnesota pushed slowly forward, as the Ninth Ohio on the right was slowly forcing the enemy, when it suddenly charged the Confederate left with bayonets and drove it back in some disorder. This success was soon followed by the Federals in hot pursuit, when, within a few miles, the enemy cavalry's attempt to make a stand was dissipated by a volley from Standart's battery. Soon the retreat generated into a panic; hundreds of muskets were scattered along the road and in the fields as were many of the haversacks of the men. This was convincing proof of the complete rout of the Confederates, since the haversacks contained their rations of corn pone and bacon; and as if to confirm the rout, General Crittenden reported that cooked rations had been abandoned by his men.[33]

Upon arrival at the enemy's Beech Grove intrenchments, Thomas

---

32. *Ibid.*, pp. 388-89.
33. *Ibid.*, pp. 389-90; *Official Records, op. cit.*, pp. 79-83.

had his division deploy in line of battle and advance to the hill at
Moulden's commanding the enemy's position. From this vantage point
Standart's and Wetmore's batteries bombarded the enemy until night-
fall, while Kinney's battery at Russell's house on the left shelled their
ferry to prevent them from crossing. The Fourteenth Ohio and the
Tenth Kentucky were placed in the advance, after coming up during
the pursuit of the enemy, in preparation for the attack at daybreak.
The Seventeenth, Thirty-first, and Thirty-eighth Ohio, under General
Schoepf, arrived at the position about the time darkness settled on
the scene.[34]

On January 20, the morning after the Battle of Mill Springs,
Wetmore's guns began firing on the ferry attempting to cross the
river with troops, and it was not long before it was abandoned and
burned by the enemy. The moving columns, with the Tenth Kentucky
and the Fourteenth Ohio in the lead, found that the intrenchments
were abandoned during the night. Among the equipment left behind
by the Confederates were eleven pieces of artillery and caissons,
battery wagons, and forges hitched up and ready to move when
abandoned, and more than 150 wagons and more than 1,000 horses
and mules. Although all of the Confederates escaped, the opposite
bank displayed evidence of their flight by the number of wagons left
behind; and since the boats used in crossing were destroyed, an
immediate chase was impossible, although during the day the Fourteenth Ohio succeeded in effecting a crossing for reconnaissance purposes and to collect enemy property left behind.[35]

In General Thomas's report to General Buell he listed 39 killed
and 207 wounded, all suffered by the Tenth Indiana, the Fourth
Kentucky, the Second Minnesota, the Ninth Ohio, and Wolford's
cavalry. Colonel McCook and Colonel Fry were among those wounded.
The Confederates lost, according to this report, 192 killed, and 89
prisoners not wounded in addition to 68 prisoners wounded, or a total
of killed, wounded, and prisoners of 349.[36] A large quantity of ammunition, commissary stores, camp tools, and garrison equipment, in
addition to six Confederate flags, were also found by the victors.
General Crittenden acknowledged in his report: "From Mill Springs
and on the first steps of my march officers and men, frightened by
false rumors of the movements of the enemy, shamefully deserted,
and, stealing horses and mules to ride, fled to Knoxville, Nashville,
and other places in Tennessee." One cavalry battalion, he reported,
lost all but twenty-five through desertion. Thomas also reported that

---

34. *Battles and Leaders, op. cit.*, p. 390.
35. *Ibid.*
36. *Ibid.*, p. 391.

among the spoils he found were copies of all orders issued by General Zollicoffer from inception of his brigade until just a few days before the battle. What is more, Thomas stated it as his belief that the rout of the enemy was so complete that the entire force was dispersed.[37]

After it was clear that the enemy had abandoned his intrenchments in great haste, Colonel Fry of the Fourth Kentucky said to Thomas: "General, why didn't you send in a demand for surrender last night?" After a moment's hesitation, Thomas replied, "Hang it, Fry, I never once thought of it." Another story relating to Thomas concerned a young slightly wounded prisoner who was allowed the freedom of the camp. When some of his captors chided him about the wholesale abandonment by his comrades of haversacks filled with rations, he replied, "Well, we were doing pretty good fighting till old man Thomas rose up in his stirrups, and we heard him holler out: 'Attention, Creation! By kingdoms right wheel!' and then we knew you had us, and it was no time to carry weight."[38]

The Battle of Mill Springs was certainly not one of the great battles of the Civil War. In terms of the number of men engaged it was indeed a small battle; but measured by the forecast it gave of the contribution by Thomas to the final victory, and by its significance as a morale factor to the North, which desperately needed the encouragement it gave, it was a most important triumph. Although the Federals were outnumbered, they outflanked and defeated the enemy in this, the first victory in the West, and the only victory of any consequence won in Kentucky during the war. If the battle did nothing else, it brought into correct focus the previously exaggerated Confederate strength. What is more, it seriously damaged the right of the enemy defense and removed about ten thousand antagonists from the immediately forthcoming operations.

In William Preston Johnston's biography of his father, Albert Sidney Johnston, he reported that General Zollicoffer crossed the Cumberland River without orders, and thus brought on the Battle of Mill Springs. This action not only disclosed the true weakness of the Confederates under Johnston, but it also interfered with his ability to launch an offensive movement in several directions.[39]

On January 28, 1862, just nine days after the triumph at Mill Springs, the Ohio Legislature authorized a vote of thanks to General Thomas and his command. General Buell expressed his gratification in the following General Order:

---

37. *Ibid.; Official Records, op. cit.,* p. 83.
38. *Battles and Leaders, op. cit.,* p. 391.
39. Van Horne, *Life of Thomas,* p. 54.

HDQRS. DEPARTMENT OF THE OHIO,
LOUISVILLE, KY., January 23, 1862.
GENERAL ORDERS
No. 4b.

The general commanding has the gratification of announcing the achievement of an important victory, on the 19th instant, at Mill Springs, by the troops under General Thomas over the rebel forces, some 12,000 strong, under General George B. Crittenden and General Zollicoffer.

The defeat of the enemy was thorough and complete, and his loss in killed and wounded was great. Night alone, under cover of which his troops crossed the river from their intrenched camp and dispersed, prevented the capture of his entire force. Fourteen or more pieces of artillery, some 1,500 horses and mules, his entire camp equipage, together with wagons, arms, ammunition, and other stores to a large amount, fell into our hands.

The general has been charged by the General-in-Chief to convey his thanks to General Thomas and his troops for their brilliant victory. No task could be more grateful to him, seconded as it is by his own cordial approbation of their conduct.

By command of Brigadier-General Buell:

JAMES B. FRY,
Assistant Adjutant-General, Chief of Staff.[40]

President Lincoln authorized the following congratulatory order to be issued to the victorious command of General Thomas:

WAR DEPARTMENT, January 22, 1862.

The President, Commander-in-Chief of the Army and Navy, has received information of a brilliant victory by the United States forces over a large body of armed traitors and rebels at Mill Springs, in the State of Kentucky. He returns thanks to the gallant officers and soldiers who won that victory, and when the official reports shall be received the military and personal valor displayed in battle will be acknowledged and rewarded in a fitting manner.

The courage that encountered and vanquished the greatly superior numbers of the rebel force, pursued and attacked them in their intrenchments, and paused not until the enemy was completely routed, merits and receives commendation.

---

40. *Official Records, op. cit.*, p. 78.

The purpose of this war is to attack, pursue, and destroy a rebellious enemy, and to deliver the country from danger menaced by traitors. Alacrity, daring, courageous spirit, and patriotic zeal on all occasions and under every circumstance are expected from the Army of the United States. In the prompt and spirited movements and daring battle of Mill Springs the Nation will realize its hopes, and the people of the United States will rejoice to honor every soldier and officer who proves his courage by charging with the bayonet and storming enemy intrenchments, or in the blaze of the enemy fire.

By order of the President:

EDWIN M. STANTON,
Secretary of War.[41]

President Lincoln's document contains magnificent praise for the soldiers under the command of General Thomas, but it is remarkable, nay shocking, in its omission of the name of the man who was the chief architect and actor in the victory. It is difficult to accept the possible explanation that the omission was due to an oversight; for throughout the nation there was joy at news of the victory and the name of Thomas was familiar to everyone. It could not be stated as the reason that there was still a lack of confidence in him; for if the first Union victory of the Civil War was not enough to erase any lingering doubt as to his loyalty, then he could never hope for recognition. Another significant omission was in the failure to give him deserved promotion promptly, during which time other generals who had as yet contributed nothing were promoted to the rank of major-general, although President Lincoln's letter was most profuse in promising just reward to those who contributed to similar successes. The promise of the document to "honor every soldier and officer who proves his courage" offered considerable basis for hope that Thomas would not be relegated to mediocrity. The recognition of his achievement in the statement that the "courage that encountered and vanquished the greatly superior numbers of the rebel force, pursued and attacked them in their intrenchments, and paused not until the enemy was completely routed, merits and receives commendation," promised something more than a most indirect reference to outstanding achievement.

Thomas was promoted to the rank of major-general on April 25, 1862, and Buell to the rank on March 21, 1862. It is true that Thomas was subordinate to Buell when Mill Springs was fought, but it is also true that Buell graduated from West Point the year following

41. *Ibid.*, p. 102.

the graduation of Thomas; moreover, Buell was not on field duty until assigned to succeed Sherman on November 15, 1861, whereas Thomas had been in active service from the beginning.[42]

Considerable speculation has revolved around the neglect of Thomas at this particular time, and it has been assumed that a remark attributed to President Lincoln—"He is a Virginian, let him wait,"— was the primary cause. This is difficult to believe, particularly since General Robert Anderson was from Kentucky, a state divided in its loyalties although remaining in the Union, and he had been entrusted with command of the Federal forces in that state. In addition, it should not be overlooked that President Lincoln was himself a Kentuckian, as was also his wife.

If Thomas had been given a promotion for his splendid victory he would have outranked both Generals Buell and Grant. The latter was promoted to the rank of major-general on February 16, 1862, although Thomas was far more experienced through continuous military service. There is every reason to believe that if he had been given the command of the Army of the Cumberland instead of Buell, the results would have been more satisfactory for the Union cause. Even at that early date in the war Thomas had displayed marked capacity as a military leader, backed by more than twenty years of devotion to his profession. The possibility for an earlier Union triumph, which the promotion of Thomas at that time might have produced, is nothing short of breath-taking when considered in relation to his subsequent successes.[43]

In refutation of the charge by both Generals Grant and Sherman that General Thomas was "too slow," that able commander proposed once more, following the Battle of Mill Springs, that East Tennessee be invaded. General Buell showed little interest in the proposal, although admittedly there was still a supply problem that, with diffi-culties of transportation, presented some argument against an im-mediate advance. General Thomas, however, was the only officer in Kentucky of high rank during the fall and winter of 1861-1862, who saw the tremendous advantage to be gained from the movement. His idea was to take twenty thousand men at a time when there were almost fifty thousand men in Kentucky, not including the home guards. The Confederates, under General Albert Sidney Johnston, had an estimated twenty or twenty-five thousand men, including the force under General Zollicoffer. The Federal forces in Kentucky continued expanding after Mill Springs, but the Confederates were unable to

---

42. George W. Cullum, *Biographical Register of Officers and Cadets of the U.S. Military Academy* (Boston, 1891), Vol. II, p. 600.

43. *Ibid.*, p. 8.

increase theirs to any appreciable extent. To add to their perplexities and problems, the Confederates were distrustful toward Tennesseeans, many of whom were loyal to the Union and needed only the invasion proposed by General Thomas to contribute greatly toward breaking up the Confederacy in that area.[44]

A testimonial in recognition of the victory of General Thomas at Mill Springs was the presentation to him of a magnificent sword by the Fourth Kentucky Volunteer Infantry Regiment. This organization performed outstandingly, not only in this battle but throughout the war. From July, 1861, to August, 1865, the regiment served continuously with the Army of the Cumberland in the field, except for a thirty-day period of leave. The scabbard of the sword is inscribed: "Presented to Major General George H. Thomas By The Enlisted Men Of The Fourth Regiment, Kentucky Volunteer Infantry." On the hilt of the sword are inscribed the General's initials, "G.H.T.," in large monogram style on the counterguard, completely studded with diamonds. The blade is completely etched and engraved with military floral and patriotic motifs, with a gold-wash background. There is a large panel lettered in gold, "Mill Springs, Kentucky—First Union Victory of the War—January 19, 1862." The case is of mahogany and contains a brass plaque inlay on the outer cover, giving the name and rank of General Thomas. The case contains the General's original buff silk saber sash and a very fancy embroidered belt and silver American Eagle buckle.[45] The author has examined this sword and found it to be exactly as described by Mr. Norm Flayderman, the owner. (Mr. Flayderman regards the sword as unique with respect to the inscription, in particular the mentioning of "First Union Victory.")

Particulars relating to the raising of money for the sword and its presentation are described in *Union Regiments of Kentucky,* a book compiled by Thomas Speed, and published in Louisville, Kentucky, in 1897:

> A pleasing incident during the siege of Chattanooga was the presentation to General Thomas, then commanding the Army of the Cumberland, of a sword ordered by the enlisted men while at Triune (Tennessee), at a cost of $1,500. No officer was allowed to contribute. When the sword was received at Chattanooga,

44. *Battles and Leaders, op. cit.,* pp. 391-92; Van Horne, *Life of Thomas,* p. 61.

45. The author is indebted to Mr. Norm Flayderman, collector of antique firearms (44 West Putnam Avenue, Greenwich, Connecticut), for the accompanying description and the pictures of the sword presented to General Thomas by the enlisted men of the Fourth Kentucky Volunteer Infantry.

many of the contributors were dead. General Thomas rode down to the regiment, which was in close column by division, the sword was presented by Quartermaster Sergeant W. R. Williams in a neat speech, to which General Thomas briefly replied, and the ceremony was over.[46]

The donation of this sword, one of the most beautiful to be found anywhere, is important in showing the great regard held for General Thomas by his men at all times. Important also is the fact that collections for it were made before General Thomas became commander of the Army of the Cumberland.

---

46. Thomas Speed, *Union Regiments of Kentucky* (New York, 1897), pp. 308-9.

CHAPTER IX

From Mill Springs to Shiloh

THE victory at Mill Springs was overwhelming and rewarding, and marked the beginning of operations that would lead across Tennessee into Mississippi in the early future. In a letter dated February 4, 1862, Congressman Horace Maynard of Tennessee advised General Thomas that on the previous day the United States Senate confirmed his nomination to the rank of brigadier general. He said further: "You have undoubtedly fought the great battle of the war. The country is still reverberating the shout of victory. The more we hear of the engagement the greater its magnitude appears. I am most gratified to learn tonight . . . that you were yourself actively engaged in pushing forward a column into Eastern Tennessee, for I know well enough that, winter though it is, rough as the ways are, you will not stop until Knoxville is in your possession and that line of railroad in your grip."[1]

Mr. Maynard evidently referred here either to the occasion when General Sherman ordered Thomas to discontinue preparations for invading East Tennessee, or to the later attempt, which was halted by the winter of 1861-1862. Nevertheless, the idea was a good one, and further support came from General George B. McClellan in his letter to General Buell of November 7, 1861, stating that ". . . you should remain on the defensive on the line from Louisville to Nashville, while you throw the mass of your forces by rapid marches by Cumberland Gap . . . in order to occupy the railroad at that point." McClellan felt that by holding a strong anchor in East Tennessee his own hand would be strengthened through curtailment of supplies to his Confederate opponent, General Robert E. Lee, in Virginia. In addition, he believed that the confidence engendered by Federal control in eastern Tennessee would encourage support from residents

---

1. *Official Records of the War of the Rebellion* (Washington, D.C., 1880–1901), Ser. 1, Vol. VII, p. 582.

of western North Carolina, South Carolina, northern Georgia, and Alabama. General Buell's refusal to accept the plan was a severe disappointment to McClellan[2] and undoubtedly contributed to prolongation of the war.

Aside from losing the Battle of Mill Springs, the Confederates lost valuable supplies and equipment; further, so many of the men left the ranks and returned to their homes that their forces almost disintegrated. Cumberland Gap was once more vulnerable to Federal attack; in fact, there is some basis for believing that an advance by General Buell at that time would have resulted in obtaining possession of the area with but little opposition. General Albert Sidney Johnston at Bowling Green realized that the destruction of his right wing at Mill Springs placed him in a perilous position. The Tennessee capital of Nashville could now be attacked and occupied by concentrating Federal troops, unless sufficient resistance could be brought against them, a rather doubtful possibility.[3]

President Lincoln had also been hopeful that the loyal people of East Tennessee might be liberated from Confederate control. In his letter of January 13, 1862, to General Buell, he expressed his strong convictions on the matter in the following language:

> I state my general idea of this war to be that we have the greater numbers and the enemy has the greater facility of concentrating forces upon points of collision; that we must fail unless we can find some way of making our advantage an overmatch for his; and that this can only be done by menacing him with superior forces at different points at the same time, so that we can safely attack one or both if he makes no change; and if he weakens one to strengthen the other, forbear to attack the strengthened one, but seize and hold the weakened one, gaining so much. . . . my idea is that Halleck shall menace Columbus and "down-river" generally, while you menace Bowling Green and East Tennessee. If the enemy shall concentrate at Bowling Green do not retire from his front, yet do not fight him there either, but seize Columbus and East Tennessee, one or both, left exposed by the concentration at Bowling Green. It is a matter of no small anxiety to me, and one which I am sure you will not overlook, that the East Tennessee line is so long and over so bad a road.[4]

The weight of competent opinion leads to no other conclusion than

---

2. *Ibid.*, Vol. IV, p. 342; Vol. VII, p. 531.

3. John G. Nicolay and John Hay, *Abraham Lincoln: A History* (New York: The Century Co., 1909), Vol. V, p. 117.

4. *Official Records, op. cit.*, Ser. 1, Vol. VII, p. 928.

that the failure to invade East Tennessee shortly after the outbreak of hostilities prolonged the war considerably.

In response to General Buell's dispatch, General Thomas reported, on January 23, 1862, that inadequate subsistence for men and animals would prevent the maintaining of a large force at Monticello, Kentucky. He stated that since the roads over which the Confederates had recently marched would be now worse for his army, particularly in obtaining forage, survival there would be impossible. In view of these conditions, he asked General Buell's permission to move down the Cumberland River with his troops, take with him sufficient subsistence and forage on flatboats, and help the main army in its drive on Bowling Green. He reasoned that since Zollicoffer's forces were now scattered, and their equipment and supplies abandoned, there would be no serious obstacle to the plan. He also suggested that General Carter's brigade be permitted to enter Tennessee to offer encouragement to the citizens by supplying them with ammunition; in the meantime, he contended, Burkesville, Kentucky, a strong position on the river, could be strengthened to prevent the enemy from getting above that point.[5]

Since General Buell was under instructions to invade East Tennessee, he disregarded the recommendations of General Thomas and requested him instead, on February 2, to advise the present condition of the roads; the present and anticipated quantities of supplies; the time required for him to reach Knoxville; the activities of the Confederates in reassembling their scattered forces; and the progress made in improving the road to Somerset. A few days later, February 6, General Buell ordered General Thomas to return to Lebanon with his division and there await further orders. On that very day another victory for the Union cause, following closely upon the victory at Mill Springs, on January 19, was won by General Ulysses S. Grant in the capture of Fort Henry on the Tennessee River.[6]

Although Federal forces were defeated in the Battle of Wilson's Creek, Missouri, on August 10, 1861, and their commander, General Nathaniel Lyon, killed, Missouri was regarded as safely within the Union fold. A Union army was assembled in downstate Illinois to aid in holding Kentucky in the Union and to regain control of the Mississippi River. In order to accomplish these objectives, it was decided to undertake a flanking movement, hitherto unparalleled in magnitude, by way of the Cumberland and Tennessee rivers.[7]

5. *Ibid.*, pp. 563-64.

6. *Ibid.*, pp. 580, 589.

7. *The Civil War Through the Camera* ("Elson's History Series" [Springfield, Mass.: Patriot Publishing Co., 1912]). Part 2, p. 2; *Official Records, op. cit.,* Vol. VII, p. 624.

General Grant wrote to General Halleck on January 20, 1862, asking permission to visit him in St. Louis. However, when he received General Smith's report, on the twenty-second, advising that Fort Henry might be captured with but two guns, he that day relayed the report to General Halleck and requested that he be allowed to seek to capture the Fort. When it was clear to Halleck that he sought to capture both Fort Henry and Fort Donelson, that request was turned down abruptly, so bluntly, in fact, that Grant felt convinced that Halleck believed him guilty of suggesting something militarily ridiculous. With the aid of Flag Officer Andrew H. Foote, who also appealed to Halleck, Grant was then given authority to move on these fortifications.

On February 2, 1862, General Grant, who had been but recently appointed to the command of all Federal forces in western Kentucky and Tennessee, left Cairo, Illinois, with seventeen thousand men, destined for Fort Henry by way of the Ohio and Tennessee rivers. Joining him in the advance on Fort Henry were seven gunboats commanded by Flag Officer Foote. After an assault by the gunboats, during which one of the large guns in the fort exploded, Fort Henry surrendered, but not before three thousand of its defenders escaped to the next scene of attack by General Grant, Fort Donelson.[8]

The victory was significant in that it was the first of many successes on Western waters that would continue until the surrender of Vicksburg, on July 4, 1863, thus permitting the mighty Mississippi to roll on, as President Lincoln stated, "unvexed to the sea." The surrender of Fort Henry was productive in trapping the Confederates under Albert Sidney Johnston at Bowling Green, and compelling him to decide promptly whether to fight in the face of almost certain defeat or to retreat.[9] Johnston, perhaps wisely for him and his cause, decided that discretion is the better part of valor, when thoroughly outnumbered, and quickly began the long journey to Nashville, February 14, 1862. No sooner had he deserted Bowling Green than Union General Ormsby M. Mitchel, advancing by land, entered the town and met with only rear-guard resistance.[10]

The next step in the opening of the Western rivers would be accomplished also by General Grant in the capture of Fort Donelson. This fort, with its eighteen thousand defenders, was besieged on February 13 by Grant in combination with the gunboats of Flag

8. M. F. Force, *From Fort Henry to Corinth* (New York: Noble Offset Printing Co.), p. 26; *The Civil War Through the Camera, op. cit.,* pp. 4-6; Fletcher Pratt, *The Civil War on Western Waters* (New York: Henry Holt and Co., 1956), pp. 32, 52-54, 57.

9. *The Civil War Through the Camera, op. cit.,* pp. 6-12.

10. *Official Records, op. cit.,* Ser. 1. Vol. VII, p. 418.

Officer Foote. After several days of desperate fighting, some of it in sleet and snow, following warm days during which many of the men threw away their winter clothing, and after heavy casualties by land and severe damage to several of the gunboats, the fort surrendered on February 16, with its remaining garrison of some fourteen thousand men. Prior to the surrender some hundreds of the defenders escaped, including the famous-to-be cavalry leader of the Confederacy, Nathan Bedford Forrest. The capture of Forts Henry and Donelson, more especially the latter, was of tremendous importance to the North. Not only did it pave the way for invasion of the western South; it also assured Federal control of Kentucky and western Tennessee. The magnitude of the achievements filled the North with great hopes for ultimate victory, just as did the Confederate victory at Bull Run encourage the South to hope that victory for it was possible. The South could ill afford to lose an army of such size as the one at Fort Donelson, since these men could neither be spared nor replaced.[11]

Prior to the investment of Forts Henry and Donelson, General Buell directed General Thomas, on February 6, to advance his division as rapidly as possible back to Lebanon and await further orders. This instruction was for the purpose of lending support to the contemplated move against the Confederates at Bowling Green, cited previously. On February 15, in order to utilize the railroad at Munfordsville, General Thomas was ordered to move his division by way of Bardstown and New Haven. He was urged by General Buell to begin the march that day and take with him the maximum of quartermaster's supplies. However, with respect to food and forage, he was to travel with a minimum of weight and to obtain at Bardstown and New Haven whatever else he might require. After heavy rains *en route* to Bardstown, regarding which Thomas reported on February 22, "It rained two days ago as I never saw it rain before," he was told to move in haste to Louisville with his division. At Louisville he embarked with his command on transports located on the Ohio River and headed for the Cumberland River to join General Buell near Nashville. This move was part of the prearranged strategy for capturing Nashville, which had been agreed upon between General George B. McClellan, successor to General Winfield Scott as commander in chief of all Federal armies; General Henry W. Halleck, commander of Western armies with headquarters at St. Louis, Missouri; and General Buell, commander of the Army of the Ohio. After taking Nashville, the Western armies were to unite with the

---

11. *The Civil War Through the Camera, loc. cit.*

Army of the Tennessee under General Grant and take possession of
the railroads crossing Alabama and Mississippi.[12] This plan was aided
considerably by the retreat of General Johnston from Bowling Green
and the surrender of Forts Henry and Donelson.

During his brief stay in Bardstown, an officer of General Thomas's
command stole a horse. When the officer was brought before him to
explain his dereliction, Thomas was so outraged that an officer would
be guilty of such conduct that he drew his sword and cut off the
officer's epaulets. He then ordered him to return the horse immediately
and in person to the owner. This incident is important in showing
the rare lack of poise by the usually imperturbable Thomas; important
because he was generally retiring, brief, direct, patient, generous,
unselfish, and approachable throughout his lifetime, but the provoca-
tion in this instance was beyond his control. Thomas was capable
of overcoming disappointment, even when passed over in promotions,
but he never let his personal feelings interfere with his determination
to carry through to the utmost of his ability whatever assignment was
entrusted to him.[13]

It is gratifying to note that during the brief march through the
principal streets of Louisville, on February 25, *en route* to their point
of embarkation, General Thomas and his command were cheered by
the extremely warm reception given them by the flag-waving citizens.[14]

On February 16, 1862, President Lincoln wrote to General Halleck,
who was at that time emerging as a leader with a strong desire for
command, regarding future plans for the divided Western armies. The
President emphasized that although Fort Donelson appeared safe,
the united effort of both himself (Halleck) and General Buell would
be required to prevent General Grant's force at Fort Donelson from
being overwhelmed by the enemy. He told Halleck further that
since the Union forces held strong positions, in addition to the railroad between Bowling Green and Fort Donelson, it would be hazardous to assume that the enemy would not risk exposing Nashville to
attack by General Buell. The President believed, apparently, that this
risk could be taken because the Confederates were capable of assembling strong defensive forces from various points in the South. This
being so, he asked, "Could not a cavalry force under General Thomas
on the Upper Cumberland dash across, almost unmolested, and cut

12. J. B. Deaterick, *The Truth About Shiloh* (Memphis: S. C. Toof and Co.,
1942), pp. 7-9.

13. W. F. G. Shanks, *Personal Recollections of Distinguished Generals* (New
York: Harper and Brothers, 1866), p. 65.

14. Judson W. Bishop, *The Story of a Regiment* (St. Paul, 1890), p. 50.

the railroad at or near Knoxville, Tennessee?"[15] Although Fort Donelson fell into Union hands the very day on which President Lincoln wrote the letter, and Nashville soon thereafter, without evident stimulus from the President's suggestions, the thoughts expressed by him displayed above-average grasp of the military problems confronting the nation and the effort needed to solve them.

Following his retreat from Bowling Green, General Johnston made his way to Nashville, some seventy miles southwest of Bowling Green on the Barron River, where he arrived on February 17 and 18, hoping there to make a stand against the oncoming Federal armies. His tenure in Nashville was destined to be short-lived, however. The main body of General Buell's Army of the Ohio was moving by flatboat down the Ohio with Nashville the objective. Thus once more the decision was presented to General Johnston to remain and fight, subjecting Nashville to the ravages of war, or evacuation of the city. In his report to the Secretary of War, Johnston stated that he abandoned Nashville on February 23, giving as his reasons that he had but eleven thousand men to face Buell's army of forty thousand, and that General Thomas with a superior force had outflanked him on the east, which, with the fall of Fort Donelson and its accessability for dispatching reinforcements against him, made his position at Nashville untenable. Johnston's report to the Secretary of War was confirmed at least in part by the arrival of the first unit of the Army of the Ohio under the command of General William Nelson, on February 24, just a day following Johnston's evacuation. The last unit to arrive, the First Division of General Thomas, which had been assigned to the rear in deference perhaps to its recent participation in the Battle of Mill Springs, completed the occupation of Nashville for the time being. Immediately following the occupation, Andrew Johnson was named military governor of Tennessee with the rank of brigadier general, and his first order of business was to establish a provisional government. Governor Johnson would become Vice President of the United States in President Lincoln's second term, and following Lincoln's assassination would become President.[16]

On the day following the fall of Fort Donelson, February 17, General Halleck wired General McClellan: "Make Buell, Grant, and Pope major-generals of volunteers and give me command in the West. I ask this in return for Donelson and Henry." For sheer brazenness in seeking reward for the performance of another, this request of Halleck, which unhesitatingly and unequivocally assumed full credit

15. *Official Records. op. cit.*, Vol. VII, pp. 425-27; *Encyclopedia Americana* (New York: American Book–Stratford Press, Inc., 1954), Vol. XVI, p. 168.

16. *Official Records, op. cit.*, p. 624; Deaterick, *op. cit.*, p. 8.

for victories he did not win, is perhaps unsurpassed. If this were not so serious in its implication of injustice, one might well marvel at and admire its expression of initiative, the equal of which, sad to relate, history does not record on the battlefield. Halleck wired McClellan again on February 20, stating: "I must have command of the armies in the West. Hesitation and delay are losing us the golden opportunity." Clearly his appeal bore fruit, as evidenced by his appointment to command large armies that floundered for many months to the accompaniment of his vacillation and incompetency.

On March 11, 1862, President Lincoln named General Halleck commander of all Federal forces in the Western theater of operations. Although he had no record of military successes, the appointment elevated him above Generals Buell, Grant, and Thomas, all of whom had proved battle records. Halleck was a text writer of some distinction on legal and military subjects. He was a graduate of the United States Military Academy and had afterward become assistant professor of engineering there. Perhaps his nickname of "Old Brains" stemmed from his literary endeavors, which, with respect to military writings, were not translated into practical success on the battlefield. On July 11, 1862, he became the commander of all United States forces, and thereafter directed from Washington the movements of the commanders in the field until relieved by General Grant on March 12, 1864.[17]

Generals Gideon J. Pillow and John B. Floyd, who turned over the command of Fort Donelson to General Simon Bolivar Buckner, the commander who surrendered it to General Grant a few days later, escaped to Nashville by boat. They arrived on Sunday morning as the people were in attendance at various churches. News of their arrival created an atmosphere of apprehension and fear, and caused immediate dismissal of the congregations. Those citizens who were possessed of the means to do so fled the city at once with the cry, "The Yankees are coming." Both press and pulpit had been proclaiming for some days that the Federals would mistreat them, and naturally some of the people believed the stories. It soon became evident that the gentlemanly conduct of both Generals Buell and Thomas, which was reflected throughout the ranks, assured the people there was nothing to fear.[18]

Shortly after his conquest of Fort Donelson, General Grant was

---

17. George W. Cullum, *Biographical Register of Officers and Cadets of the U. S. Military Academy* (Boston, 1891), Vol. I, p. 578; Force, *op. cit.*, pp. 64-65.

18. Richard W. Johnson, *Memoir of Major General George H. Thomas* (Philadelphia: J. B. Lippincott Co., 1881), p. 65.

accused of excessive drinking and all-around neglect of duty, which led to his being relieved of command. The action was taken by General Halleck, on the recommendation of General George B. McClellan, commander in chief, and General C. F. Smith was named his successor. On March 5, General Smith set up headquarters at Savannah, Tennessee, above Fort Henry, on the east side of the Tennessee River, and by the thirteenth he had four divisions with him. The attempt of General William T. Sherman of the Fifth Division to destroy the railroad and bridges near Iuka, without bringing on a general engagement, resulted in failure, through no fault of Sherman's. The attempt to destroy these facilities was prevented by the exceedingly heavy rains, storms, and high water. While advancing to Iuka, Sherman observed that the high banks at several points along the route, particularly at Pittsburg Landing, were of considerable military value. He suggested to General Smith that Pittsburg Landing, nine miles above Savannah, be occupied, since, in addition to being on the west side of the Tennessee River, the ground adjacent thereto afforded ample space for the encampment of a hundred thousand men; furthermore, the ground and general topography of the terrain permitted defense of the area by a relatively small force. Not the least of the advantages afforded by the location was the excellent opportunity it gave to move on the Confederate concentration at Corinth, Mississippi.[19]

General Buell and his army occupied Nashville until about mid-March, 1862. General Halleck's army held other strong positions, which, with General Buell's, would invite renewed aggressive action as soon as General Johnston's retreating Confederates were sufficiently strengthened, following their recent reverses. It was important that they be given no opportunity to benefit from any lack of initiative by the Federals in keeping them on the defensive. General Grant was encamped at this time at Pittsburg Landing on the Tennessee River. In accordance with agreed-upon plans, General Buell began preparations for a march toward Grant's position, there to lend any possible assistance in repelling surprise attacks. Buell ordered General Ormsby M. Mitchel to take control of the Memphis and Charleston Railroad. He himself began the march with the First, Second, Fourth, Fifth, and Sixth divisions, commanded respectively by Generals Thomas, McCook, Nelson, Crittenden, and Wood, or approximately thirty-seven thousand men. Buell assigned his newly organized Seventh Division to General G. W. Morgan with orders to advance on Cumberland Gap, if practicable, but in any case to hold the enemy in check if he

19. Force, *op. cit.*, pp. 93-95; Deaterick, *op. cit.*, pp. 15-16; *Official Records, op. cit.*, Vol. 10, Part 1, p. 27.

should attempt to advance. He arrived at Savannah on April 5, there to unite with General Halleck for a march on Corinth as soon as it might be deemed expedient.[20]

It is noteworthy that during the march Buell met with a number of delays, the most serious of which was the need for constructing a bridge across Duck River, at a point about four miles north of Columbia, Tennessee. The absence of pontoons, which in the near future would expedite the movement of troops across large bodies of water at a greatly accelerated pace, was a severe handicap to Buell. The bridge was not completed until March 29; but since Buell was not under orders to proceed in haste, and since his arrival on the battlefield of Shiloh has become controversial, it is clear that he was not to blame for the delay. Many would be the backward glances at the construction of this bridge; but despite the delay, Buell's advance troops reached the field before the first day of the battle was over, and had much to do with the Confederates' decision to retreat.[21]

The Memphis and Charleston Railroad and the Mobile and Ohio Railroad combined to make Corinth, Mississippi, an extremely important rail center leading to the Mississippi and Tennessee rivers, and to the Confederate army of northern Virginia defending Richmond. These railroads and rivers, added to the natural advantages of mountains and general terrain, explain the choice of Corinth by General Johnston as his next point of resistance. It should not be forgotten that Corinth was a vital point of operations for the Confederacy in assuring control of the area east of the Lower Mississippi. The convergence of both the Federal and Confederate armies on Corinth was in recognition of its great natural advantages of offense and defense; and these preliminary movements would have their sequence in the first large-scale battle at Shiloh or Pittsburg Landing.

A principal link in the chain of events leading to Shiloh was the sending of reinforcements from Virginia, in February, 1862, under General P. G. T. Beauregard. This hero of Fort Sumter and Bull Run was sent to help General Johnston in the defense of Tennessee. After Johnston abandoned Nashville, he retreated to Murfreesboro where he joined forces with General Beauregard and General George B. Crittenden. Late in March, General Johnston left by way of Decatur, Alabama, for Corinth, hoping there to make a stand against the oncoming Federal armies on the line of the Memphis and Charleston Railroad. In the meantime, Beauregard was concentrating troops at Corinth from points as far distant as New Madrid, Missouri, New

20. Thomas B. Van Horne, *History of the Army of the Cumberland* (Cincinnati: Robert Clarke and Co., 1875), Vol. I, pp. 97-100.

21. *Ibid.*

Orleans, Louisiana, and Pensacola, Florida. Several thousand troops from Arkansas under General Earl Van Dorn were expected to follow soon thereafter.[22]

General Grant was restored to the command of the Army of the Tennessee after General Halleck became convinced that his removal was based on groundless or at least questionable charges. Soon afterward General B. M. Prentiss arrived with the Sixth Division of Buell's army and increased Grant's force at Pittsburg Landing to about forty thousand men. General Nelson's division, also of Buell's army, arrived on April 5, and the remaining divisions of his army were expected to follow in a short time.

It is important to bring into proper perspective the roles of General Grant and Sherman in the Battle of Shiloh. Colonel Jacob Ammen, of General William Nelson's division, kept a diary in which he quoted General Grant's reply to a remark by Colonel Ammen that our troops were not fatigued and could march to Pittsburg Landing, if necessary: "You cannot march through the swamps; make the troops comfortable; I will send boats for you Monday or Tuesday, or some time early in the week. There will be no fight at Pittsburg Landing; we will have to go to Corinth, where the rebels are fortified. If they come to attack us, we can whip them, as I have more than twice as many troops as I had at Fort Donelson."[23] This statement was made at the very edge of the battle and is conclusive evidence that General Grant had some chores to do before attaining the stature of a competent general. One may assume that his long period of retirement from the army exacted its toll; and it is reasonable to conclude that this inactive period would reflect no improvement in his knowledge of the art of war, which could therefore have no other result than the retarding of his development.

Other proof that General Grant did not expect an immediate attack at Shiloh is shown by his report to General Halleck on April 5, the night before the battle, when the Confederates were about to strike his army with the fury of an avalanche: "The main force of the enemy at Corinth . . . The number of the enemy at Corinth and within supporting distance of it cannot be far from 80,000 men." To indicate Grant's confidence in the situation, proving by his own words that the Confederate attack was a complete surprise, he wrote to General Halleck on April 5, "I have scarcely the faintest idea of an attack [general one] being made upon us, but will be prepared should such a thing take place."[24] No further evidence is needed than Grant's own words to show that he was not prepared; in truth, he was completely

---

22. Deaterick, *op. cit.*, pp. 13-14.
23. *Official Records, op. cit.*, Vol. X, Part 1, pp. 330-31.
24. *Ibid.*, Part 2, p. 94.

surprised. Aside from his communications to Halleck, Grant was at Savannah, nine miles from his command, when the blow fell; this alone is some expression of the confidence he expressed to Halleck. He failed to understand that although the Confederates were about twenty miles away, they could and did advance from Corinth in a very short time. The fact that Shiloh resulted in a Union victory does not reflect great credit upon either Grant or Sherman; the simple fact is that Grant in particular was the beneficiary of that luck that so often accompanied him. At Shiloh his errors were offset by those of his enemy; but nothing can obscure the fact that he just missed defeat because of his ignoring of the elementary rules of warfare.

It is almost incredible that these West Point men ignored the basic requirement of digging intrenchments as a minimum safeguard against attack. This has been "explained" on the basis that there was little point in digging in, since they were expected to advance in a day or so. Perhaps the idea that they might have to retreat if attacked, in which event they would have provided some security, never occurred to them. Such optimism had no foundation in fact, in view of the many Federal defeats suffered up to that time. The marvel of Shiloh is that the Army of the Tennessee, made up largely of untrained and inexperienced soldiers, virtually defenseless, surprised and almost pushed by the opening attack into the Tennessee River, was able to gain the victory. The Confederates at one time were on the verge of turning back because they felt the Federals knew of their plan to attack. General Beauregard in particular insisted that the Confederates had been so clumsy and noisy in their advance that the entire Yankee force must be lying in wait for them; on this point he could not have been more wrong.[25] In reading the official and other accurate reports on the Battle of Shiloh, the wonder grows that these two men, despite their spotty records, emerged as the twin heroes of the Union victory. It is often true that much of fame is founded on misunderstanding, misrepresentation, and bias.

General William T. Sherman was in temporary command at Pittsburg Landing while General Grant was at Savannah, and he also anticipated no attack. On April 5 he reported to General Grant that "The enemy has cavalry in our front, and I think there are two regiments of infantry and one battery of artillery about 2 miles out." On that very day he again wrote to Grant: "I have no doubt that nothing will occur more than some picket firing. . . . I will not be drawn out far unless with certainty of advantage, and I do not apprehend anything

25. Bruce Catton, *U. S. Grant and the American Military Tradition* (New York: Grosset and Dunlap, 1954), pp. 83-84; Charles King, *The True Ulysses S. Grant* (Philadelphia: J. B. Lippincott Co., 1914), pp. 196-98.

like an attack on our position."[26] It is apparent that General Sherman bears much responsibility for the surprise at Shiloh. In the light of proved records, General Grant, as commander in chief, was more responsible; but Sherman, as acting commander during Grant's absence, had the implicit responsibility to safeguard his men by taking reasonable precautions. Here is another example of the effect of long absence from the army, during which they could not have kept abreast of developments in the military service.

Confederate General Albert Sidney Johnston planned his attack on Pittsburg Landing for the morning of April 5, as shown by his dispatch to President Davis on April 3: "General Buell is in motion, 30,000 strong, rapidly from Columbia by Clifton to Savannah; Mitchel behind him with 10,000. Confederate forces 40,000, ordered forward to offer battle near Pittsburg. Division from Bethel, main body near Corinth, reserve from Burnsville converge tomorrow near Monterey. On Pittsburg, Beauregard second in command; Polk left; Hardee center; Bragg, right wing; Breckinridge, reserve. Hope engagement before Buell can form junction." In this dispatch there is discernible an apprehension that contact with Federal forces is imminent, an event devoutly wished for, as General Johnston stated, before the Union armies could unite. The order to General Leonidas Polk on April 4 stated that General Breckinridge's force was ordered from a position in reserve to move "at latest at 4 A.M. tomorrow by the Ridge road to Mickey's; thence, if a road can be found in the direction of Pratt's house, on the direct road from Monterey to Pittsburg, which he will then follow until within 2 miles of General Bragg's force, where he will dispose his command en masse between the Bark road and Lick creek. At the same time you [Polk] will occupy the ground between General Breckinridge's left and Owl Creek." That the attack on the Federals at Pittsburg Landing was not made on the fifth, the date inferred from these dispatches, is explained by General Bragg's dispatch at 10 A.M. on April 4 to Generals Johnston and Beauregard: "I reached here at 8:30, ahead of my rear division. Bad roads, inefficient transportation badly managed, and the usual delay of a first move of new troops have caused the delay."[27]

General Nelson's division of Buell's army reached Savannah on April 5, and Grant reported that Buell's three oncoming divisions would be routed to Hamburg, about four miles from Pittsburg, upon arrival. Grant also reported to Buell on April 5 that the enemy in and around Corinth aggregated from sixty to eighty thousand troops. From this it is conclusive that General Grant was not pressuring General

26. *Official Records, op. cit.,* Vol. X, Part 2, pp. 93-94.
27. *Ibid.,* pp. 387, 391.

Buell to hasten his advance, a fact that disproves the argument that Buell moved slowly to his aid. In sharp contrast to this relaxed attitude, General Grant sent General Buell the following dispatch on the morning of April 6, after his return from Savannah after the Confederate attack: "The attack on my forces has been very spirited from early this morning. The appearance of fresh troops in the field now would have a powerful effect, both by inspiring our men and disheartening the enemy. If you will get upon the field, leaving all your baggage on the east bank of the river, it will be more to our advantage, and possibly save the day to us. The rebel forces are estimated at over 100,000 men."[28] Perhaps the most noticeable point in this appeal was the increase of the Confederate force from an estimated sixty to eighty thousand men, to an estimated one hundred thousand in just one day. Also there was the admission that Buell's army could "save the day to us," an admission strangely lacking in Grant's writings after the battle; in fact, the very opposite is true.

The battle opened at five o'clock on the morning of April 6, between advance Confederate troops under General William J. Hardee and Federal pickets. Grant's Army of the Tennessee was encamped in a wooded area averaging more than one hundred feet above the water of the Tennessee River. The terrain was broken and flanked on the right and on the left by creeks that did not permit turning movements; besides, the general features of the site did not render it suitable for a defensive battle. Sherman held two brigades in an advance position near the Shiloh Church, on the main road leading to the Confederate concentration point at Corinth. One of his brigades was located on the Purdy road over Owl Creek, and another occupied the extreme left to safeguard the ford of Lick Creek on the Hamburg Road. The Confederate division of General Benjamin H. Prentiss was between the right or direct road leading to Corinth, and the brigade holding the extreme left; and the two divisions of General Stephen A. Hurlbut and General W. H. L. Wallace were two or three miles to the rear at Pittsburg Landing.[29] It will be seen that these divisions were well placed to provide accessability to roads leading to Corinth; but the several forces were somewhat separated, and quick liaison for united defensive purposes was impossible. It is astonishing that defenses such as rifle pits had not been constructed to afford protection to skirmishers in withstanding an attack. Even worse was the absence of a unified command to provide over-all battle direction.

General Sherman reported to General Grant on April 10, in summarizing the battle, that although "On Saturday the enemy's cavalry

28. *Ibid.*, pp. 93-95; Van Horne, *Army of the Cumberland*, Vol. I. pp. 104-5.
29. Van Horne, *loc. cit.*

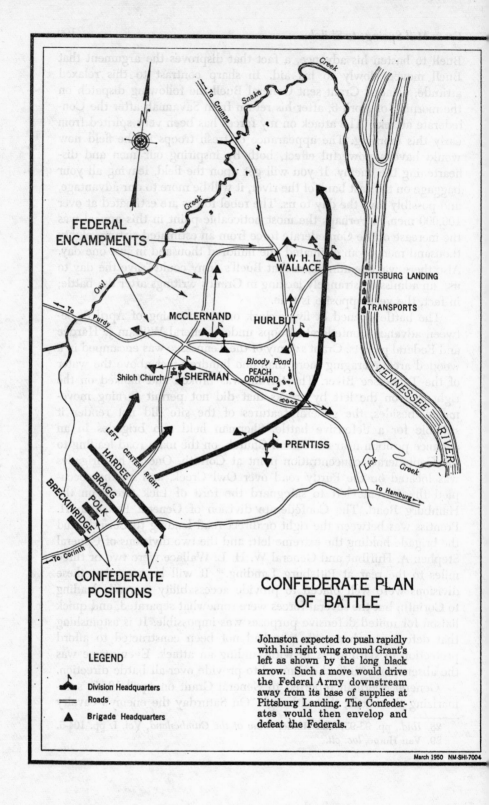

FEDERAL
ENCAMPMENTS

W. H. L.
WALLACE

PITTSBURG LANDING

TRANSPORTS

To Purdy

McCLERNAND

HURLBUT

Bloody Pond
PEACH
ORCHARD

Shiloh Church

SHERMAN

PRENTISS

TENNESSEE RIVER

HARDEE

LEFT CENTER RIGHT

BRAGG

POLK

BRECKINRIDGE

Lick Creek

To Hamburg

To Corinth

CONFEDERATE
POSITIONS

CONFEDERATE PLAN
OF BATTLE

Johnston expected to push rapidly
with his right wing around Grant's
left as shown by the long black
arrow. Such a move would drive
the Federal Army downstream
away from its base of supplies at
Pittsburg Landing. The Confederates would then envelop and
defeat the Federals.

LEGEND

⚔ Division Headquarters
═══ Roads
▲ Brigade Headquarters

March 1950 NM-SHI-7004

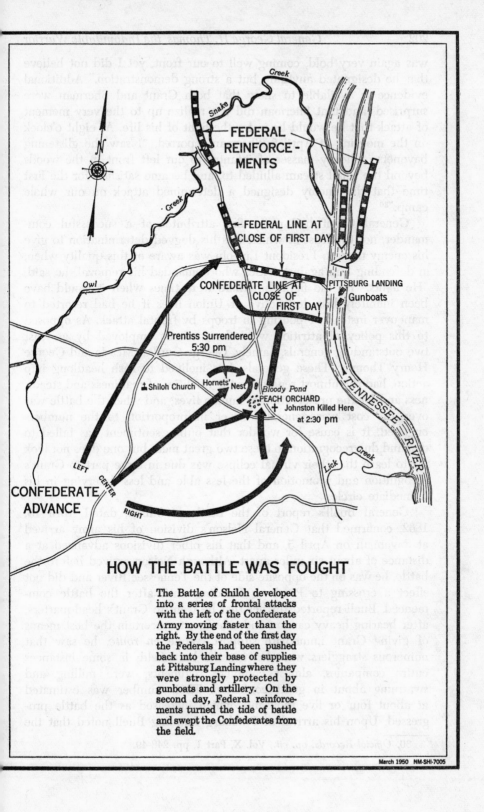

Creek

FEDERAL
REINFORCE-
MENTS

Snake

Creek

N

Creek

← FEDERAL LINE AT
CLOSE OF FIRST DAY

Owl

CONFEDERATE LINE AT
CLOSE OF
FIRST DAY

PITTSBURG LANDING
Gunboats

Prentiss Surrendered
5:30 pm

♰ Shiloh Church

Hornets' Nest

Bloody Pond
PEACH ORCHARD
Johnston Killed Here
+ at 2:30 pm

TENNESSEE RIVER

LEFT

CENTER

RIGHT

Lick

Creek

CONFEDERATE
ADVANCE

HOW THE BATTLE WAS FOUGHT

The Battle of Shiloh developed into a series of frontal attacks with the left of the Confederate Army moving faster than the right. By the end of the first day the Federals had been pushed back into their base of supplies at Pittsburg Landing where they were strongly protected by gunboats and artillery. On the second day, Federal reinforcements turned the tide of battle and swept the Confederates from the field.

was again very bold, coming well to our front, yet I did not believe that he designated anything but a strong demonstration." Additional evidence is available to show that both Grant and Sherman were surprised, and that Sherman did not realize up to the very moment of attack that he would be in for the fight of his life. At eight o'clock on the morning of April 6, Sherman reported, "I saw the glistening bayonets of heavy masses of infantry to our left front in the woods beyond the small stream alluded to, and became satisfied for the first time that the enemy designed a determined attack on our whole camp."[30]

General Grant had many fine attributes of a successful commander, not the least of which was his dogged determination to give his enemy no rest. President Lincoln was aware of this quality when, in defending him against critics who demanded his removal, he said, "He fights." He did fight; but there were times when it would have been infinitely less destructive of Union lives if he had resorted to maneuver instead of pouring in troops by frontal attack. As opposed to this policy of attrition were the methods employed by at least two outstanding generals, namely, George Gordon Meade and George Henry Thomas. These generals, less inclined to rush headlong into action, had the utmost regard for the qualities of readiness and steadiness and for the preservation of human lives; and when the battle was over the cost was generally lower in proportion to the numbers engaged. It is cause for wonder that public sentiment has failed to demand due recognition to these two great men; but one does not look far to learn that their virtual eclipse was due in large part to Grant's recognition and promotion of the less able and less deserving in his immediate circle.

General Buell's report of the Battle of Shiloh, dated April 15, 1862, confirmed that General Nelson's division of his army arrived at Savannah on April 5, and that his other divisions advanced at a distance of about six miles apart. Although Nelson arrived before the battle, he was on the opposite side of the Tennessee River and did not effect a crossing to Pittsburg Landing until after the battle commenced. Buell reported further that he went to Grant's headquarters, after hearing heavy cannon and rifle fire, to ascertain the best means of giving Grant immediate support. While *en route,* he saw that numerous stragglers were leaving the battlefield; in some instances entire companies, almost complete regiments, were milling and swarming about in great confusion. Their number was estimated at about four or five thousand, which increased as the battle progressed. Upon his arrival at Pittsburg Landing Buell noted that the

---

30. *Official Records, op. cit.,* Vol. X, Part 1, pp. 248-49.

heights above the Tennessee River were crowded with stragglers and that nothing was being done to correct the situation.[31]

General Thomas did not arrive with his division in time to engage in the battle, since his was the last division of Buell's army to leave Nashville; also, a number of mishaps slowed the march and prevented a junction with Grant. Buell reported that Thomas's division participated in the pursuit of the enemy, and that his command had already achieved honorable status by its victory at the Battle of Mill Springs.

In midafternoon, Confederate General Albert Sidney Johnston fell mortally wounded from a bullet in the leg, and bled to death in about fifteen minutes. It has been said that he could have saved his life if he had used a tourniquet to stanch the flow of blood, but he was overcome by the excitement of battle and neglected it. Thus ended the career of the soldier believed by many to be potentially the greatest commander the South had to offer. News of his death spread rapidly and created panic throughout the ranks. His loss may have been the principal reason for the Confederate defeat, since the Federals were overwhelmed in the first stage of the attack and driven back in great confusion. General William J. Hardee reported that General Johnston brought up the reserve under General Breckinridge at about eleven o'clock in the morning, turned the Union left, and drove many of them to the shelter of the gunboats. Hardee also reported that Johnston fell at about two thirty P.M., and expired at a point near where Breckinridge's men had made the successful charge only a short time before. Hardee believed that but for his death the Confederacy would have achieved a triumph unparalleled in the war. Johnston was the only full-rank, four-star American general ever killed in battle. General Beauregard, as second in command, took charge of the Confederates in the vicinity of Shiloh Church, and General Braxton Bragg, of "More grape, Captain Bragg" Mexican War fame, assumed command of the Confederate right wing.[32]

Later in the day, following a series of movements in which they were pushed back toward the Tennessee River, twenty-two hundred Federals surrendered at the Hornet's Nest, after a terrible struggle. The remnants of the Union Army prepared for a final stand on a line extending from the top of the bluff above the Tennessee to the right of Crump's Landing. Now occurred the key moment of the entire battle; with at least an hour of daylight remaining, General Beauregard ordered a cease-fire until the following morning. This order, following the splendid success of only a short time before, is one of the mysteries of the war, and cannot be explained on the basis of

31. *Ibid.*, pp. 291-96.
32. *Encyclopedia Americana*, Vol. XVI, p. 182; Deaterick, *op. cit.*, p. 24.

logical reasoning. This was the moment for the Confederates to follow up their success by pursuing the Federals while they were at a disadvantage. This was the order that saved Grant and Sherman from disgrace, and the Federal cause in the West from disaster. At the moment of Beauregard's order to cease fighting, the Union Army was defeated, but the tide of battle was now turned, and victory for the Confederates was relinquished to the Federals. The consequences of a Confederate victory here would have been great. Northern morale, not very high following many reverses since the beginning of the war, would have dropped even lower.[33]

There is nothing imaginary regarding the importance of this Union victory; for with Second Bull Run, Antietam, a virtual stalemate despite the Confederate retreat, and Fredericksburg, one of the bloodiest and least justifiable battles ever fought, all to follow in 1862, the Union cause was probably preserved at Shiloh. In fairness to Beauregard, he stated in his report of April 11 that it was after six o'clock and darkness not far away; that the chief command rested upon him; and that he was greatly prostrated and suffering from the illness that had pursued him since early in February. He also stated that officers and men were exhausted by more than twelve hours of fighting without food, and that they were worn from the march of the preceding day through mud and water.[34] Although there are two sides to this controversy, the fact remains that with Buell coming up, a factor that impelled the Confederates to attack before he could join Grant, Beauregard could not afford to stop fighting when he had the Federals reeling. Perhaps the Creator used this occasion to demonstrate that "There is a Divinity that shapes our ends, rough-hew them how we will."

Confederate General Polk's report on Shiloh is at variance with General Grant's report, in which Grant stated that the Confederates withdrew because of the destructive fire from the gunboats. In commenting on the effectiveness of the Federal fire, Polk reported that "The height of the plain on which we were, above the level of the water, was about 100 feet, so that it was necessary to give great elevation to his guns to enable him to fire over the bank. The consequence was that shot could take effect only at points remote from the river's edge. They were comparatively harmless to our troops nearest the bank, and became increasingly so as we drew near the enemy and placed him between us and his boats." To further refute Grant's report that the enemy withdrew because of the destructive fire, General Bragg reported that "their fire, though terrific in sound

33. *Official Records. op. cit.*, Vol. X, Part 1, p. 279.
34. *Ibid.*, p. 387.

and producing some consternation at first, did us no damage, as the shells all passed over and exploded far beyond our positions."[35]

Colonel Jacob Ammen's diary of the activities of his Twenty-fourth Ohio Infantry disclosed that upon his entrance to the battlefield, following a rapid march to help stem the tide of Confederate pressure on the Union lines, he observed the scene described herewith:

> In we went to a point opposite the landing at Pittsburg. . . . The northeast bank is low, the opposite bank is high—100 feet or more. The space between the top of the bank and the river, up and down half a mile or more, was crowded with men; the river was full of boats with steam up; and these boats had many soldiers on them; men in uniforms on the boats and under the river bank (10,000 to 15,000) demoralized. Signals urging us to hurry over, which I could not understand, as there were so many on the boats and under the bank not engaged of the reserve, as I supposed then. . . . On each side the boats were crowded with demoralized soldiers, so that only three or four companies could cross on a boat. On our passage over they said their regiments were cut to pieces, etc., and that we would meet the same fate, etc. The vagabonds under the bank told the same story, and yet my new troops pressed through the crowd without showing any signs of fear. In crossing the river some of my men called my attention to men with uniforms, even shoulder straps, making their way across the stream on logs, and wished to shoot the cowards. Such looks of terror, such confusion, I never saw before, and I do not wish to see again."[36]

Grant's *Memoirs* contain a most ridiculous defense of Shiloh, in an attempt to rebut criticism of his part in it. To the claim that if General Johnston had not been killed the Confederates would have been victorious, Grant replied:

> "There is little doubt that we would have been disgracefully beaten *if* all the shells and bullets fired by us had passed harmlessly over the enemy and *if* all of theirs had taken effect . . . the fact that when he was shot Johnston was leading a brigade to induce it to make a charge which had been repeatedly ordered, is evidence that there was neither the universal demoralization on our side nor the unbounded confidence on theirs which has been claimed. There was, in fact, no hour during the day when I doubted the eventual defeat of the enemy, although I was disap-

35. *Ibid.*, pp. 109, 333, 410, 466.
36. *Ibid.*

pointed that reinforcements so near at hand did not arrive at an earlier hour."[37]

In this statement Grant facetiously avoided direct comment regarding his near defeat; instead, he implied that General Buell, one of the more capable generals, who advanced to the battlefield at a pace consistent with the tenor of Grant's dispatches to him, was somehow to blame for the near defeat. In other words, although Grant's unreadiness at Shiloh was disgraceful, he attempted to pass responsibility for his own failures to the shoulders of Buell.

General Grant has come down through the years with a halo of saintly propriety that his admirers have created for him without full allowance for the trappings of earthly and human failings. Nothing shows this more clearly than Grant's own words:

General Lew. Wallace, with 5,000 effective men, arrived after firing had ceased for the day, and was placed on the right. Thus night came, Wallace came, and the advance of Nelson's division came; but none—unless night—in time to be of material service to the gallant men who saved Shiloh on that first day against large odds. Buell's loss on the 6th of April was two men killed and one wounded, all members of the 36th Indiana Infantry. The Army of the Tennessee lost on that day at least 7,000 men. The presence of two or three regiments of Buell's army on the west bank before firing ceased had not the slightest effect in preventing the capture of Pittsburg Landing."[38]

These figures are not subject to dispute; but the implication that the troops of the Army of the Tennessee decided the first day at Shiloh, instead of Buell's men and Beauregard's astonishing order to cease fire, which saved the Union Army from total defeat, is sheer distortion.

General Grant acknowledged in his *Memoirs* the arrival of Colonel Ammen's advance troops of Nelson's division of Buell's Army; but he stated that they did not arrive in time to save the day. General Buell, however, reported that when these troops arrived the condition of affairs in Grant's command was critical, that it was the decision of Beauregard to call off the fight that saved Grant from defeat, and that "had the attack [by the Confederates] been made before Nelson could arrive, with the means which the enemy had abundantly at hand, it would have succeeded beyond all question."[39] The rest of

37. U. S. Grant, *Personal Memoirs* (Hartford, 1885), pp. 188-89.
38. *Ibid.*, pp. 180-81.
39. *Official Records, op. cit.*, Vol. X, Part 1, p. 292.

the Battle of Shiloh was anticlimax. The next morning, April 7, Grant assumed the offensive with the aid of the remaining twenty-thousand men of Buell's Army of the Ohio, which came in during the night and morning and insured the Union victory. These latter reinforced his right and center, while General Lew Wallace's division reinforced his right. After both sides sent out strong skirmishing parties during the early hours of the morning, the Federals advanced in heavy force. By ten o'clock they had driven the Confederates from the Peach Orchard and the Hornets' Nest, and had gained the Hamburg-Purdy Road. At noon they were fighting once more at Shiloh Church, where the casualties on both sides were as heavy as on the day before.[40]

About two o'clock Beauregard knew that he was defeated and gave orders to withdraw to Corinth. In order to cover his retreat, he directed that a charge be made against the Union center, and placed his artillery on the ridge southwest of the Church to cover the retreat. At three o'clock the Confederate retreat was under way in leisurely fashion with full cavalry protection, leaving Grant in possession of the field.[41] This was the greatest battle of the war to date, and the losses, representing about twenty per cent of those engaged, were staggering.

General Thomas was not alone in being denied his just due by Grant and Sherman, as the foregoing so ably proves. It is sufficient to demonstrate that both of these commanders were determined to shape the record, regardless of the facts, to prove themselves deserving of credit, or, more especially in this instance, to prove themselves blameless of the incompetence they displayed at Shiloh. It is questionable whether any other battle of the Civil War so abounded in controversy, and yet was so susceptible of documentation as to refute any material distortion of the facts. It is a source of wonderment that two men in such positions of responsibility as Grant and Sherman would be so indifferent to facts that would disprove their own distorted versions of the battle. These men, with their many supporters, but these two in particular, are basically to blame for the attempts to drown the fact of their overwhelming surprise, and to deny proper credit to Buell and his men for saving them from complete destruction.

It is significant that Grant, despite indisputable evidence of it, failed to mention in his report the element of complete surprise; and although he reported that his entire line fell back "nearly half

---

40. *Shiloh National Military Park* (Washington, D.C., National Park Service), pp. 16-17; *Official Records, op. cit.*, Vol. X, Part 1, p. 293.

41. *Shiloh National Military Park, op. cit.*, p. 19.

way from their camps to the Landing," he omitted to state that his army was in chaos. Grant did report that "in late afternoon a desperate enemy attempt was made to turn our left and gain the transports, etc."; he did report that due to the difficulty of terrain for artillery, cavalry, and infantry only "necessary artillerists and a small infantry force for their support" were stationed there; he did report that "just at this moment the advance of Major General Buell's columns, part of General William Nelson's division, arrived, the two generals named [Buell and Nelson] being present"; and he did report that "an advance was immediately made and the enemy soon driven back." Singularly, he reported that "the enemy suffered terribly from demoralization and desertion,"[42] but made no special reference to his own far worse troop demoralization.

Grant's report had little comment for Buell's timely aid, other than the statement that "Buell, with a distinct army long under his command, and which did such efficient service, commanded by himself in person on the field," could report on "those of his command who particularly distinguished themselves [better] than I possibly can."[43] There is no denying, as the report proves, that Grant made little comment on Buell's activities, regardless of what he said many years later, in contradiction, in his *Memoirs*.

In his *Memoirs*, Grant reported that "Wallace came, and the advance of Nelson's division came; but none—unless night—in time to be of material service to the gallant men who saved Shiloh on that first day against great odds." It is to be wondered whether Grant included among the gallant his "four or five thousand lying under cover of the bluff, panic-stricken, most of whom would have been shot where they lay, without resistance, before they would have taken muskets and marched to the front to protect themselves."[44] Odd, indeed, that Grant reported the Confederates demoralized when such a big part of his army on the river bank would not have re-entered the fight at the point of a gun, which can only mean that there was something about Shiloh he wanted to forget. His every intention was to write his own version of the battle, hoping that the country would accept his account instead of the true facts; and, tragically for the purpose of history, that distorted version has been accepted. Sherman was, of course, far more articulate and combative in seeking to compel his version upon the country; but fortunately he did not consult Grant and obtain a general agreement on the version to be accepted,

42. *Official Records, op. cit.*, Vol. X, Part 1, pp. 108-11.

43. *Ibid.*

44. *Ibid.*; Grant, *op. cit.*, 178-80; The Buell Papers (in custody of Rice University, Houston, Texas).

a circumstance that exposed the transparency of their unidentical versions.

General Sherman would not be denied. In his feuds with publishers he challenged whatever exposed himself and Grant to the light of truth. In the same publication, *The North American Review,* in which Sherman's attempt to suppress the voice of a member of the military forces was reported, discussed elsewhere herein, Sherman stated that "General Buell did not reach the field of battle until the first day was over." Grant himself reported twenty-three years later in the *Memoirs* that he met Buell "on one occasion during the day," but that "I do not remember the hour." Grant did state in his report, as we have seen, that Nelson, of Buell's advance column, helped in repulsing the Confederates in late afternoon of the sixth. Grant also sent a dispatch to Buell on the sixth, stating that "Heavy firing is heard up the [river] indicating plainly that an attack has been made upon our most advanced position. I have been looking for this but did not believe the attack could be made before Monday or Tuesday.

"This necessitates my joining forces up the river instead of meeting you to-day as I had contemplated. I have directed General Nelson to move to the river with his Division. He can march to opposite Pittsburg."[45]

Sherman's statement regarding Buell's presence is therefore refuted, since Buell was there during the first day's action, and Grant's telegram and *Memoirs* prove that he was.

General Buell's letter to his wife on April 9, 1862, just two days after the battle, was nothing if not prophetic, as it implied much that happened afterward in denying him deserved credit for his part in it. Here it is:

> BATTLEFIELD,
> NEAR PITTSBURG, TENN.
> April 9, 1862.

MY DEAR WIFE:

I am writing you from the field, or rather in advance of the field of battle, the greatest in the size of the armies engaged that has ever been fought on this continent. Nor is it without a great result, in this, that it saved the army of General Halleck, commanded by General Grant, which otherwise was doomed to destruction.

I should not speak trustfully to anyone, unless it be to you, my wife, of the part the "Kentucky Army" had active in it. General Grant was attacked on Sunday; I arrived myself about 2 o'clock,

---

45. The Buell Papers; *The North American Review* (Dec., 1885–Feb., 1886).

and one of my divisions crossed the river about dark. It is the voice of his entire army, as far as I know, that they were lost. One of my brigades arrived in time to engage and check the enemy, then not more than 300 yards from the depot on which the army depended. Another division crossed during the night, another the next morning early; and about 6 o'clock we moved, formed for the attack.

The battle continued without cessation until evening; the enemy was driven from the field and retreated back to Corinth. I mean to state these facts very simply and briefly in my report, and let the world form its own conclusions as to what credit my troops are entitled to.[46]

The question of the acceptability of both Grant's and Sherman's *Memoirs* is constantly raised when an extended research is made affecting them. Whatever their intent may have been in seeking to give a different version of Shiloh than the facts warranted, it is particularly noteworthy that the *Encyclopaedia Britannica* reports that Grant's army had ascended the Tennessee to Pittsburg Landing and disembarked, while Buell's cooperating army moved from Nashville across country to join it:

Grant disposed his divisions in camps around the Landing rather with a view to their comfort than in accordance with any tactical scheme. No intrenchments were made; Halleck, the Union commander, was equally over-confident, and allowed Buell's leading division to march in leisurely fashion. Even so, more by chance than intentionally, Buell's leading division was opposite Savannah, nine miles below the Landing, awaiting only a ferry, on the evening before the battle. Grant, however, declined to allow it to cross, as he thought that there would be no fighting for some days. At 6:00 A.M. on April 6, 1862, near Shiloh Church, two miles from Pittsburg Landing, the Confederate Army deployed in line of battle, and advanced rapidly on the Landing, surprising and breaking up Prentiss' Union division.

At last Grant formed a connected line (5:30 P.M.) with one of Buell's brigades (Nelson's) with all troops available from his own infantry. The line was six hundred yards from the Landing and strong, and Beauregard called off the attack at sunset.

During the night Grant's detached division (Lew Wallace) and Buell's army, twenty-five thousand total, came up, and Grant took the offensive on the 7th.

---

46. The Buell Papers.

It was a Confederate failure and not a Union victory. At Shiloh Church, Bragg's rear-guard repulsed an attack by Grant and Buell for six hours before withdrawing.[47]

Thus the further stamp of authority is placed upon Grant's and Sherman's incompetence at Shiloh, as evidenced by their complete surprise, offset by Buell's unsolicited prompt arrival, although both Grant and Sherman were successful in later years in withholding deserved credit to him for his part in burying their mistakes. The reason is simple; for any credit to Buell would be an admission of their surprise. This is of all things the smallest matter for concern. What is of concern is that these two failures were able to rebound from the battle, for which they deserve little credit, with a figurative coat of whitewash, to go on to further blunders and the lion's share for the ultimate victory. Sherman did little afterward except to push Generals Johnston and Hood from Chattanooga to Atlanta with double their force; and from there he marched to the sea, with the flower of the Federal army in the West, while his march was guaranteed in Napoleonic style by Thomas. All that Thomas did was to destroy Hood's army with the inferior and insufficient forces Sherman left him for which Sherman forever branded him, the invincible, the incorruptible, the incomparable commander, with the label "slow." Grant, although more successful, did little that other Northern generals superior to himself could not have done; and certainly none can say that his policy of blood-letting before Lee reflected generalship.

The writer had occasion to hear a General Grant of another generation ridicule McClellan, as he seemingly looked down from his position on horseback in the Washington, D. C., business district. In effect, he said this: "McClellan, from this position, with two avenues of advance facing him, would not be able to make up his mind which to take." The failure to state that McClellan would probably select the route least costly in lives was obvious. The further observation could have been made that there was no national clamor for McClellan's removal because of sacrificing the lives of his men, as there was for Grant's; and the esteem of McClellan's men, who idolized him, was in distinct contrast to the feeling of Grant's men for him. Grant fell heir to the magnificent Army of the Potomac, the handiwork of McClellan; and when McClellan opposed Lee with it, he faced the best the South had to offer during the war, and not the remnants that Grant spent many months in starving into submission. Underlying all of this injustice is the element of rotten politics, the

47. *Encyclopaedia Britannica* (Chicago, 1963), Vol. XX, p. 504.

placing of favorites in power to become the judges of life and death. The story is there for all to read, how Grant and Sherman were aided in their careers by Elihu B. Washburne in the House of Representatives and John Sherman in the Senate. Soldiers wrote home of the battle, telling of the useless slaughter, and a feeling of indignation of national proportions developed against Grant after Shiloh. Senator Sherman himself wrote to General Sherman, "There is much feeling against Grant, and I try to defend him but with little success."[48]

For some unaccountable reason Representative Washburne championed Grant's promotions.

He selected Grant, and his choice was as strange as his faithful support was without parallel. Here was a man forced from the old army because of his habits, who had risen only to the rank of captain in the service, and an utter failure in all that he attempted as a means of subsistence in civil life. Through all his early military career, as a small farmer near St. Louis, as a clerk at Galena, he not only gave no evidence of ability of any sort, but no one of his associates or family ever suspected him of aught beyond the dullest common place; and yet, through good and evil report, the Hon. Elihu stood by his protege. It was a powerful support. Not only the President, but the Secretary of War, regarded Washburne as a man of sterling integrity, as well as a politician whose following among the people was so earnest that he was a power at Washington not to be neglected or slighted. Every promotion gained by Grant was really given by Washburne. Once only he faltered, and that was when he learned that, after a frightful assault on Vicksburg, Grant left his dead to rot and his wounded to writhe in agony on the outer slopes of the enemy's works for three days, under the hot summer sun of that horrible climate. Washburne sought Lincoln with the pitiable tale. He would carry the responsibility no longer. "Elihu," said the President, much moved, as he put his hand on the politician's shoulder, "it is a bad business, but we must try the man a little longer. He seems a pushing fellow, with all his faults."[49]

---

48. William T. Sherman, *The Sherman Letters* (New York: Charles Scribner's Sons, 1894), pp. 147-49; James Ford Rhoads, *History of the American Civil War, 1861–1865* (New York: The Macmillan Co., 1923), pp. 107-9.

49. Don Piatt, *General George H. Thomas* (Cincinnati, 1891), pp. 232-37; Rhoads, *loc. cit.*

This was the man who did his part well in lowering the curtain on the great achievements of General Thomas in particular, as he did also with Generals Buell and Meade, and raised the curtain on his protégés of lesser caliber, Schofield and Sheridan, among others.

> The Worldly Hope men set their Hearts upon
> Turns Ashes—or it prospers; and anon,
>   Like snow upon the Desert's Dusty Face,
> Lighting a little hour or two—was gone.
>
> The Moving Finger writes; and having writ,
> Moves on: nor all your Piety nor Wit
>   Shall lure it back to cancel half a Line,
> Nor all your Tears wash out a Word of it.
>
> OMAR KHAYYAM

CHAPTER X

"Pick and Shovel" Campaign
to Corinth, and Bragg's Advance

AFTER THE Battle of Shiloh General Halleck combined and reorganized the three armies, and the scattered forces of his Department, in the area of Pittsburg Landing. This army now consisted
of five components identified as the right wing, the center, the left
wing, the reserve, and the cavalry. General Grant was designated
to "retain the general command of the District of East Tennessee,
and reports will be made to him as heretofore, but in the present
movements he will act as second in command under the major-
general commanding the Department." This treatment of Grant
by Halleck was on a par with his earlier dealings with him. The
action was a definite demotion for Grant. In the same order General
Thomas was named commander of the right wing, or Army of the
Tennessee, consisting of his First Division of the Army of the Ohio
and four divisions from the Army of the Tennessee. In this order were
sown the seeds that would have repercussions and reverberations
throughout the military careers of both Grant and Thomas. The
command of each of these divisions was given to Brigadier
Generals William T. Sherman, Stephen A. Hurlbut, Thomas W. Sherman, Thomas J. McKean, and Thomas A. Davies. In this reorganization General William T. Sherman, destined subsequently to become
commander over General Thomas in the Chattanooga to Atlanta campaign, and in the campaign from Atlanta to the Sea, both in
1864, was subordinate to Thomas. Sherman's commission as brevet
major general was dated May 1, 1862, and that of Thomas a week
earlier, or April 25, 1862.

General Buell was named commander of the center, or Army
of the Ohio, with four divisions from that army; General Pope was
assigned to command the left wing, or Army of the Mississippi;
General John A. McClernand was assigned to command the reserves;

and General Gordon Granger, destined to bring his troops to the relief of Thomas on Snodgrass Hill during the fateful hours of the second day at Chickamauga, was in command of the cavalry.[1]

In the Northern armies during the Civil War major generals often commanded brigades and divisions, but always corps and armies, except in extreme emergencies. Grant was the only officer of higher rank, that of lieutenant general, during the war. The Confederates, on the other hand, had a number of lieutenant generals and several full generals.

The military organization of the Civil War period was substantially similar to the modern American army. A federal company at full strength consisted of 101 officers and men, although averaging from 60 to 70 men. An infantry regiment consisted of ten companies, and averaged about six or seven hundred men, while cavalry and artillery regiments consisted of twelve companies. Confederate companies and regiments were fairly comparable to the federal organization, but it is not so easy to estimate their strength. A federal brigade consisted of about five regiments each, on the average, and about three thousand men, and were numbered, in contrast to the Confederate brigades, which were named after their commander, as, for example, the Stonewall Brigade. A federal division averaged between two and three brigades, and contained from six to seven thousand men. A federal corps averaged between two and three divisions, of from fifteen to twenty thousand men, and an army comprised generally two or more corps. The 23d Corps was also named the Army of the Ohio, under General Schofield, and should not be confused with the Army of the Ohio designation in the history of the Army of the Cumberland. The latter army generally consisted of three corps, and at the period of its greatest success consisted of the 14th, 20th and 21st Corps, commanded respectively by Generals Thomas, McCook, and Crittenden.

The Department of the Cumberland was established on August 15, 1861, and comprised the states of Kentucky and Tennessee, under Brigadier General Robert Anderson of Fort Sumter fame. On October 8, Anderson was forced to retire because of ill health, on which date Brigadier General William T. Sherman succeeded him. Sherman's tenure ended on November 15, after reporting to Washington that he would need 200,000 men to accomplish objec-

---

1. Thomas B. Van Horne, *The Life of Major General George H. Thomas* (Cincinnati: Robert Clarke and Co., 1882), p. 64; George W. Cullum, *Biographical Register of Officers and Cadets of the U.S. Military Academy* (Boston, 1891), Vol. I, *passim; Official Records of the War of the Rebellion* (Washington, D.C., 1880–1901), Vol. X, Part 2, p. 144.

tives in the West, and he was replaced by Brigadier General Don Carlos Buell. The Department of the Cumberland was changed to the Department of the Ohio on November 29, 1861, and comprised the states of Ohio, Michigan, Indiana, Kentucky, and Tennessee. On October 24, 1862, the Department of the Cumberland was reconstituted to comprise Tennessee and parts of northern Alabama and Georgia. The designation was changed from the Army of the Ohio to the Army of the Cumberland, which was known as the 14th Corps, and on October 30, General Rosecrans was assigned to command the Department and Army of the Cumberland.

As commander-in-chief, General Halleck proved his incapacity for field command during the Corinth campaign. He did a creditable job in reorganizing his forces, but he lacked the aggressiveness necessary to deploy them and cope with his greatly outnumbered enemy on the battlefield. He would halt his magnificent army and establish a defensive posture at every place where he believed the hazards of battle might be met. Such extreme caution discouraged any basis for confidence by his subordinates in his ability to accomplish his objectives; it also posed the question for succeeding generations to contemplate: How could a graduate of the United States Military Academy be so lacking in the essentials for command? For that matter, the wonder is that after this most disappointing record Halleck went on to the chief command until succeeded by General Grant in early 1864. This illustration of promotion, after proved unfitness, was not unique, and it explains the early defeats of Union armies against generally outnumbered but skillfully led Confederates. Halleck in this campaign missed a golden opportunity to achieve greatness for himself and victory for his cause—victory that would surely have shortened the war. In view of the results of this campaign alone, General Halleck comes down to us with a cloud over his head that his later activities in the chief command did nothing to remove.

Halleck's extreme caution, as reflected in the slow progress to Corinth, gave subordinate commanders little chance to gain combat experience. Heavy skirmishing was encountered almost daily between formidable reconnoitering parties; but since Halleck chose to avoid full-scale action these exchanges produced but minor results. A line of intrenchments Halleck caused to be constructed made sense, after the costly lesson of Shiloh, where adequate defenses were deplorably lacking; however, this was a typical example of going from one extreme to the other.

The Federals found Corinth deserted by the weakened enemy, who, although unable to give battle or to offer defense, was able to escape with but few losses in men, arms, and supplies. This was possible because Halleck had used up thirty-seven days advancing over territory that the Confederates covered in two days while on the march to attack Grant at Shiloh.[2] One of the principal results of the campaign was the respite given the Confederates to recover from their recent reverses and to assume once more a threatening position. The benefit derived by the Federals, if any, was their occupation of Corinth without a struggle. If it could be termed a benefit, the clear-cut portrayal of Halleck as a commander without imagination, inspiration, and initiative, before an enemy far weaker in men and material, was not exploited to the country's good.[3]

Some disagreement arose between the several commanders over which one had the distinction of first entering Corinth, a point that the record does not make too clear. It is interesting to note General Halleck's communication to General Buell, referring to General Nelson's complaint to a Colonel Kelton that he, Nelson, deserved the honor, but that the newspapers gave some of the credit to both General Pope and General Sherman. Halleck was irritated by this complaint, which he construed as a reflection on his integrity, and commented that since General Sherman was the first to report to him he could only assume it was Sherman who first entered Corinth. In General Buell's report to Halleck on May 28, he stated that General McCook's division was vulnerable to attack in sight of the enemy's breastworks, located about a mile in front of the intrenchments of General Thomas. This suggests that Thomas himself had a fair claim to the honor, since he was already dug in and ready for the enemy if attacked.[4]

While at Corinth, General Thomas asked General Halleck for a transfer from command of the right wing, or Army of the Tennessee, and restoration to his former subordinate role as second in command to General Buell in the Army of the Ohio. Thomas made this request because he knew that General Grant was greatly upset by his demotion, as aforesaid, and he did not intend to perpetuate ill will against anyone, although clearly he was in no way responsible for it.[5] This magnanimity of Thomas, paradoxical as it may seem, apparently strained, rather than helped, the relations between them. The colossal bigness of this action by Thomas could have rendered Grant helpless, however willing he might have been, to offset this splendid

---

2. John G. Nicolay and John Hay, *Abraham Lincoln: A History* (New York: The Century Co., 1909), Vol. V, pp. 340-41; M. F. Force, *From Shiloh to Corinth* (New York: Noble Offset Printers, Inc.. n.d.), pp. 190-91.

3. Van Horne, *op. cit.*, p 64; Nicolay and Hay, *op. cit.*, Vol. V, p. 341.

4. *Official Records, op. cit.*, Vol. X, Part 1, pp. 626, 634.

5. Van Horne, *op. cit.*, pp. 64-65.

gesture by some act of generosity of his own. Grant, in other words, was left at a disadvantage in relation to Thomas, which he could not possibly bridge at that time. Grant's *Memoirs,* discussed on page 193, cited only this: "I was named second in command of the whole [army], and was also supposed to be in command of the right wing and reserve." He did not here mention Thomas, nor did he refer in any way to him on page 204 of the *Memoirs,* where he stated that, in addition to being second in command to Halleck, he became department commander upon Halleck's assumption of command of all the armies. It is difficult to believe that Grant's memory was so lacking in retention that he could not remember it was Thomas who replaced him, and who also removed himself from competition with him during this trying period of Grant's life. In this omission was forged another link in the chain of evidence proving that Thomas was shunted to a minor role by Grant; and that even during Grant's final days, when the *Memoirs* were written, he would not yield to Thomas, long since dead, the very minimum of credit for an unprecedentedly noble act of kindness to him.

Many have believed that Grant was the soul of generosity; but however one may seek to place him in a favorable light, and the thought has a number of possibilities, Grant was not in any sense the equal of Thomas either in character or in the profession of arms. Grant's only claim to superiority, which was often a handicap and not a virtue, was in his forever giving the enemy no rest; this falls short, however, when balanced against the inhuman slaughter of Union soldiers so relentlessly thrust against an enemy of unsurpassed courage and skill. Thomas, on the other hand, would not be coerced into committing his troops to battle before all precautions were taken to insure their safety consistent with returning them the victors. This is the record—the mute, truthful, unassailable record—and no embellishment either by Grant's admirers or his apologists, who have been caught in the web of distortion and misinformation regarding him, can successfully refute it.

Grant's personal habits, concerning which one would not commend him as an example to youth, and opposed to which Thomas shines in the full glory of recorded history as a sterling exemplar of knighthood, probably aggravated their differences. It is not difficult to perceive that Thomas had no admiration for Grant's habits; nor, for that matter, would Grant be oblivious to the lofty character of Thomas, with whom he had little basis for attachment. Thomas undoubtedly recognized Grant as weak, while Grant most likely shrank from knowledge of that recognition, which left him inferior when in the presence of Thomas. It is a matter of record that Thomas, from

West Point cadet days, was often compared with the Father of His Country, both for his nobility of character and for his presumed resemblance to him.

Grant's addiction to alcoholic beverages affected his prewar career, and General John A. Rawlins, Grant's Chief of Staff, has been given great credit for superintending the removal of this temptation from him during the Civil War. By contrast, not the slightest evidence has ever been discovered that might reflect upon the personal life of Thomas. On the other hand, Thomas certainly found nothing in Grant's record at Shiloh to excite his admiration for Grant as a military leader, but much to condemn. Thomas certainly knew that his own military record was superior to Grant's, and that since Grant was caught unawares and almost defeated at Shiloh, he, Grant, "had been weighed in the balance and found wanting." This impression was not improved by Grant's subsequent bloodletting at Cold Harbor, Spotsylvania and The Wilderness, although historians and biographers alike are much too prone to overlook the means by which the ends were derived. The means available to Grant in all of these battles, including patience and maneuver as opposed to attack and attack, would have been more productive of earlier victory and less destructive in Union lives.

On June 5, General Thomas was chosen by General Halleck to command Corinth and the surrounding area. Just five days later, however, on June 10, his request to be relieved was granted, and on June 22 he returned to the Army of the Ohio. It was not long after Corinth was occupied that the three armies, which Halleck combined for the advance thereto, returned to their respective identities, namely, the Army of the Mississippi, the Army of the Ohio, and the Army of the Tennessee.[6] General Buell was ordered by General Halleck to advance from Corinth to Chattanooga, East Tennessee, and North Georgia and, if feasible to occupy the area traversed to the fullest extent possible. This was a different version of the plan proposed by General Thomas the year before for the invasion of East Tennessee; his plan, as stated elsewhere herein, was to enter East Tennessee from Kentucky by way of Cumberland Gap. Thomas's plan would have encountered fewer obstacles to success at that time than the one now under consideration, mainly because a more substantial base would have been available in East Tennessee. The advance from Corinth was fraught with danger to communications and the disadvantage of a greatly strengthened enemy.[7]

In this movement General Buell was ordered, on June 9, 1862, to repair the Memphis and Charleston Railroad from Eastport, Missis-

---

6. *Official Records, op. cit.*, Vol. X, Part 1, p. 672.
7. Van Horne, *op. cit.*, pp. 65-66.

sippi, eastward. General Thomas J. Wood's and General William Nelson's divisions in Mississippi were also ordered eastward early in June to repair the railroad, a task that General Ormsby M. Mitchel had undertaken some months earlier. The idea was soon abandoned, however, for what was deemed the more important task of rebuilding the two railroads that led from Nashville and united at Stevenson, Alabama. This produced a fatal delay during which the advance to Chattanooga was slowed, thereby permitting the Confederate General Bragg to occupy the place unmolested. The job was most time-consuming and, in addition, required an increasing number of troops, which constantly depleted the slowly advancing army. Indeed, General Bragg was desirous of occupying a much greater area, which would mean the retaking of land lost to the Federals in Mississippi, Alabama, Tennessee, and Kentucky. With this ambitious project accomplished, the Confederates would have a line on the Ohio River both for offensive and defensive purposes.[8]

While the Confederates were concentrating at Corinth, toward which the Union forces were advancing, one of the most daring episodes of the war occurred. General Mitchel, who, as aforesaid, was repairing the railroad eastward from Eastport, had long entertained the plan of liberating East Tennessee. Mitchel knew that President Lincoln also approved such a plan; if successful it would not only strike a damaging blow at the South's resources, but control would be gained over a large segment of territory in the heart of the Confederacy, where many of the people were loyal to the Union. On April 8, 1862, the day following the two-day Battle of Shiloh, or Pittsburg Landing, he moved southward from Shelbyville, Tennessee, and occupied Huntsville, Alabama, on April 11. He next sent a detachment of troops by way of the Memphis and Charleston Railroad to establish rail communication with the victorious army at Pittsburg Landing. Still another detachment of two thousand men under General Mitchel himself moved seventy miles by railroad and stopped within thirty miles of Chattanooga.[9] Chattanooga was the key that would unlock the deadlocked stalemate between the Army of the Potomac and the Army of Northern Virginia, although not before the end of 1863, more than a year later, and not without some of the bloodiest fighting of the war.

General Mitchel could have taken Chattanooga with his small force of two thousand; by prearrangement, however, this extremely valuable point to eventual Union success in the West was avoided in deference to a plan for striking a devastating blow at Confederate

8. *Ibid.*
9. *Battles and Leaders of the Civil War* (New York, 1884), Vol. II, p. 706.

communications. On April 7, before leaving Shelbyville, General Mitchel sent a detachment of twenty-four men and their leader into Georgia to sever railroad connections, primarily the burning of bridges and the destruction of telegraph lines, between Chattanooga and points south and west. The failure of this attempt would result in much looking back to the lost opportunity of General Mitchel to occupy Chattanooga with his small force. The fearful price to be paid later placed tremendous emphasis on this decision; success of the daredevil plan would have prevented, however, the reinforcing of Corinth by the Confederates, or else would have compelled them to return to middle Tennessee.[10]

James J. Andrews, a spy in the service of General Buell, attempted to burn the bridges west of Chattanooga in March, 1862. This plan failed due to the lack of cooperation expected, but Andrews, undeterred and profiting from the experience, was anxious to make another attempt. General Mitchel approved Andrews' plan to take the detachment of twenty-four men, enter the enemy's country and capture a train. The bridges to be burned were on the northern part of the Georgia State Railroad, and one on the East Tennessee Railroad where it approached the Georgia state line. If successful, Chattanooga would have been completely isolated. At the first meeting, on April 7, 1862, about a mile east of Shelbyville, Andrews gave his twenty-four men their instructions: they were to divide into groups of three or four men each, go eastward to the mountains, and from thence southward by rail after getting well behind the Confederate lines. On the third day, or April 10, they were to meet about two hundred miles away, in Marietta, Georgia. Their agenda included blowing up of the bridges the day on which Huntsville, Alabama, was occupied; but continuous rains and accompanying muddy roads influenced Andrews to relay word to the several groups that the meeting would be held on the twelfth, this in the mistaken belief that Mitchel's entrance into Huntsville would be delayed by weather.[11]

Only twenty men were able to appear for the final briefing at the Marietta Hotel, after hazardous experiences by most of them *en route*. The next step of their itinerary was to proceed eight miles by train to Big Shanty, at the base of Kenesaw Mountain. The railroad was crowded with trains and the trains were well sprinkled with soldiers of the Confederate Army, and therefore enemies. At Big Shanty they would seize the locomotive amid a group of armed soldiers, and then be on their way. When the train stopped at Big Shanty, the conductor, engineer, and many of the passengers alighted

10. *Ibid.*, pp. 709, 716.
11. *Ibid.*, p. 710.

for breakfast, near by. The engine crew of the Andrews raiders boarded the locomotive, named the "General," uncoupled three box cars from the rest of the train, and started out, after the other raiders had succeeded in entering the box cars. So far so good, but trouble was just ahead. Rainy weather persisting throughout the trip made all trains off-schedule, thereby increasing the danger of collision. Frequent stops were necessary in order to cut telegraph lines, take up track segments, and take on fuel and water. At Etowah Station they had no time to put out of commission the old locomotive "Yonah," a factor that later weighed heavily against them. They covered the thirty miles from Big Shanty to Kingston, where, finding the road blocked, Andrews daringly ordered the track "cleared for Beauregard," a ruse that was obeyed promptly. It was still necessary to await the passing of another train before continuing. In the meantime, unknown to them, conductor William A. Fuller, and Atlanta Railway machine-shop foreman Anthony Murphy, were not far behind them, first by hand car and then on the commandeered and undamaged "Yonah," which had been left so hastily by Andrews and his men. When Fuller found himself blocked at Kingston, although at that time only about four minutes behind, he uncoupled the engine and one car from a train that had just arrived from Rome, Georgia, and with about forty men continued the chase.[12]

About four miles past Kingston the telegraph lines were again cut, and, when ready to take up a track, they heard a rapidly approaching locomotive. It was Fuller. Hastening on to Adairsville, they found a freight train waiting for an express train to pass. Fearing to delay an instant before the oncoming Fuller, they covered the nine miles to Calhoun in better than a mile a minute. At Calhoun the express was just pulling out when it noted their coming, whereupon it backed up just enough to permit entrance of Andrews' train to the sidetrack, but not enough to permit movement through the other end of the switch. After some delay and explanation, Andrews again succeeded in convincing those barring his path that he was "rushing aid to Beauregard," and not too soon to remain ahead of the oncoming Fuller. Again stopping to cut wires and hoping to destroy enough track to thwart Fuller, Andrews did his utmost to clear his path to Chattanooga and possibly beyond to Ormsby Mitchel's lines. He figured that the taking up of one rail before reaching Oostanaula Bridge might insure the success of his venture. Just at this decisive moment Fuller in his locomotive came toward them ever closer and at tremendous speed. A respite of two minutes, even one, would permit the removal of a rail and insure at least partial success of the

12. *Ibid.*, pp. 711-12.

trip. Striving to remove the rail, they succeeded only in bending it, and were compelled to rush on. One of the three cars was now uncoupled, then another, in the hope of delaying Fuller and thus increasing the distance between them. Fuller was relentless. When he encountered the box cars adrift, so to speak, he slowed his progress just enough to complete the coupling and pushed on in wild pursuit to Resaca, giving Andrews just enough time to cross the Oostanaula Bridge.[13]

Unfortunately for Andrews, he was unable to cut wires fast enough to prevent his coming being telegraphed ahead; neither could he stop long enough to damage the tracks sufficiently to stop or at least delay his pursuer. A desperate effort was made to burn the Chickamauga Creek bridge. In this attempt crossties were dropped, which did delay Fuller enough to permit the taking on of wood and water, but not enough to damage the track. How Fuller escaped disaster during his daredevil chase ranks as almost miraculous. He told later of striking a rail that had been placed skillfully on a curved section of track to derail him, but he managed to remain upright and on the rails.[14]

The chase continued past Dalton, at which point Andrews again cut wires and placed obstructions on the track in plain view of a Confederate regiment encamped not more than a hundred yards distant. With fuel running low, Andrews realized that he could not reach Chattanooga. Again the wires were cut, but the primitive tools available at this stage were inadequate to remove another rail from the tracks. One remaining hope—destruction of the tunnel north of Dalton—could not be accomplished due to lack of time. Removing the side and end timbers from their last remaining car, and dropping them on the tracks, availed little in holding off their pursuers. With but a few pieces of lumber left, they made kindling of it, set the car afire, and cut it loose, in the final hope that they might destroy a long covered bridge before Fuller reached it. Tragically for those concerned, Fuller was able to push the car off the bridge before it did too much damage. There was now nothing left but hope of escape and of eventually reaching the Union lines. Confederate pursuers subsequently agreed that their chances for escape would have been better if they had remained in a body, but Andrews thought differently and ordered the men to disperse into the woods and each attempt to save himself. They were hunted down promptly, and all were captured within a week; worse still, the two that failed to join the cause were also captured, identified, and tried as spies. The fact

13. *Ibid.*, pp. 712-14.
14. *Ibid.*, p. 715.

that they wore civilian clothing behind enemy lines was justification to their captors in holding them as spies. A court-martial was conducted, and Andrews and seven of his men were convicted and executed. The remaining fourteen were never brought to trial. Eight of these had made good their escape and returned to the North. The remaining six were held prisoners until exchanged in March, 1863, through the efforts of Secretary of War Stanton.[15]

It is understandable that General Mitchel stopped thirty miles west of Chattanooga instead of continuing on and capturing the town, since communications were destroyed and the citizens were defenseless and in panic. This condition would have been a serious handicap to occupation by any force until normal conditions were restored.

An interesting sidelight, reflecting the means employed in gaining favor, is shown by General William T. Sherman's communication of July 8, 1862, to General Halleck. He said, "I know of no man in the country able to carry it but you," meaning, of course, the burden of responsibility, although Halleck was proving to the North that he was totally unfit for field duty, if, indeed, he ever proved he was suitable for any command. On the face of it the comment was ridiculous; but Sherman's battlefield record needed bolstering, which supporting techniques like the flattery of superior officers obtained for him when his advancement could not be earned on the field of combat. Some of his later writings to Grant, in the same vein, are downright disgusting. Flattery, the device so often employed by the less capable, is perhaps somewhat universal, but no basis for it existed in this instance. In this same letter Sherman compared McClellan's movements on the James River in the Peninsular Campaign with Halleck's ignominious "pick and shovel" campaign to Corinth. This transparent attempt to seek favor with Halleck was apparently too much for Sherman himself to let stand, once he reconsidered it; he then offset his groundless claim of Halleck's ability to bear a burden not within the ability of anyone else by comparing the Corinth campaign with McClellan's, both of which were failures. If not too successful as a general, Halleck was at least a satirist or part humorist, as shown by his communication to Secretary of War Stanton: "We are now at the enemy's throat, and cannot release our grasp to pare his toe-nails."[16] So far as is known this is the only instance in the *Official Records* in which anything is expressed other than statements of fact.

General Bragg succeeded General Beauregard as commander of

15. *Ibid.*, pp. 714-16.

16. *Official Records, op. cit.*, Vol. XVII, Part 2, p. 83; Vol. XI, Part 2, pp. 128-29.

the Confederate forces at Tupelo, Mississippi, on June 20, 1862. He planned to move into East Tennessee by using the railroads, in what would be perhaps the greatest movement of troops by railroad in the history of warfare up to that time. This undertaking began in late July and was completed in early August, 1862. Starting at Tupelo, the troops moved southward to Mobile, from which point they moved northward to Montgomery, Alabama, following a short march to make rail connections, and from there by way of Atlanta, Georgia, to Chattanooga.[17]

Governor Andrew Johnson of Tennessee complained to General Halleck, on June 17, 1862, that General Buell's advance toward Chattanooga during the week or so before had left Nashville in an almost defenseless position. The Governor did not mince words when he stated: "I will say this much: this place has been left to a very great extent in a defenseless condition, thereby keeping alive a rebellious spirit that could otherwise have been put down by this time." Further, the Governor stated: "In claiming to understand the peculiar position of affairs in Tennessee I do not wish to be considered vain or egotistical: I am willing to place my reputation and all that is sacred upon the part I am called upon to act."[18] He ended this appeal for help by requesting that General Thomas and his division be sent to lower East Tennessee, where conditions were such that pro-Unionists had been compelled to conceal their true feelings as a result of secessionist demonstrations. He expressed his faith in General Thomas in the same communication: "General Thomas I believe to be truly brave and patriotic, and his sympathies and feelings are for that people." Governor Johnson, not content with complaining to Halleck, wrote to President Lincoln on July 10, emphasizing still further his conviction that conditions in his state demanded Federal military support. He said in part, "I consider the policy which has been pursued by Buell's adjutant-general here in the absence of Buell as most decidedly detrimental to the public interest. My opinion is that he is at this time in complicity with the traders here, and shall therefore have him arrested and sent beyond the influence of rebels and traders if he is not immediately removed." He told the President further: "As to an expression of public opinion, as soon as the rebel army can be expelled from East Tennessee there can and will be an expression of public opinion that will surprise you; but I am constrained to say one thing, as I said to you repeatedly in the fall, General Buell is not the man to redeem East Tennessee."[19] Thus was laid the

17. *Ibid.*, pp. 614, 660-61.
18. *Ibid.*, Vol. XVI, Part 2, p. 36.
19. *Ibid.*, p. 119.

foundation for the removal of General Buell, soon to be accomplished as the result of incessant clamoring by his political enemies, despite his commendable record as an organizer and campaigner under most difficult circumstances.

The divisions of Generals Alexander McCook and Thomas Critten-den of General Buell's command, which left Corinth and Booneville on June 11, passed the divisions of Generals Thomas Wood and William Nelson while heading toward Chattanooga, and in early July established a position at Battle Creek. The latter two divisions had been sent forward shortly before to repair the Memphis and Charleston Railroad. Once more General Thomas was given the responsibility of safeguarding the rear of Buell's army against the ever-present danger of enemy attack, particularly from the west and southwest. On June 22, General Halleck ordered General Thomas to Iuka, Mississippi, to guard the railroad between Iuka and Decatur, Alabama. Upon arrival, on June 24, he was ordered to establish headquarters at Tuscumbia, Alabama, which he reached on June 29, and to guard all railroad bridges, trestles, and telegraph lines, in addition to repairing the sixty-odd miles of the Memphis and Charleston Railroad to Decatur. This was a debatable judgment on Buell's part, since it bogged down his advance during a six-week period in a comparatively useless effort. What a pity for the Union cause that Buell was not permitted to devote his maximum energies to more strictly military objectives! Tragically for all concerned, a distressing rumor that General Bragg and thirty thousand Confederates had already occupied Chattanooga, was relayed by General Thomas to General Halleck on July 13. The reported condition of the enemy was that many were sick, more were without shoes, supplies and equipment were greatly inadequate, food and forage were at a low ebb; and the lowered morale had contributed greatly to numerous desertions in the Alabama, Mississippi, and Tennessee regiments.[20]

An error often made by historians and students of history is in assuming that the aggregate of soldiers and civilians on each side of a struggle, particularly those having the intensity of feeling of the participants in the American Civil War, are supremely devoted to their cause, come what may. Such was certainly not the case in the Civil War, nor, for that matter, has it been so in most wars. When it is remembered that many Southern people were opposed to secession but were compelled by weight of numbers to go along with the Confederacy; also when it is recalled that several Southern states left the Union by a fairly narrow vote of their legislative bodies; and that in the legislative process the individual voter had no opportunity

20. *Ibid.,* pp. 48, 49, 58, 61, 74, 84, 141; Van Horne, *op. cit.,* p. 67.

to express his personal feelings; then it is understandable that when reverses came, as they did, the individual's true feelings found expression in disgust and ultimately desertion. In his book *Fighting by Southern Federals*, Charles C. Anderson reported that 296,579 white soldiers living in the South, 137,676 colored soldiers, and approximately 200,000 Southerners living in the North, an aggregate of 634,255 Southern soldiers, fought for the North.[21] Alabama left the Union by an extremely small majority vote of its legislature. When some of these men were called upon to bear arms, it was but natural that all of them did not do so with a feeling of enthusiasm. On the long march, in the less glamorous setting of hunger, fatigue, shoddy clothing and equipment, and other disagreeable aspects of army life not seen on the parade ground, it is amazing that such a relatively small population succeeded in holding at bay an adversary several times larger and far better endowed with war-making equipment and supplies. When Napoleon declared that "An Army moves on its stomach," he meant that an army well fed and well supplied was essential to victory.

On July 15, General Buell ordered General Thomas to prepare to move promptly to Decatur, Alabama, by way of Florence and Athens, Alabama, but to await definite orders. Two days later, Buell ordered him to cross the Tennessee River at Decatur at the earliest possible moment upon his arrival there. On July 29, Buell ordered him to proceed to Decherd, Tennessee, which he reached on August 5; but on August 12 he was again ordered to McMinnville, Tennessee, where it was believed the Confederates were concentrating after their rumored withdrawal from Chattanooga. On August 16, Buell ordered him to "proceed with all possible dispatch to McMinnville and take command of the troops there and that may arrive." On the same day Buell clarified his order by stating, "I don't want your division or your train to move yet. Go only with an escort. The trains already there will suffice for the present." This later instruction was in reply to Thomas's request for permission to use a supply train operating between Murfreesboro and McMinnville, and meant that Buell wanted Thomas to take personal command at McMinnville. On August 19, the day of his arrival there, Buell ordered Thomas to prepare to march promptly, with full supplies, if necessary to counteract an enemy concentration in the Sequatchie Valley. Buell was inspired to issue this instruction upon learning that three hundred cavalry and three thousand infantry had left Chattanooga on August 18. Buell reported to him that he was concentrating both his

21. Charles C. Anderson, *Fighting by Southern Federals* (New York: Neale Publishing Co., 1912), pp. 10-11.

(Thomas's) and McCook's divisions at or near Tracy City, and sending Crittenden's division up the Anderson Road, prepared either to fight in detachments or to unite rapidly as circumstances dictated. Interestingly, Buell mentioned that he had prepared a code of rocket signals for use in his movements and for communicating information.[22]

Buell was in somewhat of a dilemma, due to the numerous rumors and facts flowing in his direction, but he was correct in deducing that General Bragg would enter the Sequatchie Valley, from which point he would be able to advance toward Pikeville in an attempt to turn the Federal left, or toward Battle Creek to attack their right. Thomas was insistent that Buell should exert every energy to meet these alternatives of Bragg's, but burdened with the cares of command he was reluctant to make a complete commitment until he was certain of Bragg's positive moves.

Although little evidence of Bragg's intentions had been revealed, it appeared that he was advancing from Chattanooga either to Nashville or Kentucky. If to Nashville, he could either move through Battle Creek, Tennessee, or Stevenson, Alabama, or through the mountains to McMinnville or Sparta, Tennessee. If his intention was to enter Kentucky, and it now appeared certain he would, he would enter through the Sequatchie Valley, as indicated, where his presence would give him the choice of moving into Kentucky or advancing to Nashville by the Northern route. Since General Buell could not yet be certain, he was under compulsion to prepare counterplans. In the meantime, events were taking form; reports began coming in from scouts and civilians that proved a movement toward Kentucky. On August 22, General Thomas at McMinnville reported to General Buell, "I have believed for the past day or two that the demonstration in this direction is intended to cover the advance of the enemy toward Kentucky." He urged Buell that day in another dispatch: "By all means concentrate here. The enemy cannot reach Nashville by any other roads across the mountain unless by Sparta. At Altamont I am positively informed that the enemy would have an equal advantage with ourselves. Here we will have a most decided advantage, and by being here, should he march to Sparta, we can meet him either there or at Allen's Ford, across Caney Creek. He is obliged to pass this place or Sparta to reach Nashville. . . . I cannot think that Bragg is coming here either by the Hill or Therman Road." Again on August 22, Thomas, in separate dispatches, informed Buell that scouts in the Sequatchie Valley reported "no enemy there"; also that since there was "neither forage nor water at Altamont, it will be as diffi-

---

22. *Official Records, op. cit.*, Vol. XVI, Part 2, pp. 156, 157, 175, 227, 264, 306, 319, 350, 371, 372.

cult for us to march across the mountains to Sequatchie Valley as for
the enemy to come either to Altamont or this place. . . . I have also
learned that Tupelo has been abandoned and most of the enemy at
that place have been sent to Chattanooga. I therefore do not apprehend any attempt to seize North Alabama."[23]

On August 23, General Buell reported to General Thomas: "There
is no possibility of our concentrating at McMinnville. We must concentrate in advance and assume the offensive or fall back at least to
Murfreesboro. I deem the former the surest, and we will act accordingly. I wish you therefore to move by a forced march to Altamont,
there to form a junction with McCook, Crittenden and Schoepf . . .
tomorrow, and any division meeting the head of the enemy's column
first must at least hold it in check until a larger force arrives. . . . I shall
probably leave here with Sill's brigade tomorrow for Tracy City to
join you." On the next day he telegraphed again to Thomas: "In
advancing to Altamont take the Hickory Creek road instead of the
Therman; that will put you on a shorter line of retreat on Murfreesboro by the way of Manchester and bring us nearer together. . . . In
the event of any reverse which makes it necessary for the whole force
to fall back do so by Manchester and Beech Grove, making a stand
to check the enemy whenever it can be done with advantage."[24]

As if Bragg could indefinitely screen his movements, Thomas
reported to Buell, on August 24, that a reconnoitering party of First
Ohio Cavalry obtained information from one or two citizens that
some two to three thousand enemy infantry were at Pikeville the day
before, and that they intended marching to McMinnville by two or
three routes. Information also furnished was that enemy pickets were
at Beersheba and in Sequatchie Valley. Thomas promised to move
by the Hickory road as directed, but his explanation, that he was
delayed until the return of his scouting parties, evidenced some
reluctance or lack of confidence in the move to Altamont. This reluctance had considerable basis, as indicated by the following dispatch
from Thomas at Altamont on August 25, at 5 P.M.: "The enemy no
nearer than Dunlap. It is reported there is one brigade there and one
at Pikesville. This . . . confirms the report of Major Laughlin, First
Ohio Cavalry, who made a reconnaissance near Spencer . . . and both
reports are confirmed by Captain Wickliffe, Third Kentucky Cavalry.
. . . Water is very scarce here, only one spring; not forage enough in
the neighborhood to last for one day. The road up the mountains is
almost impassable. General Wood has been [here] from 6 o'clock

23. Van Horne, op. cit., p. 67; Official Records, op. cit., Vol. XVI, Part 2,
pp. 391-92.

24. Official Records, ibid., pp. 399, 400, 410.

till now and he has not succeeded in getting his artillery up the road. I deem it next to impossible to march a large army across the mountains by Altamont on account of scarcity of water and forage and the extreme difficulty of passing over the road. I will therefore return to McMinnville and await further orders. As I mentioned in one of my dispatches, I regard McMinnville as the most important point for occupation of any. The occupation of McMinnville, Sparta and Murfreesboro will, in my opinion, secure the Nashville and Chattanooga Railroad."[25]

This difference of opinion between Buell and Thomas, although not in any sense a basis for ill feeling at the time or later, became a subject of discussion and controversy among historians and partisans alike. Particularly discussed has been the abandonment by Thomas of Altamont, without orders from Buell; in fact, it has been well said, he returned to McMinnville contrary to orders from Buell. None can deny that his judgment in thus returning was fully vindicated by subsequent events, since it was clear to him in advance that Altamont could not be a concentration point.

As if in confirmation of Thomas's return to McMinnville, Buell telegraphed him on August 26:

> Keep your position at McMinnville, but make nothing like a permanent establishment. Be always ready to move at a moment's notice. That Bragg is this side of the river is beyond all question; it is hardly probable that it is merely for the purpose of demonstration, and we must be prepared to concentrate promptly. Of course the passage of so large a force across the mountains is difficult, but not so much as you would suppose from the road you took. The Therman road is very good and the mountain quite easy of ascent. The descent on this side is easy enough by four roads, all diverging from Altamont, the first going by Beersheba to McMinnville, the second by Hickory Creek to McMinnville or toward Manchester, the third also to Manchester and to Decherd by Pelham, and the fourth to Cowan. The Beersheba road is excellent for a mountain road. The question is how to meet an advance which may take either of these routes through Altamont. The best positions we could take would be McMinnville, Altamont, and on the Therman road just this side of the Sequatchie Valley. We should not only be able to concentrate against an advance on that road or the Sparta road, but also threaten his flank if he should attempt to go into North Alabama by Battle Creek; a not improbable thing on many accounts. The

---

25. *Ibid.*, pp. 420-21.

difficulty of supplying ourselves on the mountain is I think the only objection to the disposition I mention.

(*Note.* The above dispatch is dated August 26, but the publisher states it should be August 27, since it was the answer to Thomas's dispatch of that date.)[26]

If the foregoing dispatch does nothing else, it shows that Buell was receptive to actions of subordinates when clearly justified by events, as was true in this instance. Thomas was not a "yes" man, and his and Buell's long friendship and harmonious relations were undoubtedly based upon mutual honesty. If to do what he knew to be wrong had led to defeat, even though subject to his command, Buell would have paid the consequences, as he eventually did, it is true; but this independent action by Thomas contributed its share in lessening his failure in the campaign.

Perhaps a contributing factor in Buell's eventual removal from command was the report from McCook on August 19 stating that the Confederates were crossing the Tennessee River in force, estimated at eighty-thousand, rations short, arms mostly poor, but crossing nevertheless. Buell advised him at once that, if satisfied that intelligence regarding Bragg's movements was correct, he, McCook, should move promptly to the Sequatchie Valley. This he did, as shown by his testimony before the Buell Court of Inquiry in December, 1862, where he volunteered information proving that he did not comply with Buell's instructions to advance into the Sequatchie Valley by the Anderson road. As it turned out, McCook's intelligence was bad, the truth or falsity of which he did not seriously attempt to verify; inasmuch as he acted upon it, its falsity was brought home to him too late to reverse his error in acting upon it. He returned to Battle Creek, his starting place, after advancing to within ten miles of his objective point, at which Anderson and Therman roads intersect.[27] No better example than this is afforded to demonstrate that the factors upon which military success depend go hand in hand with obedience to command by those charged with performance.

On August 19, General Horatio G. Wright was appointed by the War Department to command the Department of the Ohio, consisting of the states of Ohio, Michigan, Indiana, Illinois, Wisconsin, and Kentucky east of the Tennessee River. He was responsible for all of Buell's supplies, most of his rail transportation into Nashville, and his reserve troops, together with Cumberland Gap and the troops op-

26. *Ibid.*, pp. 425-26.

27. *Ibid.*, pp. 367-68; *Official Records, op. cit.*, Vol. XVI, Part 1, p. 87; *Battles and Leaders, op. cit.*, Vol. III, p. 40.

erating in its vicinity. General Kirby Smith had left Knoxville, Tennessee, on August 14, by arrangement with General Bragg, to jointly invade Kentucky. The first accomplishment of consequence by Smith was to drive the Federals under General George W. Morgan from Cumberland Gap. His next and larger accomplishment was to soundly thrash a force of six thousand five hundred men at Richmond, Kentucky, on August 30, under the command of General William Nelson. Although Smith's veteran force was larger only by several hundred, it was far superior in training and experience. On August 27, Nelson had reported to General Wright, under whose command he was then operating, that the forces in his command were undisciplined, with whom "straggling, marauding, plundering is the rule; good conduct is the exception. . . . I have ordered everybody to their camps, and shall enforce the strictest discipline." In view of these conditions it is not at all surprising that they were badly defeated, and that such setbacks did General Buell no good with the military authorities, including the ever-reliable-for-the-comment commander in chief, General Halleck. Halleck reported to General Wright on August 25, five days before Nelson's defeat at Richmond: "The Government, or rather I should say the President and the Secretary of War, is greatly displeased with the slow movements of General Buell. Unless he does something very soon I fear he will be removed. Indeed it would have been done before now if I had not begged to give him a little more time. . . . I can hardly describe to you the feeling of disappointment here in the want of activity in General Buell's large army. The Government seems determined to apply the guillotine to all unsuccessful generals."[28]

Halleck's comments were of a pattern to which the eminently successful General Thomas was not immune. Coming from Halleck, whose record in the Civil War contains not one incident to recommend him as a successful commander, and much to label him the failure he was, this was irony indeed. Halleck was noted for his constant badgering of generals who did no worse than he when entrusted with field command; most did better, if not considered successful, and by comparison Thomas and Buell were infinitely superior. It is noteworthy that Halleck needled his generals, but usually, as in this instance, he attempted to assign responsibility for it to someone else. Much as we admire President Lincoln for his performance throughout in a destined role, his elevation of Halleck to the chief command and retention in it was of all his appointments one of the least justifiable. It may be correct to state that General Buell was not above criticism; he was confused by the divided command of which he was a part,

28. *Official Records, op. cit.*, Vol. XVI, Part 2, pp. 404, 421, 435.

which was not his fault, and by often ambiguous and conflicting reports from sources that tried to mislead him, namely, General Bragg and his Southern supporters. On the other hand, Thomas's intelligence service was far more reliable than Buell's. It should be noted that General Bragg in this campaign conducted one of the most magnificent advances of the entire war, despite the oft-repeated comment that he was an incapable commander. Let it be noted also that, given a little more luck, which so-called successful commanders often need to win battles, Bragg might today deserve mention in the same breath as Lee and Jackson. To further handicap Buell, he lacked the cavalry necessary to observe the movements of his enemy, which, with his propensity to be humane to the inhabitants of enemy territory, contributed much to his failure.

On August 28, General Thomas reported to General Buell from McMinnville: "Saturday three regiments of cavalry were at Pikeville, but fell back to Robinson's Cross Roads, hearing that I was advancing on that road. . . . It was reported. . . . that Bragg was at the foot of Walden's Ridge, in the Valley of the Tennessee, with 40,000 men, awaiting train to cross the mountain. Smith will bring or send me information by tomorrow of the truth of Bragg's position. He then purposes to go toward Pikeville and endeavor to establish an express line to convey information. . . . Troops at this place can watch the direct Chattanooga road, the Dunlap and the Harrison and Pikeville roads, and by the system of expresses to be established by Smith I think I can give you intelligence of the enemy before he can cross Sequatchie Valley."[29]

It is correct to state that Generals Buell and Thomas held divergent viewpoints as to the objectives of General Bragg. Whereas Buell expected an attack on Nashville, Thomas considered such an attack extremely unlikely, either by way of the mountains, Battle Creek and Stevenson, or North Alabama. Furthermore, Thomas was unequivocal in stating his belief that Bragg's purpose was the invasion of Kentucky, which he considered should be opposed at the Sequatchie Valley route. Additionally, his proposal to concentrate troops at McMinnville would have met the danger of an advance to Nashville. Matters of this nature are always subject to the conclusion that it is individual judgment with which we are contending, and therefore that one can never be certain that an opposite or alternative judgment might have been exercised with success. What is important in this campaign, and for the record, is that the career of General Thomas is studded with consistency in doing the right thing at the right time or in having the generally superior judgment that would have brought

---

29. *Ibid.*, p. 438

earlier and more complete success. In this instance Thomas was right and Buell was wrong, as proved by events.

Bragg could not forever conceal his intentions and continue moving. On August 28, General Buell telegraphed to General Thomas that Bragg was reported already in Sequatchie Valley with the bulk of his army, and, in addition to soliciting Thomas's views on how best to cope with him, expressed the need for concentrating at Murfreesboro rather than at McMinnville. The next day Buell reported to General Halleck that two divisions in reinforcement from Grant's army in North Mississippi had not yet arrived, but that he was compelled to concentrate at Murfreesboro with an anticipated force of some thirty thousand men. Meanwhile, Bragg was seeking desperately to worm his way through the mountains without coming to blows with his opponent, while simultaneously maneuvering as though to advance on McMinnville with Nashville the ultimate objective. In this Bragg was given considerable help by Buell, although it was certainly unintentional.

On August 30, General Buell issued from Decherd a comprehensive order describing his objectives in attaining a concentration at Murfreesboro, and instructing the several units in his command concerning their specific responsibilities. This over-all plan had the underlying advantage of not only concentrating his forces in the face of threatened attack; it also gave better protection to Nashville, should that be Bragg's objective after all, and served to ease his lines of supplies and communications. The concentration was to be completed on September 5, and the several converging columns were ordered to maintain daily, and oftener if advisable, liaison for mutual purposes of attack and defense. General Thomas had trouble deciphering his copy of the order, as indicated by his dispatch of August 31 to General Buell: "Succeeded in deciphering the order for concentrating. It was a hard problem. Whoever put it up must have been asleep, as no particular route was followed and a great many words omitted." In addition to the general order, General Buell instructed General Thomas to "keep a day's march between you and the enemy," at the same time emphasizing that "it is of course highly important that you should conform to the movements of the other columns, but it is also important that you should not risk a battle."[30]

It is apparent that General Buell was not being accurately advised concerning Bragg's movements. In his dispatch of August 28 to Thomas, he stated his understanding that Bragg was already in the Sequatchie Valley with most of his force, and that because of (Buell's) inability to concentrate more than thirty thousand men in advance of

---

30. *Ibid.*, pp. 455, 463-64; *Battles and Leaders, op. cit.*, Vol. III, p. 41.

Murfreesboro, it might be necessary to fall back. Bragg actually crossed the Tennessee River at Chattanooga on August 28,[31] and it is extremely unlikely that he was able to reach the valley that day with most of his force. Be that as it may, the most significant factor in Buell's dispatch was its expression of defeatism, or the tendency to move rearward instead of forward. Buell could not have been so well advised as was Thomas, whose attitude throughout the campaign bespoke better knowledge and a much sterner fiber. Not only that; it was proved by events that Thomas's plan to concentrate at McMinnville, Sparta, and Murfreesboro would have stopped General Bragg's invasion before he advanced little more than halfway to the Kentucky line. It is reasonable to deduce from the insistence of Thomas to so assemble the Union forces that Bragg should have been stopped somewhere in the vicinity of Murfreesboro; this is a logical conclusion, since all of the advantages except the exact knowledge of Bragg's movements were with the Federals. There is some basis for believing that Thomas's insistence on this concentration area was due, as reported by historian Henry M. Cist, to his interception, on August 30, of General Bragg's dispatch of August 27 to General Sterling Price. This dispatch contained full particulars regarding his contemplated march into Kentucky, in addition to the information that General Kirby Smith had turned Cumberland Gap, after having been reinforced by two of Bragg's brigades, and was marching on Lexington, Kentucky.[32] Irrespective of the possible value Thomas may have attached to the intercepted dispatch, it at least confirmed his view of some time past that Bragg would invade Kentucky.

---

31. *Official Records, ibid.*, p. 439; *Battles and Leaders, ibid*

32. Henry M. Cist, *The Army of the Cumberland* (New York, 1882), p. 50; *Official Records, op. cit.*, Vol. XVI, Part 2, pp. 782-83.

CHAPTER XI

The Race for Louisville and
the Battle of Perryville

AFTER the several columns of General Buell's army began the march to Murfreesboro, news of General Nelson's defeat at Richmond began trickling through both to General Bragg and General Buell. General Bragg veered northwestward after crossing the Tennessee River at Chattanooga and entered Sparta on September 3, from which point he continued at a rapid rate toward Kentucky. He split his forces at Milledgeville, Tennessee, and crossed the Cumberland River at Carthage and Goldsboro, Tennessee. Uniting his forces once more at Tompkinsville, Kentucky, he proceeded to Glasgow on September 14. Thus was confirmed both the judgment of Thomas and the documentary evidence supported by the dispatch containing the enemy's invasion plans; in particular, Thomas's conclusion, that Bragg would advance by way of Sparta, was not part of Buell's thinking until September 6, when he was compelled by events to realize the truth of it. He was now aware that Bowling Green, Kentucky, which contained a small garrison and some stores, was subject to attack. He then dispatched a division to Bowling Green and another to Gallatin, Tennessee, both on September 7, for observation and report of enemy movements in the valley. General Buell himself, with six of his divisions, started with all haste to Nashville, foreseeing for the first time that he was in a race with General Bragg for Louisville, Kentucky. He well knew that Bragg, with but sixty-eight miles to cover, had a distinct advantage against one hundred and five miles he himself had to travel, particularly if Bragg could avoid losing time in battle. It was Buell's task to win this unequal race, and, if possible, compel Bragg to fight. Bragg's choice of an advance route made his progress slower than Buell's; therefore he realized that if Buell reached Louisville first he would be forced to withdraw and leave Kentucky under Federal control.[1]

---

1. *Battles and Leaders of the Civil War* (New York, 1884), Vol. III, p. 41; Henry M. Cist, *The Army of the Cumberland* (New York, 1882), pp. 56-57.

General Thomas was ordered to Nashville by rail as soon as Buell realized that Bragg seemed headed toward Kentucky. Upon his arrival, he was given command of two and one-half divisions, one of which had not yet arrived from General Grant's army, and a large number of convalescent soldiers. This was undoubtedly an expression of Buell's concern for Nashville and his confidence in Thomas. The arrangement provided for the possibility of General Bragg's retreat from Kentucky and a full-scale battle at or near Nashville. If Buell had been defeated in Kentucky, then the experienced Thomas at Nashville would have saved the troops left there by advancing to combine with Buell's main army. It was clear that Buell regarded Nashville as second in importance to insuring the safety of Kentucky, which responsibility he delegated to himself. The remainder of his command was set in motion on September 10, following receipt of information that Bragg had crossed the Cumberland River, and five days later his army was assembled at Bowling Green, Kentucky. It was here that Buell learned that the garrison at Munfordville, Kentucky, was attacked, although little was known to him beyond the bare knowledge that the enemy was repulsed at the opening of the siege on September 14. This was a delaying action in which the inexperienced but dauntless Colonel John T. Wilder of the Seventeenth Indiana Infantry defended for four days the railroad bridge at Green River. This little known but highly important achievement of Colonel Wilder and his command was instrumental in holding General Bragg's entire army at bay, thereby enabling General Buell to partially liquidate the advantage gained by Bragg at the beginning of the campaign. Colonel Wilder showed his mettle during the first day's fighting, when General Charles R. Caldwell, who eulogized him for his gallant defense, requested him to surrender. Wilder replied, "Thank you for your compliments. If you wish to avoid further bloodshed keep out of the range of my guns. As to reinforcements, they are now entering my works. I think I can defend my position against your entire force; at least I shall try to do so."[2]

Despite his firm intention to hold his position at any cost, Colonel Wilder was compelled to surrender several days later, September 17, 1862, to overwhelming numbers, estimated at about twenty-five thousand, compared with his own slightly more than four thousand men. His sacrifice was not in vain, since General Buell was given additional time in which to bring up his forces in preparation for battle. On the fourth day of the siege, General Bragg himself demanded the

---

2. *Battles and Leaders, op. cit.,* pp. 41-42; *Official Records of the Civil War* (Washington, D.C., 1880-1901), Vol. XVI, Part 1, pp. 959-62; Thomas B. Van Horne, *The Life of Major General George H. Thomas* (New York, 1882), p. 73; Cist, *op. cit.,* pp. 56-57.

surrender of the garrison, alleging that the defenders were surrounded by his entire army, and that continuance of the struggle would only result in useless loss of life. The demand was refused, with the request that Bragg afford time for consultation to consider the matter. In the council it was agreed to surrender only if Bragg would permit a personal inspection by the commanding officer of the garrison to confirm the fact that Bragg was indeed in overwhelming strength. One of the remarkable incidents of the war, and perhaps of any other war, occurred when Bragg consented to the inspection by Colonel Wilder, under escort, which proved beyond doubt that he was surrounded by the numbers claimed.[3]

Before Wilder's surrender of the garrison at Munfordville, General Buell had ordered General Thomas to move his command with all haste in the direction of Bowling Green, Kentucky, and to take with him only ambulances, ammunition, and ration wagons, the better to move more expeditiously. Thomas, pursuant to instructions, began his march on the fifteenth and reached Prewitt's Knob, more than a hundred miles distant, by the twentieth. Buell reported that after some skirmishing that evening the Confederates withdrew. Thus, from a posture of being outnumbered, Buell once more assumed the initiative, thanks to the magnificent march by Thomas. Aside from the retreat of General Bragg, which the march accomplished, the advance itself was one of the most rapid and longest of the entire war. This was Thomas at his best, the maligned and falsely labeled "slow" commander in action, proving, as did all of his actions, that in terms of the ultimate result he was never slow. It was Lincoln who said, "Hasn't he always got there on time?" in reply to Grant's charge of slowness. It is a truism that the perpetuation of this monstrous charge by writers whose responsibility it should be to present the facts, especially when such facts would refute the charge, gives them a large and discreditable share in its perpetuation. Nothing has been more revealing, in disclosing the compounding of errors relating to the Civil War, than the copying of errors by many writers from their predecessors. Neither group has performed adequate research. Small wonder it is, then, that when the average knowledgeable person is asked to name the two greatest Union generals of the Civil War, the answer is almost invariably Grant and Sherman. To the further question, "What great battles did Sherman win?", there is no answer, naturally, because he won none. Why this is so is attributable to but one fact alone, namely, that his reputation was built largely upon, and defended by, controlled sources of information.[4]

3. Cist, *ibid.*, pp. 58-59.
4. Edwin W. High, *History of the Sixty-eighth Indiana Infantry, 1862–1865*

If Buell had known that his opponent had no more than twenty-five thousand men, compared with his own force of somewhat double that number; also if he had realized that Bragg was moving ever more distant from his base of supplies into a barren country, he might have attempted to stop him when the invasion began. Thomas, it should be stressed, was well aware of Bragg's problems, and he knew that the invasion called for stopping the enemy in the vicinity of Murfreesboro. Nevertheless, this fairly bloodless race would become known as the most spectacular and, in some respects, the most magnificent campaign of the war.

Bragg and Buell conducted a foot race toward the Ohio River along somewhat parallel lines. Buell thought that he was still outnumbered, which he certainly was not, while Bragg was fairly positive that Buell outnumbered him, which he did in the ratio of something like two to one. Bragg's desire for a junction with General Kirby Smith throughout much of his advance, in order to equalize in some measure Buell's numerical advantage, can be easily grasped. For reasons each deemed justifiable, a pitched battle at full strength was avoided, although the armies were sometimes almost within range of each other's guns. This chase at a respectful distance continued apace until Buell learned of his enemy's concentration at Glasgow, Kentucky. He was on his way to do battle with Bragg on September 16, when he learned of the action at Munfordville, whereupon he directed his columns to that objective. While at Prewitt's Knob, some thirteen miles from Munfordville, Buell learned that Colonel Wilder had surrendered the garrison to General Bragg, and that all were now prisoners of war. At this time General Buell was again the victim of faulty information, apparently, since he reported his belief that the enemy numbered as many as forty thousand men, whereas available records disclose that General Bragg had no more than twenty-five thousand.

It is true that General Buell did not know for certain whether General Kirby Smith's force had combined with Bragg's, thus to present a formidable and perhaps irresistible force in his pathway. In this situation he ordered General Thomas on September 13 to exert all possible effort to advance to Bowling Green, commencing at 3 A.M. on September 15, as aforesaid. While *en route*, General Buell sent him an urgent appeal to move as rapidly as possible and unite with him in attacking General Bragg. When Thomas joined Buell on September 20 at Prewitt's Knob, he was directed to align the foremost divisions in preparation for battle. Bragg and Buell had faced each other from

September 18 to 21 in full battle array, but upon the arrival of General Thomas, and his alignment of troops in position, Bragg withdrew during the night, apparently with the realization that he was at a disadvantage, and headed in the direction of Louisville. When still some distance from Louisville, his rear guard having been forced out of Munfordville on September 21, he turned right from the main road and headed toward Bardstown, Kentucky, hoping to join the forces of General Kirby Smith in an assault on Louisville. In Bragg's report he stated that he tried for three days to draw Buell into action, but without success; accordingly, with but three days' rations remaining, he was compelled to withdraw from Kentucky.[5]

General Buell's army moved toward Louisville on what is now known as the river road. General Bragg learned upon arrival at Bardstown that Kirby Smith's forces were in pursuit of General Morgan's command at Cumberland Gap, as Morgan attempted to withdraw to eastern Kentucky. This delay to Bragg's contemplated move on Louisville was of incalculable benefit to General Buell, since he was enabled to reach that city before Bragg. It is no exaggeration to state that the general plan of the Confederates was to capture Louisville and Cincinnati and, in addition to drawing Kentucky into the Confederacy, carry the war into the North. Hindsight is always better than foresight, so, looking back, if General Bragg had passed up attacking Munfordville, he would have been able to reach Louisville some days ahead of Buell. There he would have found some twenty thousand raw Federal troops an easy prey to his army, and, with the supplies obtainable there, he would have been strengthened to the point of virtually successful resistance to General Buell. Even so, he made another equally serious mistake in turning off toward Bardstown and permitting Buell to enter Louisville. Why he gave up so much of his clear advantage is a mystery, as in an instant it changed his position from a clearly offensive posture to an undoubted defensive one, and resulted in his early withdrawal from Kentucky.[6] It is not surprising that no complaints have been found anywhere expressing the dissatisfaction of Federal authorities at the clear advantage thus given them by General Bragg.

A member of the One Hundred and First Ohio Infantry describes the entry of Buell's forces into Louisville:

> The boys were a sorry looking set—brown, dirty, ragged, long-haired, disgusted—well they surprised us. We assured them that

---

5. High, *ibid.*; *Battles and Letters, ibid.*; *Official Records, ibid.*, p. 511; Van Horne, *op. cit.*, p. 75.

6. *Battles and Leaders, ibid.*, pp. 42-43; L. W. Day, *The Story of a Regiment: The One Hundred and First Ohio* (Cleveland: W. M. Bayne Printing Co., 1894), p. 36.

while we had not lost all confidence in them, yet we could not excuse them for letting themselves run down so. They smiled a very bitter smile, hovering between pity and contempt when we informed them that each mess with *us* carried a dust brush, and that *we* should use it. They seemed to take delight in rubbing against us, and especially in turning up their blouse collars and showing what there could be seen. We were disgusted that the boys who were fighting for the old Flag, for Home and Country, and all that, should allow themselves to be in that plight. But it was not long until we "knew how it was ourselves."[7]

Anticipation in both Tennessee and Kentucky was naturally great in the wake of the advance of these two powerful opposing armies and in the possibility of a major battle. It was not known for certain, when Bragg began his advance, whether he was headed for Louisville or Nashville, and the anxiety in Tennessee was hardly diminished by information that he was headed for Kentucky. Tennessee Governor Andrew Johnson requested General Buell on September 10 to retain General Thomas at Nashville, and stated his belief that Federal forces already in Kentucky numbered not less than seventy-five thousand men. Johnson also expressed the opinion that Thomas possessed the bravery and the capacity to defend Nashville against any odds. Thomas likewise showed some concern for Nashville by informing Buell that he was leaving General Paine's division, before his own advance to the aid of Buell, to oppose any aggression in that area. President Lincoln also showed considerable concern during Bragg's advance. On September 3, he asked General Wright: "Do you know to any certainty where General Bragg is? May he not be in Virginia?" On September 8, he asked General Buell: "What degree of certainty have you that Bragg with his command is not now in the Valley of the Shenandoah, Virginia?" General Buell, while seeking to reassure the President, reported on September 10 that Bragg was "certainly this side of the Cumberland Mountains with his whole force, except what is in Kentucky under Smith." This reply did not ring with too much conviction that he could successfully cope with the fast-moving Bragg, although Buell outnumbered him in men and was far better supplied. Kentucky, perhaps more concerned than Tennessee, moved its government to Frankfort. Cincinnati and other towns along the Ohio River were placed in a state of mutual defense against a possible invasion into Ohio. Governor Oliver Morton of Indiana was desirous, meanwhile, of replacing General Buell, as indicated in his correspondence with President Lincoln. It was inevitable that these so-called western states would fear the possible con-

7. *Day, ibid.,* pp. 36-37.

sequences to themselves of an invading enemy, and Indiana certainly had ample justification in feeling a sense of fear of Bragg's army.[8]

General Buell was not in abysmal ignorance of the implications in the complaints from Governor Morton in particular, as well as from others. He reported that from the beginning Governor Morton had attempted to exercise a quasi-authority over Indiana troops after their entry into Federal service. This interference was naturally detrimental to good order and discipline. Buell stated: "The seeds of mischief, always present in his extra-official conduct toward the Indiana troops, were now being sown with a vigorous but crafty hand, in the counsels at Washington and among the executives of other States, to impair and effect my removal from command."[9] One cannot avoid a feeling of sympathy and understanding toward General Buell in this situation. Not only did he have to contend with the problems of coping with a skilled and resourceful adversary, and the additional danger, ever present, from Southern sympathizers posing as pro-Unionists; he also had to contend with the authorities in Washington who should have helped, and notably General Halleck, rather than hindered, since none of them could understand Buell's problems from such a great distance.

In General Bragg's report of the campaign he stated that, in addition to his shortage of supplies, he realized that he was in a hostile country; that even a successful engagement would seriously cripple him; and that since General Buell had the choice of another route to the Ohio River, that is, to the left, he decided to turn right to Bardstown and to request supplies from Lexington, Kentucky, to meet him upon his arrival at Bardstown. Naturally Buell was not unopposed in his march to Louisville, which the forefront of his Army of the Ohio reached on September 25, and the rear on September 29. General Charles C. Gilbert was in command of the twenty thousand green troops referred to before, which General Buell incorporated into his own regiments. On the very next day, September 30, after provisioning, Buell marched out of Louisville in pursuit of Bragg.[10] Buell himself reported that following Bragg's retreat he had but one course of action. He could not know for certain whether General Kirby Smith had effected a junction with General Bragg, although he was convinced it was virtually assured. Their combined forces, he believed, greatly outnumbered his own, and subjected Louisville to the danger of immediate attack. Since his supplies were also run-

---

8. *Official Records, op. cit,* Vol. XVI, Part 2, pp. 496-97, 500, 516, 642.

9. *Battles and Leaders, op. cit.,* pp. 42-43.

10. *Official Records, op. cit.,* Vol. XVI, Part 2, pp. 1088-92; Cist, *op. cit.,* pp. 59-60.

ning low to the point of exhaustion, and since some of his troops were without rations after reaching West Point, Kentucky, some twenty-five miles from Louisville, he felt compelled to head for Louisville. He reported also that he assigned his cavalry to outpost duty at Elizabethtown to protect his moving columns and to observe any designs of the enemy on Bowling Green.[11]

At 8:30 on the morning of September 29, General William Nelson, commander of the center corps of Buell's army, was killed by General Jefferson C. Davis, in the Galt House at Louisville. This affair, the aftermath of a quarrel in which General Davis sought an apology from Nelson for an alleged unjustified rebuke several days before, cast a deep shadow over Buell's army the day prior to his scheduled march against the enemy. Davis was from Indiana, and was presumed, by Buell at least, to have enlisted one of Buell's chief critics, Governor Morton of Indiana, in his support. In any case, Buell believed that Morton brought to bear in Davis's behalf a state feeling against the rigidity of his, Buell's, control, which only the restraining influence of discipline prevented from breaking out into serious difficulties between friends of Davis and Nelson. The incident was undoubtedly a source of deep concern to General Buell, who had high regard for General Nelson. Nelson admittedly was rough, but as a commander he was ever solicitous for the well-being of his troops, and was highly regarded by them for his many good qualities and great energy. The troops did not know Davis so well, except those in his own division, which had but recently joined Buell's army during Davis's absence. Nelson's death caused considerable indignation among the troops familiar with his many good traits.[12]

As if General Buell's collateral troubles were never to end while he was contending with Bragg, General Halleck notified him on September 24 that, pursuant to President Lincoln's orders, Major General George H. Thomas was superseding him as head of the Department of the Tennessee; accordingly, he was instructed to turn over his command and proceed to Indianapolis, Indiana, to await further orders. The day before, September 23, General Thomas was notified by Halleck of the change in command, accompanied by the injunction to exercise energy in the use of the troops entrusted to him. Halleck also instructed him: "In your movements you will pay no regard to State or department lines, but operate against the enemy; find him and give him battle. If you form a junction with any troops belonging to the Department of the Ohio, take command of them and use them." General Buell did not formally acknowledge his

11. *Battles and Leaders, op. cit.,* p. 42.
12. *Ibid.,* p. 43.

notice of removal until September 29. On September 25, apparently before receipt of Halleck's order replacing him, he wrote to him in part as follows: "It might seem useless for me to answer the frequent charges of tardiness that are made against the movements of the Army of the Ohio, though I think I could answer them with some effect. It is a mistake to suppose that Bragg has marched a greater distance than I have. He concentrated his force by railroad at Chattanooga, and from there has marched in a direct line to Bardstown, a distance of about 200 miles. My army . . . has marched some 300 miles, taking Huntsville as a center, and not including the march from Corinth. . . ."[13]

Buell's removal, in view of the communication of September 25, was probably not wholly unexpected. In this campaign there is something to say in Buell's behalf for a number of reasons, although admittedly he had not taken full advantage of his opportunities. Overlooked by the Washington authorities was the fact that Buell could not have prevented at least an attempted invasion of Tennessee and Kentucky by the Confederates. It is true that he had not risked a great battle, but he was confronted with protecting Nashville while simultaneously keeping watch on Louisville. When Bragg placed his army between Buell's army and Louisville, following Munfordville, he lost an opportunity to fight with some chance of defeating Buell. Buell could not, it seems, take tremendous risks while defending both Nashville and Louisville, and he well knew that Bragg was limited to some extent by difficulties of supply; besides, he knew that Bragg would be taking far greater risks than he until he succeeded in uniting with Kirby Smith's force, which he knew to be many miles away.

General Buell acknowledged his notice of removal and informed Halleck that he had relinquished his command to General Thomas. Things were beginning to happen, quite at variance from what was generally expected. At 11:45 on the morning of September 29, General Thomas wired an appeal to General Halleck for a reconsideration of Buell's removal. He cited, and truthfully, that since Buell's preparations were completed for moving on the enemy, he should be permitted to carry them out. He reminded Halleck that since he was not so well informed as he should be regarding plans for moving against the enemy, the matter was a source of embarrassment to him.[14] Upon receipt of this dispatch, Halleck sent a joint notification to both Buell and Thomas that the order for the former's removal was being suspended.

The request of General Thomas for Buell's continuance in command was not a refusal to accept the assignment. Rather, it was his

13. *Official Records, op. cit.,* Vol. XVI, Part 1, pp. 539, 542.
14. *Ibid.,* pp. 554-55.

intention to avert an injustice to a brother officer, more especially his superior officer, a trait exemplified many times by Thomas throughout his career. There is not the slightest reason for supposing that Thomas would not have accepted the command if Buell's removal had not been suspended. Since he eventually did become commander, it is tragic for both himself and his nation that he did not accept it at that time. His subsequent record is ample testimony to the confidence of his many friends and admirers that his acceptance would have brought an earlier end to the war. This protest is somewhat of a reminder of the one Thomas made in the fall of 1861, although in reverse order, when it was planned to replace him with General Ormsby M. Mitchel, following Thomas's recommendation that East Tennessee be invaded by way of Cumberland Gap.

In later years, Thomas denied that modesty moved him to request Buell's retention. At that time he said, "I am not as modest as I have been represented to be. . . . It was unjust to relieve him on the eve of battle, and unjust to myself to impose upon me the command of the army at such a time." There can be no doubt of Thomas's sincerity regarding his decision, since it is well established that he was anxious for an independent command. This was shown only a short time later when General William Stark Rosecrans was named to succeed Buell, at which time Thomas protested most vigorously that he outranked Rosecrans and deserved the appointment. He had supreme confidence in his ability, an asset that carried him through to victory in every engagement in which he had discretion for independent judgment and decision; therefore to ascribe lack of confidence to him in this instance, or to conclude anything beyond his simple statement, is sheer nonsense. His concept of an enlarged command, for which he felt himself capable, was through expansion and development of the troops entrusted to him, and not through succeeding to the command of troops trained by another. General Buell himself tells of Thomas's visit to his room to inform him that he would protest the removal to General Halleck, and of Buell's insistence that Thomas avoid assigning any reason for his action that could be construed as personal to Buell.[15] After this assurance, Thomas submitted his request to Halleck as aforesaid.

Shortly after General Buell's entry into Louisville and his merging of the inexperienced troops under General Gilbert into his command, he reorganized his Army of the Ohio into three corps, the First,

---

15. *Battles and Leaders, op. cit.,* p. 44; Van Horne, *op. cit.,* pp. 75-7; *Legends of the Operations of the Army of the Cumberland* (Washington, D.C.: Government Printing Office, 1869), p. 11; Donn Piatt, *General George H. Thomas* (Cincinnati, 1891), p. 171.

Second, and Third. These were commanded respectively by Major Generals Alexander McCook and Thomas Crittenden and Brigadier General Charles C. Gilbert. After his restoration to commander, General Buell appointed General Thomas as his second in command. This title was ambiguous, since he had supervision only over Crittenden's Second Corps and the related cavalry, which gave the corps two major generals, but Thomas had no authority to act as commander during Buell's absence or in emergencies.[16] One wonders whether once more Thomas was deliberately struck in the face with cold water, as it were, this time by General Buell, another time by General Grant, following his request for his own demotion and Grant's restoration to command. Certainly the mere title of second in command with no authority underlying it was small consideration for Thomas's extremely generous act in Buell's behalf. Indeed there is some basis for believing that Buell went out of his way to avoid giving Thomas anything but the title, especially since he had no authority to act in Buell's place during his absence.

At this time in the course of military events in the West, the advantages held by Bragg had slipped from his grasp into the waiting hands of Buell. Although the Confederates had captured a somewhat meaningless garrison or so, defeated some raw recruits, obtained some badly needed supplies, and raised considerable commotion among the citizens of Kentucky, they had not come to grips with the main Union army. On the other hand, General Buell had reached his main base of supplies at Louisville and, in addition, had been considerably reinforced.

On October 1, 1862, the three corps of Buell's army left Louisville by separate roads. General Joshua W. Sill, with two divisions of General McCook's corps, was ordered to move toward Frankfort to hold General Kirby Smith in check; the other columns moved to Bardstown, *en route* to which each column clashed frequently with enemy cavalry before proceeding very far from Louisville. Not only did General Sill succeed in holding Smith in check; he also interfered with some degree of success in the inauguration of the Confederate-installed Governor Hawes. General Sill was a student under General Thomas during Thomas's teaching assignment at West Point in 1853, standing third in his class of fifty-two; and it was he for whom the artillery school at Fort Sill, Oklahoma, was named. Sadly, General Sill was killed in the forthcoming Battle of Murfreesboro, then less than three months away. As Buell neared Bardstown and learned that Bragg and Smith expected to unite at Danville, he ordered McCook to march to Bloomfield by the Harrodsburg road; he ordered

16. Cist, *op. cit.*, p. 61; Van Horne, *op. cit.*, p. 77.

Thomas to advance with Crittenden's corps by the Lebanon road; and he himself, with Gilbert's corps, marched by the direct road to Perryville. While advancing, Buell was informed that Kirby Smith had crossed the Kentucky River into Salvisa, and that Bragg was assembling his forces at either Harrodsburg or Perryville. He ordered General McCook to change his course and march without delay to Perryville.[17]

On the afternoon of October 7, General Buell spotted the enemy about three miles from Perryville. He promptly ordered his cavalry and artillery forward, with two regiments in support, and pushed him back about a mile toward Perryville. Realizing that his antagonist was making preparations for battle, Buell dispatched orders at once to Generals McCook and Crittenden to begin the march to Perryville at three o'clock on the morning of October 8. McCook was instructed to form on the right and Crittenden on the left, when they should reach the scene of action, and to report to Buell for battle instructions. General McCook received his orders several hours later than expected and began marching at five o'clock, just two and one-half hours later than the designated time. Thomas, with Crittenden's corps, moved about six miles off the main road on the night of October 7 and, in combination with a number of extenuating circumstances, did not participate in the Battle of Perryville. His men had marched all day on the seventh, in heavy clouds of dust and without water, and were suffering acutely from thirst. His first consideration, orders or no orders, was the safety and comfort of his men, more especially since to ignore this consideration would have rendered the troops useless for action. He could not at once contact Buell to obtain permission to search for water, and he had the implied responsibility to do precisely as he did. It is inconceivable that General Buell, if he had been available to make the decision, would have made a different one. In any event, the loss of distance to the battlefield resulting from this slight change, due to seeking water, was no more than three miles, although the movement placed Thomas somewhat out of touch, through no fault of his own, with headquarters. The notification regarding his action, which Thomas forwarded to Buell at six o'clock on the evening of October 7, did not reach him until the next morning.[18]

17. Day, *op. cit.*, p. 41; Thomas B. Van Horne, *History of the Army of the Cumberland* (Cincinnati: Robert Clarke and Co., 1875), Vol. I, p. 184; George W. Cullum, *Biographical Register of Officers and Cadets of the U. S. Military Academy* (Boston, 1891), Vol. 1, p. 236; Cist. *op. cit.*, pp. 61-62.

18. *Battles and Leaders, op. cit.*, p. 48; *Official Records, op. cit.*, Vol. XVI, Part 1, pp. 50-51; Part 2, p. 580.

This unhappy event, unavoidable beyond the faintest trace of doubt, and so regarded by General Buell, contributed its share to the controversy that followed the Battle of Perryville. Other factors, particularly the movement of high winds, which carried the noise of battle away from the troops that were available to come to the support of the hard-pressed battle participants, are discussed later in this chapter. Not only did General Thomas report the peculiar effect of the wind on the outcome of the battle during the Buell Court of Inquiry; so also did others, in particular Major J. Montgomery, an assistant adjutant general, whose description is as follows:

A message came from the line on the left center to General Buell, and in a few moments Colonel James B. Fry, our chief of staff, called me up and sent me with an order to General Gilbert, commanding the center corps, to send at once two brigades to re-enforce General McCook, commanding the left corps. Thus I came to be a witness to some of the curious features of Perryville.

I did not know what was going on at the left, and Colonel Fry did not inform me. He told me what to say to General Gilbert, and to go fast, and taking one of the General's orderlies with me, I started on my errand. I found General Gilbert at the front, and as he had no staff-officer at hand at the moment, he asked me to go to General Schoepf, one of his division commanders, with the order. Schoepf promptly detached two brigades, and he told me I had better go on ahead and find out where they were to go. There was no sound to direct me, and as I tried to take an air line I passed outside the Union Lines and was overtaken by a cavalry officer, who gave me the pleasing information that I was riding toward the enemy pickets. Now up to this time I had heard no sound of battle; I had heard no artillery in front of me, and no heavy infantry-firing. I rode back, and passed behind the cavalry regiment which was deployed in the woods, and started in the direction indicated to me by the officer who called me back. At some distance I overtook an ambulance train, urged to its best speed, and then I knew that something serious was on hand. This was the first intimation I had that one of the fiercest struggles of the war was at that moment raging almost within my sight.

Directed by the officers in charge of the ambulances I made another detour and, pushing on at greater speed I suddenly turned into a road, and there before me, within a few hundred yards, the battle of Perryville burst into view, and the roar of the artillery and the continuous rattle of the musketry first broke upon my ear. It was the finest spectacle I ever saw. It was wholly unexpected, and it fixed me with astonishment. It was like tearing away a curtain from the front of a great picture, or the sudden bursting of a thunder-cloud when the sky in front seems serene and clear. I had seen an unlooked-for storm at sea, with hardly a moment's notice, hurl itself out of the clouds and lash the ocean into a foam of wild rage. But here there was not the warning of an instant. At one bound my horse carried me from stillness into the uproar of battle. One turn from a lonely bridlepath through the woods brought me face to face with the bloody struggle of thousands of men.[19]

Thus is recorded one of the most seemingly incredible accounts of the mysteries of Perryville, and yet one of the best documented, in consonance with the testimony of Generals Thomas and Steedman referred to elsewhere in this chapter.

As explained later, neither General Buell nor General Thomas knew of the battle until too late to participate and fully exploit its opportunities as planned. During the night of October 7, Colonel McCook was ordered with his Thirty-sixth Brigade to take possession of the creek water located about two and one-half miles from Perryville. This he accomplished after a sharp encounter with a detachment of the enemy bent on the same purpose. The water was in the bed of the stream and, although somewhat stagnant, was of great value nevertheless in relieving thirst. About two hours later, the enemy sought to regain the position, but General Sheridan ordered a brigade and a battery to disperse them. After a severe clash, with heavy losses on both sides, the enemy withdrew across the Chaplin River.

Turning again to the Confederate high command, General Bragg had left General Leonidas Polk at Bardstown with orders to withdraw slowly to Bryantsville. Bragg himself went to Lexington and there ordered General Smith and his force to Frankfort to participate in the inauguration of Richard Hawes as provisional governor of Kentucky. This event took place at noon on October 4, but by three o'clock the Confederates had begun preparations for evacuating the town. In the evening they burned the railroad bridge over the Kentucky River and destroyed the flooring and damaged the heavy timbers of the turnpike bridge. On October 5, the next day, Smith's forces had reached Versailles, a town about twenty miles north of

---

19. Van Horne, *Army of the Cumberland*, Vol. I, p. 186; *Battles and Leaders, op. cit.*, pp. 60-61; *Official Records, op. cit.*, Vol. XVI, Part 1, pp. 187-88.

Harrodsburg. The inauguration of the Confederate governor was disappointment personified to General Bragg, since it did not evoke the expected response from Kentuckians that would take their state into the Confederacy. After the inauguration Bragg realized that Kentucky was not prepared to join the Confederacy. Bragg is reported to have said, "The people here have too many fat cattle and are too well off to fight." He realized that he erred in not taking the offensive against Buell from the beginning, and working on that general's communications.[20]

General Buell must be given some credit for thwarting General Bragg's plans, in addition to preserving his army intact; in fact, he greatly strengthened it, and prevented Bragg from occupying Louisville with, of course, considerable unintentional help from Bragg himself. The farcical performance of Bragg in devoting so much valuable time and effort, including the participation of his troops in the inaugural, in what was almost destined to be a symbolic government of Kentucky, stunted his military achievements. Instead of utilizing his and Smith's forces in one supreme effort to defeat Buell, of whose presence both Confederate leaders were painfully aware, they sauntered off on this political expedition. While the ceremony of inaugurating the governor was being conducted, the booming of cannon and the dispatches that followed told Bragg that his enemy was very near, too near for comfort, so that he began a precipitate withdrawal from Frankfort as aforesaid. It is true that prominent citizens of Kentucky had assured him in June that Kentucky was ripe for an invasion, and that its people were receptive to joining his banner; he should nevertheless have used the bayonet before attempting to perform the gesture of Confederate sovereignty, which was almost foredoomed to failure.[21]

General Polk, in the meantime, was ordered by General Bragg on October 2, having been given two copies of the order in writing, to advance with his entire available force by way of Bloomfield toward Frankfort and strike Buell's army in both flank and rear. He informed Polk that Smith would attack Buell in front at the same time. When Polk received the order on the following morning, he called a council of war to discuss the new instructions; it was decided that it would be injudicious to obey them, and that instead Bragg's original instructions should be observed. Of this he informed General Bragg, in order to provide sufficient time for the withdrawal of the order to Smith to attack, advising Bragg also that his division and wing com-

20. Day, *op. cit.*, p. 41; High, *op. cit.*, pp. 22-23; *Battles and Leaders, op. cit.*, p. 602; *Official Records*, Vol. XVI, Part 1, pp. 1020, 1087.

21. *Battles and Leaders, ibid.*, pp. 600-602.

manders supported his action. He told Bragg further that he would follow the routes Bragg had indicated and would proceed toward Camp Breckinridge, the former Camp Dick Robinson, incidentally, commanded by Thomas during the second half of 1861. On October 4, following Polk's dispatch advising Bragg that he was following his original instructions, the latter ordered him to concentrate his forces at Harrodsburg. At Harrodsburg, he was informed, a brigade at Danville and the force at Camp Breckinridge would join him, as would also the troops of Generals Pat Cleburne and Kirby Smith. Bragg was not unmindful of the morale factor in this situation, for he told Polk to "keep the men in heart by assuring them it is not a retreat, but a concentration for a fight. We can and must defeat them."[22]

General Bragg gave orders for supplies, which he had ordered accumulated in Lexington, to be shipped to Bryantsville. On October 6, he advanced to Harrodsburg with his force and there met General Polk at the head of the troops that had left Bardstown on October 3. On October 7, Bragg ordered Polk to move General Benjamin F. Cheatham's division to Perryville and then, without delay, attack and rout the Federals assembled there. He was then to join Smith. These orders assumed that General Buell's command was widely scattered, with perhaps sixty miles between his right and left, which, although far from correct, might well have been the case for all practical purposes, as proved by developments during the next forty-eight hours. When the movement was completed, the Confederates in readiness for the Battle of Perryville on the following day would number about seventeen thousand men, with a distance between the right and left flanks of perhaps six miles.[23]

All of the elements were now in order for the Battle of Perryville to be waged and to go into the record as a misadventure, an encounter between two antagonists, each of whom succeeded in misleading his opponent, and each of whom, in consequence, was misled by his opponent. One of the strangest features to be brought out after the battle was that General Buell, but two and one-half miles distant from his army, did not know that a battle was fought until about four o'clock, two hours after it began, on October 8. General Thomas, on the extreme right, did not know that a battle had been fought on his left until after nightfall. His answer to the question "At what time on the day of the 8th did you become aware that the left wing was engaged with the enemy?" is most surprising:

---

22. *Official Records, op. cit.*, Vol. XVI, Part 2, pp. 887, 897, 901, 904, 905; Cist, *op. cit.*, p. 63.

23. Cist, *ibid.*; *Official Records, ibid.*, Vol. XVI, Part 1, pp. 1092, 1109, 1120.

"I did not know that a battle had been fought on the left until after night-fall, when, as I was riding to my tent, Lieutenant Fitzhugh, of General Buell's staff, overtook me and told me. This must have been about 7 o'clock." To the question "Did you hear any firing on that day; and, if so, what was the character of it?" he replied: "I heard cannonading about the time that the head of Crittenden's corps reached the position it was to take up, and I directed Captain Mack, my chief of artillery, to report to General Buell that I had arrived in position and with the head of the column, and would superintend the placing of troops in position, and requested the general to send me any orders by Captain Mack.[24]

"Captain Mack returned about 12, with a plan of the ground and directions from the general to dispose the troops in a certain manner preparatory to an attack the next morning at Perryville; . . . I asked Captain Mack if he knew what that firing was we heard on the left in front; his reply was that the report came to headquarters that it was Captain Gay, chief of artillery, reconnoitering, and the enemy were firing upon him with artillery. About 3 o'clock in the afternoon I again heard very heavy cannonading, and directed General Critten-den to send a staff officer to General Gilbert to know what that firing was. The sun was probably half an hour high when he returned. General Gilbert replied to General Crittenden by a short note, stating that he had met with some little resistance himself, but was then camping his troops for the night; that General Rousseau had been engaged—I think he said had been driven back slightly, but had regained his ground. The firing continued at intervals from about half past two till about an hour of sundown, but I am not positive."[25]

When asked, "Would such firing as that which you describe pro-ceed from the resistance of a reconnoissance?" he replied, "I do not think so; and for that reason I sent to General Gilbert to know why there was such firing." When asked, "Taking into consideration the relative distance of yours and General Buell's headquarters from the scene of this conflict and the direction of the wind, would the sound of artillery or small arms be more readily heard at General Buell's headquarters than at yours?" he replied, "I think that with as high wind blowing as there was that day the cannonading was not more distinctly heard at his headquarters than where I was. The wind was blowing very heavily." He was then asked, "Was the wind blow-ing from his headquarters toward the firing or from the firing to his headquarters?" and he replied that he thought the direction of

---

24. *Official Records, ibid.*, Vol. XVI, Part 1, pp. 50, 51, 187; Van Horne, *Life*, p. 78.

25. *Official Records, ibid.*; Van Horne, *Life, loc. cit.*

the wind was to his left from the direction of the fighting.[26] This testimony of General Thomas is singular, not only for the effect of the high wind on the battle, but also for the almost complete absence of any discussion of the wind by others.

As stated previously, General McCook's forces marched at five o'clock on the morning of October 8, with General Rousseau's and General Jackson's divisions. Rousseau's division was in the lead *en route* to Perryville, but one of his brigades, commanded by General John C. Starkweather, was dropped to the rear due to the interposition of General Jackson's division at Mackville. McCook did not await the arrival of this brigade; instead, he instructed his assistant adjutant general to post General Jackson's brigades upon arrival on a commanding position immediately to the right of the Mackville and Perryville road. He further ordered him to hold Jackson's troops in column formation for immediate movement, if necessary. He then turned over his command temporarily to General Rousseau while he reported to General Buell at headquarters. General Buell was in General Gilbert's camp on the Springfield pike, some two and one-half miles from McCook's position on the Mackville pike. At half after twelve the Confederates advanced and were soon engaged in skirmishing and artillery exchanges with the Federals. The brunt of this attack fell upon General Philip Sheridan's division, at the head of General Gilbert's corps, and also on the head of General McCook's corps marching from its position at the Russell house toward the Chaplin River.[27]

General McCook's return to his command after reporting to General Buell was met with the disappointing situation of General Rousseau's advance of the right of his line some eight or ten hundred yards; and his occupancy of a commanding ridge to the left of the Mackville and Perryville pike, against which the enemy was firing from three of his batteries. This fire was being returned by Loomis's and Simonson's artillery, but since Confederate infantry was not within sight, General McCook ordered a cease-fire in order to conserve ammunition. He then undertook a reconnaissance toward the Chaplin River in order to obtain water. Riding to the left, he located a commanding ridge about six hundred yards from, and overlooking, the river. He next brought up Generals Jackson and Terrill, showed them the water, pointed out to them his line of battle, and placed a battery on the ridge with strong supports. He next ordered General Terrill to move skirmishers down the slope when the line was formed, after which he rode back to the right of his command, some time

---

26. *Official Records, ibid.,* 187, 188; Van Horne, *Life, loc. cit.*
27. *Battles and Leaders, op. cit.,* pp. 54, 55.

around two o'clock. Two brigades of General Rousseau's division, with General Terrill's brigade, held the line of the left corps, its right on the Mackville and Perryville pike near Doctor's Creek crossing, and its left near the Chaplin River, the line running about due north and south.[28]

At this stage the brigade of Colonel Webster of General Jackson's division had not put in its appearance; however, the Confederates had engaged General Philip Sheridan's division at the head of the corps in the center only a short time before. General Robert B. Mitchell's division was coming to support Sheridan. General William P. Carlin's and Colonel William W. Caldwell's brigades of Mitchell's division were under cover to the right and rear, and Colonel Michael Gooding's brigade was north of Doctor's Creek near the river. This enabled Gooding's brigade to cover Sheridan's left while observing the distance between the two corps, or until the left corps advanced to the front. As Mitchell's division advanced to its place in the line, the enemy appeared on his right in some strength, but was repulsed by General Carlin's brigade. At about two thirty the enemy advanced all along the line. It attacked General Sheridan from its left, but it struck hardest to its right against General Rousseau, pushing everything before it. When the enemy's left struck Sheridan he was waiting for them, and he gave them a withering reception that completely repulsed them. Following this up, Carlin's brigade pushed them back in rout to Perryville, with the result that their left was turned and Carlin's brigade was in their rear.[29]

General McCook's brigades, under Rousseau, were attacked by greatly superior numbers of the enemy while moving to the front during his absence at headquarters. The advantage of attack while the troops were advancing to battle position was distinctly in favor of the Confederates. Rousseau's right brigade, or right of the left corps, was subjected to a devastating attack, while Terrill's brigade on the left, and Starkweather's, which had just reached the field, were also heavily attacked. Terrill's brigade consisted entirely of new and untried troops; it was but a few minutes therefore until they fell back in confusion, losing eight Napoleon guns. General Jackson was killed soon after the battle commenced. Only the night before, Generals Jackson and Terrill with Colonel Webster were discussing the chances of being hit in battle. Their opinion was that men would not be frightened if they would consider the doctrine of probabilities and the small chance of one person's being killed. This law certainly worked overtime for them, as all of them were killed at Perryville

28. *Ibid.*
29. *Ibid.*, pp. 55-57.

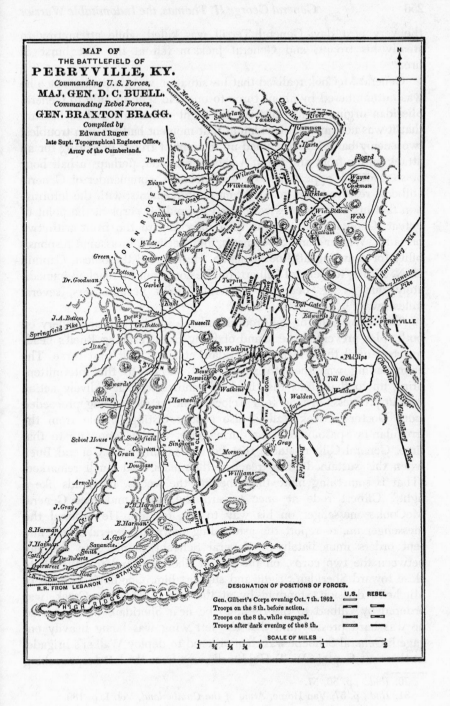

MAP OF
THE BATTLEFIELD OF
PERRYVILLE, KY.
Commanding U. S. Forces,
MAJ. GEN. D. C. BUELL.
Commanding Rebel Forces,
GEN. BRAXTON BRAGG.
Compiled by
Edward Ruger
late Supt. Topographical Engineer Office,
Army of the Cumberland.

DESIGNATION OF POSITIONS OF FORCES.

	U.S.	REBEL
Gen. Gilbert's Corps evening Oct. 7th. 1862.		
Troops on the 8 th. before action.		
Troops on the 8 th. while engaged.		
Troops after dark evening of the 8 th.		

SCALE OF MILES

1   ¾   ½   ¼   0   1   2

the very next day. General Terrill was killed while attempting to steady his troops, and General Jackson fell at the first burst of fire.[30]

General McCook realized that his situation was desperate, since he was outnumbered by about three to one. He sent an aide to General Sheridan urging him to observe the right of his line and to be sure that it was not turned. Sheridan at that moment had his own troubles; two enemy batteries were lined up in front of troops preparing for an attack on his front and flank. A short time later, perhaps a half hour or so, McCook appealed to General Schoepf, commander of General Gilbert's reserve corps, to send him reinforcements, with the information that his own reserves were used up and his corps at the point of defeat. General Schoepf was then marching to the front with two brigades, Walker's and Steedman's, and declined to assume responsibility for changing his line of march. He referred the officer, Captain H. N. Fisher, to General Gilbert, but he could not be reached immediately due to his being at General Buell's headquarters, several miles away.[31]

The topography of the ground and the sparing use of artillery on both sides prevented the sound of firing from reaching Buell's headquarters until the attack on Sheridan, at about half past three. The cannonading was then so steady, in contrast to the intermittent firing up to that time, that it clearly indicated that a lively action was in progress. Around four o'clock rapid artillery firing proceeded from Doctor's Creek Valley, also clearly distinguishable from the irregular or spasmodic firing during most of the action up to that time. General Gilbert stated that he was talking with General Buell when this sustained firing reached their ears, and Buell remarked, "That is something more than shelling the woods. It sounds like a fight." Gilbert rode at once toward the firing and met General McCook's messenger on his way to ask for aid. He ordered the messenger on, to report the astounding news to General Buell, and sent orders immediately to General Schoepf to move to the gap between the two corps, on the left of Sheridan, and to Mitchell to close toward Sheridan's right and support him. Gooding's brigade of Mitchell's division, standing by at the left of Doctor's Creek, was ordered by Gilbert to the right, to be near Sheridan, who reported he was hard pressed and that the left wing was being heavily engaged. General Schoepf was then ordered to deploy Walker's brigade. At this time Captain W. T. Hoblitzell came from the left corps seeking

---

30. *Ibid.*, pp. 56, 57.
31. *Ibid.*, p. 57; Van Horne, *Army of the Cumberland*, Vol. I, p. 189.

help, and with the information that the troops were falling back and needed help at once to save the day.[32]

The fighting at this point, as it affected Sheridan, had been increasing in intensity; but it was soon apparent that the cannonading was subsiding and, observing that General Walker's brigade had not yet deployed, General Gilbert recalled Colonel Gooding with orders to report to General McCook. With Pinney's battery of artillery, Gooding succeeded in making himself felt on the enemy's flank, which had been pushing back General Rousseau's troops toward the Russell House. Within a few minutes after Gooding's brigade went into action, Sheridan, having repulsed the Confederates, turned his guns on Rousseau's assailants across Doctor's Creek Valley. These latter, in their advance, became vulnerable to attack by Sheridan from his advantageous position, much to the relief of General McCook's right. After Sheridan opened fire, General Steedman came up with his brigade of General Schoepf's division and continued on to Doctor's Creek. The enemy was pushed back so far from McCook's front at this point as to be out of range of Steedman's infantry; however, while moving up under the fire of Sheridan's guns, Steedman stopped and opened fire on them with Smith's battery of his brigade. Following a severe encounter, the Confederate attack lost its momentum, stopped, was pushed back, and then found its line of retreat endangered. They were compelled to give up the field without taking their wounded; but in the face of superior forces they had no need for feeling humiliated, since they had acquitted themselves commendably.[33] In retrospect, it appears that the Confederate objective was to attack the left under McCook, which they assuredly did, before the greatly superior Federal forces were able to unite; and that they succeeded in performing capably before the Union armies concentrated was due in considerable measure to the mysterious circumstances and confusion that were allied with them.

General Buell reported that he had 58,000 men before Perryville was fought and that 22,000 of these were raw and inexperienced troops. His statement that not half of his total strength was engaged in the battle may be taken to mean that not more than 25,000 to 28,000 men participated. Union losses in the battle, according to Buell, were about 3,000 killed in McCook's corps, or about one-fourth of

32. *Battles and Leaders, ibid.,* pp. 57, 58; *Official Records, op. cit.,* Vol. XVI, Part 1, p. 187.

33. *Battles and Leaders, ibid.,* Van Horne, *Army of the Cumberland,* pp. 189-90.

his command numbering 12,500 men; and General Gilbert, with Sheridan's division and Mitchell's brigade, estimated at about 10,000, lost about 900 killed and wounded and some 450 prisoners, or about 1,350 men, a total loss of 4,350 men. Most of the Union regiments engaged were never under fire before; therefore, in view of all the circumstances, they may be said to have fought creditably. The Confederates, under the field command of General Leonidas Polk, General Bragg having gone to Frankfort to participate in the installation of the Confederate-sponsored Governor Hawes, lost about 3,150 men killed and wounded. In addition, Bragg reported a loss of about 250 prisoners, or a total of approximately 3,400 from his estimated total of 16,000 men engaged in the battle. These losses, both Union and Confederate, ran unusually high, more especially when considered in relation to the brevity of the engagement. General Buell's losses were about twenty per cent, while those of General Bragg were about twenty-one per cent, or substantially the same.[34]

Hostilities ended about nightfall, as aforesaid, with generally prevailing hopes that there would be a renewal in the morning. With this thought in mind, General Buell ordered General Thomas to move General Crittenden's and General Gilbert't corps forward at six in the morning of October 9, or shortly after daybreak, and attack the front and left of the enemy. General McCook was also instructed during the night to close the interval between his own right and Gilbert's left flank. Furthermore, McCook was ordered to simply hold his position while the attack was being made by General Thomas, but to be alert to any possible opportunity that might be exploited during the progress of the expected battle. The advance was made by Crittenden's and Gilbert's corps as directed, but it was soon evident that the Confederates had withdrawn during the night and headed for Harrodsburg. Anticipated enemy resistance at Harrodsburg consisted of a slight skirmish on October 13, although Federal forces occupied the town on October 11. In their retreat, it is worthy of note, the Confederates left their dead and wounded at Perryville, but otherwise they retired in good order. General Bragg, however, could not but look with dismay upon his activities in Kentucky, since he had accomplished virtually nothing; in particular, he had lost many men, and their loss had not availed him the prize of his principal objective, that of wresting Kentucky from the Union fold.[35]

It is not the purpose here to assign responsibility for Federal failures at Perryville, but rather to let the record speak for itself.

34. Cist, *op. cit.*, pp. 68, 69.
35. *Ibid.*

In assessing individual blame, particularly against General Buell, it is well to remember that he was not given the freedom of movement from Washington, particularly from General Halleck, that he needed to fully exploit his advantages. On the other hand, it is not easy to explain how Buell could have been so completely misled about his enemy's strength, when Thomas, among others, was aware of it and thought he should have fought long before he reached Louisville.

At the Buell Court of Inquiry, General James B. Steedman testified that he was encamped on the Springfield and Perryville road, about three miles from Perryville, when the battle began. He was not aware of the severity of the engagement until he moved to about three-fourths of a mile from General Rousseau's division, at which point he was within hearing distance of both musketry and artillery.[36] This testimony supports the statements of both General Buell and General Thomas that, from a few miles away, they were unaware of the magnitude of the battle until it was well under way.

General Steedman also testified that in his opinion the officers and men of General Buell's command had the utmost confidence in him until after the movement from Nashville. The men believed that their commander was reluctant, if not unwilling, to fight the enemy, whereas they felt supremely confident of their ability to take his measure. Steedman testified that when Buell stopped for something approximating two or three days at Cave City, for reasons he personally did not know, the men were impatient to attack and drive back the invaders. Furthermore, he stated that the men did not complain of the hardships they suffered; but they were disappointed at the continued marching and countermarching without meeting up with the very purpose of their presence in uniform, the enemy. Concerning his own personal feelings, Steedman said: ". . . no officer ever enjoyed to a more eminent degree the confidence of his officers and soldiers than General Buell. I know very well that I was proud to state that I belonged to Buell's army; but from the time the retrograde movement was commenced I am compelled to say I think the confidence in General Buell began to wane in the army; whether just or unjust, there was a great lack of confidence in him during the march from Nashville to Louisville." He also stated that Generals McCook, Schoepf, Mitchell, and Fry expressed their conviction that Buell should have attacked General Bragg at a number of points during his advance.[37]

Steedman testified that while at Pelham he engaged in conversation with McCook, in General Schoepf's headquarters, concerning

36. *Official Records, op. cit.,* Vol. XVI, Part 1, pp. 132-33.
37. *Ibid.,* pp. 133, 134.

the movements then under way. "McCook," he stated, "brought his hand down with considerable force on my knee, 'Don Carlos won't do,' said he; 'he won't do.' Said I, 'General, there is considerable feeling in the army on the subject.' 'O,' said he, 'George Thomas is the man, and we must have him.' I think General Buell was in the same building at the time . . . having a conversation with General Crittenden."

General Steedman also expressed agreement with General Thomas's opinion that General Buell should have concentrated his forces against General Bragg in the Pikeville and McMinnville or the Sparta area. It is the generally accepted belief that Buell was opposed to this because he believed it did not afford reasonable chances for success. Startling though it seems, General Steedman stated that some officers, including a brigadier general, some colonels, and some lieutenant colonels, believed General Buell disloyal. General Schoepf also told the Court of Inquiry that he frequently heard officers express doubt of Buell's loyalty.[38] However that may be, Buell's record discounts any such opinions, particularly his role in coming to General Grant's rescue at Shiloh or Pittsburg Landing and, in effect, turning the tide of battle in favor of the Union. It was General Lewis "Lew" Wallace of Buell's army who came with his division into the battle, and in the words of Whitelaw Reid: "He came into that action when, without him, all was lost. He redeemed the fortunes of the field, and justly won the title of the Hero of Pittsburg Landing."[39]

General Buell was a disciplinarian who, as Thomas said afterward, did much to mold the Army of the Ohio into one of the most efficient and uniformly successful military organizations in the entire history of the United States. From the mass of raw, undrilled, somewhat uninhibited, and, in many cases, illiterate troops, he fashioned them into the nucleus of that great Army of the Cumberland they soon became. The only fault of Buell, if it could be so called, was in failing to realize that the volunteer soldier would not depart from his freedom as did the professional peacetime soldier. In consequence, therefore, that liberty-loving temporary soldier, intent upon winning the war and returning to his civilian occupation, refused to become subservient, as he deemed it, to his would-be military masters. The result was bitterness toward Buell that might have been lessened or even averted if he had been alerted to it.[40]

---

38. *Ibid.*, pp. 134, 135, 182.

39. Cist, *op. cit.*, pp. 76, 77.

40. *Ibid.*, pp. 75, 76; *Official Records, op. cit.*, Vol. XVI, pp. 184-204; Piatt, *op. cit.*, p. 181.

General Thomas was an interesting if not startling witness before the Court of Inquiry. His rank of second in command to Buell after the occupation of Louisville, coupled with his request for the retention of Buell in command when Buell was faced with removal, encouraged the assumption that he would be partial to Buell if the occasion warranted it. Such was not the case, however, as the ruggedly honest soldier stated the truth. General Buell's questioning of him elicited that General Bragg, with a considerably smaller army, not only outmatched but outmaneuvered and outfought Buell's army. Furthermore, he stated that the McMinnville-Pikeville-Sparta area was the place where Bragg should have been given battle. To Buell's question whether this choice of a battleground came before or after the campaign, Thomas replied, "If you will give me your book of telegrams, I believe it will answer better than I can." As Thomas turned the pages and showed Buell that he had indeed advised him to concentrate his forces at Sparta, before Bragg reached there, no futher questioning was needed. Thomas's testimony covered the period dating from Bragg's crossing of the Tennessee River at Chattanooga, through his entrance into the Sequatchie Valley, the race for Louisville, and the Battle of Perryville, to the withdrawal of Bragg from Kentucky.[41]

Thomas was sympathetic to Buell nevertheless, regardless of the attitude of many of the officers and men of his command. He knew that Buell's path through Tennessee and Kentucky was not without great tribulation and anxiety. He knew the difficulties of faulty organization, which was the responsibility of those above him. General Halleck had planned on paper a campaign into East Tennessee that he sought to compel Buell to execute. Buell, capable and courageous, would not move his army too far from the railroad, which afforded some assurance of ready movement to wherever events might dictate. Through all of this period of travail Buell must surely have known that his removal could not be more than a few weeks away.

There is something more to be said for General Buell, while admitting that he did not stop General Bragg when he could have stopped him with very little risk of defeat. Nevertheless, as has been stated, he had the responsibility of protecting both Nashville and Louisville; and whatever else he did or failed to do in the campaign, these cities were in Union hands after Bragg's retreat. He was not far wrong in refusing to attack until his own army was north of Bragg's and the expected reinforcements from Louisville had joined him. There were three distinct times when Buell prepared his army

---

41. *Official Records, ibid.;* Piatt, *ibid.*

for action during the invasion, and, except at Perryville, the opportunity was declined by Bragg. Indeed it has been made abundantly clear that Bragg was bent on occupying Kentucky, if possible, without a major battle, and, in very truth, this he almost succeeded in doing. Bragg had every reason to feel, based upon encouragement from Confederate sympathizers, that Kentucky was ready to fall into his arms. He fully expected twenty thousand volunteers, which he was prepared to equip with arms; but the state wanted no part of the Confederacy, at least to the extent of withdrawing from a known status to an unknown one.

If the Kentucky campaign did nothing else, it at least developed intense bitterness in both armies against their commanders. We have seen already that the officers and men in General Buell's army lost all confidence in him, particularly after his failure to attack Bragg at Munfordville. In this latter decision, however, Buell was dominated by an obsession to defend and make safe not only Nashville and Louisville, but the respective areas already in Union possession. There is a point at which such avoidance of battle becomes absurd, ridiculous, and destructive of the aspirations of the country that sends men forth to battle. As General Douglas MacArthur, commander of the American forces in Korea, stated, "War's very object is victory"; and there is no known substitute for defeating the enemy short of meeting him face to face on the battlefield, unless he can be starved into surrendering. It is not so easy to understand the bitterness of Bragg's men toward him, since it has been shown that he was not only outnumbered throughout the invasion; he was also operating far from his base of supplies in a country that afforded relatively little opportunity for replenishment of his constantly diminishing material.

General Bragg's disheartenment, disillusionment, and disgust with Kentucky are indicated in his report: "The campaign here was predicated on a belief and the most positive assurances that the people of this country would rise en masse to assert their independence. No people had so favorable an opportunity, but I am distressed to add there is little or no disposition to avail of it. Willing perhaps to accept their independence, they are neither disposed nor willing to risk their lives or their property in its achievement. With ample means to arm 20,000 men and a force with that to fully redeem the State we have not yet issued half the arms left us by casualties incident to the campaign."[42]

There can be little doubt that Bragg's invasion, viewed as a purely military achievement, ended in failure; but taken in relation to its

---

42. *Official Records, ibid.,* p. 1088.

duration, during which the enemy kept a much larger army on the move and in fear and doubt as to his intentions and whereabouts, it was a thrilling and magnificent episode of the war. Bragg's disappointment, following his intense desire to "liberate" Kentucky, poses the question of what the minority, in this instance Southern sympathizers, did in the midst of their numerically superior fellow citizens of opposing beliefs. It is true that many enlisted from Kentucky, also Maryland, Missouri, and other border states, on both sides of the conflict; but it must have occurred in many instances that the line of resistance was least in joining the army of the majority, rather than leaving one's state to fight for the cause more dear to the heart.

If, in the confusion at Perryville, particularly when General Buckner's division attacked General Rousseau's right flank at right angles to the general battle line, the corps of General Gilbert and General Crittenden had turned to the left, they would have surrounded Bragg's army and engulfed it. Sadly for the Union, however, Gilbert's divisions had moved forward to bring about the situation on the left; and General Thomas, assigned to the right, could not know of the trouble on the left. General Buell, meanwhile, was too far to the rear to know the urgent need of his presence. General Crittenden had urged that he be authorized to advance in the direction of the enemy, but Thomas refused him permission because he did not have the authority in the absence of knowledge of Buell's plans. Even if Crittenden had advanced promptly, as he wished to do, he could not have aided the distraught McCook, since Gilbert's advance had left McCook's right unprotected. What was needed, as stated in part above, was a movement to the left by Gilbert's and Crittenden's corps, with Gilbert keeping in close contact with McCook's right. Out of this whole campaign, if General Thomas had been given authority that should have gone with his title of second in command, instead of being given command merely of Crittenden's corps, the results from the Battle of Perryville would surely have been vastly superior for the Union.[43]

If further proof were needed in support of General Thomas's lack of authority, it is shown by the following dispatch from General Buell's Chief of Staff, dated October 8 at 6:30 P.M.:

The First Corps [McCook's]) on our left, has been very heavily engaged. The left and center of this corps gained ground, but the right of it yielded a little. Press your lines forward as far

43. Van Horne, *Life*, pp. 80-82.

as possible to-night and get into position to make a vigorous attack in the morning at daylight. If you have got your troops into a position which you deem advantageous it will not be advisable to make a change for the purpose of complying with the general's instructions for you sent by Captain Mack. It may be as well to halt the division ordered to the center and let it wait where it is for further orders.[44]

This dispatch followed similar verbal instructions issued earlier in the day. It is extremely important to note that the dispatch contains not the slightest reference to any discretionary authority reposing in General Thomas. It ordered him simply to stand by for expected action on the following day, but as to the determination of any action he had not the remotest authority. The condition of affairs on the left was informative, but he was given no instructions to delve into the development of events.

General Bragg himself reported that he decided to withdraw from Perryville after learning that Buell's three corps were united against him. He ordered General Kirby Smith to move his force and unite with him at Harrodsburg, whence, offering General Buell battle that he stated was declined, he moved in the direction of Cumberland Gap. Upon arriving at Bryantsville on October 11, he found that the Federals had destroyed the mills and other sources from which he drew his only food supplies. In view of this and other adverse developments, and in consideration of approaching autumnal rains, which would make Cumberland Gap impassable to an army, he set both his and General Smith's columns in motion on October 13, and passed through the Gap between October 19 and 24. The condition of the Confederate army at this time, as described by General Bragg, is revealing although perhaps somewhat exaggerated:

In four weeks after passing Cumberland Gap on this memorable and arduous campaign, jaded, hungry, and ragged (as necessarily incidental to that service), this noble army was found with serried ranks in front of the enemy at Nashville better organized, better disciplined, better clothed and fed, in better health and tone, and in larger numbers than when it entered on the campaign, though it had made a march at least three times as long as that of the enemy in reaching the same point, and was moreover entirely self-sustained.[45]

44. *Official Records, op. cit.*, Vol. XVI, Part 2, p. 588.
45. *Ibid.*, Vol. XVI, Part 1, pp. 1093, 1094; Van Horne, *Army of the Cumberland*, p. 195.

General Buell could not possibly have known for certain just what Bragg's plans were; he was compelled therefore to assume that a battle might be possible. It is noted that Bragg reported he offered Buell battle after Perryville, but this is not too susceptible of confirmation. It should be remembered, however, that Buell was criticized for not pursuing Bragg, as it was felt he should, and that in consequence he was relieved of command, effective on October 24, 1862.

CHAPTER XII

Rosecrans Succeeds Buell:
Murfreesboro, the War's Turning Point

FOLLOWING the abandonment of his pursuit of General Bragg at London, General Buell placed General Thomas in chief command and retired to Louisville. On October 26, 1862, he telegraphed Thomas to assemble the two corps of Generals McCook and Gilbert at Bowling Green and to order General Crittenden to move his corps to Glasgow. General Buell had no way of knowing the intentions of the enemy nor his strength; therefore he did not discount the possibility of an attack on Nashville, since the enemy had moved promptly from Perryville. The possibility of such an attack underlay his plans for concentrating at Bowling Green; however, this did not meet with the approval of the authorities at Washington, who thought that he should enter East Tennessee. This difference of opinion was strong enough to end in the removal of Buell from his command, which was accomplished in the following order, dated October 24, 1862, from General Halleck:

> GENERAL: The President directs that on the presentation of this order you will turn over your command to Maj. Gen. W. S. Rosecrans, and repair to Indianapolis, Ind., reporting from that place to the Adjutant General of the Army for further orders.[1]

The reaction of General Buell to his displacement, at least publicly, is expressed in his communication to General Thomas dated October 29: "I judge from what appears in the papers that Rosecrans has been ordered to relieve me. Under the circumstances I am sure I do not grieve about it."[2]

Under General Orders No. 168 of October 24, 1862, the Department

---

1. Thomas B. Van Horne, *History of the Army of the Cumberland* (Cincinnati: Robert Clarke and Co., 1875), Vol. I, pp. 196-97; *Official Records of the War of the Rebellion* (Washington, 1880–1901), Vol. XVI, Part 2, p. 642.

2. *Official Records, ibid.*, p. 652.

of the Cumberland was defined as "the State of Tennessee east of the Tennessee River and such parts of Northern Alabama and Georgia as may be taken possession of by United States troops." Major General Rosecrans in the same authorization was assigned to the command of the Department.[3] Interestingly enough, General Rosecrans wrote to General Buell on October 30, stating "I know the bearer of unwelcome news has a 'losing office,' but feel assured you are too high a gentleman and too true a soldier to permit this to produce any feelings of personal unkindness between us. I, like yourself, am neither an intriguer nor newspaper soldier. I go where I am ordered; but propriety will permit me to say that I have often felt indignant at the petty attacks on you by a portion of the press during the past summer, and that you had my high respect for ability as a soldier, for your firm adherence to truth and justice in the government and discipline of your command. I beg you, by our common profession and the love we bear our suffering country, to give me all the aid you can for the performance of duties of which no one better than yourself knows the difficulties."[4]

This communication was what one would expect from one gentleman to another; unfortunately, the sentiment expressed was the exception rather than the rule. As between two former graduates of West Point Military Academy, this appeal by Rosecrans was in the finest tradition of that institution; and he knew that in addition to Buell's receiving a bad press, politics-ridden Washington, particularly at that time, did not possess the appreciation necessary to support a troubled commander in the field. Hardly a year elapsed before Rosecrans himself was replaced by the greatest soldier in the Federal army. It would be less than a month before Rosecrans would be telling General Halleck in straightforward English just how he felt about his badgering. Before Rosecrans had time enough to become oriented to the new assignment, Halleck pounced upon him, but, reacting to the bristling of the tormented Rosecrans, he recoiled with the customary resiliency of a bully.

The appointment of Rosecrans was destined to create resentment on the part of General Thomas. It was only twenty-six days before, on September 29, that Thomas had been named to succeed Buell, but, over Thomas's own objections, as stated earlier, the change in command was shelved. Thomas objected at that time because he felt that Buell should have been given the opportunity to implement his completed plans to pursue General Bragg. Naturally, Thomas felt, if he was qualified in the first instance, he should be considered this time,

---

3. *Ibid.*, pp. 641-42.
4. *Ibid.*, p. 653.

inasmuch as Buell was being definitely replaced. He promptly, and with considerable feeling, protested Rosecrans's promotion and his own assignment under him. He stated his objections to General Halleck in no uncertain terms:

> Soon after coming to Kentucky in 1861 I urged the Government to give me 20,000 men properly equipped to take the field, that I might at least make the attempt to take Knoxville and secure East Tennessee. My suggestions were not listened to, but were passed by in silence. Yet, without boasting, I believe I have exhibited at least sufficient energy to show that if I had been intrusted with the command of that expedition at that time [October, 1861] I might have conducted it successfully. Before Corinth I was intrusted with the command of the right wing of the Army of the Tennessee. I feel confident that I performed my duty patriotically and faithfully and with a reasonable amount of credit to myself. As soon as the emergency was over I was relieved and returned to the command of my old division. I went to my duties without a murmur, as I am neither ambitious nor have any political aspirations.
>
> On the 29th of last September I received an order through your aide, Colonel McKibbin, placing me in command of the Department of Tennessee, and directing General Buell to turn over his troops to me. This order reached me just as General Buell had by most extraordinary exertions prepared his army to pursue and drive the rebels from Kentucky. Feeling convinced that great injustice would be done him if not permitted to carry out his plans I requested that he might be retained in command. The order relieving him was suspended, but to-day I am officially informed that he is relieved by General Rosecrans, my junior. Although I do not claim for myself any superior ability, yet feeling conscious that no just cause exists for overslaughing me by placing me under my junior, I feel deeply mortified and aggrieved at the action taken in this matter.[5]

It is evident from this letter that General Thomas, while extremely forthright in stating his objection to an injustice, was also restrained and dignified. The weight of his argument to General Halleck was overwhelming and admitted of no rebuttal. It is noteworthy that this "homeless" general, who had no congressman or other influential person to intercede in his behalf, did not shrink from declaring his opposition to what he believed wrong. It is equally true that not once

5. *Ibid.*, p. 657.

throughout the war did he seek promotion except through his demonstrated ability.

It is worthy of comment that his reference to being relieved from command of the Army of the Tennessee did not cite that it was he, Thomas, who made the request in order to pave the way for General Grant's restoration to command. His mentioning it at all was only to prove that he had not gone out of his way to seek advantage. The truth is he had done much to subordinate his own best interests for the benefit of others; and in this instance there is no evidence to show that Grant ever acknowledged it, although there is much to show that he by-passed Thomas consistently. What particularly disturbed Thomas by this change in command was that General Rosecrans, a rank outsider to the Army of the Ohio, and also his junior, was given the command. Perhaps Thomas was also aware that while he had remained in the service since his graduation from the Military Academy in 1840, Rosecrans had been out of it since 1854; and even if Rosecrans had been his senior in rank it would have been a somewhat bitter pill to swallow.

What is difficult to believe, from the correspondence between Generals Halleck and Thomas, is that President Lincoln, in order to "justify" Rosecrans's promotion, changed the date of Rosecrans's commission from August 16, 1862 to March 21, 1862. This placed him ahead of Thomas, whose commission was dated April 25, 1862. It is not clear just why the President would resort to such an obviously dishonest act; he had the authority after all as commander in chief to make any changes in command he felt necessary. Cullum's *Biographical Register of the Officers and Cadets* of the United States Military Academy, Vol. 2, shows Rosecrans's promotion to major general on the same date as allegedly changed by the President.[6] Whether particulars of the incident are correct or not, it is a sad commentary on the system of promotion in vogue, which permitted an officer, in this instance Rosecrans, with ten years' less professional military experience, to be advanced over one with the ability of General Thomas. Rosecrans had won a minor action, at Rich Mountain, West Virginia, described later, but it had little basis for comparison with Thomas's record.

General Halleck wrote to General Thomas on November 15, 1862, in reply to his protest:

Your letter of October 30 is just received. I cannot better state my appreciation of you as a general than by referring you to the

---

6. George W. Cullum, *Biographical Register of Officers and Cadets of the U. S. Military Academy* (Boston, 1891), Vol. 2, p. 42.

fact that at Pittsburg Landing I urged upon the Secretary of War to secure your appointment as major-general, in order that I might place you in command of the right wing of the army over your then superiors. It was through my urgent solicitations that you were commissioned.

When it was determined to relieve General Buell another person was spoken of as his successor and it was through my repeated solicitations that you were appointed. You having virtually declined the command at that time it was necessary to appoint another, and General Rosecrans was selected.

You are mistaken about General Rosecrans being your junior. His commission dates prior to yours. But that is of little importance, for the law gives to the President the power to assign without regard to dates, and he has seen fit to exercise it in this and many other cases.

Rest assured, general, that I fully appreciate your military capacity, and will do everything in my power to give you an independent command when an opportunity offers.

It was not possible to give you the command in Tennessee after you had once declined it.[7]

This was the Government's thanks to the man who had given everything for the Union, his state, his family, and his friends, not omitting his faultless contribution as commander in the first Union victory of consequence at Mill Springs. In justice to Halleck, it seems clear that he had nothing to do with this slight to Thomas. In fact, there is much to suggest that Halleck thought highly of Thomas and that he was disposed to give him an independent army. It is very likely that someone more influential than Halleck, perhaps the President himself, exerted the necessary influence in favor of Rosecrans. In Don Piatt's biography of General Thomas he described a scene in which President Lincoln and several members of his Cabinet discussed Buell's successor. Secretary of the Treasury Chase was in favor of General Rosecrans for the vacancy and Secretary of War Edwin M. Stanton favored General Thomas. After listening patiently to both men, the President said, "Let the Virginian wait; we will try Rosecrans." Piatt also stated that he was in Secretary Stanton's office when he returned from the conference with the President, and that his first words were, "Well, you have your choice of idiots; now look for frightful disaster."[8] Only time, and the unsurpassed ability of General Thomas, would confirm the prophecy of Stanton; for at Chickamauga, that near-disaster,

---

7. *Official Records, op. cit.*, Vol. XVI, Part 2, p. 663.

8. Donn Piatt, *General George H. Thomas* (Cincinnati, 1891), pp. 198-99.

when dusk descended upon a field of blood and destruction that possibly just missed marking the day on which Southern independence was won, Thomas saved the day, the Army of the Cumberland, Chattanooga, and the West. Genius finally triumphed over the numerous errors of omission and commission, and by the triumph was a sorely tried nation enabled to utilize that genius in its preservation. If Thomas was the logical man to replace Buell while at Louisville, where it was first offered him while he requested Buell's retention, nothing had occurred in the interval of a few weeks to render him less eligible.

General Thomas replied to General Halleck's letter on November 21:

I have the honor to acknowledge the receipt of your letter of the 15th instant and to thank you sincerely for the kindness of its tone.

I should not have addressed you in the first place if I had known that General Rosecrans's commission dated prior to mine. The letter was written not because I desired a command but for being superseded as I supposed, by a junior in rank when I felt there was no cause for so treating me.

I have no objection whatever to serving under General Rosecrans now that I know his commission dates prior to mine, but I must confess that I should feel very deeply mortified should the President place a junior over me without just cause, although the law authorizes him to do so should he see fit.[9]

General Rosecrans possessed military skill of a high order, any argument to the contrary notwithstanding, a statement readily susceptible of proof by his record. This record should not be completely erased by one incident, that of the unfortunate dispatch to General Thomas J. Wood at Chickamauga, in which Wood was ordered to close up on Reynolds. Obedience to this order opened a wide gap in the Union line; the Confederates under General Longstreet poured through; the right and the center of the Union army were rolled up in confusion bringing to an end Rosecrans's otherwise illustrious career; and General Thomas, in salvaging what was left of the army, earned the long overdue command of the army with which he had been so long identified.

Rosecrans was a man of above-average ability in planning and executing a campaign. A native of Ohio, as were Generals Buell, Garfield, Grant, and Sherman, among others, he was graduated from West Point in 1842, fifth in a class of fifty-six, and was assigned to the en-

---

9. *Official Records, op. cit.*, Vol. XVI, Part 2, p. 663.

gineers. This class included John Pope, destined to suffer a disastrous defeat at the Second Battle of Manassas, and General Abner Doubleday, the reputed father of the great American game of baseball, among the more prominent Union generals. General Daniel H. Hill and General James Longstreet, the latter nicknamed "Old Pete" by his comrades, who graduated near the bottom of his class but was anything but third from the bottom in military achievements, were two of the better-known graduates who served in the Confederacy.[10]

The game of politics was played to the hilt during the Civil War period, and many generals owed their appointments entirely to their connections with influential politicians. Undoubtedly such influence was brought to bear upon President Lincoln in his naming of General Rosecrans to replace General Buell. Buell was not popular with men of abolitionist leanings like, for example, Governor Andrew Johnson of Tennessee, who clamored for his replacement. When General Thomas appealed for General Buell's retention in command, those who were against Buell were fortified in their suspicions that Thomas was of the same mold. Although it is not certain that President Lincoln was swayed by these people in selecting Rosecrans, it is reasonable to assume that he was considerate toward them. It has been contended that Rosecrans, a Catholic, had a wide following among Abolitionists by reason of the very fundamentals of his faith. The well-known lack of sympathy by some of the Catholic clergy toward the United States, in its armed conflict with those states leaving the Union, was believed a factor in Lincoln's selection of Rosecrans. This Catholic point of view held that the struggle was a war originating in an atmosphere of Puritanism, in which those of opposite sects were subjected to religious persecution. Having this in mind, and the knowledge that many soldiers of Irish origin were serving in the Union army, Lincoln was believed to have felt that Rosecrans's appointment would win more Catholic support. If this was the thinking of President Lincoln, it would go far in explaining the changing of the date of Rosecrans's commission to make him "senior" to Thomas.[11]

General Rosecrans had distinguished himself at the Battle of Rich Mountain, West Virginia, while serving under General George Brinton McClellan. This battle, fought on July 11, 1862, reflected great credit upon General Rosecrans. General McClellan, as chief in command, with twenty thousand troops, was hesitating over what action to take when General Rosecrans asked his permission to lead a force of two thousand men against the strongly fortified position on Rich Mountain. This point was held by General John C. Pegram and was

10. Cullum, *op. cit.*, Vol. II, p. 42.
11. Piatt, *op. cit.*, p. 200.

accessible, except by a frontal attack, only by a bridle path that lay to the rear of the Confederate position. McClellan granted the request only on condition that Rosecrans would inform him at once when he was in position, so that he, McClellan, could attack the position simultaneously in front. The element of surprise was lost, however, when the attackers were discovered. Nevertheless, they fought bravely with their muskets and succeeded in driving General Pegram and his force into the mountains. Later, as a result of this victory, Confederate General Robert S. Garnett and his entire command were captured.[12]

The victory at Rich Mountain had nationwide implications for such a small engagement, not the least of which was the catapulting of both General McClellan and General Rosecrans into national prominence. The North, hungry for victory, seized upon even this small success and acclaimed both generals as heroes. McClellan, as chief, was given undue credit, but it helped him in obtaining command of the Army of the Potomac. If Rosecrans failed to receive full recognition for his fine success, there was enough left to him to aid in his appointment to succeed Buell. It would not be too long after the appointment before General Halleck commenced his badgering, as he had done with General Buell. One wonders whether Halleck, in the peaceful environment at Washington, and looking back to his "pick and shovel campaign," might have been dissatisfied with Rosecrans and Buell because they were not using their picks and shovels in the same type of wasted effort he performed before the Confederates abandoned Corinth. Whatever may have been in Halleck's mind, he sent a dispatch to Rosecrans on December 4, 1862, and again placed the blame for his criticism on someone else:

The President is very impatient at your long stay in Nashville. The favorable season for your campaign will soon be over. You give Bragg time to supply himself by plundering the very country your army could have occupied. From all information received here, it is believed that he is carrying large quantities of stores into Alabama, and preparing to fall back partly on Chattanooga and partly on Columbia, Miss. Twice have I been asked to designate someone else to command your army. If you remain one more week at Nashville, I cannot prevent your removal. As I wrote you when you took the command, the Government demands action, and if you cannot respond to that demand someone else will be tried.[13]

12. *Ibid.*, pp. 196-97.
13. *Official Records, op. cit.*, Vol. XXII, Part 2, pp. 117-18.

That same day Rosecrans replied with a vigor that stamped him as a man of character, courage, and ability. One of the keys to understanding the reason for the lengthy duration of the Civil War is to note the instances in which Washington was able to exert pressure on field commanders to move into action before they were ready. This occurred most strikingly at First Bull Run, Second Bull Run, Fredericksburg, and Chancellorsville, in all of which battles the Federals were defeated overwhelmingly. Whether his detractors admit it or not, and conceding that he was somewhat cautious, in addition to being misinformed about the strength of his enemy, which made him overcautious, McClellan, like Thomas, would not make the mistake of being goaded into premature action. It was not without reason that General Lee is reported to have answered, "McClellan, by all odds,"[14] when asked to name the greatest general he faced.

Rosecrans's reply to Halleck, full and to the point, follows:

> Your dispatch received. I reply in few but earnest words. I have lost no time. Everything I have done was necessary, absolutely so; and has been done as rapidly as possible. Any attempt to advance sooner would have increased our difficulty both in front and rear. In front, because of greater obstacles, enemies in greater force, and fighting with better chances of escaping pursuit, if overthrown in battle. In rear, because of insufficiency and uncertainty of supplies, both of subsistence and ammunition, and no security of any kind to fall back upon in case of disaster. . . . Many of our soldiers are to this day barefoot, without blankets, without tents, without good arms, and cavalry without horses. Our true objective now is the enemy's force, for if they come near, we save wear, tear, risk, and strength. . . . If the Government which ordered me here confides in my judgment, it may rely on my continuing to do what I have been trying to do—that is, my whole duty. If my superiors have lost confidence in me, they had better at once put some one in my place and let the future test the propriety of the change. I have but one word to add, which is, that I need no other stimulus to make me do my duty than the knowledge of what it is. To threats of removal or the like I must be permitted to say I am insensible.[15]

It is doubtful if anything more straightforward and to the target, and at the same time productive of placing field commanders and Washington in proper perspective toward each other, was expressed

---

14. Robert E. Lee, Jr., *Recollections and Letters of General Lee* (New York, 1926), pp. 415-16.

15. *Official Records, op. cit.*, Vol. XXII, Part 2, p. 118.

during the whole course of the war than these magnificent words from Rosecrans.

Seventeen years later, General Rosecrans told the story of his conversation with General Thomas, following his replacement of General Buell, in his letter to the membership of the Society of the Army of the Cumberland. Excerpts from this letter, describing his experience with Thomas, are interesting and revealing, as shown below:

Having been first attracted to him when in the United States [Military] Academy, two years my senior by what I thought his remarkable resemblance to Stuart's portrait of Washington, I always retained for him both respect and friendship, substantial proofs of which were given in my recommending him for commandant of the battalion of the Virginia Military Institute, which he declined, and for Instructor of Artillery at the United States Military Academy, for which he was detailed.

On assuming command of the Army of the Ohio, at Bowling Green, October 27, 1862, it was to me no ordinary pleasure to know that one so long and greatly esteemed was the senior Major-General of that noble body of soldiers soon, and for all after time in the annals of our country, to be known as the Army of the Cumberland.

Certain that I was two years his junior in the Corps of Cadets, and believing I was six months his junior as Major-General, and not long previously having declined the command of this very army, a struggle arose in his mind between his sense of military propriety and his desire dutifully to serve his country wherever placed by superior orders. On his arrival at Bowling Green for duty, like the frank and loyal soldier and gentleman he always was, he explained his dilemma, saying to me: "There is no one under whom I would more willingly serve than yourself, but under the circumstances, which I know you appreciate, I hope you will cooperate in getting me ordered to Texas, where, with my previous knowledge of the country, I may be especially useful to the service."

I reminded him that this command came to me wholly unsought; that the interests of our country demanded self-sacrificing cooperation from all her children; that if the government had so willed, I would gladly have served under him; that, anticipating the questions of rank, it had antedated my Major-General's appointment to the 21st of March, ult.; and while thus made consonant with the proprieties of rank, the best interests of the

Nation demanded his services with that army, adding reasons to which his judgment yielded assent. Having thus secured his services with us, I offered him his choice of an independent command, or to be second and executive officer of the entire army.

You all know his choice and the sequel. How devotedly he stood by the Army of the Cumberland. How thoroughly he promoted its drill, efficiency, discipline, and that especial element and mark of its greatness and glory, its unity.[16]

General Rosecrans's letter is in conflict with General Thomas's letter of November 21 to Halleck, quoted previously, in which Thomas stated he was not aware that Rosecrans's commission antedated his. The meeting with Thomas, referred to in Rosecrans's letter, was on November 1, or twenty days prior to Thomas's reply to Halleck. Furthermore, the indignation expressed by Thomas to Halleck later, upon learning that Rosecrans's commission had been changed, proves that Rosecrans misled Thomas, or to be blunt, he was not entirely truthful in the matter. Speculation that "all's well that ends well" is one thing, but it is disappointing to realize that the maxim "The heights by great men reached and kept, were not attained by sudden flight" is not always true. Too often, as in this example, and no one can question Rosecran's ability, promotion is based upon political expediency and not otherwise.

General Rosecrans offered Thomas the role of second in command, but he was in no mood to continue in a meaningless position. Instead, he asked for a well-defined command that would give him personal responsibility for failure and personal credit for success. This Rosecrans agreed to, and on November 5 he issued, in General Orders No. 8, the notice that Thomas was assigned to the center of the army in command of five divisions under Generals Rousseau, Negley, Dumont, Fry, and Palmer. General Alexander McCook was assigned to the right wing and General Thomas Crittenden to the left.[17] This was a force that in the months to come, despite many hardships and mistakes, would write its name imperishably in the history of the United States.

In retrospect, General Thomas had received a number of discouraging and certainly undeserved setbacks, as, for example, his near replacement by General Ormsby M. Mitchel, following Thomas's

---

16. Society of the Army of the Cumberland, *Yearbook, 1879* (Cincinnati: Robert Clarke and Co., 1880), pp. 173-74.

17. Piatt, *op. cit.*, p. 202; Thomas B. Van Horne, *The Life of Major General George H. Thomas* (New York: Charles Scribner's Sons, 1882), p. 89; *Official Records, op. cit.*, Vol. XX, Part 2, p. 11.

proposed invasion of East Tennessee through Cumberland Gap. At another time, following the Battle of Mill Springs, for which he received little credit, President Lincoln nominated him for the rank of major general, but the Senate failed to confirm it. If the nomination had been approved, and on the basis of merited promotion it should have been approved, the President would have had difficulty in justifying his by-passing of Thomas by antedating the commission of Rosecrans. Thomas would then have been the unquestioned successor to General Buell.

Furthermore, his rank and his record would have been more than enough to outweigh any consideration of Grant when he was named commander in chief of all the armies in 1864. Not only would Thomas's commission have antedated Grant's, dated July 4, 1863, but Thomas would then have been in command of the Army of the Cumberland at Chickamauga. In that event there would have been no near-defeat; instead, the result would have been unquestionably a Union victory on a par with Mill Springs and Nashville. This is not speculation in any sense of the word; the stand of Thomas on Horseshoe Ridge is alone sufficient to prove his unmatched genius in facing great odds and wresting victory from defeat. What he could and would have done, acting independently and without the obstacle of near-destruction due to mistakes of others, requires little to justify faith in his ability to defeat Bragg decisively. If this great general, "the Rock of Chickamauga," did not perform the outstanding achievement of the Civil War in that engagement, the one who deserves that honor has not been named.

One does not need to dig into reams of material to prove the right of Thomas to command all the Union armies. On the record, if the fate of the nation had rested upon one battle, the leader to have been entrusted with that battle was none other than General Thomas. The mere placing of the records of Generals Grant and Thomas on the line, face upward, after Chickamauga, would have compelled the selection of Thomas. What a morsel for contemporary historians to feast upon; that is, if Thomas instead of Grant had been named commander of the Army of the Potomac! What more could be asked by the Civil War enthusiast than to speculate on the encounters between the two greatest soldiers produced on the American continent up to that time, namely, Robert E. Lee and George H. Thomas? As if to lend additional flavor to the thought, both men were stalwarts in every aspect of human life available to a soldier, and both were Virginians. If Lee was great in getting the maximum of performance from his troops by rapid movement, Thomas was equally great in standing his ground and never once yielding his position to the enemy despite the odds.

If Lee was the knight in shining armor, the gentleman, the humanitarian, the master soldier, the leader who was adored by his troops, Thomas was not less so in any particular.

The campaign of attrition so consistently followed by General Grant at the great bloodletting battles of the Wilderness, Spottsylvania, and Cold Harbor would not have been the policy of General Thomas. There is nothing in the record of Thomas to suggest, even remotely, that he would have employed tactics so productive of the awful losses in these battles. He would not have attacked until he was ready; and when the time came for him to strike it would have been with the force of a mighty sledge. That is the record. If Lee had struck first, and that is the probability, Thomas would have been prepared to counter his blows. What is certain is that he would not have been surprised, and, of all the things we know about him, he would not have been outfought nor defeated. All of this assumes the grappling of two mighty and somewhat numerically equal armies; but this assumption is unrealistic since Thomas probably would have outnumbered Lee by at least two to one, as Grant and his predecessors often did. This would have been a rare experience for Thomas, who seldom fought with odds on his side. The Army of the Cumberland, except on rare occasions, was not favored by a preponderance of numbers; and when it was so favored it was generally the advantage needed by an attacker against an intrenched defender.

The combination of Rosecrans and Thomas was an ideal one. Rosecrans was a man of unusual energy and spared neither himself nor his subordinates in performing his military duties. He set a furious pace and often worked as late as two and three o'clock in the morning. His staff members were under pressure to keep up with him, and it was not unusual for some of them to fall asleep while he wrote or pored over his maps.[18]

While at Bowling Green, after taking command of the Army of the Cumberland, he reviewed the various units of his force, a loss of time that he made up at night by working on his reports and other paperwork. The men in the ranks were at first merely receptive to him, but after learning of his industry and concern for their welfare they became enthusiastic. He was critical of their equipment, not only with respect to the lack of it, but also regarding what he could observe that was not up to his high standard. A private without his canteen was subjected to a barrage of questions, as, for example, "Where is your canteen?" or "How did you lose it?" or "Why don't you get another?" To others, for example, he would say, "You need

---

18. W. D. Bickham, *Rosecrans' Campaign With the Fourteenth Army Corps* (Cincinnati, 1863), p. 28.

shoes," or "You need a knapsack," and so on. He would usually admonish those deficient in supplies and equipment to petition their company officers for them and to go as high as the division commander if necessary. It was but natural that such interest compelled a sense of devotion and loyalty to Rosecrans that did much to maintain the high morale of his command.[19]

After General Thomas reported at Bowling Green, he became, in effect, Rosecrans's chief of staff. Rosecrans consulted him often, a matter that affected the members of the staff deeply. It was noticeable that Rosecrans showed marked respect and confidence toward Thomas, and that conversations between the two men were long and frequent. All of this had a very happy effect upon those in the ranks who did the hand-to-hand fighting, and who felt that Thomas should have succeeded Buell.

It is deserving of comment that one author, in writing of Thomas in 1863, stated in part as follows: "Most men diminish as you approach them. A few magnify, and you feel their greatness. General Thomas grows upon you. Even his physique has this peculiarity. He has a massive, full rounded, powerful form, which seems at first to absorb several inches of his six feet of stature, but it gradually expands upon you, as a mountain which you approach. His features are heavy but well-carved, with a strong, thin combative nose, cleanly cut lips and great square jaws and chin, indicating that firmness which he develops so grandly in battle. . . . He is altogether a soldier, simple in deportment and unaffected, without a soldier's vanity. He is a close observer, but a better thinker. . . . You cannot doubt his firmness. . . . No perfect history of the war of the rebellion in which Major-General George H. Thomas, of Virginia, does not figure conspicuously, can be written."[20]

General Halleck had conceived a plan of campaign into East Tennessee that did not provide adequate protection of Nashville. This demonstrated his lack of understanding of the over-all problem and confirmed General Buell's judgment in concentrating the army in reasonable proximity to Nashville. General Bragg withdrew from Kentucky to Murfreesboro, where he joined General John C. Breckinridge's command. Breckinridge had been left there to observe the movements of the garrison force posted by Buell at Nashville during Bragg's invasion of Kentucky. His force numbered about ten thousand men, in the ratio of about one-third of cavalry to two-thirds of infantry. The cavalry was commanded by Generals Joseph Wheeler and Nathan Bedford Forrest. The principal inconvenience from these

19. *Ibid.*, pp. 29-30.
20. *Ibid.*, pp. 31-32.

capable commanders was in the occasional interruption of Federal communications between Nashville and the North.[21]

Nashville was somewhat in a state of siege during Bragg's Kentucky invasion, a period in which frequent skirmishing occurred between garrison pickets and scouting parties from Murfreesboro. Lieutenant Colonel A. Van Schrader established a system of well-supervised pickets and blockhouses. These were strong enough to discourage attacks by the Confederates. Nevertheless, General Forrest obtained permission from General Bragg to attack Nashville with his three thousand cavalry and General Roger Hanson's four thousand infantry, and on November 6 they made a demonstration by way of the Murfreesboro pike. They succeeded in driving forward the Federal pickets, but an order came from Bragg to stop the action as the infantry was about to attack. Forrest was greatly disappointed; in fact, he was furious at being ordered to withdraw from an action that held such great promise of success. Nevertheless, in obedience to orders he withdrew after some skirmishing with the Nashville outposts.[22]

General Bragg's commitment of the ten thousand troops under General Breckinridge to watch Nashville was believed by many to be a serious mistake, since these troops would have been of considerable aid in his invasion. It was felt that his force, with these troops, would have given him a superiority over General Buell's command in the ratio of something like three to two. Bragg was perhaps correct, however, in avoiding a fight for Nashville, since Southern sympathizers in the territory occupied by Federal troops would have been subjected to rough treatment. This would not have been enough to compensate for a temporary occupation of Nashville.[23]

The Louisville and Nashville Railroad was restored as far as Mitchellville; General John H. Morgan's cavalry had damaged the railroad from there to Nashville. General Thomas was instructed to advance General Dumont's and General Fry's divisions to Gallatin, at which point they arrived on November 12 to complete repairs to the railroad into Nashville. For several weeks his troops were occupied in repairing the tunnel south of Mitchellville, but during that time he was also engaged in transporting supplies by wagon, a distance of thirty-five miles, to Nashville.[24]

In the meantime, General Crittenden crossed the Cumberland River and established a position at Silver Springs. On November 18,

---

21. Henry M. Cist, *The Army of the Cumberland* (New York, 1882), p. 78.
22. *Ibid.*, pp. 79-80.
23. *Ibid.*
24. *Ibid.*, pp. 77-79; Van Horne, *Cumberland*, Vol. I, p. 211.

he moved leisurely toward Nashville, and General Dumont, with two brigades, advanced to Gallatin, while General Scott's brigade marched from Glasgow to Hartsville. General Rosecrans had already established his headquarters at Nashville on November 9, although he did not arrive in person until November 20, preparatory to concentrating his army and marching on the enemy near Murfreesboro. The Confederate cavalry was actively seeking to disrupt Rosecrans's plans for moving to Nashville, in particular to interfere with the movement of supply trains, annoy outposts, and overwhelm weak and isolated detachments. In addition to these several kinds of interruption, General Bragg's cavalry was able to cover the main objectives of his army. Ignorance of Bragg's plans did not prevent Rosecrans from making headway with his own, despite these attempts to interfere with him. His forces were moved nearer to Nashville, even before railroad communications were re-established between Nashville and Louisville.[25]

On December 7, Hartsville was the scene of a severe and humiliating defeat for the Union forces. Colonel John H. Morgan, the great Confederate cavalry leader, with a force variously estimated at from fifteen hundred to four thousand men, attacked the Thirty-ninth Brigade, numbering about two thousand seven hundred men. After a fight lasting about an hour and a quarter, in which casualties on each side were estimated at more than one hundred and fifty, the entire Federal force was captured. This detachment, under the command of Colonel A. B. Moore, had been assigned by General Thomas to guard the ford of the Cumberland River and to watch and report on Confederate activities on the Lebanon road.[26]

Morgan planned for a complete surprise, but reports of his movements are many and contradictory. It is generally agreed that he was in the Union camp before being discovered, a point needing little confirmation in view of his complete success. This disgraceful incident is attributable either to faulty or nonexistent picketing or to the failure of the pickets to perform their assigned responsibilities. When first discovered, Morgan's men were marching toward a ravine at the foot of the hill on which Moore's troops were posted, a circumstance that does not appear to have made the Confederate move a complete surprise. Although the reports are confusing in the extreme, it appears that Colonel Moore lacked a plan or comprehension of the minimum requirements for safeguarding his command. Apparently nothing had

---

25. Van Horne, *ibid.*, pp. 211-12.

26. Frederick Phister, *Statistical Record, Campaigns of the Civil War* (New York: Jack Brussel, a reprint, no date), p. 215; *Official Records, op. cit.*, Vol. XX, Part 1, p. 45; Van Horne, *Cumberland*, Vol. I, 214; Cist, *op. cit.*, p. 82.

been done to protect his position; neither does it appear that he had done anything to resist an attack. In addition to these serious drawbacks, a portion of the troops did not exhibit the elementary subjection to discipline and good order necessary to success. It goes without saying that this disgraceful conduct brought questioning from both General Halleck and General Rosecrans. Rosecrans interrogated Thomas twice on December 7, asking for an explanation of the disaster. Thomas replied that the 104th Illinois Infantry suffered over eighty casualties, whereas the other two regiments, the 106th and 108th Ohio Infantry, suffered insignificant losses, indicating that the latter two regiments behaved badly. General Halleck naturally reported the President's concern in his dispatch of December 9, demanding a prompt reply from Rosecrans, assigning responsibility.[27]

In justification of the presence of troops at Hartsville, General Rosecrans told Halleck of the lack of cavalry and the need for garrisoning the far-flung lines of communication. This force was sufficiently strong to cope with the enemy if minimum security measures had been employed. Rosecrans failed to give the names of those responsible, but Halleck, not to be denied, demanded in his dispatch of December 10 that he do so, and stated that whoever was responsible would be punished. Colonel Limberg and Captain Good of the 108th Ohio, both of whom escaped capture, reported to Rosecrans, as a basis for his reply to Halleck, "that Federal artillery did nothing to disturb the enemy; that only two companies of skirmishers turned out; that infantry stood in line of battle at 'ordered arms' and allowed the enemy to dismount and advance, as skirmishers, within 100 yards before they commenced firing. The artillery allowed the enemy's mountain howitzers, and probably two other pieces, to move up into position without disturbing them. It was finally brought out of the woods, and fired a few shots, with little effect, as the enemy advanced in line of skirmishers. Closing in, our troops soon fell into confusion, ran to their camp in a crowd, where the enemy's artillery played on them and they soon hoisted a white flag and surrendered. The behavior of the Second Indiana Cavalry seems to have been as spiritless as their picketing. The enemy exchanged their Austrian for our Springfield rifles and drove their prisoners across the river, waist deep, and retreated so hastily that, when support came up, a light battalion of cavalry chased them across the river and recaptured three of the thirty wagons they had captured." Rosecrans estimated that the enemy force aggregated twenty-five hundred men.[28]

---

27. Van Horne, *Cumberland*, Vol. I, pp. 214-15; *Official Records, op. cit.*, Vol. XX, Part 1, pp. 41-45.

28. *Official Records, ibid.*, p. 44; Van Horne, *Cumberland*, p. 215.

It is of more than passing interest to note that Lieutenant Colonel Gustavus Tafel, commanding the 106th Ohio Infantry, in his report on Hartsville to General Rosecrans, gave the distinct impression that the enemy wore the uniform of the United States. After reporting that Colonel Moore, the camp commander, had surrendered, he stated: "At this juncture men came riding up, wearing United States uniforms, waving their hats and telling us to surrender like the rest; but I cried out to the men not to listen, and that General Dumont was near with reinforcements. The men accordingly made another stand, but were quickly surrounded by the then otherwise wholly disengaged aggregate force of the enemy."

In another report, Captain Carlo Piepho, commander of the 108th Ohio Infantry, stated that there were no outposts posted, where needed, to warn of the approach of the enemy, and that his command was equipped with the totally worthless Austrian rifle.[29] If this report is correct, and it is the official record as reported by the regimental commander, it goes some distance in lightening the blame attaching to Brigade Commander Moore. Furthermore, the statement of Lieutenant Colonel Tafel of the 106th Ohio would have some bearing also in softening the blame on Colonel Moore. Wearing the uniform of your enemy while engaged with him in mortal combat is not looked upon by civilized nations as in the best tradition of chivalry.

The Hartsville raid was undoubtedly a source of extreme embarrassment to General Thomas, although he was not in the slightest particular responsible for it. The highly political nature of the appointment of officers, particularly up to and including the rank of colonel, was one of the worst evils army commanders were called upon to face. Thomas knew that his own staff organization was weak, as also did Rosecrans; only several weeks previously, Rosecrans asked Halleck's permission to reorganize his own staff, but such authority was not received. Political considerations outweighed military necessity, and all because the Administration was responsive to the demands of Congressmen, Senators, friends of supporters of those holding public office, and others who sought and obtained rank for those having little or no military experience.

After repairs to the Louisville and Nashville Railroad were completed on November 26, the following month was devoted to assembling supplies and equipment preparatory to the advance of Rosecrans's army on the enemy at Murfreesboro. General Thomas, having performed magnificently in repairing the railroad and in forwarding equipment and supplies, moved his command, the center of the Army of the Cumberland, to Nashville on December 22. There he

---

29. *Official Records, ibid.,* pp. 58-60.

concentrated the divisions of Generals Johnson and Negley, and General Walker's brigade of General Fry's division, under his personal command. The other components of his force, General J. J. Reynolds's division and the remaining two brigades of Fry's division, were guarding the Louisville and Nashville Railroad. Thomas's remaining division, under General R. B. Mitchell, was assigned to garrison duty at Nashville.[30]

General McCook and his three divisions, commanded respectively by General Richard W. Johnson, Jefferson C. Davis, and Philip H. Sheridan, were at Nashville; also General Thomas L. Crittenden and his three divisions, under Generals Thomas J. Wood, John M. Palmer, and Horatio P. Van Cleve, had moved to Nashville and were located along the Franklin, Nolensville, and Murfreesboro turnpikes. General Rosecrans was aware that General Bragg's two corps, under Generals Leonidas Polk and Kirby Smith, were at or near Murfreesboro, both fully protected by outposts; also that General William J. Hardee was on the Shelbyville and Nolensville turnpike, between Triune and Nolensville, with an advance guard at the latter place.[31]

On December 26, General Rosecrans ordered the three wings of his army, consisting of the right, the center, and the left, under Generals Alexander McCook, George H. Thomas, and Thomas L. Crittenden, to move toward Murfreesboro. Crittenden's brother, Confederate General George B. Crittenden, was defeated by General Thomas at Mill Springs on January 19. General McCook advanced to Triune on the Nolensville pike; General Thomas on the Franklin and Wilkinson pikes; and General Crittenden on the Murfreesboro pike. The objective of Rosecrans was to turn the Confederate right flank under Hardee at Triune. When General Bragg became aware of Rosecrans's purpose, he recalled Hardee to Murfreesboro; meanwhile, Generals McCook, Thomas, and Crittenden continued toward Murfreesboro.[32]

When General McCook resumed his advance on December 27, he discovered General Hardee's army lined up in preparation for battle. A heavy fog made friend and foe alike indistinguishable at one hundred and fifty yards, and an engagement more than ordinarily hazardous. Since his cavalry had fired upon his own infantry, McCook ordered a halt until the fog lifted around noon. Johnson's and Sheridan's divisions pursued Hardee's force and bivouacked that night at Wilson's Creek, but not before repairing the bridge damaged

30. Cist, *op. cit.*, pp. 81, 87.

31. *Ibid.*, p. 87.

32. *Ibid.*, pp. 87-88; *West Point Atlas of American Wars* (New York: Frederick Praeger, 1959), p. 77.

by Hardee's withdrawing troops. After ascertaining that Hardee had continued to Murfreesboro, McCook left Colonel Philemon P. Baldwin at Triune, on December 29, to protect his own right flank, while he continued with the rest of his force toward Murfreesboro on the Bole Jack road.[33]

As General McCook neared Murfreesboro and observed that the Confederates were in a position to give battle, he arranged his own troops accordingly and encamped for the night. On the morning of December 30, McCook's entire command, including the brigade left to guard the bridge at Triune, advanced by way of the Wilkinson pike until his forward troops encountered Confederate pickets. The troops deployed immediately, with Sheridan's left on the right of the Wilkinson pike and to the right of General James S. Negley's division on the left of the turnpike. Davis's division occupied a position on Sheridan's right, and Johnson's division was to the right of Davis, whose division was the extreme right of the army. McCook's skirmishers clashed almost immediately with enemy skirmishers and pushed them slowly back, with a loss of about seventy-five men in Sheridan's division and about two hundred in Davis's division. Despite these Union losses, disclosure of the entire Confederate position was made by sundown and may be regarded as some justification for these casualties. One of the important occurrences of the day was the considerable damage to Federal supply trains by Confederate cavalry, which rode around the whole Union army.[34]

General Bragg had established a defensive position, including light intrenchments, about two miles west of Murfreesboro. His right, under General Breckinridge, rested on the right of meandering Stones River and curved slightly beyond the right of the Lebanon pike. His left and center, commanded respectively by Generals Hardee and Polk, extended beyond the left of the Franklin road, from a point where the Nashville and Chattanooga Railroad intersected. His left was on the eastern side of Stones River and his center on the western side, on what is known as the West Fork of that river. Several bridges spanned the river, which, in addition to the many fords available, provided ready movement across it. It was realized that rising waters might isolate the troops under General Polk from the remainder of General Bragg's army. The area was dominated by a number of hills north of Murfreesboro and east of the river occupied by General Breckinridge. There were a number of clearings between the river and Overall Creek, but most of the ground was covered with heavy woods and scrub-cedar growth, which afforded cover while

---

33. Cist, *ibid.*, p. 89; *Atlas, ibid.*, p. 78.
34. Cist, *ibid.*, p. 90; *Atlas, ibid.*

providing somewhat limited troop movements. Bragg's reason for selecting this location is unclear, but it is possible that he desired to avoid the endangering of Murfreesboro while having the advantage of launching an offensive or defensive movement. He knew as early as December 26 that his opponent was advancing against him, the knowledge of which impelled him to select a battle site; also he ordered cavalry commanded by Generals Joseph Wheeler, John A. Wharton, and John Pegram, and three infantry brigades with artillery support, to delay Rosecrans until his own army was united.[35]

Since the expected Union attack did not develop on December 30, General Bragg ordered an attack on that army to be launched on the morning of the thirty-first. General Hardee's corps on the left, less Breckinridge's division, was to move southward, cross Stones River with support from Wharton's cavalry, and roll up the Union right flank under McCook. General Bragg's purpose was to push Rosecrans's entire army against the river, bottle it up, and probably capture the whole force.[36]

A meeting of corps commanders was held at Rosecrans's headquarters in the cedars near the Murfreesboro pike on the night of December 30, there to receive final instructions on the plan of battle. The plan was for General Crittenden on the Union left to move with his two divisions across the river and seize and occupy the ground held by General Breckinridge. This done, his artillery could sweep the entire Confederate position. McCook was ordered to open up on the Confederate center directly to his front, and thus prevent them from crossing from their position on the western side of the river. Rosecrans's center, under General Thomas, including General Palmer's division, was to make limited attacks in the center until General Crittenden had General Breckinridge surrounded. Crittenden was instructed to continue his advance, take Murfreesboro, and then move westward on the Franklin pike as rapidly as possible; if feasible he was to drive Breckinridge as far as Salem in the hope of cutting off his retreat and destroying him utterly. Following this movement, an over-all Union assault on the Confederate army would complete the work of destruction. McCook, for his part, also was ordered to build a series of campfires beyond his own right in order to give the impression of larger bodies of Union troops. It was through this plan that Rosecrans hoped to pin Bragg's army between the Federals and the river. Corps commanders were reminded that the Union strategy depended for success upon McCook's ability to hold his position for at least three hours; if he

35. Cist, *ibid.*, pp. 90, 99; *Atlas, ibid.*
36. Cist, *ibid.*, p. 99; *Atlas, ibid.*, pp. 78-79.

Major General George H. Thomas. (*From the Library of Congress*)

Diorama of Snodgrass Hill. The site on which General Thomas won the nickname of the Rock of Chickamauga, September 20, 1863. The diorama was made by Philip Braunstein of Rockville, Maryland. (*Owned and photographed by the author*)

Major General George H. Thomas. Painting by George Dury was authorized by the Tennessee Legislature in 1866. It hung in the State Capitol at Nashville for many years until it was restored in early 1963. (*Courtesy of the Tennessee State Library and Archives, Nashville, Tennessee*)

The Battle of Shiloh, Tennessee. The action depicts an engagement on April 7, 1862, when a Union regiment captured a Confederate battery. Generals Grant and Sherman were caught napping by the Confederates under General Albert Sidney Johnston, but nevertheless they luckily emerged the victors. (From the Library of Congress)

The Battle of Stones River or Murfreesboro, Tennessee, December 31, 1862, and January 1 and 2, 1863. Here the Union forces under General Rosecrans defeated the Confederate forces under General Bragg. General Thomas, in command of the Union center, reorganized the badly shattered forces in the midst of the battle, thus turning the tide when everything seemed lost. (From the Library of Congress)

The Battle of Chickamauga, September 19 and 20, 1863. A technical defeat for the Army of the Cumberland, but Thomas averted disaster on the afternoon of the 20th by his heroic stand on Snodgrass Hill and won the title of the Rock of Chickamauga. (*From the Library of Congress*)

The Battle of Missionary Ridge, November 25, 1863. With Sherman's forces bogged down, Grant called upon Thomas to attack the center of the ridge in hopes of creating a diversion to relieve the pressure on Sherman. The small figure is that of General Grant, and to his rear and left are Generals Granger and Thomas, standing on Orchard Knob, captured by Thomas's troops on November 23, 1863. (*From the Library of Congress*)

The Battle of Lookout Mountain (famed as the Battle Above the Clouds). Fought and won by General "Fighting Joe" Hooker, under General Thomas, November 24, 1863. (From the Library of Congress)

The Battle of Missionary Ridge, November 25, 1863. The Army of the Cumberland, under Thomas, was ordered to take the first rifle pits and never stopped until it had gained the heights and compelled the Confederate defenders to retreat in rout. Thomas's command has been given credit in this assault for one of the most magnificent feats of arms in military history. (*From the Library of Congress*)

The Battle of Resaca, May 13–15, 1864. During the march to Atlanta, this battle was the first major accomplishment of the Atlanta campaign, and forced Confederate General Johnston to begin his long series of magnificent retreats ending in the loss of Atlanta. (*From the Library of Congress*)

The Battle of Kenesaw Mountain. The assault by Sherman, opposed by Thomas, was fore-doomed to failure. Several thousand needless casualties were suffered, and not one small bene-fit was gained. (*From the Library of Congress*)

The Battle of Atlanta. The death of General James B. McPherson on July 22, 1864, near the end of the Atlanta campaign, is depicted. (*From the Library of Congress*)

The Battle of Nashville, December 15 and 16, 1864. Confederate General Hood's Army of Tennessee was virtually destroyed by Thomas and his hastily organized and inexperienced forces. This was the most devastating defeat suffered by an army during the entire Civil War. (*From the Library of Congress*)

The Heights of Monterey. A Mexican War battle, September 21–23, 1846, in which Thomas was brevetted for gallantry. (*From the Library of Congress*)

The Battle of Buena Vista, February 22 and 23, 1847, during the Mexican War, in which Thomas was again brevetted. One of the great battles of American history, in which the artillery of Thomas and O'Brien did much to earn victory for the American forces. (*From the Library of Congress*)

Major General Robert Anderson. He received the first Confederate attack of the Civil War at Fort Sumter. He selected Generals Sherman, Buell and Thomas to serve with him in Kentucky, each of whom commanded the Army of the Cumberland, in turn, following General Anderson. *(From the National Archives)*

Lieutenant General Braxton Bragg, Confederate States of America. He commanded the Army of the Tennessee and narrowly missed winning the war's greatest victory at Chickamauga by failing to follow up the opportunity created by a disastrous break in the Union line. Thomas's stand on Snodgrass Hill did much to wrest victory from Bragg. *(From the National Archives)*

Major General John M. Brannan. His troops opened the Battle of Chickamauga and were among the last to cease fighting. *(From the National Archives)*

Major General Don Carlos Buell. He succeeded General Anderson to the command of the Army of the Cumberland, but was relieved after the Battle of Perryville for not pursuing a sufficiently aggressive campaign during General Bragg's invasion of Kentucky. *(From the National Archives)*

Major General Jacob D. Cox. A splendid division commander who performed outstandingly in the Franklin and Nashville campaigns. An able historian of the Civil War, he was accused of authoring, in collaboration with General Schofield, the infamous letter (New York *Tribune,* March, 1870), which sought to give Schofield undeserved credit for planning the Battle of Nashville, and denying just recognition to General Thomas. *(From the National Archives)*

Major General Thomas L. Crittenden. A brother of General George Crittenden, Confederate commander defeated at the Battle of Mill Springs, Kentucky, January 19, 1862, by General Thomas. As commander of the 21st Corps at Chickamauga, Thomas Crittenden was court-martialed, but exonerated, following the rout of his troops in that action. *(From the National Archives)*

Major General Jefferson C. Davis. An able division commander and commander of the famous 14th Corps, he served creditably throughout the war. Davis was never brought to trial for the killing of General William Nelson, after Nelson's failure to apologize for an alleged insult. *(From the National Archives)*

Major General James B. Fry. He was Chief of Staff under General Buell, and is noted for his debunking of Sheridan's claim that he returned with his command to the field of Chickamauga following the rout. The War Department refused to silence him in a dispute with Sherman over an article by Fry, published in the *North American Review* of December, 1885, and referred to in the text. *(From the National Archives)*

Major General Kenner Garrard. After transferring from the Army of the Potomac, he distinguished himself in the Army of the Cumberland during the Chattanooga and Atlanta campaigns. *(From the Library of Congress)*

Major General James A. Garfield. He was Chief of Staff to General Rosecrans when both left the field of Chickamauga, although he returned to General Thomas on Snodgrass Hill. Elected President in 1881, he was assassinated by Charles Guiteau, a disappointed office seeker, shortly after taking office and died some months later. *(From the National Archives)*

Major General John B. Gordon, Confederate States of America. An able corps commander under General Lee, he served with distinction in a number of engagements fought by the Army of Northern Virginia. He gave one of the finest appraisals of Chickamauga to be found. *(From the National Archives)*

Major General Gordon Granger. He served during the siege of Corinth under General Halleck, became a corps commander, and distinguished himself by moving to Thomas's aid at Chickamauga. He served with distinction during the Chattanooga campaign, especially at Missionary Ridge. *(From the National Archives)*

Major General Henry W. Halleck. He wrote books on military and other subjects, a principal reason, perhaps, for his nickname of "Old Brains." A proven failure as a field commander, he was nevertheless President Lincoln's military adviser and general-in-chief until General Grant's accession to the chief command. *(From the National Archives)*

Lieutenant General John Bell Hood, Confederate States of America. He fought with distinction at Gettysburg and at Chickamauga, sustaining severe wounds. He succeeded General Johnston during the Atlanta campaign, but his reckless offensive actions could not stay the Union advance. His army was all but destroyed by General Thomas at Nashville and never reappeared as a fighting unit. *(From the Library of Congress)*

Major General Joseph Hooker. An able corps commander, he suffered the most complete Union defeat of the war at Chancellorsville when commanding the Army of the Potomac. He fought with conspicuous success under General Thomas in the Chattanooga battles and under Sherman in the Atlanta campaign. *(From the National Archives)*

Major General Oliver Otis Howard. The assault by General "Stonewall" Jackson on his 11th Corps did much to bring defeat to General Hooker at Chancellorsville. Nevertheless, he was an inspirational and successful corps commander, particularly under Thomas in the Chatttanooga campaign and under Sherman in the Atlanta campaign. *(From the National Archives)*

Major General Erasmus D. Keyes. A long-time friend and former commander of General Thomas during their early days in the army. He has left some fine comments regarding the high character of Thomas. Served wtih distinction in the Army of the Potomac. (From the National Archives)

Major General Judson Kilpatrick. A leading Civil War cavalry commander who fought with distinction in a number of major engagements, including Gettysburg. Served with Sherman in the March to the Sea, in which he commandeered the best animals, leaving Thomas with insufficient and inadequate cavalry to fight against Hood. (From the National Archives)

Major General John A. Logan. Among the best of the political generals of the war. He fought with Grant at Fort Donelson, at Vicksburg, and with Sherman in the Atlanta campaign. (From the National Archives)

Lieutenant General James Longstreet. One of the superior corps commanders, "Old Pete" was known as Lee's war horse. His war record was as long as the proverbial arm. Following his famous breakthrough which wrought near-disaster on the Union Army of the Cumberland, he was repulsed by Thomas on Snodgrass Hill. Only the mighty stand by Thomas saved the day. (From the National Archives)

Major General James B. McPherson. He served under Grant at Vicksburg and did well in the Atlanta campaign as commander of the Army of the Tennessee. He was killed approaching Atlanta, following his attempt at escape when asked to surrender. (*From the National Archives*)

Major General James B. McPherson. He served under Grant at Vicksburg and did well in the Atlanta campaign as commander of the Army of the Tennessee. He was killed approaching Atlanta, following his attempt at escape when asked to surrender. (*From the National Archives*)

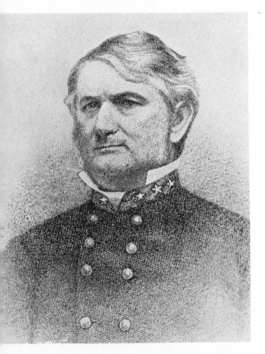

Lieutenant General Leonidas Polk, Confederate States of America. A West Point graduate, corps commander, and former Bishop in the Episcopal Church, he was killed at Pine Mountain, in the Atlanta campaign, on June 14, 1864. (*From the National Archives*)

Major General William S. Rosecrans. One of the best strategists in the Union Army, he succeeded General Buell as commander of the Army of the Cumberland. His unfortunate and mistaken order at Chickamauga, that General Wood close up on Reynolds, led to the rout of his right and center, and brought about his replacement by General Thomas. (*From the National Archives*)

Major General Lovell H. Rousseau. He fought with distinction at Perryville and Stones River, and led a successful expedition into Alabama in late 1864. He was noted for his ability to hold his troops together under maximum adversity. *(From the National Archives)*

Lieutenant General John M. Schofield. His most notable victory was at Franklin, Tennessee, November 30, 1864, where the Confederate losses, particularly of general officers, were staggering. He was saved from disaster at Spring Hill, just prior to Franklin, by Generals Stanley and Wilson, with help from Confederate lapses. He is better known for his bitter and unreasoning enmity toward General Thomas, whom he sought to replace before the Battle of Nashville. *(From the National Archives)*

Lieutenant General Philip H. Sheridan. He was one of the great cavalry leaders of the Civil War and a splendid division commander. He performed valiantly at Murfreesboro, Missionary Ridge, in the Shenandoah Valley, and in the Army of the Potomac under General Grant, but had a bad day at Chickamauga, September 20, 1863, following the breakthrough. *(From the National Archives)*

Lieutenant General William T. Sherman. His fame rests principally on the Atlanta campaign, fought in the main by General Thomas's Army of the Cumberland, which comprised two-thirds of Sherman's force. He was an excellent raider, but his battle record made no contribution to his fame. *(From the National Archives)*

Major General William F. Smith. He brought relief to the starving horses and men of the Army of the Cumberland cooped up by the Confederates at Chattanooga, by opening the Cracker Line. He fought well in the Army of the Potomac at Antietam, Fredericksburg and elsewhere. *(From the National Archives)*

Major General David S. Stanley. Along with aid from General James H. Wilson, he saved Schofield from disaster at Spring Hill just prior to the Battle of Franklin. Stanley accused General Jacob Cox of writing the infamous letter, published in the New York *Tribune*, falsely crediting Schofield with planning the Battle of Nashville, which was exclusively an achievement of General Thomas. *(From the National Archives)*

Major General James B. Steedman. He marched with General Granger to the aid of General Thomas at Chickamauga, September 20, 1863, and fought heroically to repel the Confederates under General Longstreet. *(From the Library of Congress)*

Brigadier General Ferdinand Van Derveer. A valiant fighter at Perryville, he played a conspicuous part at Chattanooga. His was the last organization to cease firing at Chickamauga and the first on the firing line at Missionary Ridge. *(From the Library of Congress)*

Major General Gouverneur K. Warren. The statue on Little Round Top at Gettysburg commemorates his contribution to the Union victory there in seizing that site in advance of the Confederate attempt. Exonerated by a Court of Inquiry after his death, he had been unjustly accused by Sheridan of slowness in bringing up his troops in the Battle of Five Forks. *(From the Library of Congress)*

Colonel John T. Wilder. Famed for his organization of mounted infantry, he was also noted for equipping his mounted men with the celebrated Spencer repeating rifle. This weapon wrought havoc on the Confederates at Hoover's Gap, June 24, 1863, during Bragg's retreat from Tennessee. *(From the National Archives)*

Major General James H. Wilson. Perhaps the greatest cavalry leader produced on this continent, he was certainly the greatest Union leader of the Civil War and one of the noblest soldiers. His intimate acquaintance with General Thomas, and his excellent writings after the war, contributed much in establishing detailed proof of Grant's mistreatment of Thomas. *(From the National Archives)*

Major General Thomas J. Wood. A superior division commander whose withdrawal from the line under orders from Rosecrans enabled the Confederates to break through and roll up the Union center and right at Chickamauga. He was heroic at Missionary Ridge and in the Atlanta campaign, as well as at Franklin and Nashville. *(From the National Archives)*

General Robert E. Lee, Confederate States of America. The famous commander of the Army of Northern Virginia, his genius prolonged the war immeasurably until his surrender to Grant at Appomattox. *(Painting in West Point Military Academy Library)*

Lieutenant General Ulysses S. Grant. Victor at Forts Henry and Donelson, Shiloh, Vicksburg, and in the final campaign against General Lee ending at Appomattox. His enmity toward Thomas became one of the greatest injustices in American history. (*Painting in West Point Military Academy Library*)

The Thomas home, rear view. The room to the right of the chimney is the Thomas birthplace. Located near Newsoms, Virginia, several miles north of the North Carolina border in Southampton County. (*Photograph by the author*)

The Thomas home, front view. The venerable oak tree which stood when George Thomas was a boy. (*Photograph by the author*)

The schoolhouse on the Thomas property. The present owner, Mrs. Henry Miles, told the author it had been used by George and other children in the neighborhood. (*Photograph by the author*)

Lee and Gordon's Mills. In the vicinity of the Chickamauga battlefield, it was an important site in connection with the battle. (*From the National Archives*)

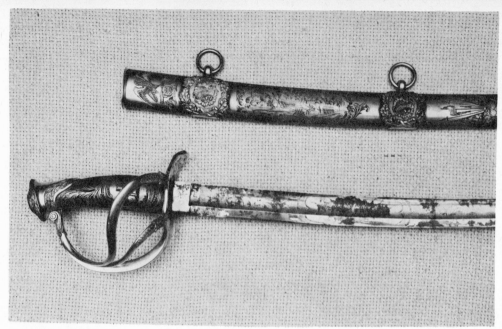

Sword and scabbard. Presented to Thomas for services in the Mexican War by citizens of Southampton County, Virginia. Now in possession of the Virginia State Library, Richmond, Virginia. *(Photograph courtesy of the Virginia State Library)*

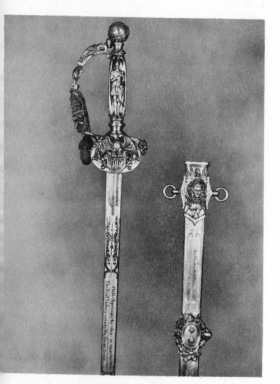

Sword and scabbard. Presented by enlisted men of the Fourth Kentucky Volunteer Infantry in honor of General Thomas's victory at Mill Springs, Kentucky, January 19, 1862, the first Union victory of the war. *(Photographs courtesy of Norm Flayderman, dealer in antique fire-arms, Greenwich, Connecticut, present owner of the sword)*

Statue of General Thomas. Erected by his comrades in 1879 at Thomas Circle, Washington, D.C., this is the only monument erected to his memory. *(Courtesy of National Park Service, Department of the Interior)*

Final resting place of General George H. Thomas. The Kellogg family burial ground located in Oakwood Cemetery, Troy, New York. (*Photograph by Van Arnam Studio, Troy, New York*)

could not hold against the dash of the Confederates, his withdrawal was to be made slowly, stubbornly, and as costly as possible to the Confederates. McCook indicated his belief that he could hold Bragg, which is all that was to be expected of him.[37]

General Crittenden's advance on December 26 to Lavergne had been timed to permit General McCook to arrive at Triune, referred to earlier, and to permit General Thomas to move in support. General James Negley's division was joined by General Rousseau's division at Stewartsboro on December 28. On the following day Negley crossed the ford at Stewart's Creek, about two miles southwest of, and two miles above, the Nolensville pike bridge, and advanced about eight miles in support of Crittenden's force. Here he established a position within three miles of Murfreesboro. Early on the morning of December 30, Crittenden moved his division into position on the extreme left of the line of battle under spirited enemy fire. Negley's division moved obliquely to the right of General Palmer's division; later, these troops moved through a thick cedar growth several hundred yards wide to the Wilkinson crossroads, and during this operation enemy skirmishers were repulsed with considerable loss. General Rousseau's division, less General Starkweather's brigade, had been left at Stewartsboro to observe and report on enemy movements. Upon being ordered forward, he bivouacked for the night to the rear of Negley's division, with his left resting on the Murfreesboro pike.[38]

During the night of December 30, General Bragg shifted General Pat Cleburne's division to his right. General Rosecrans ordered his troops under Generals Van Cleve and Wood to move up during the night preparatory to crossing the river in the morning. Their order to advance was not received until the following morning. The movement of General Cleburne's command was discovered by one of General Wood's brigade commanders, and General Crittenden was informed accordingly, although no counteraction was taken. General McCook and General Johnson appear to have been satisfied with their extreme right, particularly McCook, in view of his failure to change his dispositions as suggested by General Rosecrans before the battle commenced. General Rosecrans expressed his doubts to McCook regarding the position McCook occupied, but he did not order him to make the necessary changes, a factor that would weigh somewhat heavily on the results of December 31. That night, McCook's right rested in the cedar woods, from which both officers and men cut boughs to use as beds during the night, and slept under

37. *Atlas, ibid.*, p. 78.
38. Cist, *op. cit.*, pp. 92-93; *Atlas, ibid.*, pp. 78-79.

blankets in a drenching rain.[39] For all of the men, both Union and Confederate alike, this convenience was primitive enough, although it was a seeming luxury to many who "laid them down in their last sleep." The events on the opening day of battle would bring into sharp focus Rosecrans's lack of wisdom in strengthening his left for offensive purposes while weakening his right for defensive purposes. In addition, it would disclose that subordinate commanders without the gift of instinct for command are capable of undoing the best-laid plans, and Rosecrans's plan was well-conceived.

General Bragg's objective was to push the Union right and center under McCook and Thomas, respectively, against Crittenden's left near the river, prevent its escape and sever communications with Nashville. This would cut off the base of operations and supplies for Rosecrans's army and constitute a long stride forward in capturing Nashville. The armies were about equal in numbers, except that the Confederate cavalry was much stronger and more efficient, the latter a factor that gave them a definite superiority in observation and nuisance value. The plan of battle of each commander was identical, that is, each planned to strike his opponent's right, the time factor alone being different. Bragg set the time for attack at daybreak, but Rosecrans ordered that his men eat breakfast and attack at seven o'clock.[40] It is interesting to contemplate the possible result if both commanders had begun their attack simultaneously; but it requires little imagination to realize that the spectacle would have been somewhat in principle like a wheel revolving in clockwise motion. In that event, Bragg would have driven from his left flank toward the right flank of the Union army, which is what he actually did; Crittenden on the left flank of the Union army would have advanced toward the Confederate right flank, which he also did, but about a half hour after Bragg's attack began. Whether the unison of these attacks would have had any material bearing on the over-all result is conjectural; but viewed from present-day, air-reconnaissance facilities, weak spots could have been promptly noted and perhaps at once corrected.

The Confederate attack began near the Widow Smith House at six thirty on the morning of December 31. The divisions of Generals John P. McCown and Pat Cleburne of General Hardee's corps advanced against Generals August Willich's and Edward N. Kirk's brigades of General Richard W. Johnson's division of General McCook's right wing. General Willich was captured and General Kirk mortally wounded in the ensuing struggle, and both brigades suffered tremendous losses. Willich was away from his command at

39. Cist, *ibid.,* p. 101.
40. *Ibid.*

division headquarters when the Confederates struck, a possible major contribution to the Confederate success in the early hours of the struggle. General Johnson was not on the line nor near enough to his troops to give them orders when the attack came, since his headquarters was about a mile and a half to the rear. His report of the battle stated that his two advanced brigades were commanded by "two gallant and experienced officers," but significantly he made no reference either to his presence or absence from the front line of battle, and he has been regarded generally as negligent at that time. Willich's troops were eating breakfast when attacked, and, although there has been some debate regarding it, they appear to have been at least somewhat surprised. Nevertheless, the Confederate attack was devastating, aided in part also by the relatively thin disposition of troops insufficiently supported.[41]

Although Johnson's men fought bravely, they withdrew too far to the west upon retiring to permit the making of a unified stand. His reserve brigade, under the command of Colonel Philemon P. Baldwin, was at headquarters, perhaps a mile and a half distant, when disaster struck the brigades of Generals Kirk and Willich. Baldwin succeeded in preparing his men for battle just before the enemy in great numbers appeared at close range on his front and on his left, which was extended beyond the extreme Union right. His infantry and artillery met the enemy and with a most destructive fire checked them in front, although their left continued advancing against his right. Four pieces of artillery posted near the woods also poured a withering fire into the advancing foe; but the overwhelming superiority of the enemy finally compelled Baldwin to retire to the railroad for reforming just in time to avoid being surrounded and captured.[42]

The victorious advance of McCown and Cleburne continued in its somewhat semicircular path, and next struck the division of General Jefferson C. Davis. Davis formed a new line, with his right brigade under General Post almost at right angles to his former position, and completed his dispositions in preparation for the attack. Baldwin, already battered and reformed, took position in the line to await another attack. The tide of McCown's and Cleburne's troops fell upon the front and rear both of Baldwin's and Post's brigades at a time when two brigades of General Jones M. Withers ran head-on into two brigades under Generals William P. Carlin and William E.

41. Cist, *ibid.*, pp. 105, 134; *Official Records, op. cit.*, Vol. I, Part 1, pp. 192, 193, 296; Ezra J. Warner, *Generals in Gray* (Baton Rouge: Louisiana State University Press, 1959), p. 199.

42. *Official Records, op. cit.*, Vol. XX, Part 1, p. 337.

Woodruff. Not stopping there they advanced until they encountered General Joshua W. Sill's brigade of General Sheridan's division.[43]

The realignment of Post's brigade had the effect of giving to the two remaining brigades of Davis's division, and also Sill's brigade, the equivalent of a division front. At this point the Confederates again attacked, and again Baldwin was compelled to withdraw; but Post repulsed the enemy on his front, and Carlin, Woodruff, and Sill compelled them to withdraw from their front with great loss. After reforming and receiving fresh reinforcements from General Benjamin F. Cheatham's division, the enemy once more advanced, only to be repulsed and driven back to their intrenchments. General Sill, who had fought bravely and well, was killed; and although his brigade withdrew, it reformed immediately for battle. Meanwhile, Cleburne renewed the attack on Post's brigade and was beaten back. The two brigades of Carlin and Woodruff were almost perpendicular to Sheridan's division and, with Woodruff's left and Sill's right, formed what was in effect a right angle. The Confederates attacked a third time with four brigades under Cheatham, this time realizing that if they could take the point of this angle they would be in a commanding position to rake both Union forces simultaneously. Post was again attacked by McCown and Cleburne and compelled to fall back to the Nashville pike. This withdrawal exposed Carlin's right and encouraged the enemy to again attack, this time in overwhelming numbers, after first circling to their own right and bearing down in massed columns on Davis's division. Carlin stubbornly resisted this latest attack until almost surrounded, and his brigade in imminent danger of capture; he then retreated to the edge of the woods.[44]

General Woodruff also fell back at this time, but turned and compelled his pursuers to retreat beyond his original position. He also withdrew into the cedars when he was unable to obtain support. General Davis was reforming once more the remnants of his forces, but before Woodruff reached this new line, Carlin's men opened fire on the advancing Confederates. Davis then ordered a withdrawal back across the Wilkinson pike. Woodruff, in the meantime, charged again and drove the enemy back until, his ammunition having become exhausted, he withdrew to the Murfreesboro pike.[45]

Up to this time Davis had, for all practical purposes, protected the right of the Union line under Sheridan, and both divisions had repulsed two enemy attacks, although Davis's division was badly

---

43. *Official Records, ibid.,* pp. 192-93; *Battles and Leaders of the Civil War* (New York, 1884), Vol. III, pp. 618-19; Cist, *op. cit.,* p. 108.

44. Cist, *ibid.,* pp. 108-9.

45. Van Horne, *Life,* p. 93; Cist, *ibid.,* p. 109.

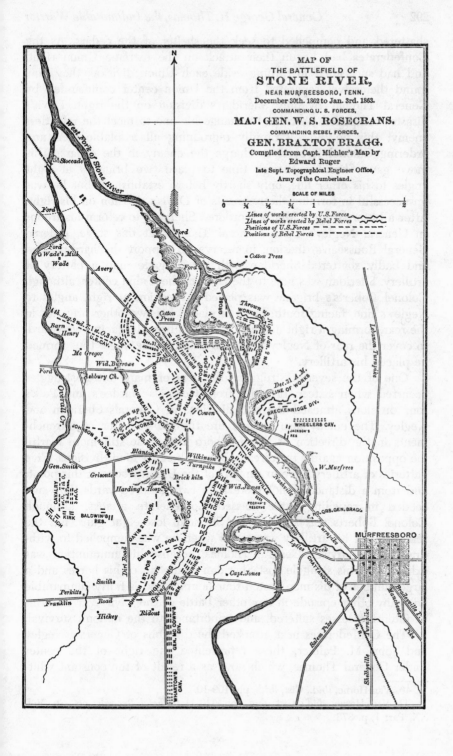

MAP OF
THE BATTLEFIELD OF
STONE RIVER,
NEAR MURFREESBORO, TENN.
December 30th. 1862 to Jan. 3rd. 1863.
COMMANDING U. S. FORCES,
MAJ. GEN. W. S. ROSECRANS.
COMMANDING REBEL FORCES,
GEN. BRAXTON BRAGG.
Compiled from Capt. Michler's Map by
Edward Ruger
late Supt. Topographical Engineer Office,
Army of the Cumberland.

SCALE OF MILES

0   ¼   ½   ¾   1   2

Lines of works erected by U.S.Forces
Lines of works erected by Rebel Forces
Positions of U.S.Forces
Positions of Rebel Forces

shattered and compelled to seek the shelter of the cedars. As the Confederates had begun their attack on the extreme Union right, and had succeeded in turning aside each Union division, they now found themselves separated from the Union center commanded by General Thomas by only Sheridan's division on the right. Davis's disaster compelled Sheridan to change his line to meet the relentless enemy; this he did by rapidly regrouping all available men and ordering Colonel Roberts to charge the enemy in the cedars. This move gave Sheridan enough time to place two brigades at right angles to his other line, only shortly before established, but he was unsuccessful in forming the remnants of Davis's division on his right. After a bitter struggle McCook ordered Sheridan to reform his troops on General Negley's right. General Thomas, at this stage, ordered General Rousseau's division, in reserve, to support the hard-pressed and badly shattered Sheridan with two brigades and a battery of artillery. Sheridan was now to the right of the Union center, although Colonel Roberts's brigade was placed in position at right angles to Negley's line, facing south; he then placed his two other brigades in the rear, forming a right angle to Roberts's brigade, facing westward, to cover the rear of Negley's two lines, and in the angle thus formed he placed his artillery.[46]

One of the severest struggles of a day of many bitter struggles occurred when sixteen brigades from Generals Hardee's and Polk's four divisions attacked the two divisions of Generals Sheridan and Negley. The enemy also opened fire from the shelter of intrenchments in the direction of Murfreesboro and made still more fearful the opposition against the already outnumbered Union divisions. Five batteries of artillery were in support of the Union troops at this point; and from a distance of not more than two hundred yards they succeeded in repelling three massed Confederate attacks, although Colonel Roberts was killed. Here Sheridan lost eight guns, but the remainder of his artillery was saved when he was compelled to withdraw, as he advised General Thomas, because his ammunition was exhausted. This struggle cost Sheridan nearly all of his horses and a large number of his men, lasted four hours,[47] and is fairly comparable with any other episode in any other battle of the Civil War in terms of intensity, losses suffered, and importance to the nation's survival.

The Confederates next attacked the divisions of Generals Negley and John M. Palmer; these represented the right of the center under General Thomas, which now, as a result of the constant whit-

---

46. Van Horne, *ibid.*, Cist, *ibid.*, pp. 109-10.

47. Van Horne, *ibid.*; Cist, *ibid.*, pp. 110-11; *Official Records, op. cit.*, Vol. XX, Part 1, p. 373.

tling away of the Union right since the battle began, was the extreme right of the entire army. General Thomas was in command here and knew that if the point at which the Nashville pike approached Stones River should fall into Confederate hands the battle would be lost; he realized also that the extreme left flank of the Union army under General Crittenden's command on the east side of the river would be isolated and perhaps destroyed.

The withdrawal of Sheridan created the great crisis of the battle. Here was the moment supreme, the fateful point at which the Confederate tide would either continue to certain victory and probable recovery of Tennessee, or ebb in retreat and perhaps defeat. The Army of the Cumberland was in one of the gravest crises of its existence, and it did not appear that it would be able to extricate itself. The work of many months of effort was hanging on the fate of the next few hours; and the end result might very well determine whether the nation itself would remain "half slave and half free." This is not inconceivable, since the nation, after a number of bitter and overwhelming defeats, was worn and weary from the struggle. Another defeat here, as at Fredericksburg only eighteen days before, December 13, 1862, when the Union suffered one of the most one-sided defeats in the history of the United States, would have been a blow from which it might not have had the will to continue. As the poet Longfellow so well put it in his story of the midnight ride of Paul Revere, "The fate of a nation was riding that night," so at this little stream, on December 31, George Henry Thomas, the loyal Virginian, rose up to bar the path of victory to his fellow Southerners and saved the Union army. This was the moment climactic, as at Thermopylae where Leonidas held back the Persian hordes, when the dauntless, the inimitable, the ever-resourceful George Thomas would wrench victory from defeat and go on to greater if relatively unrecognized laurels.

It was at this critical point in the battle that General Thomas ordered the brigades of Colonels John F. Miller and Timothy R. Stanley, of Negley's division, to fall back to avoid possible annihilation or capture. When Stanley withdrew, however, the effect was to expose the right of General Palmer's division and compel General Charles Cruft's brigade to retire, this due to his unprotected left flank. Both of General Negley's and General Rousseau's flanks were also left unprotected, and both were soon almost completely surrounded by the Confederates. The Confederates continued their advance in high spirits, after their opening successes in turning aside the divisions of Johnson, Davis, and Sheridan, and next attacked the divisions of Rousseau, Negley, and Palmer. Colonel William Grose's brigade of General Palmer's division faced to the rear to confront the enemy, and General Negley's division fought stubbornly as they retired, while General Rousseau's division fought in several directions during this phase of the fighting.[48]

This desperate situation called for the ultimate in generalship, and General Thomas was more than equal to the occasion. He knew that the only way to save the center, and the entire army for that matter, was to establish a new line connecting General Crittenden's left wing and General McCook's scattered forces on his right with his center. This required, and he was well equipped to perform it, one of the most difficult maneuvers ever performed on any battlefield. He had first to establish a new and temporary line before he could succeed in forming a permanent one. He assembled all of his artillery on the high ground selected for the permanent line, and then posted part of his infantry on the low ground in front of the artillery to resist the expected advance of the Confederates. This infantry was under the command of General Rousseau in the rear of the cedars, and was the temporary line. There then ensued the heaviest fighting of the day, and the losses on both sides were tremendous. When the Confederates advanced they were subjected to a withering fire and mowed down like "chaff which the wind driveth away." General Thomas then made his center secure after reforming his line, thus saving the day when everything but hope and determination stood in the way of a smashing Confederate victory.[49]

Just before the Union artillery was placed, the Confederates charged in dense masses, with blood-curdling yells, against the force of General Horatio P. Van Cleve. They came on, four lines deep, but were met by musket fire from General Rousseau's and Colonel John Beatty's troops and by double-shotted canister from the artillery. The Confederates were in the open, and the gunners contesting their advance could take dead aim on them; but no human being could withstand the horrible punishment meted out to them, and they were compelled to withdraw with frightful losses. After being rallied in the cedar growth, they advanced once more, this time with fresh troops in support, in an attempt to dislodge the Union defenders from the Round Forest, the name given to the site by the Confederates; but they were again repulsed and forced to retire. Not to be denied, or so at least they hoped, they advanced four more times and were as many times repulsed. Colonel Oliver L. Shepherd's regular brigade lost six hundred men of a total number engaged of one thousand five hundred and eighty-six, or more than

48. Van Horne, *ibid.*, p. 94; Cist, *ibid*, p. 111; *Official Records, ibid.*
49. Van Horne, *ibid.*; Cist, *ibid.*, pp. 112-13; *Official Records, ibid.*

forty per cent. The Pioneer Brigade, commanded by Captain St. Clair Morton, was also conspicuous in this operation in covering the moving troops with musketry and artillery fire. As a result of the herculean effort made by General Thomas, ably supported by his subordinate commanders and their men, the divisions of Generals Rousseau, Negley, and Palmer were established in a good defensive line, which enabled them to withstand any further assaults from the Confederates.[50]

The aggregate of reports on the Battle of Stones River are many and varied; what is most important, they do not admit of a sequential narrative that details the events in the order in which they occurred. The battle itself was so confused due to the impossibility of controlling the events that unfolded as the several stages progressed that the reports submitted inevitably chronicle what at best results in a somewhat confused story of what took place. The movements of the various units on and off the field of battle are impossible to describe with certainty in the order in which they occurred. For this reason, the operations of General Rosecrans, which are clearly a phase of the battle that had little to do with the difficulties confronted by McCook, Davis, and Thomas until the day was fairly well spent, are treated as a separate phase of the action. For the same reason, the operations of McCook, Davis, and Thomas, already described, have lent themselves quite clearly and logically to separate treatment.

From his headquarters behind General Crittenden's Corps, where he could observe and direct the action, General Rosecrans gave the order to advance at seven in the morning of December 31, as planned. This attack was different from the Confederate attack on the Union right wing under McCook, heretofore discussed, in that Crittenden's corps was under the necessity of crossing the river and advancing a couple of miles before engaging the Confederate right wing under General Breckinridge. Two of General Van Cleve's brigades crossed the river according to plan without encountering serious opposition, and General Thomas J. Wood's division had reached the river preparatory to crossing in support of General Van Cleve. The sound of battle from the Union right was regarded as confirmation of Rosecrans's plan to engage the Confederate left and prevent a shifting of large reinforcements to Breckinridge's support. After the lapse of perhaps an hour a messenger came hurriedly from General McCook entreating General Rosecrans to send reinforcements in relief of his right wing.[51] It is puzzling that McCook did not give details of affairs to permit his commander in chief to properly evaluate

50. Van Horne, *ibid.*; Cist, *ibid.*, pp. 113-17.
51. *Battles and Leaders, op. cit.*, Vol. III, p. 623; Cist, *ibid.*, p. 112.

his situation in relation to the over-all engagement. Why, when his extreme right under General Johnson was routed, he did not advise Rosecrans accordingly is beyond understanding. It is readily understood that Rosecrans, in the absence of a full disclosure of the facts, would interpret the request for reinforcements at face value. It is not enough to argue that Rosecrans knew McCook asked for reinforcements; it should be remembered that Rosecrans realized McCook would be faced with difficulties and that he needed reinforcements; but when McCook's situation jeopardized the whole army, that fact should have been explained to Rosecrans.

Interpreting McCook's request quite literally, Rosecrans instructed the staff officer: "Tell General McCook to contest every inch of ground. If he holds them we will swing into Murfreesboro and cut them off." When a second messenger to Rosecrans conveyed the true state of affairs, he realized that he must abandon his original plan of battle and make the necessary dispositions to save his army. He ordered an immediate suspension of Van Cleve's crossing of the river to the extent of diverting two brigades to McCook's relief. He next directed General Wood to suspend his plan to cross the river and to prepare at once to move to the new line on the right; in the meantime, Wood was told to hold General Milo S. Hascall's brigade in reserve. He then ordered General Van Cleve to be placed to the right of General Rousseau and General Wood to send Colonel Harker's brigade to attack the Confederates on Van Cleve's right, as indicated heretofore in discussing the critical situation in the Round Forest, from which point the battle turned in favor of the Union.[52]

In the face of this new line of battle, established as a result of the fighting in the Round Forest, the Confederates were confronted with the need for reinforcements. General Bragg's large numerical superiority, although extremely successful against the Union right, was now, as a result of gathering resistance to his repeated assaults, in large measure dissipated. At the time when the Union center under General Thomas succeeded in standing firm and rebuilding a new line, General Hardee requested reinforcements of General Bragg. Bragg had used about three-fifths of his army against the Union right flank under McCook, and had continued in its arc still more to the right until it struck Thomas's center. When such a large segment of Bragg's army eventually recoiled in defeat with heavy losses and disorganized ranks, the only hope for Confederate victory was in using the remaining reserves against Rosecrans's left. This he sought to do by sending General Leonidas Polk with four brigades from the east side

52. Van Horne, *Life*, p. 94; Cist, *ibid.*

of the river. At this time the Union left was held by General Palmer's division, and General Hascall's and General George D. Wagner's brigades of General Wood's division; in addition to these Colonel Schaefer's brigade was to the rear in support. In this attempt Bragg failed to overcome the Union left and had to abandon the offensive altogether.[53]

In the evening, General Starkweather's brigade of General Rousseau's division and General Walker's brigade of General Fry's division came upon the field; however, as General Negley's two brigades were then in reserve in the center, the first-mentioned troops were assigned to support General McCook and later relieved General Crittenden's corps, that the latter might resume its designated place in the Union line.[54]

One of the surprising incidents of the first day at Stones River was the spectacle of entire regiments of soldiers of the Army of the Cumberland running in panic from the scene of conflict. The rear of a line of battle often contains a number of those who are unable to withstand the horrors of combat, and many of these are so overcome with disgust that their courage fails them in their hour of greatest need. It has been said many times that one of the greatest fears of a soldier is that he may not be able to suppress his fear in the hour of supreme trial. Equally surprising is the fact that the Union line was restored and the tide of battle turned, despite these wholesale withdrawals of soldiers from the front line of battle. Nothing can detract from the spirit of the Army of the Cumberland when, after being decisively thrashed in the opening stages of the battle, due in great measure to its being overwhelmed by numbers and to the lack of will to resist of some of the defenders, it was able to persevere and end the day with a good chance for final victory. General Rosecrans's address to the troops on the day of battle is as follows:

> The General Commanding desires to say to the soldiers of the Army of the Cumberland that he was well pleased with their conduct yesterday.... He now feels perfectly confident with God's grace and their help, of striking this day a blow for the country, the most crushing, perhaps, which the rebellion has yet sustained. Soldiers! the eyes of the whole nation are upon you; the very fate of the nation may be said to hang on the issues of this day's battle. Be true, then, to yourselves, true to your own manly character and soldierly reputations; true to the love of your dear

53. Van Horne, *ibid.*, pp. 95-96.
54. *Ibid.*, p. 96.

ones at home, whose prayers ascend this day to God for your success. Be cool. I need not ask you to be brave. Keep ranks. Do not throw away your fire. Fire slowly, deliberately—above all, fire low, and be always sure of your aim. Close readily in upon the enemy, and when you get within charging distance, rush upon him with the bayonet. Do this, and victory will certainly be yours. Recollect that there are hardly any troops in the world that will stand a bayonet charge, and that those who make it, are sure to win.[55]

This appeal of General Rosecrans and his own lofty spirit were transmitted to the rank and file of his army, and can be stated without regard to the number that gave way in Hardee's attack on McCook's right, when the shock of superior numbers and the incomplete control by subordinate commanders made the outcome doubtful. If this had not been so there could not have been the complete wresting of victory from almost certain defeat.

Although there were many acts of individual heroism and outstanding performances on this bloody field, none equaled in importance the achievement of General Thomas when he reformed the center of the line while subjected to attack in front, flank, and rear, and established liaison with the remainder of the army; this he did under intensive musketry and artillery fire. Although he had but five brigades of his command on December 31, he was able with these, and other units obtained hastily in that critical period, to completely secure the entire Union battle line against everything the Confederates were able to bring against it.[56]

An informal gathering of leading Union officers was held at McCook's headquarters in a cold, dimly lit cabin, in the rear of the battlefield, on the night of December 31. After discussing the principal events of the day and appraising results in terms of their next action, that is, whether to retreat or fight in the morning, Generals Crittenden and Thomas expressed emphatic objection to retreating. There are several versions of just exactly what took place, but there is general agreement regarding the final decision to fight, in which Thomas cast the strongest vote. It has been told that before the decision to fight Rosecrans asked the opinion of each officer present, during which Thomas, wearied from the hard day, was resting on an improvised seat. General Rosecrans asked Surgeon Eben Swift if he had sufficient transportation with which to remove the wounded from the battlefield, clearly implying an intention to retreat. Dr.

55. Bickham, *op. cit.*, p. 202.
56. Van Horne, *Life*, pp. 95-96.

Swift replied that there were five or six thousand wounded men to consider, and that a fairly large number might be able to walk; however, he thought there were enough vehicles to provide for the badly wounded. When General Rosecrans asked General Thomas, "Will you protect the rear on the retreat to Overall's Creek?" he replied, "This army can't retreat!" That clinched it for the remainder of the group, particularly General Philip H. Sheridan, one of the great heroes of the battle who, when he heard Thomas's decision, spoke emphatically to the same effect; in so doing, along with General Crittenden as aforesaid, the army held its ground. Thomas had apparently made up his mind before the meeting began that the army should not retreat; and although he is reported to have dozed off several times during the meeting, when the subject of retreat was mentioned he voiced his opposition.[57]

Another account of the meeting is to the effect that Rosecrans polled the officers, purposely avoiding asking Thomas for his opinion until the others stated their views. Then, "General Thomas, what have you to say?" Thomas, so the story goes, rose slowly to his full height and, buttoning his overcoat preparatory to leaving, replied, "I know of no better place to die than right here." Rosecrans at this point told his officers, "If you are not attacked by six o'clock [in the morning] you will open the fight promptly, posted as you are, and move on to Murfreesboro. Clear the field yet tonight of all wounded and see to it that your ammunition is well up; we will whip this fight tomorrow."[58]

Still another account, this one more especially emphasizing the intention of Rosecrans to retreat, as told by Crittenden, is given herewith:

> After the fight on the night of the 31st a number of general officers were assembled by Rosecrans' order, including McCook, Thomas, Stanley, and myself. There was some talk of falling back, I do not remember who started the subject, but I do remember that I expressed the opinion that my men would be very much discouraged to have to abandon the field after their good fight of the day, during which they had uniformly held their position. I spoke of the proposition as resembling the suggestion of General Wool to General Taylor at Buena Vista, when Taylor responded: "My wounded are behind me, and I will never pass

57. Van Horne, *Life*, pp. 96-97; Piatt, *op. cit.*, pp. 211-12; *Atlas, op. cit.*, p. 82.

58. *Military Order of the Loyal Legion, Indiana War Papers* (Indianapolis, 1898), pp. 174-75.

them alive." Rosecrans called McCook to accompany him on a ride, directing us to remain until their return. McCook has since told me that the purpose of this ride was to find a position beyond Overall's Creek to which the army might retire. Upon approaching the creek Rosecrans, perceiving mounted men moving up and down with torches, said to McCook: "They have got entirely in our rear and are forming a line of battle by torchlight." They returned then to where we were, and Rosecrans told us to go to our commands and prepare to fight or die. The explanation of the torches is that the men were making fires, and the torches were firing-brands being carried from one point to another by cavalrymen. I had received an order from General Rosecrans not to allow the men to make fires; but upon looking out of my quarters I discovered that the fires were already made from one end of my line to the other. I sent Rosecrans word that as the men were cold and were not being disturbed by the enemy, and as it would take all night to put out the fires, we had better leave them. The men would have suffered very much if they had stayed all night without fire.[59]

General Rosecrans, not to imply in any sense that he withheld the events of the December thirty-first night meeting, probably did not feel it important to discuss within the limitations of his report the details underlying his decision to remain and fight.

New Year's Day, January 1, 1863, dawned clear and cold following a night of rain in which supreme efforts were made to strengthen the Union position. Such effort was not in vain, since General Bragg had sent out his cavalry at daybreak to probe the Union lines for weak spots of attack. Being unable to find a vulnerable spot was disappointing to him indeed, but intrepid Joe Wheeler found plenty to keep himself occupied, including the capture of a large wagon train of supplies for use by Rosecrans's army. Such activities were annoying, but supplies and ammunition were not stopped, and the day ended with little action, and with both armies substantially as they were at the end of December 31.

Late on the afternoon of January 2, after a period of but random firing since the fighting of December 31, a heated action occurred on the east side of the river. General Crittenden had sent General Van Cleve's division, now commanded by Colonel Samuel Beatty, Van Cleve having been wounded, with instructions to occupy the hill dominating the two fords close to the Union right. General Bragg was concerned at this movement of Union troops, considering it a

---

59. *Battles and Leaders, op. cit.,* Vol. III, pp. 633-34.

menace to the position held by General Leonidas Polk, and decided
to drive them back across the river. He gave the task to General
Breckinridge, under protest, who regarded it as impossible of accomplishment. Although he undertook to follow orders, nevertheless he took the time to ride to General William Preston and state
his views regarding the order in the following language:

"General, this attack is made against my judgment and by
special orders of General Bragg. Of course we all must try to do our
duty and fight the best we can; but if it should result in disaster and
I be among the killed, I want you to do justice to my memory and
tell the people that I believed this attack to be very unwise and tried
to prevent it."[60]

Breckinridge commanded about forty-five hundred men in the
advance commencing about four o'clock in the afternoon. Consisting
of two lines, the first line advanced with fixed bayonets under orders
to deliver one volley before using the bayonet. General Crittenden
was riding on the Nashville pike with his chief of artillery, Major
John Mendenhall, when they observed the Confederate advance.
Mendenhall at once began concentrating all available guns on an
elevation at McFadden's Ford on the west side of Stones River.
General Crittenden reported that when he saw the Confederate advance he turned to Mendenhall and said, "Now, Mendenhall, you
must cover my men with your cannon." "Without any show of
excitement or haste, almost as soon as the order was given, the
batteries began to open, so perfectly had he placed them. In twenty
minutes from the time the order was received, fifty-eight guns were
firing upon the enemy. They cannot be said to have been checked
in their advance—from a rapid advance they broke at once into a
rapid retreat. Reinforcements soon began to arrive, and our troops
crossed the river, and pursued the fleeing enemy until dark." Before
Mendenhall's batteries began their deadly work, Colonel Beatty's
division had been driven from its position to the bank of the river.
It was at this stage of the action that the artillery began its work.
Despite the repulse by the first line, the second line came forward,
reinforced by some of the units of the damaged first line, and was
also driven back.[61]

During the artillery barrage against the retreating Confederates a
remarkable event occurred. Colonel John F. Miller, of Negley's division, Thomas's command, noting the retirement of the enemy from the

60. *Atlas, op. cit.*, p. 82; Alexander F. Stevenson, *The Battle of Stone's River*
(Boston, 1884), p. 132.

61. *Atlas, ibid.*, pp. 82, 83; *Official Records, op. cit.*, Vol. XX, Part 1, pp.
374, 451, 785-86.

Federal artillery fire, reported that a number of the pursuing regiments were mixed together. In the meantime, Thomas noted that Colonel Beatty's troops might need help and promptly ordered Negley's troops to advance to their support if necessary. Obedience to this order in a roundabout manner forms an example of initiative that often seems to accompany American troops in times of crisis. Colonel Miller actually carried out Thomas's order by taking command without direction from Negley, who was not immediately available, and attacked Breckinridge's troops with seven regiments he assembled on the spot. General Davis moved promptly to support Colonel Miller, with the result that together they held and fortified a key position that forced the Confederates in retreat to Murfreesboro. In this closing phase of the Battle of Stones River General Bragg's objective was primarily to capture and hold a position that endangered his own. The scope of the encounter went far beyond his intention, when his troops pursued Colonel Beatty's force and brought on pursuit of themselves by the forces of Colonel Miller and General Davis. The result was to compel Bragg to withdraw, as the dominating position of the Federal artillery made his further stay on the battlefield impossible. Furthermore, a heavy rain that began falling during the night continued into the next day and made the field impassable for artillery, in addition to raising the water in Stones River to near-flood stage.[62]

Bragg's retreat to Murfreesboro, conducted with skill and aided by the rain, which worked in reverse by preventing Rosecrans's pursuit of him, followed the main road into the town. There he left his wounded and continued to Tullahoma, some forty miles from the battlefield. Rosecrans may be said to have won a battle in which the wills of the opposing commanders exercised full play. Although Bragg fought a resourceful and courageous battle, and narrowly missed winning one of the most convincing victories of the war, his defeat was in no sense an indication of inferior generalship. On the field opposed to him were a number of generals whose abilities were above average, including Sheridan and Thomas; and not to be ignored was the fact that these officers commanded men whose exploits would be repeated on other battlefields. If there is any inclination to disparage Bragg's effort at Stones River it should be asked (except at Chickamauga under orders from Rosecrans), when, during the Civil War, was a field yielded to the enemy on which George H. Thomas

---

62. *Atlas, ibid.*, p. 82; *Official Records, ibid.*, pp. 374, 434-35; Piatt, *op. cit.* p. 213; John G. Nicolay and John Hay, *Abraham Lincoln: A History* (New York, 1909), Vol. VI, pp. 292-93.

was a participant? Rosecrans made no serious attempt to follow Bragg, although he did order Thomas to proceed to Murfreesboro. Thomas entered the town on March 5 with his entire command, preceded by General Stanley's cavalry. The losses on both sides were about twenty-four thousand, including killed, wounded, and missing, although the Confederates are estimated to have lost slightly fewer than half that number, or about eleven thousand five hundred men.[63] In terms of the number of men engaged, the estimates indicating an aggregate of between forty and forty-five thousand men on each side, the losses were approximately about three to every ten men.

It is understandable that when news of the victory at Stones River, slim as it was, reached the North, there was great jubilation. General Rosecrans rose sharply with the tide of enthusiasm into the front rank of military leadership. It silenced for a time the personal animosity between members of the President's Cabinet and Secretary of War Stanton, a bitterness that had been rekindled when Rosecrans was placed in command of the Army of the Cumberland as successor to Buell. It is told that Secretary of the Treasury Salmon P. Chase, a chief sponsor of Rosecrans to replace Buell, and despite the protests of Secretary Stanton, whose choice was Thomas, could not suppress his exuberance over the victory. Stanton disliked Rosecrans and felt that Chase's attitude was not only insupportable but also a personal affront. "You see," said Chase to Stanton during a cabinet meeting, "my friend has justified all I urged on you in his behalf." "If you knew as much about Stones River as I do," growled Stanton, "you would not feel so cocksure of your friend. But for George H. Thomas, the man I wanted to head that army, Stones River, instead of being a victory, would have been a defeat." Chase responded, "Come now, Stanton, be just. We selected Rosecrans, and Rosecrans had the sagacity to select Thomas. Then, you know, nothing is so successful as success."[64] Regardless of whatever else has been said in criticism of Stanton, he had the disposition and the determination to win; and this exchange with Secretary Chase illustrates that earnestness in seeking success for the Union cause, while demonstrating that Chase appeared more concerned for an appointment for his friend Rosecrans.

Stanton was far from being alone in having a high opinion of Thomas; unfortunately space does not permit more than a few

---

63. Van Horne, *Life*, p. 99; *Atlas*, *ibid.*, p. 83; *Official Records*, *ibid.*, pp. 374-75.

64. Piatt, *op. cit.*, p. 214.

illustrations to reflect the general esteem in which he was held by his contemporaries, and by a long succession of authorities, for his outstanding contribution at Stones River.

In discussing the critical moment on December 31, when McCook's right was rolled up and the Confederates swept irresistibly toward the center held by Thomas, Fletcher Pratt, the well-known writer and authority on military subjects, had this to say:

> When he [Rosecrans] did realize it [the rout of McCook], he ordered a couple of divisions back across the river from Crittenden, but things were then so bad that the men jammed in the loop of the river would have been cut to pieces like the Romans at Cannae, if the line, now back to the Nashville pike and cramped at a frightening angle, gave way.
>
> It did not give way; Thomas held it. Before anyone else he realized what was happening; perceived that the Rebel attack could sweep McCook's wing back for a long distance without serious damage, but that if the point where the Nashville pike approached the river were lost, everything was lost and Crittenden would be cut off. He rushed nearly all the artillery of the center to this point—a cedar clump on a hill, the Round Forest. Sheridan, falling back from the Rebel masses, was ordered to direct his own guns thither; the cannon of Negley's and Van Cleve's fresh divisions were hurried out to the new right wing, where another bit of high ground gave them an enfilade into the flank of any force crossing the Nashville pike.

As if to prove still more the fighting characteristics of this very great soldier, he added the following regarding the deportment of Thomas at Stones River:

> He always had an eye to the value of formal effects, and as usual when a battle was toward, that morning had climbed into the nearest thing to a full-dress uniform that the camp afforded. Now, all togged out like a Christmas tree, he rode the line, bellowing in a voice audible to every man within a hundred yards that help was coming, all they had to do was keep down and shoot low. "Fighting under Thomas was like having a wall in front of you or a battery to cover you." He was the most conspicuous object on the field, and hardly any man, perceiving how he rode untouched through the storm, but lost some of that sense of personal danger which makes troops break. Nor was personal courage all that Thomas offered by his pres-

ence; if a spot were really weak, the reappearance of the general was infallibly followed by reinforcements.[65]

Another comment demonstrates the great credit given Thomas for his conduct in the Battle of Stones River:

> The Union right being broken, the howling masses of the enemy were hurled in successive charges, with fearful impetuosity, against the devoted center. They were flushed with success and confident of victory. Calm and unmoved General Thomas stood amidst the fearful conflict, always in front cheering and inspiring his troops by his presence and example. As the angry billows of battle rolled back and forth among the dismal cedar glades, gloomy and painful suspense long obscured the fortunes of the day. With a constancy that never faltered, a devoted heroism that was insensible to danger, Thomas continued to cheer his men, repulsing every charge, and finally held his position. . . . Thomas stood like an immovable statue, master of the position.[66]

W. H. T. Squires, a native Virginian, and author of a number of subjects relating to his state, praised Thomas highly in his book *The Days of Yester-Year*. Squires was one of the very few Virginia authors in the past hundred years who have even mentioned Thomas's name; most authors have purposely omitted any mention of him in writing of leading Virginians, because he fought for the Union.

> In that bloody duel between Rosecrans and Bragg for possession of Tennessee, the sword of Thomas won the day. The Confederates smashed the right wing of the Union army. From dawn until nightfall Thomas, in the center, repulsed the repeated and almost superhuman efforts of the victorious Confederates to break through his line. Had it not been for Thomas, Murfreesboro might have changed the entire fortunes of the war.[67]

While paying tribute to the skill of both Rosecrans and Thomas, the following comment gives credit to Thomas for turning defeat into victory:

65. Fletcher Pratt, *Eleven Generals* (New York: William Sloane Associates, 1949), pp. 189-90.

66. C. J. Wood, *Reminiscences of the War* (no publisher, no date).

67. W. H. T. Squires, *The Days of Yester-year* (Portsmouth, Va., 1928), p. 191.

It was the supreme test for Rosecrans, and whatever his previous faults may have been, he bore himself well. He hurried up ammunition, which was much needed at many points; directed the formation of new lines and the posting of fresh batteries; and whenever the emergency permitted, he took himself to the battle front where his presence reanimated his sorely beset soldiers. In spurring from one part of the field to another, his aide-de-camp and much-loved companion, Lieut.-Colonel Julius P. Garesche, was beheaded by a cannon ball, and his blood sprinkled the uniform of his commander. . . . Upon Thomas now fell a burden of tremendous weight. He had early perceived the displacement of Sheridan and had sent two brigades of Rousseau's division to reenforce that commander and support his right. Then he turned to face one of the most dangerous and furious efforts made by the foe during the whole day. . . . To give way here would be fatal, for back of Thomas and of what was left of the right wing Rosecrans was hastily arranging a new battle-line to hold the Nashville pike.

The commander of the center seemed ubiquitous. Though his charger never broke out of the slow pace that had given its master the nickname of Old Slow Trot, Thomas was apparently in all places at once; now directing the firing to repulse a charge, now placing a regiment in line, and again marking a point to which his troops must retire and take up the fight anew.[68]

The consistency with which the so-called name generals avoided giving Thomas just credit was maintained by General Philip H. Sheridan, a friend of both Grant and Sherman and a beneficiary of their favor. Although Sheridan fought valiantly at Stones River, it was the circumstance of his troops giving way, with others, that imperiled the center and created the situation that General Thomas stabilized and corrected. That was one of the most crucial moments of the war, one that Sheridan could never forget. How strange that Sheridan's *Memoirs* give no credit to the genius of Thomas there, the one man without whose achievement Sheridan and the whole Union army would have suffered devastating defeat! We shall see that Sheridan was equally silent about Chickamauga on Sept. 20, 1863, the day that he might have wished to forget, since he had the worst day of his career; instead, he was critical of Thomas who again saved him and the army.

Apart from any consideration of individual performance at the

68. Wilson J. Vance, *Stone's River* (New York: Neale Publishing Co., 1914), pp. 49-50.

Battle of Stones River is the appalling fact that so few Americans realize the great effect the battle had on the outcome of the war. The tendency to regard only those battles fought on the perimeter of the Confederacy, or adjacent to the Potomac River, as important is difficult to comprehend. Perhaps this is so because these battles were fought between and around the respective seats of government; and the excess of population in this area helped in circulating the fallacy of greater importance than was possible in the more sparsely settled Mississippi Valley, Chattanooga, and other areas in the then so-called West. This tendency also included a general oversight of the United States Navy's operations on western rivers, a major factor in wearing down the South and restoring the Union.

Another factor often overlooked was the low estate into which the national morale descended when the Battle of Stones River was fought. The years 1861 and 1862 were disastrous for the Union cause, as the Confederate armies, under their able leaders, defeated the Northern armies in most of the important battles. The corresponding spirit of despair that inevitably followed those defeats was somewhat reversed after the Confederate retreat at Stones River.

The Army of the Cumberland consistently brought victories, despite criticism from those who could not perform so capably. Although the Army of the Potomac, despite its splendid composition, won few battles and suffered devastating defeats, the Army of the Cumberland won all important battles except Chickamauga, and the result there is debatable. That army was also successful in holding Kentucky in the Union and was instrumental in returning Tennessee to the Union, the first state to do so.

The Army of the Cumberland and other armies in the West also produced most of the famous generals of the war, among whom were Buell, Rosecrans, Thomas, Grant, and Sherman. It will be recalled that although Grant ended his military career with the Army of the Potomac, he first came into prominence at Fort Henry, Fort Donelson, and Vicksburg. In the aggregate, the generals of the Army of the Potomac did not compare in ability with those of the West, but General Meade, the victor of Gettysburg, was a cool, capable, and above-average commander, perhaps the best, and Generals Hancock and Hooker were among its more capable corps commanders, although Hooker met one of the worst defeats in American history at Chancellorsville. General Hancock, who is credited with having selected the site at Gettysburg, and did much to bring Federal victory there, was one of the ablest corps commanders on either side, although he was not entrusted with an independent army command.

Last but not least, General McClellan was the ablest organizer in the Union Army, and he must be given credit for building the Army of the Potomac; it should be said also that if McClellan did not win a spectacular victory at Antietam, it was a most important one. Furthermore, it should be emphasized that McClellan suffered no disastrous defeats; he would not be bullied into sacrificing his men needlessly; and he managed to maintain his army intact while avoiding serious defeat. On the contrary, Generals McDowell, Pope, and Burnside commanded at First Bull Run, Second Bull Run, and Fredericksburg, three of the worst Union defeats; and without reflecting upon the successes of Generals Jackson and Lee, it is a fact that much of their success was built upon the poor generalship of these Northern commanders.

CHAPTER XIII

Respite at Murfreesboro: Tullahoma and Prologue to Chickamauga

GENERAL Robert E. Lee's retreat after the Battle of Antietam on September 16 and 17, 1862, in which his army was outnumbered by more than two to one, discouraged recognition of the Confederacy by Great Britain in particular among the European powers. Emperor Napoleon the Third was on the throne of France at the time and was casting covetous glances toward North America. The time for direct action had not yet arrived, but in June, 1864, Napoleon's puppet, the Austrian Archduke Maximilian, was established as emperor of Mexico at Mexico City. This distinct threat to our security was removed after the end of the Civil War, when the United States Government reminded the French that their occupation of Mexico was in violation of the Monroe Doctrine. More than one European power would have welcomed the breaking up of the Union; and it is but realistic to conclude that but for the Northern victory other nations would have attempted to gain a foothold elsewhere in this hemisphere.

Great Britain, somewhat less reluctant to take the extreme step of intervention, gave great material support to the Confederacy, despite outwardly amicable relations with the United States. This was shown by the construction of large vessels in British shipyards for the Confederate States for use in breaking the blockade of Southern ports by the United States. British merchants sold goods, including arms and other essential war material, that helped the South immeasurably; and from British citizens British bankers raised large sums of money that they lent to the South. Shares in British-built blockade runners were sold to Britons with relative ease; in brief, Great Britain did everything short of actually declaring war to maintain the division of the Union.

The British working classes, even those most vitally affected by the stoppage of cotton shipments to their mills as a result of the blockade, it should be noted to their everlasting credit, were deeply sympathetic to the harassed North. In strange contrast, William Ewart Gladstone, later British Prime Minister, expressed the general attitude of the British Cabinet in these words:

We know quite well that the people of the North have not yet drunk of the cup—they are still trying to hold it far from their lips,—which all the rest of the world see, they, nevertheless, must drink of. We may have our own opinions about slavery; we may be for or against the South; but there is no doubt that Jefferson Davis and other leaders of the South have made an army; they are making, it appears, a navy; and they have made,—what is more than either,—they have made a nation. We may anticipate with certainty the success of the Southern States, so far as their separation from the North is concerned.[1]

All of this is intended to make crystal clear that Great Britain wanted but a set of suitable conditions on which to base recognition of the Confederacy. The hypocrisy of Gladstone's assertion that the South was building a navy is transparently evident, since his nation was the chief instrument in that effort. It is needless to comment on the failure of his prophecy—that of the establishment of the Confederate States of America as a permanent nation—but it is important to observe that the battles waged on the soil of the United States, whether North or South, were vital in establishing the truth or falsity of his statement. No battles were more significant in this particular than Antietam, fought three weeks before Gladstone made his prediction; and Stones River, fought less than three months after the speech, was equally important in discouraging recognition of the South.

After the bloody defeat of the Army of the Potomac at the Battle of Fredericksburg, Virginia, December 13, 1862, jubilation among the British well-to-do rose accordingly. If Stones River, fought less than three weeks later, had resulted in another Confederate victory, British recognition would have almost surely followed; Stones River, therefore, fairly assured the maintenance of the Union intact. Stones River was, in other words, the turning point; and General George H. Thomas, by his heroic stand at the Round Forest, following the rolling up of the Union right, saved the battle and the Union.

Except for one mistake at Stones River, that of failing to provide an adequate defense on his right, the better to withstand the Con-

---

1. John Morley, *Life of Gladstone* (New York, 1911), speech at Newcastle, England, Oct. 7, 1862.

federate attack, General Rosecrans displayed great skill in conception and execution. This mistake, however unfortunate, placed him on the defensive immediately; and during the rest of the battle he had little opportunity to regain the initiative thus lost. Any reasonable hope of launching a sustained attack was forgotten in the tremendous effort to avoid serious defeat. This error cost Rosecrans the opportunity to win a decisive victory and to begin an earlier advance on Chattanooga, the vitally important starting point for an advance to the Atlantic Ocean by way of Atlanta, Georgia. The Chattanooga campaign, from August through September, 1863, would have begun earlier, while offering a greater and more immediate hope for success. This judgment rests on the premise that the Confederates would not have had the time to restore their shattered forces. On the contrary, the Federals would not have needed so much time as they eventually did to revitalize their forces.

One of the difficulties preventing an early advance on Chattanooga, aside from the need for rebuilding the Union army, was the lack of adequate transportation. The Louisville and Nashville Railroad, on which so much depended for shipment of supplies, ammunition, and other equipment to Murfreesboro, was in almost constant need of repair due to Confederate cavalry raids. The railroad superintendent reported that, during the year commencing July 1, 1862, "the road had been operated for its entire length only seven months and twelve days; all the bridges and trestleworks on the main stem and branches, with the exception of the bridge over Barren River and four small bridges, were destroyed and rebuilt during the year. Some of the structures were destroyed twice and some three times. In addition to this, most of the water stations, several depots, and a large number of cars were burnt, a number of engines badly damaged, and a tunnel in Tennessee nearly filled up for a distance of eight hundred feet."[2]

The route of advance from Nashville to Chattanooga was through an area intensely loyal to the Confederacy. The citizens were active, intelligent, and ready to give their all to obstruct a foe dedicated to returning them to the Union. Home guards and civilians of every age group able to bear arms made the lot of stragglers from the Federal army an unhappy one. Even the women of the area were belligerent and uncooperative, an attitude reflected upon every occasion by the heaping of ridicule and insults on the "Yankees." This antagonism was expressed in more violent form by male civilians as well as by members of the Confederate military. Large numbers of soldiers were therefore required to safeguard the railroad and the

2. Henry M. Cist, *The Army of the Cumberland* (New York, 1882), p. 138.

depots containing ordnance, equipment, and foodstuffs from capture or destruction.

Following his entry into Murfreesboro on January 5, 1863, General Thomas was ordered to place his command on the Woodbury, Bradyville, Manchester, and Shelbyville roads. General McCook placed his men from the Shelbyville pike across the Salem pike, with his right resting on Stones River. General Crittenden placed his force, beginning with the left of Thomas's position, the better to protect the Liberty and Lebanon turnpikes, with his left extending to Stones River.[3]

The Army of the Cumberland was reorganized effective January 9, 1863, when the three wings were renamed the Fourteenth, the Twentieth, and the Twenty-first Corps, commanded respectively by Generals Thomas, McCook, and Crittenden.[4]

The most important project to occupy the attention of Rosecrans during the first six months of the year 1863 was the construction of elaborate fortifications. Strong earthworks were built on the high ground between Murfreesboro and Stones River on each side of the Louisville and Nashville Railroad and the Nashville pike. The next few months were spent in perfecting the individual soldier and in equipping him for the battles to be faced in fulfilling his responsibility. The months seemed interminably lengthy, and Secretary of War Stanton expressed impatience at what he regarded as unnecessary delay in vanquishing the enemy. General James A. Garfield, chief of staff to General Rosecrans, was also impatient to move, although Thomas and most of the other generals were in agreement with Rosecrans that all plans should first be completed.[5]

On January 25, 1863, Forts Henry and Donelson, including the Cumberland River, were transferred from the command of General Grant to General Rosecrans. The Cumberland River was important as a major artery of supply, but the principal one was the railroad.[6]

After General Bragg's retreat from Murfreesboro, he established headquarters at Shelbyville and moved part of his army to Tullahoma. At Tullahoma he erected strong fortifications and earthworks, after which he went into winter quarters. General Bragg assigned Generals Van Dorn and Wheeler to defend the front and flanks of his army, Van Dorn to the left, with headquarters at Columbia, and Wheeler

3. Thomas B. Van Horne, *History of the Army of the Cumberland* (Cincinnati, 1875), Vol. I, p. 287.

4. *Official Records of the War of the Rebellion* (Washington, 1880–1901), Vol. XXIII, Part 2, p. 36.

5. Van Horne, *op. cit.*, Vol. I, p. 288.

6. *Official Records, op. cit.*, Vol. XXIII, Part 2, pp. 11-12.

to the right. Wheeler had under him such notables as Generals Morgan, Wharton, and Martin, while Forrest was assigned to General Van Dorn. On January 26, Bragg ordered Wheeler to capture Fort Donelson. Wheeler then requested Forrest to move with his brigade and four pieces of artillery by the river road to the Dover area. Dover was the strong point of the Federals, rather than old Fort Donelson. Wheeler himself moved by a road to the left with about twenty-five hundred men.[7]

When General Rosecrans learned through his scouts that Wheeler was on the move he ordered General Jeff Davis and his division, with two brigades of Colonel Robert H. Minty's cavalry, to advance by the Versailles Road and strike Wheeler at the rear. As a precautionary measure, General James B. Steedman was ordered to observe Wheeler's movements in the direction of Triune. Davis ordered Minty to advance with his cavalry through Unionville and Dover, at which latter place he captured some three hundred and fifty men. Davis himself moved to Eaglesville with his infantry. Both Generals Davis and Steedman combined their forces at Franklin; but Wheeler, advancing rapidly, marched between the two forces in pursuit of him and, on February 3, fell upon Colonel Abner C. Harding's Eighty-third Illinois Infantry at Dover, some six hundred men, with his greatly superior force of approximately four thousand men.[8]

Two unsuccessful charges by the Confederates having been repulsed, Colonel Harding ordered his men to countercharge, which resulted in the capture of more than forty men. Wheeler retreated with a loss of more than seven hundred killed, wounded, and captured. Harding lost about one hundred and twenty-six killed, wounded, and captured, having been aided considerably by fire on the Confederates from six gunboats conveying eighteen regiments of infantry and equipment to reinforce General Rosecrans. Following the engagement the boats continued with the reinforcements to Nashville. These troops were under the command of Generals George Crook, Absolom Baird, and Charles Gilbert. General Crook, in February, moved his force to Carthage, Tennessee, on the Cumberland River, to observe Confederate movements as far removed as Rome, Georgia, while General Gilbert took his brigade to Franklin, Tennessee.[9]

A surprising communication from General Rosecrans—General Order No. 16 of February 10, 1863—called attention to reports coming

7. *Ibid.*, pp. 39, 41, 46; Cist, *op. cit.*, pp. 138-40.

8. *Official Records, ibid.*, p. 46; Cist, *ibid.*, p. 140; Frederick Phister, *Statistical Record, Campaigns of the Civil War* (New York: Jack Brussel, a reprint, no date), p. 283.

9. Cist, *ibid.*, pp. 140-41; *Official Records, ibid.*, p. 46.

to him that Confederate soldiers appeared in battle in Federal uniforms. Furthermore, they had been reported as even carrying the United States flag in order to complete the deception. In view of these violations of recognized rules of warfare, Rosecrans enjoined all patriotic citizens and soldiers to apprehend the guilty whenever possible and to insure their well-deserved punishment. On that date also General Joseph J. Reynolds submitted a lengthy report to General Thomas, in which he described the types of injustice to loyal residents of Tennessee. Thomas had been solicitous for some time concerning the unfortunate people who were forced involuntarily into Confederate service or, alternatively, to avoid such service had fled to the hills or other hideouts available to them. Those fortunate enough to escape military service were often aided by friends and relatives who brought them food and other necessities. General Reynolds stated that as his men passed the houses of the persecuted loyal men their women and children gave them a hearty welcome and requested them to stay. He reported also that these people were generally illiterate and timid and understood little regarding the sectional strife; however, they could not accept the arguments of their wealthier and better-informed neighbors, who insisted that they support a Government that had oppressed them, and that they repudiate the Government they knew and loved. Thomas referred Reynolds's letter to Washington on February 18, and on March 5 General Halleck instructed General Rosecrans that he had free rein in punishing hostile citizens according to the customs and usages of war.[10]

General Gilbert, who in February had moved his brigade to Franklin as aforesaid, ordered Colonel Coburn, on March 2, with five infantry regiments and three cavalry detachments under Colonel Thomas J. Jordan, and a battery of artillery, almost three thousand men in all, to observe Confederate activities around Columbia. It was hoped that this force would combine with another detachment proceeding from Murfreesboro and ascertain the whereabouts of the Confederates. Confederate commander General Van Dorn had in mind the establishing of outposts and picket lines near Franklin and Triune and the shifting of his headquarters from north of Duck River to Spring Hill.[11]

Colonel Jordan struck the Confederates, arrayed in line of battle, with his cavalry and artillery and forced them to retreat to Spring Hill. Realizing that he faced a much larger force, Colonel Coburn requested of General Gilbert that he be permitted to with-

10. *Official Records, ibid.*, pp. 53-56.

11. *Ibid.*, Vol. XXIII, Part 1, pp. 85-93; Phister, *op. cit.*, p. 326; Cist, *op. cit.*, p. 141.

draw, but this was refused; instead, Gilbert ordered him to advance. There is some confusion here, inasmuch as General Gordon Granger reported to General Rosecrans, on March 6, 1863, that Colonel Coburn did not keep General Gilbert advised, nor did he approach the Confederates with due caution to learn their true strength before attacking a well-defended foe three or four times his own number. Nevertheless, the next morning Coburn met the enemy lined up for action near Thompson's Station. General Forrest, with a battery, was on the far right near Colonel Samuel C. Armstrong's brigade. On Coburn's left a Texas brigade under J. W. Whitfield, with two guns on each side of Columbia Road, rounded out a total of ten thousand men under General Van Dorn's command. Coburn deployed his infantry across the turnpike to the right and ordered an advance at 9:30 on the morning of March 5. The charge was executed according to plan, but at about one hundred and fifty yards Armstrong's and Whitfield's brigades opened a withering fire on them and compelled their withdrawal.[12]

After a half hour's brisk exchange of firing, Coburn withdrew and ordered Jordan and his cavalry to cover his retreat. General Van Dorn tried twice to surround Coburn's forces before succeeding, but General Forrest and his men were checked enough to enable Coburn to remove his artillery. Coburn was simply overwhelmed, his loss in killed, wounded, and prisoners being approximately twenty-four hundred. This setback compelled General Gordon Granger to order the troops of General Baird to move to Franklin by rail, while he himself moved his own headquarters there and assumed command in person.

General John H. Morgan's cavalry suffered a severe defeat at Vaught's Hill, near Milton, Tennessee, at the hands of Union Colonel A. S. Hall's two brigades of General Joseph J. Reynolds's division. Morgan's losses included ninety-five killed, three hundred and fifty wounded, and twenty prisoners. Again on April 3, Morgan met defeat, this time at Liberty, Tennessee, when opposed to General David S. Stanley. This engagement began when General Stanley attacked Morgan's command and compelled it to fall back to the main army. He then struck with part of his force and turned Morgan's left flank. Morgan soon yielded at every turn before withdrawing, although his officers strove desperately but unsuccessfully to rally their men.[13]

---

12. *Official Records, ibid.,* Vol. XXIII, Part 2, p. 112; Vol. XXIII, Part 1, 85-93; Cist, *ibid.,* p. 143.

13. *Official Records, ibid.,* Vol. XXIII, Part 1, pp. 153-55; Cist, *ibid.,* pp. 143-44.

On April 7, General Rosecrans assigned a brigade to Colonel Abel D. Streight for the purpose of disrupting enemy communications and destroying property. This force, partly mounted, moved from Nashville through Clarksville to Fort Henry, and from there by ship to Eastport, Mississippi. Despite the best effort to supply all men with animals, only four-fifths of the men were mounted. On April 21, he left Eastport and, passing through Tuscumbia three days later, arrived at Moulton, Alabama, on April 26. Leaving Moulton on April 28, he continued through Day's Gap on Sand Mountain toward Blountsville. On April 30, his rear guard was attacked at Day's Gap by General Forrest's cavalry, after the latter had ridden night and day to repel Streight's advance. Continuing to Streight's camp, Forrest attacked him with artillery to open the encounter. Streight at once dismounted his command on a hill crest and awaited the oncoming Forrest, when, at the proper moment, he charged and drove the Confederates back at all points. Forrest lost about seventy-five men killed and wounded, while Streight lost about twenty, in addition to a number of horses. At about three o'clock that afternoon Forrest again attacked but again losing heavily, during an encounter lasting until dark, he withdrew once more.[14]

At noon on May 1, Streight and his men reached their planned destination at Blountsville. After burning all the wagons but one, and after placing the ammunition on mules in addition to giving the men the maximum they could conveniently carry, his men once more began to move. Skirmishing with the Confederates commenced at three o'clock, almost as soon as they broke camp, and they continued marching until midnight. Resuming their march on May 2, with skirmishing by the rear guard, they entered Gadsden and destroyed a large quantity of enemy provisions. An expected steamer for transporting a detachment of the command to Rome, Georgia, having failed to appear, Streight's problems increased rapidly, the most serious of which was the physical exhaustion of men and animals. To prevent the capture of stragglers, the march was slowed considerably. On May 2, also, General Forrest attacked Streight's command while the horses were being fed at Blount's farm, and he was again repulsed, despite a continuing skirmishing with Streight's rear guard. The main force crossed the Coosa River, after holding Forrest in check at Blount's farm until dark; but tragically for the Federals, the river was so high that the men were unable to prevent the ammunition from getting wet. One fortunate occurrence was the burning to the ground, by a detachment from Streight, of the Round

---

14. *Official Records, ibid.,* pp. 285-93; Cist, *ibid.,* p. 146.

Mountain Iron Works, one of the principal manufacturing plants for munitions in the Confederacy.[15]

On May 3, while preparing breakfast, Forrest again attacked and demanded the surrender of Streight under a flag of truce. Although at first he refused to consider the demand, Streight held a conference with his officers. It was decided that the damaged ammunition and the exhausted condition of his men made further resistance impossible. Streight was permitted to make a personal examination of Forrest's artillery before surrendering his force of almost fifteen hundred men.

General Thomas was not idle during Colonel Streight's expedition. He ordered General Reynolds on April 20 to proceed to McMinnville with three brigades of infantry, Colonel Minty's cavalry, and Colonel Wilder's mounted infantry. There he substantially accomplished his mission of destroying the railroad, in addition to burning all the bridges, cars, locomotives, and other railroad equipment, including the depot at McMinnville. He also captured a large quantity of supplies besides taking about one hundred and eighty prisoners and six hundred animals. A companion event occurred on April 27, when Colonel Lewis Watkins attacked the Texas Legion, posted near Van Dorn's main army at Spring Hill, capturing one hundred and twenty-eight men, over three hundred animals, and camp equipment, without losing a single man.[16]

While the Army of the Cumberland was devoting its time to recouping its losses after the Battle of Stones River and preparing for the campaign to take Chattanooga, another bitter exchange of correspondence developed between General Halleck and the authorities in Washington, on the one side, and General Rosecrans, on the other. This was but a repetition of the bitterness resulting from Halleck's earlier badgering of Rosecrans to get his campaign under way after Buell was relieved. At that time, as stated previously, General Rosecrans showed rare courage and manhood in refusing to be bullied into hasty action; in fact, he told Halleck in straight language that if he was not satisfied with his, Rosecrans's, performance he could replace him. This time he was no less direct and to the point in telling Halleck where he stood than he had been previously, when he retorted that his effort in seeking victory was not dependent upon the hope of personal reward but upon the hope of reuniting his divided country.

On March 1, 1863, Halleck sent the following letter to General Rosecrans:

15. Cist, *ibid.*
16. *Ibid.*, p. 147.

"There is a vacant major-generalcy in the Regular Army and I am authorized to say that it will be given to the general in the field who first wins an important and decisive victory."[17]

Historian Henry M. Cist reported that General Grant received the same offer, but that he very quietly folded it and put it by for possible future reference, and apparently quite indifferent to its contents, he proceeded with his plans for taking Vicksburg without offering any comment or protest. Rosecrans was of a different mold. He was stunned by an offer implying that he would do more for his country under the incentive of a promotion or bonus, in this case a major general's commission, if he would but win a battle that he might not otherwise seek without the offer of a reward. It goes without saying that Rosecrans was most industrious and, as always, was doing his utmost to prepare his army for successful accomplishments when Halleck made his insulting offer. The response of Rosecrans on March 6 was prompt and seething with indignation:

> Yours of the 1st instant, announcing the offer of a vacant major-generalcy to the general in the field who first wins an important and decisive victory, is received. As an officer and a citizen, I feel degraded to see such auctioneering of honor. Have we a general who would fight for his own personal benefit, when he would not for honor and the country? He would come by his commission basely in that case, and deserve to be despised by men of honor. But are all the brave and honorable generals on an equality as to chance? If not, it is unjust to those who probably deserve most.[18]

In the Civil War, which abounded with incompetent political generals who commanded and led men, often to needless death, this stand by Rosecrans must have had a beneficial effect. Although it brought no thaw in the cool relationship between Halleck and Rosecrans, there is nothing to indicate that Halleck took punitive action against him. This exchange of correspondence was an accurate portrayal of the characters of both men, as shown by the over-all records of each. One notes with sadness that in this type of incident the lofty objectives of the Civil War were obscured by the evil shadows of those who, in utmost charity, were weak, stumbling, and often incapable human beings. The wonder of it all is that beyond such examples as this were the great majority who lived, fought, and died to save the Union. It is not because of the weaknesses of those who trod the stage in the Civil War drama that Americans

---

17. *Official Records, op. cit.*, Vol. XXIII, Part 2, p. 95.
18. *Ibid.*, p. 111.

have been held by an ever-increasing interest; rather, it is in the strength of those who gave their all unselfishly that we, in looking back, see ourselves as we prefer to believe we would have been.

Rosecrans, despite his fatal mistake at Chickamauga, referred to earlier and to be discussed later in the account of that battle, was a great general and deserved a much better fate than he received. Apart from his generalship, he was also a noble figure in the best sense of the term. The Army of the Cumberland was commanded from the beginning by men of high character and ability, including Generals Robert Anderson, Don Carlos Buell, William S. Rosecrans, and George H. Thomas.

An interesting sidelight on the Army of the Cumberland while at Murfreesboro concerned the difficulty of General Rosecrans in obtaining supplies and ordnance. In a letter to Halleck, dated February 1, 1863, he requested that Halleck be not wearied of his importuning him for badly needed arms, particularly revolving arms, and stated that no mode of recruiting will so promptly strengthen his army. Then he made a final appeal, "Will you please aid me to get the arms? Even installments, to show that they will come some day, will answer. We must create military ardor." On the very next day, February 2, he wrote to Secretary of War Stanton, stating that Halleck regarded his request for arms as a complaint. He told Stanton that he was speaking for the country when he asked for men properly mounted and equipped with which to carry out his responsibilities, as though the fulfillment of such responsibilities would not imply the need for such means of performing them. General Halleck was a most difficult man and his subsequent removal from the chief command created little surprise.[19]

General Rosecrans issued a circular letter to his generals on June 8, 1863, requesting their answer to three questions concerning the military situation affecting the Army of the Cumberland. In brief, these questions were "(1) From the fullest information in your possession, do you think the enemy in front of us has been so materially weakened by detachments to Johnston or elsewhere that this army could advance on him at this time with strong reasonable chances of fighting a great and successful battle? (2) Do you think an advance of our army at present likely to prevent additional reenforcements being sent against General Grant by the enemy in our front? (3) Do you think an immediate or early advance of our army advisable?"

General Thomas replied that he had no reason to believe that the Confederates were materially weakened, and reliable reports

---

19. *Ibid.*, pp. 31-34.

from his scouts and officers indicated that an advance might bring on a battle in which the opposing forces would be equal. He stated his conviction that unless a decisive victory could be gained, Federal communications would be under continuing Confederate cavalry attack. Thomas also reported that in his opinion an advance would give the Confederates the alternative of falling back to Chattanooga, enabling them to demonstrate sufficiently to hold the Federals in check, while luring them away from their base of supplies and communications. Thomas advised strongly against an advance at that time; instead, he recommended holding the army in readiness for an opportune moment, meanwhile threatening Bragg from a position of strength and impressing him with the danger of sending reinforcements to General Johnston in Mississippi. Finally, as to the argument that Bragg, reinforced, might attack the Army of the Cumberland in its formidable position, Thomas stated, "I will simply say that I should be most happy to meet him here with his reinforcements."[20]

Rosecrans's plan followed pretty generally Thomas's proposals. Repeated cajoling and prodding from Washington, and anxiety by General Grant who was besieging Vicksburg, an anxiety that found expression in his entreaties to Halleck and Rosecrans that Bragg be attacked, did not deter Rosecrans from his purpose of keeping General Bragg uncertain of his intentions. This strategy was designed not only to hold Bragg in his immediate front and under his control, but also to retain his army intact near his base of supplies in the event of Grant's defeat. General Bragg figured, no doubt, that his occupation of Middle Tennessee was preferable to being driven from the state; however, Rosecrans wanted Bragg in Tennessee, to prevent his union with General Pemberton at Vicksburg. Opposed to this judgment, which was shared by everyone of Rosecrans's corps and division commanders, were Secretary of War Stanton and Generals Grant and Halleck, all of whom were far removed from the scene.[21]

General Rosecrans, despite his decision to delay advancing until more favorable conditions developed, began preparations that had all of the indications of an early offensive. He made various dispositions, including the shifting of troops to afford the best possible defense in case of attack, meanwhile completing preparations to advance when opportune. On June 23, following receipt of news that Grant's prospects for success before Vicksburg were very good, he ordered an advance on Tullahoma and Shelbyville. In the meantime, General Ambrose E. Burnside was making serious gestures, as though he intended attacking in the Cumberland Mountains. General Thomas

20. *Ibid.,* pp. 413-14.
21. Cist, *op. cit.,* p. 151.

had given him detailed data regarding the routes from Kentucky into East Tennessee, also informing him of the natural advantages and obstacles of such a movement, including the attitude of the inhabitants. At this time a communication went from Burnside to Rosecrans stating that General Lee seemed to be moving north with a view to invading Pennsylvania and Ohio. He also gave his opinion that Lee's main army was still (June 17, 1863) between the Blue Ridge and Bull Run Mountains. Burnside, at Cincinnati, had some reliable sources of information apparently not available to General Hooker, the man chiefly concerned, who did not seem to know where Lee was much of the time during his advance to Gettysburg.[22]

When the Army of the Cumberland began its advance on June 23, Confederate General Polk's corps was strongly defended at Shelbyville behind heavy intrenchments constructed during the long period since the Battle of Stones River. Shelbyville, some twenty-odd miles south of Murfreesboro and the same distance north of Tullahoma, contained a large number of pro-Unionists. These sympathizers were subjected to considerable embarrassment and distress from Confederates who used every opportunity to make life difficult for them. General Bragg's right was at Wartrace with General Hardee's troops, which held the important passes at Liberty, Hoover, and Bellbuckle gaps. His extreme right was guarded by cavalry at McMinnville, while his cavalry, under Forrest, with headquarters at Columbia, posed a threat to Franklin. General Polk also posted an advance force at Guy's Gap, with his main army in supporting distance.[23]

The Confederate base of supplies at Chattanooga was the main supply source for the region south of Duck River. The area south of that river is a mixture of rocky ranges of hills and very rough terrain. The hills form a natural division between fertile mid-Tennessee and the country comprising an uneven plateau known as the "barrens," between the hills at Duck River and the Cumberland Mountains. Tullahoma, located on the McMinnville branch of the Nashville and Chattanooga Railroad, was the principal Confederate supply depot. Duck River, a narrow, deep stream having limited means of crossing it, was in close proximity to this depot and a large Confederate camp not far away. The main roads ran southward through the hills toward Tullahoma and Confederate communications. Manchester pike passed through Hoover's Gap to the "barrens" by a canyon known as Matt's Hollow. The Wartrace road coursed through Liberty Gap, whence it led into the road along the railroad through Bellbuckle Gap, while the

---

22. *Official Records, op. cit.,* Vol. XXIII, Part 2, pp. 261-62, 436.

23. *Ibid.,* Vol. XXIII, Part 1, p. 403; Van Horne, *op. cit.,* Vol. I, p. 303; Cist, *op. cit.,* pp. 154-55.

road to Shelbyville ran through Guy's Gap.[24] With this setting in mind, General Rosecrans began his offensive movement, seeking to finesse General Bragg's army of forty-odd thousand men from its long-established position.

Aware of Bragg's great strength at Shelbyville, Rosecrans realized that even if Bragg should be defeated he could retreat by an easily defended road. He decided therefore to ignore Bragg's intrenchments at Shelbyville completely, invite a battle on ground of his own choosing, and compel Bragg to retreat, if possible, by a less-desirable road. This was a large undertaking and required a reshuffling of the most advanced troops from the left to the right of his main position. Rosecrans's plan was to appear to attack Shelbyville; he therefore ordered General R. B. Mitchell and his cavalry to move from Triune and drive Bragg's cavalry back on his infantry. Sharp skirmishing at Eagleville, Rover, and Unionville followed. Rosecrans then personally demonstrated with cavalry from his left, and, in the meantime, dispatched infantry to Woodbury to draw Bragg's attention from Shelbyville. General Gordon Granger and his corps, with General Brannan's division of General Thomas's corps, advanced from Triune to Salem, and Rosecrans's entire army was beginning to move in what would prove to be one of the finest strategic campaigns of the war.[25]

General McCook and his Twentieth Corps marched by the Shelbyville pike on June 23 toward Liberty Gap. General Sheridan's and General Davis's divisions camped for the night at Millersburg, and General Richard W. Johnson's division continued its march to Liberty Gap. Five companies of the Thirty-ninth Indiana Infantry were attacked by the Confederates in the vicinity of the gap; General Willich then advanced and pushed Confederate skirmishers to the hill crests on both sides of the entrance to the gap. It was not feasible to take the position by direct assault; therefore a part of Colonel John F. Miller's brigade went into action, and, after both Confederate flanks were enveloped, drove them through the narrow depression between the hills. This movement resulted in the securing of a gateway through the natural defenses of Bragg's army.[26]

On June 24, General Thomas advanced from Murfreesboro by the Manchester pike with the divisions of Generals Reynolds and Rousseau, to seize and hold Hoover's Gap. This was one of the four gaps into which Rosecrans poured his artillery and wagon trains through

---

24. Cist, *ibid.; Hammond's World Atlas* (New York, 1953), p. 86.

25. Cist, *ibid.,* pp. 156-57; Van Horne, *op. cit.,* Vol. I, p. 303; *Official Records, op. cit.,* Vol. XXIII, Part 1, pp. 405-8.

26. *Official Records, ibid.,* pp. 462, 465, 486; Van Horne, *ibid.;* Cist, *ibid.,* pp. 158-59.

the Cumberland Mountains. Hoover's Gap was strongly defended by Confederate cavalry and infantry. Thomas's force comprised the advance of Rosecrans's army and, it should be noted, was to occupy the key role in the ultimate outcome of the campaign. Thomas ordered Colonel John T. Wilder's "Hatchet Brigade," Reynolds's division, sometimes known as the "Lightning Brigade," comprising about four thousand mounted infantry, to clear the gap of enemy troops for the advance of his main force. Wilder encountered the Confederate cavalry about seven miles from Murfreesboro and drove them back on their reserve force. He followed up this advantage by advancing quickly through the three-mile gap, much to the delight of the defenders, who expected to overwhelm them. When the Confederates realized, all too late, that Wilder's men were holding their fire until well within range of them, their jubilation vanished. Wilder's men then opened fire on the enemy with the new and revolutionary Spencer breech-loading, seven-shooter, repeating rifle, a small-arms weapon that had no counterpart in warfare up to that time.[27]

Lieutenant Colonel Gilbert C. Kniffen clearly outlined the advance through Hoover's Gap:

> Colonel John T. Wilder, in command of his splendid brigade of mounted infantry, was ordered to "trot through the gap," pushing the Confederate pickets before him, while Thomas was directed to follow as closely in his rear as possible. Wilder obeyed his orders literally, paying no attention to the frequent stands made by the retiring pickets, but, driving them back upon their reserves—who in turn fell back upon Stewart's division, posted on the Garrison Fork—he pushed on to Elk River in rear of Tullahoma. General Stewart sent Bushrod Johnson's brigade forward, and a brisk fight ensued. The head of Thomas' column was six miles to the rear, but Wilder's plucky regiments used their Spencer rifles to such good purpose as to hold their ground until Reynolds' division secured possession of the bridge, when Stewart, finding that the movement was really an advance in force, that the Gap he was posted to guard was lost, and that a heavy infantry column was crossing the bridge, fell back upon the main line.[28]

The Confederates here outnumbered the Union forces by about four or five to one, but the superiority of the Spencer rifle was so great that fire power was in favor of the attackers by a wide margin. In addition to the Spencer rifle, the remainder of Reynolds's division,

---

27. Cist, *ibid.*, p. 159.

28. *Battles and Leaders of the Civil War* (New York, 1884), Vol. III, p. 636; Fairfax Downey (in *Ordnance*, July–August, 1960), pp. 64-65.

with regular muskets and some artillery, were used against the Confederates. The yelling of the combatants, the intense excitement and confusion wrought by the surprising Spencer rifle, in addition to the normal uncertainties of battle, created a scene hardly to be described.

The Spencer rifle was an invention of Christopher Miner Spencer, a New Englander with a bent for mechanics and a lust for travel. He moved from place to place, working on first one thing, then another. Perhaps the most important work he did was with Colt's Firearms Company, in Hartford, Connecticut. At Colt's he repaired defective pistols, yet in this area of limited opportunity to expand his ideas he conceived the plan of the repeating rifle that bore his name. Seeking to introduce his valuable rifle to the armed forces, he met with little success until he obtained an audience with General Rosecrans and members of his staff while occupying Murfreesboro. It was here that Colonel Wilder saw the great potentiality of the rifle, and succeeded in placing an order for four thousand of them for delivery to his brigade. The Spencer rifle would be heard from again; first, in an engagement at Hanover, Pennsylvania, June 30, 1863, just before Gettysburg, under the direction of General George A. Custer, of doubtful fame in being ambushed and killed by Sioux Indians at the Battle of the Little Big Horn; second, in the Battle of Gettysburg; third, in the Battle of Chickamauga; and, finally, in the Atlanta and Nashville campaigns.[29]

General Crittenden left General Horatio P. Van Cleve's division at Murfreesboro on June 24, and advanced with General Wood's and General Palmer's divisions to Bradyville. General Granger and General Brannan moved their divisions from Salem to Christiana. General Stanley left Murfreesboro with General John B. Turchin's cavalry division to reinforce General Robert B. Mitchell at the junction of the Salem and Christiana roads. On June 25, Crittenden continued to Holly Springs; Brannan united with Thomas at Hoover's Gap; General Reynolds brushed with the Confederates during much of the day; and that night General Rousseau moved up to attack the enemy at Beach Grove on June 26. Stanley pushed the enemy from Guy's Gap and then joined Granger's corps, Mitchell's division, and Minty's Brigade at Christiana for operations on the right flank. Part of Colonel Eli Long's brigade of Turchin's division united with Crittenden at Holly Springs.[30]

29. J. O. Buckeridge, *Lincoln's Choice* (Harrisburg, Pa.: The Stackpole Co., 1956), pp. 38, 46, 49, 50, 51-53; *The American Gun* (Dec. 1, 1960), Vol. I, pp. 19-20; Van Horne, *op. cit.*, Vol. I, pp. 30-34; Cist, *op. cit.*, pp. 159-60.

30. Cist, *ibid.*, pp. 160-61; Van Horne, *ibid.*, Vol. I, p. 304; *Official Records, op. cit.*, Vol. XXIII, Part 1, pp. 405-8.

During the late afternoon of June 25, the Confederates attacked Liberty Gap, expecting to force General Johnson to withdraw. Johnson's occupation of the gap the day before, as stated previously, encouraged Bragg to presume that Rosecrans would advance his main army through it. Several attempts by Bragg to dislodge Johnson resulted in his losing eight hundred and fifty men killed and wounded, while Johnson lost two hundred and thirty-one killed and wounded.[31]

On June 26, Thomas marched toward Fairfield and came in contact with the Confederates on the high ground north of Garrison Creek. Incessant rain during the night of the twenty-fifth rendered an advance almost impossible, but they were ready to march by ten thirty in the morning. At four that morning Brannan's division joined Thomas for an expected attack. At eight in the morning Negley's division occupied a position in support. The divisions of Brannan and Rousseau operated against the Confederate left and Reynolds advanced against their right and front and pushed them back toward Fairfield.[32] Following their retreat, the enemy hoped to make a determined resistance by enfilading troops of General Thomas from the high position on his right; however, this attempt was prevented by Colonel Moses B. Walker's brigade, in cooperation with some Second Division regulars under Major Sidney Coolidge, who forced the enemy from this new position. Thomas pursued the enemy with his Fourteenth Corps and arranged his troops on a line from the Fairfield road to within five miles of Manchester. Generals McCook and Granger remained at Liberty Gap and Christiana, respectively. General Crittenden's move toward Manchester was impeded by bad weather, which made marching conditions extremely difficult.[33]

Thomas's Fourteenth Corps was now dispersed in advance of Hoover's Gap to insure concentration of Rosecrans's main army on the Confederate left. In this position he sought to compel the Confederates either to dispute the Union advance or to abandon their position entirely. Moving promptly to exploit the opportunity, McCook's corps left Liberty Gap on June 27, and marched through Hoover's Gap toward Manchester to the rear of Thomas's command. Thomas also began moving his force early on the morning of June 27—the divisions of Rousseau and Brannan to Fairfield, with Negley's division in support, and Reynold's division to Manchester. Finding that the enemy had left Fairfield, the divisions of Rousseau, Brannan,

31. Van Horne, *ibid.*, pp. 304-5; *Official Records, ibid.*, pp. 404-8.

32. Phister, *op. cit.*, pp. 304-5; Cist, *op. cit.*, pp. 159-62.

33. Van Horne, *op. cit.*, Vol. I, p. 305; *Official Records, op. cit.*, Vol. XXIII, Part 1, pp. 405-8.

and Negley continued to Manchester, where the entire Fourteenth Corps was concentrated.[34]

Stanley's reserve corps, with his cavalry in advance, left Christiana for Guy's Gap, and there encountered the Confederates. Minty's brigade and Mitchell's division drove the Confederates from the gap and compelled them to retreat to their intrenchments about four miles north of Shelbyville. Here they met resistance from General Joe Wheeler, although he was compelled to leave his intrenchments and withdraw to Shelbyville. Mitchell attacked Wheeler at this point and, turning his right, blocked his retreat. His artillery and about five hundred of his men were captured, while Wheeler himself barely escaped by swimming Duck River with the rest of his command. General Bragg, it developed, withdrew his forces from his main defenses during the day, which comprised the first step in Rosecrans's plan to push Bragg back to his defenses on the Tennessee River.[35] This was a day of tremendous importance to Rosecrans, not only because of the minimum losses suffered, but also because it proved to Union followers that the Army of the Cumberland was capably led. The augury for future success by this fine army was also not lost upon the followers of the Confederacy, who realized that their cause was losing ground.

Early on the morning of June 28, Thomas ordered Wilder's brigade to disrupt rail communications south of Decherd, and Colonel John Beatty's brigade was ordered to move to Hillsboro to support Wilder. Thomas also ordered Rousseau's and Brannan's divisions to advance toward Tullahoma with the aid of some regiments from the divisions of Reynolds and Sheridan. Wilder arrived at Decherd at eight o'clock that evening and soon began damaging railroad installations, including about three hundred yards of track, and the depot and water tank. Withdrawing at the approach of enemy infantry, they continued next day damaging railroad facilities at University, but withdrew toward Anderson and Tantallon after dividing the force. Finding the Confederates too strong to make attack advisable, the brigade again united at University and arrived at Manchester at midday on June 30.[36]

On June 29, the three corps of Thomas, McCook, and Crittenden advanced toward Tullahoma, while Stanley arrived at Manchester, thus completing the concentration of the Army of the Cumberland for the final step against Tullahoma. Crittenden's command, which had

---

34. Van Horne, *ibid.*, pp. 305-6.

35. *Ibid.*, p. 306; *Official Records, op. cit.*, pp. 538-41.

36. Van Horne, *ibid.*, p. 307; *Official Records, ibid.*, pp. 457-61; Cist, *op. cit.*, pp. 164-65.

been marching a distance of some twenty miles since June 26, had a fearful time negotiating the rain-soaked roads, averaging only about five miles daily.[37]

Learning from a civilian, on June 30, that Bragg had abandoned Tullahoma, Thomas ordered Steedman to make reconnaissance in force; taking with him his own brigade and two regiments of Reynolds's division, he sought to establish the accuracy of the report. This force entered Tullahoma about noon and found the place deserted, except for a few stragglers. Upon being informed of the evidence of Bragg's retreat, Rosecrans ordered his troops to begin immediate pursuit. The forces of Rousseau and Negley intercepted the Confederate rear guard at Bethpage Bridge and engaged in a sharp skirmish that resulted in the enemy's retreat, after darkness made fighting impossible. The rain-swollen streams, particularly the Elk River, and the generally bad conditions of the roads, prevented a rapid pursuit of Bragg, and he escaped otherwise unmolested into the Cumberland Mountains.[38] Naturally the bad weather that was a distinct benefit to Bragg was equally a detriment to Rosecrans. The net result of Bragg's retreat was to return control once more of Middle Tennessee to the Army of the Cumberland. In this short campaign of about twelve days, rain fell almost constantly, and the troops, aside from being wet and uncomfortable, suffered the inconvenience of eating rain-soaked food.

Rosecrans's strategy, which forced Bragg to give up his strong defenses and retreat toward Chattanooga with relatively little difficulty, was due largely to his own skill in conception and that of his able subordinates in execution. Great credit attached also to the unconquerable spirit of his men, so ably exhibited during the Battle of Stones River. This campaign, which recovered so much territory with the loss of less than six hundred men in killed, wounded, and missing, seems not to have been appreciated by Secretary of War Stanton. In reply to Stanton's dispatch of July 7, advising Rosecrans of the surrender of Vicksburg on July 4, and prodding him with the remark that "You and your noble army now have the chance to give the finishing blow to the rebellion," General Rosecrans once more gave the type of manly reply characteristic of him. Bristling with indignation at the absence of even the barest mention of his outstanding achievement, perhaps the most brilliant and least bloody of the war, Rosecrans told Stanton, "You do not appear to observe the fact that this noble army has driven the rebels from Middle Tennes-

37. Cist, *ibid.*, p. 165; Van Horne, *ibid.*, p. 307.

38. Van Horne, *ibid.*, pp. 307-8; *Official Records, op. cit.*, pp. 402-3, 428; Cist, *ibid.*, p. 166.

see, of which my dispatches advised you. I beg in behalf of this army that the War Department may not overlook so great an event because it is not written in letters of blood. I have now to repeat that the rebel army has been forced from its strong intrenched positions at Shelbyville and Tullahoma, and driven over the Cumberland Mountains."[39] One can understand Stanton's anxiety in appealing to Rosecrans for a continuance of his aggressiveness toward Bragg; however, to ignore completely the barest mention of Rosecrans's bloodless victory showed a lack of understanding of the tremendous accomplishment by the one man from whom such understanding was most expected.

Confederate losses during the Tullahoma campaign, seldom ascertainable with any degree of accuracy, are unknown, although more than sixteen hundred men were taken prisoner. In retrospect, the campaign was similar in some aspects to the movement by these opposing forces during the Kentucky-Tennessee campaign of the summer of 1862, which ended in the Battle of Perryville. General Bragg's decision to retreat from the Tullahoma area without fighting a general engagement left the Union Army pretty much in control of the Tennessee River and the railroads in central Tennessee. Thus a great stride forward was accomplished toward the eventual capture of Chattanooga, the gateway to Atlanta, and the key to certain defeat of the Confederacy. Chattanooga was of incalculable value to the Confederates, and its possession by the Federals would mean the severing of the direct line of communication between the Mississippi River and the Atlantic Ocean. Furthermore, there would then be no means afforded for cooperation between the eastern and western sides of the Allegheny Mountains other than by a roundabout route through Atlanta.[40]

With Bragg in retreat and on the defensive, Rosecrans began preparing for another campaign that afforded Bragg no respite. During these days of watchful waiting and of preparation, the Union cavalry was occupied largely in drawing supplies from the occupied territory. The diversion of these supplies from the Confederate armies to the National armies soon began to have a telling effect in tightening the stranglehold that meant death to their cherished hopes for independence.

At the conclusion of the Tullahoma campaign, the two armies began preparing in great earnestness for a renewal of the struggle. Bragg occupied Chattanooga and the mountains above and below the

---

39. Cist, *ibid.,* p. 170; *Official Records, ibid.,* Vol. XXIII, Part 2, p. 518.
40. Walter Geer, *Campaigns of the Civil War* (New York, 1926), p. 194.

city, while Rosecrans occupied the western foot of the Cumberland Mountains, from McMinnville on the left to Winchester, almost directly south, on the right. Hardly three weeks after the close of the Tullahoma campaign, General Halleck resumed his systematic badgering of the commander of the Army of the Cumberland. One might well wonder at the abuse administered to these uniformly successful commanders by Halleck, as contrasted with the relative absence of pressure on commanders of the Army of the Potomac, whose results were not remotely comparable. On July 24, 1863, Halleck warned Rosecrans that he should remain no longer inactive, since "the patience of the authorities has been completely exhausted"; furthermore, he advised Rosecrans that but for his (Halleck's) intervention "you would have been removed from the command. . . . I am well aware that people at a distance do not appreciate the obstacles and difficulties which they would see if nearer by; but, whether well founded or without any foundation at all, the dissatisfaction really exists, and I deem it my duty, as a friend, to represent it to you truly and fairly; and I think I ought to do so, if for no other reason, because it was at my earnest solicitations that you were given the command."[41] Once more in evidence is Halleck's whiplash, or reminder, that but for him Rosecrans, a most able general, would not have been given the command; more to the point, there is in Halleck's cajolery the clear implication that assumption of command is a one-sided arrangement from which benefit can come only to the one in command. What nonsense! The degree of success achieved by commanders of the Army of the Cumberland in the face of this abuse is nothing short of amazing.

41. *Official Records, op. cit.*, Vol. XXIII, Part 2, p. 552.

CHAPTER XIV

To "The Valley of the Shadow"

THE brilliance of General Rosecrans in forcing General Bragg to withdraw from the strong defenses of Shelbyville and Tullahoma, despite continuous rain and mud, did much to relieve the Confederate strain on Union-held Nashville and Murfreesboro, and stamped him as a strategist of the first rank. The historian Henry M. Cist placed him at the head of the list by labeling him the greatest strategic general of the war.[1] Whatever might be his precise place, none can debate his greatness in planning a campaign. His achievement in advancing on his opponent at full strength and striking in the rear of his communications was the factor that compelled General Bragg to retreat to Chattanooga. This movement ended almost on the hour with General Grant's capture of Vicksburg, on July 4, 1863, and some thirty thousand prisoners, which resulted in the opening of the Mississippi River to the Gulf of Mexico and established the western boundary of the Confederacy. General Lee's defeat at Gettysburg, on July 3, 1863, reduced Confederate hopes of victory by invading Northern soil. Gettysburg, Vicksburg, and Tullahoma, remarkable for their simultaneity, were cause for the greatest Fourth of July rejoicing in American history and rank second in importance only to the signing of the Declaration of Independence, for which the day is celebrated.

After these great victories there still remained the intact South, a phalanx of states that would not be broken until the Chattanooga campaign, soon to follow, ended in Union success. Tullahoma therefore, although a splendid achievement, postponed the decision that was to be made on the battlefield. The major question was whether General Rosecrans would be compelled to lay siege to Chattanooga or, alternatively, succeed in maneuvering General Bragg into giving up the stronghold as he had done at Shelbyville and Tullahoma. The latter eventuality would once more merely postpone the inevitable

---

1. Henry M. Cist, *The Army of the Cumberland* (New York, 1882), pp. 168-71.

showdown between General Bragg and General Rosecrans, which, as history records, occurred at Chickamauga, Lookout Mountain, and Missionary Ridge.

Concealment was a primary element necessary to insure success of the undertaking, once the advance on Chattanooga was decided upon. Not least in importance was the need for accumulating supplies and equipment; also vital was the need for a thorough knowledge of the terrain to be traversed and the condition of routes of passage over mountain ranges that must be crossed. There was the additional factor of maintaining intact the important lines of communication. No basis exists for speculation whether General Rosecrans and his subordinate officers were idling about or indulging in flights of fancy as opposed to their complete devotion to preparing for the forthcoming campaign. The authorities in Washington, whether they actually thought so or not, acted consistently as though they believed field commanders, particularly those leading the Army of the Cumberland, were less than bright and aggressive. Everyone familiar with the problems confronting General Rosecrans knew that supreme efforts were being made to advance and defeat the enemy wherever he could be found.

Once preparations were completed the formidable problem of crossing the Cumberland Mountains, followed by the even more difficult one of crossing the Tennessee River, would have to be solved before the Confederates would be encountered. There was also the difficulty of repairing the Nashville and Chattanooga Railroad and obtaining additional reinforcements from Union forces to the east and west of Rosecrans's army. Then, too, delay was necessary while the corn crop ripened to supplement subsistence stores.[2]

After General Rosecrans had completed his problem of supply he turned his attention to the crossing of the Tennessee River. His acceptance of General Thomas's suggestion that railroads be utilized in combination with water whenever possible raised the question of crossing either above or below Chattanooga. General Thomas favored crossing at some distance below Chattanooga, thereby avoiding Confederate resistance while relieving the overburdened rail line, a plan that was adopted in principle. An aid in this plan was the supply depot that had been established at Stevenson, Alabama, a short time after the Army of the Cumberland occupied Tullahoma. A huge accumulation of supplies had to be concentrated in advance of the forthcoming campaign, as stated previously, although all of it was not required at Stevenson. General Rosecrans decided to utilize a branch

---

2. Thomas B. Van Horne, *History of the Army of the Cumberland* (Cincinnati, 1875), Vol. I, p. 310.

railroad running east from Cowan, Tennessee, to Tracy City, Tennessee, at the elevation of the Cumberland plateau, to provide supplies to the left of his army, another factor contributing to his delay in moving at once against General Bragg. Such utilization of railroads confirmed General Thomas's opinion that the war could not have been won without their use by the military forces.[3]

The ever-impatient authorities in Washington, chiefly through their spokesman General Halleck, were a source of considerable annoyance to General Rosecrans. In his reply of June 11, 1863 to General Halleck's communication of the same date, reminding him that "I deem it my duty to repeat to you the great dissatisfaction that is felt here at your inactivity," he wrote in part as follows:

> My preliminary infantry movements have nearly all been completed, and I am preparing to strike a blow that will tell; but, to show you how differently things are viewed here, I called on my corps and division commanders and generals of cavalry for answers, in writing, to these questions: 1st. From your best information, do you think the enemy materially weakened in our front? 2d. Do you think this army can advance, at this time, with reasonable prospect of fighting a great and successful battle? 3d. Do you think an advance advisable at this time?
>
> To the first, eleven answered no; six yes, to the extent of 10,000. To the second, four yes, with doubts; thirteen no. To the third, not one yes; thirteen no.
>
> Not one thinks an advance advisable until Vicksburg's fate is determined. Admitting these officers to have a reasonable share of military sagacity, courage and patriotism, you perceive that there are graver and stronger reasons than probably appear at Washington for the attitude of this army. I therefore counsel caution and patience at headquarters. Better wait a little to get all we can ready to insure the best results, if by doing so, per force of Providence, observe a great military maxim, not to risk two great and decisive battles at the same time. . . . I must have such thorough grounds (for success) that when I say "forward," my word will inspire conviction and confidence, where both are now wanting.[4]

Rosecrans's reply in explanation of his seeming delay apparently had its good effect, at least for a time, although Halleck attempted

---

3. Thomas B. Van Horne, *The Life of Major General George H. Thomas* (New York, 1882), p. 67.

4. *Official Records of the War of the Rebellion* (Washington, 1880-1901), Vol. XXIII, Part 1, pp. 8-10.

to maintain his position by reminding Rosecrans that "councils of war never fight," a most ridiculous statement in view of the facts. This reference to Rosecrans's polling of his commanders would seemingly render mute and bereft of council any officer seeking the opinions of his subordinates, a position that no commander before the enemy could tolerate. It did not take long for Rosecrans to reply to Halleck in convincing language:

> . . . you say you do not see how the maxim of not fighting two great battles at the same time applies to the case of this army and Grant's.
>
> The same maxim that forbids, as you take it, a single army fighting two great battles at the same time (by the way a very awkward thing to do), would forbid this nation's engaging all its forces in the great West at the same time, so as to leave it without a single reserve to stem the current of possible disaster.
>
> We ought to fight here if we have a strong prospect of winning a decisive battle over the opposing force, and upon this ground I shall act. I shall be careful not to risk our last reserve without strong grounds to expect success.[5]

The foregoing illustrates the difficulties confronting Rosecrans before Tullahoma, an attitude that was renewed in the waiting period after its capture. On August 5, General Halleck ordered General Rosecrans to set his army in motion against the enemy, ignoring in the order the reasons given by Rosecrans for the delay as well as the local conditions that might make such an order impossible of success. Rosecrans attributed this order to Secretary of War Stanton, in a letter to the 1879 Reunion of the Army of the Cumberland, in which he stated that "I read to them [his corps commanders] an order from General Halleck, by that unprincipled Secretary of War, who, a few weeks previously, had announced to gallant Rousseau, our bearer of dispatches, his hostility to our command, and recklessness of consequences to the country, saying he wouldn't send us 'another d——d man.' This was nothing less than that the Army of the Cumberland should be forthwith put on its march, and never halted until it had crossed the Tennessee into Georgia." Additionally, to emphasize the absurdity of the order, Rosecrans stated that he had reminded the Washington military hierarchy that to achieve success in the campaign it would be necessary to take twenty days' rations, that growing corn should be matured sufficiently to afford food for men and animals, and that the Confederates should be completely deceived as to the place of crossing the Cumberland Mountains and the Tennessee River.

5. *Ibid.*, pp. 8-9.

Furthermore, General Thomas, as spokesman, expressed the unanimous agreement of those present by stating emphatically, "That's right! Stand by that, and we will stand by you to the last."[6]

Rosecrans had established headquarters at Winchester where was stationed also General McCook's Twentieth Corps. Thomas was at Decherd with his Fourteenth Corps, and Crittenden was at McMinnville with his Twenty-first Corps. The cavalry was commanded by General D. S. Stanley and was busily engaged observing Confederate movements. This was the disposition of the Army of the Cumberland on the eve of its advance toward Chattanooga.

The Confederate Army also comprised three corps commanded by Generals Leonidas Polk, D. H. Hill, and Simon Bolivar Buckner, in addition to two cavalry corps commanded by Wheeler and Forrest. Bragg was reinforced by Walker's corps from Mississippi, and by Longstreet, who had arrived with his corps from the Army of Northern Virginia during the night of September 19 in time to perform a tremendous part in the outcome of the Battle of Chickamauga on the twentieth.

As in the Tullahoma campaign, General Rosecrans planned once more to conceal his intentions from General Bragg and perhaps again maneuver him from his position, this time from Chattanooga. He decided to send General Crittenden's corps from McMinnville across the Cumberland Mountains (average height, 2,200 feet) and Walden Ridge (average elevation, 1,300 feet) into the Tennessee Valley opposite Chattanooga. This movement was fraught with great difficulty through the thirty-mile-wide Cumberland Mountains and Walden Ridge's fifteen-mile width. Rosecrans hoped to encourage General Bragg into expecting an attack in that direction while with his main army he would cross the Tennessee River near Bridgeport, Alabama, about thirty-five miles below Chattanooga. This accomplished, he would move across the twenty-mile-wide Raccoon mountain range lying south-southwest of Chattanooga and the fifteen-mile-wide Lookout mountain range to the rear of Chattanooga, both of which averaged about 2,200 feet in height. The reaching of this objective would place squarely up to General Bragg the decision whether to defend Chattanooga or to retreat to protect his lines of communication. General Rosecrans hoped that General Crittenden's diversion would convince General Bragg that Crittenden was seeking a junction with General Burnside's force coming out of Kentucky into East Tennessee.[7]

---

6. Society of the Army of the Cumberland, *Yearbook, 1879* (Cincinnati, 1880), pp. 174-75.

7. Van Horne, *Cumberland,* pp. 311, 312; H. V. Boynton, *The Chickamauga National Military Park* (Cincinnati, 1895), pp. 15-16.

General Crittenden's corps moved on August 16 from Hillsboro, Manchester, and McMinnville toward the Tennessee Valley north of Chattanooga. Colonel Minty's cavalry advanced through Sparta and Pikeville, and in a spirited skirmish with Confederate cavalry at Kingston drove them across the river. Continuing his operations, Minty created the illusion of considerable movement for a distance of about thirty miles above Blythe's Ferry. General Crittenden's three divisions, commanded respectively by Generals Wood, Palmer, and Van Cleve, occupied the Sequatchie Valley at Anderson, Dunlap, and Pikeville. General Crittenden then ordered General Hazen's brigade of General Palmer's division and General Wagner's brigade of General Wood's division to enter the Tennessee Valley by way of Walden Ridge and join Colonel Wilder's mounted infantry of General Reynolds's division of the Fourteenth Corps. Tents were pitched along the crests of the ridges; fires were built at night and bugles blown both morning and night near the fords for a considerable distance up the river; and sawed-off pieces of lumber were floated down the river—all to create the illusion of a grand movement by the main army. Needless to say, in all of this General Bragg was completely deceived; first, as shown by his withdrawal of the infantry brigade defending the Tennessee River at Bridgeport and shifting it to Rosecrans's expected crossing; and second, in addition also to moving General Buckner from East Tennessee to defend the river, his little-delayed abandonment of Chattanooga.[8]

In the meantime, Generals Thomas and McCook crossed the Cumberland Mountains to the Tennessee River, where they were awaiting developments from General Crittenden's Twenty-first Corps. Generals Reynolds and Brannan with their divisions were at the mouth of Battle Creek, and Generals Baird and Negley were stationed near Bridgeport. General McCook's Twentieth Corps was near Stevenson, Alabama, where his right was protected by cavalry. General Rosecrans's front now extended over a distance of some one hundred and fifty miles and presented to General Bragg a most threatening and formidable adversary.[9]

An unusual and interesting sidelight in connection with the movement of Rosecrans's army was the presence in the ranks of Little Johnny Clem, John Lincoln Clem, Company C, Twenty-second Michigan Infantry. Johnny tried to enlist in the Third Ohio Infantry, also the Twenty-second Michigan Infantry, but was rejected because of his youth. Not discouraged, Johnny ran away and caught up with the Twenty-second Michigan after they marched too far away for him to be sent home. He was made a drummer boy, but could not, of course,

8. Van Horne, *Cumberland*, pp. 313, 314; Boynton, *ibid.*, pp. 17-18.
9. Boynton, *ibid.*, p. 18.

keep up with his comrades; therefore, when he became too tired on the long march, he would be carried in the saddle of a mounted officer. He was paid from collections donated by officers of the regiment but was finally placed on the payroll in May, 1863, after he became twelve years old. He served in the Battle of Shiloh, or Pittsburg Landing, where a shell demolished his drum, and where he was given the nickname by which he is best known, "The Drummer Boy of Shiloh." He then began carrying a musket, which had been reduced in size to accommodate his small stature, in response to his complaint, "I did not like to stand and be shot at without shooting back." At Chickamauga he took his place in the line while serving in General Granger's reserve corps, which came to support General Thomas in the desperate action on Snodgrass Hill. When a mounted Confederate colonel called upon Johnny to surrender during the action, he shot and killed him instantly. For this achievement General Rosecrans put him on the Roll of Honor and assigned him to duty at the headquarters of General Thomas. He was wounded at Chickamauga, where he was surrounded and taken prisoner, but managed to escape before reaching prison camp. While being hospitalized he was promoted to lance sergeant, although still only twelve years of age. When the war ended he sought admission to West Point Military Academy, but was rejected for lack of educational qualifications. Nevertheless, in 1871, President Grant gave him a lieutenant's commission and he was assigned to the Twenty-fourth Regular Infantry. Eventually he rose through the ranks, and upon his retirement in 1916 he was a major general. He had reached the ripe old age of 85 upon his death in San Antonio, May 13, 1937, having been born in Newark, Ohio, August 13, 1851. He is buried in Arlington National Cemetery, Washington, D.C.[10]

The crossing of the Cumberland Mountains over narrow, winding trails, in many instances, was but one of a number of difficulties besetting Rosecrans's army. His men were compelled to construct bridges over the Tennessee River ranging in length from one-fourth of a mile at Caperton's, Alabama, to more than one-half a mile at Bridgeport, Alabama. The bridge at Caperton's was transported by railroad and unloaded in the wooded section near by. At this location the soldiers assigned the task of installing it were enabled to simulate the operation without enemy detection. At daybreak on August 29,

10. *Photographic History of the Civil War* (New York, 1957), Vol. VIII, p. 192; Benson J. Lossing, *A Pictorial History of the Civil War in the United States* (Elgin, Pa., 1885), Vol. III, p. 141; Bell I. Wiley, *The Life of Billy Yank* (Indianapolis, 1952), pp. 297, 298; Frederick H. Dyer, *A Compendium of the War of the Rebellion* (New York, 1959), Vol. III, p. 1291.

fifty boats containing fifty men each were rowed to the southern bank. The bridge was laid promptly, following the dispersal of a small opposing cavalry force. General Davis's division crossed the bridge and went into camp at the foot of Raccoon Mountain, and on September 2 crossed with his and General Johnson's divisions. Still later, September 4, General Davis occupied the pass at Winston's, over Lookout Mountain, some forty miles south of Chattanooga. General Stanley's division of cavalry crossed a day later and entered Broomtown Valley.[11]

General Sheridan's division crossed the Tennessee River at Bridgeport, after laying pontoons, and proceeded to Valley Head. General Negley's division, Thomas's corps, crossed with General McCook, and General Baird, also of Thomas's corps, crossed with Sheridan. Generals Brannan and Reynolds, Thomas's corps, crossed at Battle Creek and Shellmound, mainly on rafts and in canoes, but a number of the men swam across with the aid of small improvised rafts to transport their clothing and equipment. Once the entire Fourteenth and Twentieth Corps had crossed the river, General Crittenden sent his remaining force in the Sequatchie Valley to Battle Creek, where they also crossed on September 3 and 4 on rafts and other means utilized by Generals Brannan and Reynolds. General Crittenden was near Wauhatchie, just below Chattanooga, on September 6, where, for the first time, General Bragg must have realized the imminent presence of Rosecrans's army. Just three days later, September 9, a small force of General Crittenden's corps ascended to the top of Lookout Mountain and observed that General Bragg had abandoned Chattanooga. General Thomas, meanwhile, crossed Lookout Mountain with his command on September 8 to Stevens' Gap, about twenty-six miles south of the abandoned city.[12]

Part of General Woods division followed the Ninety-second Illinois Mounted Infantry of General Wilder's brigade into Chattanooga on September 9. The divisions of Generals Palmer and Van Cleve marched to the north point of Lookout Mountain and followed after General Bragg, but camped for the night in Rossville Gap. Bragg's army had left Chattanooga on September 7, from where he retreated to Lafayette behind Pigeon Mountain. General Wilder's brigade crossed Friar's Island on September 8, and General Hazen's brigade crossed there on September 10; meanwhile, General Wagner's brigade crossed the river directly opposite the city and entered it on the afternoon of September 9. It is important to note that the first unit to enter Chattanooga, the Ninety-second Illinois, was part of General

---

11. Van Horne, *Cumberland*, Vol. I, p. 314; Boynton, *op. cit.*, pp. 17-19.
12. Van Horne, *ibid.*, pp. 314-15; Boynton, *ibid.*, p. 19.

Reynolds's division of General Thomas's Fourteenth Corps.[13] This serves as another refutation of the time-worn falsehood that General Thomas was slow.

The campaign, which, begun on August 16, resulted in General Bragg's evacuation of Chattanooga on September 7, only twenty-two days later, was a duplication, although somewhat enlarged, of the Tullahoma campaign. The success achieved in overcoming natural disadvantages of terrain and water, added to the inevitable military difficulties, was one of the most notable of the war, if not the most important.

Confederate General William W. Loring asserted some time before Appomattox that it was apparent that the Chattanooga campaign spelled the end of the Confederacy. He stated that "not a man in the Confederacy felt that the Union had really accomplished anything until Chattanooga fell."

When asked, "You do not mean to say, general, that Vicksburg and Gettysburg were nothing?", he replied, "The loss of Vicksburg weakened our prestige, contracted our territory, and practically expelled us from the Mississippi River, but it left the body of our power unharmed. As to Gettysburg, that was an experiment; if we had won that battle the government at Washington would, perhaps, have tendered peace with a recognition of the Confederacy. Our loss of it, except that we could less easily spare the slaughter of veteran soldiers than you could, left us just where we were."

Continuing the conversation, General Loring was asked, "But in the latter part of 1863 some of your people lost hope?" He replied, "Not exactly that, but they experienced then for the first time a diminution of confidence as to the final result." Further, he stated that it was the fall of Chattanooga, in consequence of the Chickamauga campaign, and the total defeat of General Bragg's efforts to recover it, that caused the loss of confidence in Confederate success.

Regarding the reason Chattanooga was held to be so important, he replied, "As long as we held it, it was the closed doorway to the interior of our country. When it came into your [the Union's] hands the door stood open, and however rough your progress in the interior might be, it still left you free to march inside. I tell you that when your Dutch General Rosecrans commenced his forward movement for the capture of Chattanooga we laughed him to scorn; we believed that the black brow of Lookout Mountain would frown him out of existence; that he would dash himself to pieces against the many and vast natural barriers that rise all around Chattanooga; and that then the Northern people and the government at Washington would per-

---

13. Van Horne, *ibid.*, p. 316; Boynton, *ibid.*, pp. 19-20.

ceive how hopeless were their efforts when they came to attack the real South."

To another question, "But the capture of Chattanooga convinced you that even the real South was vulnerable, did it?" he commented, "Yes, it was only a question as to whether we could beat back your armies by sheer force of desperate fighting, and as you largely outnumbered us, and our resources were every day diminishing, the prospects to the thinking part of our people looked gloomy indeed." To a final remark, "But, general, there are people in the North who regard the Chickamauga campaign as a failure for the Union cause," he said, "Ah! We would gladly have exchanged a dozen of our previous victories for that one failure."[14]

This judgment finds general support from competent military authorities. Chattanooga was undoubtedly the key to the unlocking of the Confederacy, of which Chickamauga was an extremely important first step. Richmond, on the other hand, was a holding action in effect, perhaps more accurately a stalemate, in proof of which the record of Union battles lost is cited. It was not until after Chickamauga, which prevented General Bragg's retaking Chattanooga, followed by the battles of Orchard Knob, Lookout Mountain, and Missionary Ridge, in November, 1863, and still later the clinching Battle of Nashville, in December, 1864, that the Confederacy was first cracked, then opened, and finally broken. Paramount in all of these battles was the towering, unmatched figure of General Thomas, whose achievements dominated them as did no other commander in any of the other battles of the Civil War. One shudders at the thought of the Union's peril if General Thomas, the strong Virginian, had not been in the Army of the Cumberland from the very beginning; his absence in almost any of these important battles might have made the difference, but his absence in all of them surely would have made it.

When General Rosecrans realized that he had won another virtually bloodless campaign, after Bragg's retreat from Chattanooga, he planned immediate pursuit in the hope of bringing on a general engagement. He summoned Thomas to his headquarters on the morning of September 9 to discuss his plan; however, in the summons he directed Thomas to prepare his entire command to move promptly in pursuit. The ambiguity between the summons to discuss the matter and his order to prepare for pursuit is readily apparent. In the dis-

---

14. H. V. Boynton, *Chattanooga and Chickamauga Campaigns* (reprint of Boynton's wartime letters to the Cincinnati *Gazette*), (Washington, 1888), pp. 2, 3; Ezra J. Warner, *Generals in Gray* (Baton Rouge: Louisiana State University Press, 1959), p. 193.

cussion, Thomas expressed in strong terms his opposition to the move, based on sound military considerations, chief of which was that he would be required, in crossing the mountains, to split his forces.[15]

The dispersal of the Army of the Cumberland was not a compelling argument to Rosecrans against the plan, since the several corps, he believed, could be united within a day or two, if necessary. Also, the mountains offered concealment of the movement of the Fourteenth and Twentieth Corps through Lookout Valley; and furthermore, the Twenty-first Corps was capable of holding Chattanooga while protecting the south and east entrances with help from the brigades on the north bank of the Tennessee River. It was clear from General Bragg's withdrawal to Lafayette that he had no present intention of returning to contest Chattanooga. The Federal force's domination of all roads to the west of Lookout Mountain, which roads converged on the only road that crossed the tip of that mountain abutting the Tennessee River a few miles from Chattanooga, discouraged any thought Bragg might have had of retracing his steps. There was nothing to prevent concentration of the entire Union Army, which, in view of Rosecrans's occupancy of the city, left the question of thorough preparation by that general as the next step.

Thomas advised Rosecrans to defer pursuit of the Confederate Army until supplies could be replenished and communications firmly established between Bridgeport and Nashville. This accomplished, Thomas reasoned, success in the advance against General Bragg would be more certainly assured; furthermore, the gains already made would be rendered more secure by waiting until preparations were completed. Rosecrans adhered to his decision to follow Bragg promptly, thus ignoring the good counsel and advice of his able subordinate. There soon followed the series of incidents that exposed the Army of the Cumberland to the danger of being destroyed piecemeal. As the movements of his forces disclosed, once the advance was in full swing, Thomas's judgment would return to jolt Rosecrans with considerable emphasis that, but for a series of compensating errors by Bragg's subordinate commanders, the Army of the Cumberland would have suffered a terrible defeat.

After the meeting with General Thomas, General Rosecrans issued the following directive:

September 9, 1863

Major-General Thomas,
Commanding Fourteenth Army Corps:

The General commanding has ordered a general pursuit of the

---

15. Van Horne, *Life,* p. 104.

enemy by the whole army. General Crittenden has started to occupy Chattanooga and pursue the line of Bragg's retreat. Our forces across the river from Chattanooga have been ordered to cross and join General Crittenden in the pursuit. General Mc-Cook has been ordered to move at once on Alpine and Summerville. The General commanding directs you to move your command as rapidly as possible to Lafayette and make every exertion to strike the enemy flank, and if possible cut off his escape. Colonel Wilder's brigade has been ordered to join you at Lafayette.[16]

In effect, this order stated that the entire Army of the Cumberland was scattered, as one corps was in the rear of the Confederate Army, another was near the center, and a third was to the left of it. Viewed in entirety, the three corps were in an extremely dangerous situation relative to the main Confederate Army. That these corps were saved from annihilation forms one of the most nearly miraculous episodes of the Civil War, which, as aforesaid, was made possible only because of a series of offsetting blunders. Perhaps in this circumstance there was that Divine intervention that would not brook destruction of the American Union. Whatever may be the evaluation of the remarkable series of coincidences that saved the Union Army, the genius of General Thomas in foreseeing these dangers, and his forthrightness in opposing the decision that brought the dangers into reality, combined with his indispensable skill in extricating the army from its peril, stamps him still more indelibly as the outstanding Union general of the war. This unmatched ability was so inborn in him that, rather than creating jealousy, it served only to bolster the faith of his brother officers in him. There was a deep confidence in every undertaking of General Thomas, and it is worth mentioning that one of his biographers, Donn Piatt, gives an unusual explanation for it.

In the brief but stormy campaign [Tullahoma] conceived by Rosecrans but made practicable by Thomas, our hero exhibited those high qualities as a soldier that lifted him head and shoulders above the epauleted crowd on either side. He was making the noble army that he subsequently said made him, and now, putting his men to their first test of excellence, he felt assured that his orders would be executed with promptness and precision, if such lay within the bounds of human possibility. Riding silent at the head of his column, he kept himself in touch with the

16. *Ibid.*, pp. 104-8.

forces under his command, and every part of the wide and shifting movement was under his immediate control. The entire army moved as a huge but perfect machine at his will, and his mind took in and held every part, and the aides dashing to and from him bringing reports and carrying orders continued without interruption the story of a grand plan being successfully executed[17]

The feeling cannot escape the reviewer of the exemplary life of General Thomas that there was something of the Divine in the man, and that his reputation for honorable dealings in all his affairs with his fellow men came, not from coincidence, but from a sound faith. It was more than mere chance that impelled him to follow the far more difficult path of devotion to the Union when all of his immediate family, friends, and neighbors chose otherwise. His principal biographer, Thomas B. Van Horne, tells us that he was a firm believer in the Christian religion, and that during his last few years he felt a deep sense of obligation to its precepts. Furthermore, we are informed that a public profession of his faith near the close of his life was prevented by the inconveniences that crowded in upon him. He contemplated uniting with the Protestant Episcopal Church at Louisville, Kentucky, in 1869, but considered himself unable to perform such a solemn duty with the degree of calmness and freedom from worldly care that such a step required.[18] Nevertheless, no biographer is called upon to tell the story of a life that expressed more devotedly the teachings of the Master of Galilee.

A young aide once asked General Thomas if he believed in an overruling Providence.

"Most assuredly," he replied. The aide persisted, "I would like to know, then, why He is not on our side." The reply, again in the same vein, was characteristic: "Are you satisfied such is not the case?" Not convinced, the aide then said, "Why, it looks that way, General, if the Almighty is interfering. We are getting the worst of it all the time. Where God is there is the majority, you know." General Thomas replied, "I am not prepared, my young friend, to throw any light upon that matter. I have never made religion a study, and I am not equipped for its discussion. I never was tempted to question what came to me so sweetly, and so full of consolation and comfort, any more than I would

17. Donn Piatt, *General George H. Thomas* (Cincinnati, 1891), p. 358.
18. Van Horne, *Life,* p. 459.

doubt and question the love of my mother. I know that it is here, and I know that it is Divine because it is good."[19]

The character of General Thomas, as exemplified by his refusal to resort to strategems, treachery, deceit, and the many other devices employed by ordinary humans in wresting so-called success from other struggling mortals more deserving, is proof positive that he was, with God's help, "The master of his fate and the captain of his soul." There was something in General Thomas of a piece far removed from selfish ambition, when he refused, time and again, to accept a promotion that he felt would be unjust to his superiors. His supreme loyalty to his superiors was unswerving, even when he himself did not agree with their judgment; and it mattered not that time vindicated his own better judgment in a number of important instances, as described in this work.

General Bragg displayed sound judgment in locating his main army at Lafayette, following his retreat from Chattanooga. He believed that General Rosecrans commanded about seventy thousand men, exaggerated, and General Burnside at Knoxville another twenty-five thousand, a force that rendered him incapable of protecting his communications, depots, and workshops. His right extended to Pigeon Mountain, about three or four miles south of Lee and Gordon's Mill. From this position he observed the advance of General Rosecrans, the Fourteenth Corps under General Thomas, moving down Lookout Mountain. The usual information as to his enemy's movements was also furnished by Confederate citizens along the routes on which the Federals were advancing, until they reached McLemore's Cove by way of Stevens' Gap. General Crittenden's Twenty-first Corps was at Rossville, about twenty miles distant from McLemore's Cove, which placed him within about five miles of Chattanooga. General McCook's Twentieth Corps was in the area of Summerville and Alpine, between forty and fifty miles away, and was therefore not within supporting distance. The scattering of the three corps of Rosecrans's army was due to their following the widely separated trails over Lookout Mountain. General George Crook's cavalry had advanced meanwhile to within three miles of General Bragg's army at Lafayette.[20]

It did not take long for General Bragg to perceive that the Union forces were separated, and he began prompt efforts to destroy each

---

19. Piatt, op. cit., p. 359.

20. Frederick Phister, Statistical Record, Campaigns of the Civil War (New York, Jack Brussel, no date), p. 277; Official Records, op. cit., Vol. XXX, Part 1, pp. 47, 52-54; Vol. XXX, Part 2, pp. 22, 23; Van Horne, Cumberland, op. cit., Vol. I, p. 317.

one before they could unite. Whatever ideas he may have had when retreating to Lafayette, during which time General Rosecrans assumed that he was planning to retreat to Rome, Georgia, he now saw a golden opportunity to regain his lost ground. He ordered General Thomas C. Hindman, at midnight of September 9, to march at daybreak from Lee and Gordon's Mill to Davis' Crossroads, where the road from Lafayette, through Dug Gap and Stevens' Gap, intersects. At the same time he ordered General D. H. Hill to send the division of General Pat Cleburne from Lafayette to unite with General Hindman at the Crossroads. This combined force was then to attack General Thomas's Fourteenth Corps advancing from Stevens' Gap. Time was of the utmost importance, and success demanded prompt execution of General Bragg's orders; however, General Hill reported that General Cleburne was ill, and that felled timbers had so obstructed the gaps that it would require at least a day for them to be removed before the advance could be continued.[21]

General Hill's delay prevented the interception and probably certain defeat of General Negley's division at Stevens' Gap, since General Baird was unable to arrive at the foot of the mountain until ten o'clock the night of September 10. Upon learning that General Hill could not complete his assignment, General Bragg ordered General Buckner and his two divisions, at ten o'clock on the morning of the same day, to join General Hindman in an attack on General Negley. Hindman stopped three miles north of Davis' Crossroads, where General Buckner joined him in the afternoon, thereby seemingly cutting off the escape of General Negley, only a short distance away. General Hindman considered his force outnumbered and awaited the arrival of General Hill. The position of General Negley was indeed perilous, since he was exposed to attack on both flanks and in front. This had come about following Negley's arrival at McLemore's Cove, a spot formed by a spur of Lookout Mountain curving eastward and inclining northward on the eastern side of Chickamauga Creek, where it is parallel with the Creek, Missionary Ridge, and Lookout Mountain. Here Negley skirmished with Confederate troops and drove them back a distance of some three or four miles. From this action Negley had moved forward, skirmishing heavily once more until he reached the opening at Dug Gap in Pigeon Mountain, through which the direct road to Lafayette passes, which was the route of the Fourteenth Corps.[22]

During General Negley's advance he had received conflicting

21. *Official Records, ibid.,* Vol. XXX, Part 2, p. 28; Cist, *op. cit.,* p. 185.
22. *Official Records, ibid.;* Cist, *ibid.,* pp. 185-86; Van Horne, *Cumberland,* Vol. I, pp. 318, 319.

reports as to the movement of possible reinforcements, realizing meanwhile that his situation was indeed critical. General Baird's division had crossed the mountain during the day, and Negley was assured that this force would support him in the morning. General Bragg had moved his headquarters to Lafayette on the night of September 10, the better to insure a successful attack on General Negley. He also ordered General Walker's corps and General Cleburne's division to unite at Dug Gap for the attack. At eight o'clock on the morning of September 11, General Baird's division joined General Negley at Davis' Crossroads. At daybreak, also on September 11, General Bragg joined Cleburne, where, despite Bragg's repeated orders, General Hindman failed to attack until the middle of the afternoon. During the delay, Generals Baird and Negley, by masterful maneuvering in the face of sharp fighting, withdrew from their dangerous position. The prompt arrival of General Thomas's two divisions of Generals Brannan and Reynolds made certain the safety of the Union center, and accordingly averted what might have been the most dangerous moment in the history of the Army of the Cumberland.[23]

General Rosecrans, disappointed at what he regarded as the slow movement of General Thomas's force, sent him the following dispatch at about 10 P.M. on September 10:

> The general commanding directs me to say that General Negley's dispatch forwarded by you at 10 A.M. is received. He is disappointed to learn from it that his forces move tomorrow morning instead of having moved this morning, as they should have done, this delay imperiling both extremes of the army. Your movement on Lafayette should be made with the utmost promptness. You ought not to encumber yourself with your main supply train. A brigade or two will be sufficient to protect it. Your advance ought to have threatened Lafayette yesterday morning. . . .

Thomas's reply, at 8 P.M. on September 11, gave the reason why he had not pursued his advance as promptly as expected. It is important to note that General Thomas had been advised by Negley on September 9 that large Confederate forces, comprising three or four divisions consisting of infantry, artillery, and cavalry, moved to Dug Gap the night before. From this it was apparent they were preparing to resist the advance of the Fourteenth Corps; therefore General Thomas ordered General Negley to concentrate at the foot of Look-

---

23. Van Horne, *ibid.*, pp. 319, 320; *Official Records, ibid.*, Vol. XXX, Part 2, p. 29; Cist, *ibid.*, p. 186.

out Mountain and to prepare for the march on Lafayette the following day. Thomas reminded Rosecrans that if Negley had marched
on Lafayette as ordered by Rosecrans he would have met a severe
defeat. It is true also that if it had not been for the delay on the part
of the Confederates Negley's defeat would have been inevitable.[24]
Negley's dispatch gave General Thomas no alternative but to be
cautious in the face of a formidable assembling of enemy forces.

Thomas was so concerned by the news from Negley that he made
a personal visit to him at Dug Gap. There he learned that a captured
soldier from the Thirty-second Mississippi Regiment warned Negley
that if he advanced he would be surely beaten. It was at this point
that General Thomas ordered Generals Baird, Brannan, and Reynolds
to concentrate, in the hope of driving the Confederates beyond Pigeon
Mountain. Here Thomas expressed regret that he did not have
Wilder's brigade, as he believed he could have seized Dug and Cat-
lett's gaps before the Confederates reached there. General Thomas
then ordered Negley to hold his forces in readiness, but not to advance unless he heard firing from General Reynolds's advance. In
the latter eventuality, he recommended that General Baird support
Reynolds while he, Negley, remained ready to support them while
also watching Dug Gap and being prepared to resist any advance
of the enemy in that direction.[25] In effect, this position by General
Thomas amounted to disobedience of orders; but General Bragg
had prepared a trap for him and his Fourteenth Corps, which fact
Thomas was aware of almost from the beginning, and but for which
the Army of the Cumberland would have faced destruction in one-
two-three order. The commander in chief, General Rosecrans, could not,
at first, seem to get it into his mind that his great subordinate had
diagnosed General Bragg's plan, and that his initiative in circumvent-
ing it had saved his army. In a dispatch to General McCook, at 10:00
P.M. on September 11, General Rosecrans acknowledged that Bragg's
main army, it was "nearly certain," has concentrated in heavy force
in the vicinity of Lafayette.[26]

It appears that General Rosecrans could not face the reality of
Bragg's concentration, since on September 12, in reply to two dispatches from General Thomas during the previous night and at four
o'clock that morning, he said, "After maturely weighing the notes,
the general commanding is induced to think that General Negley
withdrew more through prudence than from compulsion."[27]

24. *Official Records, ibid.,* Vol. XXX, Part 3, pp. 485, 511, 534.
25. *Ibid.,* pp. 510, 511, 535.
26. *Ibid.,* p. 541.
27. *Ibid.,* pp. 564, 565.

General Bragg's plan for intercepting and overwhelming the divisions of Generals Baird and Negley was sound but, of course, disappointing, since only the element of luck was lacking to make it a complete success. Undaunted, he then planned to attack General Crittenden's Twenty-first Corps, comprising at that time the Union left. He therefore ordered Generals Walker and Polk to advance their corps in the direction of Lee and Gordon's Mill. On September 12, Bragg ordered Polk to attack Crittenden on the morning of September 13, realizing that Crittenden had been weakened by the sending of one of his divisions to Ringgold. He also refused Polk's request for reinforcements, and followed his refusal by again ordering him to attack, reminding him that he outnumbered Crittenden, and that General Buckner's corps would move within supporting distance of him.[28]

Since the Confederate rear guard was no farther south than Lee and Gordon's Mill on September 11, and their left was established in a good position near that location, General Rosecrans realized with some tardiness that Bragg might be concentrating for an all-out attack. He therefore began immediately to change from pursuit to defense, since it was apparent that Bragg was not heading for Rome, Georgia, as he had believed, and now hoped to combine his three corps between Chattanooga and the Confederate army. Rosecrans knew that events of the next few days would most likely decide the fate of his own army, a reasonable viewpoint in the light of gathering forces. On the eleventh also, General Halleck telegraphed Rosecrans to ascertain the truth of the rumor that Bragg was sending reinforcements to Lee's Army of Northern Virginia. If Halleck feared that such was the case, it is fairly conclusive that General James Longstreet's corps, which had been several days *en route* by railroad to reinforce General Bragg, had slipped away from Lee's army without his knowledge.[29] This is a serious reflection on the intelligence-gathering forces of the Federal authorities, and throws some of the burden of responsibility for Rosecrans's troubles on them and away from him. Time and again, Rosecrans failed to receive cooperation and needed support, particularly with respect to cavalry, as shown by repeated appeals to Washington and the resultant criticism of him in asking for what he needed to bring victory.

On the morning of September 13, Bragg learned that Crittenden's corps had not been attacked as ordered. He also learned that Crittenden's corps was now united, that it had crossed Chickamauga Creek

28. *Ibid.*, Vol. XXX, Part 2, p. 29; Cist, *op. cit.*, p. 187.

29. *Official Records, ibid.*, Vol. XXX, Part 1, pp. 54-55; Part 3, p. 530; Cist, *ibid.*

(River), and that it occupied a good defensive position at Lee and Gordon's Mill. Once more swallowing his disappointment, Bragg ordered his forces, including newly arrived reinforcements from Mississippi and Virginia, to cross Chickamauga Creek at six o'clock on the morning of September 18 at Reed's Bridge. His plan was to get between the Union army and Chattanooga, attack Crittenden on the Union left at Lee and Gordon's Mill, and push it back on the Union center at Stevens' Gap in McLemore's Cove.[30] This done, the Army of the Cumberland would have been forced into the mountains and rendered considerably ineffective, if not destroyed.

General Crittenden's movements east of Chattanooga near Ringgold, with Minty's cavalry and Wilder's mounted infantry, permitted concentration at Lee and Gordon's Mill, to which point Thomas's Fourteenth Corps extended from Stevens' Gap, which he held. Thomas was there awaiting the arrival of McCook's Twentieth Corps by way of Lookout Mountain. After he had crossed Lookout, however, he decided to recross it to its western base, in the hope of taking from there the road to Stevens' Gap; but after doing so and learning of a good road at the summit, he ordered Generals Johnson and Davis to retrace their steps and push rapidly with their commands to Stevens' Gap. These repeated mountain marches delayed his union with Thomas until darkness fell on September 16, when he and General Stanley's cavalry entered McLemore's Cove through Dougherty's Gap. General Crittenden had been moved near the Fourteenth Corps and held a good position at the southern spur of Missionary Ridge, where he also awaited the arrival of McCook. Following this move, on September 17, the three corps were in supporting distance. On the following day, Crittenden's corps was returned to Lee and Gordon's Mill along the Lafayette road, there to await the expected advance of Bragg's Confederate column.[31]

On the night of the seventeenth, Bragg issued the following order preparatory to the movement of his forces across the Chickamauga, commencing at six o'clock on the morning of the eighteenth:

1. Johnson's column [Hood's], on crossing at or near Reed's Bridge, will turn to the left by the most practicable route and sweep up the Chickamauga, toward Lee and Gordon's Mills.

2. Walker, crossing at Alexander's Bridge, will unite in this move and push vigorously on the enemy's flank and rear in the same direction.

3. Buckner, crossing at Thedford's Ford, will join in the move-

30. *Official Records, ibid.*, Vol. XXX, Part 2, pp. 30-31.

31. *Ibid.*, Vol. XXX, Part 1, pp. 54-55; Part 2, p. 31; Cist, *op. cit.*, p. 187.

ment to the left, and press the enemy up the stream from Polk's front at Lee and Gordon's Mills.

4. Polk will press his forces to the front of Lee and Gordon's Mills, and if met by too much resistance to cross will bear to the right and cross at Dalton's Ford, or at Thedford's, as may be necessary, and join in the attack wherever the enemy may be.

5. Hill will cover our left flank from an advance of the enemy from the cove, and by pressing the cavalry in his front ascertain if the enemy is reinforcing at Lee and Gordon's Mills, in which event he will attack them in flank.

6. Wheeler's cavalry will hold the gaps in Pigeon Mountain and cover our rear and left and bring up stragglers.

7. All teams &c., not with troops should go toward Ringgold and Dalton, beyond Taylor's Ridge. All cooking should be done at the trains. Rations, when cooked, will be forwarded to the troops.

8. The above movements will be executed with the utmost promptness, vigor and persistence.[32]

During the eighteenth, Minty's cavalry brigade was attacked at Pea Vine Creek, three miles from Reed's Bridge, by General Bushrod Johnson's three brigades and General Robertson's brigade of General John B. Hood's division. Wilder's mounted infantry was also attacked at Alexander's Bridge by General William H. T. Walker's corps, and both he and Minty were driven back to the Lafayette road. This action delayed Johnson's arrival at Jay's Mill until four o'clock in the afternoon, when, after General John B. Hood assumed command, the entire force marched toward Lee and Gordon's Mill. Minty and Wilder both withdrew, and Wilder bivouacked a short distance from Hood's command. General Edward C. Walthall's brigade of General St. John R. Liddell's division suffered more than one hundred casualties on the afternoon of September 18, in a struggle with Colonel Wilder's repeater-equipped riflemen for Alexander's Bridge; the latter, how-ever, had dismantled the bridge, although under enemy fire, and rendered it useless. Walthall then crossed the Chickamauga at Byram's Ford, a mile downstream, and bivouacked about three-fourths of a mile west of Alexander's Bridge. The divisions of Generals Stewart, Preston, Benjamin Cheatham, and William Walker, with part of Hood's division, crossed the Chickamauga during the night and were in battle formation at seven o'clock on the morning of the nineteenth.[33]

---

32. *Official Records, ibid.*, Vol. XXX, Part 2, pp. 30, 31.
33. Boynton, *Military Park*, pp. 31-32; Cist, *op. cit.*, p. 189.

Generals Stewart and Preston were on the Confederate left near Hall's Ford; General Bushrod Johnson was in the center; General Hood was on the right; General Cheatham was in reserve; and General Walker was moving from the rear to the right of the front line. These troops were about a thousand yards east of the Lafayette road, prepared to attack Crittenden's three divisions on the west side of that road, with the right resting on Lee and Gordon's Mill.

General Rosecrans's order to General Thomas included the posting of General Negley's division at Crawfish Springs, in replacement of two divisions of General Crittenden's corps. General Thomas, convinced that General Bragg's army was crossing the Chickamauga, marched the remaining divisions of his corps all night, after posting Negley's division at Crawfish Springs and resting two hours with his men. The situation just before and during Thomas's march is very well described by Boynton in his series of letters to a Cincinnati newspaper:

That night [September 18] was to cover the inversion of an army. About four o'clock Thomas started his whole corps from Pond Spring toward Crittenden, McCook following him. This was doubtless interpreted by Bragg as closing in on Crittenden; but it was far more than that.

As soon as night shut the columns in they were pressed rapidly to the left. Negley, as he drew near to Crittenden, was moved to the Chickamauga in front of Crawfish Springs.

This prevented a night attempt to cut the column by occupying the roads intersecting at this point. Meantime Thomas, with his other three divisions, pushed on. It was a long, weary night. Heavy flanking forces streamed along parallel to the road, and well out toward the river. There were constant interruptions to continuing movement, causing frequent halts of the infantry. The night was cool, and, as the commands stopped, the men warmed themselves by starting fires in the fences. The result was that toward midnight the trains were everywhere driving between two continuous lines of fires, and the men on either side, or in the road, had constant facilities for warming themselves. It was a tedious and most fatiguing night, but at daylight the vitally important task was done. . . . And so at sunrise the Union right, instead of resting far up the Chickamauga from Crittenden's position, as Bragg expected to find it, had become the left of Rosecrans's army, and Crittenden was the right. More than this, Rosecrans had established his lines two miles beyond Bragg's right, and between it and Chattanooga. The victory of concentration had been followed by the equally important success of inverting the army and thus thrusting its columns between the enemy and the objective of the campaign. These second stages of the movement deserve to take rank with the matchless strategy with which it was inaugurated.

It was a difficult and dangerous movement, where two armies, intent on battle, were only separated by such a stream as the Chickamauga, which was everywhere easily fordable above Lee and Gordon's. But General Thomas, who led this column, is the one commander of a great army of whom it can be said with accuracy that, from the first of the war to the close, no movement of his miscarried.

The building of fires is reminiscent of General Washington when, seemingly caught in a trap by the British after his glorious victory at Trenton, New Jersey, on December 26, 1776, during the American Revolution, he left his campfires burning, escaped the trap and fought and won the Battle of Princeton, January 3, 1777.[34]

An interesting comment on the night march of Thomas and his men is given by Fitch, in his *Echoes of the Civil War:*

How many of these took up that march of the dead the next day, and the next, the return of casualties of that awful battle alone discloses! These victims of the coming battle marched with an eager tread and as careless swing as those who survived. They were as merry, they made as light of the coming conflict as their more fortunate comrades who do not lie in the National Military Cemetery at Chattanooga. What a wonderful preventive of misery this is! This human inability to penetrate the future, even for the infinitesimal period of one day. Think of the despair, the dread that would have seized every soldier in that long line had it been apparent to him just who would be killed or wounded on the morrow, just who were then marching straight to death! Despair would have weakened those who were the doomed, and utter unhappiness through sympathy, those who survived. . . .

The peaceful woods lying in profound darkness said not a word to the passing regiments of these awful future events. As if in pity for those over whom the Angel of Death was then hovering, the spirit of the forest breathed the same monotonous

34. Michael H. Fitch, *The Chattanooga Campaign* (Wisconsin Historical Commission, 1911), pp. 77-79; Boynton, *Campaigns,* pp. 25-28; John Richard Alden, *The American Revolution* (New York, 1954), p. 110.

murmur it always had. We marched along in blissful ignorance of what the next two days would bring forth.[35]

General McCook's corps made slow progress on September 18, and was compelled to bivouac at Pond Spring, near Crawfish Springs, when darkness fell, although he had begun his movement that morning. With General Baird's division in the lead of Thomas's column, the utmost secrecy was maintained during the march; with the enemy on the other side of the Chickamauga but a short distance away, they would have been forewarned by any unusual sounds and would certainly have sought to reach Thomas's objective ahead of him. General Hill's corps and Wheeler's cavalry were posted on the east side of the Chickamauga to prevent the advance of the Fourteenth and Twentieth Corps. After leaving Crawfish Springs, Thomas's advance continued, later followed by McCook's corps, over a little-used road leading to the Lafayette road opposite the Kelly farm.[36]

On the route to Kelly's was a dwelling in the middle of a clearing known as the Widow Glenn's house. A few small farms throughout this thickly wooded battlefield were owned by simple folk whose names would never have been heard of outside their immediate environment but for the battle that lifted them to fame as enduring as the Battle of Chickamauga itself. Names like Snodgrass, Brotherton, Dyer, Viniard, the Widow Glenn, among others, will be remembered because of their relation to the ground over which Americans struggled to the death against each other, in two days of the bloodiest and most unrelenting struggle ever waged on the North American continent. One can only ask: Why should this have happened, and what good could come from it?

Although the head of the Confederate column was but three or four miles away when Thomas arrived at Kelly's farm, he lay down under a spreading tree near a dilapidated-looking house to catch a few moments of rest. As he gathered some blankets about himself, he requested his aide not to let him sleep more than an hour. Barely fifteen minutes had gone by when he was awakened by Colonel Dan McCook and informed that he had burned a bridge over which a Confederate brigade had just crossed, and that if given enough troops he would be able to capture it.[37] (This will be discussed at length as the battle unfolds.)

General Thomas has been described thus while on this historic

---

35. Michael H. Fitch, *Echoes of the Civil War* (New York, 1905), pp. 131-34.

36. Fitch, *Chattanooga*, pp. 77-80.

37. Fitch, *Echoes*, p. 136.

night march by one who saw much of him during the night. "There was about him, at all times, the very atmosphere of solid merit and reserve strength. As he rode beside General Baird, attended by the two staff corps, there was no indication that he was conscious of his high position. His modesty was always conspicuous. No one in the long line of march stretching for miles behind him could see in this unpretentious officer the true hero of the coming conflict, who would be known in the future as 'The Rock of Chickamauga.' "[38]

We have seen that General Thomas, followed by General McCook, marched from McLemore's Cove by the Crawfish Springs road to its intersection with the Lafayette road at Kelly's farm. General Brannan's division passed this junction to McDonald's farm by seven o'clock, also on the morning of September 19, and continued to Jay's Mill near Forrest's cavalry position. General Baird occupied a position in support of Brannan between the Kelly and Poe houses, facing east. General Steedman's division of General Granger's reserve corps was posted at Rossville, after having bivouacked near Jay's Mill during the night of September 18, and skirmished with Forrest's cavalry at daybreak on the nineteenth. General Negley's division was at Glass' Mill facing Breckinridge across the Chickamauga, and General Reynolds's division on the Crawfish Springs road was following Thomas's column. General McCook's corps at that time was at Crawfish Springs, about five miles from Kelly's farm.[39] This was a far different situation from what General Bragg realized on September 9, when Thomas entered McLemore's Cove. Bragg knew on that day that Rosecrans's army was pursuing him in the belief that he, Bragg, was retreating. Bragg's force was then united in front of the center held by Thomas, and he also knew that Rosecrans's three corps were widely dispersed and vulnerable to possible destruction, one by one, before they could combine. Now, after Bragg lost a number of golden opportunities, the three corps had succeeded not only in escaping from their dangerous situation, but were ready to give battle with a united front.

---

38. Fitch, *Chattanooga*, pp. 81-82.
39. Boynton, *Military Park*, pp. 32, 34.

CHAPTER XV

Chickamauga, "River of Death," September 19

As introduction to this, the bloodiest and most bitterly fought battle in the entire history of the United States, no better description of the epic is to be found anywhere than the one below. The general theme of this estimate of the great struggle will be found in at least two sources, one of which is in *Reminiscences of the Civil War,* by Confederate General John B. Gordon. Although General Gordon did not participate in the battle, he was a keen student of the war in which he was a most capable subordinate of General Robert E. Lee in the Army of Northern Virginia.

An American battle which surpassed in its ratio of carnage the bloodiest conflicts in history outside of this country ought to be better understood by the American people. Sharpsburg, or Antietam, I believe, had a larger proportion of killed and wounded than any other single day's battle of our war; and that means larger than any in the world's wars. Chickamauga, however, in its two days of heavy fighting, brought the ratio of losses to the high-water mark. Judged by the percentage in killed and wounded, Chickamauga nearly doubled the sanguinary record of Marengo and Austerlitz; was two and a half times heavier than that sustained by the Duke of Marlborough at Malplaquet. . . . Or if we take the average percentage of loss in a number of the world's greatest battles—Waterloo, Wagram, Valmy . . . we shall find by comparison that Chickamauga's record of blood surpassed them nearly three to one. It will not do to say that this horrible slaughter in our Civil War was due to the longer range of our rifle nor to the more destructive character of any of our implements of warfare; for at Chickamauga as well as in the Wilderness and at Shiloh, where these Americans fell at so fearful a rate, the woodlands prevented the hostile lines from seeing each other at great distances and rendered the improved arms no more effective than would have been rifles of short range. Some other and more reasonable explanation must be found for this great disparity of losses in American and European wars. There is but one explanation—the personal character and the consecrated courage of American soldiers. At Chickamauga thousands fell on both sides fighting at close quarters, their faces at times burnt by the blazing powder at the very muzzle of the guns.[1]

When everything is considered, this description would have to be given to the struggle that was so destructive in human lives.

Although the above estimate was made of a battle fought in the early part of the latter half of the last century, the validity of it cannot be questioned after the Russo-Japanese War of 1904–1905 and World Wars I and II of 1914–1918 and 1939–1945. In the light of well-established statistics and authoritative estimates, General Gordon might well have stated in fewer words what his description so clearly implied, namely, that Chickamauga, in terms of its duration and numbers engaged, was the bloodiest and most bitterly fought battle in the history of the world. He might also have stated the conviction more strongly that it is a sad commentary that the American people have so little understanding of the importance of Chickamauga, rather than it "ought to be better understood by the American people." Another aspect of the battle that should not escape the attention of the American people is the dominant part in it of Major General George H. Thomas. The almost certain result of the battle without Thomas is left to the judgment of the beneficiaries of a united country, but the expression should permit repetition. The American people should understand who it was that guided the fortunes of the Union in the important Battle of Chickamauga and why the battle was so important to its preservation.

Generally accepted figures regarding numbers of men engaged and casualties suffered at Chickamauga, although not claimed by authorities to be accurate, are substantially as stated here. The total Union losses, including killed, wounded, and missing, were 16,179 of an estimated fifty thousand participating. The Confederates, whose figures are far more unreliable due in part to a number of their units failing to report, lost about 18,000 in killed, wounded, and missing. Both Union and Confederate losses are believed to represent about

---

1. *Michigan at Chickamauga, Chattanooga and Missionary Ridge* (Lansing, Mich., 1899), p. 61; John B. Gordon, *Reminiscences of the Civil War* (New York, 1908), pp. 199-200.

33 per cent of the total number of men engaged. Longstreet lost about 44 per cent, most of them on September 20, as the bulk of his corps did not become engaged until the twentieth. Even more appalling were the losses of General Steedman's reserve corps on the afternoon of the twentieth which, in about four hours of fighting, lost 49 per cent in killed and wounded alone. Most of the Union divisions and other units under General Thomas on Snodgrass Hill during the afternoon of the twentieth averaged in losses from 40 to 50 per cent.[2] Surprisingly, followers of Civil War history believe that Gettysburg had the greatest ratio of losses. In comparing great battles of the war it should be remembered that Confederate losses were not generally reported with as much accuracy as were losses of Union forces. Nevertheless, it is generally accepted that at Gettysburg the aggregate of killed, wounded, and missing in the Army of the Potomac was about 23,000, whereas the Army of Northern Virginia is estimated to have lost about 20,500. In the latter figure a number of Confederate units are not included; but assuming it to be reasonably accurate, and the number of Confederates actually engaged estimated to be 60,000, a figure that also does not include reports from a number of units, the Army of Northern Virginia lost about 30 per cent in three days. Since the number of Union men reported in or ready for action at Gettysburg is estimated at about 77,000, the estimated losses of 23,000 reflect a ratio of about 30 per cent also.[3] In other words, average losses at Gettysburg of 30 per cent in three days were less than the average of 33 per cent at Chickamauga in two days.

Any attempt to describe in complete detail and with reasonable accuracy the principal events of a great battle such as Chickamauga is almost certain to result in failure. This battle in particular consisted of a number of individual engagements in which subordinate commanders fought much of the time in complete isolation from the central command, and therefore upon their own initiative and responsibility. For this reason alone it is impossible to discuss the over-all battle in terms of a single engagement. An account seeking to portray the several phases of the struggle separately is almost certainly affected by the naturally subjective viewpoint of the individuals operating in their respective areas. The describing, for example, of the activities of a regiment, a brigade, a division, or even a corps would, by the sheer magnitude of the detail required, be out of place in a biographical work. Nevertheless, in discussing Chicka-

---

2. *Encyclopedia Americana* (New York: American Book–Stratford Press, Inc., 1954), Vol. VI, p. 454; *Official Records of the War of the Rebellion* (Washington, 1880-1901), Vol. XXIII, Parts 1 and 2; Vol. XXX, Parts 1, 2, 3 and 4.
   3. *Battles and Leaders of the Civil War* (New York, 1884), Vol. III, p. 384.

mauga, the normal scope or range of description is exceeded in this book for two very important reasons. First, the average student of Civil War history will be afforded the opportunity to know that Chickamauga ranks second to no other battle of the war in any respect whatever; second, greater details will show that without its results national unity would have been, as stated previously, extremely doubtful. Not to be overlooked is that many Americans will be made aware for the first time that General Thomas was the dominant figure of the battle from beginning to end, and that the mere nickname of "The Rock of Chickamauga" does not do full justice to that unexcelled general. Perhaps General Rosecrans himself best summed up the battle when he reported to his troops:

> Neither the history of this war nor probably the annals of any battle furnish a loftier example of obstinate bravery and enduring resistance to superior numbers, when troops, having exhausted their ammunition, resorted to the bayonet so many times to hold their position against such odds as did our left and center on the afternoon of the 20th of September, at the battle of Chickamauga.[4]

Many of the fields presently dotting the area of the battlefield were covered with trees and thick foliage during the battle, although otherwise the general appearance of the topography remains little changed.

The present field east of the McDonald house on the Lafayette road, and north of the road to Ringgold, Georgia, was considerably more wooded during the battle than at present. North of the Viniard house and east of the Brotherton house, thick woods occupied what is now cleared ground. Snodgrass Hill proper remains very much today as it was when the battle was fought, although most of the cleared ground at the foot of it was woodland at that time. Brock field was surrounded by a considerably greater wooded area than today, which also can be said for the fields near the Winfrey house. Jay's Mill vicinity, to a depth of some two hundred yards, was also wooded area during the battle.[5] This description does not, of course, purport to cover the changes made by the markers and monuments erected on the battlefield to commemorate the hallowed locales of heroism and death of the participating forces, and to identify battle positions of the various units.

Familiarity with the composition of the country beyond the

---

4. *Official Records, op. cit.,* Vol. XXX, Part 1, p. 78.

5. H. V. Boynton, *The Chickamauga National Military Park* (Cincinnati, 1895), pp. 29-31.

immediate battlefield perimeter over which one-eighth of a million Americans, brother against brother, marched in the epic two-day struggle, is indispensable to a basic understanding of the battle.

The Chickamauga River, sometimes referred to, perhaps more accurately, as Chickamauga Creek, was given its name by the Indians who once inhabited the area. The name, interpreted, means River of Death, whether for some reason known to themselves we do not know; but there can be no doubt that the name was prophetic of the great battle fought by white men not far from its banks. In fact, the battlefield proper is hardly a mile from the stream itself. The source of the river is in Catoosa County, Georgia, at the northern end of McLemore's Cove and several miles east of Pond Spring. This is where the river begins flowing in a northeasterly direction also, at a distance of about twenty miles from the battlefield. Oddly enough, McLemore's Cove and Pigeon Mountain to the south of the battlefield lie in somewhat the same northeasterly direction, as though following the river. Glass' Mill, located about five miles northeast of Pond Spring on the eastern side of the river, three miles east of Crawfish Springs and four miles south of Lee and Gordon's Mill, was an important point *en route* from the south to the battlefield.[6]

Lee and Gordon's Mill is on the west side of the river, where it bends to the east at the spot where the main road between Lafayette, Georgia, and Chattanooga crosses the stream, about half the distance between the towns. On both sides of the river north of the mill the ground is somewhat level, although in some places the banks are high and quite steep. For some distance east and northeast of the mill on the west side of the stream the ground is also high and steep. A number of fords and bridges spanned the water, of which, for purposes of the battle, Alexander's and Reed's bridges were the scenes of more action than most of the other crossings. Dalton's and Tedford's fords, to the south of the mill, were nearest to it. Alexander's Bridge was about three miles northeast of the mill, while Reed's Bridge, about six miles west of Ringgold, was about three miles north of Alexander's Bridge and perhaps six miles northeast of it.[7]

Pea Vine and Chickamauga creeks lie virtually in one valley. Between Lee and Gordon's Mill and Rossville, the many farms were encircled by clearings on both sides of the road, although the ground between was largely wooded. The roads from Alexander's and Reed's bridges, as also from Dalton's, Tedford's, Lambert's, and Byram's fords, cut through this wooded area into the main road,

---

6. *Ibid.*; John B. Turchin, *Chickamauga* (Chicago, 1888), p. 56.
7. Turchin, *ibid.*

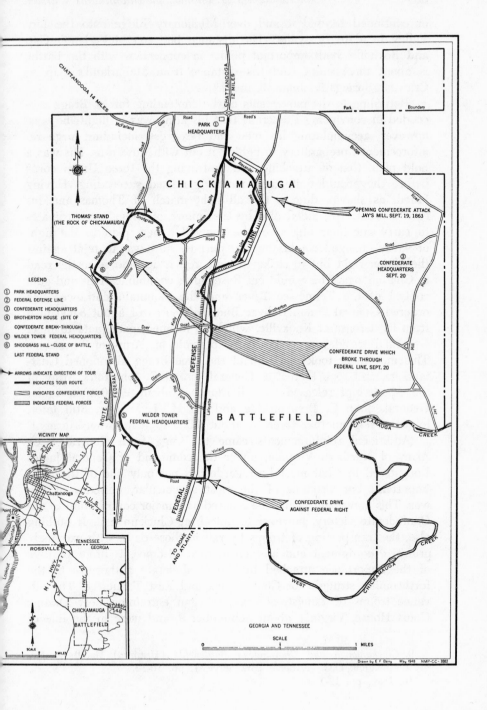

CHATTANOOGA 14 MILES

CHATTANOOGA 12 MILES

Park   Boundary

Road   Reed's

Road   PARK ①
            HEADQUARTERS

McFarland   Gap

Alexander Rd.

Bridge

C H I C K A M A U G A

N

OPENING CONFEDERATE ATTACK
JAY'S MILL, SEPT. 19, 1863

THOMAS' STAND
(THE ROCK OF CHICKAMAUGA)

SNODGRASS   HILL

②

Road

Road

③
CONFEDERATE
HEADQUARTERS
SEPT. 20

⑥

LEGEND

① PARK HEADQUARTERS
② FEDERAL DEFENSE LINE
③ CONFEDERATE HEADQUARTERS
④ BROTHERTON HOUSE (SITE OF
   CONFEDERATE BREAK-THROUGH)
⑤ WILDER TOWER FEDERAL HEADQUARTERS
⑥ SNODGRASS HILL – CLOSE OF BATTLE,
   LAST FEDERAL STAND

Dyer   Road

④

Brotherton

Road

Road

CONFEDERATE DRIVE WHICH
BROKE THROUGH
FEDERAL LINE, SEPT. 20

ARROWS INDICATE DIRECTION OF TOUR
        INDICATES TOUR ROUTE
        INDICATES CONFEDERATE FORCES
        INDICATES FEDERAL FORCES

Glenn   Road

⑤
WILDER TOWER
FEDERAL HEADQUARTERS

B A T T L E F I E L D

CHICKAMAUGA   CREEK

VICINITY MAP

Chattanooga

Alexander

Vineyard   Road

CONFEDERATE DRIVE
AGAINST FEDERAL RIGHT

U.S. HWY. 27

U.S. HWY. 11

U.S. HWY. 41

Point Park

Lookout   Mountain

TENNESSEE
GEORGIA

ROSSVILLE

Missionary   Ridge

ST. HWY. 27

TO ROME
AND ATLANTA

WEST   CHICKAMAUGA   CREEK

CHICKAMAUGA
BATTLEFIELD

ST. HWY. 148

SCALE
0   1   2 MILES

GEORGIA AND TENNESSEE

SCALE
0   1   MILES

Drawn by E. F. Berry   May 1948   NMP-CC- 7002

or continued beyond it and over Missionary Ridge onto the Dry Valley Road to Rossville.[8] The distance between McFarland's Gap and Rossville, both important points in connection with the battle, is about three miles, and the distance from McFarland's Gap to Crawfish Springs is about six miles.[9]

Returning to the movements of the contending forces, Bragg succeeded in convincing Rosecrans that his army was in flight; he was, however, accumulating his men and resources, including large reinforcements, preparatory to fighing it out with Rosecrans. His was a bold plan, that of attacking and destroying the three Union corps before they could unite, and narrowly missed succeeding. Having failed, as shown, due to the all-night march of Thomas and his Fourteenth Corps, aided also by the failure of Bragg's subordinates to carry out their objectives, he evolved a new plan in the light of vastly changed conditions. His purpose now was to feint against the Union right but to strike the left, roll it up, and seize the road to Chattanooga. This would cut Rosecrans's communications and gain control of the Tennessee River and the mountain entrances. He ordered General Simon Bolivar Buckner's corps of about 8,000 men from its defense of Knoxville, which he deemed inadequate to meet General Burnside's army head on, to rejoin his Army of Tennessee. This movement took place about the time Bragg abandoned Chattanooga, and soon thereafter General Joseph E. Johnston's Army of the Mississippi released two divisions of about 9,000 men under Generals John C. Breckinridge and W. H. T. Walker. Still later, Johnston sent another force of about 2,500 to help Bragg's army.[10]

Additional reinforcements came to Bragg from General Lee's Army of Northern Virginia, under the command of General James Longstreet, in what must be regarded as not only one of the most important, but also one of the most spectacular, episodes of the war. This movement cannot be ignored as a major contribution to the Confederate victory, however technical, at Chickamauga. If nothing else, the transporting of troops by rail in those days, with extremely primitive equipment and at such a great distance, is proof positive of the importance attached by the Confederate authorities to the forthcoming struggle for Chattanooga and East Tennessee. The advance troops of Longstreet's corps began entraining near Orange Court House, Virginia, about September 9, and were in the line of

---

8. *Ibid.*, pp. 56-57.

9. *Chickamauga and Chattanooga Battlefields* (Historical Handbook No. 25; Washington, D.C.: National Park Service), pp. 10-13.

10. *Ibid.*, pp. 12-13.

battle at Chickamauga on September 19. One observer noted that the troops, while going through Kingsville, South Carolina, lay in rows on flat cars, with heads covered and apparently fast asleep. It is estimated that about 9,000 men, comprising three brigades, arrived in time for the first day's fighting, although none of the artillery arrived in time for the battle, and Longstreet did not arrive in person until about midnight of the nineteeth.[11] Many writers have noted that Longstreet was extremely disappointed at Bragg's failure to send him an escort or other contact, in order to expedite his progress to the battlefield and to accord him the courtesy expected by one undertaking such a trying ordeal.

General D. H. Hill reported that after the Battle of Gettysburg, Longstreet suggested to Lee that Bragg be reinforced from Lee's army; further, that when Longstreet began his movement General Lee saw him off and entreated him, "General, you must beat these people," to which Longstreet replied, "General, if you will give your orders that the enemy, when beaten, shall be destroyed, I will promise to give you victory, if I live; but I would not give the life of a single soldier of mine for a barren victory." Lee replied, "The order has been given and will be repeated."[12]

Early on the morning of September 19, as stated previously, Colonel Dan McCook reported to General Thomas, not long after Thomas's arrival at Kelly's field, that he had burned Reed's Bridge the night before, and that a Confederate brigade had become isolated on the west side of the river. Little did he realize that General Walker's entire corps was across and in readiness to attack the Federal left. McCook asked permission of Thomas to attack and capture this brigade if possible, a suggestion that seemed reasonable under the circumstances. General Thomas had received conflicting information regarding movements of the Confederates and had acted upon such information according to his judgment. Not trusting to chance on this new information from Colonel McCook, he ordered General Brannan to leave one of his brigades to support General Baird, and with the other two to reconnoiter in the vicinity of the burned bridge and, if possible, capture it. This order was to have a tremendous impact on the events of the next forty-eight hours, since the initiative thus displayed proved that Rosecrans's forces, under the immediate guidance of Thomas, had indeed snatched control of the battle from Bragg. The spearhead of this control reposed in the hands of Thomas's Fourteenth Corps, consisting of

11. *Battles and Leaders, op. cit.*, Vol. III, p. 652.
12. *Ibid.*

the two divisions of Generals Baird and Brannan,[13] and ignited the fuse that was to become the Battle of Chickamauga. This burden was not to be laid down until after sundown of the following day, when Thomas himself ordered the tattered remnants of his command to withdraw to Rossville. Well it was that George H. Thomas was on the field during the conflict; and words could give no greater tribute to his importance than these: "General Thomas, who now held the key position was, for a slow and stubborn fight, one of the best corps commanders in either army, perhaps the very best." From this moment of Thomas's seizure of the golden choice of freedom of action, "there was not so much counter-action as Bragg had intended, partly because Thomas delivered vigorous counter-blows whenever there was opportunity; but there was fierce and persistent action all along the line,"[14] as the details hereinafter disclose.

Although each commander was in considerable doubt as to the movements of his opponent, and although the two armies had been maneuvering at a fairly close distance during the preceding twelve days, General Thomas, a downright genius for diagnosing the intentions of his adversaries, knew that a number of Confederates were west of the river.[15] He knew also that his own detached command and the other two corps of the Army of the Cumberland were not far away. In addition, perhaps for the first time in the experience of the Army of the Cumberland, telegraphic communications existed between Thomas at Kelly's field, Rosecrans at the Widow Glenn house, and Granger and his reserve corps at Rossville.

The Union line on the morning of September 19 was parallel to the road to Chattanooga, between Lee and Gordon's Mill, a distance of about five miles. This line, running somewhat from west to east, was formed by the divisions of Generals Wood, Van Cleve, and Palmer of Crittenden's corps, and the divisions of Baird and Brannan of Thomas's corps, as mentioned previously. The divisions of Generals Negley and Reynolds had not arrived on the field when the battle opened, while the division of General R. W. Johnson of McCook's corps had reached Crawfish Springs and was soon followed by the divisions of Generals Jeff Davis and Sheridan, also of McCook's corps.[16]

13. Thomas B. Van Horne, *History of the Army of the Cumberland* (Cincinnati, 1875), Vol. I, p. 333; *Battles and Leaders, op. cit.,* Vol. III, p. 649.

14. Van Horne, *ibid.;* Rossiter Johnson, *Fight for the Republic* (New York, 1917), p. 224.

15. Van Horne, *op. cit.,* Vol. I, p. 333.

16. Boynton, *op. cit.,* pp. 27, 34; *Battles and Leaders, loc. cit.*

At daybreak on the nineteenth the three brigades of General Forrest's cavalry were sent to protect the Confederate right and rear from General Gordon Granger's cavalry posted along the Chickamauga near McAfee's church. Soon after seven o'clock, General John T. Croxton's brigade of Brannan's division attacked Forrest at Jay's Mill, so that the initiative thus displayed resulted in the outflanking of Bragg, a boomerang, in fact, since it was his objective to outflank Rosecrans. Bragg's army was backed against the Chickamauga, where there was no escape except at the fords and bridges. Here was the moment ideal for Thomas, a situation made to order for a quick hammer blow so characteristic of him. Thomas hoped to dispose of Forrest's one division with his two divisions and to defeat reinforcements one by one as they came to support Forrest. He wanted General Palmer to attack Forrest in front while he attacked him in flank, and requested Rosecrans to order Crittenden to advance from Lee and Gordon's Mill to join in the attack at Alexander's Bridge. By this strategy, he stated to Rosecrans, "We can, I think, use them up." Rosecrans refused to believe that the Confederates were across the river, rejected the plan, and ordered Thomas to establish a strong position. Tragically, the initiative so recently held by Rosecrans was by this misconception returned to Bragg. Doubtful of his ability to maintain a defensive position, Thomas ordered Reynolds to support him without delay, and requested Crittenden to spare him another division, if possible, also without delay.[17]

About eight o'clock General Van Derveer's brigade had joined in the fighting as the action increased in intensity all along the line. Colonel John M. Connell's brigade also went into the action, and the Battle of Chickamauga was in full swing, at a point about two and one-half miles to the right at which Bragg had planned to begin it. Forrest's men fought dismounted with such vigor that they were at first thought to be infantrymen. In response to Forrest's appeal, on foot, the brigade of Colonel Claudius Wilson was sent to his aid from Alexander's Bridge and placed in position on Croxton's right. Soon afterward, Forrest again appealed for reinforcements, this time following Van Derveer's attack, and Colonel Matthew Ector's brigade was rushed to him from Alexander's Bridge to meet this danger. At this point Forrest had lost about one-fourth of his command.[18]

17. *Official Records, op. cit.,* Vol. XXX, Part 1, pp. 124-26; *Indiana at Chickamauga* (Indianapolis, 1900), pp. 14-15; Van Horne, *op. cit.,* Vol. I, p. 333; Boynton, *op. cit.,* pp. 27-34; *Battles and Leaders, op. cit.,* Vol. III, p. 649.

18. *Indiana, op. cit.,* p. 15.

The fortunes of battle favored first Croxton and then Wilson, and both fought with equal ferocity; Van Derveer, however, was successful in clearing the Confederates from his front. When Thomas first heard the noise of battle from Croxton's men, he rode forward to ascertain the nature of the action and then sent General Baird's division in support. Baird, resting at Kelly's field after marching all night with Thomas, responded promptly and moved eastward into action. He at once relieved Croxton with King's brigade and placed Scribner's brigade to the right of King on Wilson's flank. He soon ordered King to change front to the south, but before the movement could be executed, Walthall's and Govan's brigades of Liddell's division attacked both King and Scribner, drove them back in disorder, and captured ten pieces of artillery. At this point reinforcements were close at hand, and the state of General Brannan's position permitted the use of Van Derveer's and Connell's brigades in attacking the pursuing Confederates; this attack with the bayonet was so successful that King's artillery was recaptured. The loss of this artillery originally was attributed largely to the difficulty in moving it in the wooded and broken terrain. It is worthy of note that General Thomas requested and placed these reinforcements on his own initiative. When assured that the Confederate army was in his front, he asked the then unengaged General Crittenden to support him, and General Palmer's division was sent to him at once. Additionally, General Rosecrans sent Richard Johnson's division of McCook's corps a little later, and General Reynolds's division followed soon thereafter.[19]

Shortly after the battle opened, a struggle began at Glass' Mill between Negley's and Breckinridge's artillery that lasted for about three hours. This action took place on the Confederate left, about nine miles away, and was ended by both sides withdrawing to the center of the battle action.

General D. H. Hill, in discussing this opening phase of the battle, referred to clouds of dust rolling down the valley caused by the retirement of Federal troops from this scene of action to support the left of their line. He said, "This was the time to have relieved the strain upon our right by attacking the Federal right at Lee and Gordon's. My veteran corps . . . would have flanked the enemy out of his fortifications at this point, and would by their brilliant onset have confounded Rosecrans in his purpose of massing upon his left; but Bragg had other plans." Hill said further: "The great commander is he who makes his antagonist keep step with him. Thomas, like

---

19. Van Horne, *op. cit.*, Vol. I, pp. 334-35; *Indiana, op. cit.*, p. 15; Boynton, *op. cit.*, p. 35.

the grand soldier he was, by attacking first, made Bragg keep step with him. He who begins the attack assumes that he is superior to his enemy, either in numbers or in courage, and therefore carries with him to the assault all the moral advantage of his assumed superiority."[20]

The shifting of brigades and divisions into and out of the line resulted in a considerable realignment from the one that began the day's action. General Cheatham's five brigades, comprising the main Confederate reserve, moved into the struggle, with three brigades in its front line and the other two comprising its second line, on a mile-wide front. He succeeded in pushing back Starkweather's brigade as it was pursuing Govan from the field. The center of Cheatham's forces was now at Brock's Field and the left about four hundred yards from the Lafayette Road. At about twelve thirty he became engaged with General Richard Johnson's and Palmer's divisions *en route* to support Thomas, but his right and center were compelled to retire after about two hours of bitter fighting, and following the relief of his first line by his second line. Palmer, moving from Lee and Gordon's Mill to aid Thomas, marched by the Lafayette road to the Poe house where, hurriedly forming by brigades in echelon, he advanced to Brock field. At this time there existed a considerable interval between the forces of Thomas and Crittenden, but Bragg made no attempt to exploit this golden opportunity to outflank them. His plan had been to surround Crittenden, in the belief that his left rested at Lee and Gordon's Mill.[21]

Turning attention to the extreme left of the Union line, Van Derveer, who had done magnificent work in the Battle of Mill Springs, closed the fighting in that area by prompt and determined action. Colonel Connell had at first given support to Croxton, after which he supported Van Derveer with two regiments and a battery of artillery. When Van Derveer observed that Forrest, under cover of the woods, had formed in four lines on the crest north of his, Van Derveer's, left, he changed directions at once and with his men, as well as his own and Connell's batteries, advancing at full speed, turned toward the crest to which Forrest was heading. He then ordered the left to move back slowly until his ten pieces of artillery opened up on Forrest's oncoming column. Firing double-shotted canister at a distance of about forty paces, these guns raked Forrest's lines. Despite this terrific fire, Forrest's men continued advancing until within range of the riflemen, when, finding this unendurable, they withdrew to Jay's Mill to reform their torn lines. Walker's men

---

20. *Battles and Leaders, op. cit.*, Vol. III, p. 651.
21. Van Horne, *op. cit.*, pp. 335-36; *Indiana, ibid.*, pp. 15-17.

also reformed behind Cheatham's lines, and at about midafternoon both Walthall and Govan went into action for a short time.[22]

At about three o'clock, General Richard Johnson formed his lines, with his forward position near Reed field, where he remained inactive until darkness came. General Reynolds arrived at the Poe house at about one o'clock, and at this time sent General John B. Turchin's and King's brigades to Palmer's left and right respectively, as Palmer's men had run out of ammunition. Stewart's three brigades entered the southern corner of Brock field shortly after noon, with Clayton's brigade leading, followed by Brown's and Bate's brigades. Van Cleve, with two brigades, reached Brotherton field from Lee and Gordon's Mill, at about midafternoon and before Stewart arrived on the field, in time to repel the advance of Cheatham's left brigade and capture its battery of artillery. Stewart's men, Clayton's brigade, retaliated by driving Van Cleve across the Lafayette road at the Brotherton house, to beyond the Dyer field and thence to the tan yard. Bate's thrust against the Union line at the Poe house compelled it to withdraw to as far south as the Brotherton house. Next, Hazen's and Grose's brigades of Palmer's division returned to the Lafayette road. General Turchin's brigade attacked the Forty-fourth Alabama of Law's division at Brock field and compelled it to withdraw. Law's other regiments were in action farther south, on the right of Bushrod Johnson's division, and both then moved across the Lafayette road.[23]

When the fighting on the left had stopped, General Thomas ordered Baird and Brannan to withdraw to the glade east of the McDonald farm, from which point he dispatched Brannan to strengthen the line at Dyer field. As both Brannan and Negley reached Dyer field, the latter having marched from Glass' Mill, Stewart withdrew without a struggle and entered the woods east of the Lafayette road. Meanwhile, Bate's brigade, continuing in the direction of the Poe house, encountered Reynolds with his hastily assembled infantry, including Palmer's forces, with twenty guns, established on an elevation at the north end of Poe field. This was a force too strong for him, and, as he advanced on the field, he was soon repulsed and compelled to retire. This ended the fighting for the day on the Union center.[24]

Throughout the afternoon a severe struggle occurred at the Viniard house, on the Confederate left, commencing at about one o'clock.

---

22. Boynton, *op. cit.*, p. 36; *Indiana, ibid.*, pp. 15-16.

23. Van Horne, *op. cit.*, Vol. I, 337-38; *Indiana, ibid.*, p. 16; Boynton, *op. cit.*, p. 37.

24. Van Horne, *ibid.*; *Indiana, ibid*; Boynton, *ibid.*

About an hour before, Jeff Davis's brigades, commanded by Carlin and Heg, arrived at Rosecrans's headquarters at the Widow Glenn house. Rosecrans ordered Davis to proceed at once to the Viniard house to explore the Confederate positions. There was danger here that the Confederates would succeed in placing a large force in the breach between Thomas and Crittenden before reinforcements could be brought up. Crittenden had strengthened his own position on the left with Beatty's and Dick's brigades, after leaving one of Van Cleve's brigades at Lee and Gordon's Mill. Van Cleve soon formed on Reynolds's right, when Davis arrived with the brigades of Carlin and Heg. Davis placed his artillery on high ground in an open field east of the Lafayette road, and soon became heavily engaged. He resisted fiercely, but was compelled to yield ground, however grudgingly, until Wilder's mounted infantry came to his support. This formidable organization, the famous "Lightning Brigade," equipped with the Spencer seven-shooter rifle, enabled both Van Cleve and Davis to withstand greatly superior numbers seeking to divide the Fourteenth and Twenty-first corps.[25] It has been said that Longstreet told Wilder after the war that the fire from his Spencer rifles was so great that General Bragg thought an entire corps was attacking his left.

General Barnes's brigade of Van Cleve's division arrived in haste from Lee and Gordon's Mill and occupied a position in support of Davis's right. When General Wilder's brigade moved to Davis's left from its position in observation of the Confederate left, the whole Union line swung against General Bushrod Johnson's division and a brigade of Preston's division. This line was pushed to the west side of the fields back of the Viniard house, after gaining control of the house, but the Confederates in turn were soon forced back before they succeeded once more in recovering the ground just won. In one of these exchanges Wilder enfiladed the Confederates with two pieces of artillery, inflicting considerable loss of life on them and forcing them back."[26]

By four o'clock Davis's division was badly mauled from the see-saw struggle, but Buell's and Harker's brigades arrived from Lee and Gordon's Mill and, with other available brigades, restored the right of his line. Harker, moving to Davis's left, joined in this action, and the fighting once more became intense. Wilder's enfilading of Bushrod Johnson's division compelled it to retire to the Viniard farm north of the Lafayette road. Harker had advanced rapidly northward along the Lafayette road with two of his regiments, crossed to the

---

25. Van Horne, *ibid.*, Vol. I, pp. 336-7; *Indiana, ibid.*; Boynton, *ibid.*, p. 38.
26. Van Horne, *ibid.*; Vol. I, p. 337; *Indiana, ibid.*, pp. 17-18.

west of it, and struck the right brigade of Bushrod Johnson's division. This brigade attacked Van Cleve's left in the field back of Brotherton field, and compelled it to withdraw to the woods east of the Lafayette road. General Phil Sheridan arrived at this time from Crawfish Springs, and, going into action with Bradley's brigade on Buell's right, pushed the Confederates back. This was the most bitterly fought action of the nineteenth, a battle in itself, as shown by the large number of killed and wounded on both sides, and near sundown the Confederates withdrew from this part of the field. The Union forces held the line of the Lafayette road from Lee and Gordon's Mill to the Brotherton house.[27]

After a lull of short duration, following this decisive repulse of the Confederates, a severe action developed along the lines of Generals Johnson and Baird, about a mile east of the Brotherton house. During the afternoon Baird had moved in support of Johnson's left near the Winfrey house. Cheatham, behind the high ground east of Winfrey's, had rained artillery fire on Johnson's line since about three o'clock.[28]

After the several brigades of Walker's division yielded to the severe pounding by Baird and Brannan, General Bragg ordered General Pat Cleburne's division, then on the east side of the Chickamauga, to attack them from the direction of Jay's Mill. Responding promptly, his men waded across the stream with water up to their shoulders and, after a rapid march, reached Jay's Mill at six o'clock. He attacked both Baird and Brannan immediately, and the resulting contest ended only after complete darkness had settled, during which the participants were able to continue only by following the flash of the guns. This fighting lasted about an hour, during which General Cheatham's two right brigades gave full support to Cleburne, until both Baird and Brannan withdrew to the Kelly house for the night. Cleburne's men, including the wounded, wet clothes notwithstanding, rested on the cold ground without fires to await the morning.[29] The total gain in the day's operations was the firm establishment of the Army of the Cumberland between the Confederates and Chattanooga, a technical Union victory.

The Lafayette Road along or near which the broken lines of each army were rallied and reformed, and across which the surging currents of fire had repeatedly rolled, became the "bloody lane" at Chickamauga.

The remorseless war-god at this hour relaxed his hold on the

27. Van Horne, *ibid.*; *Indiana, ibid.*
28. Van Horne, *ibid.*; *Indiana, ibid.*, p. 18; Boynton, *op. cit.*, pp. 38-39.
29. Van Horne, *ibid.*; *Indiana, ibid.*: Boynton, *ibid.*

two armies whose life-blood had been flowing since early morning. Gradually the mighty wrestlers grew weary and faint, and silence reigned again in the shell-shivered forest. It was, however, only a lull in the storm. On the extreme Union left the restless Confederates were again moving into line for a last tremendous effort. The curtain of night slowly descended, and the powder-blackened bayonets and flags over the hostile lines were but dimly seen in the dusky twilight. . . . "Enough of blood and death for one day!" was the language of the bravest hearts which throbbed with anguish at the slaughter of the 19th and with anxiety as to the morrow's work.[30]

As though this brief summary reflected the ultimate in human slaughter, the following day's carnage would be so terrible as almost to completely eclipse that of the nineteenth.

Those of us who are the beneficiaries of the death struggle that was Chickamauga are prone to think of the battle only in terms of the printed page that seeks to portray its results. Words convey woefully little in bringing to the reader the indescribable plight of the participants, North and South, many of whom lay on the cold and uncomfortable ground with torn and bleeding bodies. Sick and wounded, and those who would participate in the blood bath on the morrow, needed water, medicine, comfort, perhaps a prayer for their departing spirit. Their clothing was inadequate to warm their chilled bodies, those unable to help themselves, as they lay listening to the building of breastworks by Union soldiers from felled trees and undergrowth. For those able to prepare for the day that would end the slaughter was the uncertainty that its sunset would find them in the land of the living. These were the breastworks that would salvage for Union arms the token of victory and leave the attackers frustrated, bewildered, and almost barren of hope. As General D. H. Hill so correctly stated it: "It seems to me that the élan of the Southern soldier was never seen after Chickamauga—that brilliant dash which distinguished him was gone forever. He was too intelligent not to know that the cutting in two of Georgia meant death to all his hopes. He knew that Longstreet's absence was imperiling Lee's safety, and that what had to be done must be done quickly. . . . He fought stoutly to the last, but, after Chickamauga, with the sullenness of despair and without the enthusiasm of hope. That 'barren victory' sealed the fate of the Southern Confederacy."[31]

Where is the American who can read the results at Chickamauga

---

30. John B. Gordon, *op. cit.*, pp. 203-4.
31. *Battles and Leaders, op. cit.*, Vol. III, p. 662.

or, for that matter, any other of the Civil War's battles, and remain unfeeling at the awful suffering and death, the price paid for a united country? What American can avoid a sense of pride in the knowledge that these men, both North and South, fought with an intensity of purpose unsurpassed in the history of the human race? The only basis for exultation by any American is in the knowledge that we have but "one nation under God, indivisible, with liberty and justice for all."

Thomas's Fourteenth Corps was extremely fatigued from the long night march of the eighteenth and nineteenth and the continuous fighting on the nineteenth, which should be kept in mind when appraising the tremendous ordeal further endured on the twentieth. On the night of the nineteenth, Rosecrans held a council of war attended by his division and corps commanders. Thomas was so completely exhausted from his exertions of the previous forty-eight hours that he would occasionally fall asleep while Rosecrans was receiving reports from his other commanders. Each time he was awakened to give answer to some question asked by Rosecrans he would offer the same advice, namely, "I would strengthen the left," meaning, of course, that it was imperative that the road to Chattanooga be defended at all hazards. Each time, Rosecrans would ask the same question in reply, "Where are we going to get the men from?" Rosecrans leaned heavily on Thomas, his able second in command, and wherever the peril happened to be on any field, there was Thomas in command, and there was success. The mental strain experienced by Rosecrans during the long campaign of five weeks, particularly the last two, undoubtedly had its bad effect upon the nervous system and reflexes of this brilliant man, and, in consequence, this bore heavily on his below-standard efforts just before and during the Battle of Chickamauga.[32]

All during the night and early morning of the twentieth the two armies ministered to the wounded and buried the dead; reorganized and consolidated the shattered remnants of fighting units; strengthened and made more secure their assigned positions; and finally went to rest and sleep, many for the last time.

The men of Thomas's corps labored, as did no other force that night, constructing defenses. The comment that "General Thomas had wisely taken the precaution to make rude works about breast high along his whole front, using rails and logs for the purpose," denotes the saving feature of the forthcoming struggle. "The rails and logs ran at right angles to each other, the logs keeping parallel to the proposed line of battle until the proper height was reached.

---

32. *Indiana, op. cit.,* p. 18.

The spaces between these logs were filled with rails, which served to add to their security and strength. The spade had not been used."[33] This is not at all surprising; rather, it would have been more surprising by far if Thomas had not done the utmost to insure success.

During a visit to the several commanders, before hostilities commenced on the twentieth, Rosecrans asked Thomas some questions regarding certain aspects of the battle of the nineteenth. Uncharacteristic of Thomas, he was somewhat carried away when discussing a brilliant charge made by his men, and exclaimed zestfully, "Whenever I touched their flanks they broke, general, they broke." When his glance met that of a listener, he seemed to have realized that his enthusiasm was out of bounds, and he blushed like a woman. This momentary display of enthusiasm by Thomas refutes the oft-repeated contention that he was cold and reserved; rather, it proves the opposite, and he would have been less than human if he had not reacted with satisfaction to the telling of the incident. That he was extremely self-disciplined is certain, as evidenced by his composure and coolness under the excitement and danger of battle. It was said of him in after years, "Until I had seen at Chickamauga repeated instances of his imperturbation, I did not believe that human nature was capable of it." In another instance at Chickamauga, Thomas was sitting with an aide at a spot within range of enemy shellfire when a shell passed between the two officers. An exchange of faint smiles was made between them when, shortly thereafter, another followed the same course. This was no time for further smiling, and Thomas said to his companion, "Major, I think we had better retire a little."[34] None can deny that this was coolness of the highest order, but he had the sense of propriety and awareness of peril to avoid endangering his life unnecessarily.

---

33. *Battles and Leaders, op. cit.,* Vol. III, p. 654.

34. W. F. G. Shanks, *Personal Recollections of Distinguished Generals* (New York, 1886), p. 67.

CHAPTER XVI

Sunday, the Lord's Day, and Death Compounded, September 20

SEPTEMBER 20, 1863, was the Sabbath, the day designated as the one among seven that should be remembered and kept holy. Perhaps even more important was the command that "Thou shalt not kill," but, perhaps again, God may not have meant that one should not kill for a "cause." It was a day on which the civilians of Chattanooga, but a few miles away, were asking Divine aid for whatever "cause" the worshiper espoused, there can be little doubt. It was a day on which the great majority of the participants, there could be no doubt, were offering up to God an appeal for their own and their country's safety. Sunday is like any other day when two armies meet, and Sunday was the day of the week on which several of the great Civil War battles were fought, either entirely or in part, including First Manassas or Bull Run, Mill Springs, Shiloh, Chickamauga, and Chancellorsville.

All Union troops saw action on the nineteenth except General Sidney Post's brigade, which had been assigned to protect supply trains, and General William Lytle's brigade, which had been held at Lee and Gordon's Mill. The Confederate divisions of Breckinridge, Hindman, and Kershaw, Preston's brigades commanded by Kelly and Gracie, and Gist's brigade of Walker's division, quite a large force, had seen either little or no action on the nineteenth, and comprised a most formidable force. It is needless to say that Rosecrans had no idea that such a large number of fresh troops, in addition to reinforcements brought by Longstreet and others, would face his tired veterans. It has been shown that the Union army was exhausted from its excessive exertions on the eighteenth and nineteenth, whereas the Confederates had suffered little inconvenience and fatigue. Somewhat as an offset to this advantage of the Southerners, the Union army occupied uniformly higher ground, as at Snodgrass Hill and the Widow Glenn house.[1] Regardless of General Bragg's apparent advantage, there was little comfort for him in the over-all outlook, since his plan of battle had to be revised, and may be said to have met with failure on September 19.

Although General Bragg's reserves were almost intact after the nineteenth, which left him in an apparently better position than Rosecrans, he was in no position to feel complacent regarding the outcome of the fighting yet to be done. His plans had been for the most part thrown out of hand, and, in general, it is fair to state that he was repulsed. One of the most damaging blows to his plans was the shifting of Crittenden's corps from the left of the Union line, and the replacement of it by Thomas. Also his lines that had enveloped the Union flank were, in turn, outflanked and the right half badly beaten. The advantages he once held were not productive of the success expected of them. When the battle commenced, Rosecrans had been under great difficulty in placing his units in position, and often there was no support on either the right or the left of divisions and brigades. Bragg's dream of breaking the Army of the Cumberland into fragments, by forcing its left on its center and smashing it back into the mountains, was a complete failure. This summing up can be interpreted in no other way but as a decided setback for him.[2]

The Confederate objective of seizing and utilizing the Lafayette road to get between the Union Army and Chattanooga was fundamentally the same on the twentieth, despite the failures of the day before. After the arrival of Longstreet with his reinforcements, Bragg transferred all his infantry to the west side of the Chickamauga. He then divided his army into two wings and assigned General Leonidas Polk to the command of the right and General Longstreet to the command of the left. Polk was instructed to send his divisions into action from the right to the left, while Longstreet was ordered to await the outcome of Polk's attack and send his divisions into combat in similar fashion. Bragg gave Longstreet the impression that he had been skirmishing heavily in attempting to bring his men into the line of battle, but the truth is that some of the brigades were reduced by as much as one fourth in an action that far exceeded the bounds of mere skirmishing.[3]

---

1. W. F. G. Shanks, *Personal Recollections of Distinguished Generals* (New York, 1866), p. 70; Thomas B. Van Horne, *History of the Army of the Cumberland* (Cincinnati, 1875), Vol. I, pp. 340, 343; *Indiana at Chickamauga* (Indianapolis, 1900), p. 19.

2. Van Horne, *ibid.*, pp. 341-43.

3. Van Horne, *ibid.*, p. 343; John G. Nicolay and John Hay, *Abraham Lincoln: A History* (New York, 1909), Vol. VIII, p. 91; John Wyeth, *Life of General Nathan Bedford Forrest* (New York, 1899), p. 264.

General Polk bitterly disappointed Bragg by not attacking as ordered, but the heavy fog that lay over the battlefield during the early hours of the twentieth might well have been the reason for the delay. Unable to endure the anxiety any longer, Bragg went in person to ascertain the trouble, only to learn that Polk not only was not on the field in person, but that he had not made preparations for battle. General Bragg had learned, however, that beyond Thomas's left flank the Lafayette road to Chattanooga was not defended. Thomas was keenly aware of this deficiency, since he had requested of Rosecrans that Negley's division be assigned to close the gap, and his anxious appeal to Negley elicited the promise that he would soon come to his aid. General Absolom Baird's division was unable to reach far enough to close this gap without weakening its own position, a matter that Baird had brought to the attention of Thomas the night before. Rosecrans, in riding along the line at daybreak, ordered Negley to join Thomas immediately; meanwhile, he directed General McCook to correct his right, since it extended too far beyond the crest, and to move Davis's division to the left and close it compactly.[4]

It is reported that in later years Bragg spoke with considerable bitterness of Polk's delay in attacking. Although ordered to do so at dawn, it was nine o'clock before he got under way. Bragg complained that but for this failure Confederate independence might have been won. Polk was not the only one to come in for Bragg's criticism, as he also reproached Cheatham, Breckinridge, and Longstreet.[5] There seems little on which to differ with Bragg in this criticism of Polk, but his placing of blame on Longstreet is impossible to comprehend. The only thing to be said against "Old Pete" is that he failed to dislodge the greatest defensive fighter in American history in the person of General George H. Thomas. Bragg's complaint that Southern independence might have been won but for Polk's failure, it is interesting to note, is a comment that assumes great importance in the light of Thomas's defense.

General Bragg was not immune to criticism himself, particularly by his own subordinates. General Forrest, after having been sent to oppose General Burnside in East Tennessee, received an order to turn over his command to General Wheeler. Forrest was not informed that the purpose was to strengthen Wheeler in an attack on the rear of the Federal Army, and he reacted accordingly. He sent Bragg a letter charging him with duplicity and lying, and promised to come to

---

4. Van Horne, *op. cit.*, Vol. I, p. 344; Henry M. Cist, *The Army of the Cumberland* (New York, 1882), pp. 201-2.

5. Van Horne, *ibid.*; Cist, *ibid.*

headquarters and say verbally what he wrote in the letter. Forrest went to Bragg, as promised, refused to take his hand in greeting, and, furiously moved, said, "I am not here to pass civilities or compliments with you, but on other business. You commenced your cowardly and contemptible persecution of me soon after the battle of Shiloh, and you have kept it up ever since. You did it because I reported to Richmond facts, while you reported damned lies." Continuing, he told Bragg that "You have played the part of a damned scoundrel, and if you were any part of a man I would slap your jaws and force you to resent it. You may as well not issue any more orders to me, for I will not obey them." True to his word, Forrest went to Jefferson Davis, following which he was given an independent command in West Tennessee.[6]

General McCook ordered General Lytle's brigade to move up promptly from Lee and Gordon's Mill and unite with a force from Viniard's farm on the elevation back of the Widow Glenn house. Sheridan's and Wood's divisions of Crittenden's corps were in position back of the Brotherton property. Thomas's corps, spreading across to the east side of the Lafayette road, between the Poe and Kelly places, extended around the east and west sides of Kelly's field, about half the distance to the Lafayette road. On the evening before, Thomas had aligned his divisions to afford greater compactness and strength, with Baird's, Johnson's, and Palmer's divisions east of the road, and Brannan's and Reynolds's divisions west of it. The formation consisted of two brigades from each division, in two ranks, on the battle line, and one brigade from each division in reserve. This is where General Thomas expected Negley's division, then on Brannan's right, west of Brotherton field, to be placed on Baird's left, to form the extreme left of the Union line. Wilder's mounted infantry brigade and Harrison's regiment of mounted infantry occupied the high ground back of Sheridan's divisions in the rear of the Brotherton property.[7]

General Bragg's line overlapped the Union right by an entire division, and by a division and two brigades on its left, in addition to Forrest's dismounted cavalry division. The Union line was protected by crudely placed trees, rocks, rails, and other defenses in the vicinity of Kelly's field, but elsewhere there was little cover except at Snodgrass Hill.

---

6. Van Horne, *ibid.;* Cist, *ibid.*

7. Van Horne, *ibid.*, Vol. I, p. 343; *Official Records of the War of the Rebellion* (Washington, 1880–1901), Vol. XXX, Part 1, pp. 69-70, 137; Thomas B. Van Horne, *Life of Major General George H. Thomas* (New York, 1882), p. 127.

The Confederate right, beyond the far left of the Union line, in division order beginning with Forrest's two cavalry divisions under Pegram and Armstrong, was east of Cloud's. Later that morning, Forrest captured the Union hospitals near by. Breckinridge, Cleburne, and Stewart with their divisions occupied the lines east of Poe field and east and south of Kelly's field, where they fought fiercely but without success until about one o'clock. Walker's two divisions under Liddell and Gist were behind Breckinridge, and Cheatham's five brigades were in reserve to the rear of Cleburne. Gist's division was repulsed at about noon, and Liddell's division was also forced back. Bushrod Johnson formed a central line of three divisions about seven hundred yards east of Brotherton field, with Law's and Kershaw's divisions directly back of him. Hindman was to the left of Johnson and Preston was on the far left, east and south of Viniard's and past the Union right. Stewart's division was on the right of Longstreet, and Cleburne's division was to the left of Polk's. The position to the fronts of Stewart and Johnson was defended by hastily improvised barricades consisting mainly of logs and other immediately available material.[8]

Colonel Joseph B. Dodge's brigade of Johnson's division was shifted to Baird's left just before the battle commenced; but this extended Baird's flank to only about half the distance to the Lafayette road, and created a dangerous situation. Thomas sought unsuccessfully to obtain another division to close this opening, which was north of McDonald's house on the Lafayette road. In the meantime, Breckinridge advanced at nine thirty from about seven hundred yards east of the glade in front of Baird. Hurriedly, General Beatty's Brigade was ordered into the breach, but his numbers were inadequate and the line was stretched very thin. The consequences to his command were disastrous, as will be shown.[9]

General Polk's failure to attack at daylight, commencing on his right, to be followed by Longstreet's divisions taking up the fight to the left, was a serious blow to Bragg's plans, and a great boon to Rosecrans. General D. H. Hill, commanding Polk's right, stated that he was not informed of Bragg's order to attack until some time after it should have begun.

Breckinridge's division, consisting of Helm's, Stovall's, and Adams's brigades, advanced against Baird's position. Part of Helm's brigade was caught in a crossfire from Baird's right during the advance and suffered tremendous casualties, although a force comprising about

---

8. H. V. Boynton, *The Chickamauga National Military Park* (Cincinnati, 1895), p. 43.

9. *Ibid.*, p. 44.

two and one-half regiments gained the rear of the Union line to the Lafayette road. Beatty's brigade defended at McDonald's over an area allotted a division, and although his troops were badly shattered, Beatty himself withdrew to Snodgrass Hill until the end of the battle. Helm was killed, and his brigade withdrew with the loss of about one-third of its strength. Stovall's and Adams's brigades, on Breckinridge's center and right, respectively, continued advancing to the Lafayette road, from where they passed the Union left to its rear a distance of several hundred yards; despite this, Forrest's dismounted cavalry and another division farther on still overlapped the Union flank.[10]

Stovall's and Adams's brigades moved to Kelly field, where the former attacked Baird's left and met repulse. General Stanley's brigade of Negley's division moved rapidly to dispute Adams's advance and succeeded in checking it after severe fighting. Stanley was then ordered to reinforce Thomas's left on Snodgrass Hill. Meanwhile, Stovall recovered from his temporary setback and reached the north end of Kelly's field. Adams likewise resumed the advance after Stanley's withdrawal. At this stage, the Union left appeared to be hemmed in and cut off; Van Cleve's, Wood's, and Davis's forces were placed in the line to await the expected attack of Breckinridge; and Cleburne attacked on the east of Kelly's field as Stewart attacked from the east and south. Van Derveer's brigade advanced to the left in two lines from out of the woods north of the Kelly house, and formed about one hundred yards in front of Stovall. The first line of this brigade, consisting of two lines, fired a full volley into Stovall's force, and he was immediately checked. Next, the rear line rose from its prone position, charged Stovall anew, and compelled him to retreat after the first line came to its support. The importance of Van Derveer's brigade at this critical time averted disaster to the Union left almost as though by a miracle; however, the cost in men, and the disabling of all but two of the horses, attests to the devastating fire to which they were subjected in this brief attack.[11]

It should be stated also that Adams was compelled to withdraw after his flank became exposed to an enfilading fire. During the struggle, the four divisions surrounding the field were under bitter attack by Cleburne and Stewart. Although these attacks were most determined and sustained, the low Union defenses successfully resisted by the expedient of passing loaded rifles from those who were not able to fire to those who were. The Confederates here experienced, according to statements of their own officers, an unbroken stream of

10. *Ibid.*, p. 45; Van Horne, *Cumberland*, Vol. I, pp. 345-46.
11. Van Horne, *ibid.*, pp. 346-47; Boynton, *op. cit.*, pp. 45, 47.

fire, testifying to the reason they were unable to take the Union
works. The Union left was saved by this action of Brannan's brigade
under Van Derveer; and Bragg's formidable attack failed in its
sweep by divisions from his right to his left. Cleburne lost about
five hundred men in a few minutes, and Breckinridge's left brigade
was almost destroyed, including the loss of several line officers.[12]

At Rosecrans's council of war on the night of the nineteenth it was
stipulated that General Brannan's division would be held in reserve
to support Thomas, if needed. Without Thomas's knowledge, however, this division was placed in the line at Poe field before dawn.
When Thomas sent for Brannan to reinforce him as agreed, Brannan
was being subjected to attack by Stewart. Realizing the seriousness
of the situation, Brannan at once conferred with Reynolds, both of
whom agreed that Stewart should be faced, and that Rosecrans should
be informed and asked for a decision. In partial satisfaction of
Thomas's request, Brannan ordered Van Derveer's reserve brigade
to him, with the result stated above.[13]

During Van Derveer's successful action, Longstreet's three divisions
moved from the woods east of the Brotherton house and through
a breach in the Union line, a movement fraught with calamity for the
National Army. Shortly before Brannan was ordered to report to
Thomas, General Negley's division was replaced by Wood's division
at the Brotherton house. Concluding that Brannan would promptly
obey the order, Rosecrans ordered Wood to close up rapidly on
Reynolds and support him. Since Brannan had not left the line, and
since Reynolds was in a position to Wood's left, Wood moved at once
to the rear of Brannan toward Reynolds's position. This was the
moment when Longstreet struck with lightning suddenness and effect;
and whether Longstreet saw the opportunity, or whether he was
simply the beneficiary of coincidence by just stumbling into it, the
calamity to the Union army was great.

General Thomas had sent an aide, Captain Sanford C. Kellogg, to
report to General Rosecrans that he was heavily pressed and needed
help. While on his mission, the aide noted what he thought was a big
gap in the line between Reynolds and Wood, and reported it to Rosecrans upon arrival. What Kellogg failed to notice was that Brannan's
division, although not so far in front as were the others, had
retired only a short distance to the rear, but not out of line, as he had
thought. Rosecrans, not being on the scene, sent an order to General
Wood: "The general commanding directs that you close up on

---

12. Van Horne, *ibid.*; Boynton, *ibid.*
13. Van Horne, *ibid.*, p. 347; Cist, *op. cit.*, p. 206; Van Horne, *Life*, pp.
135-37; *Official Records, op. cit.*, Vol. XXX, Part 1, p. 103.

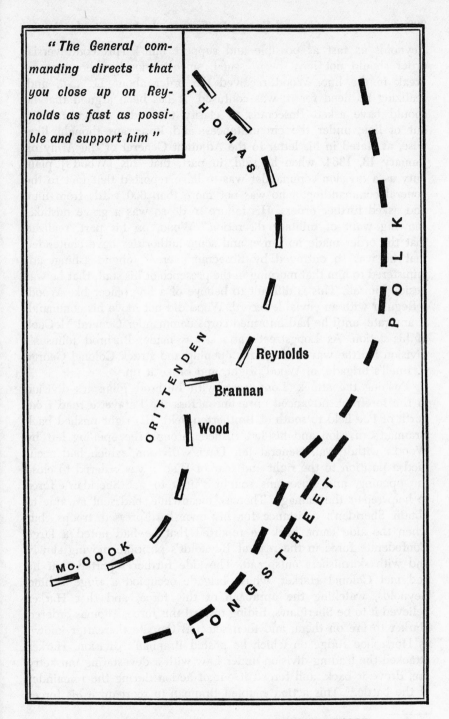

"*The General commanding directs that you close up on Reynolds as fast as possible and support him*"

THOMAS

POLK

CRITTENDEN

Reynolds

Brannan

Wood

LONGSTREET

Mc.COOK

CHICKAMAUGA: THE FATAL ORDER TO WOOD

Reynolds as fast as possible and support him." This controversial order should not have been issued, since obviously there was no break in the line. Wood received the order about 11 A.M., and, realizing no need for it, was confused. It has been argued that he should have asked Rosecrans to clarify the order before moving out of line, under the circumstances; and Rosecrans thought likewise, as stated in his letter to the Adjutant General of the Army on January 13, 1864, when he said, in part, that "his [Wood's] plain duty as a division commander was to have reported that fact to the general commanding, who was not more than 600 yards from him, and asked further orders. His failure to do so was a grave mistake, showing want of military discretion." Wood, on his part, realized that the order made no sense; and some authorities have contended that he was so outraged by Rosecrans's cruel tongue-lashing, administered to him that morning in the presence of his staff, that he was beside himself. This is difficult to believe of a fine officer like Wood, a Regular with an enviable record. Wood did not move his command, at any rate, until he had informed corps commander General McCook of his action. As Longstreet's attack was made, Bushrod Johnson's division led the way through the opening and struck Colonel George P. Buell's brigade, of Wood's right, and broke it up.[14]

Pushing the attack, Longstreet, with Bushrod Johnson's division in the forefront, advanced on a line across the Lafayette road from north of Poe field to south of Brotherton field. His right pushed back Brannan's division and his left rushed through the opening left by Wood's withdrawal. General Jeff Davis's division, which had occupied a position to the right and rear of Wood, was ordered to close the opening, and Rosecrans sought vainly to get Sheridan's force to help repair the damage. Thomas, meanwhile, had sent an aide to obtain Sheridan's assistance for his own hard-pressed troops, but when the aide came back he reported that he had noted a large Confederate force in the rear of Reynolds's position, moving slowly and with skirmishers outspread. The aide further reported that he had met Colonel Harker, whose brigade occupied a ridge behind Reynolds, watching the approach of this force, and that Harker believed it to be Sheridan's. Riding toward this force, Thomas ordered Harker to fire on them, and then selected the site thereafter known as Horseshoe Ridge on which he posted Brannan's division. Harker attacked the leading division under Law with a devastating musketry fire, drove it back, and forced it out of action during the remainder of the battle.[15] This action enabled Brannan to reorganize his forces

14. Van Horne, *Cumberland; Indiana, op. cit.,* p. 21.
15. Cist, *op. cit.,* pp. 207-8; *Indiana, ibid.*

behind Harker on Snodgrass Hill, as stated, and then align his troops with Harker's.

Thomas went to the crest of the hill on the front, where he met Wood and his command. Wood confirmed that the advancing troops were Confederates, whereupon Thomas ordered him to establish a line next to Brannan and resist the advance as long as possible. He had barely time to place his men on Brannan's left before they were attacked fiercely; but fortunately the attack was repulsed, although repeated again and again with the same result. Thomas had taken the important step, after selecting the site of Horseshoe Ridge, of placing artillery on the spurs to the rear.[16]

In the Union rout following the breakthrough, which extended from the Dyer field to the Vittitoe house and was stopped at Snodgrass Hill, as we have seen, the Confederates achieved their only significant success during the battle. There is no minimizing the importance of the success, however, for on it turned the Confederate victory, though technical it may be regarded. Following the breakthrough, Buell's and Beatty's brigades were badly shattered and complete batteries were captured. Scattered detachments fought independently, including the Eighty-second Indiana, under Colonel Morton C. Hunter, on the south and east sides of Snodgrass Hill. When he reached the hill, Hunter declared, "I will not retreat another inch," and he kept his word. There he stood, and with help from scattered groups, representing largely the units that had left the field, and supported by some artillery, he held on until darkness came. Stanley's brigade of Negley's division occupied a position between Harker and Brannan, and Negley also sent about eight hundred men of the Twenty-first Ohio before abandoning the field, which Brannan placed on his extreme right. Negley's departure from the field without orders remains clouded in confusion and debate, and a Court of Inquiry seeking reasons for his conduct did not clarify the matter. His division had performed capably when acting separately, as did Beatty's brigade, when it went to the aid of Baird at 8:00 A.M., and Stanley's brigade, in giving valuable and badly needed aid to Thomas earlier in the day. Negley himself had been given orders to assemble all available artillery to the rear of the line and post it on the elevation overlooking Baird's left. After collecting about fifty guns they were sent instead to the ridge, which General Gordon Granger's troops would later occupy on the right of Brannan, with considerable support from the infantry. Here General Negley, before any action occurred, ordered his entire command to retire to the rear, and they then moved to Rossville.[17]

---

16. Cist, *ibid.*; *Indiana, ibid.*
17. Boynton, *op. cit.*, pp. 49, 52; *Indiana, ibid.*, p. 102.

Negley stated in his report of the battle that after he sent the Twenty-first Ohio to aid General Brannan he was seeking a position for the artillery he had collected when he learned of the breakthrough by Longstreet. He learned further, he stated, that Rosecrans, McCook, and Crittenden had left the field, and thus he felt it all important to save the artillery. Proceeding to within two miles of Rossville, where he found the first open ground on which troops could be assembled and reorganized, he also found General "Little Phil" Sheridan, subsequent hero of "Sheridan's Ride," with about 1,500 troops. He said that Sheridan, quoting him, was seeking to proceed to Rossville, but that he "respectfully suggested" that he move "to the support of General Thomas, stating that I would join him with all the troops I had collected." He stated further that he conversed with Generals Davis and Sheridan and Colonel Ducat, and it was decided to go to Rossville to prevent enemy possession of the cross-roads, at which point Sheridan would move to support Thomas by way of the Lafayette road. He stated that after reaching Rossville at dark, and there rapidly reorganizing the available troops, he learned that Granger had reinforced Thomas, that he was safe, and that he was retiring to Rossville. He learned also that General Sheridan halted several miles from Rossville.[18]

Negley does not indicate why he left the field without orders, although, as will be explained later, General Thomas was shocked to learn that he was not occupying his assigned position. Neither did he attempt to reconcile his arrival at Rossville, when darkness had settled over the area, with the time he departed from the battlefield, some four hours or more earlier. There is nothing said regarding the plight in which he left Thomas, during which Granger and Steedman arrived in time to offset the damage his departure would otherwise have caused. Omitted completely is any reference to the possibility that his presence on the field, where the bullets were flying, might have enabled Thomas to hold the battlefield; but perhaps any such reference would have been too much to expect. Conceivably, Negley was dazed from battle fatigue, as apparently other officers were, notably Rosecrans and Sheridan.

The action of Sheridan in the rout is anything but inspiring. It has been mentioned that Sheridan, a friend of Grant, rose through that friendship eventually to head the United States Army, with the rank of Lieutenant General, held only by Washington, Grant, and Sherman before him. Sheridan, the "Litttle Phil" of his chief sponsor, Grant, and member of the most powerful and longest-lived military dynasty

---

18. Boynton, *ibid.,* p. 52; *Official Records, op. cit.,* Vol. XXX, Part 1, pp. 330-31, 338.

in the history of the United States, had a bad day at Chickamauga. Sheridan did his part well in drawing a curtain over the incomparable deeds of Thomas, as did his fellow members of the dynasty, namely, Sherman, Schofield, and Grant; and nothing proves this so well as the occasional reference to the alleged "slowness" of Thomas by this group, which created the false legend that consigned to virtual anonymity this mighty soldier of the Union cause. It has been shown previously that the memoirs of these generals give little, if any, credit to Thomas for his great service to his country. Any credit given is more often canceled by qualification and innuendo, as in Grant's reference to Thomas's defensive ability, when he was tremendous from any standpoint.

Colonel Gates P. Thruston lends support to Negley's report in describing some of his experiences during the Union rout. He reported that when he struck the Dry Valley road he "found Sheridan and Davis, with remnants of their five brigades. General Phil was furious. Like the great Washington on several occasions, he was swearing mad, and no wonder. The devoted Lytle and the truest and bravest had fallen in vain resistance around him. His splendid fighting qualities and his fine soldiers had not half a chance. He had lost faith." Reaching Snodgrass Hill, Thruston reported to General Thomas. He said that "He was intently watching the conflict near the crest, a few steps in rear of the battleline. . . . I reported briefly the situation on the right. Thanking me, he requested me to try to bring up Sheridan's and Davis's troops to aid his right." Continuing, Thruston reported: "Unfortunately Sheridan's and Davis's force had drifted down the road toward Rossville. Hastening after them, we found they had already entered the narrow road or defile at McFarland's Gap. I tried to halt the rear of the column, but without success. . . . I rode furiously through the thicket, alongside, and appealed to officers. 'See Jeff, Colonel?' they said. 'See Phil?' Some old trudger in the ranks called out, 'We'll talk to you, my son, when we get to the Ohio River!" Finally reaching the head of the column, Thruston found Davis, Sheridan, and Negley about half the distance between the field and Rossville. After a hasty conference, Davis ordered a right-about at once and went briskly to the front, but, in the words of Thruston, "Sheridan was still without faith. He may have thought there was danger at Rossville, or that his troops had not regained their fighting spirit. He insisted on going to Rossville. Darkness would catch him before he could reach the field from that direction. Negley was vacillating; he finally went to Rossville."[19]

---

19. *Battles and Leaders of the Civil War* (New York, 1884), Vol. III, p. 665.

If the reader is still in doubt regarding Sheridan's part at Chickamauga and of his prejudice toward Thomas, as referred to in an earlier chapter, his statement that "I have always thought that, had General Thomas held on and attacked the Confederate right and rear from where I made the junction with him on the Lafayette road, the field of Chickamauga would have been relinquished to us, but it was fated to be otherwise," will suffice. What Sheridan should have stated was, in justice to the truth, that if he had returned and helped Thomas, the hindsight suggestion referred to would have been a step in the direction of its implementation.[20]

In Sheridan's report of the battle he stated: "On reaching the Dry Creek Valley road I found that the enemy had moved parallel to me and had also arrived at the road, thus preventing my joining General Thomas by that route. I then determined to move quickly on Rossville and form a junction with him on his left flank via the Lafayette road. This was successfully accomplished about 5:30 P.M." Regarding this, General Thomas reported that he sent an aide to notify General Reynolds to begin the movement at 5:30 [from Snodgrass Hill], the time Sheridan reported his junction with Thomas's left at Rossville, several miles away.[21] It would have taken the aide some time to deliver the order to Reynolds, and it would have required some time for Reynolds to get ready to withdraw, perhaps at least a half hour altogether, but with Rossville still several miles away. In other words, it would have been impossible for Sheridan to have formed a junction with Thomas's left at 5:30. Sheridan's statement is simply not correct; and assuming for the sake of being extremely charitable toward him that he sought a junction with Thomas, his low-blow insinuation that Thomas might have done better is of a piece with the then current injustice to a great man. Moreover, this incident is but one of a lengthy series of injustices that have resulted in minimizing for a century the deeds of the greatest soldier in the Union Army.

Some famous men left the field of Chickamauga, the most prominent of whom were General Rosecrans, commander in chief, General Garfield, chief of staff, and Generals Crittenden and McCook, corps commanders of the center and right. In fairness to all it should be emphasized that, but for the mistaken order to General Wood, Chickamauga might have been the greatest Union victory of the war. What these men could have done to avert or to minimize the disaster is anyone's guess, but from available evidence they were caught up in an irresistible tide.

---

20. Philip H. Sheridan, *Personal Memoirs* (New York, 1892), Vol. I, p. 289.
21. *Official Records, op. cit.,* Vol. XXX, Part 1, pp. 254, 581.

Another famous man to leave the battlefield was Charles A. Dana, a civilian, the Assistant Secretary of War, who was on a tour of inspection with the Army of the Cumberland. In his dispatch to Washington, Dana described the great confusion prevalent in the retreating Union center. He reported that he never saw anything to crush the mind so much as that scene, and that in the confused rabble he was caught and swept away with part of Rosecrans's staff. Some of the officers drew their swords in attempting to check the panic, but when a few stragglers were about to form a nucleus on which to reassemble, a crashing shell would undo the good work and send the cowards once more on the run. He reported that he rode twelve miles to Chattanooga at a gallop, and found the road glutted with baggage wagons, artillery, ambulances, Negroes on horseback, field and company officers, and wounded men limping along. Union refugees from the surrounding country were leading their wives and children, with mules running at large, squads of cavalry, and every element that could be a part of the rout of a great army, including a major general commanding a corps. This was the situation in which only a part of that fleeing general's corps remained in support of the left under the magnificent old hero, General Thomas, and the Marshall Ney of the Civil War, General Gordon Granger.[22]

Dana reported that although Rosecrans bore no part of the afternoon's success, when the army was saved, he lost some of his popularity with the soldiers, whose idol was naturally Thomas, and he himself shared their feeling. Further, the general organization of the army was inefficient and its discipline defective due to his failure to punish those who needed it; additionally that his incapacity for command asserted itself in his insistence on personally directing every department of his army.[23]

When Rosecrans arrived at Chattanooga after leaving the field of destruction, he rode up to Department Headquarters and was assisted from his horse. His appearance was that of a man broken in spirit, who was trying to bear up by supreme effort, after receiving a terrible blow that he did not fully understand. He had suffered great privation for more than a week, however, and during the past twenty-four hours had eaten but little. The sight of his army collapsing about him, after a most brilliant campaign of maneuver and near-catastrophe during the recent past, was evidently the climactic event to outwit his nervous system. When he received Garfield's dispatch informing him that he was then with Thomas, who was holding on

22. James H. Wilson, *The Life of Charles A. Dana* (New York, 1907), p. 264.
23. Shanks, *op. cit.*, p. 273.

with seven divisions and a number of smaller forces, he exclaimed, "Thank God!" Waving the dispatch above his head, he said, "This is good enough; the day isn't lost yet." Turning to his two retreating corps commanders, Crittenden and McCook, Rosecrans reminded them that their place was on the battlefield. Unfortunately, neither commander was able to reach the field before the contest was ended.[24]

General Granger, that rough-and-ready officer who fought like a demon, and whose tongue had an edge like a razor, was no respecter of rank when it came to stating a truth. The famous reporter William F. G. Shanks, in his *Personal Recollections of Distinguished Generals,* stated that General Thomas sent Granger to report to Rosecrans the situation at Chickamauga. Granger found Rosecrans and had little trouble in convincing him that he should accept Thomas's ideas. Sitting at a table, with Granger following his preparation of the order to Thomas to fall back, Rosecrans began preparing a detailed list of the way in which the withdrawal should be conducted. Uppermost in Rosecrans's mind, apparently, was the thought of deceiving the Confederates into believing that, through these elaborate instructions, some mastermind move was in contemplation. Impatient at the delay, and aware that Thomas was eminently qualified to handle the situation, Granger interrupted him with: "Oh, that's all nonsense, general! Send Thomas an order to retire. He knows what he's about as well as you do."[25] Rosecrans made no protest, tore up the order, and wrote a new one, which conveyed all that Thomas needed to know.

Returning to the debacle created by the mistaken order, the five brigades on the right of Brannan's line were shattered in the breakthrough and driven to McFarland's Gap. Davis's and Sheridan's divisions, seeking to stem the tide, were attacked in front and on the right by Hindman, and on the left by Bushrod Johnson. Hindman's three brigades overlapped both of Davis's flanks and forced him to retreat in disorder; but this situation was made worse when Davis collided with Sheridan's troops as they were moving to support Thomas. General Lytle was killed there while leading his brigade in an attempt to stem the attack. Both Davis and Sheridan retreated over the spurs of Missionary Ridge to McFarland's Gap, as stated, to reorganize their shattered forces. Hindman moved his force to Bushrod Johnson's left, near the Vittitoe house, before joining in the attack on Thomas's men on Horseshoe Ridge. During this encounter, Wilder's brigade and the Thirty-ninth Indiana moved to the Widow Glenn house and charged the left of Hindman's column with Spencer seven-

24. Cist, *op. cit.,* p. 226.
25. Shanks, *op. cit.,* p. 273.

shooter repeating rifles. The five regiments equipped with this rifle led the Confederates to believe they were opposed to a considerably larger force.[26]

Hood's divisions inclined rapidly toward the Snodgrass house, as part of the left of Longstreet's crashed through the Union line, by way of Dyer field and the near-by woods. Bushrod Johnson veered to the ridge to the west side of Dyer field, capturing fifteen guns, and continued on preparatory to attacking the Union left on Snodgrass Hill. Longstreet was showing evidence of his awareness of near-victory by the reckless manner in which he poured troops against Snodgrass for the grand clean-up, but this would be frustrated by canister and musketry from the defenders. Johnson formed a line at the base of Snodgrass Hill, when joined by one of Hindman's brigades, about half the distance to the Snodgrass house, and established liaison with the left of Kershaw's brigade, which extended still more the Confederate line running to the Snodgrass house. Humphrey's brigade, also of Kershaw's division, comprised the right of the Confederate line and was in position to assault Harker's position to the left of Brannan. The right of the Union line was made up of three brigades and a battery of artillery, on the crest of Horseshoe Ridge, above the powerful Confederate concentration at the base of the hill.[27]

Following the repulse of Gist's and Liddell's divisions at Kelly field, there was little action there between one o'clock and sundown. The opposing forces were alerted to possible further action, but were occupied in listening to the flow of battle on Snodgrass. Repeated assaults were made between two and three o'clock by Bushrod Johnson's and Kershaw's divisions, aided by Anderson's brigade of Hindman's division, but without success. Before three o'clock, about half of Brannan's men had exhausted their ammunition and were preparing to resist further attack with the bayonet. Bushrod Johnson's left was advancing on the crest from which General Negley withdrew, when unexpected help came for the hard-pressed defenders.[28]

The Battle of Chickamauga abounds with claims and counterclaims, with tales of heroism and incompetence, as perhaps no other battle of the Civil War. One of the most enduring and least plausible stories is in relation to the advance of General Granger's reserve force to aid Thomas at the most critical moment on Snodgrass Hill. Steedman, subordinate to Granger, has been credited with insisting to

26. *Official Records, op. cit.*, Vol. XXX, Part 1, pp. 252-53; Donn Piatt, *General George H. Thomas* (Cincinnati, 1891), pp. 428-31; *Indiana, op. cit.*, p. 22.

27. *Battles and Leaders, op. cit.*, Vol. III, p. 655; Boynton, *op. cit.*, p. 53.

28. Van Horne, *Cumberland*, Vol. I, p. 348; Boynton, *ibid.*, p. 55.

Granger that he would march to the relief of Thomas, orders or no orders, despite Granger's warning that he might be subject to court-martial. This is a good story, but it gives too much credit to Steedman and little to Granger, although both performed most capably during the action. In General Steedman's report, he stated that at 11:30 A.M. General Granger ordered him to move to the battlefield, after becoming satisfied, from the sustained heavy firing, that the left of the Union line was being punished severely. Furthermore, General Granger himself reported that he "determined to go to his [Thomas's] assistance at once."[29]

There is no basis for withholding from General Steedman the maximum of credit for his superior performance after reaching Snodgrass. Nevertheless, there is no justification for implying that Rosecrans, a superior commander, would have tied down his reserve and rendered it incapable of performing its whole duty, particularly when its presence would avert disaster. To refute this over-credit to Steedman, General Rosecrans instructed General Granger, at 10:00 P.M. on the nineteenth, to hold his force in reserve on the twentieth and directed him "to post his command on the eastern slope of Missionary Ridge to support either McCook or Thomas." This order clearly gave Granger discretion in using his reserve, although admittedly he marched without orders from the commander in chief, who was not on the field at the time. Additionally, at one o'clock on the afternoon of the nineteenth, Thomas requested Granger to let him know the state of affairs with him, indicating further that Thomas was placing reliance on Granger's reserve, if needed.[30] This exchange of communications appears to refute the story that Steedman was subject to court-martial for moving to the relief of Thomas; but more especially it would have been ridiculous for Granger, under the circumstances, to have suggested such a possibility.

Once the decision was made, Granger and the two brigades under Steedman marched toward the sound of battle. The other brigade, under Colonel Dan McCook, was left to guard the Ringgold road near McAfee's church. Continuing past a Confederate force under General Forrest with but minor skirmishing, Granger relayed orders to Dan McCook to keep the Lafayette road clear and insure that the open fields from that point, about two miles from the battlefield, remained under Union control. The intent there was to afford as much protection to Thomas as possible, and McCook brought up his brigade and held his position until late that night.[31]

---

29. *Official Records, op. cit.*, Vol. XXX, Part 1, pp. 854, 860.
30. *Ibid.*, pp. 69, 127.
31. Cist, *op. cit.*, p. 209.

Thomas's Fourteenth Corps, with help from various units and groups from the Twentieth and Twenty-first Corps of McCook and Crittenden, continued to draw in their lines on Snodgrass Hill as their numbers were reduced by death and disability. Thomas had with him altogether during the long and fateful afternoon about five divisions and, in addition, the two brigades brought up by Granger and Steedman.[32]

Continuing toward the scene of action, the while subjected to random firing from Confederate batteries, which they elected to ignore in deference to the more important objective of aiding Thomas, they came within view of the peerless leader of the defenders. Noting the thick cloud of dust in the distance, from his position in rear of the line of battle of his re-formed right, the thought uppermost in Thomas's mind was whether they were friends or foes. An officer near him, General Thomas J. Wood, suggested that the column could be infantry, in view of the low dust clouds, and might be Granger's reserve, whereas, if the dust clouds were higher, it might suggest Forrest's Confederate cavalry. Thomas was visibly nervous, something unusual for one to note in him. If the oncoming column was one of Union troops, the safety of his position was assured, but if it was an enemy column the day might be lost. Wood reiterated, "Don't you see the dust rising above them ascends in thick mist clouds, not in spiral columns as it would be if the force were cavalry?"[33]

Not content with just waiting, Thomas sent Captain Johnson of the Second Indiana Calvalry to ride out and ascertain the identity of the approaching force. The moment was one of the great ones in American military history. As Johnson came closer, he saw that they were Federals. Moving nearer, he asked, "Whose troops are these?" "Mine, sir," was the General's reply. "General, may I inquire your name?" "I am General Steedman, commanding the First Division of the reserve corps." "And I am serving on the staff of General Thomas, who directed me to ascertain who you were, as an approach from this quarter was unexpected." As the force drew near to Snodgrass Hill, Steedman rode up to General Thomas. After the usual exchange of greetings, Thomas said, "General Steedman, I have always been glad to see you, but never so glad as now. How many muskets have you got?" "I have 7,500 muskets, general." "It is a good force," replied Thomas, "and needed very badly."[34] This situation is somewhat com-

32. Van Horne, *Cumberland*, Vol. I, 348.

33. Shanks, *op. cit.*, p. 68.

34. J. T. Woods, *Steedman and His Men at Chickamauga* (Toledo, 1876), pp. 48-50; *Military Essays and Recollections* (Chicago: Illinois Commandery, Military Order of the Loyal Legion of the U.S., 1891), Vol. I, p. 244.

parable to the Battle of Waterloo, when the Duke of Wellington, nearing defeat by Napoleon, exclaimed, "Would to heaven that Blücher or night would come!"; and Blücher came and turned the tide of battle that brought victory to the duke.

In Thomas's report of the battle, he stated that when he learned from General Wood that the Union right and center had met with disaster, at about two o'clock, he directed him to align his force with Brannan's and confront the Confederate attacks. He ordered Steedman to take position on Brannan's right, which order was obeyed promptly, "as if on drill," where, fighting his way to the crest of the hill, he moved his artillery forward and drove the enemy down the slope. This new force revived the flagging hopes of those who had stood their ground, and every attack thereafter was repulsed all along the line until nightfall. The ammunition was reduced to about two or three rounds per man, but, fortunately for all, Steedman had brought along enough to raise the average to about ten rounds per man. Until this supply was available, the men had been reduced to emptying the cartridge boxes of the dead and wounded; and Thomas had ordered those completely out of ammunition to fix bayonets.[35]

When Steedman's men arrived on the scene, General Thomas was standing entirely alone under a clump of dead trees, coolly directing the movements of the men who, as their ranks grew thinner, closed around him. Thomas had noticed that the key position, which should have been held at all costs, had fallen into Confederate hands. The loss was stunning, but, not shaken, he merely said, "General Negley's command occupied that ridge a short time ago, and why he abandoned it I do not know. The enemy are now posting a battery there and will soon enfilade our position with the fire of its guns." He told Steedman, "You must take that ridge."[36] which Steedman did, at the cost of tremendous casualties on both sides.

Fortunately for the Union defenders, General Van Derveer arrived with his brigade at about 2:30, the approximate time that Steedman entered the battle. Coincidentally, Van Derveer also moved without orders at the sound of the guns, and reaching the ridge on Steedman's left reinforced Brannan's battered ranks. He then relieved Brannan's men and fought on until darkness. Determining to hold the position, and fixing bayonets after their ammunition was exhausted, he compelled the Confederates to withdraw. He then retired to Rossville after Thomas gave the order.[37]

35. *Official Records, op. cit.,* Vol. XXX, Part 1, p. 253; George W. Skinner (comp.), *Pennsylvania at Chickamauga and Chattanooga* (William Stanley Ray, 1897), p. 238.

36. Woods, *op. cit.,* p. 51.

37. *Official Records, op. cit.,* Vol. XXX, Part 1, pp. 430-31.

Around three o'clock, two brigades of Hindman's division formed to the left of Johnson near the Vittitoe house preparatory to a new attack. Next, Johnson reached Vittitoe's and planted two batteries, but all other attempts at breaching the Union line ended in failure. Also at three o'clock, Preston's division marched from Hall's Ford to Snodgrass Hill by way of the Brotherton house where, at about four thirty, it relieved Kershaw's brigade. Preston then advanced on Stanley's and Brannan's positions, with Johnson and Hindman advancing at the same time. A salient in Stanley's line was taken by Gracie's brigade, but after some of the hardest fighting of the day the position was given up.[38] The repeated and unsuccessful Confederate attacks on Horseshoe Ridge, from about two o'clock until sunset, have never been surpassed on any battlefield, if indeed they have ever been equaled. A testimonial to their valor were the heaps of dead and wounded strewn across the slopes over which they could not advance. It would be supremely unjust not to give equal credit to the doubly outnumbered American defenders of the North under Thomas, who would not give up the position they chose to hold against their American assailants of the South, who would not give up until there was no hope.

Confederate General Gordon expressed Horseshoe Ridge well, perhaps better than most, when he reported:

In the furious tempest there now came one of those strange, unexpected lulls; but the storm was only gathering fresh fury. In the comparative stillness which pervaded the field its mutterings could still be heard. Its lightnings were next to flash and the thunders to roll around Horseshoe summit. Along that crest and around Snodgrass House the remaining troops of Rosecrans' left wing planted themselves for stubborn resistance—one of the most stubborn recorded in history. To meet the assault of Longstreet's wing, the brave Union General Brannan, standing upon this now historic crest, rallied the remnants of Croxton, Wood, Harker, Beatty, Stanley, Van Cleve, and Buell; but up the long slopes the exulting Confederate ranks moved in majestic march. As they neared the summit a sheet of flame from Union rifles and heavy guns blazed into their faces. Before the blast the charging Confederates staggered, bent and broke; reforming at the foot of the slope, these dauntless men in gray moved again to still more determined assault upon the no less dauntless Union lines firmly planted on the crest.

Through the blinding fires they rushed to a hand-to-hand conflict, breaking here, pushing forward there, in terrible struggle.

---

38. *Ibid.*, Part 2, pp. 304-5: Boynton, *op. cit.*, pp. 55, 56.

Through clouds of smoke around the summit the banners and bayonets of Hindman's Confederates were discovered upon the crest, when Gordon Granger and Steedman, with fresh troops, hurried from the Union left and, joining Van Derveer, hurled Hindman and his men from this citadel of strength and held it till the final Union retreat. With bayonets and clubbed muskets the resolute Federals pierced and beat back the charging Confederates, covering the slopes of Snodgrass Hill with Confederate dead. . . The woods caught fire from the flaming shells and scorched the bodies of dead and dying.

At the close of the day the Union forces had been driven from every portion of the field except Snodgrass Hill; and as the sun sank behind the cliffs of Lookout Mountain, hiding his face from one of the bloodiest scenes enacted by human hands, this heroic remnant of Rosecrans' army withdrew to the rear and then to the works around Chattanooga, leaving the entire field of Chickamauga to the battered but triumphant and shouting Confederates.[39]

General Gordon captured much of Horseshoe Ridge in words, perhaps as accurately as any such scene has ever been captured; and as he portrayed the mighty heroism and the awful agony, he saw that these were Americans, not just enemies. There is hope in this, that all of us may see in like objectiveness the deeds of valor so gloriously displayed by men whose basic differences stemmed largely from their place of birth.

With fullest credit to the unnumbered heroes of both sides in the conflict, there had to be some leadership, and there was in the persons of Generals Longstreet and Thomas. Both "Old Pete" Longstreet and "Old Pap" Thomas had something to ignite and unite in men, and it was something extraordinary and priceless, namely, the ability to inspire the confidence of men to follow them into the jaws of death. One participant of Snodgrass recalled seeing Thomas on that fateful afternoon when "his ranks had been heavily pressed—in places they were broken—the enemy had followed his advantage and his bullets were cutting the leaves from the trees above the General's head. On his old familiar steed he sat; not a muscle of his face moved while he issued orders to restore the line in the quiet conversational tone that politeness prescribes for a ladies' drawing-room. It was the discipline of a lifetime concentrated on a moment. There is no figure in military history more sublime than that of General Thomas in

---

39. John B. Gordon, *Reminiscences of the Civil War* (New York, 1905), pp. 209-10.

the midst of this line of fire that nearly encircles the Horseshoe Ridge, not only wrenching victory from the brink of defeat, but in that awful hour making amends for the sins of a whole campaign; for Halleck's misconceptions and blunders at Washington; for Rosecrans' excessive confidence that, in the face of his foes, scattered his army over sixty miles when it should have occupied six; for the failure of Burnside to cooperate from Knoxville; or of Grant from Vicksburg.

"It has been said of Thomas, 'His was the equal mind that was never lost in disaster, the unconquerable will, the steadfast purpose, the dauntless courage, the limitless resources.' Such is the description of leadership of The Rock of Chickamauga, the type of man of whom Shakespeare spoke in such eloquent words, 'He was a man, take him for all in all, and I [we] shall not look upon his like again.' "[40]

Almost one hundred years after Chickamauga, General Douglas MacArthur, the great commander of World Wars I and II, speaking at West Point Military Academy to the members of the 1962 graduating class, had this to say of the American soldier:

> And what sort of soldiers are those you are to lead? Are they reliable? Are they capable of victory?
>
> Their story is known to all of you. It is the story of the American man at arms. My estimate of him was formed on the battlefields many, many years ago, and has never changed. I regarded him then, as I regard him now, as one of the world's noblest figures; not only as one of the finest military characters, but also as one of the most stainless.
>
> His name and fame are the birthright of every American citizen. In his youth and strength, his love and loyalty, he gave all that mortality can give.
>
> From one end of the world to the other, he has drained deep the chalice of courage.
>
> In memory's eye I could see those struggling columns of the First World War, bending under soggy packs on many a weary march, . . . driving home to their objective, and for many, to the judgment seat of God. . . . They died unquestioningly, uncomplaining, with faith in their hearts, and on their lips, that we would go on to victory.

What a testimonial to the American soldier, coming from one of the greatest of soldiers!

General Thomas reported that at four o'clock General Garfield, Rosecrans's Chief of Staff, accompanied by several officers, gave him

---

40. Skinner, *op. cit.,* p. 238.

the first reliable information concerning the disintegrated Union right and center. Thomas reported also that soon afterward Rosecrans sent him a dispatch instructing him to assume command of all forces and, with Generals Crittenden and McCook, establish a strong and threatening position at Rossville. Clearly, this was an order from Rosecrans to retreat. In addition, Rosecrans promised to send rations and ammunition to Rossville, and to join him after examining the terrain at Chattanooga. General Thomas determined to hold his position until nightfall, if at all possible, and then distributed the remaining ammunition as he had promised his commanders some time before.[41]

Much controversy has raged over the question whether Thomas withdrew to Rossville before or after darkness fell, although Thomas's report clearly indicated that it was dark. As if to confirm that darkness came to the battle area early at the time of Thomas's order to withdraw, his order to Reynolds to begin the movement was issued at 5:30, after he had stated he was determined to hold on until darkness if at all possible. It has been shown heretofore that, from the time the order was issued until it was feasible to start, it would inevitably have been dark soon after that time at Chickamauga on September 20. In the mountainous area around Chattanooga, night comes early in September, and the sun had already set behind the background of dense foliage and woodland. In confirmation of the lateness of the hour when Thomas's troops retreated from Snodgrass Hill, the following quotation from battlefield Marker No. 21, entitled "Close of the Battle, Sept. 20, 1863, 7:30 P.M." is given:

> At dusk the right of Brannan's line rested to the left of this position near the monument of the 35th Ohio facing southeast. The right of Kelly's brigade of Preston's division being discovered to the right rear of that position, the 35th Ohio was hastily brought to this ground to confront it, facing southwest. Trigg's brigade of Preston's division was then discovered half way down the slope to the right of this tablet. The 35th was thereupon moved still farther to the right and formed on a curved line to face both Kelly's and Trigg's positions. At this juncture the 9th Indiana was reported by Gen. Brannan to the commander of the 35th Ohio to re-enforce his line. A movement of the Confederates called out a volley which was responded to by them and was then followed by their withdrawal. This was the last firing of the battle. The 68th Indiana, Captain Edmund Finn, and the 101st Indiana, Maj. George W. Steele, both under the command

---

41. *Official Records, op. cit.* Vol. XXX, Part 1, p. 253.

of Lieutenant Colonel Thomas Doan of the 101st, were soon reported to the commander of the 35th Ohio, and were posted by him along the crest to the right of this position to cover the withdrawal. The 101st being to the extreme right, Vanderveer's brigade with the 9th Indiana was then withdrawn by segments from left to right, and after a short interval the 68th and 101st Indiana, in the order named, followed, covering the movement.

When it is remembered that the Chickamauga battlefield was dedicated in 1895, at a time when many of the participants of the battle were still living and in attendace at the dedication, the accuracy of the foregoing marker may be assumed.

The darkness of the woods was something that oppressed the spirit, an indefinable feeling that could not be averted and yet could not be explained. Men who were in the battle often spoke of it afterward as though that fatal nickname of Chickamauga, "The River of Death," hovered over their spirits and left them with an eerie feeling. Perhaps this was part of what overcame Rosecrans, of whom it was said that afterward the shadow of Chickamauga was discernible on his face. Perhaps the extreme physical exhaustion of many of the men who fought the battle gave them a reaction to the battlefield area that otherwise they would not have felt. Aside from being exhausted, there was little water for many of them, and for a period of twenty-four hours many had not eaten at all. Perhaps the uncertainty of the morrow, which would have applied equally on both the nineteenth and the twentieth, overcame their spirits and left its mark upon them until their dying day. There was something else that went with Chickamauga as with no other battle: the destruction and damage to human lives on a scale not hitherto experienced in the annals of war must have had an enduring effect upon all who took part in the battle.[42]

How realistically is described one soldier's reaction! The men sank to rest where their ranks had formed but there was no rest. Shots on the picket line were not especially disturbing until they became all too frequent. Then the loud screeching of a random shell, sounding as if a clarion call to battle, rends the air and frays the nerves. The dead-tired soldiers rise once more to the command of "attention," and the order to move renews again the action that will bring more suffering and death. Under the open skies, with your opponent in plain sight, fighting is bad enough, but at night, in woods so dense that the skies cannot be seen, when it is impossible to distinguish

---

42. Skinner, *op. cit.*, p. 236.

friend from enemy, and the sound from many thousands of rifles is blended with the screeching shells, then is the most horrible of all moments in battle.[43]

After giving the order to Reynolds to withdraw, Thomas left his position behind General Wood to tell Reynolds personally the point at which to form the new line to protect the retirement of his remaining troops to Rossville. While passing through the open woods to Reynolds's position, several soldiers informed him that a large force of Confederates was in the woods and proceeding in his direction. He at once directed Reynolds to form his line perpendicular to the Rossville road and to charge the Confederates on his front. General John Turchin's brigade struck this force with great fury and routed them while taking about two hundred prisoners. Turchin's and Willich's brigades then covered the withdrawal of the army divisions of Generals Wood, Brannan, and Granger. Johnson's, Baird's and Palmer's divisions and Cruft's and Grose's brigades were attacked while retiring, but were able to withdraw to Rossville with but few losses. Generals Thomas, Garfield, and Granger proceeded to Rossville and preparations were begun immediately to place the town in a state of defense.[44]

General Garfield sent a message to General Rosecrans from Rossville at 8:40 P.M., saying, "General Thomas has fought a most terrific battle and has damaged the enemy badly. . . . From the time I reached the battlefield [3:45 P.M.] till sunset the fighting was by far the fiercest I have ever seen. Our men not only held their ground, but at many points drove the enemy splendidly. Longstreet's Virginians have got their bellies full. Nearly every division in the field exhausted its ammunition, got supplies, and exhausted it again. . . . On the whole, Generals Thomas and Granger have done the enemy fully as much injury to-day as they have suffered from him, and they have successfully repelled the repeated combined attacks, most fiercely made, of the whole rebel army, frequently pressing the front and both flanks at the same time." Garfield stated further that General Rosecrans's order to retire to Rossville was received a little after sunset and communicated to Generals Thomas and Granger, and that they were moving back; he also stated that they were in good shape and would be in a strong position before morning. He said, "I hope you will not budge an inch from this place, but come up early in the morning, and if the rebs try it on, accommodate them."[45] This

43. *Ibid.*
44. *Official Records, op. cit.,* Vol. XXX, Part 1, pp. 145, 253-54.
45. *Ibid.,* p. 145.

indicates quite clearly that if General Bragg had elected to fight on the twenty-first he would have had his hands full.

Assistant Secretary of War Charles A. Dana, who was caught in the rout from the battlefield when Longstreet broke through Wood's vacated position, reported to Secretary of War Stanton at four o'clock: "My report to-day is of deplorable importance. Chickamauga is as fatal a name in our history as Bull Run." Dana was incoherent, and understandably so. He had been in a stampede unparalleled on any prior American battlefield. Fortunately, his report did not reckon fully with the ability of General Thomas to hold on. At eight o'clock, after news of the stand by Thomas and his heroic men, Dana reported that "my dispatch of four o'clock proves to have given too dark a view of our disaster. Having been myself swept bodily off the battlefield by the panic-struck rabble into which the divisions of Davis and Sheridan were temporarily converted, my own impressions were naturally colored by the aspect of that part of the field. . . . only those two divisions were actually routed. . . . Thomas, with the remainder of the army, still holds that part of the field."[46] More will be heard later from Dana, who, it will be found, exerted great influence in the appointment of Thomas to succeed Rosecrans in command of the Army of the Cumberland.

"Well did General George H. Thomas earn that day the grand name of The Rock of Chickamauga, and when, in the coming centuries, posterity makes up the final judgment of the ability of the soldiers, in the light of opportunity and conditions, it will show, on the immortal Roll of Honor, not a single name above that of the heroic figure whose personal character was as spotless as his genius was exalted."[47] Eulogies such as this, to the greatness of General Thomas, are to be found with little effort throughout the vast store of reference material available; but strangely, perhaps paradoxically, this estimate does not find its way into the general histories that frequently accord overfull measure of credit to Generals Grant and Sherman.

Although it had its origin in one of the most unjust criticisms imaginable, President Lincoln paid to General Thomas one of the finest tributes, following his achievement at Chickamauga, to be found anywhere. On September 23, just three days after the battle, a reputedly chronic critic and self-appointed advisor, wired the President a telegram.

---

46. *Ibid.*, pp. 192, 193.
47. *The History of Our Country* (Philadelphia, 1890), Vol. I, p. 1077.

"Will Buell's testamentous Executor George Thomas ever let Rosecrans succeed? Is Bragg dumb enough to punish Thomas severely and disgracingly?" This story comes down to us from a cipher clerk in the War Department, in a letter to General George H. Thomas, dated May 27, 1867:

"I have had in my possession since the day it was written a telegram penned by our late loved President. Its history is this:—

"Robert A. Maxwell, a Quixotic individual resident of Philadelphia, has, during the war and since, humored a propensity for addressing numerous dictatorial and sensational dispatches to the President, his cabinet and prominent officers of the Government. On receipt of one of these dispatches—a copy of which I enclose also—President Lincoln came to the Department and handed me his reply marked 'cypher.' He lingered in the office while I was preparing it for transmission and when nearly ready he remarked, 'I guess on the whole, Mr. Tinker, you need not send that—I will pay no attention to the crazy fellow. I put it into my pocket and have preserved it as a precious autograph, hoping some time to be honored with an opportunity to present it to you in person to whom I feel it justly belongs, a priceless tribute to a noble hero whose dauntless courage on that fatal day saved the Army of the Cumberland.

"It gives me profound pleasure to hereby make the presentation." This was Lincoln's letter that was never sent:

"I hasten to say that in the State of information we have here, nothing could be more ungracious than to indulge any suspicion towards Gen. Thomas. It is doubtful whether his heroism and skill exhibited last Sunday afternoon, has ever been surpassed in the world.

"A. Lincoln"[48]

Another tribute expressive of the general respect held for Thomas by Confederate officers acknowledges his outstanding ability. "The attack of the right wing having partly broken down, the enemy in front of Polk was not held to their own, but were in large numbers free for a masterly movement by that fine soldier, General George Thomas. . . . He was one of the ablest of their soldiers, perhaps none equaled him, and I heartily wish he had been anywhere else but at Chickamauga."[49] Still another eulogy to him recognized the important contribution he made, not only at Chickamauga, but also on

---

48. David H. Bates, *Lincoln in the Telegraph Office* (New York, 1907), p. 169.

49. G. Moxley Sorrel, *Recollections of a Confederate Staff Officer* (New York, 1905), p. 186.

other fields. "It was General George H. Thomas of Virginia who stood like a rock between the Union Army and destruction at Chickamauga, and at Chattanooga and Mission Ridge dealt the Confederacy blows from which it never recovered. The same general had previously saved the Union army at Mill Springs and Murfreesboro, and shattered Hood's army to pieces at Nashville. A distinguished Confederate has said that those two men, Andrew Jackson and George H. Thomas, dug the grave of the Confederacy."[50] The reference here to Jackson is presumed to relate to his strong pro-Union sentiments and actions during his terms as President, during which he expressed opposition to nullification. Some Southern states, notably South Carolina, as early as 1832 were talking of secession, and Jackson strongly insisted that the Union was indissoluble. (This is expanded in the Epilogue to include an excerpt from the famous speech of Confederate Vice President Alexander H. Stephens before the war, in arguing against the withdrawal of his native Georgia from the Union; also the words of the famous artillery officer of the Army of Northern Virginia, after the war, General E. P. Alexander, and his commander, General Longstreet, expressing gratitude that the Union was not dissolved, are given.)

"Only God and George H. Thomas saved the Union wreck. Not all of the battlefield knew of the rout of the center. The rest rallied about this Virginian Loyalist who took command of the shattered lines on Snodgrass Hill. The right was routed, the center fleeing in confusion, but the left stood stoutly, in an arc of 270 degrees about the defense of Rossville Gap. There is a conventional picture, cast into the iron markers of the Chickamauga battlefield, that after Rosecrans' right and center had been routed, 'the Rock of Chickamauga' rallied on Snodgrass Hill, Granger marched to the sound of the guns, and the bleeding Union forces, not at bay, actually won the final chapter of the battle."[51] This estimate is substantially correct, inasmuch as the Confederates were unable to attack the Union forces the next day or the next, in exploitation of their claimed success. General Benjamin F. Cheatham is reported to have stated after the war that, but for the breastworks constructed by Thomas during the night of the nineteenth, the Confederates would have been the victors before noon on the twentieth.

When General Garfield was on his way to Washington following his election to the House of Representatives, he was given a dinner

---

50. *William and Mary Quarterly* (1907–1908), Vol. XVI, No. 2, pp. 118, 119.

51. George F. Milton, *Conflict: The American Civil War* (1941), pp. 290, 291.

in Baltimore by the Honorable Henry Winter Davis. In discussing Chickamauga, a subject still very much in the minds of the people at the time, Garfield said: "It was not a defeat, but a great victory, only we at headquarters did not know it. It was about three in the afternoon, when riding with Rosecrans toward Chattanooga, that the continuous roar of a battle on the center and left struck us as indicating an obstinate defense, and I suggested the propriety of my riding back and ascertaining the conditions of affairs on Thomas' front. . . . The road was crowded with fugitives, men, ambulances, and wagons. . . . No one inexperienced in such a rout can conceive of the disorganization and wild dismay of such a mass. I succeeded at last, and I shall never forget my amazement and admiration when I beheld that grand officer holding his own with utter defeat on each side and such wild disorder in his rear. He had the moment before repulsed a terrific assault and his unmoved line of bronzed veterans stood by their guns as grim and silent as a line of rock. Thomas' greeting to me was as quiet as if on parade, and, on my asking him as to the situation, he replied, 'We have repulsed every attack so far, and can hold our ground if the enemy can be kept from our rear.' "[52]

After Steedman's appearance with the reserve and his splendid attack on the Confederates, Garfield reported that "we saw the enemy hesitate, waver, fall back, and disappear, as at the same moment a terrific assault was made on our front. . . . As to the anxiety I speak for myself, my heart was in my mouth, but for Thomas, from first to last he stood unmoved, receiving reports and giving orders, as if the situation were not utterly desperate. Once only he exhibited any feeling. We were moving along the line to encourage the men and to make inquiry regarding the ammunition, when Thomas approached a man whose coolness and courage he had noticed, and shaking the brave fellow's hand, thanked him for his gallant conduct. The man stood embarrassed for a second, and then exclaimed, 'General Thomas shook that hand; if any fellow ever tries to take it I'll knock him down.' "

Garfield went on to say that from then on "Pap" Thomas became in the hearts and mouths of the men "the Rock of Chickamauga." "That rock is his pedestal of honor, and so long as the memory of the terrible conflict, which cemented in blood our people as a nation, remains, that monument will grow clearer and brighter against its background of warclouds; and the able, grand, silent, untainted man will be fairly worshiped when the little tin gods now rattled about among the groundlings are forgotten. . . . If these, the popular beliefs

52. Donn Piatt, *Memories of the Men Who Saved the Union* (New York, 1887), pp. 230-32.

and facts agreed on, were to be settled by the partisans who rule to-day, Thomas would have but scant justice, as little after death as they accorded him in life. He won his laurels on the blunders of the men who are the heroes of the hour, and they can be recognized only in obscuring him. Fortunately these noisy worshipers make but a part of the American nation, while amid the English-speaking people, of which these blind devotees are a small minority, history will speak, and the history to which he appealed will do his memory justice."[53]

These are the words of one of our martyred Presidents, a major general who knew General Thomas intimately through long service in the Army of the Cumberland, although his prophecy as to eventual justice to that great Virginian, and even greater American, is just beginning to reach fulfillment.

Although during the Mexican War both Generals Bragg and Thomas served together with conspicuous success, General Bragg refused to recognize a communication from General Thomas during the Battle of Chickamauga on the ground that he wanted nothing to do with one who had been unfaithful to his native state. Nevertheless, there is ample evidence to show that Bragg thought affectionately of Thomas, and would refer to him as "Old Tom."[54]

One of the most unusual aspects of Chickamauga was the departure of both commanders from the field during the afternoon of the twentieth, and the conducting of activities of both armies by the second in command, namely, Longstreet and Thomas. Both were regarded highly by their men, and both may be said to have controlled the battle during that fateful afternoon. The result of their encounter refutes the oft-repeated claim that Thomas never faced an able commander; and if there was a better corps commander in either army than "Old Pete" Longstreet, his name does not come to mind. One noted authority stated that "with the exception of Lee and Johnston, no one in the Confederacy showed the same ability in the command of an independent army as Thomas."[55] After the death of Stonewall Jackson, Longstreet was Lee's most trusted lieutenant. The comparison of Thomas and Longstreet is clear cut in favor of Thomas on this occasion, since Longstreet could not budge Thomas from his position, despite greatly superior numbers. The claim has been made also that eulogists of General Thomas were so emotional in advancing his right to consideration that his deeds were exaggerated out of proportion to the true facts. Nothing in the record supports any other

---

53. *Ibid.*

54. *Battles and Leaders, op. cit.*, Vol. III, p. 658.

55. James Ford Rhodes, *History of the American Civil War* (New York, 1923), p. 302.

conclusion but that he was deliberately passed over when the laurels were distributed; that mediocre and less capable men were given commands that should have been given to him; and that those entrusted with the responsibility of granting promotions were often influenced either by political or other considerations unrelated to merit. What General Thomas did for his country shines like a beacon throughout reliable reference material, which is readily available to those who seek the truth.

General Van Cleve's division continued to Chattanooga after the withdrawal from the battlefield, but the remainder of the Union Army occupied Rossville, the right of Mission Ridge, and Lookout Mountain near by. This left the two opposing forces in the same relative position as before the battle, despite the terrible casualties of both, with the Union forces blocking Bragg's entry into Chattanooga. At midnight on the twenty-first, the Union Army occupied Chattanooga and the adjacent area, and by noon of the twenty-second had established rifle pits all along the lines for their defense.

Rosecrans's force at the beginning of the battle was estimated to approximate sixty thousand. At that time a force of about two thousand occupied the city, while about three thousand were detailed to guard supply trains. This left about fifty-five thousand available for battle. Bragg's force is not so easy to determine, but he reported that almost thirty-nine thousand were available for duty after the battle; this force, added to the estimated losses in battle of about eighteen thousand, indicates that fifty-seven thousand men began the battle for Bragg, or a force slightly larger than Rosecrans had available for duty.[56]

In the campaign from Tullahoma to the closing scene of the Battle of Chickamauga, the genius of George Thomas was strikingly demonstrated many times. When it is recalled that this ability was so great as to shade the activities of his commander in chief, Rosecrans, and that he dominated the battle from beginning to end, the proof is unmistakable. His ability to change posture from defense to attack, and vice versa, was the factor that time and again saved the Army of the Cumberland. The first important instance occurred when he advised Rosecrans to defer pursuit of Bragg until supplies and communications were adequate. More emphatically he urged that the several corps remain within supporting distance of each other. The advice went unheeded, but the wisdom of it was not long in becoming exposed.

Bragg grasped the opportunity to attack each corps separately,

---

56. Boynton, *op. cit.,* p. 58.

but failure on the part of his subordinates to carry out his plans served to neutralize Rosecrans's mistake. The prompt ordering of Brannan's and Reynolds's divisions by Thomas to support Negley and Baird, when both were seemingly entrapped, averted one of the most potentially disastrous moments in the history of the Army of the Cumberland. In this instance Rosecrans rebuked Thomas for his apparent slowness in advancing Negley's division to Lafayette, as ordered; but Thomas had diagnosed Bragg's intentions to destroy the Union Army piece by piece, and so informed Rosecrans. Not until then did Rosecrans realize the situation, and that Thomas had averted disaster to the army and saved himself from disgrace.

The next instance of magnificent performance on the part of Thomas took place when he marched all night on September 18, arriving at Kelly's field in readiness for battle on the morning of the nineteenth, after learning that Bragg's army was crossing the Chickamauga. This was followed, after his arrival at Kelly's field, by ordering Brannan to Reed's Bridge, the spark that seized the initiative from Bragg and began the Battle of Chickamauga.

Uppermost of Thomas's achievements, the stand on Snodgrass Hill ranks in majesty with Bunker Hill, the Alamo, and other epic incidents in military history, and has already been discussed in some detail.

Finally, there was the incident that occurred when the troops were withdrawing to Rossville, in which General Turchin, by order of Thomas, charged into the Confederates to permit the column to proceed to Rossville in comparative safety.

In short, General Thomas possessed the rare quality of not only recognizing sudden and unexpected danger in whatever form it might appear; he also had the ability, undoubtedly achieved by forethought and instinct, to cope with it successfully. These difficulties encountered, often due to the failures of others, were usually disposed of as if he knew beforehand they would be met, and thus made preparations to solve them.

It has been said many times that the uniformly greater success achieved by the Army of the Cumberland and other Western armies was due to the inferior quality of the opposition faced. "Comparisons of this kind are of little value, since, in each army, Eastern and Western troops were intermingled. When Longstreet's corps, which had been counted the flower of Lee's army, on the afternoon of September 20, led by such division commanders as Hood and Kershaw, surged up against the semicircle of men of whom Thomas was the center, with ranks thinned, and ammunition reduced, with few cannon and no reserves, everything gone but manhood and the ground they stood on, it recoiled from those invincible lines as completely baffled and broken as when, nearly three months earlier, the remnants of Pickett's men, mowed down by the fire of a hundred guns, and assaulted front and flank, drifted back from the heights of Cemetery Ridge and gave up the field at Gettysburg. Nor, later still, did the same troops meet any better success in their attempt to capture Knoxville. These are the only occasions when any of Lee's troops encountered the armies of the West. The result was not encouraging."[57]

One of the factors overlooked by those who argued that Western soldiers were generally not so good as those in the East was the quality of superior leadership in Western armies. The observation is made with the qualification that the Washington authorities often circumscribed the authority of field commanders and rendered them incapable of success. This was particularly true in the days of General McClellan, when, surprisingly, a large part of his army was reserved for the defense of Washington. McClellan, an above-average commander, protested vigorously against the decision by Washington to have him reserve some fifty thousand troops to insure the safety of Washington and the Shenandoah Valley. One noted authority states that McClellan left 78,456 men behind him when he undertook the Peninsular Campaign,[58] quite a formidable force, which would have surely turned failure into success. The trouble with commanders of the Army of the Potomac was not always due to the authorities in Washington, however, as the records of Pope, Burnside, and Hooker attest.

---

57. Henry Stone, *Some Federal and Confederate Commanders* (Boston, 1895), p. 183.

58. William Swinton, *Campaigns of the Army of the Potomac* (New York, 1882), p. 92.

CHAPTER XVII

The Siege of Chattanooga

By midnight of September 20 the Union Army, temporarily under the command of General Thomas, was in the vicinity of Rossville, except Van Cleve's division and some smaller units that were sent to Chattanooga. Food, medical supplies, and ammunition were rushed as fast as possible from Chattanooga. On the morning of September 21, Crittenden's corps occupied Missionary Ridge, north of Rossville Gap; Thomas's corps occupied Rossville Gap and the road to McFarland's Gap; and McCook's corps, the mounted infantry, and the cavalry occupied the Chattanooga Valley to Lookout Mountain. Little action took place during the twenty-first, other than skirmishing with Forrest's and Wheeler's cavalry, and that night the army moved into and about Chattanooga. McCook's corps held a position on the right; Thomas held the center, or weakest part of the defense; and Crittenden's corps held the left.[1]

On September 22 the Union line was protected by rifle pits. General Thomas was confident on the twenty-third that he would be able to hold his position until reinforcements arrived, but he requested General Granger's cavalry to support him. Dana, however, was not so confident as Thomas, and held out little hope for success, as indicated by his many communications to Secretary of War Stanton over a period of forty-eight hours. General Bragg left the field of Chickamauga on the afternoon of the twenty-first and marched by way of Ringgold Bridge and Mission Mills toward Chickamauga Station. On the morning of September 22, the advance under General Cheatham reached Shallow Ford, whence they took the direct road to Chattanooga. On September 23, Bragg ordered a combined movement on Chattanooga, with his right wing along the Shallow Ford and Mission Mill roads and his left wing along the Rossville road.

---

1. H. V. Boynton, *The Chickamauga and Chattanooga Military Park* (Cincinnati, 1895), p. 90.

Cheatham's division established a line at the foot of the ridge west of the spot crossed by the Shallow Ford road. General Hindman's division was to the left of Cheatham's, with General Walker's division in reserve to the rear of Hindman. General Hill's corps crossed the ridge on the Mission Mill road.[2]

General Longstreet's left wing advanced by the direct road from Rossville, reached the Watkin's house at eleven o'clock on the twenty-third, about two miles from Chattanooga, and formed its line near the foot of Lookout Mountain to the left of Hill's corps.[3]

On September 24, a formidable Union reconnoitering force learned of the position occupied by Bragg's army. When General Rosecrans realized that General Bragg had a strong force on Lookout Mountain, he withdrew McCook's corps from its position on the right to Moccasin Point, not far from Chattanooga and in plain view of General Bragg on Lookout Mountain. The Confederate line on the right ran through Orchard Knob and was in proximity to the Union position. Meanwhile, Wheeler's cavalry was ordered on a raiding expedition against Union supply lines, on which he destroyed about three hundred wagons at Anderson's Crossroads in the Sequatchie Valley. These supply lines were limited to mountain roads over Walden's Ridge and the Cumberland Mountains, after Longstreet's occupation of the heights on the south side of the Tennessee River commanded the road on the north of the river. It was only a matter of days before rations and forage were so reduced that it was necessary to limit quantities to both men and animals.[4]

The movements by the rival forces prepared the stage for the events that were to unfold during the next sixty days in the struggle for Chattanooga. The town was in somewhat of a state of siege almost from the beginning of the Union occupancy, although it was not completely surrounded. General Bragg sought to restrict the flow of supplies and force Rosecrans's thirty-five thousand men into abandonment or surrender. His failure to assume a more aggressive posture in pursuing his objective, particularly the occupation of the eastern side of the Tennessee River, was clear indication of the weakened condition of his army after Chickamauga. Another matter engaging his thoughts was the likelihood of Federal reinforcements, a preoccupation that soon became a reality. General Burnside at Knoxville was in no position to send any; however, Washington, which prior to

2. *Ibid.*, p. 92.

3. *Ibid.*, pp. 92-93.

4. *Ibid.*; Michael H. Fitch, *The Chattanooga Campaign* (Wisconsin Historical Commission, 1911), pp. 156, 159; John Fiske, *The Mississippi Valley in the Civil War* (Boston, 1900), p. 283.

the battle appeared little concerned with East Tennessee, now realized that aid should be sent with all haste.[5]

Reinforcements were not long in coming. Two corps under General "Fighting Joe" Hooker, commanded respectively by General Oliver Otis Howard and General Henry W. Slocum, were sent from the Army of the Potomac. General William T. Sherman's Fifteenth Corps was sent from the Army of the Tennessee. Cavalry and artillery under Colonel E. M. McCook were sent from Bridgeport to oppose Wheeler's cavalry in the Sequatchie Valley, and they arrived in time to witness smoke from the burning embers of the three hundred wagons destroyed. He pursued and overtook the marauders, capturing some soldiers and about eight hundred mules. Wheeler continued to McMinnville, captured the arsenal there, burned supplies, and moved toward Murfreesboro, where a concentration of cavalry under General Crook and Colonels E. M. McCook and R. B. Mitchell prevented his destruction of the town. Although he was driven away before he could destroy the railroad, he was successful in destroying the telegraph lines.[6]

To add to the problems of the Union forces cooped up in Chattanooga, heavy rains increased supply problems. The roads were so deep in mud that many of the underfed animals dropped in their tracks, and died. As a result, trips took longer, were inevitably far fewer in number, and resulted in ever-diminishing supplies of much-needed sustenance for troops and animals. Artillery horses, having been given the least forage because deemed more expendable, died much earlier than the other animals; as a result, the artillery arm of the services became virtually immobilized. More than ten thousand animals died during the several weeks, and the military authorities were confronted with one of two alternatives, that is, retreating, which would invite almost certain renewal of the fighting, or remaining in their state of near-starvation, with the possibility of eventual surrender anyway.

In view of the difficulties at Chattanooga, Washington was greatly alarmed lest the Army of the Cumberland disintegrate. Charles A. Dana was well known for his propensity to publicize flaws of character and ability in others, although his evaluations were not without flaws themselves and some of his defects of character were not unnoticed. Suffice it to state that his habit of criticism and faultfinding did little to build and preserve morale among those entrusted with responsibility. Dana was an extremist in drawing hasty and un-

5. Fitch, *ibid.*, pp. 156-58.
6. *Ibid.*, pp. 159-60; *The Chickamauga and Chattanooga Battlefields* (Washington, D.C.: National Park Service, 1961), p. 27.

reliable conclusions, an example of which bore bitter fruit to Rosecrans through his pressuring dispatches to Washington. He left no one in Washington in doubt that Rosecrans deserved the role of scapegoat for Chickamauga. If Lincoln and Stanton had not yet decided for themselves just what should be done about Rosecrans, Dana did not hold back in commenting on Rosecrans's ability whenever he felt it might be helpful in reaching a decision.[7]

It was inevitable that Chickamauga caused considerable soul searching, as well it should have done, where the safety of men and the nation was concerned. Generals Rosecrans, McCook, Crittenden, and Negley, among others, had performed in a manner that left much to be desired in the minds of most of the authorities. Such conduct demanded an exhaustive and painstaking review of their conduct during the recent campaign. Rumors spread rapidly and far and wide that Rosecrans was to be relieved and that General Thomas would replace him. The well-known sensitivity of Thomas, when the subject of succeeding his superior officer was broached, was again reflected in his declaration that he would not accept the command if offered.[8]

Prior evidence of the disinclination of Thomas to replace his superiors came when he requested and obtained permission to continue in his then present command after orders had been issued for him to replace General Buell. Before that, following his replacement of General Grant, it has been shown that Thomas requested Grant's restoration to his former role, although this meant that Thomas suffered a reduced command. Now he was again refusing to accept promotion after the following dispatch of September 30, from Secretary of War Stanton, was made known to him:

Mr. CHARLES A. DANA:

On Monday the President's order was sent to Rosecrans removing Crittenden and McCook, ordering them to Indianapolis for a court of inquiry, consolidating their corps, and appointing General Gordon Granger commander of the consolidated corps. If Hooker's command gets safely through, all that the Army of the Cumberland can need will be a competent commander. The merit of General Thomas and the debt of gratitude the nation owes to his valor and skill are fully appreciated here, and I wish you to tell him so. It was not my fault that he was not in chief command months ago.[9]

7. Fiske, *op. cit.*, pp. 283, 284.
8. Thomas B. Van Horne, *The Life of Major General George H. Thomas* (New York, 1882), p. 151; Fiske, *op. cit.*, pp. 283-84.
9. *Official Records of the War of the Rebellion* (Washington, 1880-1901), Vol. XXX, Part 3, p. 946.

When Dana received this dispatch he assumed that it represented President Lincoln's thinking and informed Thomas accordingly. Thomas expressed to Dana his deep appreciation, but emphasized that much as he desired an independent command he could not consent to relieve Rosecrans.[10]

Dana wrote to Stanton on October 8 that Thomas would gladly accept any command out of the department to which he might wish to assign him, but that he would not do anything that would give rise to the suspicion that he had intrigued against Rosecrans. Besides, he stated, Thomas had as perfect confidence in the capacity and fidelity of Rosecrans as he had in General Buell before him.[11]

On September 28, Secretary of the Navy Gideon Welles told President Lincoln that it would not do to send any one of our generals from the East to replace Rosecrans, and that he doubted if he had any one suitable for that command the equal of Thomas. Thomas was a capable general, had undoubted merit, and was a favorite with the men.[12]

Since the rumors and discussions were known to almost everyone, Rosecrans was fully aware of their implications. He knew also that a meeting was held in Thomas's headquarters participated in by Dana, Wood, and McCook and that Thomas had rejected it.[13] It was realized by Thomas that Rosecrans's path was no bed of roses, and that he had labored under political pressures from Washington, which had retarded his activities, and that he might be dealt with similarly if he took the command. He was sickened by the cheap political conniving that often underlay military operations, and he wanted no part of it. Furthermore, he was in agreement with Rosecrans's objective in holding Chattanooga and fully believed that he should be retained in command, Chickamauga notwithstanding. It is true that he had disagreed with Rosecrans in not combining his three corps at Chattanooga and in not establishing completely adequate communications with Nashville, but these matters did not materially alter Thomas's opinion of Rosecrans, nor did it affect his loyalty to him.[14]

Reverting to the appointment of Rosecrans to command the Army of the Cumberland as successor to Buell, it is true that Thomas objected most strenuously to the move, but that objection was undeniably valid, since Thomas was then, as he was when ultimately named

10. Van Horne, *op. cit.*, p. 151.

11. *Ibid.*, p. 152.

12. Gideon Welles, *The Diary of Gideon Welles* (Boston, 1911), Vol. III, p. 446.

13. Troy *Times*, April 6, 1870.

14. Van Horne, *op. cit.*, pp. 152, 153.

commander, the logical person for the assignment. Additionally, Thomas was more familiar with the workings of the Army of the Cumberland, aside from having the greater right to the command by virtue of his record, than anyone else. Now, however, he repudiated any thought of personal advantage and thought only of the good of the country. It was not until after Rosecrans himself insisted that Thomas take the command, arguing that his refusal to take it "would be no relief to him [Rosecrans], and it would subject the Army of the Cumberland to possible abuse of a commander who could have no just conception of its worth" that he agreed to accept the command. In the first meeting with Dana after his appointment, Thomas said, "Well, you have got ahead of me this time, and I have no option but to obey orders; but I assure you, I never obeyed an order more reluctantly than this one."[15]

General Order Number 337 of the War Department, dated October 16, 1863, relieved General Rosecrans and designated General Thomas to succeed him. In the same order General Grant was named commander of the Military Department of the Mississippi, comprising the departments and armies of the Ohio, the Cumberland, and the Tennessee. General Thomas reported that his army consisted of 154,289 men and 274 pieces of artillery, and was made up of the Fourth Corps, formerly the Twentieth and Twenty-first Corps, and the Fourteenth Corps; three divisions of cavalry; the local garrisons of Middle Tennessee; and the Eleventh and Twelfth Corps from the Army of the Potomac under the over-all command of General Joseph Hooker. He reported further that his animals were dying by hundreds daily and that, although suffering from food scarcity, the men realized the importance of not giving up Chattanooga.[16]

General Thomas announced his assumption of command in the following order dated October 20, 1863:

> In obedience to the orders of the President of the United States, the undersigned hereby assumes command of the Department and Army of the Cumberland.
>
> In assuming the control of this army, so long and ably commanded by Major General Rosecrans, the undersigned confidently relies upon the hearty cooperation of every officer and soldier of the Army of the Cumberland, to enable him to perform the arduous duties devolved upon him.

---

15. *Ibid.*, p. 153; Donn Piatt, *General George H. Thomas* (Cincinnati, 1891), p. 446.

16. Official Records, *op. cit.*, Vol. XXX, Part 4, p. 404; *Report of the Joint Committee on the Conduct of the War* (Washington), p. 117; Van Horne, *op. cit.*, pp. 153, 154.

The officers on duty at the various departments of the staff, at these headquarters, will continue in their respective places.

All orders heretofore published for the government of this army will remain in full force until further notice.

GEORGE H. THOMAS
Major-General U.S. Vols.[17]

This order was in keeping with the character of General Thomas in that it contained no bombast, no vainglorious reminder of things past, present, or future, nothing to reflect aught but praise upon retiring General Rosecrans, and with a humble appeal to his officers and men to continue giving him the support necessary to perform his responsibilities.

The mutual respect General Rosecrans and General Thomas held toward each other was further disclosed in General Rosecrans's order of October 19, which stated in part:

Major-General George H. Thomas, in compliance with orders, will assume the command of this army and department. The chiefs of all the staff departments will report to him for orders.

In taking leave of you, his brothers in arms, officers and soldiers, he congratulates you that your new commander comes to you not as he did, a stranger. General Thomas has been identified with this army from its first organization. He has led you often in battle. To his known prudence, dauntless courage, and true patriotism, you may look with confidence that under God he will lead you to victory. The general commanding doubts not you will be as true to yourselves and your country in the future as you have been in the past. . . .

W. S. ROSECRANS,
Major-General.[18]

It was a sad leave-taking for Rosecrans and, for that matter, the army he commanded, for, there is no doubt, there was great affection between them. It is well to recall that but for a mere slip, that of the mistaken order that removed General T. J. Wood from the line and precipitated the catastrophe that drove the right and center of the Army of the Cumberland from the field, Rosecrans might well have won a glorious victory.

On October 18, General Grant assumed command at Louisville, Kentucky. Apparently concerned for the safety of Chattanooga, be-

17. Van Horne, *ibid.,* p. 157.
18. *Official Records, op. cit.,* Vol. XXX, Part 4, p. 478.

cause of Rosecrans's expressed fear that it might not be held, Grant started for the front at once. He wired General Thomas on the nineteenth to "Hold Chattanooga at all hazards. I will be there as soon as possible. Please inform me how long your present supplies will last, and the prospect for keeping them up." The reply from Thomas was immediate and to the point:

CHATTANOOGA, TENN.,
October 19, 1863.

MAJOR-GENERAL GRANT:

Two hundred and four thousand four hundred and sixty-two rations in store-houses; ninety thousand to arrive tomorrow, and all the trains were loaded which had arrived at Bridgeport up to the 16th—probably three hundred wagons. I will hold the town till we starve.

G. H. THOMAS,
Major-General.[19]

The promise to "hold the town till we starve," coming from a man of the known temperament of Thomas, was, if such a thing were possible, an understatement. Grant knew that the promise would be kept, if there was any possibility of doing it. This promise is in the same category as "I have just begun to fight," uttered by John Paul Jones when his ship was sinking, while engaged with the British man-of-war *Serapis;* and just begin he did, for, despite the odds, Jones won the engagement, the first American naval victory of the Revolutionary War.

After arriving at Bridgeport, Alabama, General Grant headed for Chattanooga, about thirty miles distant, by way of Walden's Ridge. Due to the heavy rains that made the roads a series of quagmires in spots, added to the physical discomforts from an injured leg and the weather, Grant and his party were not expected to reach their destination until late on the night of October 23. His horse fell again, this time while descending the mountain, and his leg was injured still more. When he arrived it was necessary to lift him from the saddle, but despite the discomfort he was surprisingly composed and alert.[20]

Following a light supper, General Thomas invited a number of general officers to his headquarters, including his own staff, and a very interesting as well as prominent group was assembled. It appears that for some time after the members had settled down General Thomas was observed to be sitting very quietly, as was also General

19. *Ibid.,* pp. 450, 479.
20. Horace Porter, *Campaigning With Grant* (New York, 1897), p. 3.

Grant, when a member of General Thomas's staff called his attention to the wet condition of General Grant's clothing and suggested that he be invited to step into an adjoining bedroom to change to dry apparel. Perhaps General Thomas was so preoccupied that he neglected to observe the normal civilities expected of a host. It may well be that Thomas was so apparently lacking in forethought for the moment, out of consideration of the fact that General Grant was his superior, and he quite naturally expected him to display the initiative regarding anything he might desire. Once his attention was called to it, however, Thomas responded in his usual gentlemanly manner and offered Grant the opportunity to avail himself of conveniences. Grant thanked him politely, but refused to improve his personal comfort. The only concession he made was to light a cigar and draw closer to the fire to dry his clothing. This narrative, by Horace Porter, is slightly at variance with the one by General James H. Wilson, an admirer of both Grant and Thomas. It is inconceivable that Thomas would have deliberately acted as he did for the purpose of showing his dislike of Grant, although there was no love lost between them throughout the war and afterward. General Wilson made no mention of Grant's refusal to accept Thomas's belated hospitality.[21]

Porter and Wilson were roommates at West Point. Wilson had accompanied Grant's party from Louisville and reported that when they arrived at Stevenson, Alabama, Grant met a number of army officers, including General Rosecrans. He noted that Grant regarded Rosecrans as a man of ability, although somewhat insecure and pretentious, and Rosecrans felt that Grant was "a fool for luck," rather than a great leader.[22]

Wilson and Dana left Bridgeport ahead of Grant and reached Captain Porter's headquarters in Chattanooga at midnight. Wilson's first realization of the state of things in the beleaguered town was when he found the garrison reduced to short rations and each animal on two ears of corn daily, with no hay. This situation emphasized to him the importance of reopening the supply line. The morale of the troops, for all that, was found to be good, and their military position was regarded as impregnable, subject only to a continuous food and ammunition supply.[23] The approaching winter weather, added to the difficulties of supply, made the situation a desperate one, although hope was far from lost. Nevertheless, Washington was keenly aware that unless supplies were increased very soon the plight of the

---

21. *Ibid.*, p. 4; James H. Wilson, *Under the Old Flag* (New York, 1911), Vol. I, p. 273.

22. Wilson, *ibid.*, pp. 262-65.

23. *Ibid.*, pp. 268-71.

defenders of Chattanooga would be desperate, and had ordered General William F. "Baldy" Smith, an outstanding army engineer, to report to General Thomas, in order to solve the supply problem.[24]

The problem of morale among the officers was also a serious one, following the recent campaign, and General Thomas addressed himself to its solution with promptitude. A number of changes were made by General Thomas personally, and Generals McCook and Crittenden were haled before a court of inquiry for examination into their conduct during the Chickamauga campaign. Nineteen officers were recommended for promotion; sixteen left the Army of the Cumberland for various reasons; and many remained in command without change in status. An example of General Thomas's exercise of skill in handling different personality problems is afforded by his method of resolving General John M. Palmer's request to transfer General Absolom Baird from his command. Palmer had succeeded General Thomas as commander of the old Fourteenth Corps, and complained afterward that he wanted a replacement for Baird, whom he regarded as cantankerous. Thomas suggested that Palmer wait until "we have a battle; then if you want Baird relieved I will do it." After several battles during the Atlanta campaign, Thomas asked Palmer, "How about relieving Baird?" Palmer replied, "No, Baird is a fighter—he devils the Rebs more than he ever did me."[25] It is worthy of note that Thomas thought very highly of Baird, and the two were together during the march of September 18 and 19, when Thomas's corps marched all night to Kelly's field, preceding the opening of the Battle of Chickamauga.

Thomas would have none but the most capable officers serving under his command, and every man was assigned to duty as nearly as possible in accordance with his abilities. He appointed General William D. Whipple, a brave and capable officer having many of the same attributes and characteristics as himself, as his chief of staff. Thomas had no political rewards and debts to offer and to pay off; also no relatives or mere self-seekers could gain foothold in his organization. For these reasons it was never necessary to apologize for the misconduct or mistakes of incompetent or irresponsible people.[26]

The new commander was methodical, painstaking, and thorough. He was so much devoted to rules of conduct that he berated the

24. *Ibid.*, p. 271.

25. John M. Palmer, *Personal Recollections* (Cincinnati, 1901), pp. 198, 199.

26. Richard W. Johnson, *Memoir of Major General George H. Thomas* (Philadelphia, 1881), pp. 115, 116.

enemy at Chickamauga because "they are fighting without any system." He liked to see things done as they should be done, whenever that was possible, and he desired completeness in all things, even to the point of display in his camp service and equipage, as shown by his Negro attendants and silver tableware. It is said that General Sherman sought to discourage this seeming luxury on the part of General Thomas during the Atlanta campaign, but met with little or no success. There is some evidence that notwithstanding Sherman's surface objections he was fond of availing himself of the comforts that Thomas was equipped to offer him. Thomas did not indulge in this apparent display out of a sense of superiority, but because it was a part of his nature to like good things. It is important to note that Assistant Secretary of War Charles A. Dana reported that "order prevails instead of universal chaos," a reference to Rosecrans's somewhat indifferent system, which reflected his more nervous temperament. Nevertheless, to those who knew him personally, Thomas was never cold and, as General Oliver Otis Howard stated, "His smile of welcome was pleasant and most cordial. As a general, Thomas is calm and cautious; does everything by rule, leaves nothing to chance. He makes his arrangements for a battle with caution and foresight, and is sure to have every column and division move with clock-work regularity, and strike at the proper time and place. Nothing disturbs or unnerves him."[27] Perhaps this is what Thomas's critics referred to when erroneously accusing him of slowness. His perfect military record proves that his methodical attention to detail paid rich dividends in lives saved and battles won.

General James H. Wilson's first impressions, after meeting with General Thomas, are left to his own words:

I had never seen him before, but Dana, who presented me, had fully described him and his imperturbable sangfroid and courage during the campaign and battle of Chickamauga. My mind had therefore become strongly prepossessed in his favor, and I was ready to greet him as an able and reliable commander. . . . I was not prepared to see in him so many of the external evidences of greatness. Six feet tall, of Jovelike figure, impressive countenance, and lofty bearing, he struck me at once as . . . the traditional Washington in appearance, manners, and character more than any man I had ever met. He expressed a modest confidence in being able to make good his hold on Chattanooga,

27. *Personal Recollections of the Rebellion* (New York Commandery, Military Order of the Loyal Legion of the U. S.; New York, 1891), Vol. I, p. 301; W. F. G. Shanks, *Personal Recollections of Distinguished Generals* (New York, 1896), p. 64.

and at once inspired me with faith in his steadiness and courage. . . . Later, when I came to know him better, he not only confirmed the impression of perfect self-reliance he gave me on that occasion, but made it clear that the need of supervision from any source had never presented itself to his mind.[28]

In this observation by Wilson perhaps lies the secret of the coldness that existed between Grant and Thomas. Thomas was supremely confident in his own abilities, as shown by the habitual calmness he displayed under the stress of great crises; and this confidence could not be concealed in the presence of Grant, toward whom he must have felt, as stated elsewhere herein, that he was undeserving of the high responsibility and rank given him.

The consistency with which men of character and ability observed and commented enthusiastically upon the greatness of Thomas is striking. No figure on either side during the Civil War has been the subject of more favorable comments than he, and not one figure was more deserving of such comments in the light of the ineradicable record. The lone exceptions, the Grant dynasty, are equally as surprising for their hostility toward his heroics as are the almost universal eulogies heaped upon him by both friend and foe alike. The imperishable record made by Thomas, which was for so long shielded by the curtain of military power wielded by these men, could not be long concealed once the *Official Records* and other equally reliable data were brought to light. More and more the continuing outpouring of books in recent years has helped to chip away the wall of silence concerning his achievements, and exposed the too-long-suppressed proof of his greatness. In particular, the savagery of General Grant's continuing and generally baseless attacks on Thomas, which had for their undoubted purpose the ruining of his military reputation, will be treated hereinafter in considerable detail, particularly in connection with the Battle of Nashville.

The change in command, the accession of General Thomas to the leadership of the Army of the Cumberland, occurred at perhaps the most trying time in the history of that army. The army had just suffered the greatest losses in its history, coupled with its only defeat, although the greater losses suffered by the Confederates constituted a price they could not afford to pay. The specter of either starvation or surrender confronted him and threatened his chances of holding Chattanooga, although the morale factor was satisfactory.

At the risk of repetition, a review of the precise situation in which

---

28. Wilson, *op. cit.*, Vol. I, pp. 272-73.

the two opposing forces found themselves at Chattanooga during the near-starvation period for the Federal Army is in order. The Union forces were hemmed in on the north by the Tennessee River, although a pontoon bridge and two ferries offered routes of escape, if necessary. Lookout Mountain formed an obstacle on the west, and Missionary Ridge, lying to the east and south of Chattanooga, was occupied by the Confederates. The Confederates controlled all railroads into the town, and by means of their artillery and riflemen were able to stop traffic on the Tennessee River. Additionally, the Confederates controlled the only road north of the river, which led to the nearest Union supply base at Bridgeport. The only road available to the Union forces was the one over Walden's Ridge through the Sequatchie Valley to Bridgeport.[29]

On October 19 General Thomas informed General Hooker that he, Thomas, had been appointed the new commander by order of President Lincoln. He stated that it was the President's desire to exercise haste in preparing to move as instructed by General Rosecrans, and to leave the railroad properly guarded. Rosecrans's instructions covered the concentration at Bridgeport of as much as could be spared from protecting the railroad between that place and Nashville, to be ready to move promptly toward Chattanooga upon receipt of orders, and until then seek to establish rail and water communications with Chattanooga. However, no plans had been formulated to give General Hooker needed support from Chattanooga, a prerequisite to which required obtaining possession of the left side of the Tennessee River.[30]

In order to relieve the beleaguered army, it was decided to open the Tennessee River and the roads to Bridgeport. Although final plans had not been completed between Generals Rosecrans and Chief Engineer Smith of the Army of the Cumberland, it is clear that they had discussed the relieving of Chattanooga, "and had partially planned the movement which was left to me [Thomas] to be completed when I assumed command, namely, to open a short route of supplies from Bridgeport." This is another example of General Thomas's fairness in giving full credit to others, as of course he should have done, instead of attempting to appropriate credit to himself, as others might have done. When the project was completed, General Thomas reported: "To Brigadier General William F. Smith, Chief Engineer, should be accorded great praise for the ingenuity which

29. *Battlefields, op. cit.*, pp. 25, 27; *Official Records, op. cit.*, Vol. XXX, Part 3, p. 485; Part 4, p. 445.

30. Van Horne, *op. cit.*, p. 154; *Official Records, ibid.*, Vol. XXX, Part 4, pp. 465, 467.

conceived, and the ability which executed, the movement at Brown's Ferry."[31] This plan required fifteen hundred men, who were drawn from General Hazen's brigade. These men, with the crewmen, were to board pontoons at night, move past Lookout Mountain, and land on the left side of the Tennessee River immediately above Brown's Ferry.

Following General Grant's arrival at Chattanooga, Generals Thomas, Smith, and other personnel present, with the aid of a large map, pointed out to Grant the location of the various troop organizations and briefed him regarding the general situation. Of particular concern was the plan for relieving food and supply shortages. Grant sat silently, completely absorbed in the discussion, until all had completed the briefing. He then became quite animated and began asking questions so pertinent that he made a profound impression on all present. His questions implied a determination not only to open the supply line, but also to take the offensive immediately.[32] It will be recalled that the plans were begun by Rosecrans and Smith, that they had the approval of General Thomas, and that General Grant, in effect, was acquiescing in plans already completed by others.

Brown's Ferry in 1863 was but a few miles below Chattanooga, across the narrow neck of Moccasin Point. It was on the old stage road to Nashville, and had the advantage of being out of range of the Confederate artillery posted on Lookout Mountain. It was estimated that if General Hooker could move from Bridgeport to Brown's Ferry by the south side of the river, boats would be able to move near it and the distance by wagon reduced to six or eight miles. Additionally, a wagon road would be open to Bridgeport on each side of the river.

The order of October 19 from General Thomas to General Hooker could not be implemented at once, however, as his wagons did not arrive until about a week later. It was also important that the movements be made simultaneously from Bridgeport and Chattanooga. General Thomas was to seize Brown's Ferry, while General Hooker was to cross the river at Bridgeport, move to Wauhatchie and Brown's Ferry by way of Whiteside's, and occupy Lookout Mountain.

On the morning of October 24, Generals Grant, Thomas, and Smith, with their party, made a reconnaissance in the vicinity of Brown's Ferry, the river below Chattanooga, and the hills on both

---

31. Van Horne, *ibid.,* pp. 155, 156; *Report of the Joint Committee, op. cit.,* p. 118; *Battles and Leaders of the Civil War* (New York, 1884), Vol. III, pp. 714, 715.

32. Van Horne, *ibid.,* p. 157; Porter, *op. cit.,* pp. 4, 5.

sides of the river, in quest of a final determination of the supply problem. The result was that General Grant expressed his approval of the plans already made.[33]

Fifty pontoons, each with a capacity of twenty-five men in addition to the crew, and two flat boats, one capable of carrying forty men, the other seventy-five, were prepared at Chattanooga. The pontoons were equipped with oars and trained crews were to operate them. On the night of October 26, the fifteen hundred men and one hundred crewmen, sixteen hundred in all, entered the boats at the Chattanooga landing. At three o'clock on the morning of the twenty-seventh, all of the boats under command of General Hazen, General Smith accompanying, rowed to the north shore and began to descend the river.[34]

The scheduled time for starting, in order to reach Brown's Ferry at daybreak, was based on observations made of logs floating from the town to that point. During the whole distance of seven miles the boats moved unobserved under the shadows of trees on the north bank, surprised enemy pickets at the ferry, and hastily occupied the position and near-by points. The boats were then rowed across the river to move the remainder of the troops under Turchin, comprising his brigade, the remainder of Hazen's brigade, and the artillery; all of this force had moved across the peninsula (Moccasin Point) to the wooded hillside as security to the pontoons, in the event of failure to land or to join them if successful, which they did. At daybreak the crossing was complete, and the work begun of making their position secure by the felling of timbers and the construction of the bridge. Everything was then in readiness to await the coming of Hooker's column that evening, since the Tennessee River, from Bridgeport to Chattanooga, was in Union hands.[35] The surprising feature of the operation was that little or no Confederate resistance was encountered.

General Hooker crossed the Tennessee River at Bridgeport at daylight on October 28, with the Eleventh Corps and General Geary's division of General Hooker's Twelfth Corps, *en route* to Brown's Ferry. Moving with caution, in the realization that Longstreet's men in Lookout Valley might oppose his advance, he arrived at Brown's Ferry at five o'clock in the afternoon and went into camp near by. Geary's force was posted at Wauhatchie, about three miles to the rear, as protection to the main body. Longstreet reported

33. *Battles and Leaders, op. cit.,* Vol. III, p. 714; *Official Records, op. cit.,* Vol. XXXI, Part 2, pp. 27-31.

34. Van Horne, *op. cit.,* p. 158; Boynton, *op. cit.,* pp. 101-3.

35. Boynton, *ibid.*

that his attention was called to the Federal movement by a dispatch messenger who reported that the advance was being made along the base of the mountain, including artillery and infantry. It was planned immediately to capture Geary's rear guard that night, some fifteeen hundred troops, and Bragg promised Longstreet to use McLaws's and Jenkins's divisions for the work.[36]

The night was clear and cool, with a bright moon overhead, and it was hoped that the assignment could be completed before daylight, in order to permit the divisions to withdraw to the mountain under cover of darkness. After waiting until near midnight, Longstreet, seeking to learn the reason for the delay in getting started, found that McLaws's division had not been ordered to participate. Believing that the movement had been countermanded, Longstreet returned to his headquarters, only to realize later that Jenkins was going through with the plan. He then gave Jenkins three other brigades to support him as deemed necessary. At about one o'clock in the morning this force swooped down upon Geary's division from three sides. It would have been a complete surprise but for a warning shot fired by a sentinel in time for the sleeping men to be awakened. Although exhausted from their twenty-five-mile march, they entered the combat with spirit and dash and drove the attackers back after a three-hour struggle. It was the Confederate plan to first attack and destroy Geary's force, and then attack Howard's Eleventh Corps about three miles away. Longstreet had sent a small force to occupy a hill overlooking Howard's position at the rear of his camp, but Howard's order to Colonel Orland Smith to attack the hill with his brigade resulted in its capture at the point of the bayonet. The Confederates were dislodged at all points and compelled to retreat from the valley at dawn, with the loss of about five hundred compared with the Federals' loss of about four hundred and twenty.[37]

General Thomas complimented General Hooker's troops in the following words: "The bayonet charge of Howard's troops, made up a steep and difficult hill over two hundred feet high, completely routing the enemy from his barricades on the top, and the repulse by Geary of greatly superior numbers who attempted to surprise him, will rank among the most distinguished feats of arms of the war."[38]

General Grant telegraphed to General Halleck on October 26

36. *Battles and Leaders, op. cit.,* Vol. III, p. 720; James Longstreet, *From Manassas to Appomattox* (1896), pp. 474-77.

37. *Battles and Leaders, ibid.,* p. 720; Longstreet, *ibid.*

38. Henry M. Cist, *The Army of the Cumberland* (New York, 1882), p. 242.

that General Thomas had authorized plans for getting control of the Tennessee River between Lookout Mountain and Bridgeport, and that success in the venture would fully resolve the supply problem. On October 28 he reported that the plan was progressing satisfactorily, and that he regarded the question of supplies as settled. In both dispatches Grant was as careful as was Thomas in claiming no credit for himself. On his part, Thomas fully agreed with Grant's intention to take the offensive against Bragg next, although he did not necessarily agree with him as to the time it should commence.[39] This offensive would become one of the most spectacular as well as one of the most controversial in the military history of the United States, particularly with respect to the various claims and counterclaims of supporters and admirers of the several leading participants, chiefly Grant and Sherman. This will be discussed at some length in the succeeding chapter in relation to the several battles around Chattanooga in November, 1863.

---

39. Van Horne, *op. cit.*, p. 159; *Official Records*, *op. cit.*, Vol. XXXI, Part 1, p. 56.

CHAPTER XVIII

Battles Around Chattanooga:
The Key to the Confederacy

GENERAL GRANT learned on November 7 that General Bragg had dispatched a force under General Longstreet into East Tennessee to capture Knoxville and defeat General Burnside's army or force it to retreat into Kentucky. He then ordered Thomas to create a diversion by attacking the northern end of Missionary Ridge with the strongest available force. After succeeding in this move, Thomas was to threaten, and attack if necessary, Bragg's concentrations between Dalton, Georgia, and Cleveland, Tennessee.[1]

That General Thomas was aware of Burnside's vulnerability to attack is indicated by his message of November 2, 1863, to General Grant: "If the enemy designs turning Burnside's flank, as suggested by him, why would it not be good tactics for Burnside to fall back on Kingston, and so concentrate his troops as to force the enemy to march for Kentucky by Cumberland Gap? In the meantime send two divisions of Sherman's corps by Nicholasville, and march from those two points to the Cumberland to intercept his farther advance into Kentucky. By this move Burnside would be on the enemy's flank, and the forces here so far in his rear that he could not hope to escape." Grant did not accept Thomas's recommendations, since he had other plans, but strong logic underlay the conception, and adoption would have seriously curtailed Bragg's initiative at that time.[2]

When General Thomas received the order to make the diversionary attack on Missionary Ridge, he was shocked into the realization that obedience to it would produce complete defeat. He called

1. Thomas B. Van Horne, *The Life of Major General George H. Thomas* (New York, 1882), p. 160; *Official Records of the War of the Rebellion* (Washington, 1880–1901), Vol. XXXI, Part 3, p. 73.

2. *Official Records, ibid.*, Vol. XXXI, Part 3, p. 16.

General William F. Smith, his chief engineer, into conference immediately to inform him of the implications of the order and to discuss its impracticability. General Smith's report of the incident states, "From General Grant's order of November 7th the following extract is made:

"'. . . I deem the best movement to attract the enemy to be an attack on the north end of Missionary Ridge with all the force you can bring to bear against it, and, when that is carried, to threaten, and even attack if possible, the enemy's line of communication between Dalton and Cleveland. . . . The movement should not be made one moment later than tomorrow morning.'"

In his explanation, Smith said that this order from General Grant represented a complete change from the plan proposed by himself, as telegraphed by Assistant Secretary of War Dana to Secretary of War Stanton on November 5, part of which follows:

"'. . . Grant and Thomas considering plan proposed by W. F. Smith to advance our pickets on the left to Citico Creek, about a mile in front of the position they have occupied from the first, and to threaten the seizure of the northwest extremity of Missionary Ridge.'"

The change referred to by Smith resides in the words "to be an attack on the north end of Missionary Ridge with all the force you can bring to bear against it," in lieu of the proposal by Smith merely to "threaten the seizure." Further, Smith stated, "When it is remembered that eighteen days after this Sherman with six perfectly appointed divisions failed to carry this same point of Missionary Ridge, at a time when Thomas with four divisions stood threatening Bragg's center, and Hooker with nearly three divisions was driving in Bragg's left flank [Bragg having no more strength than on the seventh], it will not be a matter of surprise that the order staggered Thomas. After the order had been issued I sought a conversation with General Grant for the purpose of inducing a modification, and began by asking General Grant what was the plan prepared by General Thomas for carrying out the order. To this General Grant replied, 'When I have sufficient confidence in a general to leave him in command of an army, I have enough confidence in him to leave his plans to himself.'" This discouraged further conversation on the subject.[3]

In discussing the problem with Thomas, Smith stated that Thomas feared the order from Grant related to the telegraphic dispatch from Dana to Stanton on November 5, and said, "If I attempt

3. *Ibid.*, Vol. XXXI, Part 2, pp. 29-32; *Battles and Leaders of the Civil War* (New York, 1884), Vol. III, pp. 715-16.

to carry out the order I have received, my army will be terribly beaten. You must go and get the order revoked." Without replying to this, Smith suggested that they study the ground over which the order would be implemented. After an hour, more or less, noting the extreme of Bragg's campfires on Missionary Ridge, and becoming certain that Thomas with his force could not outflank Bragg's right without endangering communications with Chattanooga, Smith reported to Grant that no movement could be made in that direction until Sherman arrived. Grant at once countermanded the order pending the combining of Sherman's Army of the Tennessee with the Army of the Cumberland.[4] This is one of the best examples in proof of the superior ability of Thomas in comparison with Grant. For those who are prone to regard Grant as the superior, it is only necessary to ponder the result if Thomas had obeyed the order without question. On the other side of the order it is well to remember that this is the type of "slowness" with which Grant maliciously branded Thomas, and opposed to which, it must be assumed, Grant's destructive speed is an exemplification.

In Grant's official report he stated simply that "after a thorough reconnaissance of the ground, however, it was deemed utterly impracticable to make the move until Sherman could get up, because of the inadequacy of our forces and the condition of the animals then at Chattanooga"; but Grant never forgave Thomas for this difference of opinion. In Badeau's biography of Grant, and in Grant's *Memoirs,* his disapproval of the conduct of his great subordinate is indicated. This was General Grant, who took it out on a great man, his superior in every aspect of their careers but that of the man-bestowed bauble of rank. To those who dismiss this incident as prejudice by ardent admirers of Thomas, let it be emphasized that it is completely documented fact.[5] Thomas was a towering man, physically and in greatness. Grant, a little man in size, and in many of the attributes of character, inevitably reacted normally when in the presence of, or in any way in contact with, General Thomas. No one likes to feel inferior; and no rank that could have been bestowed upon Grant was able to bridge their differences and convince him that he was actually the superior of Thomas. In this statement undoubtedly lay the basic difference that divided them.

We have seen that Grant was overmatched by Thomas in military ability. There remains now another facet of Grant's character, that of appropriating credit for the work for which Thomas deserved

---

4. *Battles and Leaders, ibid.,* p. 716.

5. *Ibid.;* John G. Nicolay and John Hay, *Abraham Lincoln: A History* (New York, 1909), Vol. VIII, pp. 30-31; Van Horne, *op. cit.,* p. 161.

the credit. General Smith, who arrived in Chattanooga on October 3, was authorized by Rosecrans to find some way to shorten the distance to the railroad at Bridgeport; and he is responsible for the statement concerning Grant's assumption of credit due Thomas.

General Smith stated that on October 19 he made a survey, and on October 20 he reported his plan to General Thomas, who had just relieved General Rosecrans, and that Thomas approved it on October 22, following two days of study and discussion. Before the meeting between Generals Grant, Thomas, Smith, and others on October 24 at Brown's Ferry, Assistant Secretary of War Dana had sketched to Secretary Stanton the plan of the whole movement. Dana declared further that General Thomas had to put the plan before General Grant for his approval, the plan that Thomas had determined upon, and that it was proper for Grant to go to Brown's Ferry before he gave his approval; but there is not the slightest reason for doubting that Thomas would have made the same move, with the same men, and with the same results, if General Grant had remained in Louisville.[6]

Continuing, General Smith stated that "General Thomas was a man who observed strictly the proprieties and courtesies of military life; and had the plan 'for opening the route to Bridgeport,' and the orders for its execution, emanated from General Grant, Thomas would hardly have noticed the subject. . . ." Further, "At some future time I may have an opportunity of doing justice to the memory of General George H. Thomas, whose comparatively early death was so great a loss to the country. The civil war developed no higher character than his, viewed in all its aspects, either as soldier or civilian. There are no clouds on it to mar the brightness of his glory. General Grant's narrative is in text and inference so unjust to the memory of the late Major General George H. Thomas that it is proper to make a statement of facts taken in the main from official papers." This has been stated already in connection with Grant's countermanded order; however, the matter of injustice referred to in General Grant's narrative is as follows: "That night [October 24, the day he looked over the plan for use of Brown's Ferry] I issued orders for opening the route to Bridgeport—a 'cracker line,' as the soldiers appropriately termed it. They had been so long on short rations that my first thought was the establishment of a line over which food might reach them."[7]

It would be naive indeed to conclude that Grant suffered a lapse of memory concerning an incident so important as the breaking of the

---

6. *Battles and Leaders, op. cit.,* Vol. III, p. 714.

7. *Ibid.,* pp. 685, 715.

siege of Chattanooga. Grant was supreme commander in the West, and as such must be presumed to have had knowledge of important events and the extent to which he may or may not have participated in them. No other conclusion is possible than that this incident, one of a number in which Grant was unjust to Thomas, was designed to accomplish a double purpose: he wanted to appropriate credit to himself, and at the same time accomplish the downgrading of Thomas, one of the greatest military figures in American history. This incident is one of the many contributions to the "Grant Legend," the aura of superiority and invincibility that Grant and his friends did much to build up in paving the way for his candidacy and election to the Presidency. Many defenders and apologists for Grant have protested the criticism of his injustice to Thomas with the argument that the Thomas admirers sought to give too much credit to him. This one example is sufficient to stamp Grant's unfairness to Thomas as an outrage, and no better documentation than the cited references is needed to prove its authenticity.

On November 21, General Grant telegraphed General Halleck that he had ordered a movement two weeks ago, referring to the order of November 7 to Thomas to attack Missionary Ridge, later countermanded, but that it was impossible to move artillery. He reported also that it was necessary to await the arrival of Sherman's animals for use in placing the artillery in position. "I have never felt such restlessness before as I have at the fixed and immovable condition of the Army of the Cumberland," a statement perhaps accurate to a degree, although Grant must have conveniently forgotten the mess at Shiloh due to his own failings as a commander. Adam Badeau, Grant's generally discredited and rejected biographer and eulogist, ascribed the failure to attack Missionary Ridge to the "shortcomings" of General Thomas. This is another of the baseless falsehoods that have served for so long to cast a cloud over that incomparable general. It has been demonstrated that both General Smith and General Thomas had correctly evaluated the danger inherent in carrying out Grant's order, and that Grant countermanded it when the danger was presented to him by General Smith. In view of facts so incontrovertible, one would have difficulty in believing that General Thomas would be named the goat; however, Badeau had no difficulty in making the following groundless, and of course harmful, statement:

> But Thomas announced that he had no horses to move his artillery, and declared himself entirely and absolutely unable to move, until Sherman should arrive to cooperate. Grant was,

therefore, forced to leave Burnside to contend against superior forces. . . . A prompt movement on the part of the commander would undoubtedly have had the effect to recall Longstreet, but now, it was possible that the troops sent into East Tennessee might succeed in overthrowing the occupation which was so important.[8]

The foregoing is typical of the misrepresentation to be found in Badeau's *Military History of U. S. Grant.* Its chief claim to distinction is in its overcredit to Grant and its chipping away at the reputations of others in order to accomplish that end.

Following the seizure of Brown's Ferry and the laying of a pontoon bridge across the Tennessee River at that point, and Hooker's successful advance from Bridgeport and his gaining possession of the south side of the river at Raccoon Mountain and in Lookout Valley, the way was prepared for the Union Army to reopen a short supply line between Chattanooga and Bridgeport. This was the rail end of the supply line. The "Cracker Line" ran by boat up the Tennessee from Bridgeport to Kelly's Ferry. Above Kelly's Ferry the current of the river was so swift as to render it unnavigable to some of the boats. At this point the "Cracker Line" left the river and crossed Raccoon Mountain by road to Brown's Ferry. At Brown's Ferry the line crossed the river on the pontoon bridge, crossed Moccasin Point, again crossed the river and into Chattanooga. The successful completion of these operations, with little interference, is convincing evidence that the Confederates were in a weakened condition.[9]

It is apparent that General Bragg, from his position on Missionary Ridge and Lookout Mountain overlooking Union-occupied Chattanooga, was influenced by one or both of two convictions: either he considered his position impregnable or he was completely lacking in awareness of the incoming reinforcements, which combined to insure his defeat and compel him to retreat.

General Sherman arrived in person at Chattanooga, on November 15, 1863, ahead of his Army of the Tennessee. Grant's plan was to use this force in an effort to turn the right flank of Bragg's army. This would be the grand spectacle, the opening phase, which comprehended the wresting of Missionary Ridge from the Confederates to their right flank at Tunnel Hill. The Army of the Cumberland under

---

8. *Official Records, op. cit.,* Vol. XXXI, Part 3, p. 216; Van Horne, *op. cit.,* pp. 162-63; Donn Piatt, *Memories of the Men Who Saved the Union* (New York, 1887), pp. 238-39; Adam Badeau, *Military History of U.S. Grant* (New York, 1881), Vol. I, pp. 463, 464.

9. *The Chickamauga and Chattanooga Battlefields* (Washington: National Park Service, 1961), p. 32.

Thomas was to be relegated, in effect, to a more or less spectator role.[10]

The opportunity for large-scale maneuvers has seldom if ever been provided in a more magnificent setting than in the great natural coliseum of Chattanooga, or under circumstances more difficult. This was particularly so in respect to the Union forces that were compelled to advance against natural mountain barriers, in front of a formidably intrenched foe determined to defend his native soil. The unsurpassed bravery exhibited by the men of the Army of the Cumberland, nevertheless, would be the main factor in the capture of these strongholds from a gallant enemy. Courage, however, was not an exclusive attribute of either side, as illustrated by the story of young Sam Davis of the First Tennessee Infantry of the Confederate Army.

General Grenville M. Dodge was ordered by General Grant to move his Sixteenth Corps from Corinth, Mississippi, in order to reinforce the Union forces at Chattanooga. While *en route,* Dodge was greatly concerned in the knowledge that General Bragg was obtaining advance information on his troop movements. This information was furnished General Bragg by the Coleman Scouts, of which Sam Davis was a member. General Dodge was sure that someone in his own official family, a traitor, was leaking the information to the enemy. Suffice it to state that General Dodge assigned a number of troops to the task of putting a stop to it, and that in due course Sam Davis was captured by the Seventh Kansas Cavalry. In his shoes was found an incriminating letter that fastened the guilt on him.[11]

Sam Davis was told that as a spy his life would be spared only if he would disclose his informant; otherwise he would suffer the penalty of death. Sam spurned the offer, despite appeals by his captors, who were reluctant to carry out the penalty, and he was hanged on the morning of November 7, 1863, at the tender age of twenty-one. Such fidelity naturally made him a martyr among his fellow soldiers and countrymen and inspired admiration of men everywhere. Aside from the heroism of Sam Davis, the wonder is whether he died with the secret of an undisclosed Civil War Benedict Arnold in his heart. This is not at all implausible, for it will be remembered that Sam Davis died because he would not disclose the name of the person or persons giving him Union secrets.

On November 18, 1863, General Grant ordered General Thomas

---

10. *Battles and Leaders, op. cit.,* Vol. III, p. 720; *Official Records, op. cit.,* Vol. XXXI, Part 1, p. 712; Part 2, p. 79.

11. Mabel Goode Frantz, *Full Many a Name* (Jackson, Tenn., 1961), pp. 96-105.

to prepare to attack the Confederates on Missionary Ridge on the twenty-first. The general plan was for Sherman to cross the Tennessee River below the mouth of the Chickamauga with his Army of the Tennessee and one division from Thomas's Army of the Cumberland. Thomas was instructed to cooperate in the movement by concentrating his remaining troops in the Chattanooga Valley on his own left; also he was to leave only enough troops to defend fortifications and to reserve a division to move wherever needed. He was expected to join Sherman by advancing well toward the north end of Missionary Ridge and, if possible, move simultaneously with him. After uniting and carrying the Ridge, communications were to be established linking the two armies by roads on the south bank of the river. This plan superseded Grant's countermanded plan of November 7.[12]

General Grant's order in brief was for Thomas to combine with Sherman by advancing toward the north end of Missionary Ridge and moving as promptly as possible in step with him in order to force the Confederates from the Ridge. This done, communications were to be formed between the two forces by roads on the south bank of the Tennessee. It was emphasized by Grant that Sherman was to carry the heights from the northern extremity of the Ridge to about the railroad tunnel before Bragg could combine against him, but beyond this instruction Grant gave no specific order or plan of battle. On this point Grant reported that not being provided with a map, which would give names of roads and other locations, definite instructions from him were impossible.

Regardless of General Grant's order to attack on the twenty-first, delay in the arrival of Sherman's army in sufficient force compelled a postponement to the twenty-fourth. Rain and muddy roads *en route* from Bridgeport slowed his advance, in addition to the movement of supplies. To add to the difficulties, on the twenty-second the pontoon bridge at Brown's Ferry broke and prevented General Osterhaus's division from crossing. Osterhaus was then ordered to join General Hooker in Lookout Valley.[13]

Assistant Secretary of War Dana had accused Sherman of blundering, in moving his forces from Bridgeport, with his large trains brought from West Tennessee following in the rear of each division, instead of moving his troops and artillery first. It was felt that the movement together complicated perplexities and delayed Grant in his planned attack against Bragg.

During the delay, Thomas completed preparations for battle. He

---

12. Van Horne, *op. cit.*, p. 167; H. V. Boynton, *The Chickamauga and Chattanooga National Military Park* (Cincinnati, 1895), p. 111.

13. Boynton, *ibid.*

ordered General Wood's division to form the moving column and directed General Jeff Davis's division to unite with Sherman as Grant desired. Thomas placed Howard's division between the Brown's Ferry and Chattanooga bridges; he then located his artillery on the heights north of the Tennessee River; and he assigned Colonel Long's cavalry brigade to protect Sherman's left flank, after which Long was to move against Confederate communications at Knoxville. Thus far complying strictly with Grant's instructions, Thomas suggested to him, on November 22, following the third postponement of the proposed attack on Bragg, that the attack be made on the twenty-third, before Bragg learned of the plan. He also suggested that Howard's force be used by General Sherman in lieu of his two divisions in Lookout Valley, and that these two divisions and Hooker's force be pitted against Bragg's left flank on Lookout Mountain simultaneously with Sherman's attack on Bragg's right on the north end of Missionary Ridge.[14] Thomas reasoned that this demonstration by Hooker would aid Sherman significantly and contribute to over-all success.

When Thomas made this suggestion, Bragg's right occupied a position opposite the intrenched Union left east of Chattanooga, or several miles from the northern end of the ridge. His four divisions were on the summit and on the western slope of Missionary Ridge, on the line across Chattanooga Valley to Lookout Mountain; and he was not aware that both Sherman and Thomas planned to attack his right flank. Stevenson's division held the summit of Lookout Mountain, and Cheatham's and Walker's divisions held the front slope of the mountain. If Grant had adopted Thomas's suggestion, the latter, with four divisions, and Sherman, with five divisions, a total of nine, would have attacked Bragg's five divisions with great expectation of overwhelming them. Furthermore, if Sherman had crossed the Tennessee on the night of November 22, Thomas would have joined in the attack; only one of the divisions opposing Sherman on the twenty-fifth would have occupied Missionary Ridge; and Bragg's right flank would have been far south of the tunnel. Also Hooker, with four divisions to use against Bragg's left, would have faced Cheatham's and Walker's divisions from the face of Lookout Mountain and rendered inoperative Stevenson's division at the top of Lookout, just as he did on the twenty-fourth. This plan would have brought Union victory on the twenty-third by the use of all of Grant's thirteen divisions, since conditions were much more favorable then than later. Grant insisted on awaiting another day the expected arrival of Sherman's remaining force, but

14. Van Horne, *op. cit.*, pp. 170-72; *Battlefields, op. cit.*, p. 33.

Bragg was far weaker and more overextended on the twenty-third; accordingly he would not have been able to combine his entire force on Missionary Ridge for final defense as he did later.[15]

On the night of November 22, a Confederate sentinel turned deserter informed General Sheridan that General Bragg was about to withdraw. With this information, General Grant decided to await Sherman no longer, and if Bragg was withdrawing to attack him at once. On November 23, Grant ordered Thomas to drive in the enemy's pickets and ascertain whether the Confederates still occupied the valley in force. This order reflected a change in Grant's plan, since he substituted the Army of the Cumberland for Sherman's Army of the Tennessee.[16]

The costly delay of Sherman was causing both General Grant and General Thomas uneasy moments. Thomas, however, prepared for any eventuality (one of his dominant characteristics) and not simply for a reconnaissance by ordering five divisions, Wood's and Sheridan's of the Fourth Corps, Schurz's and Steinwehr's of the Eleventh Corps, and Baird's of the Fourteenth Corps, to make preparations for immediate action. In addition, he ordered General Granger to stand by in readiness for action with the remainder of his Fourth Corps. This preparation by Thomas marked the first material change from Grant's plan. Grant's order for a reconnaissance, a relatively minor operation, was implemented by Thomas in full preparation for battle, if occasion required, and made it possible for results that vitally affected the successful outcome of the Chattanooga operations. It is interesting to note that the Confederates observed this shifting of troops with considerable detachment, apparently believing it nothing more than a review of troops.[17]

At about two o'clock General Wood, in obedience to orders, advanced and held the strong outpost of the Confederate line at Orchard Knob, before Missionary Ridge, but only after a hard fight. Sheridan's division, on Wood's right, dashed forward soon afterward and occupied the base of the knob at both the right and rear; and the Eleventh Corps advanced to Citico Creek, which operation disclosed that the Confederates were in considerable strength. It is thus far clear that these dispositions by Thomas paved the way, as aforesaid, for the Union victory, and that he in effect took control of the Chattanooga battles. His consistency in dominating battles was not broken in this one, although Grant had intended that Sherman take

15. Van Horne, *ibid.*, pp. 171-72.

16. *Ibid.*, p. 173; Boynton, *op. cit.*, p. 113; *Battles and Leaders, op. cit.*, Vol. III, p. 721.

17. Van Horne, *ibid.*; Boynton, *ibid.*, pp. 113-14.

the leading part, due either to his genuine lack of confidence in the Army of the Cumberland after Chickamauga, or, what is more likely the case, because he wanted Sherman to gain the victory.[18]

This success by Thomas compelled the Confederates to withdraw Pat Cleburne's and Bushrod Johnson's divisions from the Knoxville operation to bolster Missionary Ridge. On November 23 also, General Marcus Wright's brigade of Cheatham's division was ordered to guard the Shallow Ford Road and railroad bridges over the Chickamauga, and to proceed to the mouth of the Chickamauga to resist any Union attempt to cross the Tennessee River. When he reached the lower railroad bridge he was attacked from the opposite side of the Chickamauga by part of Sherman's forces. That night, November 23, Walker's division was withdrawn from the line between the eastern base of Lookout Mountain and Chattanooga Creek and sent to the far right of General Bragg's army. Bragg placed it on Missionary Ridge, with the right more than one mile from the north end of the Ridge; and thus Walker's division formed the extreme right of the Confederate line. Jackson's brigade of Cheatham's division and Cummings's brigade of Stevenson's division moved from Lookout Mountain to replace Walker's division.[19]

When General Thomas observed General Wood's flags planted on Orchard Knob he signaled to him: "You have gained too much to withdraw; hold your position and I will support you." He then ordered Howard's force to join Wood's left and Baird to form on Sheridan's right. General Grant was able to report to General Halleck: "General Thomas' troops attacked the enemy's right at two o'clock to-day, and carried the first line of rifle-pits running over the knoll, 1,200 yards in front of Fort Wood, and low ridge to the right of it. . . . The troops moved under fire with all the precision of veterans on parade. Thomas' troops will intrench themselves, and hold their position until daylight, when Sherman will join the attack from the mouth of the Chickamauga, and a decisive battle will be fought."[20] This dispatch confirmed Grant's intention to give priority to Sherman in carrying the major phase of the battle.

Grant stated in his report that "Thomas, having done on the 23rd with his troops in Chattanooga what was intended for the 24th, bettered and strengthened his advanced positions during the day, and pushed the Eleventh Corps forward along the south bank of the Tennessee River, across Citico Creek, one brigade of which, with Howard in person, reached Sherman just as he had completed the

18. Van Horne, *ibid.;* Boynton, *ibid.*

19. Van Horne, *ibid.*, p. 176; Boynton, *ibid.*, pp. 114-16.

20. *Official Records, op. cit.*, Vol. XXXI, Part 2, p. 24.

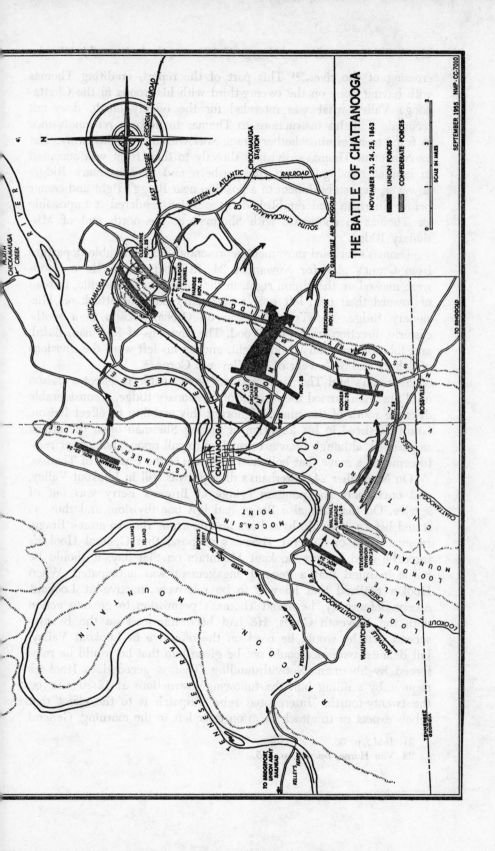

THE BATTLE OF CHATTANOOGA

NOVEMBER 23, 24, 25, 1863

UNION FORCES

CONFEDERATE FORCES

SCALE IN MILES
0   1   2

SEPTEMBER 1955   NMP-CC-7010

crossing of the river."[21] This part of the report, crediting Thomas with having done on the twenty-third with his troops in the Chattanooga Valley what was intended for the twenty-fourth, does not reconcile with his instructions to Thomas to make a reconnaissance in force to ascertain whether Bragg was withdrawing his army. The movement of Thomas's divisions directly to their front was accepted in lieu of moving toward the northern end of Missionary Ridge; however, the establishment of a position near Bragg's right and center before Sherman had established his position rendered it impossible for Thomas to cooperate with Sherman at the north end of Missionary Ridge.

Thomas's forward movement represented a considerable departure from Grant's plan for November 24. In other words, these troops were massed on the Union right, in the direction of Rossville, instead of toward their own left nearer Sherman's point of attack on Missionary Ridge. Wood's center was on Orchard Knob in a southeasterly direction from Fort Wood. The divisions of Sherman, Baird, and Johnson were on Wood's right, and on his left were the divisions of Schurz and Steinwehr of the Eleventh Corps.[22]

Sherman's and Thomas's divisions were unable to effect a liaison until Sherman carried the summit of Missionary Ridge, a considerable distance south of the tunnel. Ignoring this inability to effect liaison, Grant persisted in his intention of having Sherman open the attack as planned, although he was compelled to call upon Thomas for reinforcements, a move that bolstered Sherman at the expense of Thomas.

On November 24, Osterhaus's division was still in Lookout Valley, and once more the pontoon bridge at Brown's Ferry was out of service. On that day also Bragg had lost one division, and thus, as stated before, it would have been an opportune time to attack Bragg. In evaluation of General Thomas's proposal that General Hooker's force be used against Lookout Mountain on that day, it should be borne in mind that a general engagement was anticipated. When Hooker realized that he was to be relatively inactive at Lookout except defensively, he asked Thomas's permission to go into action with the Eleventh Corps. He had been informed on the twenty-second that he would be used on the offensive in Lookout Valley, but definite assurance could not be given him that he would be reinforced by Sherman. Notwithstanding, Thomas acceded to Hooker's request by sending him the following instructions at 12:30 A.M. on the twenty-fourth. "Intercepted rebel dispatch is to the effect that rebels expect us to attack them on their left in the morning. General

---

21. *Ibid.*, p. 33.
22. Van Horne, *op. cit.*, p. 175.

commanding desires that you make demonstrations early as possible after daybreak on point of Lookout Mountain. General Grant still hopes Wood's division will get across to join Sherman, in which case your demonstration will aid Sherman's crossing. If Wood can't cross you can take the point of Lookout if your demonstration develops its practicability."[23]

Late on November 23, General Grant gave Hooker instructions that were to the same effect as those given by Thomas. After the capture of Orchard Knob, and the breaking of the bridge at Brown's Ferry required the shifting of Osterhaus's division to Hooker on Orchard Knob instead of to Sherman at the north end of Missionary Ridge, this plan was necessary.[24]

Thomas's order gave Hooker discretionary power as to the time and manner of demonstrating against Lookout, a matter that insured a good relationship between the two men. His conception of the attack on Lookout was brilliant, as was also his execution, and one of the most spectacular exploits of the war.

Hooker's warm relationship with Thomas was in sharp contrast to the coldness between himself and Grant. This latter relationship may have been due in some measure to the fact that Hooker only recently was commander of the Army of the Potomac. General Howard reported that when Grant was to arrive by rail from Nashville to Stevenson, Alabama, Hooker sent an officer of his staff with a spring wagon to meet him and to conduct him to his own quarters. Grant was lame at the time, due to his horse's fall, a short time earlier. When Hooker's aide reported to Grant that he would escort him to Hooker's headquarters, Grant stated with emphasis: "If General Hooker wishes to see me he will find me on this train." Hooker lost no time in reporting to Grant and extending his courtesies in person.[25]

Grant respectfully declined Hooker's offer of hospitality as he was going with Howard to Bridgeport. Howard was solicitous concerning the bare comforts he could give Grant in the common wall tent they shared. Howard, noting that Grant's eyes rested upon a liquor flask hanging against the tent, said, "That flask is not mine. It was left here by an officer, to be returned to Chattanooga; I never drink." Grant replied promptly, "Neither do I," which answer was stated with much seriousness. Howard stated that Grant at that time was

---

23. *Ibid.*, pp. 176-78; *Official Records, op. cit.*, Vol. XXXI, Part 2, p. 106.
24. *Battles and Leaders, op. cit.*, Vol. III, p. 721.
25. *Personal Recollections of the Rebellion* (New York Commandery, Military Order of the Loyal Legion of the U.S.; New York, 1896), Vol. I, pp. 245-49.

free from every appearance of drinking, and that he was glad to note his clear eye and face refuted the falsehoods that envy and rivalry had set in motion since the Battle of Shiloh. That night Grant remarked that he had no sympathy for grumbling officers of rank dissatisfied with their commands, nor with those who were selfishly ambitious.[26] It is presumed that Grant's reference was to Hooker.

It is probable that since Grant had no prior dealings with Hooker he was influenced adversely against him by his friend, William T. Sherman. It is a matter of record that Sherman held a low opinion of Hooker's military capacity, as stated in one of the Sherman letters shortly after Hooker's defeat at Chancellorsville: "I know Hooker well and tremble to think of his handling one hundred thousand men in the presence of Lee."[27]

Hooker had some misgivings concerning the possibility of success at Lookout Mountain, believing that it meant almost certain defeat; but regardless of his so expressing himself to Thomas, no change was made in the original plans.

Perhaps the most generally recognized account of the Chattanooga battles, particularly by those who participated in them or were privileged to witness them, is the one by General Joseph S. Fullerton. This account first appeared in the May, 1887, issue of *The Century Magazine* and subsequently was published in the third volume of *Battles and Leaders of the Civil War*. With some supplementation this account has been used here in portraying these battles.

November 24 began with a cold, drizzling rain and with thick mist clouds hovering on Lookout Mountain. Whitaker's brigade of Cruft's division advanced to Wauhatchie at daybreak, and by eight o'clock had crossed Lookout Creek there, the closest point at which it could be forded. The mist clouds served as a cloak for their movements, which were not observed by the Confederates. When they were discovered, however, the Confederates withdrew from the summit, changed front, and formed a new line, with their left at the palisade and their right at the heavy works in the valley at the creek crossing. Whitaker's brigade, in advance, drove back Confederate pickets and moved rapidly up the mountain to the foot of the palisade. This brigade established a firm foothold with its right, faced left in front, with its left joined to Geary's division. Geary moved along the mountainside and through the valley to cover Harker's crossing.[28]

---

26. *Ibid.*, pp. 246-47; R. S. Thorndike, (ed.), *The Sherman Letters* (New York, 1894), p. 250.

27. Oliver Otis Howard, *Autobiography* (New York, 1907), Vol. I, p. 459.

28. *Battles and Leaders, op. cit.*, Vol. III, p. 721; Henry M. Cist, *The Army of the Cumberland* (New York, 1882), p. 249.

In the meantime, Grose's brigade was engaging the Confederates at the lower road crossing, and Wood's brigade of Osterhaus's division was building a bridge a half mile up Lookout Creek. Geary arrived at the bridge at about eleven o'clock in the morning, just as it had been completed, and when Osterhaus and Grose were crossing, Hooker's entire force was now fully combined, with his line extending down the mountain to the valley where Osterhaus and Grose had just crossed. When Hooker gave the command to move up the mountain, Thomas's artillery at Moccasin Point opened fire on the Confederate rifle pits at the foot of the mountain and on the works planted on the Craven House plateau. Hooker's guns on the west side of the creek also opened up on the Confederate right, followed by an assault by Osterhaus and Grose.[29]

After two hours of fighting up the mountainside, over and through gullies, hurdling large rocks and fallen trees, the Confederate earthworks were carried and the occupants driven back. At this time, 2:00 P.M., Hooker's ammunition was about used up, and with the thick clouds to contend with he found further advance impracticable, and called a halt. He had, however, taken all Confederate works on the east side of Lookout, established communications with Chattanooga, and now commanded the Confederate line of defense in Chattanooga Valley. When he reported to Thomas that his ammunition was gone, Thomas sent each soldier of Carlin's brigade with as much as he could carry, so that by five o'clock Hooker's men were ready to continue their work.[30]

This movement by Hooker was not known definitely by Grant that morning, and Sherman had no idea of it whatever. Bragg also was completely in the dark regarding the attack, since Hooker was to attack only if there was a very good chance for success, after making a mere demonstration.

Sherman's men at the north end of Missionary Ridge and Thomas's men at the center followed the sound of artillery and musketry from Hooker's action in Lookout Valley. They felt considerable concern in the knowledge that a battle they were unable to see was in progress above them. When the wind created a rift in the clouds, and the retreating Confederates were exposed to view, a mighty shout, heard above the roar of battle, went up from thirty thousand throats below. As the sun set, the clouds disappeared, exposing Lookout to view in the clear, cool evening. The campfires of the two armies, less than two miles apart, extending from the base of Lookout to the summit, gave the appearance of burning lava; and none who

---

29. *Battles and Leaders, ibid.;* Cist, *ibid.,* p. 250.
30. *Battles and Leaders, ibid.,* p. 722; Cist, *ibid.,* p. 251.

witnessed the scene could ever forget it. Between these two opposing armies musket flashes glowed like giant fireflies. The next morning before daybreak, eight men of the Eighth Kentucky Infantry scaled the palisade and ran up the Stars and Stripes. The Confederates retreated during the night;[31] but one cannot but wonder whether, in the entire Confederate host remaining to witness their former flag, there were some who felt some pride at seeing their once-loved symbol of national unity flying in the breeze.

Hooker's success was the result of splendid planning, aided of course by the element of surprise, rather than of overpowering force. This was the famous "Battle Above the Clouds," a somewhat erroneously descriptive nickname in view of the fact that there was a heavy mist instead of clouds. This success by Hooker, for which he deserves much honor, turned the Confederate left flank, although the absence of a general battle on that day permitted Bragg to reinforce his right.

General Grant made no change in his original plan of having Sherman attack Bragg's right on Missionary Ridge. General William F. Smith, who conceived the plan of opening Brown's Ferry to Federal supplies, directed the crossing of Sherman's troops at north Chickamauga Creek, in and near which one hundred and nineteen pontoons had been secretly placed. After dark on November 23, Colonel James Barnett, chief of artillery of the Army of the Cumberland, protected Sherman's crossing with six-gun batteries on the foothills and a battery of siege guns on the north side of the Tennessee River. Commencing at midnight of the twenty-third, Smith and his men had completed the 1,350-foot bridge by eleven o'clock the next morning, promptly following which Sherman's artillery and Ewing's division crossed over. Sherman reported that he doubted whether the history of war could show a bridge of such length laid so noiselessly, so rapidly, and so well.[32]

At one o'clock on the afternoon of the twenty-fourth, as Hooker rounded the front of Lookout Mountain, the roar of the battle inspired Sherman's Army of the Tennessee as Sherman gave them the command "Forward!" At half-past three o'clock his troops took the hill at the extreme right of Bragg's line, presuming it to be the north end of the ridge, and soon thereafter they captured another hill a short distance away. Both hills were separated by a deep depression near

---

31. *Battles and Leaders, ibid.,* pp. 722, 723; Cist, *ibid.*

32. *Battles and Leaders, ibid.,* p. 723; James H. Wilson, *Heroes of the Great Conflict* (Wilmington, 1904), pp. 74-79; *Official Records, op. cit.,* Vol. XXXI, Part 2, p. 573.

fortified Tunnel Hill, their objective, on which rested Bragg's principal right-flank defense.[33]

On the night of November 24, as mentioned earlier, Hooker's fires lighted Lookout Mountain, and off to the left, extending far above the valley, at the north end of Missionary Ridge, which Sherman had just captured, Sherman's fires were lighting the surrounding area. The Army of the Cumberland troops, although elated by the successes of Sherman and Hooker, were naturally apprehensive that they might not have an opportunity to share in the victory.[34]

On the night of November 24, General Grant ordered Sherman to attack the Confederates at dawn on the twenty-fifth, believing that he had taken Tunnel Hill the day before. Thomas was ordered to cooperate with Sherman, and Hooker was instructed to be ready to advance into Chattanooga Valley to hold the road leading to the summit. This was the only time in Thomas's experience in the Civil War that he had not been designated to bear the chief responsibility in battle plans. When Grant learned on the twenty-fifth that Sherman had not captured Tunnel Hill the day before, he revised his orders, instructing Hooker to carry the pass at Rossville and operate on Bragg's left and rear concentrated on Missionary Ridge, and in the valley at the east foot. During the night of the twenty-fourth, Cheatham's and Stevenson's divisions withdrew from Lookout Mountain, and after a night march reinforced Bragg's right at dawn on the twenty-fifth.[35]

On the morning of the twenty-fifth Generals Grant and Thomas chose Orchard Knob as headquarters from which to observe and direct the battle. General Sherman began the assault on Tunnel Hill at sunrise, but after a number of attempts to capture it had resulted in failure, he stopped operations; this was sometime early in the afternoon. The Federal armies had risen at dawn, on a bright and sunny day. Sherman's movements could be observed by the occupants of Orchard Knob as he tried to turn Bragg's right at the tunnel. After passing at that point the railroad ran northeastward to the Chickamauga and crossed a bridge controlled by Confederate General Polk. Sherman seriously threatened the bridge, which he shelled until about ten o'clock from twelve hundred yards away. At about eleven o'clock, General John E. Smith's men were advancing on the tunnel, and a furious action began by a charge on Smith's battery stationed on the hill above the tunnel. After a desperate struggle, during which

---

33. *Battles and Leaders, ibid.*
34. *Ibid.*
35. *Ibid.;* Cist, *op. cit.,* p. 252.

the attackers came within forty yards of the battery, they were compelled to withdraw with heavy losses. Reforming their lines, the most serious action of the day occurred, beginning at one o'clock, when another attack was made on the tunnel. This attack also failed, one and one-half hours later, after the Confederates were reinforced; and Sherman's men were compelled to retreat with heavy losses in prisoners, in addition to the loss of eight colors from his regiments.[36]

At about one o'clock, Sherman sent a dispatch to Grant inquiring "Where is Thomas?" Thomas replied promptly, "I am here. My right is closing in from Lookout Mountain towards Missionary Ridge." At one o'clock Hooker reported that he would be delayed an hour repairing the bridge at Chattanooga Creek. Actually, Hooker was delayed three hours due to the repairing of bridges damaged by the Confederates. After occupying Rossville he advanced against the south end of Missionary Ridge and promptly carried it. Continuing northward, he confronted Stewart's division on the summit defending earthworks built by the Army of the Cumberland on September 23, after the retreat from Chickamauga. Cruft's division drove the Confederates from the defenses they themselves had constructed. Hooker's time and effort had been well spent; but since the sun was about to disappear, he lacked sufficient time to join Sherman at the north end of the ridge, about six miles away.[37]

Under the personal command of General Thomas were the four divisions of Generals Baird, Wood, Sheridan, and R. W. Johnson of the Army of the Cumberland. These divisions extended from Orchard Knob to a point opposite the center of the ridge. Baird's division was on the left, Johnson's on the right, and between them were the two divisions of Wood and Sheridan occupying the lines they had taken at Orchard Knob on November 23. Sherman's movement against Tunnel Hill ended in failure early in the afternoon, as already stated, and Hooker's success had not yet become apparent. There was no time to lose if Bragg was to be driven from the ridge before darkness fell. At half-past three Grant changed his battle plan by ordering Thomas's entire line to advance in unison and take the rifle pits at the base of the ridge. This was to be a demonstration whose purpose was to relieve the pressure on the hard-pressed Sherman at Tunnel Hill, by compelling Bragg to divert troops to confront Thomas. The order in Sheridan's division was: "As soon as the signal is given

36. Edwin H. High, *History of the Sixty-eighth Indiana Infantry* (1902), pp. 144-46.

37. *Ibid.;* Cist, *op. cit.,* pp. 252-53; *Official Records, op. cit.,* Vol. XXXI, Part 2, pp. 44-46; *Battles and Leaders, op. cit.,* Vol. III, p. 723.

[the rapid firing of six guns on Orchard Knob] the whole line will advance, and you will take what is before you."[38]

The valley between Orchard Knob and Missionary Ridge was studded with small timber. The ground on Baird's right and Wood's front was wooded, but the fronts of Sheridan and Johnson were fairly well cleared. Extending in front of the rifle pits, which were visible from Orchard Knob, the ground was covered with felled trees to a depth of some four or five hundred yards. The approaches to the rifle pits were commanded by Confederate artillery, and good visibility provided for both direct and enfilading fire from the rifle pits. From this point to the summit the distance was about six hundred feet. The side of the ridge was broken by gullies completely devoid of timber. About half the distance to the top of the ridge was another line of rifle pits, while on the summit were additional lines supported by fifty pieces of artillery.[39]

At about 3:40 the signal guns were fired, followed promptly by twenty thousand men in brigade formation, with double skirmishers in front and reserves in the rear, advancing to the attack. The large siege guns in the Chattanooga forts were heard above the roar of the lighter artillery, as the Confederate rifle pits began firing, and soon the entire front was an inferno. The Federals continued advancing over difficult obstructions, in the face of a murderous fire, broke through the Confederate defenses in several places at bayonet point, and killed and captured a large number of the defenders. This assault threw the rest of them into a state of panic and immediate flight toward the top of the ridge, with the loss to them of many more prisoners and a quantity of small arms. Thus was successfully completed the order to take the first rifle pits, but the momentum of the victors would not end there.[40]

These men of the Army of the Cumberland had a score to settle, a blot to erase, the stigma of defeat at Chickamauga to avenge, and they would not be denied. Stopping only long enough to re-form, and obeying an overwhelming impulse to advance as if in obedience to orders, they continued after the fleeing Confederates. Perhaps the sight of the retreating defenders gave them an irresistible urge to follow them, perhaps not; but without thought of support to their flanks they rushed headlong, regiment by regiment, until they reached the summit.[41]

---

38. James H. Wilson, *Life of John A. Rawlins* (New York, 1916), pp. 171-73; Cist, *ibid.*, p. 253.

39. *Battles and Leaders*, *op. cit.*, Vol. III, p. 724; Cist, *ibid.*

40. Cist, *ibid.*, p. 254.

41. *Ibid.*, 254, 255.

General Grant, from his position on Orchard Knob, turned quickly and angrily to General Thomas and asked, "Thomas, who ordered those men up the Ridge?" When Thomas replied, "I don't know, I did not," Grant turned to General Granger and asked of him, "Did you order them up, Granger?" "No," replied Granger, "they started up without orders. When those fellows get started all h——l can't stop them." Grant, mumbling that someone would suffer if the move failed, then turned and continued watching the ridge.[42]

Granger then ordered General Fullerton, his chief of staff, to "Ride at once to Wood, and then to Sheridan, and ask them if they ordered their men up the ridge, and tell them, if they can take it, to push ahead." As Fullerton was leaving, Granger said, "It is hot over there, and you may not get through. I shall send Captain Avery to Sheridan, and other officers after both of you." When the message was delivered to Wood, that officer said, "I didn't order them up; they started up on their own account, and they are going up, too! Tell Granger, if we are supported, we will take and hold the ridge!"[43] General Sheridan also reported, "I didn't order them up, but we are going to take the ridge." Sheridan then waved his flask at a group of Confederate officers at the top, with the exclamation, "Here's at you!" At that moment two guns in front of Bragg's headquarters were fired in Sheridan's direction. "Ah! that is ungenerous; I shall take those guns for that!"[44] He lost no time in carrying out his threat.

The men struggled upward, fighting as well as they could while seeking the best possible footing and alignment. Sixty flags were advancing up the hill as Bragg was moving large numbers of men from his right to the center, while exhorting others to hold their ground. The movement was too rapid; before Bragg's men could reach the center from their position opposite Sherman the summit was lost. Artillerymen from the top of Missionary Ridge were lighting the fuses of shells and rolling them down the hill by the hundred, but the Union men advanced. At six different places Sheridan's and Wood's men swept over the top, with Sheridan first, near Bragg's headquarters, where he captured the two guns he had threatened to take.[45]

Johnson soon followed on Sheridan's right; Baird captured the works on Wood's left almost at once, arriving just in time to oppose the Confederates Bragg had shifted from his right to support his center. After a sharp struggle that lasted until darkness fell, Baird

42. *Battles and Leaders, op. cit.,* Vol. III, p. 725.
43. *Ibid.*
44. *Ibid.*
45. *Ibid.,* pp. 725-26; Cist, *op. cit.,* p. 255.

drove the Confederates back beyond a high point that he at once took over.[46] Wood recalled in after years that, when General Fullerton relayed his reply to General Granger, Grant said, "If Wood fails, he'll pay for it."[47]

Bragg's shattered army had abandoned Missionary Ridge before sundown and left behind their thickly strewn dead and wounded. The joyful shouts of the victors then went up in a mighty roar, including the wounded who forget their misery long enough to enjoy the triumph, although many wept. Sheridan, however, was not yet through for the day. He descended the ridge with two brigades on the Mission Mills road and located the Confederate rear posted on a second hill. After a warm encounter these were dislodged with the loss of many prisoners and a pair of guns.[48]

General Granger reported to General Thomas at seven o'clock that he might be able to cut off a large number of Confederates leaving Sherman's front, if he could make a quick thrust at them, and that he was undertaking the movement. Guides were not available until midnight, when Sheridan again set his force to moving; however, the Confederate rear guard was crossing the bridge when he arrived. His pressure on them was so great that they burned the bridge before all had crossed; as a result several hundred additional prisoners were captured.[49]

Charles A. Dana, Assistant Secretary of War, was quite beside himself in reporting the events of the twenty-fifth to Washington. At four thirty that afternoon he wrote: "Glory to God. The day is decisively ours. Missionary Ridge has just been carried by a magnificent charge of Thomas's troops, and rebels routed." Later that day he wrote, in part, that "the heights which Thomas carried by assault are at least 500 feet above Chattanooga Valley, with an inclination of at least 45 degrees, and exceedingly rugged and difficult." Again, Dana reported on November 26, in part, "The storming of the ridge by our troops was one of the greatest miracles in military history. No man who climbs the ascent by any of the roads that wind along its front can believe that 18,000 men were moved up its broken and crumbling face unless it was his fortune to witness the deed. It seems as awful as a visible interposition of God."[50] What no one should lose sight of in reviewing the battle was the mighty effort displayed by Sheridan and Wood in particular, who seemingly must

---

46. *Battles and Leaders, ibid.*, p. 726.
47. *High, op. cit.*, p. 150.
48. *Battles and Leaders, op. cit.*, Vol. III, p. 726.
49. *Ibid.*
50. *Official Records, op. cit.*, Vol. XXXI, Part 2, pp. 68, 69.

have interpreted their orders loosely enough to entertain the idea of taking the summit. Authorities are not agreed on this point; but the overwhelming opinion is that the action from the first line of rifle pits was spontaneous and unordered.

General Thomas told in after years that after the battle, at the top of the hill, he talked with some of his old soldiers who always took liberties with him. When he attempted to compliment them for the gallant assault they had just made, one of them said, "Why, General, we know that you have been training us for this race for the last three weeks." Hardly knowing how to respond, he noted a steamboat approaching Chattanooga, and said, "We have trained you as long as we want to; there come the rations."[51]

A good example of Sherman's technique in seeking credit for himself is in his *Memoirs*, relating to the advance of his Army of the Tennessee for the relief of Chattanooga. He described his long-delayed arrival at his destination and his hearty welcome by "Generals Grant, Thomas, and all, who realized the extraordinary efforts we had made to come to their relief."[52] In this statement Sherman did not lose the opportunity to dramatize his achievement, a trait deeply anchored in his nature. Of course, the beleaguered defenders of Chattanooga were glad to welcome him; but Sherman in this account failed to relate the complete story. This story should have included an account of his delay in arriving due to his advancing with his slower-moving supply trains.

Continuing, Sherman described the magnificent view of the panorama of Chattanooga. "Lookout Mountain, with its rebel flags and batteries, stood out boldly, and an occasional shot fired from Wauhatchie or Moccasin Point gave life to the scene. . . . All along Missionary Ridge were the tents of the rebel beleaguering force; the lines of trench from Lookout up toward the Chickamauga were plainly visible; and rebel sentinels, in a continuous chain, were walking their posts in plain view, not a thousand yards off. 'Why,' said I, 'General Grant, you are besieged,' and Grant replied, 'It is too true.'" Grant then told Sherman that mules and horses of Thomas's army were so starved that they could not haul his guns; that forage, corn, and provisions were so scarce that the hungry men stole the few grains of corn that were meant for the favorite horses; and that Thomas's army was so demoralized that it was feared the men could not be gotten out of their trenches to take the offensive. Sherman stated that the Army of the Cumberland had been so long in the

51. Van Horne, *op. cit.*, p. 426.

52. William T. Sherman, *The Memoirs of William T. Sherman* (New York, 1891), Vol. 1, p. 361.

trenches that Grant wanted his troops to take the offensive, after which Grant had no doubt the Army of the Cumberland would do well.[53]

Sherman's recital of Grant's plan for the use of his Army of the Tennessee, instead of Thomas's Army of the Cumberland, is surprising for its seeming implication of superiority of his troops, particularly since his troops failed miserably in the assignment while Thomas's men performed in a manner to forever stamp them as magnificent. It was perhaps better for the Union that Sherman's troops were selected, since, as a result, the Army of the Cumberland was infuriated to an irresistible heat, in consequence of which Missionary Ridge was captured at much less cost in lives than was expected.

It is small wonder that the Army of the Cumberland felt humiliated by the secondary role, and that they were inspired to charge all the way up Missionary Ridge in vindication. Sherman's comment, after being saved by the greatest single achievement of the war and by the men his statement disparaged, also many years after the death of the great hero who saved both himself and Grant from humiliating defeat, is manifestly unjust. History would soon lose its flavor if dependent upon this type of deceptive narrative. Nevertheless, it shows once again the extremes resorted to by members of the military clique in advancing themselves and discrediting others.

Sheridan's and Wood's two center divisions lost thirty-one per cent of their artillery; several thousand small arms; over twenty-three hundred killed and wounded; and thirty-eight hundred prisoners in the estimated one hour of fighting. Sherman lost seventeen hundred killed and wounded in two days, of which about thirteen hundred were from his own three divisions. The result of the battle was to pave the way for the march to Atlanta in early 1864 and the cutting in two of the Confederacy by the end of that year.[54]

General Bragg, in commenting on the action of his troops at Missionary Ridge, said, "A panic, which I had never before witnessed, seemed to have seized upon officers and men, and each seemed to be struggling for his personal safety, regardless of his duty or his character."[55]

On this great day for the Union, November 25, 1863, Chickamauga was avenged and General George Thomas and his men wrote an imperishable chapter in the history of their country. Grant, the chief in command, and Sherman, his great friend, to whom he gave every opportunity to carry off the laurels, emerged with little of actual

---

53. *Ibid.*
54. *Battles and Leaders, op. cit.*, Vol. III, p. 726; Cist, *op. cit.*, p. 258.
55. *Battles and Leaders, ibid.*, p. 727.

glory to themselves, although biased writers have accorded both of them credit earned by Thomas, Hooker, Sheridan, Wood, Baird, and others. Thomas and his troops earned almost all the honor the field could give, and they it was, not Sherman and his men, who gave the Confederates the worst defeat received by them in the war to date. Regardless of Grant's effort to give Sherman the credit for Missionary Ridge and of Grant's friends to give him, Grant, credit for the victory, he had little to do with it. It was Hooker who reported that, when Grant was discussing the battle, he said, "D—n the battle! I had nothing to do with it."[56]

Thus we find Grant disclaiming with emphasis any credit for the victory, which is, of course, correct. Official records and other reliable supporting data, including reports and statements of participants and witnesses, give deserved credit to Thomas. It was not long before Grant's political sponsors and supporters began to build him up for the Presidency. Subordinate commanders, who wished to appropriate to themselves a high ranking in the war, did much to foster the falsehood that Thomas was slow. In this series of battles it was the "slow" Thomas, not the implied speedy Grant and Sherman, who made the principal contribution to victory. Logically, therefore, it must be concluded that "slow" generals are successful. No better opportunity was afforded during the whole war than at Chattanooga to demonstrate superior generalship; and it was Grant and Sherman, particularly the latter, who were "weighed in the balance and found wanting." It is plain that when these men were built up at the expense of Thomas, naturally the last was the chief loser. Long overdue credit to Thomas is within the power of his countrymen, the beneficiaries of his genius, who have the choice of accepting fact or continuing to accept fiction.

The Grant Legend persists to the very hour of this writing, a legend that is the only motivation for this "labor of love"; without this legend, which rests in great part upon the structure of injustice to Thomas, there would be no need to right the wrong of undercredit to Thomas and overcredit to Grant and Sherman. In a recent advertisement appeared a scene featuring the Battle of Lookout Mountain. In the narrative accompanying this scene it was stated that the Army of the Cumberland, under Grant, was told to probe, then rest. It has been shown that Hooker, under the command of Thomas, captured Lookout Mountain, and that Thomas, not Grant, commanded the Army of the Cumberland. It has been shown also that Hooker

---

56. Clarence E. Macartney, *Grant and His Generals* (New York, 1953), p. 15; Lloyd Lewis, *Sherman, Fighting Prophet* (New York, 1932), p. 323.

was given discretionary authority by Thomas, not by Grant, to do as he did; therefore any credit to Grant, with none to Thomas and Hooker, is sheer distortion. It would be unbelievable that such misinformation can find its way into accepted reading matter if, indeed, we did not see it. As in all of the major battles in which he participated, Missionary Ridge included, the striking characteristic of Thomas to dominate, in order words, to become the chief architect of victory, or, as at Chickamauga, to avert disaster, is undeniable.[57]

Concerning Sherman's assignment at Tunnel Hill, which was designed to double up Bragg's right flank or drive him from his line of supply and compel his retreat, both he and Grant died believing that Sherman's unsuccessful attack there was due to Bragg's withdrawal of troops from his center, opposite Thomas. It has been shown that General Baird, at the summit of Missionary Ridge, fought Confederate troops that had been shifted from Sherman's front, the exact opposite of Grant's and Sherman's mistaken impression; therefore Thomas's attack did create a diversion that helped, rather than damaged, Sherman; and correspondingly, Thomas was further handicapped by this withdrawal, rather than being helped, as they are thought to have believed. Confederate reports cited elsewhere also support the statement that not one Confederate soldier was removed from his position before Thomas's front to oppose Sherman.[58]

General Grant reported that "discovering that the enemy in his desperation to defeat or resist the progress of Sherman was weakening his center on Missionary Ridge, determined me to order the advance at once. Thomas was accordingly directed to move forward his troops, constituting our center." This statement is in conflict with Grant's report, in which the statement is made that Baird's division, Fourteenth Corps, was sent to Sherman's aid, but when Sherman reported to him that he had all the force necessary Baird was assigned to a position on Thomas's left. It is entirely clear from this that Sherman felt confident of holding his position, or, stated differently, that Bragg was not withdrawing from Thomas's front to oppose Sherman.[59]

At the close of the battle, Grant wrote to Sherman: "No doubt you witnessed the handsome manner in which Thomas's troops carried Missionary Ridge this afternoon, and can feel a just pride, too, in the part taken by the forces under your command in taking, first, so much

---

57. High, *op. cit.*, p. 128.

58. Wilson, *Heroes*, pp. 77-78; *Official Records, op. cit.*, Vol. XXXI, Part 2, pp. 748-49; *Society of the Army of the Cumberland, 1892* (Cincinnati, 1893), p. 9.

59. *Official Records, ibid.*, p. 34.

of the same range of hills, and then in attracting the attention of so many of the enemy as to make Thomas' part certain of success."[60] In view of all the facts, this statement of Grant's is almost incredible and could have no other result, regardless of its intent, than to give credit to Sherman, when none was due him, and deprive Thomas of credit, to whom all credit was due. No better illustration than this can be presented, nor is it needed, to show the teamwork of Grant and Sherman in downgrading Thomas and upgrading themselves.

In support of the statement that no Confederates were withdrawn from Thomas's front, the testimony, from the *Official Records,* by the chief Confederate opposing Sherman, is as follows: "It is but justice for me to state that the brunt of this long day's fight was borne by Smith's [Texas] brigade and the Second, Fifteenth, and Twenty-fourth Arkansas [consolidated], of Govan's brigade, together with Swett's and Key's batteries. The remainder of my division was only engaged in heavy skirmishing. The final charge was participated in, and successful, through the timely appearance and gallant assistance of the regiments of Cumming's and Maney's brigades, before mentioned." That portion of the force under Sherman that was engaged fought splendidly and suffered heavy losses. Astonishingly, it is nevertheless true that of the seventeen brigades under Sherman during the entire day only six of them faced Cleburne. In other words, eleven brigades did not see action at any time; and "neither histories, memoirs, nor reports, give any explanations of these remarkable facts."[61]

Chattanooga was distinctive for a number of reasons. First, it was the scene of Lookout Mountain, the famous "Battle Above the Clouds," an outstanding and spectacular achievement; second, it was also the scene of the generally regarded most spectacular and magnificent charge in military history, the assault and capture of Missionary Ridge; third, present on the battlefields were the four best-known and reputedly most capable generals of the war, namely Grant, Sheridan, Sherman, and Thomas; and fourth, participating in these operations were troops from the three principal armies of the Union, the Army of the Cumberland, the Army of the Potomac, and the Army of the Tennessee.

Just before the unordered victory charge of the Army of the Cumberland at Missionary Ridge on November 25, General Thomas observed a suitable site for the location of a national cemetery. This spot was later utilized for the purpose. During the period of preparing the ground, General Thomas provided troops for the work

---

60. *Ibid.,* p. 45.
61. *Ibid.,* p. 752; Cist, *op. cit.,* pp. 96, 99.

and made frequent trips to the cemetery to note progress and to offer suggestions. He insisted that the dead be buried with the utmost care and that their graves be beautified. Through his initiative this cemetery became the ideal for national cemeteries in the West and was the example for improvement of those in the East.[62]

In discussing the plan of burial with General Thomas, the chaplain asked whether the dead should be buried by states. Hesitating a moment, Thomas replied with emphasis, "No, no. Mix them up; mix them up. I am tired of state-rights."[63] After seeing the cost in human lives during almost three years of warfare, in which the rights of every citizen, both North and South, were submerged to the objective of victory, any theoretical concept of state rights lost much if not all of its meaning for him.

It is true that Missionary Ridge ended too late in the day for a general pursuit of the Confederates, but the wonder is that General Grant did not order a fast and resolute follow-up with, for example, the eleven brigades under Sherman that, as has been noted, never saw action during the twenty-fifth. There is every evidence that Grant could not decide the course of action that would have exploited his great advantage over Bragg. Immediately after the battle he reported that "I shall pursue Bragg tomorrow and start a heavy column up the Tennessee River the day after."[64] It seems clear that Grant lacked aggressiveness here, a trait that he hounded Thomas for allegedly not possessing before the Battle of Nashville.

After the action at Missionary Ridge, General Grant directed Thomas to begin a strong reconnaissance at 7 A.M. on the twenty-sixth, in order to ascertain the position of Bragg's forces. If in full retreat, Thomas was to follow them with his entire force, except Granger's corps, which was being sent to Burnside's relief at Knoxville. He also informed Sherman that "the next thing now will be to relieve Burnside," and that "My plan is to move your forces out gradually, until they reach the railroad between Cleveland and Dalton."[65] There can be no doubt that Grant was in no hurry to follow up his advantage with the energy required, nor is there room for doubt that he was more concerned for Burnside at Knoxville than for his adversary, who posed great danger to him and who was vulnerable to a resolute follow-up blow.

General Howard reported that his corps crossed the Chickamauga at 5 A.M. on the morning of the twenty-sixth and that he had over-

---

62. Van Horne, *op. cit.*, pp. 212, 213.
63. *Ibid.*
64. *Official Records, op. cit.*, Vol. XXXI, Part 3, p. 247.
65. *Ibid.*, Part 2, p. 45.

taken Davis's division at 7 A.M., although Davis had started earlier in pursuit. When arriving at Chickamauga Station at noon two guns were captured, also corn, flour, and ten pontoons; however, large quantities of flour and corn were still burning. General Sherman arrived at this time and the pursuit continued. Just before dark Davis's force encountered the enemy's rear guard, but after deploying two of his brigades the enemy was compelled to withdraw. Howard encamped there for the night.[66]

In the meantime, Generals Hooker and Palmer had been delayed by the destruction of bridges across the Chickamauga and Pea Vine Creek. Although his infantry crossed, Hooker's artillery was unable to come up until later. The combined forces separated at the junction of the road east of Pea Vine Creek, Hooker taking the right toward Ringgold, and Palmer the left road to Graysville. Palmer overtook Bragg's rear guard at 9 P.M. of the twenty-sixth and compelled it to withdraw from Graysville before midnight. The next morning Hooker and Palmer joined forces, Hooker coming in from the west and Palmer from the north. General Bragg assumed a fighting stance at the cut where the railroad runs through Taylor's Ridge. Hooker attempted to silence enemy guns with small arms, although he did not succeed. Pat Cleburne, the dauntless Confederate fighting man, was to reckon with here; and when Hooker made two attempts to get into his rear he was thwarted both times. When Hooker's guns arrived Cleburne withdrew; but he had delayed the pursuers long enough to enable Bragg's main force to continue its retreat. When General Grant arrived at Ringgold he gave the order to discontinue the pursuit.[67]

In Hooker's report of the campaign, he stated that "the greatest difficulty I experienced with my new command, and the one which caused me the most solicitude, was to check and curb their disposition to engage, regardless of circumstances, and, it appears, almost of consequences. This had also been the case on Lookout Mountain and on Missionary Ridge. Despite my emphatic and repeated instructions to the contrary, a desultory fire was kept up on the right of the line until the artillery arrived, and you will see by the reports of commanders that, under cover of elevated ground between my position and our right, several small parties advanced to capture the enemy's battery and harass his flank at the gap. It is with no displeasure I refer to these circumstances in evidence of the animation of the troops, neither is it with a feeling of resentment, for of

66. *Ibid.*, p. 350.
67. *Ibid.*, pp. 320-22; Van Horne, *op. cit.*, p. 201.

that I was disarmed by an abiding sense of their glorious achievements. It has never been my fortune to serve with more zealous and devoted troops."[68] What Hooker could not say was that he was a splendid corps commander and that he had the personal magnetism to command and lead troops. Not to be overlooked is the fact that these men were of the Army of the Cumberland and of the Army of the Potomac that, given proper leadership, did as well-led American troops have always done.

At Knoxville, Sherman reported, Burnside was completely invested and had only enough provisions with which to sustain twelve thousand men until December 3. Although eighty-four miles distant, Sherman, who had been assigned to the command of all troops moving to the relief of Knoxville, made all possible haste. Altogether, Sherman had thirty thousand troops, in addition to the crack cavalry corps of the Army of the Cumberland, on the move against Longstreet's force opposing Burnside. The cavalry was moving against him from the west, while the remaining force was coming from the south. Sherman succeeded in getting a few units into Knoxville on December 3, and Longstreet, perceiving that he was on the verge of being surrounded, wisely retreated northward toward Virginia.[69] From all indications the Knoxville affair was largely a tempest in a teapot and diverted troops from the real issue, that of assailing Bragg.

---

68. *Official Records, ibid.*
69. *Ibid.,* pp. 577-82.

CHAPTER XIX

The Atlanta Campaign:
From Chattanooga to Kenesaw

DURING the winter of 1863–1864 the Army of the Cumberland occupied a number of widely scattered points in middle and eastern Tennessee. The chief activities included the repairing of railroads, building of bridges, improving fortifications, and generally bringing equipment and facilities into a state of readiness for the forthcoming offensive operations. During this time there was ever present the danger that the Confederates, concentrated at Dalton, Georgia, might attempt to break through the Union line at some weak point and cause considerable disruption of installations, forces, and plans.

General Thomas had the responsibility, after the Knoxville situation was relieved, of feeding and supplying the armies of the Cumberland, Ohio, and Tennessee. As one of his major duties, he handled almost the entire staffwork incident to the three armies, and General Grant exercised over-all command, with headquarters at Nashville.[1] As if to put his patience to a test, General Thomas was also responsible for the distribution of rations. General J. G. Foster, successor to General Burnside, complained that he could not undertake an offensive movement due to the meager supplies being sent him by Thomas; however, the situation for Thomas was no bed of roses. On January 13, 1864, in reply to Foster's appeal for more rations, Thomas stated, "From the condition of supplies here I do not know how you can be supplied from this place with anything like half rations. The railroad management is unequal to the emergency, and as that management is not under my control, I cannot say how we shall succeed after the road is opened to that point. My animals are dying from starvation, too. And seeing this inevitable state

1. The John N. Hough Papers (descendant of Alfred Lacey Hough, aide to General Thomas from 1863 till his death).

of affairs, I have decided to starve with them until we can better their condition as well as our own. My only hope is that we can stand it longer than the enemy."[2] It requires no imagination to realize that Thomas was having a pretty rough time of it, and that he was very much depressed over it.

Of course, the underlying reason for the food and supply shortages was the bad condition of the railroads, which General Thomas strove desperately to remedy. The work of repairing and rebuilding these railroads was under the control of John B. Anderson, military director of railroads for the Department of the Cumberland. There was something wrong with this arrangement, as indicated by General Thomas's dispatch to General Grant, in which he reported that of 1,200 workmen hired to repair the railroads Anderson accepted only 500 of them with reluctance, although all were badly needed. After a lengthy series of dispatches to Generals Grant and Halleck, Thomas succeeded in having a successor, Daniel C. McCallum, a superintendent of the Erie Railroad, appointed military director of railroads of the Department of the Cumberland. Colonel McCallum had been serving previously as the director of military railroads in Virginia. It was not long before McCallum had the roads in considerably better running order; by February 15 the railroad from Chattanooga to Loudon was operating in good order, and all the way to Ringgold toward the end of March.[3] Apart from his many other qualifications, General Thomas was a most capable railroad administrator. The period of service since the war's beginning, during which he utilized railroads to the maximum extent possible, made him the most highly efficient military officer in the Federal armies for that type of work.

In early February, General Grant revoked his orders to General Thomas to conduct operations in East Tennessee but to concentrate against General Joe Johnston's forces at Dalton. This was intended as a diversion in favor of General Sherman, who was seeking to force General Polk from Meridian, Mississippi, destroy that place's effectiveness as a rail center, and "march on Mobile," Alabama. During this operation, General Schofield and his Army of the Ohio would keep General Longstreet busy, while General Thomas and his Army of the Cumberland would give General Johnston enough to do to prevent his interference with the plan. Sherman started his move on February 3. General William Sooy Smith, who was to destroy General Forrest's force of some four thousand cavalrymen, left Memphis a

2. *Official Records of the War of the Rebellion* (Washington, 1880–1901), Vol. XXXII, Part 2, p. 82.

3. *Ibid.*, pp. 43, 63, 88, 89, 111, 131, 143, 248, 395.

few days later with about double Forrest's force. After disposing of Forrest, Smith was to join Sherman at Meridian. After waiting five days for Smith, Sherman returned to Vicksburg on February 28, where he learned that Forrest had defeated Smith decisively.[4]

On February 12, General Grant asked General Thomas, "Should you not be required to go into East Tennessee, could you not make a formidable reconnaissance toward Dalton, and, if successful in driving the enemy out, occupy that place and complete the railroad up to it this winter?" Thomas informed Grant that an advance on Dalton would be successful if he could have Logan's division. Grant was uncertain whether he wanted to go through with the plan, as indicated by his reply to Thomas, in which he stated that "Logan's troops started yesterday morning [February 11]. If I decide not to make the move at present into East Tennessee, I will send them back, unless you require them to aid in advance on Dalton."[5] General Thomas was held up by heavy rains for more than a week; but in the meantime he forwarded General Grant a complete reconnaissance report of the situation, including the statement that no troops had been sent away from Johnston's command, except one infantry brigade.[6] This series of exchanges between Generals Grant and Thomas is important for its effect upon the relationship between them. Although Grant's *Personal Memoirs,* in alluding to his order to Thomas "to take Dalton," ends on a somewhat conciliatory note, the wording in his comment is unmistakably antagonistic. This is what he wrote:

> On the 12th of February I ordered Thomas to take Dalton and hold it, if possible; and I directed him to move without delay. Finding that he had not moved, on the 17th I urged him again to start, telling him how important it was, that the object of the movement was to cooperate with Sherman, who was moving eastward and might be in danger. Then again on the 21st, he not yet having started, I asked him if he could not start the next day. He finally got off on the 22d or 23d. The enemy fell back from his front without a battle, but took a new position quite as strong and farther to the rear. Thomas reported that he could not go any farther, because it was impossible with his poor teams, nearly starved, to keep up supplies until the railroads were repaired. He soon fell back.
>
> Schofield also had to return for the same reason.[7]

---

4. William T. Sherman, *The Memoirs of William T. Sherman* (New York, 1891), pp. 390-95.

5. *Official Records, op. cit.,* Vol. XXXII, Part 2, pp. 373, 429.

6. *Ibid.,* p. 434.

7. U.S. Grant, *Personal Memoirs* (Hartford, 1885), p. 357.

It did not matter to General Grant, apparently, that within a week the information given him by General Thomas had been verified, and that the *Memoirs,* written many years later, and after General Thomas had reposed in death also for many years, would reveal him as a man of deep resentment toward a man who gave everything there was to give for his country.

On February 28, General Thomas reported to General Grant that General Butterfield, at his direction, had recently examined the line between Chattanooga and Nashville, and that Butterfield believed that a force of six thousand men, including two regiments of cavalry, would be adequate to guard the line. He reported further that two thousand infantry and two thousand cavalry would be adequate to guard the line between Nashville and Decatur, and that a total force of six thousand infantry and two thousand cavalry could guard both lines. Finally, he reported his belief that if permitted the use of the Fourteenth and Fourth Corps in front, with General Howard's corps in reserve, he would be able to move along the line of the railroad and overcome all opposition as far at least as Atlanta. There is plenty of aggressiveness displayed by Thomas in this suggestion; moreover, if it had been adopted at that time the war would have been shortened by a number of months.[8] Suffice it to say that General Grant had his own ideas for the campaign, as will be shown.

On March 17, Generals Grant and Sherman met in Nashville and planned a combined campaign against the two main Confederate armies of Generals Lee and Johnston. Grant had but recently received the appointment to command all Federal armies, with the rank of lieutenant general, as partial reward for his overcredit for the victories around Chattanooga. Sherman was to command the Western armies, at Grant's suggestion, to be known as the Military Department of the Mississippi. On March 18, General James B. McPherson was named to succeed Sherman as commander of the Army of the Tennessee. This arrangement, regardless of pro and con arguments, gave promise of greater coordination between the Union forces in the East and West. It was agreed that in early May Sherman would move against General Johnston and that Grant would move against Lee, both moves to be made simultaneously.[9] The appointment of a junior in rank to Thomas, in this instance Sherman, was the second time he was side-tracked. He outranked Sherman on the basis of his appointment as a major general on April 25, 1862, whereas Sherman's appointment dated

---

8. *Official Records, op. cit.,* Vol. XXXII, Part 2, p. 489; John McElroy, Address on General Thomas (in Congressional Library).

9. Jacob D. Cox, *Atlanta* (New York, 1882), p. 19; Thomas B. Van Horne, *History of the Army of the Cumberland* (Cincinnati, 1875), Vol. II, p. 24.

from May 1, 1862. To suggest that Thomas was indifferent to the slight is absurd, since Thomas wanted recognition as well as anyone else, more particularly since, as in this instance, he was more deserving of it.

In discussing the matter with another officer, Thomas said, "I have made my last protest against serving under juniors. I have made up my mind to go on with this work without a word, and do my best to help get through with this business as soon as possible." He had not at any time lost a movement or a battle, from the opening engagement at Mill Springs through the campaign of Chattanooga. The country was well aware of his achievements, in particular his stand at Chickamauga, and he was acclaimed throughout the Northern states as a great leader. He had maintained the high standing of the Army of the Cumberland, which was begun with General Buell's rigid training schedule; and his army idolizd him, from the highest ranking officers to the privates in the ranks.[10]

The by-passing of Thomas would have been less conspicuous if the junior, Sherman, had brought to the appointment a record to recommend it. Sherman, equally with Grant, had been surprised at Shiloh, a surprise that was due to the neglect of minimum requisites of an officer of his rank. Sherman had failed at Chickasaw Bayou, before Vicksburg, and had failed in his assaults on Vicksburg. At Chattanooga, his was the one failure of the three armies engaged; and it was the diversion by General Thomas and his army that salvaged that failure and saved both Sherman and Grant from condemnation. It should be emphasized that the failures of Sherman were not due to a want of courage and energy on the part of the men under his command.[11]

On April 4, General Grant informed Sherman that he wanted him to move against Johnston and destroy him and his war-making potential. Grant instructed him further to travel light and to subsist on the country; additionally, he was to use the railroads sparingly, except for transporting materials and supplies of war.[12] This meant that to the greatest extent possible his men would be on the march. Inherent in Grant's instructions was the purpose to prevent either Johnston or Lee from sending reinforcements to the other during the forthcoming campaign.

Generals Sherman and Thomas then held a conference at Chattanooga at which Thomas suggested that McPherson's Army of the

---

10. Donn Piatt, *General George H. Thomas* (Cincinnati, 1891), pp. 519, 520.

11. *Ibid.*

12. Sherman, *op. cit.*, Vol. II, p. 25.

Tennessee, with Schofield's Army of the Ohio, demonstrate against Johnston's army at Dalton by the direct roads to Buzzard's Roost Gap and from the direction of Cleveland. At this time he would advance his Army of the Cumberland through unguarded Snake Creek Gap and attack Johnston's communications between Dalton and Resaca. After this had been accomplished, Johnston would be compelled either to retreat eastward through poorly supplied country or to stand his ground at Dalton and suffer almost certain defeat. Thomas's plan was overruled, just as the quite similar proposal made to General Grant was also overruled. Sherman contended that he needed his Army of the Cumberland to form a reserve for the other two armies, namely, the Ohio and the Tennessee, and to serve as a rallying point from which these armies could operate. Sherman's plan, it should be noted, might have been effective in a more level country, but it was the hilly North Georgia terrain through which the plan was carried out. Sherman did adopt so much of Thomas's suggestion as to send a smaller force through Snake Creek Gap, but with a different purpose in view. In a direct advance the main force, in this instance Thomas's Army of the Cumberland, would encounter the strongest opposition, while the smaller forces, moving independently, would be unable to achieve decisive results.[13]

Sherman's force totalled 98,357 men. The Army of the Cumberland in the center consisted of 60,733 men; the Army of the Tennessee on the right contained 24,065 men; and the Army of the Ohio on the left numbered 13,559 men. These forces included 6,000 cavalrymen, and 4,600 artillerymen with 254 pieces of artillery. Thomas's force comprised about sixty per cent of the total; and his men consisted of about two-thirds infantry and the remainder cavalry, artillery, and miscellaneous services.[14]

The Army of the Cumberland consisted of three infantry corps, namely the Fourth, the Fourteenth, and the Twentieth, commanded respectively by Generals Howard, Palmer, and Hooker. Each corps consisted of three divisions. Howard's division commanders were Stanley, Newton, and Wood; Palmer's were Johnson, David, and Baird; and Hooker's were Williams, Geary, and Butterfield. In addition to the infantry, there were two cavalry divisions in Thomas's army, commanded by General Edwin M. McCook and General Kenner Garrard.

---

13. Van Horne, *op. cit.*, Vol II, pp. 24-25; Cox, *Atlanta*, p. 31; Piatt, *op. cit.*, pp. 497-98; Thomas B. Van Horne, *The Life of Major General George H. Thomas* (New York, 1882), p. 221.

14. John G. Nicolay and John Hay, *Abraham Lincoln: A History* (New York, 1909), Vol. IX, pp. 1-4; Jacob D. Cox, *Military Reminiscences of the Civil War* (New York, 1900), Vol. II, p. 201.

A third division of cavalry under the famous Judson Kilpatrick belonged to the Army of the Cumberland, but served during the campaign with the Army of the Tennessee.

It would have been surprising if the other two army commanders, McPherson and Schofield, with much smaller armies, had not complained to Sherman at the wide difference in numbers between Thomas's army and theirs. When they did complain, Sherman expressed his real evaluation of the worth of his favorite "whipping boy" by answering, "I keep you on the flanks in order that if anything happens to either of you I would have 'Old Thom' left; and as you both know, nothing could budge him."

An interesting letter has come to light, that emphasizes the completeness of the source material available to Thomas B. Van Horne, which material was furnished by General Thomas with the request, "I wish you to write a narrative history of the Army of the Cumberland." This letter, from the War Department, Publication Office, War Records 1861–65, dated February 15, 1879, and addressed to General Buell (The Buell Papers), is self-explanatory as to the completeness of the data furnished Van Horne by General Thomas:

GENERAL:

I am charged with the preparation, for publication, of the official records of the War of the Rebellion, and am anxious that such publication shall set forth all the important military correspondence of that war. The records, particularly for 1861, and of the Western commands in 1862, are by no means complete. Van Horn[e] has published some of your correspondence that cannot be found on the files of the War Department, and I write to request that you allow me to use such official records, originals or retained copies, as may be in your possession. They shall be returned to you, if so desired, and all express charges will be defrayed by this office. Much of your correspondence I now have, but I wish to be sure that I have all of it that you consider important.

(Signed) ROBERT N. SCOTT

This letter is important enough to show the completeness of General Thomas's records during the tenures of Generals Buell, Rosecrans, and Thomas, in comparison with the recognized *Official Records*. Intensive research by this author has confirmed that the material available to Van Horne was more complete, at least in respect of some of the matters checked, than the *Official Records*. For this reason considerable reference is made by the author to Van Horne's *History of the Army of the Cumberland,* more especially in connection with the Atlanta campaign. Considerable reliability was also placed upon the Atlanta campaign by General Jacob D. Cox for the very good reason that the work is highly regarded by historians generally. In addition, which undoubtedly underlies the reason for its excellence, General Cox, a division commander in Schofield's Twenty-third Corps, made a splendid contribution to the success of the campaign and was therefore familiar with the events that occurred.

General Joseph Johnston was at Dalton and the near-by area with his Army of Tennessee, at which point he succeeded General Bragg on December 27, 1863, following the latter's defeat at Missionary Ridge on November 25. General Bragg stopped for the night at Dalton, following his retreat from Chattanooga, and when he realized that he was not being pursued he decided to remain for the time being. He began at once to strengthen his position, which was continued throughout the winter, and offered some confidence to the defenders that they could withstand a formidable attack. General Thomas, it has been commented upon elsewhere herein, was once a subordinate to Bragg in the Mexican War, and had been but recently placed in command of the Army of the Cumberland.[15]

General Grant telegraphed General Sherman on April 28 that his offensive against General Lee would begin on May 4, and that he, Sherman, should begin his advance against Johnston on May 5. Sherman was delayed and unable to begin his advance until May 6. Thus was begun the combined stroke that, it was hoped, would toll the death knell of the Confederacy. Johnston's army consisted of two corps under Generals John B. Hood and William J. Hardee aggregating fifty-five thousand men, which, with an additional fourteen thousand under General Polk and scattered forces aggregating seven thousand, gave him a total strength of seventy-five thousand men. Johnston's position was a strong one; and Sherman decided, as did Thomas in February, that a direct frontal assault should not be attemped against him.[16]

Johnston's intelligence-gathering services were aware that Sherman's April movements suggested an intent to attack, but General Bragg believed otherwise. As recently as May 2, General Bragg felt convinced that Sherman's activities were merely demonstrations de-

15. Cox, *Reminiscences,* Vol. II, p. 197; Lloyd Lewis, *Sherman, Fighting Prophet* (New York, 1932), p. 308; Van Horne, *Cumberland,* Vol. II, pp. 11-14.

16. Van Horne, *ibid.,* pp. 44, 47-51; Nicolay and Hay, *op. cit.,* Vol. IX, p. 4; *The Civil War Through the Camera* (Elson's History Series [Springfield, Mass., 1912]), Vol. XIII, pp. 2-4; Cox, *ibid.,* Vol. II, p. 197.

signed to cloak his real purpose. On May 1, Sherman wired Grant that Thomas would concentrate at Ringgold; McPherson's army was already *en route* to Chattanooga; and Schofield, at Charleston, would proceed to Cleveland. Further, he reported that Thomas would advance to Tunnel Hill, Schofield to Catoosa Springs, and McPherson to Villanow.[17]

Dalton was well defended from attack on the Chattanooga Road. Mill Creek meanders through the Chattanooga Mountains at Rocky Face by a crooked gorge flanked by steep cliffs known as Buzzard's Roost. The western side of Rocky Face is an almost perpendicular wall, and in the Mill Creek Gorge projecting spurs enfilade the entrance like bastions. North of the gorge a large spur from the ridge extends downward to the east, where it joins a smaller but parallel ridge; and from the lower ridge a line of heavy earthworks ran to Cooyehuttee Creek. The summit and sides of Rocky Face were defended by a continuous line of batteries, and formed an imposing obstacle to an aggressor. Mill Creek had been dammed in order to form a water barrier or defense of the gorge.[18]

About three miles north of Mill Creek Gap, Rocky Face and Tunnel Hill break off into small but separated hills. Here, near Catoosa Springs, the more open country formed a connection between the Union center at Ringgold, Georgia, and its left moving from Cleveland.[19]

Johnston's main army, still at Dalton since Bragg's retreat from Chattanooga, expected and hoped for an attack by Sherman against Rocky Face Ridge. Sherman realized that the position was too strong, however, and began to demonstrate or feint at several points in the hope that Johnston might be diverted from interfering with McPherson's move against Ship's Gap and Villanow, and later to Snake Creek Gap near Resaca.[20]

In order to mislead Johnston into believing that his design was to attack Snake Creek Gap, Sherman ordered General Geary's division to advance up Chatooga Mountain, near Dug Gap, at the point where the road from Lafayette to Dalton extends from Mill Creek Valley. Chatooga Mountain and Rocky Face Ridge are separated by Mill Creek at Buzzard's Roost, from which point Chatooga extends southward. Although he failed in four attempts to reach the summit, and

---

17. *Official Records, op. cit.*, Vol. XXXVIII, Part 4, p. 1; Nicolay and Hay, *op. cit.*, Vol. IX, p. 9; Joseph E. Johnston, *A Narrative of Military Operations* (New York, 1874), p. 302.

18. Cox, *Reminiscences*, Vol. II, pp. 199-200: Nicolay and Hay, *ibid.*, Vol. IX, pp. 9-10.

19. Cox, *ibid.*; Nicolay and Hay, *ibid.*

20. Cox, *ibid.*, p. 200; Van Horne, *Cumberland*, Vol. II, p. 47.

was compelled to withdraw beyond gun range after losing heavily, the action was regarded generally as justified.[21]

On May 7, Thomas and his Army of the Cumberland advanced toward Tunnel Hill. This was resisted by a show of force against General Palmer's Fourteenth Corps, with infantry and artillery, until Howard's troops appeared, and the enemy was compelled to withdraw to Buzzard's Roost. On the same day General Hooker advanced to Trickum and began observing Buzzard's Roost on the left and Villanow on the right.[22]

On May 9, Harker's brigade, Newton's division, Fourth Corps, advanced along Rocky Face Ridge about one and one-half miles from the Confederate signal station. There he was compelled to stop in the face of enemy obstructions. Soon skirmishers from General Wood's, General Davis's, and General Butterfield's divisions advanced and pushed the defenders back to their intrenchments at Buzzard's Roost, and the three divisions advanced to the entrance. In the afternoon, Johnson's and Baird's divisions advanced to Davis's support, and Butterfield's division joined General Hooker's force.[23]

The Army of the Cumberland became heavily engaged on the east, north, and west at Buzzard's Roost. Considerable feinting and sparring took place on May 9 and 10; in the meantime, Hooker, at Trickum, supported McPherson's advance through the gap. Hooker sent a division to widen the road through the gap for facility of movement of both men and trains. Other support included Kilpatrick's cavalry and Williams's division of the Twentieth Corps. In the prolonged demonstrating, which sought to prevent a concentrated attack on McPherson, a number of troops were killed and wounded.[24]

McPherson's passage through Snake Creek Gap took place on May 9, and he arrived at strongly fortified Resaca at about two in the afternoon. As there were no roads through the forest to the railroad, and also since his flank was exposed to attack from Dalton, he withdrew to the gap. Without cavalry support, McPherson feared to march eastward to destroy the railroad and at the same time to leave his flank exposed, as aforesaid. When Johnston learned that two corps were at Resaca, he sent General Hood with three divisions to oppose them.[25]

21. Cox, *ibid.*, p. 110; Van Horne, *ibid.*, pp. 48-49; *Official Records, op. cit.*, Vol. XXXVIII, Part 4, pp. 79, 83, 84.

22. *Camera, op. cit.*, Vol. XIII, p. 5; Van Horne, *ibid.*, p. 47; *Official Records, ibid.*, p. 47.

23. *Official Records, ibid.*, p. 102; Van Horne, *ibid.*, pp. 47-49.

24. *Official Records, ibid.*, pp. 83, 84; Van Horne, *ibid.*, 48-50.

25. *Official Records, ibid.*, pp. 104, 105; Van Horne, *ibid.*, pp. 50-52; Cox, *Atlanta*, p. 35.

Sherman, disappointed that McPherson had not broken Johnston's rail communications, was compelled to change his plans, although he spared McPherson's feelings. He had hoped that Johnston could be held at Dalton, within convenient accessibility to Federal services, and that McPherson would damage his communications enough to compel him to fight there. He had also instructed McPherson to hold Snake Creek Gap and attack Johnston's flank, or his railroad at any point between Tilton and Dalton. McPherson was warned to attack Johnston in flank, if he fell back slowly along the railroad, since a slow pursuit would weaken his own forces as the enemy was being strengthened. He was assured that he would be given full support. When Sherman found that McPherson's only accomplishment was his position at the gap, he ordered an attack through that point.[26]

Control of Snake Creek Gap rendered simple the job of turning Dalton by a force strong enough to weaken Johnston's communications, or capable of furnishing enough of a force to risk an engagement with Johnston's whole army. All of the Confederate defenses north of Dalton could be by-passed while the attackers enjoyed the relative security of the mountains. If Johnston's forces had been large enough to hold his positions north of Dalton, and the lower mouth of the gap, he could have withstood an attack by 100,000 men. Unfortunately for him, however, he was compelled to retreat to preserve his communications.

General Johnston recalled Hood's three divisions from Resaca, after McPherson had retired from there, and his army was united once more at Dalton on May 11. The next morning, Howard's corps and Stoneman's cavalry appeared before him as the remainder of the Union forces were moving toward Snake Creek Gap. At ten o'clock, an enemy force moving in the direction of Newton's left had such serious implications that Wood's division was ordered to his support. The enemy drove back Newton's skirmishers and then withdrew, after apparently establishing whether the Union forces were on his front seeking to threaten Resaca. Johnston was ever alert to the possiblity of being outflanked and kept a constant vigil on Sherman's movements, as well he should have. After he became convinced, on May 12, of Sherman's intended flank movement, he withdrew his artillery and infantry to Resaca that night and assigned his cavalry to cover the movement. At nine o'clock the next morning, Howard's troops entered Dalton and soon began pursuit of Johnston. Hooker's corps also moved on the Resaca road to support McPherson.[27]

---

26. *Official Records, ibid.*, pp. 39, 112, 113, 125; Van Horne, *ibid.*, Cox, *ibid.*, pp. 50-51.

27. Van Horne, *ibid.*, p. 52; Cox, *ibid.*, 40-41.

Johnston's retreat to Resaca put a crimp in Sherman's plans, as he had hoped to hold him at Dalton until his own forces passed through Snake Creek Gap. Whatever opportunity was available to Sherman to realize his objective was lost between May 9 and the morning of May 13. Johnston, however, was unaware until the twelfth of Sherman's extensive plan to outflank him. He had no way of knowing the number of Union troops entering the gap, and it was this lack of knowledge that made its success possible. Johnston would have been compelled to fight at a considerable disadvantage if McPherson and the forces coming behind him had moved rapidly into position on May 12 between Resaca and Tilton.[28]

The most striking aspect of McPherson's failure was the lost opportunity to defeat Johnston and end the campaign at the very beginning. This failure, which was ultimately Sherman's failure, recalled the plan, referred to previously, presented by General Thomas to General Sherman. The plan called for the armies of the Ohio and the Tennessee to hold Johnston at Dalton by commencing an attack on Buzzard's Roost, while he with his Army of the Cumberland would march through Snake Creek Gap, cut Johnston's communications between Dalton and Resaca, and force him either to fight or retreat to the east. Sherman's original plan was to feint toward Resaca and thus hold Johnston at Dalton, putting it up to him either to fight or to retreat. If he should have given up Dalton, then Sherman would have attacked him during his withdrawal.

The opening operations established the pattern for the entire campaign. Generally the defenders held fortified positions as long as possible, during which every opportunity to inflict damage to Sherman's forces was exploited to the full. Retreat was the alternative when the Union forces could no longer be contained and when necessary to save their lines of communication.

The Battle of Resaca

At nine o'clock on the morning of May 13, Howard's troops, learning that Johnston had abandoned Dalton during the previous night, drove the cavalry from the town and entered it. Howard then began prompt pursuit, captured a number of prisoners, and encamped about eight miles from Resaca. Johnston entered Resaca on the morning after General Loring left the town to hold McPherson in check

28. Van Horne, *ibid.*, pp. 52-53.

and enable Hood's and Hardee's corps to form, following their retreat from Dalton.[29]

Kilpatrick's cavalry accompanied Hooker on the road to Resaca; also Palmer's corps advanced toward Resaca from Snake Creek Gap, closely followed by Schofield and the others, except for Howard's corps and Stoneman's cavalry which were stationed near the Resaca end of the gap. When near the railroad Palmer encountered the Confederates and engaged them from about noon until dark. Butterfield's division of Hooker's corps supported Palmer's right during this action, and Schofield's two divisions supported his left. General Howard then moved close to Resaca, and after establishing communications learned that his right was about a mile from Schofield's left.[30]

Johnston's position at Resaca, as at Dalton, was strong, with Camp Creek in front and strong earthworks close to the town to defend the Oostanaula River and to safeguard his possible retreat. Polk's corps formed the left of his line, with his left flank on the Oostanaula, Hardee's corps in the center, and Hood's on the right flank, with his right resting on the Connasauga River. His outer defenses comprised strong redoubts and rifle trenches on naturally defensible ground. Part of his force was distributed in the inner defense line, but the main part of it occupied the fortified hills north and west of the town.[31]

Sherman ordered a pontoon bridge laid across the Oostanaula River at Lay's Ferry, toward Calhoun, before risking contact with Johnston's army. This project had a twofold purpose, the first of which was to cross the river and threaten Calhoun, the second, for a cavalry force to advance from Villanow toward Rome, cross the river, and break the railroad communications between Calhoun and Kingston.[32]

General McPherson crossed the river near the mouth of Camp Creek on May 14, drove Polk from the hills dominating the railroad bridges from the west, and established a position close by. The next move was to swing the entire line from Hooker's left, which was formed the previous evening, to the far left of the Union line. This movement was performed with Johnson's right as a pivot or the right of the Fourteenth Corps, and with each division advancing until it contacted the Confederates.[33]

When Johnson's right came close to the Confederate position, the

---

29. Van Horne, *ibid.* p. 64; *Official Records, op. cit.,* Vol. XXXVIII, Part 1, p. 141; Cox, *Atlanta,* p. 41.

30. Cox, *ibid.,* p. 40; Van Horne, *ibid.*

31. Cox, *ibid.,* p. 42; Van Horne, *ibid.,* p. 65.

32. Cox, *ibid,* p. 43; Van Horne, *ibid.*

33. Cox, *ibid.,* pp. 43-46; Van Horne, *ibid.*

divisions to his left contacted their adversary successively. General Baird's division was on Johnson's left and Davis's division was in reserve. On the morning of May 14, General Thomas ordered General Howard to form his corps on Schofield's left and advance by the main road to Resaca. Newton's and Wood's divisions moved toward Schofield's left, and Stanley's division toward the Confederate right, on the Fulton and Resaca roads. When Newton reached Schofield's left, Wood's division changed direction to the left on a road between Newton's and Stanley's divisions.[34]

Johnson's division advanced on open ground under sharp artillery and infantry fire, which forced it to withdraw to shelter, after which it poured a steady stream of projectiles into the Confederates. Baird's left and Schofield's right experienced difficulty in maintaining liaison with the rapidly moving troops to their left as they advanced into the woods and were forced to withdraw from the steadily increasing artillery and rifle fire.[35]

Mitchell's brigade of Davis's reserve division moved rapidly to the left to cover Turchin's retreat, and was soon hotly engaged, while Turchin's brigade was re-forming on the elevation west of Camp Creek. Newton's, Wood's, and Stanley's divisions established liaison before reaching the enemy as Howard's corps was converging; and as the joining of the roads constantly shortened the battle lines, most of Newton's division dropped back in reserve on Schofield's right. When Schofield's left won the position on its front, Newton supported his left center and held secure all ground captured. Wood aligned his division with Newton's and forced the enemy from his rifle pits, while Stanley took position on the left of Wood. With artillery support the advance was maintained as the Confederates were compelled temporarily to abandon their defenses.[36]

With this setback, General Stanley noted General Johnston preparing to attack Sherman's left flank. General Howard, with his reserves used up, obtained needed troops from General Thomas's Twentieth Corps to protect the imperiled flank. Stanley's reserves were exhausted in maintaining the overlapped line. Simonson's battery was effectively preventing the line from being doubled up by Stevenson's, Stewart's, and Walker's troops, when Williams's division advanced to support the battery, and soon the devastation wrought by the battery prevented the flanking movement. Johnston sent Walker to Calhoun after learning the next morning that Federal

34. Van Horne, *ibid.*
35. *Ibid.*, p. 66.
36. Cox, *Atlanta*, pp. 44-46; Van Horne, *ibid.*, pp. 66, 67.

infantry were crossing the Oostanaula River by pontoon bridge near that town.[37]

The day ended satisfactorily for the Union forces, and orders were given for a general advance on the morning of the fifteenth. Schofield's troops were moved from the center to Hooker's left. Preparations for the attack were not completed until noon, at which time the Twentieth Corps advanced with General Geary on the left, General Butterfield on the right, and General Williams in reserve. General Hooker sent Williams to protect the left flank from an advance by General Hood before the advance was completed. The ground over which Williams advanced was hilly and alternately wooded and open, and he formed his brigades on hills west of and parallel to the railroad, with batteries planted to command the front line.[38]

The Confederates in front of Hooker were intrenched on hills with spurs protruding in every direction possible; and batteries were located to enfilade the attackers. Geary's and Butterfield's divisions captured the nearest hills after a brisk advance and in the presence of heavy artillery and musketry. Butterfield's division, with two supporting brigades, drove away the operators of a bothersome battery, but were unable either to remove the guns or remain with them. Moving to defensible ground they succeeded in firing on the enemy and preventing the capture of the guns; that night the guns were taken by a detachment of the Fifth Ohio Infantry.[39]

The whole line had become engaged between Howard's right and Hooker's left, during which heavy skirmishing and artillery action continued along the entire front of Thomas's Army of the Cumberland. Howard's steady artillery and musketry fire on the attacking Confederates prevented the shifting of troops to support the force opposing Hooker, although he was unable to hold any point of the enemy line. Despite repeated assaults in front of Williams's position near the railroad, the Confederates could not penetrate the line against his artillery. A long cleared field lay in front of Williams's and Geary's position near two hills and a gully, and adjacent to a woody hill on which rested the Confederate line. On the right of the field were wooded hills that extended to the captured battery. Around five o'clock Stevenson's division left the main line and charged in column to capture the hills.[40]

Stevenson was repulsed by a heavy fire from Williams's and Geary's divisions and his leading regiments almost destroyed. This ended the

37. Cox, *ibid.*, pp. 44, 45; Van Horne, *ibid.*, p. 67.
38. Cox, *ibid.*, pp. 46, 47; Van Horne, *ibid.*, p. 68.
39. Cox, *ibid.*, p. 47; Van Horne, *ibid.*, pp. 68, 69.
40. Cox, *ibid.*; Van Horne, *ibid.*

general struggle. Johnston had ordered the evacuation of Resaca, although he was observed on the day before sending supplies to the rear. He moved from Resaca on the night of the fifteenth, after two days of struggle, and when confronted by the danger of disruption to his communications.[41]

The Union forces entered Resaca on the morning of May 16, and General Sherman gave orders for prompt pursuit of Johnston's army. Resaca was dissimilar in many respects to Dalton, although the two forces were engaged in heavier fighting at Resaca, which naturally resulted in greater casualties. The losses of the Army of the Cumberland reported by General Thomas aggregated about thirty-five hundred killed, wounded or missing.[42]

Etowah and Alatoona

The first requirement in Sherman's pursuit of Johnston was the laying of pontoon bridges at and above Resaca. McPherson's force crossed the Oostanaula at Lay's Ferry, and Howard's at Resaca, during May 16. On May 17, the three armies advanced toward the enemy. Stubborn rear-guard fighting by the Confederate cavalry and artillery slowed Sherman's advance considerably. Their resistance was strengthened by three lines not far apart, which enabled them to withdraw from one line to the other only as fast as they were compelled to relinquish their position. This helped them to cover the rear of their army while two lines of their rear guard were covered.[43]

On the evening of May 17, the Fourth Corps, in two columns, pushed the Confederates so strongly that, an action appearing imminent, the lines were increased to battle strength. Artillery was used liberally, but darkness closed the activities, and Johnston withdrew from his strongly intrenched position. He was hoping that through some mistake by his opponent he might gain an advantage without a battle. Sherman was too wary in this kind of warfare to fall into a trap; he hoped, rather, to compel Johnston either to fight north of the Etowah River, divide his army, or abandon Rome or Alatoona. If Johnston held these towns, Sherman hoped to break his railroads and compel him to fight. General Thomas was ordered to send Davis's division to Rome from Resaca to support the cavalry on the right.[44]

On May 18, the armies advanced, and that night the Fourth and

41. Cox, *ibid.;* Van Horne, *ibid.,* p. 70.
42. Van Horne, *ibid.*
43. Cox, *Atlanta,* p. 51; Van Horne, *ibid.,* p. 71.
44. Cox, *ibid.,* pp. 50-53; Van Horne, *ibid.,* pp. 71, 72.

Fourteenth Corps camped near Kingston. At eight o'clock on the following morning, with Stanley's division of the center column leading, they moved in the direction of Cassville. About halfway to Cassville a Confederate six-gun battery of artillery fired on him from an elevation, but withdrew after being fired on in turn by infantry and artillery. Following an advance of four miles, Stanley was again stopped by the enemy arrayed in two lines. After Howard's artillery opened and compelled the first line to retreat, the Fourth Corps occupied the position. Hooker's corps joined Howard's at this point, after having sparred with the enemy between Adairsville and Cassville. Skirmishing continued until dark, when the several forces bivouacked for the night. During the day Schofield came close to Cassville, and McPherson advanced from Woodland to Kingston.[45]

Johnston had determined to fight at Cassville after being reinforced; Hood, however, under orders to attack, mistakenly believing that the columns on the east had turned his position, delayed attacking until too late to overwhelm Howard's advance columns. Johnston would have still offered battle, but deferred to the opinion of his chief lieutenants. That night he withdrew, crossed the Etowah River on May 20 with all of his equipment, and took over a strong position at Alatoona Pass. Sherman's hope to compel General Johnston to give battle north of the Etowah had gone glimmering.[46]

General Davis, meanwhile, had been ordered to support Garrard's cavalry movement down the west bank of the Oostanaula. He was then to find a ford or crossing for Garrard's artillery and equipment, thus freeing the cavalry for operations against Johnston's flank. No crossing was located, however, and Garrard returned to Resaca; but Davis, believing he was justified in taking the initiative, advised General Thomas of his plan to go through with his instructions and, pursuing the enemy, drove him into his fortifications at Rome. The next morning, the Confederates left the town too hurriedly to destroy the valuable iron works, machine shops, large quantities of stores, and six pieces of artillery.[47]

General Sherman did not at first follow Johnston beyond the Etowah. Instead, he made a detour to the right, in order to turn Alatoona or to work on Johnston's communications at either Marietta or the Chattahoochee River. Johnston called for reinforcements from Mississippi and the Southwest as his overextended supply line and losses had seriously depleted his fighting strength. After resting his

45. Cox, *ibid.*, p. 53; Van Horne, *ibid.*, pp. 72-73.

46. Cox, *ibid.*; Van Horne, *ibid.*, p. 73.

47. *Official Records, op. cit.*, Vol. XXXVIII, Part 1, pp. 627-28; Cox, *ibid.*, p. 55.

army for several days, on May 23 Sherman ordered an advance south of the Etowah; the Army of the Tennessee crossed at Conasene Creek; General Thomas's Army of the Cumberland crossed four miles below Kingston; and General Schofield's Army of the Ohio at Etowah Cliffs on the left of Thomas. General Blair, with two divisions and a brigade, was ordered to advance from Huntsville, Alabama, to Rome and Kingston.[48]

On May 24, at daybreak, Thomas ordered Geary's division, Hooker's corps, to hold the Alatoona Road near Alatoona, and cover the left flank of the Twentieth Corps until relieved by Schofield. The rest of the Twentieth Corps was ordered to follow McCook's cavalry to Burnt Hickory. McCook arrived there at about 2:00 P.M., after skirmishing for several miles, and intercepted a carrier with a dispatch from Johnston stating that his army was heading toward Dallas and Powder Springs. Later, General Thomas confirmed that Johnston had anticipated Sherman's plan in time to place his army across his path near Dallas.[49]

New Hope Church

At eleven o'clock on the morning of May 25, Geary's central division of the Twentieth Corps met a considerable force about five miles north of Dallas. After a heavy exchange the Confederates were driven back. These were the advance troops of Hood's corps, with Hardee's close behind. This was a critical situation, and General Hooker at once ordered a defensive posture on a hill, besides ordering up General Williams's and General Butterfield's divisions, several miles distant. He then informed General Thomas of the situation. These divisions arrived in late afternoon, went into action promptly, and drove the enemy back about one and one-half miles to New Hope Church. Here they were stopped by artillery, and General Geary's attempt to dislodge the defenders was unsuccessful. Johnston's army was strongly posted and under cover across Sherman's path in readiness to give him battle.[50]

Sherman, believing that he was on Johnston's right flank, determined to turn it. He sent McPherson to dislodge the enemy in front of him and, if unsuccessful, to move to the left. McPherson did not

---

48. Van Horne, *Cumberland,* Vol. II, p. 74; Cox, *ibid.,* pp. 56, 57.

49. Van Horne, *ibid.,* p. 75; Cox, *ibid.,* pp. 67-68; *Official Records, op. cit.,* Vol. XXXVIII, Part 4, pp. 299-300.

50. Van Horne, *ibid.,* pp. 75, 76; Cox, *ibid.,* pp. 70-72.

move to the left as expected, and the opportunity to pass beyond Johnston's right was lost.[51]

On the night of May 25, the Fourth Corps, ordered by General Thomas to support Hooker, formed on his intrenched left near the enemy. Davis's division, having left Rome on the twenty-fourth, was in supporting distance, but Johnston's and Baird's divisions were delayed by the trains and were still in the rear. On the twenty-sixth, the armies were concentrating. McPherson moved to Dallas and Schofield was ordered to the left of Thomas in an effort to turn Johnston's right, the cavalry covering the extreme left, right, and rear of the army. Hooker's corps kept its position of the night before; but the Fourth Corps occupied a line of hills somewhat at right angles to Hooker's corps and posed a more direct threat to the Confederates. Schofield, on Howard's left, covered the road between Alatoona and Dallas by New Hope Church, and both skirmished into position within firing range of the main forces.[52]

On the morning of May 26, General Thomas ordered General Davis to locate Johnston's left flank and establish communication with McPherson. He advanced on the Burnt Hickory Road and, after dispersing pickets from the town, deployed on the east of the Marietta Road. McPherson and his Army of the Tennessee soon formed abreast of him and extended across the Villa Rica Road. Johnson's division of the Fourteenth Corps formed in the rear of the Fourth Corps during the afternoon, and the two armies were in liaison and ready for action. Hardee's corps was on Johnston's left, Hood's on the right, and Polk's in the center.[53]

Sherman ordered McPherson to establish liaison with Hooker's right, a move that would enable his entire line to advance by the left flank, beyond Johnston's right, and get between him and the railroad. As it turned out, McPherson was unable to effect a junction with Hooker. He also ordered Howard and Hooker to demonstrate, and to make a strong attack on Johnston's right. For this purpose Generals Sherman and Thomas gave their closest attention. Howard was to make the attack; but both Thomas and Howard, realizing that the attackers would be subject to a crossfire of artillery and musketry, agreed that Howard would move his column to the left and strike the Confederate flank.[54]

Wood's division of the Fourth Corps was chosen to make the

---

51. Van Horne, *ibid.*, p. 77.

52. *Ibid.*; Cox, *Atlanta*, p. 73.

53. Van Horne, *ibid.*, pp. 77-78; Cox, *ibid.*; *Official Records, op. cit.*. Vol. XXXVIII, Part 4, p. 316.

54. Van Horne, *ibid.*, p. 78; *Official Records, ibid.*, p. 326.

attack on May 27, with Johnson's division of the Fourteenth Corps on the left and McLean's brigade of the Twenty-third Corps on the right. This column formed to the far left and to the rear of the Twenty-third Corps, with Wood's division in column six lines deep, and Johnson's division in brigade front on the left. Howard moved a mile to the east and ordered Wood to turn his division to the south and advance; but the strength of the enemy was such that the attackers moved eastward another mile. Here, Generals Howard and Wood decided to attack after discovering the Confederate defenses failed to cover the entire front. Wood's division, Hazen's brigade, opened the attack at five o'clock in the afternoon with great energy; but, being hard-pressed and without support, Wood sent Scribner's brigade to help his left. Scribner soon halted to make dispositions to cover his flank, but at this stage it was apparent that the attack had failed.[55]

General Pat Cleburne's reserves, to the accompaniment of an enfilading fire, raked Wood's left and forced it back, while his right underwent a crossfire of artillery and musketry fire. McLean had not given the support expected, and as both of Wood's flanks were being steadily liquidated under the severe fire, Howard ordered the column to withdraw. Both Johnson's and Wood's divisions withdrew slowly and thus were enabled to take their wounded with them. General Johnson's loss was relatively small, although he himself was wounded severely. Wood lost about fourteen hundred killed, wounded or missing, and the Confederates lost an estimated four hundred and fifty.[56]

Although the assault was repulsed with heavy losses, a position of value in later movements was established on the Confederate right. The operation demonstrated that Johnston would be alert to any attempt to outflank him, a characteristic in evidence throughout the campaign. Johnston probed Sherman's lines in search of a weak spot at which to deal a lethal blow, and was planning an attack for May 29. Sherman was awaiting McPherson's move to the left to join Hooker before himself attacking Johnston's position. General Hood was chosen to deliver the Confederate attack, which was to be followed by the remainder of his army from right to left. When he noted that his opponent was intrenched, Hood withheld attacking and asked for instructions. The element of surprise to the Unionists was now certainly lost, and the attack was therefore abandoned. The Confederates demonstrated throughout the twenty-ninth along the entire front as a feint to conceal their movement against McPherson.

---

55. Van Horne, *ibid.,* pp. 77-78; Cox, *Atlanta,* pp. 76-79.
56. Van Horne, *ibid.,* pp. 79-80; Cox, *ibid.,* p. 79.

That evening, Hardee's corps attacked McPherson as he was closing in on the Union center; but he had not gone far from his defenses and repelled the attack with considerable loss to the Confederates. In this action, McPherson did not change his position, and the remainder of the line remained fairly stable. One of Stanley's brigades was placed between Schofield and Wood, and Mitchell's brigade of Davis's division dug in about half the length of the three-mile interval toward Hooker's position. Mitchell also cut roads to his rear to permit ready closing of the right wing upon the center at New Hope Church.[57]

During the month of May, the Army of the Cumberland lost 8,774 killed, wounded and missing. On the other side of the ledger, some 1,500 prisoners were captured and about 500 deserters surrendered.

General Sherman held his armies in front of Johnston near Dallas, since his main objective in moving to the right was to turn Johnston's flank. He had ordered General Blair to ascertain the Confederate strength at Alatoona Pass, but by June 1, Blair was a considerable distance to the rear. It was not until June 8 that Blair reached Alatoona, which completed the assembling of all the armies. After a number of attempts, General McPherson succeeded in dislodging himself from the position that had held the attention of the enemy for so long, so that now the united forces could move by the left flank. General Sherman then ordered General Garrard, on June 1, to the east end of Alatoona Pass, and General Stoneman to the west, both divisions arriving at Alatoona that night.[58]

A number of adjustments were made in the Union forces at the end of May, including the relieving of some of the divisions and the shifting of others. On June 2, Hooker was shifted to Schofield's left and Baird went to Johnson's left. These three commands then made a right circle and forced back Confederate skirmishers and their main army from the roads to Ackworth and Alatoona. The Union line was extended farther to the left on June 4 and 5, and continued moving closer to Johnston's front. When he realized that Sherman's shift to the left opened the way to Ackworth, he occupied the hills and mountains north and west of Marietta. On the sixth, General Thomas's Army of the Cumberland went into position southwest of Ackworth; General Hooker was near the junction of the Sandtown road and the road to Burnt Hickory and Marietta; Palmer was on Hooker's left; and Howard's corps was at Durham's house about three miles from Ackworth. A rest of several days until June 10 was ordered by

---

57. Van Horne, *ibid.*, pp. 79-81; Cox, *ibid.*, pp. 79, 80, 87.
58. Van Horne, *ibid.*, pp. 81, 82.

Sherman for the armies, during which period Alatoona was strengthened as a base of supplies.[59]

On June 9, the First Cavalry, having observed the Confederates in force on Pine Mountain, formed a heavy line three miles in front of Hooker's position. The next day, Palmer's corps advanced to the southeast before Pine Mountain and gained an elevation within artillery range, on a line with Palmer; and on the eleventh, Palmer and Howard moved slightly to the left flank until Palmer's left adjoined McPherson's right at the railroad. It was now evident that Johnston's line ran from a group of hills at Kenesaw Mountain to Lost Mountain as the base of a triangle, and with Pine Mountain as the apex, fortified in front. His natural defenses of ravines and thick woods offered little encouragement to the invading army.

On June 14, the Fourteenth Corps and the left of the Fourth Corps advanced about a mile, with the right of the Fourth near Pine Mountain and in liaison with the Twentieth Corps. General Leonidas Polk was killed that day while studying the movements of Sherman's forces. He was engaged in conversation with Generals Johnston and Hardee, while standing on an elevation, and could see plainly the blue columns moving eastward from them, while the Federal advance guard felled trees and built trenches at their very feet. A Federal order was given the artillery to fire on any officers in gray who seemed to be observing their operations. While Hardee was illustrating the danger of one of his divisions being cut off by the Federal advance, a cannon ball struck General Polk in the chest. General Polk was a bishop in the Episcopal Church, although educated at West Point, and exhorted many of his fellow Louisianians to follow him into the Confederate service. Just a few days before his death, General Polk administered the sacrament of baptism to both General Hood and General Johnston. General Hood, crippled from wounds received at Gaines' Mill, Gettysburg, and Chickamauga, was unable to kneel, and was compelled to lean forward on his crutches. General Polk's death was a tremendous shock to the entire Confederate Army. The valor displayed by these three men, Polk, Hood, and Hardee, excites the admiration of everyone who can regard bravery and endurance as virtues.[60] During the night of June 15 the Confederates were forced from Pine Mountain by the left of the Union line, from where they retreated to the Kenesaw-Lost Mountain intrenchments.

General Sherman ordered Schofield to threaten Lost Mountain, McPherson to threaten Kenesaw Mountain, and Thomas to attack the Confederate center. Schofield carried the line on his front, which was exposed by the withdrawal from Pine Mountain; McPherson captured a hill on his front; and Thomas pushed ahead one and one-half miles at the center. Other gains were made almost to the main Confederate defenses, and Johnston withdrew from six miles of his defenses to a new line across Mud Creek in the direction of Marietta.[61]

On June 17, Thomas ordered his army to advance. The Fourth and Twentieth Corps and the right of the Fourteenth Corps advanced southeastward over the abandond defenses of Johnston, and found a line of skirmishers deployed before a group of hills running southwest from Kenesaw Mountain. The advantage of terrain enabled the skirmishers to resist until after dark, when, having been driven across Mud Creek, they failed during the night in their attempt to dislodge the intrenched Fourth Corps. A segment of the Confederate main-defense line was taken and held by General Wood's and General Newton's divisions on the morning of the eighteenth, ably supported on the left by General Baird. After dark, Newton's division gained a decisive advantage by digging in less than a hundred yards from the Confederate defenses. General Thomas ordered an attack for the morning of the nineteenth on Johnston's weakened position, but he retreated during the night.[62]

General Thomas advanced his Fourth Corps on the morning of the nineteenth and, pushing across Noyes' Creek, stopped on the west bank. Later, the Twentieth Corps formed on the right of the Fourth, while the Fourteenth advanced to the base of Kenesaw Mountain, with its right joining the left of the Fourth. The Confederates, Hood's corps, were in position near Marietta on the northeast; Loring's corps held Kenesaw Mountain; and Hardee's corps was spread from Kenesaw to the Lost Mountain-Marietta road. His lines were visible from the base of Kenesaw Mountain to the southwestern hills; and from his salient on Kenesaw his flanks were positioned to protect Marietta and his communications.[63]

The Union armies, pressing ever forward toward Atlanta despite three weeks of rain, would soon compel Johnston to fight or be forced back to the defenses of Atlanta. Sherman next put the Army of the Cumberland in motion to the right and held the Army of the Tennessee east of the railroad in readiness to move to the right also if occasion required.[64]

---

61. Van Horne, *ibid.*, p. 87.
62. *Ibid.*, pp. 87-88.
63. *Ibid.*, p. 88.
64. *Ibid.*, pp. 88, 89.

On June 20, a readjustment of the line resulted in establishing complete liaison between the three Union armies, although not without some heavy skirmishing. On the morning of the twenty-first, after aiding in taking and fortifying a hill that had been lost the previous day, General Wood won an elevation that permitted the right of the Fourth Corps to advance about five hundred yards. General Hooker succeeded in placing his corps abreast of General Howard's right, against tremendous resistance. This was the signal for General Johnston to take action by moving Hood's Corps from his right to his left, but his three charges against Wood during the night ended in failure.[65]

Hood's transfer left only Wheeler's cavalry to confront the Army of the Tennessee; but McPherson, misled by Wheeler's deceptive activity, believed that Wheeler's position was strengthened rather than weakened by Hood's removal. Johnston gained temporarily by concealing the actual state of his right, and repelled all efforts to turn his left, but his dislodgment was in sight. Sherman's plan was for McPherson to advance, when possible on the railroad and the main Marietta road, and push the Confederates back or, failing in that, establish a position on the ridge dominating those roads. In the meantime, Thomas's Army of the Cumberland, moving toward Schofield's Army of the Ohio, which sought contact with Johnston's left flank, would compel a weakening of the line beyond his ability to prevent a breakthrough. Hood's transfer to the left not only defeated Sherman's plan, but enabled Hood to attack Hooker before McPherson realized he had withdrawn from his front.[66]

Sherman next planned an attack for June 22 on Johnston's left. Schofield was ordered to cross Noyes' Creek, join Hooker toward Marietta, and deploy south of the Marietta-Powder Spring road. Then the remainder of Thomas's line would advance to conform with Hooker and Schofield. McPherson would press the enemy before him to cover Big Shanty, while having his rear in readiness to support Thomas if necessary.[67]

At 3 A.M., a detachment of Geary's division compelled the enemy to abandon a hill about a mile in front of the center of the Twentieth Corps. The entire division then intrenched on a commanding ridge, and was soon joined by Williams's division on the right and Butterfield's on the left. Although the line of the corps was somewhat irregular, each division held a separate hill with natural defensive

---

65. *Ibid.,* pp. 89, 90.
66. *Ibid.,* p. 90.
67. *Ibid.*

advantages. When the Twentieth Corps was fully established, General Howard advanced and formed liaison with it.[68]

When Williams's division reported to Hooker at 3 P.M. that Hood was massed in front, he was instructed to dig in at once. Hood dashed from the woods to attack before defenses could be dug, but notwithstanding he was driven back by a most destructive canister fire. Two more attempts by Hood to break Hooker's line ended in failure, and with heavy losses, due in large part to the devastating efficiency of Hooker's artillery.[69]

General Thomas sent reserves to Hooker's support as early as possible, after the pattern of the action had been established. Hood's assault from Johnston's left compelled a revision of plans; therefore the problem was presented either of turning his flank or of forcing his lines. General Thomas suggested to General Sherman that McPherson attack Marietta from the east side of Kenesaw Mountain, with support from his Army of the Cumberland; Sherman, however, refused to consider it as he had another idea, to be tragic for the men of Thomas's Army of the Cumberland, and one of the worst mistakes of the war. On the twenty-fourth, Sherman announced to his army commanders that he would attack Johnston's position, a decision to which Thomas raised firm objection. General Sherman's avowed purpose was to show Joe Johnston that he, Sherman, could assault also. When Thomas received the order two days later to attack on the twenty-seventh, he handed the order to General Whipple, his adjutant general, with the comment, "This is too bad." When Whipple asked, "Why don't you send a written protest against the assault?" Thomas replied, "I will not do it. I have protested so often against such things in this command that if I protest again Sherman will think I don't want to fight. But he knows my views."[70] This was one of Sherman's worst mistakes; but what is particularly noteworthy is that Thomas, whom Sherman often berated in print for his "slowness," sought to spare his men from needless slaughter. If Thomas had the good judgment to foresee disaster when Sherman could not, whence the credit to Sherman and the discredit to Thomas in the distorted pages of history?

The Kenesaws are two mountains. When observed from the north they give the appearance of blending into one, in the form of a great human foot with a high instep. The larger is about six hundred feet in height and may be considered the ankle; the smaller, from about

---

68. *Ibid.*, p. 91.

69. *Ibid.*

70. *Ibid.*, p. 92; Society of the Army of the Cumberland, *Yearbook, 1893* (Cincinnati, 1894), p. 118.

one hundred to one hundred and fifty feet lower in height represents the instep and the foot. The crest of Little Kenesaw down the instep is perhaps a thousand feet, from which point the descent is gradual to the south as far as the low mounds, where the Burnt Hickory and Marietta roads cross. The Marietta road curves around the north end of Big Kenesaw, then moves in a southeasterly direction through Marietta, about three miles below the mountain. Johnston's army was forced back until it held the two Kenesaws at the top. His line on the right was at right angles to the main body, and crossed the railroad while covering Marietta. From Little Kenesaw on the left his army extended toward the Chattahoochee, and covered the railroad on that end.[71]

General Thomas chose the divisions of Generals Davis and Newton of the Fourteenth and Fourth Corps to make the attack, and after several adjustments were made to the lines, including some replacements, preparations wre complete. At 8 A.M. on the twenty-seventh, Morgan's brigade and Davis's division occupied earthworks prepared by Whittaker's brigade of Stanley's division. Stanley had moved to the left to support Newton, and Baird's division was in support on Davis's right. Hooker's force was in reserve in support of Palmer's and Howard's corps. Colonel Dan McCook and Colonel J. G. Mitchell were to the rear of Morgan's intrenchments preparatory to attacking salients in the Confederate defensive system. Newton's division was aligned with Harker's and Wagner's brigades. After a fifteen-minute artillery assault on their objective, McCook's and Mitchell's brigades moved from their intrenchments under a devastating artillery and musketry fire to the enemy's works some six hundred yards distant. Let it be said that despite the heavy fire rained on them they advanced to a position under the Confederate guns, although exhaustion and enemy fire had taken their toll and they were compelled to halt.[72]

Johnston's works were concealed by woods protected by numerous types of obstruction, which made the lot of the attackers, despite their bravery before an enemy capable of admiring it, an almost certain defeat. At 10:45 in the morning, General Thomas informed General Sherman that "General Harker's brigade advanced to within twenty paces of the enemy's breastworks, and was repulsed with canister at that range, General Harker losing an arm. General Wagner's brigade of Newton's division, supporting General Harker, was so severely handled that it is compelled to reorganize. Colonel Mitchell's

---

71. *Society, ibid.*, p. 117.
72. Van Horne, *Cumberland*, Vol. II, p. 93; Cox, *Atlanta*, pp. 121-124.

brigade of Davis' division, captured one line of rebel breastworks, which they still hold. McCook's brigade was also very severely handled, nearly every colonel being killed or wounded. Colonel McCook wounded. It is compelled to fall back and reorganize. The troops are all too much exhausted to advance, but we hold all we have gained."[73]

The plight of the attackers was desperate. It was humanly impossible to take their objective, but to remain there incurred great risk and further losses. Even worse, retreat meant even greater losses, perhaps complete destruction. In this period of danger General Thomas ordered Davis to fortify his position. Tools were sent forward promptly and earthworks were dug within a few yards, but not without considerably greater losses.[74]

Newton's troops advanced with less disclosure of movement, but being held up by obstacles and entanglements, under a murderous fire that they were powerless to avert, they were compelled to withdraw. The loss of almost sixteen hundred men killed, wounded, or missing, by Davis and Newton, was almost seven times greater than the 236 lost by the Confederates. The tragedy of it all was that it served no useful purpose, although General Thomas stated that the men went to their work with the greatest coolness and gallantry; nevertheless, no excuse can be presented to remotely justify it.[75]

While Davis and Newton were attacking the center, the armies of the Ohio and the Tennessee under Schofield and McPherson were active on both flanks. McPherson employed a part of his army against Little Kenesaw, but confined his action to demonstration only. Schofield made some progress at Olley's Creek, which was a first step in another movement to the right flank. At 11:45 A.M. Sherman instructed Thomas in the following dispatch: "McPherson's column reached near the top of the hill through very tangled brush, but was repulsed. It is found almost impossible to deploy, but they still hold the ground. I wish you to study well the position, and if it be possible to break the line, do it; it is easier now than it will be hereafter. Hold fast all you make."[76] This dispatch has been construed as a conditional order for another assault, as well it might, in view of the order to break the line if possible.

At 1:30 P.M., Sherman sent another dispatch to Thomas inquiring whether, in view of McPherson's and Schofield's deadlocked situation,

73. *Official Records, op. cit.*, p. 608.

74. Van Horne, *Cumberland*, Vol. II, pp. 93-94; Cox, *Atlanta*, pp. 122-125.

75. Van Horne, *ibid.*, pp. 94-95; Cox, *ibid.*, pp. 125-127.

76. Van Horne, *ibid.*, p. 94; Cox, *ibid*, p. 124; *Official Records, op. cit.*, p. 609.

Thomas could carry any part of the enemy's line today. This was answered at 1:40 P.M. in the following dispatch:

> Davis' two brigades are now within sixty yards of the enemy's intrenchments. Davis reports that he does not think he can carry the works by assault on account of the steepness of the hill, but he can hold his position, put in one or two batteries, tonight, and probably drive them out tomorrow morning. General Howard reports the same. Their works are from six to seven feet high and nine feet thick. In front of Howard they have a very strong abatis. Davis' loss in officers has been very heavy. Nearly all the field officers in McCook's brigade, with McCook, have been killed or wounded. From what the officers tell me, I do not think we can carry the works by assault at this point to-day, but they can be approached by saps and the enemy driven out.[77]

This was typically Thomas, stating the situation clearly, although at variance with the decision to assault this most formidable position. Just a little later, however, Thomas answered another dispatch from Sherman, this time in unequivocal language:

> We still hold all the ground we have gained, and the division commanders report their ability to hold it. They also report the enemy's works exceeding strong; in fact, so strong that they cannot be carried except by immense sacrifice, even if they can be carried at all. I think, therefore, the best chance is to approach them by regular saps, and if we can find a favorable position to batter them down. We have already lost heavily to-day without gaining any material advantage; one or two more such assaults would use up this army.[78]

Sherman was adamant in seeking some way to salvage a success from this so wicked and useless slaughter. After two bloody failures, he contemplated another assault at 5 P.M., but here is where Thomas let him have the following opinion: "The Army of the Cumberland has already made two desperate, bloody, and unsuccessful assaults on this mountain. If a third is ordered, it will, in my opinion, result in demoralizing this army, and will, if made, be against my best judgment, and most earnest protest."[79] It is correct to state that this ended the slaughter for the day, although it did not end Sherman's unceasing effort to justify his terrible mistake. Sherman reported to Thomas his opinion as to the losses suffered by saying that "I regret

77. *Official Records, ibid.,* pp. 609-610; Piatt, *op. cit.,* p. 545.
78. *Official Records, ibid.,* p. 610.
79. Piatt, *op. cit.,* p. 547.

beyond measure the loss of two such young and dashing officers as Harker and Dan McCook. McPherson lost two or three of his young and dashing officers, which is apt to be the case in unsuccessful assaults. Had we broken the line to-day, it would have been most decisive, but as it is our loss is small compared with some of those East. It should not in the least discourage us. At times assaults are necessary and inevitable. At Arkansas Post we succeeded; at Vicksburg we failed. I do not think our loss to-day greater than Johnston's when he attacked Hooker and Schofield the first day we occupied our present ground."[80]

This dispatch shows that Sherman was doing some soul-searching, although beyond doubt he was not yet ready to state publicly that the assaults should not have been made. At 9 P.M. he asked Thomas whether he was willing to risk the move on Fulton, stating also that it would bring matters to a crisis, and that Schofield had secured the way. He was aware, as this dispatch indicated, that there was an opportunity for flanking General Johnston out of position. Nevertheless, General Thomas replied in a few well-chosen words: "What force do you think of moving with? If with the greater part of the army, I think it decidedly better than batting against breastworks twelve feet thick and strongly abatised."[81] General Schofield had sent an earlier dispatch to Stoneman calling attention to the possibility of turning Johnston's position by flank movement in order to salvage the little that had been gained.[82]

In order to show the extremes to which General Sherman could go in removing from his own shoulders the responsibility that was his, and in passing to the shoulders of another, in this instance Thomas, the blame for his reprehensible deed, the following will suffice:

> The assault I made was no mistake; I had to do it. The enemy and our own army and officers had settled down into the conviction that the assault of lines formed no part of my game, and the moment the enemy was found behind anything like a parapet, why everybody would deploy, throw up counter-works, and take it easy, leaving it to the "old man" to turn the position. Had the assault been made with one-fourth more vigor, mathematically, I would have put the head of George Thomas's whole army right through Johnston's deployed lines on the best ground for go-ahead, while my entire forces were well in hand on roads converging to my then object, Marietta. Had Harker and McCook

80. *Official Records, ibid.,* p. 611.
81. *Ibid.,* p. 612.
82. *Ibid.,* p. 622.

not been struck down so early, the assault would have succeeded, and then the battle would have all been in our favor on account of our superiority of numbers, position, and initiative."[83]

The content of this dispatch to General Halleck on July 9 is nothing less than a jumble of words having for their objective the glossing over an unforgivable failure. "Had the assault been made with one-fourth more vigor," Sherman reported, implying that the brave men who fought against hopeless odds, and in the face of almost certain death, might have exerted one-fourth more energy and thereby assured victory. Not a word from Sherman regarding the responsibility for giving an order against the advice of his peerless subordinate, General Thomas. Rather, the implication is clear that Sherman wanted to brand him with responsibility for the failure of the attack. Then Sherman further alibied, "Had Harker and McCook not been struck down so early, the assault would have succeeded, . . ." But this alibi is noteworthy for not placing the blame upon himself for their and their comrades' death. The morality involved in his insinuation that Thomas and the Army of the Cumberland, and also McPherson and his Army of the Tennessee, might have done better is there for all the world to judge. What more is needed to show how Sherman, in too many instances, reaped credit to which he was not entitled, although the pages of this work contain many, and far from all, similar examples? Perhaps the most incredible aspect of this series of dispatches is that a man of Sherman's rank would presume to ignore the available facts, substitute his own version, and hope that his version would be accepted. Oddly enough, the generally biased and often distorted versions relating to Sherman have been accepted by a public too little interested to concern itself with the truth.

On June 28, General Grant informed General Sherman "that the movements of your army may be made entirely independent of any desire to retain Johnston's forces where they are." With this discretionary power, which widened Sherman's latitude for offensive action, he prepared promptly to strike at Johnston's communications. In order to accomplish this, he was compelled temporarily to forego the railroad; and he decided, if his action resulted in Johnston's abandonment of Marietta, to move in upon the road to his rear; but if Johnston remained in Marietta, to strike it between him and the Chattahoochee bridge.[84]

---

83. *Ibid.*, Part 5, pp. 91-92.

84. *Ibid.*, Part 4, p. 629; Cox, *Atlanta*, pp. 124, 131-32; Van Horne, *Cumberland*, Vol. II, p. 94.

During June, considerable effort was more or less wasted by the Confederate cavalry and sympathizers in putting the railroad below Dalton out of commission. Since his supplies had been accumulated in such volume as to justify abandonment of the railroad, Sherman on July 1 ordered his armies to the right in order to turn the position he had failed to take by direct assault. General Thomas was ordered to hold the intrenchments below Kenesaw to Olley's Creek and watch enemy movements until McPherson advanced to the right to threaten Johnston's rear. McPherson advanced on July 2, and the next night Johnston withdrew his entire army, which movement was proof positive of Sherman's mistake in judgment in ordering the frontal attack on Kenesaw. General Thomas followed him with his Army of the Cumberland on the direct road to Atlanta, after having first assembled at Marietta. The Confederate rear guard was encountered about four miles from Marietta and compelled to withdraw behind its strong, previously prepared position. General Thomas promptly formed his army, and by midnight had it close to the enemy's lines. General Sherman's order to his entire army, to pursue Johnston's force across the Chattahoochee bridge, found him already secure behind his defenses. He held his position at Ruff's Station, with his left against McPherson, until Hood's and Loring's troops crossed the Chattahoochee. He then assigned Hardee to the intrenchments on the right of the river to cover the bridges. Sherman, realizing that his troops were dog-tired to the point of exhaustion, welcomed the opportunity thus afforded to rest them and replenish his supplies.[85]

The willingness of General Thomas to expose himself to risk, perhaps, more correctly, to avoid the appearance of entertaining fear for his personal safety, was in evidence several times during the campaign. On one of two such occasions, during the movement to the Chattahoochee, he accompanied other officers to the picket line to establish the force of the enemy. On the line was a log cabin, to which the officers went after securing their horses to the rear. Openings between the logs provided poor protection, and a volley from the enemy inspired all but General Thomas to dash for their horses. General Thomas walked back slowly, although a clear target for enemy bullets, stopped at a gate in the rear, faced the enemy, and walked leisurely to his horse. He would not show fear.[86]

---

85. Cox, *Atlanta*, pp. 132-133; Van Horne, *Cumberland*, pp. 95-96.
86. Van Horne, *Life*, p. 237.

CHAPTER XX

The Atlanta Campaign: From Kenesaw
to the Capture of Atlanta
and the Battle of Peachtree Creek

GENERAL Joe Johnston, believing that two Federal corps had crossed the Chattahoochee and intrenched, withdrew Hardee's corps on the night of July 9 and burned his bridges behind him. He posted his army on high ground south of Peachtree Creek to block, or at least delay, the Union Army's advance on Atlanta, until his defenses, under construction for the use of state troops, were completed between the Decatur and Marietta roads. He would then attack with his main force at the most exposed flank. He was confident that his defensive methods since the beginning of the campaign had resulted in the loss of at least five times as many casualties to his adversary than was the case; he felt that with the fortifications at Atlanta to fall back upon he could, for the first time, take the offensive against Sherman's force on a nearly equal basis. The only thing wrong with this was that Sherman's losses were not nearly so great as he believed; in truth, they were hardly greater than his own conceded losses of ten thousand killed and wounded. There was therefore little change between his fifty thousand and the one hundred thousand Sherman commanded before Resaca.[1]

Sherman's outlook, apart from his anxiety over the danger from Forrest's cavalry, although that great leader was some distance away in Mississippi, was promising as he contemplated Atlanta, his next objective. Sherman was on the move from Decatur to Opelika to sever rail communications and thereby stop shipments of supplies between Atlanta and the states west of it; and General Stoneman's

---

1. Jacob D. Cox, *Atlanta* (New York, 1882), p. 141; Thomas B. Van Horne, *History of the Army of the Cumberland* (Cincinnati, 1875), Vol. II, pp. 109-10; *Battles and Leaders of the Civil War* (New York, 1884), Vol. IV, pp. 312, 313.

cavalry force was on a mission that sought the same objective near Atlanta. General Grant, meanwhile, had reached the conclusion that delay was dangerous, in view of the possibility of the reinforcement of Johnston by twenty thousand Confederates from the Shenandoah Valley; therefore, on July 16, he ordered Sherman to begin his advance to Atlanta on the following day.[2]

General Schofield's Army of the Ohio had crossed the Chattahoochee River at Phillip's Ferry; General Howard's corps was on the south side of the river before Power's Ferry; and on the morning of July 17 General McPherson's Army of the Tennessee crossed at Roswell and continued toward the Augusta Railroad near Decatur. His travel distance was several times greater than the distance Thomas had to cover and the danger to the right flank was considerable; but the bulwark of success was the Army of the Cumberland, under its great commander General Thomas, whose task it was to hold at bay the Confederate Army. Sherman knew that he could rely upon that leader of unsurpassed courage, skill, and steadiness. General Schofield next moved toward Cross Keys, and Palmer's and Hooker's corps crossed the Chattahoochee at Pace's Ferry. General Wood's division had moved down the left side of the river and, joining the Fourth Corps, then on to Burkhead. Garrard's cavalry was with McPherson and Stoneman, and McCook guarded the river and roads below the railroad.[3]

On July 17, the armies of Sherman had executed a complete revolution or wheel to the right, with the pivot on the Fourteenth Corps under General John Palmer. The night of the seventeenth the Army of the Cumberland encamped along Nancy's Creek, a branch of Peachtree Creek, after forcing skirmishers to withdraw from along the Chattahoochee. On the eighteenth, the Army of the Cumberland advanced until Palmer's right was at the junction of Nancy's and Peachtree creeks and Howard's corps was at Buckhead. General Schofield had neared Decatur, and General McPherson had destroyed a section of the Augusta Railroad several miles east of Decatur. This operation was planned to combine the armies on September 19, either on the edge of or in Atlanta.[4]

On July 19, the Fourth Corps, General Wood's division in front, reached Peachtree Creek on the Buckhead and Atlanta road and discovered that the bridge was destroyed. Here the Confederates had constructed heavily manned fortifications on the high ground beyond

---

2. Cox, *ibid.*, p. 146; Van Horne, *ibid.*, 110.

3. Cox, *ibid.*, pp. 146-47; Van Horne, *ibid.*, p. 111; *Battles and Leaders, op. cit.*, Vol. IV, p. 313.

4. Cox, *ibid.*; Van Horne, *ibid.*; *Battles and Leaders, ibid.*

it. General Wood repaired the bridge that afternoon, crossed the stream, and dislodged the enemy. General Stanley crossed the creek at the north fork against stout opposition; and to the right General Davis's and General Geary's divisions fought their way across, with Mitchell's division supporting the action near the close of the operation. At nightfall, three of Thomas's columns had been successful in crossing Peachtree Creek, which, considering the marshy landing ground, was a major achievement. The troops on the south side of the creek dug in during the night, and early on the twentieth the remainder of the Army of the Cumberland also crossed. Sherman's basic objective now was to determine Johnston's intent regarding Atlanta. His first move to that end was to order two divisions of the Fourth Corps to close a wide interval between General Thomas's left and Schofield's right; although this move did not wholly correct the gap, it gave greater strength to the left. Following Stanley's and Wood's shift to the left, facing Atlanta, an interval of about two miles still existed between Thomas's left and Schofield's right on the Buckhead road. Thomas was in a difficult situation here, as the nature of the ground restricted movement except to the left, and that only by roundabout movements rearward.[5]

General Williams crossed Peachtree Creek and occupied an elevation beyond Geary's position and one taken by Johnson's division on the left of the Fourteenth Corps, although separated by a depression in the terrain. At ten o'clock on the morning of the twentieth, General Geary formed his division on the hill to the left of General Williams, and posted his men several hundred yards in advance of it. General Newton later formed his division on the Buckhead road, a distance of a division from Geary's left, opposite which interval Ward's division of Hooker's corps was concealed behind a hill. General Newton covered his position with rails and timber, and placed Wagner's brigade on the left of the road; Kimball's brigade was placed on the right, with a battery of four guns between them. General Geary placed Candy's brigade on the left of the road, with his battery of guns, and Jones on the right facing a wooded area, with Ireland's brigade behind Jones.[6]

Welcome news for the Union armies came with the appointment of General John B. Hood to succeed General Joe Johnston as commander of the Army of the Tennessee on July 17. Hood, although a brave soldier, was reckless and inclined to plunge headlong into battle regardless of consequences. His appointment to succeed Johnston

---

5. Cox, *ibid.*, pp. 151-63; Van Horne, *ibid.*, pp. 111, 112; *Battles and Leaders, ibid.*

6. Cox, *ibid.*, p. 154; Van Horne, *ibid.*, pp. 112, 113.

was no doubt interpreted by him as a mandate to shift from defense to offense. The change in command was no great surprise, since it was well known that the Confederate authorities and the people were restive under Johnston's Fabian policy of withdrawing before Sherman's forces. None can doubt, however, that Johnston was a wily and resourceful foe, who exploited to the utmost the disadvantage against him in numbers and material. President Davis did not like Johnston, and apparently believed that he should have been more successful in Georgia than General Lee was in Virginia, a point that Johnston did not fail to make clear to him. When it is remembered that Johnston was outnumbered by something like two to one throughout the campaign, he must be given great credit for keeping his army intact and inflicting almost equal losses on his opponent.[7]

General Johnston had planned to attack Sherman at Peachtree Creek, prior to his replacement, hoping to drive him into the creek after it had become evident to him that he could no longer postpone full-scale action. His intention was to attack Sherman's three armies and turn their flanks by breaking through the lines. He did not know that the several armies were at that time separated and most vulnerable to assault. General Hood was faced at once with the golden opportunity of striking individually the widely separated armies of the Ohio and the Tennessee from the Army of the Cumberland. This latter force had just crossed Peachtree Creek without Newton's and Geary's divisions, which extended the flanks between the forks of Peachtree; it then advanced, with its weakened left thrust forward close to the hills on which Hood's force was prepared to attack, and its right wedged between Hood's defenses and Peachtree Creek. Hood then sent some soldiers into the Union lines to report that there were no heavy Confederate troop concentrations within two miles, after recalling his skirmishers to make it appear he was making a complete withdrawal. When the Federals sent out reconnaissance forces to develop the situation on their front, and ascertained that there were no skirmishers opposing them, it seemed certain that the deception was complete. It was, although the attack, when it did come, was a complete failure.[8]

At 3 P.M. on the twentieth, the Confederates, with the advantage of surprise thus afforded, rushed from the woods. One division attacked Newton's left; one passed his left flank near Clear Creek; and another attacked his right flank. The division on his left was driven back to the woods by Newton's division, and next, the division on his

---

7. Cox, *ibid.*, pp. 148-49; Van Horne, *ibid.*, p. 113; *Battles and Leaders, op. cit.*, Vol. IV, p. 313.

8. Cox, *ibid.*, p. 155; Van Horne, *ibid.*

front was compelled by Wagner's and Kimball's brigades to withdraw with heavy losses. These two brigades then changed front at
right angles and opposed the third division. This last division advanced between Newton and Geary, in the belief that a large opening existed in the line, and faced east to oppose Newton. Ward's division moved from its concealment; and the skirmish line, comprising
the Twenty-second Wisconsin and the One hundred and thirty-sixth
New York, contained the assault until the entire division occupied a
hill to the right and rear of Newton. Ward's unexpected appearance
caused confusion in the ranks of the enemy when, with rapidly
diminishing numbers due to the concentrated fire leveled at him, he
was compelled to retreat. Ward then moved to an elevation, between
Newton and Geary, commanding some six hundred yards of open
terrain, and thus discouraged an immediate attack while he began
strengthening his position. When the attack first began on Geary's
line, the Confederates moved on him in front and rear, since Williams
was not completely aligned. When Geary was compelled to change
his front to the right and form in liaison with Williams, only five
regiments and his artillery were on his first line. Williams, hearing
firing on his left when moving his artillery to dislodge the enemy,
was compelled to deploy in haste. Knipe's brigade was placed on
the right, Robinson's on the left, and Ruger's in reserve. He then
formed his batteries to command both flanks and front, and held
three sections in reserve. Soon thereafter the Confederates attacked
with great force, after moving unobserved through the undergrowth. In
response to heavy firing on his right, Williams reinforced Knipe with
the Twenty-seventh Indiana and, with help from the Forty-sixth
Pennsylvania, the enemy was compelled to withdraw. Even stronger
attacks were made on the left, but Robinson's brigade, the batteries,
and Geary's line combined to completely repel the Confederates here
also.[9]

Although the entire Confederate line had been disclosed, it did
not succeed in reaching Palmer's Fourteenth Corps. The attack
spanned the front from Newton's front to Colonel Anson McCook's
brigade, Johnson's division, Fourteenth Corps; however, Hood,
although repulsed, did not give up. He again attacked on the same
general front by first assaulting Newton's left with a view toward
rolling it up.[10]

General Thomas used a battery of Ward's artillery, which he
personally directed against the attackers. Ward was unable to move

9. Cox, *ibid.*, pp. 155, 156; Van Horne, *ibid.*, pp. 113, 115; *Battles and
Leaders, op. cit.*, Vol. IV, p. 314.

10. Cox, *ibid.*, p. 157; Van Horne, *ibid.*, p. 115.

his guns across the ravine; but a battery that had been left near the bridge was the one used by Thomas with great damage to the enemy. Combined with Newton's guns, they again repelled the Confederates. The engagement continued until 6 P.M., when, the Union defense having been strengthened, the Confederates sullenly abandoned their effort to breach the line. Artillery, in this Battle of Peachtree Creek, was used so effectively that the Confederates did not succeed in capturing a single Federal gun.[11]

The divisions of Generals Wood and Stanley were engaged in a spirited action in which considerable artillery was used by the Confederates, during the afternoon and evening of the twentieth. Compelling enemy outposts to move back, they came within sight of the main defenses. General Stanley, after dispersing enemy pickets, crept close to the Confederate defenses. That night, the Confederates withdrew to the formidable defenses of Atlanta. General Wood advanced his right the next morning, and during July 21 the entire Army of the Cumberland moved closer to the Confederate defenses. The Fourteenth Corps fortified its position west of the railroad; the Twentieth from the railroad to the Buckhead road; and the Fourth from the Buckhead road to Schofield's right. The Army of the Cumberland was now united and in liaison. Thomas's position was such that strong batteries, capable of firing within the city of Atlanta, were mounted at convenient points outside it.[12]

In this action, four divisions and one brigade wrote an imperishable record. The Army of the Cumberland performed the major role in repelling a force that sought to begin by this attack the destruction of the three Union armies, a force, incidentally, that outnumbered them in the ratio of about five to one. Hood, as the new commander, had put his every ounce of energy into stopping Sherman's advance and saving Atlanta, but he took a terrible beating, principally at the hands of Thomas. Under advantages seldom enjoyed on a battlefield, Johnston and Hood were defeated by less than one half of the Army of the Cumberland, clearly demonstrating that Johnston's Fabian policy was more successful than an offensive one. The defeat could bring no encouragement to the Confederate cause; and if the handwriting was not seen at Chattanooga, there was no doubt of it after Peachtree Creek. General Thomas's direction of artillery, at which he was a master, was ably joined by General Hooker; and both were at crucial positions when most needed to contribute a major share to the bril-

11. Cox, *ibid.*, pp. 155, 158; Van Horne, *ibid.*, pp. 115, 116; *Battles and Leaders, op. cit.*, Vol. IV, p. 314.

12. Cox, *ibid.*, pp. 154-60; Van Horne, *ibid.*, p. 117; *Battles and Leaders, ibid.*, p. 313.

liant results. This same able direction, evident in varying degrees throughout the chain of command, inspired the troops to heroic achievement. As usual, Confederate losses are unavailable, but General Hooker's estimate of forty-four hundred in opposing his Twentieth Corps, was used by General Sherman in his *Memoirs;* and General Hood, in using Sherman's book, did not take exception to the estimate. Losses of the Army of the Cumberland were about seventeen hundred.[13]

General Hood struck the Army of the Tennessee, at about noon on July 22, as it was drawing close to Atlanta, and, although he gained an advantage at first, he was defeated with heavy losses. General James B. McPherson, commander of the Army of the Tennessee, was killed while making changes to preserve his left flank. He had ordered the trains and hospitals removed from an opening through which the Confederates were advancing, and had just received dispatches from General Blair appealing for help when, hastening to Blair's line by the road that had just been clear, he was struck. After galloping about a hundred yards along the road, he had run into Cleburne's men advancing through the opening, and when he raised his hat, as if in salute, when called upon to surrender, he turned to gallop away, and was fired upon and mortally wounded. In a short time the tide of battle turned; and the ground on which he fell was recaptured, and his body recovered before it was yet cold.[14]

On July 22 also, General Rousseau, who was on the move from Decatur to Opelika, arrived at Marietta after raiding through Alabama and Georgia and destroying thirty miles of railroad, a number of bridges, railroad facilities, and considerable supplies and material. After the raid he joined the forces closing in upon Atlanta.[15]

The Siege and Fall of Atlanta

As the forces of General Sherman undertook the siege of the citadel of Atlanta, the pattern of offense and defense remained substantially unchanged. All day on July 21 the armies of the Cumberland and of the Ohio were occupied in digging intrenchments for skirmishers very close to the defenders.

All railroads into Atlanta had been rendered useless except the

13. Cox, *ibid.,* pp. 158, 159; Van Horne, *ibid.,* pp. 115, 116.

14. Cox, *ibid.,* 168, 169; Van Horne, *ibid.,* pp. 117, 118; *Battles and Leaders, op. cit.,* Vol. IV, pp. 317, 319.

15. Van Horne, *ibid.*

one between Macon and Atlanta, and its control by Union forces would compel Hood to evacuate the city. Accordingly, General Sherman moved the Army of the Tennessee from the left to the right, in order to reach Macon from his right, and also sent five thousand cavalry under General Stoneman and four thousand under General McCook to unite at Lovejoy's Station and destroy it. After this operation, Stoneman was authorized to seek the liberation of ten thousand prisoners at Macon and twenty thousand at Andersonville. The basic purpose was to compel the Confederates to abandon Atlanta and fight or to submit to a siege.[16]

On the morning of July 27, McCook destroyed two and one-half miles of track at Palmetto Station on the West Point road. After continuing his widespread destruction of railroad property and capturing about 850 prisoners, he moved to Lovejoy's Station; but when he became surrounded at this point by rapidly assembled enemy forces that had been thwarted from reinforcing Atlanta by his damage to the railroad, he fought his way through and reached Marietta with a loss of about 500 of his own men and the 850 prisoners. Stoneman fared even worse. He was also surrounded and captured with 750 of his men, although the rest of his force escaped. The most regrettable aspect of these cavalry operations was that the Federal prisoners were not released.[17]

On July 27, General Howard succeeded General McPherson as commander of the Army of the Tennessee. His selection by-passed General Hooker, senior corps commander, and General John A. Logan, senior corps commander of the Army of the Tennessee. Hooker was senior to both Sherman and Thomas, but Sherman had little esteem for him. Sherman only recently, following Hooker's report of an action on June 22, in which Hooker expressed concern for his right flank, thus implying that Schofield had not properly supported him, had occasion to become irritated with him. Sherman decided, after investigation, that the implication was unjust to Schofield, concluding that an officer of Hooker's experience should have been above such conduct; also Sherman felt that Hooker should have performed better himself. Logan, on the other hand, although having a strong political background, had won his spurs through actual performance on the battlefield. He had a reputation, however, for finding fault with orders given him and could usually be relied upon to suggest that a different order should have been given.[18]

16. Cox, *op. cit.*, p. 182; Van Horne, *ibid.*, p. 123.

17. Van Horne, *ibid.*, p. 124.

18. Cox, *op. cit.*, pp. 178, 179; Van Horne, *ibid.*, pp. 114, 115; *Battles and Leaders, op. cit.*, Vol. IV, pp. 319, 321; Walter A. Herbert, *"Fighting Joe" Hooker* (Indianapolis, 1900), pp. 285-88.

In all of this it should not be forgotten that, although Hooker suffered perhaps the worst defeat of the Civil War at Chancellorsville, he was not helped by the Eleventh Corps under Howard. This corps, it has been shown, was caught by Stonewall Jackson's surprise attack, with guns stacked and when ready to partake of a meal, and cut to pieces. Although it is generally agreed that both Hooker and Howard were jointly responsible for the defeat, Howard, who was not with his men when the attack came, had the mistaken judgment that an attack was out of the question when there was plenty of reason for him to be on the alert. Then, too, in fairness to both, Hooker was one of the best corps commanders in the Union Army, as indicated by his consistent success throughout his career. His one mistake was Chancellorsville. Howard, on the other hand, had a record marred by failure until he joined Sherman's March to the Sea. Looking at their records, Hooker was the logical choice; and it is not surprising that he resigned in disgust at this degradation.

The Army of the Tennessee was moving to the right on July 27, and the next morning took position on the right of General Thomas's Army of the Cumberland, with its line inclining to the south. General Davis's force made a detour by way of Turner's Ferry, to Howard's right, in order to attack the Confederate flank if an attempt was made to advance. General Hood's two corps, commanded by Hardee and Lee, attacked with great force in order to disrupt the arrangement threatening them, but they were thrown back with considerable slaughter. The Army of the Cumberland was ordered to make a diverson, but General John D. Morgan of Davis's division was unable to find a direct road and did not join in the demonstration. Hood's men were sickened by the appalling losses; but he felt that his appointment to succeed Johnston demanded offensive action and that was the thing he meant to do.[19]

Reconnaissance by the Fourteenth and Twentieth Corps disclosed that Hood's lines on the right were strong, but that his left was over-extended. On July 30, the pickets of the Twentieth Corps made a bold dash to higher ground and captured a number of prisoners, while on the thirty-first, General Davis reconnoitered toward the Macon Railroad and found the enemy in earthworks about a mile from it. Considerable sparring was done by both armies during the next thirty days, in addition to which rifle pits were constructed and other defensive gestures made by Sherman's armies while being subjected to artillery and musketry fire.[20]

19. *Battles and Leaders, ibid.,* pp. 319, 320; Cox, *ibid.,* p. 183; Van Horne, *ibid.,* p. 124.

20. *Battles and Leaders, ibid.,* p. 321; Cox, *ibid.,* p. 186; Van Horne, *ibid.,* pp. 125, 126.

After Hood's third failure on the offensive he went on the defensive. Sherman once more faced the decision either to attack or try a turning movement. Hood's army at this point was still intact, despite tremendous losses, and as much out of reach as at any time since the campaign began. President Davis must have been compelled to draw upon his ingenuity to explain his order to Hood to resume the defensive after having replaced Joe Johnston for his consistently defensive posture. Nevertheless, Sherman extended his line to the right still farther in an effort to get within artillery range of the Macon Railroad and force a showdown. Thus he kept his right very strong and his whole line firm enough to threaten Atlanta from the north and prevent a build-up against his advancing right.[21]

On the morning of August 6, General Johnson's Fourteenth Corps held its own line and the line held by the Twenty-third Corps, after it shifted beyond what appeared to be the Confederate left flank. Schofield's Army of the Ohio, the Twenty-third Corps, tried to breach the Confederate line; but after being stopped by obstructions, and trying to break through at some unprotected point, he learned that Hood's lines reached beyond Utoy Creek. Schofield reported to Sherman that he could not make headway due to lack of cooperation from Palmer and his Fourtenth Corps, and following a lengthy correspondence and repeated insistence Palmer's resignation was accepted. Surprisingly, General Thomas readily accepted the resignation, as he had Hooker's resignation earlier, and more surprising still, both Hooker and Palmer thought highly of Thomas.[22] One of Palmer's possible difficulties was that, not being a West Pointer, he was resented by subordinate commanders who were, and therefore perhaps did not give him their full cooperation.

General Sherman told General Schofield on the night of August 6 that "there is no alternative but for you to continue to work on that flank with as much caution as possible, and it is possible the enemy may attack us or draw out." He told General Thomas, "Instead of going round East Point, I would prefer the enemy to weaken, so we may break through at some point, and wish you to continue to make such effort. I will instruct General Howard to do the same at the head of Utoy Creek, his right." General Thomas opposed this plan, an assault on heavily defended works, due to the heavy price in casualties it would entail and to the limited hope for success. He told Sherman, "I will keep the attention of the enemy fully occupied by threatening all along my front; but I have no hopes of breaking

---

21. *Battles and Leaders, ibid.*, p. 319; Van Horne, *ibid.*, pp. 126, 127.

22. John M. Palmer, *Personal Recollections* (Cincinnati, 1901), pp. 212-20; Van Horne, *ibid.*, pp. 128, 129.

through his lines anywhere on my front, as long as he has a respectable force to defend them. My troops are so thinned out that it will be impossible to form an assaulting column sufficiently strong to make an attack sure."[23] No better example is afforded to show the concern of Thomas for the lives of his men and the relative indifference or disregard of Sherman. This is undoubtedly what Sherman chose to regard as "slowness" on the part of Thomas. There is no doubt that Sherman, when he leveled this unfair charge, was at a point of frustration, and like a petulant boy unable to have his way, or to whom things are not to his liking, chose to blame someone else. In this case, since he did more than anyone else with his largest army, Thomas was the whipping boy or goat. The injustice is there for all who would take the time to note; Thomas was anything but slow; and Sherman was anything but a good general as proved by his record. As it has been noted with considerable pain, Thomas saved Sherman's military hide on so many occasions that the wonder of it is that Sherman, not Thomas, is the more famous.

Although the point has been referred to elsewhere, it is important to cite the letter of June 18, from Sherman to Grant, in which he said, "My chief source of trouble is with the Army of the Cumberland, which is dreadfully slow. A fresh furrow in a plowed field will stop the whole column, and all begin to intrench. I have again and again tried to impress on Thomas that we must assail and not defend; we are the offensive, and yet it seems the whole Army of the Cumberland is so habituated to be on the defensive that, from its commander down to the lowest private, I cannot get it out of their heads."[24] No sharper blade, no more cruel charge, no greater display of ingratitude has come out of the Civil War, a war that reeked of injustice, or "man's inhumanity to man," than this example of Sherman's treachery toward Thomas. Thomas bore the brunt of the campaign to Atlanta; he opposed that unpardonable mistake of drenching Kenesaw Mountain with human blood, the blood of the gallant men of Thomas's Army of the Cumberland; he obeyed his orders implicitly, although oftentimes when he knew the orders should not have been given; and he was the guiding spirit that brought the victory; yet Sherman, because he was the untruthful commander these unfair charges prove him to have been, is the national hero who broke the back of the Confederacy, when he deserves little credit for it. Thomas, none other, broke the back of the Confederacy. Reading the words of

---

23. Van Horne, *op. cit.*, Vol. II, pp. 129-30; Cox, *op. cit.*, pp. 194, 195.

24. *Official Records of the War of the Rebellion* (Washington, 1880–1901), Vol. XXXVIII, Part 4, p. 507; The Society of the Army of the Cumberland, *Yearbook 1893* (Cincinnati 1894), pp. 111, 112.

Sherman without thinking, one might get the erroneous idea that here was some modern Hannibal, or perhaps a Caesar, discussing a stumbling corporal instead of the mightiest military figure the North brought into action. Sherman was resorting to alibi and nothing else, since, if Thomas had been even slightly deserving of his vicious attack, he would have sought his replacement. This he could not have afforded, since he knew that Thomas was the best. It should not be lost sight of, however, that Sherman's falsehoods bore their share in creating animosity between Grant and Thomas, and because Grant and Sherman were buddies, whose philosophy was "All for one, one for all, that is our device,"[25] the tragedy of Thomas resulted.

This charge of Thomas's slowness had never appeared until Sherman's letter to Grant. "In every campaign, and in every battle in which he was a factor, he had shown the wise haste that is expressed in the homely proverb, 'Make haste slowly.' He was not rash or impulsive; he saved armies and the lives of his men. He first made sure that he was ready—the first duty of a great captain—and then he went ahead with such energy that all went before him."[26]

On August 7, General Schofield forced Hood to abandon the intrenchments on Hood's left, but since these were not part of his main-defense line, no added danger to his control of the Macon Railroad resulted. The Fourteenth Corps captured the rifle pits in front of the former position of the Twenty-third Corps and there constructed a line close to the enemy. Sherman continued through August 8, 9, and 10 his effort to extend his line to the right, in order to control the Macon Railroad; additionally, his heavy guns were hurling shells into the city of Atlanta night and day for the purpose of damaging machine shops and supplies vitally needed for Hood's army.[27]

It should be stated here that during the early days of August, when Sherman was anxious to destroy the railroad and prevent Hardee's forming a junction with Hood in Atlanta, he ordered Thomas to accomplish that operation. The order directed that Thomas "move early in the morning down to Jonesboro, or the enemy wherever he may be, breaking up the railroad as you move south. I do not believe anybody recognizes how important it is to destroy this railroad. Should it appear the enemy is trying to make a junction round by the east we must strike him in motion." It was apparent that this order came too late to strike the enemy in motion, since the Army of the Tennessee was no longer in danger. On the day of the order, Thomas

---

25. Alexander Dumas, *The Three Musketeers,* Chapter 9.
26. The Society, *op. cit.,* p. 112.
27. *Official Records, op. cit.,* Vol XXXVIII, Part 4, p. 507; Cox, *Atlanta,* p. 194; Van Horne, *op. cit.,* Vol. II, p. 130.

begged to be permitted to attack the enemy passing not more than two miles to his front, but the request was denied. At about 7:00 P.M., Thomas requested permission to use his Army of the Cumberland against the railroad east of Fayetteville, there to confront and hold the enemy at Jonesboro, "for, if true," reported Thomas, "that General Howard has repulsed the enemy and inflicted heavy loss upon him the move on Fayetteville would be eminently beneficial." Sherman replied at nine that night that since he had already given orders to Schofield and Stanley to move down the railroad, breaking it up, until they contacted Baird and Davis at Jonesboro, he thought it best to adhere to that plan until the enemy's game was developed, or when Sherman was between Hood and the railroad. This plan was very much like the one offered by Thomas for going through Snake Creek Gap early in the campaign and offered similar good prospects of success.[28]

General Wheeler, the great Confederate cavalry leader, sought to destroy Sherman's communications with a force of about ten thousand troopers, between August 10 and 20, and Sherman was compelled to retaliate by sending his own force against the railroad south of Atlanta. On the afternoon of the fourteenth, Wheeler began his strike, and at three o'clock in the afternoon, Steedman at Chattanooga learned that he was headed for Dalton. Steedman reached Dalton at midnight, heard that Wheeler had captured it, and awaited daylight. It was not correct, the rumor of Dalton's fall, as indicated by the sound of heavy firing proceeding therefrom, and Steedman marched at once toward the town and expelled the attackers. Continuing northward, however, Wheeler damaged slightly the railroad at Graysville, moved to the northeast, and proceeded to middle Tennessee for a union with other forces.[29] It is important to note that Sherman's communcations suffered little damage from the many forays against them.

On August 16, Sherman, realizing that he could not flank Hood from Atlanta, planned once more to disrupt his communications while awaiting the result of General Kilpatrick's raid to Fairburn. The day before, August 15, Kilpatrick had compelled General William Jackson's cavalry to leave Fairburn, after which Kilpatrick destroyed railroad facilities, telegraph lines, and the railroad proper for a distance of about twenty-three miles. On the eighteenth, with about five thousand troopers, he continued his sweep until, too hard pushed to continue, he returned to McDonough and Decatur.[30]

---

28. The Society, *op. cit.*, pp. 141, 142.
29. Van Horne, *op. cit.*, Vol. II, pp. 131, 132; Cox, *Atlanta*, p. 196.
30. Van Horne, *ibid.*, pp. 132, 133; Cox, *ibid.*, pp. 195, 196.

The Battle of Jonesboro and the Fall of Atlanta

During the several actions by Kilpatrick's cavalry, Sherman's forces continued to shell Atlanta. General Stanley resorted to feinting on his left in the hope of misleading the enemy into believing an attack would be made there. Since, however, Kilpatrick did not damage the railroads as much as hoped, General Sherman ordered his army to move by the right flank. This formidable operation would be directed against enemy communications instead of his defenses. It was feared that a direct attack on defenses would result in too many casualties, a point on which, as we have seen, General Thomas agreed.

The Fourth Corps was assigned to an elevation behind the Twentieth Corps on August 25, in order to cover the retirement of the Twentieth Corps to the far side of the Chattahoochee; to hold the railroad bridge, and the bridges at Pace's and Turner's ferries; and to protect supplies of material. On the twenty-sixth, Garrard's cavalry covered the movement of the corps rearward, and the Fourth's movement to the high ground along Utoy Creek. The Fourteenth Corps, now under General Davis, moved on the right of General Stanley at Utoy Creek during the night of the twenty-sixth. The Army of the Tennessee also moved to Sandtown during the night, leaving Schofield's Twenty-third Corps unchanged.[31]

On the twenty-seventh, the Fourth Corps moved to Mount Gilead Church and skirmished with enemy cavalry *en route*. The Fourteenth Corps remained unchanged, since it was necessary that each corps cover another until beyond reach of the enemy. In late afternoon, the Fourteenth Corps moved to its camp near Red Oak, soon followed by the Fourth, when both were in line across the West Point Railroad, facing east. Howard's Army of the Tennessee was above Fairburn, and Schofield's Twenty-third Corps was on the same road below East Point. That evening and the next day about twenty miles of railroad were destroyed. The Macon Railroad, however, from Jonesboro to Atlanta, was of greater importance as a base for strategic moves, and on August 30 the armies marched toward it in the rear of Atlanta.[32]

The Fourth and Fourteenth Corps formed a line near Couch's House, inclining to the northwest, and went into camp, although some skirmishing was done by the lead division of each corps. Here it was learned that an enemy force was at Morrow's Mill on Crooked Creek, about a mile from Stanley's left. General Thomas was in contact with General Howard's army, but not with Schofield's. Sherman ordered

---

31. Van Horne, *ibid.*, p. 140; Cox, *ibid.*, pp. 196, 197.
32. Van Horne, *ibid.*, p. 141; Cox, *ibid.*, pp. 198, 199.

Thomas to send Stanley's corps to Rough and Ready to contact Schofield, and to send a force from the Fourteenth Corps to "feel for the railroad." Baird, having been sent, reported that enemy trains were moving eastward to Jonesboro, and that Hardee's and Lee's corps had passed to that point.[33]

The leading detachment of General Baird's division reached the railroad on the afternoon of August 30, about four miles from Jonesboro, and, although far in advance of the other columns, he decided to hold it. The Fourth Corps joined the Twenty-third Corps at the railroad and established a barricaded line on the road southeast of Rough and Ready, facing Jonesboro. Other troops continued moving up, and General Howard was attacked by Hardee's and Lee's corps during the later afternoon. These activities established the general situation. Two of Hood's corps were at Jonesboro; it was uncertain as yet whether Stewart's corps had left Atlanta; but as the enemy was in strong force at Jonesboro, Sherman moved to that place with the intention of getting between Stewart and the other two corps. Assuming that Stewart would leave Atlanta, Sherman asked Thomas to direct General Slocum's Twentieth Corps to reconnoiter toward Decatur and observe enemy movements there. The stage was seemingly set for the capitulation of Atlanta, and on September 1 General Sherman ordered his entire army to move on Jonesboro.[34]

General Howard's Army of the Tennessee was already at Jonesboro; General Davis and his Fourteenth Corps formed on Howard's left; but General Schofield's Twenty-third Corps and General Stanley's Fourth Corps were much delayed due to the far greater distance required to travel and to the destroyed railroad. General Garrard's cavalry was in the rear; and General Kilpatrick's cavalry was ordered to move down the west bank of the Flint River to threaten the railroad below Jonesboro, while General Blair's corps, Army of the Tennessee, was sent in the same direction. General Davis occupied Blair's position, and at once sent General Carlin's brigade to reconnoiter the railroad on which General Stanley was moving. This brigade met strong opposition, but held on until a hill was captured beyond Moker's Creek, which permitted the enemy's defense to be attacked to advantage. General Thomas arrived on the scene and suggested a plan of action. General Davis rushed his column to the hill just captured and deployed for action. Carlin's other brigade formed on Edie's brigade, and Morgan's division formed on Carlin's right. General Baird's division was in the rear of Carlin's left at the railroad. General Stanley then formed on the left of Carlin, and Kimball's two

33. Van Horne, *ibid.*, pp. 141-42.
34. *Ibid.*, pp. 142-43; Cox, *Atlanta*, pp. 202-3.

brigades were ordered to deploy and push the enemy with vigor on the left of the railroad.[35]

Two brigades of the Fourteenth Corps and General Morgan's division were selected to make the attack. The Confederate position was in a wooded ridge, about one thousand yards distant. At 4:00 P.M. the advance, preceded by an artillery bombardment, began over rough and marshy ground. Within about four hundred yards of the enemy the line was stopped to make some needed readjustments, although only Edie's brigade, which captured part of the objective, suffered serious casualties. Baird sent Este's brigade forward to support Edie, and at five o'clock the lines advanced once more, the action then becoming general, and good progress was made. Morgan's division jumped over the fortifications to its front and captured the defenders at bayonet point.[36]

Este's brigade on the right captured the position on its front, but the left was compelled to halt before a terrible fire until reinforcements arrived. Moore's brigade on Carlin's left was held up for a time, but finally won its objective. The Fourth Corps, but for the obstacle of thick foliage and enemy skirmishers, which slowed Kimball and Newton, who did not arrive until 5:00 P.M., might have resulted in the capture of Hardee's corps. This was the most successful assault, nevertheless, of the entire campaign. More than one thousand prisoners were taken during the attack and about the same number surrendered or were captured during the night.[37]

It was too late to pursue the retreating Confederates, and the victors bivouacked in the captured defenses. Hardee withdrew to Lovejoy's Station that night, and the following morning the Confederates were pursued by all but the Fourteenth Corps, which was left to inter the dead and collect abandoned materiel. Reaching Lovejoy's Station at noon on September 2, the Fourth Corps deployed for action against an enemy occupied in fortifying a line across the railroad a mile to the north. At 3:30 P.M., General Stanley's Fourth Corps, and Howard's Army of the Tennessee joined in attacking the Confederates. Stanley, believing that Howard's force would hold the enemy and enable him to reach the Confederate right flank, advanced his center and left. The route of advance was so broken and difficult to traverse that Wood's and Kimball's divisions, Fourth Corps, did not reach the position until 6 P.M. Wood was wounded and compelled to relinquish his command, although one of his brigades won its objective but could not hold it. Kimball's command was swept by

35. Van Horne, *ibid.*, p. 143; Cox, *ibid.*, pp. 202-6.

36. Van Horne, *ibid.*, pp. 144, 145; Cox, *ibid.*, pp. 206-7.

37. Van Horne, *ibid.*, pp. 145-46; Cox, *ibid.*, p. 206.

artillery, the order to charge was revoked, and both divisions dug in. Sherman believed that it was too late to intercept Stewart's corps, retreating from Atlanta to McDonough, and that it was inadvisable to attack Hood further.[38]

During the night of September 1 the explosion of Hood's ammunition indicated his abandonment of Atlanta. General Henry Slocum, observing movements from his position at the Chattahoochee River, reconnoitered following the explosion, and when his advance neared the city on September 2 the mayor formally surrendered it. Slocum occupied the city with seven brigades shortly afterward, and found that, aside from twenty pieces of artillery and some hundreds of small arms, Hood had destroyed about everything he could not take with him, including eight locomotives and eighty-one cars of ammunition and supplies.[39]

On September 3, Sherman declared the campaign at an end, and ordered his armies to rest in Atlanta pending indications of further enemy action. Since Hood's army held intrenchments at Lovejoy's Station, Sherman's army did not occupy Atlanta at once. The Fourth Corps joined the Fourteenth Corps at Jonesboro on the morning of September 6, and on the eighth the army encamped outside the city. In summary, therefore, Atlanta was won after a series of maneuvers that did not include a large-scale engagement, although Kenesaw was quite bloody and utterly unproductive of a single benefit, while Peachtree Creek, Jonesboro, and several lesser engagements were severe enough to result in relatively large losses.[40]

Although the fall of Atlanta brought great jubilation to the North, the main objective, as in all wars, the enemy's army, was still intact. The end was not yet, nor would it be until after the soon-to-be-fought decision at Nashville, to be followed in turn by the March to the Sea, which was assured by the result at Nashville. The one thing that victory did not and could not bring was the elimination of the bitterness that brought on the struggle. Only time, and many years of it, would neutralize the intensity of feeling held by the vanquished, but nothing would completely erase it.

During the Atlanta campaign the Army of the Cumberland performed the dominant part, and naturally so, since it was considerably larger than the armies of the Ohio and the Tennessee combined. Tragically enough, these armies did not enjoy the spirit of rivalry to the exclusion of the human compulsion to appropriate complete credit to themselves and their respective commanders. This rivalry

---

38. Van Horne, *ibid.*, pp. 146-47.
39. Van Horne, *ibid.*, p. 147; Cox, *Atlanta*, pp. 204-5.
40. Van Horne, *ibid.*

rose to the surface and resulted in many claims and counterclaims, which all the effort of ensuing years could not eliminate nor in many instances fully resolve. The battles for possession of Chattanooga, when these armies were brought together for the first time, including detachments from the Army of the Potomac, undoubtedly precipitated this rivalry. It has been shown that the Army of the Cumberland indisputably rose to the heights in that campaign, to carry off the major share of the honors; and nothing better proves this fact than the charge of the Army of the Cumberland up Missionary Ridge to relieve the pressure on Sherman and his Army of the Tennessee. The Cumberlanders were out to prove that when Grant ignored them, because they were regarded as not quite adequate, and also because Sherman was to be given the honor of gaining the victory, he made one tremendous mistake, and this was proved. Not only did the Army of the Cumberland win the battle; they also won the undying animosity of the Army of the Tennessee, which was saved from defeat by the Army of the Cumberland that they despised. Some have contended that underlying this rivalry were the differences in composition of character between Sherman and Thomas. That may be correct; but Sherman was often barbed in his remarks regarding the Cumberlanders, although they were the backbone of his army in his March to the Sea. Sherman's true estimate of them is shown, however, in his selection of the famous Fourteenth Corps, which was the handiwork of Thomas, to march with him to the sea.

General James H. Wilson, perhaps the greatest cavalry leader developed by this country, delivered a most remarkable address many years after the Civil War had ended. In paying tribute to the gallant hosts on both sides of the conflict, he said this:

> And I am sure, my comrades, you will sympathize with those gallant heroes, who in so many battles measured their prowess against yours, in unavailing and unsatisfied strife, and finally laid down their arms proudly claiming that they were "outwearied rather than overcome," if they now desire before it is too late to measure not only their prowess but their patriotism and loyalty, with yours, under a common flag and against a common foe! What man of you with red blood in his veins would not like to see them once more in "battle's magnificently stern array," with muskets gleaming, sabers flashing, amidst "the cannon's opening roar," and over all the warrior's fixed determination to do or die, but this time side by side with you under the starry flag, the common emblem of Liberty and Union to every American citizen?[41]

---

41. The Society, *op. cit.*, p. 44.

Continuing, Wilson pointed out that he knew personally almost every one of the corps commanders and army commanders on both sides of the conflict, including McClellan, Grant, Sherman, Sheridan, Meade, and Thomas under whom he served. In this association he was able to study their characters and peculiarities, not only as soldiers and generals, but as men and citizens as none but a comrade could know them. His knowledge of these men was such that he could appraise them with considerable accuracy. In Wilson's own testimony to his qualifications to judge men, he cited further his knowledge of the history of other times and other lives. He remarked upon the three periods in our first hundred years' history that produced, first, Generals Washington, Greene, and Lee; second, Generals Scott, Taylor, Worth, and Wool; and third, Grant, Meade, Sherman, and Thomas. Then:

And now having said so much for the great men that all Americans love to honor, may I not emphasize the lesson I would teach, and have you teach to your sons, by dwelling awhile upon the life and character of one who, if not the most unfortunate among them, was the most modest, most steadfast, the most deserving—"the noblest Roman of them all?" Need I in the presence of his surviving comrades give him further name or description? Ah! my fellow soldiers, I see that you recognize his stalwart form, his eagle eye, his calm and lofty demeanor, his imperial presence! You know him by his heroic attributes, and so long as life lasts you can never forget him. [Cheers.]

But bear with me yet a while. He has not altogether escaped envy, jealousy and misrepresentation, which are the unconscious tribute ignoble souls offer to those above them. His motives have been questioned, his actions have been impugned, even his honors have been claimed by others, but in every case his assailants have been put to confusion and discussion has served but to exalt his character and intensify the admiration of his countrymen! In no single instance did he feel called upon to break silence or to write a word in his own behalf, but calmly and serenely he stood upon his record, confident that it would vindicate him in the end, and nobly has it justified his faith. His friends and comrades throughout the land—those who knew him best—were swift to defend his good name, to ascertain the facts and to write them into history, till now he stands spotless and alone, while those who would have injured him deny their complicity or claim that they were entrapped into the work of detraction.[42]

---

42. *Ibid.*, pp. 44-64.

One may dispute Wilson's assertion that the name of Thomas stands spotless and alone, but there is no disputing that all who knew Thomas, and they were almost without exception, other than the little group of Grant and Sherman in particular and Sheridan and Schofield, recognized him as one of the greatest of the Union generals. In all of this one wonders whether his detractors, if they could live again, would rest on the record each actually deserved, instead of the record, part of which they sought to take from Thomas, they did not deserve. The facts of the official and other records are so overwhelming that we can speculate with some confidence that the correct record, however much curtailed, would be preferable to a questionable one.

Wilson very carefully reminded his hearers that he was not saying who was the greatest, but in the following assumption he clearly showed that Thomas deserved that honor.

And who can blame him if, looking back over their past lives, he should have said to himself then or afterward, as when actually superseded in chief command by Grant at Chattanooga: "I graduated higher than this man, went into a higher branch of the service, gained greater distinction, won more brevets, led a more studious and creditable life, am a better soldier, a more rigid disciplinarian and a more successful organizer, and I am at least his equal in deserts and success as a general. If he captured Fort Henry and Fort Donelson, I won the battle of Mill Springs, and helped to save his army afterward at Shiloh. If he captured Vicksburg, I won the battle of Chickamauga and saved Chattanooga." Far be it from me to intimate that he ever did say this to any human being. I only suggest that he may have felt it, and if he did feel it, who can blame him for it? Who can blame him if he went even further in his reflections and said to himself: "I did not need this man's supervision. I not only held Chattanooga for him, but, with the Army of the Cumberland, I was mainly instrumental in winning the battle of Missionary Ridge?" Who can blame him if still later, with heightening indignation, he said to himself: "For that matter, I did not need Sherman's supervision either. I held my own and did my part throughout the Atlanta campaign, and afterward furnished forth the holiday march to the sea, with the bulk of my seasoned veterans, and the pick and choice of my transportation, while I was sent back to Nashville to organize an army from the scattered detachments of three departments with which to make head against the oncoming and valiant host that for six months had withstood the onset of a hundred thousand men?"

Who can blame him if he finally grew impatient at the repeated outcries which came from the headquarters of the armies in the East [Grant and Halleck], while with watchful and incessant care, with due deliberation and imperturbable coolness, with the consummate art of a master, he stayed the progress of the invader, gathered in his detachments, and while marching and fighting, welded them around the Fourth Corps, and the handful of cavalry which happily they had left him, into an invincible army?

Who can blame him if in the midst of all his labors, and after he had with consummate skill concentrated his forces at the great strategic center of his theater of operations, organized his army, remounted his cavalry, and completed his arrangements all within an incredibly short time, to strike a fatal blow, and was delayed from striking it only by the hand of Providence—by the rains, the inclement blasts and frosts, which covered the country with a glaze of ice over which it was impossible to move with safety, or to fight with success, he cried out after the meeting with his corps commanders on the memorable 10th of December, for the first time in his honorable life, with indignation which he would have been base to conceal, "Wilson, they treat me as though I were a boy! [This reference was to Grant and Halleck.] They do not seem to think in Washington that I know enough to plan a campaign or to fight a battle. Now, if they will let me alone, I'll show them what we can do. You know that we shall win this battle and that we shall fight as soon as it is possible!" I shall never forget his flashing eye, the firm set of his jaw, the grim determination of his countenance or the majestic attitude of his person, when he uttered those impressive words.[43]

The marvel of all this is that the foregoing is but one of many testimonials to the greatness of Thomas, although none knew him better than Wilson, and that regardless of its transparent inaccuracy the Grant Legend persists to such an extent that Grant and his stanch friend Sherman, a detractor of Thomas in his own right, are the principal authors of the downgrading of the achievements of Thomas. Those two, Grant and Sherman, as has been abundantly shown in these pages, distorted and twisted the facts, presumably for but one purpose, to hawk the lesser claims of themselves, and somewhat secondarily to withhold from Thomas what was his due, because it was their way of getting even with their real superior. Another marvel is that Thomas, under the tremendous burden of abuse, criticism,

---

43. *Ibid.*

and badgering, was able to surmount the on-the-spot difficulties and complete preparations for the most magnificent feat of arms of the entire war. What a man he was!

One famous historian of the Civil War, in discussing the mysterious hold that Grant had upon the people of the United States, said that the American people did not know him as he really was; that he had a place in the hearts of the nation he does not deserve; that it is impossible to get the American people to measure his true worth; that his own judgment, formed many years before, has been strengthened by time and the light that history has thrown on the man; and that this is not the first time a people has worshiped an idol of clay.

Henry Stone, another historian, had this to say: "The publication of the Official Records will alone afford means of learning the truth. Meantime, a whole generation has grown up, whose chief sources of information about the great events in which he [Thomas] bore so leading a part are the partial and imperfect accounts given by Grant and Sherman; Grant, misled by those to whom he entrusted the collection and arrangement of the records; Sherman by his own prejudice, and his amazing indifference to historic truthfulness."[44]

Sherman himself gives an inkling of the moral climate in which he operated when discussing the July 22 operations, the only engagement of importance during the Atlanta campaign in which the Army of the Cumberland did not perform a dominant part. It was the destiny of Sherman's old Army of the Tennessee to dominate the battle, and Sherman stated that "I rode over the whole of it [the battlefield] the next day, and it bore the marks of a bloody conflict. The enemy had retired during the night inside of Atlanta, and we remained masters of the situation outside. I purposely allowed the Army of the Tennessee to fight the battle almost unaided, save by demonstrations on the part of General Schofield and [General] Thomas against the fortified lines to their immediate fronts. and by detaching, as described, one of Schofield's brigades to Decatur, because I knew that the attacking force could only be a part of Hood's army, and that, if any assistance were rendered by either of the other armies, the Army of the Tennesse would be jealous."

Thus we have from Sherman's own pen, the *Memoirs*, that there was jealousy on the part of his old Army of the Tennessee, and that he deferred to that jealousy regardless of the consequences to the army as a whole. The reference to Grant's assignment of what both he and Sherman regarded as the choice role at Missionary Ridge, when all available evidence indicated Sherman was to obtain all the

44. Henry Stone, *Some Federal and Confederate Commanders* (Boston, 1895), p. 190.

credit and the glory, is appropriate now. Although we have seen that the plan boomeranged, and that Thomas and his men of the Army of the Cumberland were called upon to extricate both Grant and Sherman from their dilemma, the result of which was the miracle of Missionary Ridge, the proof is there for all to note that Sherman's and Grant's philosophy was to help each other, and they did, to the detriment mainly of Thomas, but of others as well. Sherman continued, "Nobly did they do their work that day, and terrible was the slaughter done to our enemy, though at sad cost to ourselves . . ."[45] Perhaps good generalship and less selfishness would have reduced the casualties he described, if he had utilized the other forces available to him.

It should not be forgotten that this tremendous campaign was fought in the main by the Army of the Cumberland, although none can withhold due credit to the other splendid men and officers of the armies of the Ohio and the Tennessee. The Army of the Ohio lost 2,909; the Army of the Tennessee lost 8,441; and the Army of the Cumberland lost 21,032, all including killed, wounded, and missing, or a grand total of 32,382. Further, the three armies took 12,984 prisoners, of which the Army of the Ohio captured 1,090; the Army of the Tennessee 3,305; and the Army of the Cumberland 8,589. Almost all of the losses in the Army of the Cumberland were wounded officers and men, and the greatest loss in the Army of the Tennessee occurred on July 22, above referred to, when they were surprised by the enemy. Every gun captured by the army was taken by the Army of the Cumberland while losing but one to the Confederates. Every assault made on the defenses of the enemy was made by the Army of the Cumberland, except that by the Army of the Ohio at Resaca, two divisions only; the minor assault at Resaca by one of General Logan's divisions of the Army of the Tennessee; and the relatively light assault by another division of the Army of the Tennessee at Kenesaw Mountain.[46]

Although General Thomas did not remain long in Atlanta after its capture, it is interesting to learn that one of his former subordinates, Horace Porter, made a pleasant visit to him in his quarters at the Leyden House on Peachtree Street. This house was surrounded by a broad porch supported by fluted columns, on which the friends evidently held their conversation. Among other things discussed was the Chickamauga campaign, and this recalled to General Thomas an amusing incident concerning a mule. The General, in referring to it,

45. William T. Sherman, *The Memoirs of General William T. Sherman* (New York, 1891), Vol. II, p. 82.

46. The Society, *op. cit.*, p. 148.

asked, "Do you remember that jackass that looked over the fence one day when we were passing along a road near the Tennessee River? He pricked up his ears and brayed until he threatened to deafen everybody within a mile of him; and when he stopped, and a dead silence followed, a soldier quietly remarked, 'Boys, did you hear him purr?' I thought that was about the loudest specimen of a purr I had ever heard." Then Thomas lay back in his chair and shook with laughter at the recollection, a reaction that demonstrated he was more full of fun than was generally believed. Porter told also how, at Murfreesboro a year earlier, a piano was obtained and musical entertainment was had at general headquarters during the evening. Thomas was a regular attendant at these meetings, at which songs were sung and during which he would beat time to the music with his foot. When amusing songs were sung or other incidents occurred, Thomas would laugh heartily.[47]

One of the contributing factors in the success of General Thomas throughout his military career was his highly developed intelligence service. It has been seen that his scouts obtained information concerning movements of the Confederates, particularly during Bragg's invasion of Kentucky, when Thomas was often enabled to diagnose enemy movements and make strong recommendations to General Buell. Buell must have wondered, although he had an intelligence service of his own, how his able second in command was able to make such accurate suggestions concerning General Bragg's movements, at a time when he, Buell, was uncertain of his own moves to counteract them. In the Atlanta campaign General Joe Johnston must also have been in a quandary at the frequency with which his movements were counteracted by Thomas. There is not the slightest doubt that Thomas had a highly developed instinct for self-preservation, and that he utilized every known technique or means to insure the safety of his army. This has been shown in the instances in which he was always able to offer adequate defense to counteract any unexpected development; also, let it be emphasized that he was just as alert to insure that he could throw whatever force was necessary to turn the tide in favor of his superiors when needed on the offensive, as, for example, at Stones River and Chattanooga.

Both General Grant and General Sherman relied upon the knowledge furnished by Thomas; in fact, Thomas briefed each of them regarding his information, and they were able to place great reliance upon it. Through his policy of establishing relay signal stations at regular intervals, he was able to transmit information for the use of his

47. Horace Porter, *Campaigning With Grant* (New York, 1897), p. 295.

advancing infantry. These stations enabled his men to observe enemy movements at a considerable distance and to relay them through the several stations to the ultimate users. Through his scouts, loyal informants, and deserters he obtained much valuable information that enabled him to know pretty much what was going on. His success in averting surprise attacks is proof positive that he knew generally what his enemy was doing. Then there were fast couriers, and of course the telegraph, which he employed to the utmost in deriving intelligence of his enemies.

General Don Carlos Buell, although he retained agents, relied greatly upon the advice and suggestions of Thomas, which were generally more reliable than his own. It is well established that General Buell approved statements of expenditures from his agent for such items as the purchase of horses; the acquisition of forage for horses; regular salary to the agent during his period of service; travel expenses to and from Paducah, Louisville, and Cincinnati; alcohol and related shipping costs; advance money for the purchase of a horse in the South, including other expenses that may be incurred by six men; and purchase of revolvers, also five horses, presumably enough to outfit all six men, the other horse to be purchased in the South, as noted. A minister was to receive $210 for helping to organize two expeditions to blow up two bridges; and the agent agreed to pay each man performing the destruction of the railroad bridge on which the Charleston and Memphis Railroad crosses the Tennessee River at Decatur, Alabama, the sum of $3,000 each, or $12,000. The destruction was to be accomplished by fire or other means, and one or more spans falling into the water would be assurance of their success. The destruction of the Bridgeport bridge, for whatever reason, would be accomplished at just half the price of the Decatur bridge, or $6,000. Although this agent knew General Thomas, as indicated by the correspondence, there is nothing thus far disclosed to show that there was any relationship between them. It is not at all surprising, however, that the agent wrote of Thomas in such a way as to suggest he had great respect for him.[48]

It is not surprising to learn that General Thomas's scouts were reported in the Shenandoah Valley, a clear indication that he was observing the movements of Sheridan's and Grant's forces in the absence of cordial relations with those commanders.[49]

In the campaign just closed, although little is generally known of the great contribution General Thomas made toward its success, we

48. The Buell Papers (at Rice University, Houston, Texas).
49. *Official Records, op. cit.*, Vol. XLVI, Part 2, p. 894.

have seen that he and his men accomplished the major feats of arms that brought victory. It is correct and, in fact, imperative to state that General Thomas rendered no decision or approval that ended in failure, nor did he reject any plan that resulted in success. Whenever he advised and such advice was not accepted, his judgment was vindicated by the outcome; and in every case the result proved that his plan would have succeeded.

CHAPTER XXI

From Atlanta to Franklin

WHEN Atlanta fell into Federal hands, it did not mean that the war
was rapidly coming to an end, or that it was necessarily the beginning
of the end. As events soon disclosed, however, it was a great stride
forward, particularly because of the impact on Confederate resources
and manpower. In other words, it was the whittling away of assets
tangible and intangible, including confidence and morale, especially
at this time, rather than a defeat on the battlefield, that offered a
clue as to the final outcome. Of course it is true that as Confederate
confidence fell the opposite effect occurred in the North. Nevertheless, the Confederate Army was still intact and presented a real danger
in the West. Atlanta itself did not possess the strategic importance
of Chattanooga, for example, although it did have considerable importance as a manufacturing center for war materiel for the Confederate armies. It was far removed from Sherman's base of supplies,
and any contemplated aggressive action southward from that city
meant the abandonment of his northern supply center. It could be
said that on the whole the chief benefit from its capture was the de-
pressing effect it produced upon the Southern people. After all, here
was an enemy army in the very heart of the South, from which location that enemy could spread itself in other directions and take over
still more of the Southern states.

The next problem for the Union military authorities was the utilization of the armies to make further inroads on the Confederacy, with
a view toward bringing hostilities to a speedy end. The Confederate
authorities realized that their people were beginning to lose confidence, if they had not already lost it. With this in mind, the Confederate strategists sought to concentrate all available troops for a
master stroke against General Sherman and his communications. General Hood was charged with this responsibility; and to aid him in the
effort all available troops along the Mississippi were to be transferred
to his command. Underlying this move was the hope that sufficient

strength could be mustered from new recruits and from deserters returning to the fold for a supreme attempt at recovering much, if not all, of the lost ground. Some of the Confederate leaders, notably General Beauregard, had suggested earlier that the large Southern cities be evacuated, so that a great army might be assembled for an advance into the North. It is not understood how this operation would be helped by abandonment of the cities. This would be perhaps the last full-scale opportunity for settling the war and, at worst, obtaining independence, quite apart from the further objective of bringing to the North some of the realities of war. Beauregard had attempted previously to cross to the eastern side of the Mississippi, but had been deterred by General Edward R. S. Canby and his Army of the Gulf.[1] This latest plan was intended, therefore, to bring to Northern cities the devastation visited upon Southern cities, and, in addition, to replenish the meager supplies of the Confederacy. This, in effect, was the responsibility of General Hood to accomplish, but it would end in failure at the Battle of Nashville.

Uppermost in the minds of Confederate authorities was the quick reversal of discouragement among their people; to substitute for the prolonged stature of defense, with all its uncertainties about where the aggressor would strike next, a position of offense that would give them the choice of action. The South by now was a nation of depleted manpower, due in great measure to the exacting toll of the battlefield, including not only the dead but the living, who were unable to sustain themselves independently. To add to this manpower loss was the reduced economic opportunity brought in war's wake, which would increase the difficulties of those still able to work. In all of this reposed one dominant factor; these were Southerners, indeed Americans, fighting for what they believed was right, to whom the word "surrender" was unthinkable. The outlook for them, grim as it appeared to others, would not swerve them from their purpose to fight to the bitter end; and that is what they did. Even Grant at Appomattox did not defeat his adversary on the battlefield, or in one dramatic feat of arms. This was accomplished by attrition, and only after Lee's army was so reduced in numbers and supplies that fighting was no longer possible; but was Lee's army compelled to capitulate in open battle? Never! It is little wonder that the actors and the actions in this mighty drama have a grip upon the imagination of succeeding generations, a grip that grows and will continue to grow until courage and love of country cease to be.

Generals Grant and Sherman were thinking of extending their

---

1. Thomas B. Van Horne, *The Life of Major General George H. Thomas* (New York, 1882), p. 251.

gains beyond Atlanta while the Confederate plan for a Northern invasion was being developed. General Hood began his offensive action in late September by striking at Sherman's communications in Georgia, while General Forrest sought to break his communications in Tennessee. Meanwhile, General Sherman's army had become somewhat reduced temporarily, due to the numerous furloughs of men and officers to visit their families, so that this offensive activity by the Confederates was not entirely welcomed. In late September, Sherman sent General Newton's division of the Fourth Corps and General Morgan's of the Fourteenth Corps to Tennessee to oppose Forrest. General Forrest had been driven to the west by Generals Granger, Rousseau, and Steedman, thus rendering the other two divisions unnecessary for that purpose; however, they did supplement the force being built up to oppose Hood's army, and they did stand ready to preserve Sherman's communications. In these movements the initial steps were taken leading to the never-to-be-forgotten campaign of Thomas, which ended in the destruction of Hood's army, an event that was not foreseeable at that time.[2]

The threat to Northern communications was of sufficient importance to suggest to Sherman the wisdom of ordering Thomas back to Chattanooga. About the time he arrived there, on September 29, his telegraphic communications with Sherman were broken and the situation in Georgia was clouded. On September 30, Hood crossed the Chattahoochee and spread his wings to embrace the capture of Ackworth, Big Shanty, Dalton, and Tilton, familiar names in Sherman's march to Atlanta; he also spread considerable alarm, which prompted Sherman to take up the chase by ordering five corps to intercept him. This left one corps at Atlanta. Thomas, at Chattanooga, did not have enough men in Tennessee to cope with the enemy, certainly not enough to do more than slow him down. In this dilemma, which was a completely unanticipated occurrence, the Washington authorities sent troops from the North to Thomas, but not many. They did send plenty of suggestions, an always plentiful and seemingly inexhaustible supply, in fact, which had no value as a substitute for needed troops.[3]

A salty exchange of correspondence developed between Generals Hood and Sherman just before Sherman's occupation of Atlanta. On September 7, Sherman notified Hood that in the interest of the United States the citizens of the city should be removed, and that those desiring to go north and those desiring to go south be permitted to go whichever way they preferred. He offered to furnish necessary

---

2. Jacob D. Cox, *Atlanta* (New York, 1882), pp. 222, 223.
3. Van Horne, *op. cit.*, p. 253.

transportation and food for those desiring to go north, and for those going south he offered transportation by cars and wagons as far as Rough and Ready, including their clothing, furnishings, and other needed effects. Sherman pointed out as the basis for his letter that Atlanta was no place for women and children, and that he had no desire to send any of them north if Hood would assist in sending them south.[4] Hood's reply was prompt, and with considerable emphasis, citing his lack of an alternative, he accepted the offer. He did not fail to state his attitude in the following paragraphs:

> And now, sir, permit me to say that the unprecedented measure you propose transcends, in studied and ingenious cruelty, all acts ever brought to my attention in the dark history of war.
>
> In the name of God and humanity I protest, believing that you will find that you are expelling from their homes and firesides the wives and children of a brave people.[5]

Sherman's reply of the tenth was highlighted by these comments on Hood's letter:

> You style the measures proposed "unprecedented," and appeal to the dark history of war for a parallel, as an act of "studied and ingenious cruelty." It is not unprecedented; for General Johnston himself very wisely and properly removed the families all the way from Dalton down, and I see no reason why Atlanta should be excepted. Nor is it necessary to appeal to the dark history of war, when recent and modern examples are so handy. You yourself burned dwelling-houses along your parapet, and I have seen to-day fifty houses that you have rendered uninhabitable because they stood in the way of your forts and men. You defended Atlanta on a line so close to town that every cannon-shot and many musket-shots from our line of investment, that overshot their mark, went into the habitations of women and children. . . .
>
> I say that it is kindness to these families of Atlanta to remove them now, at once, from scenes that women and children should not be exposed to. . . .
>
> In the name of common sense, I ask you not to appeal to a just God in such a sacrilegious manner. You who, in the midst of peace and prosperity, have plunged a nation into war—dark and cruel war—who dared and badgered us to battle, insulted our

---

4. *Official Records of the War of the Rebellion* (Washington, 1880–1901), Vol. XXXIX, Part 2, pp. 414-15.

5. *Ibid.*, p. 415.

flag, seized our arsenals and forts that were left in the honorable custody of peaceful ordnance-sergeants, seized and made "prisoners of war" the very garrisons sent to protect your people against Negroes and Indians, long before any overt act was committed by the (to you) hated Lincoln Government; tried to force Kentucky and Missouri into rebellion . . . ; turned loose your privateers to plunder unarmed ships; expelled Union families by the thousands, burned their houses, and declared, by an act of your Congress, the confiscation of all debts due Northern men for goods had and received! Talk thus to the marines, not to me, who have seen these things, and who will this day make as much sacrifice for the peace and honor of the South as the best-born Southerner among you! If we must be enemies, let us be men, and fight it out as we propose to do, and not deal in such hypocritical appeals to God and humanity. God will judge us in due time, and he will pronounce whether it be more humane to fight with a town full of people at our back, or to remove them. . . ."[6]

Hood's reply of the twelfth simply prolonged, but did not settle, the issue, as, of course, nothing could but the resort to arms. In addition to the exchange between Hood and Sherman, the mayor and two city councilmen submitted a letter to Sherman in which they cited specific instances of suffering and the inconvenience to which his executed order would further subject them, but Sherman was adamant in his stand and would not revoke his original order.[7]

When General Grant was informed that Hood had recaptured Dalton and had continued to Lafayette, he assumed that his objective was Chattanooga. He advised Thomas to withdraw his garrisons from the railroad between Columbus and Decatur. Thomas, however, most immediately concerned, did not share Grant's view; rather, he believed Hood would skirt around that city, choosing to avoid fortifications and their risk of high casualties in favor of the more promising advance through northern Georgia. He had high hopes of inspiring the citizens and his troops to a renewed interest in the war, and to eventually meet Sherman in a general engagement; in this latter hope, however, he was to meet disappointment. Thomas sent Schofield with Newton's and Morgan's divisions to check Hood in his expected move from Lafayette. Later, when he moved as though to attack Bridgeport, Thomas directed Schofield to advance to Caperton's Ferry, a move that Sherman frowned upon. Nevertheless, Hood's objective was Gunter's Landing, where he hoped to cross the Tennessee River, capture

6. *Ibid.*, p. 416.
7. *Ibid.*, pp. 417-19.

Bridgeport and Stevenson, and defeat Thomas, a large assignment, which no one succeeded in doing throughout the war, then head for Kentucky by way of Nashville. If Hood had completed his plan, the garrison at Caperton's would have been subject to capture and Thomas's instructions to Schofield would have been correct. Sherman, on October 17, wired Schofield that he should not move on Caperton's, that his original instruction to move to Lookout Valley was correct, and that General Thomas should be informed of Sherman's views. Of course, the movement was wasted, but only because Hood changed his plans. Before he reached Gunter's Landing, Hood discovered that Forrest would be unable to join him for a march on Nashville, and he decided to go on to Decatur.[8]

While Hood was on his expedition he sent the following communication to the commander at Resaca: "Sir: I demand the immediate and unconditional surrender of the post and garrison under your command, and, should this be acceded to, all white officers and soldiers will be paroled in a few days. If the place is carried by assault, no prisoners will be taken." This surprising demand was answered by the commander, Colonel James B. Weaver, in part as follows: "Your communication of this date [October 12] just received. In reply, I have to state that I am somewhat surprised at the concluding paragraph, to the effect that, if the place is carried by assault, no prisoners will be taken. In my opinion I can hold this post. If you want it, come and take it." Hood was undoubtedly bluffing, since he made no serious attempt to take it. His losses previously apparently discouraged him from making the attempt.[9]

While on the subject of cruelty, it would be remiss not to mention that before Sherman's march through the Carolinas, when Columbia was burned, and concerning which there has been much controversy whether the Union or Confederate troops fired it, the following exchange, herewith in part only, took place between Generals Halleck and Sherman:

Halleck's communication of December 18 to Sherman: "Should you capture Charleston, I hope that by some accident the place may be destroyed, and, if a little salt should be sown upon its site, it may prevent the growth of future crops of nullification and secession."

Sherman's reply of the twentieth, also in part, contained this reference to Halleck's comment regarding Charleston: "I attach more importance to these deep incisions into the enemy's country, because

---

8. John B. Hood, *Advance and Retreat* (New Orleans, 1880), pp. 266-67; Van Horne, *op. cit.*, pp. 253-54.

9. William T. Sherman, *The Memoirs of General William T. Sherman* (New York, 1891), Vol. II, pp. 154-55.

this war differs from European wars in this particular: we are not only fighting hostile armies, but a hostile people, and must make old and young, rich and poor, feel the hard hand of war, as well as their organized armies. I know that this recent movement of mine through Georgia has had a wonderful effect in this respect. Thousands who had been deceived by their lying newspapers to believe that we were being whipped all the time now realize the truth, and have no appetite for a repetition of the same experience. To be sure, Jeff. Davis has his people under pretty good discipline, but I think faith in him is much shaken in Georgia, and before we have done with her South Carolina will not be quite so tempestuous.

"I will bear in mind your hint as to Charleston, and do not think 'salt' will be necessary. When I move, the Fifteenth Corps will be on the right of the right wing, and their position will naturally bring them into Charleston first; and, if you have watched the history of that corps, you will have remarked that they generally do their work pretty well. The truth is, the whole army is burning with an insatiable desire to wreak vengeance upon South Carolina. I almost tremble at her fate, but feel that she deserves all that seems in store for her.

"I look upon Columbia as quite as bad as Charleston, and I doubt if we shall spare the public buildings there as we did at Milledgeville."[10]

The important point here is not whether Sherman authorized the burning of Columbia as a necessary act of war, or whether the Confederates burned it to prevent supplies from falling into Union hands, or for whatever reason. The entire incident has been repeatedly denied by both sides; but why Sherman would express his attitude toward its destruction by proclaiming the effectiveness of his Fifteenth Corps in that kind of work and then falsify his report regarding it is beyond logical reasoning. Later, in the *Memoirs*, Sherman said that "In my official report of this conflagration, I distinctly charged it to General Wade Hampton, and confess I did so pointedly, to shake the faith of his people in him, for he was in my opinion boastful, and professed to be the special champion of South Carolina." Sherman also stated that a number of investigative groups had sought to assign responsibility for Columbia's destruction, one of which settled the point, in effect, namely, that its destruction "did not result from the acts of the General Government of the United States—that is to say, from my army."[11] If Sherman burned Columbia, and his *Memoirs* indicate that such was his intention, why was he not man enough to admit it? In

10. *Ibid.*, pp. 222-28; Thomas B. Van Horne, *History of the Army of the Cumberland* (Cincinnati, 1875), Vol. II, pp. 304-5.

11. *Ibid.*, p. 287.

any event, Halleck's letter, cited above, planted the idea in Sherman's mind if it was not there before.

General Hood threatened Decatur on October 26, a move he termed a "slight demonstration" to cover the advance of his troops toward the West. But for the fact that Thomas had retained a garrison there, regardless of Grant's advice to withdraw it, Hood would have gained control of the Tennessee River at Decatur. As it transpired, Thomas was enabled to send reinforcements from Chattanooga and forestall Hood's plan there, an excellent illustration of his ability to anticipate and counter the moves of his enemy. Perhaps his famed intelligence service was functioning at its usual high standard, and he was making his moves on the basis of fact and not intuition. In any case, Hood decided that Decatur was too formidable for him and proceeded toward Tuscumbia for reinforcements. There he established a supply line to Corinth and completed plans for entering Tennessee. This placed him close to Nashville and to his supplies at Corinth, and, what was equally important, his reinforcements from Mississippi were more accessible to him there than was the case at the beginning of the campaign.[12]

After many attempts by Sherman to obtain Grant's permission to turn his back on Hood and march with his armies of the Cumberland, the Ohio, and the Tennessee to the Atlantic, it was granted on November 2. Grant had wondered only the day before whether, since Hood had advanced so far north, it would not be well to first dispose of him before undertaking his march, since with him out of the way "you can go where you please with impunity. If you can see the chance for destroying Hood's army, attend to that first and make your other move secondary." Still, when he authorized the movement the next day, he said, "I really do not see that you can withdraw from where you are to follow Hood without giving up all we have gained in territory. I say, then, go on as you propose." It is important to note that the authorization was given by Grant after duly noting that "With the force, however, that you have left with General Thomas, he must be able to take care of Hood and destroy him."[13] It passes understanding that Grant would run the somewhat needless risk of losing the territory already won by hard fighting in permitting Sherman to march to the sea. It is well to note that during Sherman's march he avoided fortified positions and adhered mainly to convenient routes of travel. All the more surprising is the fact that both Grant and Sherman were surely aware that Confederate plans comprehended the assembling of a large force for the invasion of the North, including the force from

12 Van Horne, *Life*, pp. 254-55.

13. *Ibid.*, p. 255; Sherman, *op. cit.*, Vol. II, p. 166.

Mississippi. It was Sherman's idea to even reduce the force holding this trans-Mississippi force in check.[14]

The March to the Sea was begun at a time when Hood's army was farther north than it was before the beginning of the Atlanta campaign in May, 1864, but also when it would relinquish more of Georgia than was gained during that campaign. Sherman did not contend that the march was purely military or strategic; rather, it was to prove, in his words, "the vulnerability of the South." He stated to Grant that on the basis that General Thomas can hold the line of the Tennessee and assume the offensive as against Beauregard, it was his purpose to so act against the material resources of the South as to negate Davis's boasted threats and promises of protection. Further, "if we can march a well appointed army right through this territory, it is a demonstration to the world, foreign and domestic, that we have a power which Davis cannot resist."[15] Sherman also said, "I considered this march as a means to an end, and not as an essential act of war. . . ."[16]

General Thomas was strongly opposed to Sherman's moving with his entire field forces to the Atlantic, once General Hood established himself at Florence, Alabama. He also expressed his opposition to being left behind with inferior and inadequate manpower. He made a proposal to General Sherman shortly after the fall of Atlanta on the basis that, since Sherman had no further use for him, he be permitted to "take my little command and go eastward to the sea." Sherman's answer was that he could not approve without first discussing the matter with General Grant, which he promised to do while making repairs to the army, but Thomas heard nothing more concerning it until "his little army was ordered to face Hood—the only effective organization in the southwest—while Sherman took his army to encounter the Georgia militia under Cobb." On October 17, Thomas had telephoned to Sherman to express the hope that he would "adopt Grant's idea of turning Wilson loose, rather than undertake the plan of a march, with the whole force through Georgia to the sea, inasmuch as General Grant cannot cooperate with you as at first arranged." This latter statement referred, apparently, to a plan of cooperation discussed by Grant and Sherman at a point in Georgia or South Carolina. When that plan was considered, Sherman stated, "Hood is not going to enter Tennessee"; in fact, he had made no promise of troops for the defense of that state.[17]

On October 18, Thomas wired Sherman that he was prepared to

---

14. Van Horne, *Life,* p. 260.
15. *Ibid.,* p. 257.
16. Sherman, *op. cit.,* Vol. II, p. 220.
17. Van Horne, *Life,* pp. 255-56.

carry out his instructions, should Hood enter Tennessee, and that General Wilson would carry a duplicate of his views on Sherman's plan of operations. One thing Thomas emphasized was "that he did not wish—to be left in command of the defense of Tennessee, unless Sherman and the Washington authorities deem it necessary."[18] Well, the Washington authorities did deem it necessary; and no matter what Grant and Sherman may have had in mind when they left him to face Hood, the fact is inescapable, regardless of the bitter correspondence between Grant and Thomas later, that they reposed supreme confidence in his ability to handle Hood, and the confidence was not misplaced. In order to bring the actual situation into focus, it is imperative that Sherman's campaign be recognized in its correct relation to the assignment of Thomas to hold Hood in check. Foremost in both Grant's and Sherman's minds was that their reputations were on the line; in short, if anything went wrong with Thomas in Tennessee, that is, if he was cuffed by Hood, the March to the Sea would show them both to be stupid for leaving Thomas alone to fight it out with him. Their many moments of anxiety, as revealed through the correspondence between Grant and Sherman during the march, but more especially Grant's jitters before Nashville was fought, were proof positive that everything depended upon Thomas back in Tennessee. Hood's defeat not only would relieve Sherman and Grant of anxiety, but would also put the completion of the war right on General Grant's doormat. If Sherman had been compelled to return from his campaign, Thomas would not have been in the least affected in Tennessee, the exact opposite of what would have occurred if Thomas had been defeated.

Sherman took with him the cream, the very best troops, almost, but not quite, without exception, to engage in a jamboree, a virtually bloodless campaign to the sea, leaving Thomas to face Hood's army, which he, Sherman, had been unable to bring into action.

The number of troops left to Thomas with which to face Hood, not including those scattered throughout the states of Alabama and Tennessee, aggregated about twenty-five thousand. Van Horne estimated that there were about twenty-two thousand infantry and about forty-three hundred cavalry, or more than twenty-six thousand. Sherman estimated his own force as fifty thousand. Important to a consideration of the number was the quality of troops left to Thomas. Aside from the Fourth Corps, which Sherman regarded highly, Thomas had little to brag about. Of course, he had a nucleus in Wilson's cavalry, which had to be greatly increased before he could do battle with Hood, and Schofield's Twenty-third Corps, which, although satisfac-

18. *Ibid.*, p. 256.

tory, was not in any sense the equal of the Fourteenth and Twentieth Corps of Thomas's Army of the Cumberland that Sherman took along with the Fifteenth and Seventeenth Corps.[19] The biggest disappointment in this assignment of troops was that Thomas was left without his famous Fourteenth Corps. By every moral right this corps should have gone to Thomas, since he had been the organizer and commander of the first brigade; afterward he commanded the division that included that brigade; the corps that included the First Division; and finally the Army of the Cumberland, which included the Fourteenth Corps. He would understandably have a deep attachment for this corps, perhaps the finest in the Federal service, since it had more to do with his fame as a military leader than any other organization. Thomas has been credited with maintaining that he organized his men into a fighting unit and that they were responsible for his success.

Sherman clothed Thomas with complete authority, as early as October 26, to command troops not in the presence of himself. On October 23 he wrote to Thomas, "I believe you are the man best qualified to manage the affairs of Tennessee and North Mississippi. I can spare you the Fourth Corps and about five thousand men not fit for my purpose, but which will be well enough for garrison duty in Chattanooga, Murfreesboro and Nashville. What you need is [sic] a few points fortified and stocked with provisions, and a good movable column of twenty-five thousand men that can strike in any direction."[20] This instruction is important in demonstrating, by Sherman's own admission, that about five thousand men were not fit for his purpose, meaning of course that they were actually far less fit for Thomas, who must fight battles with the only formidable Confederate force while Sherman was undertaking his much less exacting campaign. The Twenty-third Corps under Schofield was given to Thomas as perhaps an afterthought, but in the light of Schofield's well-documented venom toward his superior in command, his former instructor at West Point, it would have been infinitely more desirable if he had remained with Sherman. The full story of Schofield will be given later in this work; but it is very probable that Sherman, who could mix with the best in rough-and-tumble, would have been able to handle him. On the other hand, perhaps such difficulty would not have been met by Sherman, because Schofield would have been smart enough to know that he could not wedge himself between Grant and Sherman, as he has been accused of doing with respect to Thomas.

19. Van Horne, *Cumberland*, Vol. II, pp. 183, 186; Richard W. Johnson, *Memoir of Major General George H. Thomas* (Philadelphia, 1881), pp. 175-76; Van Horne, *Life, op. cit.*, pp. 260-61.

20. *Official Records, op. cit.*, Vol. XLV, Part 2, pp. 56, 71, 85.

In his dilemma, brought about by his inferior numbers and the considerable percentage of troops whose enlistments approached expiration, Thomas asked for and received some men from General Rosecrans in Missouri. These, with some additions from recruitment and from other sources, increased his effective infantry strength to some thirty-two thousand men. His troops were so thinly dispersed that he was unable seriously to interfere with one of General Forrest's most successful raids. Before the Fourth and Twenty-third Corps were sent to Thomas, Hood was in possession of the line at Florence, the line regarding which Sherman, in his dispatch to Thomas on October 19, stated, "If you can defend the line of the Tennessee in my absence of three months, it is all I ask." All that he asked was quite an order. The Fourth Corps reached Chattanooga on October 29, and was dispatched at once to Athens, Alabama, after Hood had made a crossing of the Tennessee River. On that same day Thomas asked for the aid of gunboats to cooperate by going up the Tennessee River to obstruct and, if possible, prevent further movement across the river at that point. Schofield arrived at Nashville on November 5 with the advance of his Twenty-third Corps, and his entire force was sent to Johnsonville at once to oppose Forrest's cavalry, some sixty-odd miles to the west of Nashville. He reached there as soon as possible, but Forrest, having already come and gone, a characteristic for which he was famous, Schofield was ordered to leave a force there and join the Fourth Corps at Pulaski, Tennessee, as originally directed, and assume full command.[21]

General Thomas was under no misapprehension concerning his ability to prevent Hood's crossing the Tennessee, and that his defense of the river west of Stevenson was contingent upon the prompt receipt of promised reinforcements. He could not get the desired help from the gunboats due to the shallow depth of the river, and his best hope was that he could slow Hood enough before he could concentrate for a decisive battle. His strategy was to place the Fourth and Twenty-third Corps in the way of Hood's forward movement and to utilize his cavalry well in advance of his own forces. Thomas had the further anxiety of not knowing whether Hood would make a turning movement toward Huntsville, Alabama; he could not, therefore, withdraw his troops from Decatur, Alabama, and from the Nashville and Chattanooga Railroad. He did, in the circumstances, move all available troops from Chattanooga to that railroad at Stevenson, and awaited events.[22]

In late October, Sherman had urged upon Thomas the necessity

21. Van Horne, *Life*, pp. 263-65.
22. *Ibid.*, pp. 265-66.

for holding Decatur, inasmuch as its possession would aid in co-operation between gunboats on the Tennessee River and the land forces. A little later, November 12, telegraphic communication was destroyed between Sherman and Thomas by enemy action; but the principal highlights of their exchange of communications on the eleventh are important in connection with the events that followed. On that date, Thomas informed Sherman that prisoners reported two Confederate corps had crossed the Tennessee River and one still remained on the other or southern bank; also that their troops were in great need of clothing, particularly shoes, although they were hoping for replenishment of these supplies. They also reported that the railroad was repaired to Cherokee, some fifteen miles from Tuscumbia, Alabama, that they were fortifying, presumably meaning Cherokee, and that rumors were that they were contemplating an advance on Nashville. Thomas advised additionally that General Stanley reported the water still very high at Pulaski, Tennessee, which might carry away the enemy's pontoon bridge. He reported also that deserters alleged that Georgia troops were deserting out of disgust with events, and that there were not many enemy troops at Corinth, but that Beauregard apparently intended making that place his base, judging from the stream of supplies being sent there on the Mobile and Ohio Railroad. Finally, Thomas reported that General A. J. Smith's reinforcements had not yet arrived, although expected daily.[23]

General Sherman's reply expressed disbelief that Beauregard would move against Nashville from Corinth as a base at that late stage of the war, but offered the comment, "If he does you will whip him out of his boots. But I think you will find commotion in his camp in a day or two. Last night we burned Rome, and in two days more will burn Atlanta, and he must discover that I am not retreating, but on the contrary, fighting for the very heart of Georgia." He said further, "About a division of rebel cavalry made its appearance this morning south of the Coosa River, opposite Rome, and fired on the rear-guard as it withdrew. Also two days ago some of Iverson's cavalry—about eight hundred—approached Atlanta from the direction of Decatur, with a section of guns and swept around toward Whitehall and disappeared in the direction of Rough and Ready. These also seem to indicate that Beauregard expected us to retreat. . . . Tomorrow I begin the movement laid down in my Special Order No. 115, and shall keep things moving thereafter. By tomorrow morning all trains will be at or north of Kingston, and you can have the exclusive use of all the rolling stock. By using detachments of recruits and dismounted cavalry in your fortifications, you will have Schofield and Stanley and

---

23. Sherman, *op. cit.*, Vol. II, p. 169; Van Horne, *Life*, pp. 266-69.

A. J. Smith, strengthened by eight or ten new regiments and all of Wilson's cavalry, you could safely invite Beauregard across the Tennessee, and prevent his ever returning."[24] It is well to note Sherman's reference to the troops that Thomas would have, particularly detachments of recruits for use against Hood.

It is once more pertinent to note that Sherman's *Memoirs* were inaccurate, this time in regard to his exchange of dispatches with Thomas on November 11, concerning which he reported that Thomas stated he had heard of the arrival of A. J. Smith's two divisions at Paducah; but reference to Thomas's dispatch discloses that he said not a word about Smith other than that he had not yet arrived, the exact opposite of the statement Sherman attributed to him. In a letter to General Grant, Sherman stated, "I myself am somewhat astonished at the attitude of things in Tennessee. I purposely delayed at Kingston until Thomas assured me that he was ready; and my last dispatch from him of the 12th of November was full of confidence, in which he promised me that he would ruin Hood if he dared to advance from Florence, urging me to go ahead and give myself no concern about Hood's army in Tennessee." Examination of Thomas's dispatch of the twelfth reveals that Thomas did not assure Sherman he was all ready; neither did he urge Sherman to go ahead nor did he promise unconditionally to ruin Hood, that promise stating that "I believe I shall have men enough." Well, he did not have men enough; and although Van Horne attributes Sherman's mistakes to not having the necessary dispatches before him, the wonder is that a man in his position would make so many mistakes throughout his *Memoirs*. Further, Thomas made a heavy qualification in his dispatch of the twelfth when he stated, "If he does not follow you, I will then thoroughly organize my troops, and, I believe, shall have men enough to ruin him unless he gets out of the way very rapidly."[25]

There is not the slightest doubt that any promise made by General Thomas was dependent upon expected reinforcements, and he knew when the dispatches were exchanged of his inability to face Hood until reinforcements were received and organized. As early as October 25 he had reported to both Grant and Sherman that if Rosecrans's expected troops arrived the following week he would have no further fears. As we have seen, he somewhat anticipated that Hood might follow Sherman, in which case he was prepared to follow him, or, if Hood did not follow him, he, Thomas, would probably meet him in southern Tennessee. Suffice it to cite that when Sherman left Kingston and broke his telegraphic connections with Nashville, Thomas was on his own

24. Van Horne, *ibid.*
25. *Ibid.*, pp. 269-70.

initiative, that is, he had the prerogatives of an independent commander.

During the early days of November, Hood was busily engaged in improving the bridges over streams on the route of his expected advance, so that on November 19 his preparations were completed. On the contrary, Thomas was having the utmost difficulty in obtaining needed horses and equipment for his cavalry; in addition, many of his men were going home after completion of their enlistments, and although new men were coming in, they were fewer in number than those who departed. In the meantime, word was received that General A. J. Smith's command would leave St. Louis about November 10 for Paducah, Kentucky, and that upon arrival he would telegraph Thomas to that effect. Also, Thomas was advised that some men had left for Paducah on November 6, and more were to follow that night. This information from Grant was very encouraging, but the fact remains that reinforcements were long overdue, and Thomas did not have enough men and resources to prevent the invasion of Tennessee. Hood had been cutting a daring swath to the rear of the Federal forces, and was successful in capturing several garrisons to the front also following its heading toward the north. On the site of General Bragg's former concentration of men to face Rosecrans, he established a camp, and went from there westward to continue his aggressive actions. This move was so serious that General Thomas, who had been promised so much in the way of men to repel any attack, was now unable to assemble as few as thirty thousand men to stop Hood's advance on Nashville without seriously endangering the important points over which a number of battles had been fought.

It can be readily perceived that this situation into which Thomas was placed, by the failure to provide needed troops and equipment, endangered the success of the entire plan of Grant and Sherman, including the March to the Sea. From this situation developed the bitter condemnation of Thomas by Grant and his followers, a matter for which the authorities, not Thomas, were entirely responsible.

Aside from the immediate danger to Thomas, General Hood was expecting reinforcements from the west side of the Mississippi under the command of General E. Kirby Smith. These added troops would have given Hood a tremendous superiority; but General Edward Canby, assigned to just such responsibility, was active in patrolling the Mississippi by steamers and in protecting the crossings with troops, and successfully thwarted Kirby Smith's movement eastward. This latter move, by Canby, must be regarded as the key to the Nashville campaign, and the one that, but for its success, would have raised serious doubts that Thomas could have defeated Hood at Nashville.

One of the factors favoring Canby was his interception of a dispatch to General Smith from President Davis ordering Smith to cross the Mississippi; and of course Canby was put on notice to guard against the movement.[26]

Author Van Horne reported that he talked with General Canby in Portland, Oregon, a short time before his murder in 1873, by Modoc Indians, while engaged in a conference with them. Van Horne noted that he had traced an intimate connection between Canby's operations on the Mississippi River and those of General Thomas in Tennessee in November and December, 1864, in defeating the Confederate plan of operations, and that historians appeared to have overlooked this connection. Canby replied that such a connection did exist, and that his efforts were directed to preventing the Confederate crossing of the Mississippi. Canby laughingly observed that the intercepted dispatch from President Davis was in code, which he then produced, but that he could not then decipher it.[27]

General Halleck in Washington was aware that the Confederates were planning to overwhelm Thomas in Tennessee, as indicated by his dispatch of November 6 to General Grant, in which he reviewed his awareness of Confederate activities. This plan, to move all available troops into Tennessee and then northern Mississippi against Federal forces there, was an ambitious, if not a desperate, one. Specifically, Hood hoped to defeat Schofield and Thomas before they could unite, capture the Federal base at Nashville, and, after selecting a point at which he could cross the Cumberland River and avoid Union gunboats, march into Kentucky. From this point he would threaten Cincinnati and augment his depleted forces with recruits from Kentucky and Tennessee. Of course, this plan was formulated before Sherman had begun his march to Savannah; and if Sherman made his march, Hood hoped to move through Tennessee and Kentucky and strike Grant before Sherman could reach Virginia.[28] The success of this plan was sidetracked in the main, at first by Canby's success against Kirby Smith, and later by Thomas's defeat of Hood at Nashville, as will be seen. Of course, too, Hood was not so certain that his plan had the approval of Richmond authorities; besides, the accumulation of needed supplies delayed him in beginning to implement it, which, added to Smith's failure to join him, caused him to lose almost a month.[29]

---

26. Van Horne, *Cumberland*, Vol. II, pp. 179-80.

27. George W. Cullum, *Biographical Register of the Officers and Cadets of the U. S. Military Academy* (Boston, 1891), Vol. 3, p. 134; Van Horne, *Life*, pp. 273-74.

28. Matthew F. Steele, *American Campaigns* (Washington, 1931), pp. 560-61; *Battles and Leaders of the Civil War* (New York, 1884), Vol. IV, pp. 425-28.

29. *Battles and Leaders, ibid.*

General Hood reported that when his forces reached Florence his army had somewhat recovered from the despondency that usually overcomes an army addicted to constant retreating. Further, he reported, "The enemy, having for the first time divided his forces, I had to determine which of the two parts to direct my operations against. To follow the forces about to move through Georgia under Sherman would be to again abandon the required territory to the forces under Thomas, with little hope of being able to reach the enemy in time to defeat his movement, and also to cause desertion and greatly impair the morale, or fighting spirit, of the army, by what would be considered a compulsory retreat. I thought the alternative clear that I should move upon Thomas. If I succeeded in beating him, the effect on Sherman's movement would not be great and I should gain in men sufficiently to compensate for the damages he might inflict. If beaten I should leave the army in better condition than it would be if I attempted a retrograde movement against Sherman."[30] Hood was certainly correct in his conclusion that if he had beaten Thomas the effect of Sherman's movement would not have been great; and no better testimony is needed than the evidence of worry by both Grant and Sherman when Thomas would not move until ready.

Hood's advance created great apprehension in the North; and although belated all-out efforts were made to hasten reinforcements to General Thomas, he was still very much outnumbered. When the advance began, General Stanley's Fourth Corps was at Pulaski, Tennessee; General Jacob Cox's division of the Twenty-third Corps was north of Pulaski; and scattered forces were covering a number of points on Duck River and the Confederates near Florence, Alabama. After sending two brigades left by Schofield at Johnstonville to Duck River, Thomas instructed Schofield on November 19 to prepare to fight at Pulaski "if the enemy advanced to that point, or cover the railroad and assemble his forces, numbered at about eighteen thousand infantry and about four thousand cavalry, at Columbia, Tennessee." He also instructed him that if an attempt should be made to turn his right flank, General Hatch should cover the forts and ferries across Duck River and hold them during the concentration at Columbia. Thomas and Schofield agreed that the weather was so bad that Hood would hardly begin his advance in it; but that hardy commander began to advance that day. He turned Pulaski in short order by marching on the roads west of the town; but the Fourth Corps and General Cox's division marched during the night and arrived at Columbia ahead of Hood, although not in time to prevent his turning it. Schofield placed his infantry on the south bank of Duck River near the

---

30. Hood, *op. cit.*, p. 327.

town and constructed fortifications, while General James H. Wilson's cavalry was stationed at a number of points along the river to observe enemy movements.[31]

General Thomas suggested to Schofield on November 24 that if he could not hold Columbia he had better withdraw to the north bank of Duck River. Furthermore, he noted that from the description he had received previously he presumed the line was short enough to permit Schofield and Stanley to hold it and also to furnish a reserve. The next day, November 25, he advised Schofield to hold some cavalry on the south side of the river, should he be required to move to the north bank as suggested in his dispatch of November 24, so as to delay Hood's advance on the Chattanooga Railroad as long as possible. On November 27, Thomas informed Schofield that he was sending him all available reinforcements; and that night Schofield crossed to the north bank of the river.[32]

It was Hood's purpose to feint with two cavalry divisions and hold Schofield at Columbia while he moved seven divisions of infantry and the remainder of his cavalry to the rear of Schofield and defeat him. That it failed is one of the more surprising incidents of the war, although the first part of the action was a success, due in great part to Schofield's disregard of Thomas's instructions to move promptly to the north bank of the river, if it became clear he could not hold Columbia. In other words, Schofield failed to move to the north bank until the turning movement was in full swing.[33] It is probably the case that Schofield was so imbued with confidence in his ability to evaluate Hood's character that he felt he could anticipate what his next move would be. This confidence, which stemmed from their days together at West Point, was probably unjustified, and almost led to Hood's success.

General James H. Wilson, that brilliant twenty-seven-year-old cavalry leader working with General Thomas, was no mere boy in mental capacity. In his assignment of watching Hood for a possible turning movement, as we have seen, he reported to Generals Thomas and Schofield on November 28 that Hood was moving to turn the position. Schofield reported, "The enemy has crossed in force a short distance this side of Lewisburg pike, at noon to-day, and has driven our cavalry back across the river on that pike at the same time. . . . Wilson has gone with his main force to learn the facts and drive the enemy back, if practicable." At this time Schofield did not believe that enemy in-

31. *Official Records, op. cit.*, Vol. XLV, Part 1, pp. 339-42, 944; Van Horne, *Life*, p. 277.

32. *Official Records, ibid.*, pp. 1017, 1036, 1085.

33. Hood, *op. cit.*, p. 283.

fantry had pushed the cavalry back, but a little later he thought Hood commanded from forty to sixty thousand effectives in the ratio of three of infantry to one of cavalry. General Thomas, highly disturbed at the thought of an enemy greatly in excess of the troops at Schofield's disposal gaining access to his rear, with all the danger to the Union cause in the West such an incident would entail, sent him the following telegraphic instructions:

3:30 A.M., Nov. 29, 1864

I have directed General Hammond to halt his command at Spring Hill and report to you for orders, if he cannot communicate with General Wilson, and also instructing him to keep you well advised of the enemy's movements. I desire you to fall back from Columbia and to take up your position at Franklin, leaving a sufficient force at Spring Hill to contest the enemy's progress until you are securely posted at Franklin. . . . General A. J. Smith's command has not yet reached Nashville; as soon as he arrives I will make immediate disposition of his troops and notify you. Please send me a report as to how matters stand upon your receipt of this.[34]

Schofield's reply was prompt, advising that the enemy's cavalry had made a crossing in force on the Lewisburg pike, and that Wilson had reported the infantry crossing at Huey's Mill, about five miles from that place. If it should prove true, he promised, he would act as Thomas instructed earlier, that is, fall back from Columbia and contest the enemy's progress. General Wilson stated in his official report that it was clear on the night of November 29 that the Confederate cavalry had crossed the river, and that he was heading for the Lewisburg pike, which information was forwarded to Schofield at 8 P.M., including the fact that Forrest's cavalry had not made its appearance. From prisoners he derived information that Forrest had crossed the river at Huey's Mill, perhaps the same force that Schofield had reported earlier. Wilson suggested that with this knowledge the Federal infantry should reach Spring Hill by 10:00 A.M. on the twenty-ninth. Wilson reported that he deemed Schofield's infantry would be afforded ample time to move by the Franklin pike to Spring Hill, or to any other intermediate point, ahead of the enemy, as the latter was moving by poor roads made worse by recent hard rains. Wilson would perform a holding action as long as possible on the Lewisburg pike with his entire force.[35] Enough is known here to suggest that Wilson

---

34. *Official Records, op. cit.,* Vol. XLV, Part 1, pp. 1107, 1135, 1137.
35. *Ibid.,* pp. 558, 559, 1137.

completed his instructions to observe enemy movements and to report on the situation as he revealed his intentions. It is also beyond doubt that General Thomas gave Schofield instructions to withdraw from Columbia at once and take position at Franklin.

Thomas wired Schofield on the night of the twenty-ninth, assuming that his instructions to him at three thirty that afternoon had been fulfilled, informing him that Wilson had given him a complete run-down on enemy activities. This included the news that Forrest was thought to be considering attacking Nashville while the infantry would move on Franklin, that is, Schofield, and attempt to turn his flank. He instructed Schofield to cross the Harpeth River at Franklin, should he find such to be the case, and then to retire along the Franklin pike to Nashville while covering his wagon train and the railroad. Thomas also informed Schofield that agreeably to his desires he had ordered General Cooper to withdraw from Centerville by the Nashville road, crossing Harpeth River at Widow Dean's house, and to report to Schofield from that place for further orders.[36]

When this dispatch was sent, General Wood's division, with General Kimball's not far behind, were nearing Spring Hill, although two enemy divisions were to their rear and they were nearing seven enemy divisions of infantry and all of the enemy's cavalry. On the morning of November 29, General Stanley advanced toward Spring Hill with his wagons and reserve artillery, while the other Union forces held the river crossings. Stanley's leading brigade arrived at Spring Hill in time to intercept Forrest on his way to take control of the Mount Carmel road and cut off the retreat of the Union forces. The Confederate turning movement was now indicated, and Wood's division reported that Hood's infantry were crossing Duck River on their way to Spring Hill. Kimball's division remained on the south side of Rutherford's Creek as insurance against an attack on the flank, while Stanley continued to Spring Hill. General Hood had by this time gained Schofield's rear, and everything looked lovely to him. His feint with two of Lee's divisions at Columbia, followed by his own advance with Cheatham's and Stewart's corps and one of Lee's divisions that was moving on Spring Hill, gave every appearance of success. Forrest's cavalry, meanwhile, followed General Wilson until opposite Spring Hill, when it turned into that place; but at this point, about 11:30 A.M., Wilson learned that Stanley's and Wagner's divisions were only about two miles from Spring Hill, and coming strong. Stanley, on his part, aware of the situation, advanced hurriedly and compelled Forrest to withdraw, as stated, after which he ordered Wagner to assign

---

36. *Ibid.*, pp. 1138, 1139.

two of his brigades to protect the trains and guard the town, and with the other observe from a wooded elevation, less than a mile distant, the enemy from that point.

Hood, meanwhile, had not been idle. He placed four divisions of Stewart's infantry at the Rutherford Creek crossing *en route,* about two and one-half miles from Spring Hill, to prevent Schofield's escape to Murfreesboro, and was himself moving on Stanley's corps with Cheatham's corps. This was an excellent opportunity for Hood, as Schofield's forces were somewhat dispersed; General Cox's division was opposite Columbia on the Duck River; Kimball's division had joined Wood's division, both of which now faced to the east to contest the enemy from Huey's Mill; half of Ruger's division was some distance down Duck River and without orders to join the main forces; and the other half of the division was at Rutherford Creek crossing on the Franklin pike. To confront these scattered forces, Hood had seven divisions and his entire cavalry within easy supporting distance near Stanley's division at Spring Hill, just as Wilson's dispatch had predicted. During most of the day Colonel Post reported Hood's movements from his location on Duck River; these reports, that Hood was moving north from Huey's Mill, had been sent often and promptly, but Schofield did not act upon the information until about 3 P.M., according to his official report, when he became convinced that he would not be attacked on Duck River, and that the Confederates were advancing two corps to Spring Hill. He stated that he then gave orders for the withdrawal of his troops after dark, and took Ruger's troops with him to Spring Hill to establish communication with General Stanley, followed by the head of his main column.[37]

At the same time, 3 P.M., that Schofield began to be aware of Hood's purpose, Hood was observing the lone division under General Stanley at a distance of about two miles, but Stanley was a distance of eight miles from his nearest support. He at once ordered General Cheatham to move to Spring Hill with his corps and to hold the road, after which he would be given aid from the several divisions approaching. Surprise of surprises, General Stanley was not attacked seriously from noon until 7 P.M., although Hood's cavalry and other forces were in near proximity to him. In late afternoon, General Pat Cleburne's division opened an attack on Bradley's brigade but was repulsed, although two attempts were made to dislodge him and but one regiment could be spared to reinforce him. Cleburne's advance was greeted with heavy firing from General Stanley's eight pieces of artillery posted near the town, together with an enfilading fire from

---

37. *Battles and Leaders, op. cit.,* Vol. IV, pp. 444-46; *Official Records, op. cit.,* Vol. XLV, Part 1, pp. 341-42.

Colonel John Lane's advancing troops. Normally, one would expect that with such a preponderance of numbers the Confederates would have overwhelmed Stanley, but Hood quoted General Cheatham as stating that Stanley appeared to be too strong unless Stewart formed on his right.[38] It is the general impression that Hood did attempt to bring up Stewart's corps on Cheatham's right on the Franklin road, but approaching darkness dissipated the attempt. This missed golden opportunity of Hood's, according to his own statement, was due to the disobedience of a subordinate. Be that as it may, if Hood had crushed Wagner's division, the escape of Schofield's army south of Spring Hill would have been impossible without the benevolent aid from Confederate commanders. There is no doubt among these leaders that something went wrong with them and right for Union forces; and the combined Confederate failures that produced Union success in eluding this entrapment and to enable them to go from there to tremendous victory at Franklin will go down as the campaign of lost opportunities.[39]

It should be remembered that the Union forces were outnumbered, and that their escape from defeat for that reason alone is something to cause surprise. Despite the mistakes of the Confederates, the wonder is that any of the Union forces escaped and eluded the ten divisions, plus cavalry, that were capable of pouncing upon them, not omitting two more divisions to the rear. The key to the escape, perhaps, was the failure of Hood's forces to dispose of General Wagner's division, the event that enabled the troops south of Spring Hill to escape.[40]

General Wilson stated that General Schofield, in discussing his escape and giving him thanks and the credit for it, commented, "If you had not succeeded in doing that, our victory here would have been in vain, for with Forrest upon our flanks and rear it would have been impossible for us to have withdrawn our train, artillery and troops from this position." Wilson further commented that he regretted to state that however Schofield may have felt at that time he entirely forgot to express it in his official reports, and had little to say of it in his memoirs, *Forty-six Years in the Army*.

In General Schofield's communication to General Wilson, following the Battle of Franklin, he stated, through his aide, the following:

> The major-general commanding directs me to acknowledge receipt of your communication, per Colonel Wharton, of 5 P.M.

---

38. *Battles and Leaders, ibid.*, p. 445; *Official Records, ibid.*, p. 342; Hood, *op. cit.*, p. 286.

39. *Battles and Leaders, ibid.*, pp. 446-47.

40. *Ibid.*, pp. 449, 450, 451; Steele, *op. cit.*, p. 566; Hood, *op. cit.*, p. 286.

He tenders his compliments and thanks. We have whipped them at every point. The general directs me to say that he will withdraw to Brentwood tonight, but will leave the pickets out till near daylight to guard the fords, etc. He desires you to remain with your command till daylight and watch the river closely, then fall back on the flanks of the rear guard. It is barely possible he may not withdraw tonight, in which case, of course, you must retain your position. He desires you to ascertain definitely, then, before moving whether the troops are gone.[41]

Painstaking reference to Schofield's *Forty-six Years in the Army* discloses little by way of compliment to either Wilson or, as stated elsewhere in this work, his eminently superior commander Thomas, the military latchet of whose shoes Schofield was not fit to tie. Schofield's facility in the use of the personal pronoun "I" placed him in the front rank of that cult, perhaps the very best, and nowhere in the book does one get the impression that his use of the pronoun ever tired him; in fact, if it were possible one might suspect that the use of the word was his exclusive copyright. Schofield had the dominant characteristic, developed to a remarkable if not disgusting degree, of cultivating and flattering the prominent, or those highly placed, whose favor might prove a steppingstone to his advancement. His meteoric rise owed much to this characteristic. We have noted his failure to obey the instructions of General Thomas, which almost, and but for Confederate compensating lapses would have, brought Union disaster. He was indeed fortunate to escape with his military hide; and but for the grand soldier and gentleman whom he maligned, General Thomas, he probably would have been dismissed for incompetency. He had the sheer effrontery to criticize Thomas's report for not placing more of the laurel wreath upon his brow for Franklin and Nashville, after all but encompassing the defeat of the army. Indeed, his slighting of Wilson, who helped to preserve him for later use with Generals Grant and Sherman, for whatever value that may have had, the record alone discloses; at best, this conduct was not inconsistent with the procedure employed by the military dynasty of which he was a one-fourth, if not prominent, part.

To return to the escape of Schofield's army following Hood's apparent entrapment, when three and one-half divisions were about to be absorbed by Hood's overwhelming numbers, Confederate leaders are agreed that a grand opportunity was lost, but are much in dispute as to the cause. General Cheatham stated that one of his staff

41. James H. Wilson, *Under the Old Flag* (New York, 1911), Vol. II, pp. 54-55; *Official Records, op. cit.,* Vol. XLV, Part 1, p. 1179.

officers, Major Bostick, returned to headquarters after placing General Edward Johnson's division in position near the pike, and related that he had heard stragglers passing northward on the pike. This was about midnight, when a note came from Major A. P. Mason, Hood's assistant adjutant general, reporting that Hood, having knowledge of the stragglers, it behooved someone to take care of the situation. Mason then sent Bostick to instruct Johnson to "go to the pike and cut off anything that might be passing." After a while Bostick returned with the information that he and Johnson had ridden close to the pike, where they found everything quiet and no one passing; therefore Johnson's division was not moved.[42] This story alone would seem to reconcile the Confederate lapse, but there are other versions.

General Cheatham reported that he received the warning note from Major Adams regarding the stragglers and acted accordingly; but the next day, after General Hood had told Governor Harris that he blamed Cheatham for not making the night attack, Major Mason drew Governor Harris aside and gave him the startling information that Cheatham was not to blame, since he, Mason, had not sent him the order: "I fell asleep again before writing it." Of course, Harris told Mason he should inform General Hood of it, but although he promised to do so, nothing disclosed indicates that he did. Here we have Cheatham admitting he received an order that the supposed sender admits he did not send. Whom to believe?[43]

Years later, it is told, Governor Harris wrote a letter to Governor Porter of Tennessee explaining what occurred at Spring Hill on that very important night. This letter, written in 1887, throws some light on the ability of General Hood to have such an important command. In reporting the contents of this letter it is important to any appraisal of General Hood to recall that he was a man who had given all but his life for the Confederacy. He lost a leg at Chickamauga and previously, at Gettysburg, was wounded in the arm. The wonder is that he was not compelled to take some responsible but less exhausting assignment. Here is the letter:

General Hood, his Adjutant General Major Mason, and myself, occupied the same room at the residence of Captain Thompson, near the village. Late at night we were aroused by a private soldier, who reported to General Hood that, on reaching the camp near Spring Hill, he found himself within the Federal lines; that the troops were in great confusion, a part of them marching in the

---

42. Stanley F. Horn, *The Army of Tennessee* (Indianapolis, 1941), p. 390; Hood, *op. cit.*, p. 289.

43. Horn, *ibid.*

direction of Franklin, others had turned toward Columbia, and that the road was blocked with baggage-wagons and gun-carriages, rendering it impossible to move in order in either direction. Upon receipt of this report, General Hood directed Major Mason to order General Cheatham to move down on the road immediately and attack the enemy. General Hood and myself remained in bed. I went to sleep, and I suppose that General Hood did the same. At daylight on the following morning we learned that the Federal army had left Spring Hill and was being concentrated at Franklin.[44]

The Confederates were asleep, which story is the most susceptible of acceptance, and General Schofield, the one person who dared not sleep, did not. Some rumors were to the effect that General Hood was drunk; but whether he was or was not, this was not at the usual Confederate standard of vigilance.[45] If General Hood partook of alcohol to numb the pain in his body, it would not have been in the least surprising; as stated, the surprising factor in the entire muddle was that Hood was given the command at all.

---

44. *Ibid.*, pp. 391-92.
45. *Ibid.*, p. 392.

CHAPTER XXII

Franklin and Nashville

HOOD's lost opportunity at Spring Hill was the great blow of the campaign for him. He had the unusual privilege of moving but a few hundred yards and firing into the troops and trains of his enemy as they crept stealthily along his own front. At Spring Hill there was a bridge too narrow for wagons traveling in opposite directions to pass each other. That night, Schofield led his corps into Franklin, leaving General Stanley and his corps, with the army trains, in front of Hood. Stanley, the unquestioned hero of the engagement at Spring Hill, skillfully moved his trains over the narrow bridge under protection of a line of troops the entire distance to Franklin, and preserved his corps and the vehicular equipment entrusted to him from enemy capture. In all of this Hood was not fully alert to what was transpiring. If he had ordered an advance against Stanley, who was weighted down with his trains and other equipment, not to omit being outnumbered, he would have won a great triumph. That he did not attempt it defies belief; and his failure to do so must be reckoned as a decision of the Almighty who has His own purposes.

Colonel Emerson Opdycke, who, with Colonel John Lane, had been assigned to cover the baggage trains and perform as rear guard, fought a tremendously important successful delaying action against Hood the greater part of November 30, as Hood's army advanced to Franklin. General Thomas had no expectation of fighting at Franklin, particularly for the reason that he had been unable to assemble his forces; and on the night of November 29 he ordered Schofield to withdraw from Franklin to Nashville if the Confederates demonstrated toward Franklin. General Thomas had done everything possible to round up an army with which to confront General Hood on a somewhat equal basis; but although he had sought reinforcements from Kentucky and Indiana, no help of consequence was available.[1]

---

1. *Official Records of the War of the Rebellion* (Washington, 1880–1901), Vol. XLV, Part 1, pp. 1138, 1139; Thomas B. Van Horne, *The Life of Major General George H. Thomas* (New York, 1882), p. 287.

The Battle of Franklin began on the afternoon of November 30, after Schofield had personally directed the repairing of the bridges for passage of his artillery to the north bank of the Harpeth River. He left General Jacob Cox in command of the Twenty-third Corps to guard the river crossing of his own and Stanley's Fourth Corps. General Cox utilized three divisions to encircle Franklin, which were Ruger's and Reilly's of his own corps and Kimball's of Stanley's Fourth Corps. Wood's division advanced to the north bank of the Harpeth River also, in order to protect the flanks in the event the enemy tried to cross the river above or below Franklin. This division was in an exposed position about one mile from the intrenched line. Colonel Opdycke objected to the danger inherent in this exposure and was permitted to move his brigade inside the lines, where he posted it at the key point of the line, the rear of Carter's Hill. The wisdom of this request would pay rich dividends later, when, as the only reserve, it saved the situation when the line gave way at Carter's Hill.[2]

Colonel John Lane later also objected to his own position in front of the line, although on a hill some distance from the main line; here he noted that the enemy, forming for action, would surely overwhelm his force unless he changed to a better position. He was directed to form on the right of Colonel Joseph Conrad's brigade of Wagner's division. Colonel Lane became convinced early in the afternoon that General Hood was planning to attack, and reported his observation to General Wagner. The latter then notified General Stanley, by messenger, in the presence of General Schofield, although nothing was done about the two brigades in advance of the main line.[3]

If General Thomas did not expect a battle at Franklin, neither did Generals Schofield and Stanley, both of whom were engaged in conversation at 4 P.M., more especially so late in the day. It is a fact that General Hood was not given to attacking intrenched lines, except for feinting at Columbia, for which reason it seemed that he had no better excuse for attacking the intrenchments at Franklin. Meanwhile, the wagon trains were moving fast across the river toward Nashville, another factor that would seem to have discouraged Hood from attacking at that time. Hood was not one who was susceptible of scientific prediction, however, and having prepared his forces for an attack by his center, he struck the two brigades in front, those of Lane and Conrad. Conrad's brigade received the first big blow from Hood's attack and fled through the defenses, which were abandoned by the defenders and immediately occupied by the enemy. Lane's left

---

2. *Battles and Leaders of the Civil War* (New York, 1884), Vol. IV, p. 452; Van Horne, *ibid.*, pp. 287-90.

3. *Battles and Leaders, ibid.;* Van Horne, *ibid.*, pp. 288-90.

was exposed by Conrad's departure and he fell back at once, followed closely by the pursuing enemy, to the safety of the intrenchments at the right of the Columbia road. Here the men turned and fired into the front troops of the enemy, after which they formed a triple line in the deserted trenches. It so happened that these brigades, in falling back, became a screen for the pursuers, and some that followed Conrad passed to the rear of Carter's Hill, or key point in the line. From then until late at night the Confederates assaulted a number of times on the entire line, but more especially at Carter's Hill, where the action was galling. It so happened that Carter's Hill was as close to the bridges over Harpeth River as the right flank, and almost as close as the left flank. The enemy captured two batteries here and fired them right and left, when Hood's heavily massed troops were approaching in haste, their objective being the opening created by Conrad's withdrawal. At about one hundred yards within this breach, or opening, was Opdycke's reserve, mentioned earlier.[4]

Here was where Opdycke's request to move to a more sheltered, or less exposed, position paid rich dividends. Not waiting for orders, he and his men sensed that they could save the situation, and they did. As Opdycke was about to give the order to fill the gap, he saw that his men already had bayonets fixed for a charge. Rushing forward they drove back the enemy in desperate hand-to-hand fighting, pushing him completely off Carter's Hill, and saving the army while recapturing the lost batteries. General Stanley, in the meantime, following the roar of battle, galloped to the scene, but too late to order Opdycke's brigade to advance. General Cox also intended ordering Opdycke to move into the opening they voluntarily filled, but the brigade had already taken its own action. Cox's judicious use of men at his disposal was of great value in repulsing the Confederates; and in combination with the bravery and devotion of men and officers the day was won for the Union. Stanley again, and of course Cox, did conspicuous service at Franklin, although Stanley had a horse shot from under him and was himself wounded.[5]

While the infantry action was taking place, General Forrest's cavalry crossed the Harpeth River, no doubt with the intention of capturing Schofield's vehicles; but General Wilson's troopers fought so energetically that he was driven off, and gave no more trouble that day. The battle ended with complete success for the Union line; and although their losses were much lower than the Confederates, they were estimated at about twenty-four hundred.[6]

4. *Battles and Leaders, ibid.;* Van Horne, *ibid.*, pp. 291-92.

5. *Battles and Leaders, ibid.;* Van Horne, *ibid.*

6. *Battles and Leaders, ibid.;* Frederick Phister, **Statistical Record** (New York, no date), p. 218.

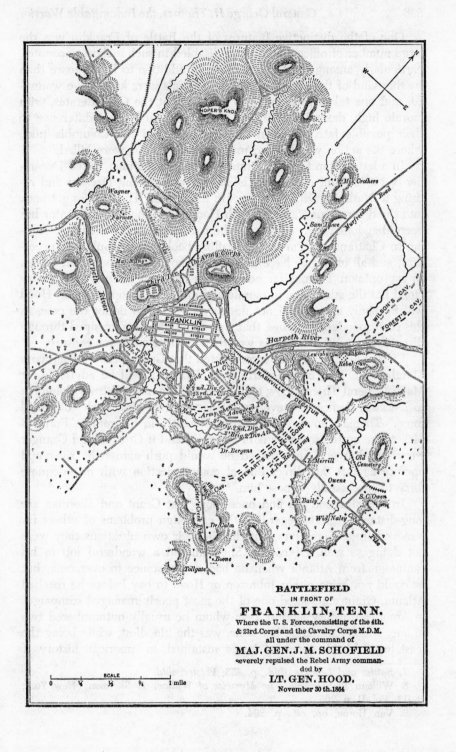

BATTLEFIELD
IN FRONT OF
FRANKLIN, TENN.
Where the U. S. Forces, consisting of the 4th.
& 23rd. Corps and the Cavalry Corps M.D.M.
all under the command of
MAJ. GEN. J. M. SCHOFIELD
severely repulsed the Rebel Army command-
ed by
LT. GEN. HOOD.
November 30th. 1864

One of the distinctive features of the Battle of Franklin was the large number of officers killed and disabled in such a short encounter, particularly among the Confederates. In addition to losing more than six thousand of the rank and file, six generals were killed, five wounded, and one taken prisoner. It is evident that the Confederates, with morale high, dashed madly into action with supreme indifference to their possible fate. Between the gin-house and the Columbia pike, where the action was hottest, most of the generals were killed.[7]

In a letter from General Grant to General Sherman, dated December 3, 1864, Grant criticized Thomas for abandoning Decatur and retiring to Nashville with his army. He stated that "Thomas has got back into the defenses of Nashville with Hood close upon him. Decatur has been abandoned and so have all the roads, except the main one leading to Chattanooga. Part of this falling back was undoubtedly necessary, and all of it may have been. It did not look so, however, to me. In my opinion Thomas far outnumbers Hood in infantry. In cavalry Hood has the advantage in morale and numbers. I hope yet that Hood will be badly crippled, if not destroyed."[8] It is no doubt the case, as this correspondence implies, that Grant and Sherman gossiped through dispatches, and that Thomas was their favorite topic for censure.

First of all, it should be remembered that Grant, prior to Sherman's March to the Sea, informed Halleck, "I think it will be advisable for Major General Thomas now to abandon all the railroad from Columbia to Decatur, thence to Stevenson. This will give him much additional force." Thomas, however, thought differently in his reply: "Forrest's pickets are on the south bank of the river, and if Croxton and Granger were withdrawn, I am satisfied he would push across the river and operate against our direct line of communication with no adequate force to successfully oppose him."[9]

In this situation we find once more that Grant and Sherman are long-distance experts regarding the campaign problems of others far removed from themselves, but that in their own situations they were not doing so well. Of course, Sherman did a wonderful job in his campaign from Atlanta when he had no resistance to overcome; but he could not bring either Johnston or Hood to bay before he reached Atlanta. Grant conducted one of the most poorly managed campaigns in American history against Lee, whom he usually outnumbered two to one, which campaign, bar none, was the bloodiest, while being the least justifiable, in terms of losses sustained, in American history, if

7. *Battles and Leaders, ibid.*, p. 453; Phister, *ibid.*

8. William T. Sherman, *The Memoirs of William T. Sherman* (New York, 1891), Vol. II, p. 205.

9. Van Horne, *op. cit.*, p. 294.

not in the entire history of civilized nations. It is strikingly the fact
that no one else, certainly not the Confederate opposition, but Sherman, Grant, and their favorites ever said that Thomas was slow; in
fact, without exception, when the Confederate leaders said anything
about him, it was in eulogy or that they wished he had fought with
them.

Of all the ridiculous things said against Thomas, none equals in
groundlessness Sherman's communication of December 16 to Grant;
and no general of the Civil War, including General Burnside of
Antietam and Fredericksburg record, had a less enviable battle record
than Sherman. This is what he wrote:

> Why he did not turn on him at Franklin after checking him
> surpasses my understanding. Indeed, I do not approve of his
> evacuating Decatur, but think he should have assumed the of-
> fensive against Hood from Pulaski, in the direction of Waynes-
> burg. I know full well that General Thomas is slow in mind and
> in action, but he is judicious and brave, and the troops feel great
> confidence in him. I still hope he will out-maneuver and destroy
> Hood.[10]

Nothing in Sherman's blast is more reprehensible than his remark
concerning Thomas's mentality; and he was quick to salvage for Thomas a modicum of ability to offset his baseless insinuation by conceding
that he was judicious and brave. Does not judgment require mentality?
Thomas was so far superior to both Grant and Sherman, a matter of
proved record, that both combined were no match for him in military
ability. They outmatched him only in their capacity for injuring their
fellow soldiers; and no instance has been found in which Thomas
spoke evilly of anyone, although, as proved on the scene at Chattanooga, he showed up both Grant and Sherman as blundering incom-
petents, both of whom he bailed out from disgrace. That is the record,
which goes far beyond the false and malicious statements of either or
both of them. As if Chattanooga, particularly at Missionary Ridge, did
not prove the incompetence of both Grant and Sherman, while demonstrating Thomas's superior qualifications, then the seal was placed
upon it by Thomas at Nashville, as we shall see.

General Jacob D. Cox, a most capable division commander, was
not a Thomas admirer in any sense of the word, but he did describe
him after his first meeting, while in the Atlanta campaign, where he
also met Sherman. Cox stated that Thomas was also tall, as was
Sherman, with an air of dignified quiet and deliberation. "His countenance was almost impassive and the lines of his brow gave an air of

10. Sherman, *op. cit.*, p. 266.

sternness. His part in the conversation was less, his words much fewer and less expressive, but always clear and intelligent. His manner was kindly but rather reserved, and one felt that his acquaintance must be gradually cultivated. His reputation for cool intrepidity and stubborn tenacity could not be excelled, and no soldier could approach him without a deep interest and respect that was not diminished by his natural modesty and demeanor. Better acquaintance with him made one learn that his intellect was strong and broad, and his mind had been expanded by general reading, with some special scientific tastes beyond his military profession. He was a noble model of patriotic devotion to country, and of the private virtues that make a great citizen."[11] Nothing there to suggest that General Thomas was of less than normal mentality, as Sherman's comments by and large so often implied; in fact these remarks leave one with the impression that there was little more that could be said in favor of Thomas. It would be remiss not to state that Cox, in eulogizing Sherman, reported, "In conversation he poured out a wealth of original and striking ideas from a full experience, observation and reading.[12] This sounds like Sherman; he talked so much that he did not translate his words into battle victories; and psychologists of today would regard it as indicating instability and nervousness, both of which might suggest unfitness for command.

General Cox made another comment regarding Sherman; one worthy of more than passing notice: "I soon acquired an undoubting conviction that of all the men I had met, he was the one to whose leadership in war I would commit my own life and the lives of my men with most complete confidence."[13] This is surprising indeed, and it is a matter of wonder whether Cox ever heard of the useless sacrifice of life at Kenesaw Mountain, a needless slaughter that Thomas strongly opposed. There were no incidents of that nature in the career of Thomas, a fact well confirmed by the devotion of his men for him. There was no such devotion for Sherman.

The statement in Sherman's communication to Grant that Thomas should have pursued Hood at Franklin overlooks one important particular. General A. J. Smith was not available in time to fit into Thomas's plan as hoped; and it was necessary to plan without him, which meant that a general engagement must be avoided at all hazards, or until the forces were more nearly equal. Whether this was right or wrong it would be difficult to say; and Thomas was not

11. Jacob D. Cox, *Military Reminiscences of the Civil War* (New York, 1900), Vol. II, pp. 204-5.

12. *Ibid.*, pp. 203-4.

13. *Ibid.*, p. 204.

superior to Hood in infantry, as asserted by Grant in his letter of December 3 to Sherman, without abandoning the local garrisons. There was too much hanging in the balance for Thomas for one moment to become careless; and those who have criticized him here do so without considering that Sherman had the troops that should have been left with Thomas. All of the experting done by Grant and Sherman in particular ignores the fact that all major battles fought outside the area of Chattanooga showed a preponderance of numbers by Union forces. No such excess fell to the lot of Thomas's army.

If Thomas had elected to ignore the possibility of fighting a general engagement at Pulaski, he would have risked losing control of the railroad through Athens, Huntsville, and Decatur, and seriously impaired his chances of holding what had been gained during many weary months of struggle. It was wise, therefore, for Thomas to move the troops from Decatur to the Nashville and Chattanooga Railroad in order to hold it as he thought best and as he was directed to do. It was his purpose, not to invite Hood to attack him at Nashville, but rather to await the proper moment when his chance for victory was definitely good.

On November 30, General Thomas's dispatch to Schofield stated: "It will take Smith quite all day to disembark, but if I find there is no immediate necessity to retain him here, will send him to Franklin or Brentwood, according to your circumstances. If you can prevent Hood from turning your position at Franklin, it should be held; but I do not wish you to risk too much."[14] This dispatch, on the very day of the Battle of Franklin, shows that Smith's men were not available, and, of course, Hood would not just sit about and wait until Schofield received reinforcements, as it would appear from Grant's and Sherman's criticisms.

Schofield's reply to the foregoing, at noon, stated: "I am satisfied that I have heretofore run too much risk in trying to hold Hood in check, while so far inferior to him in infantry and cavalry. The slightest mistake on my part, or failure of a subordinate, during the last three days might have proved disastrous. I don't want to get into so tight a place again; yet, I will cheerfully act in accordance with your views of expediency, if you think it important to hold Hood back, as long as possible. When you get all your troops together and the cavalry in effective condition, we can whip Hood easily, and, I believe, make the campaign a decisive one; before that the most we can do is husband our strength and increase it as much as possible. I fear the troops which were stationed on the river below Columbia

14. *Official Records, op. cit.*, Vol. XLV, Part 1, p. 1169.

will be lost. I will get my trains out of the way as soon as possible, and watch Hood carefully. Possibly I may be able to hold him here, but do not expect to be able to do so long."[15] If nothing else, this dispatch from Schofield confirms the condition of his own and that of Thomas's forces before Nashville, and constitutes at once a rejection of Grant's insistence that Thomas was ready to attack Hood before he did.

General Thomas asked General Schofield, also on the thirtieth, whether he was capable of holding Hood at Franklin for three days longer; also he asked what Wilson thought he could do to help Schofield in holding Hood, after informing him that Smith's command had arrived but with one division still behind. Schofield replied, "I have just received your dispatch asking whether I can hold Hood here three days. I don't believe I can. I can doubtless hold him one day, but will hazard something in doing that. He now has a large force, probably two corps, in my front, and seems prepared to cross the river above and below. I think he can effect a crossing tomorrow, in spite of all my efforts, and probably tonight, if he attempts it. A worse position than this for an inferior force could hardly be found. I will refer your question to General Wilson this evening; I think he can do very little. I have no doubt Forrest will be in my rear tomorrow, or doing some great mischief. It appears to me that I ought to take position at Brentwood at once. If A. J. Smith's divisions and the Murfreesboro garrison join me there, I ought to be able to hold Hood in check for some time. I have just learned that the enemy's cavalry is already crossing three miles below. I will have lively times with my trains again."[16]

General Wilson also advised a concentration at Nashville, but, as we have seen, he could not have ordered a concentration below there or until General Smith's arrival, at which time Thomas asked for Schofield's opinion whether he could hold Hood three days. General Thomas had hoped to fight Hood as early as expedient from the time the campaign began; and if his orders had been obeyed he would have kept his inferior forces astride Hood's forces, hoping for a chance to give him battle more nearly on his own terms. Any contention that Thomas should have fought elsewhere than at Nashville implies strongly that he should have fought without Smith's reinforcements; that he should have abandoned the important garrisons to give him needed equality of numbers to confront Hood; and that his concentration should have been made at Pulaski or Columbia, or anywhere else, before Hood's intentions were disclosed. What Thomas did was

---

15. *Ibid.*, pp. 1169-70.
16. *Ibid.*, p. 1170.

to transfer the garrison at Decatur to Stevenson, based upon his own best basis for judging. His intention was to insure that if Hood went for the Nashville and Chattanooga Railroad, it, and the important points on its route, would be safeguarded. General Steedman, entrusted with the responsibility of protecting the railroad, kept pace with Hood as the latter made his advance toward Nashville, and reached that city on December 1.[17]

This serious problem of contesting Hood's invasion of Tennessee was one that in the beginning Thomas did his utmost to avoid. First, he did not want the command of forces contesting Hood's army; second, he did not approve of Sherman's campaign to the sea, which left Hood free to move about almost at will, or until a formidable army could be brought against him. There was also a distinct possibility that Hood might successfully overcome Thomas's army; and logically so, because Hood commanded veteran troops that outnumbered those of Thomas, which had been in large part collected from various sources. Certainly some of them were Sherman's rejects. Despite all of this, Thomas, great soldier that he was, and he was to prove himself even more indelibly during the next few weeks, turned to his task with that so characteristic determination, and won. It will be borne in mind that Thomas fought two forces, the one on his front and the one at his back in Washington, headed by General Grant, aided and abetted by Secretary Stanton, with apparently little if any assistance from General Halleck. Of the two opposing forces it would perhaps be correct to assume that he was prepared to face Hood's army with infinitely greater chances for success than he could confront the forces at his back.

At the risk of repetition, it should be remembered that General Thomas virtually declined the command of forces to oppose Hood, upon Sherman's March to the Sea. He was aware of the difficulties confronting him, after knowing that Sherman was taking the élite of the army to wage a bloodless campaign, as Sherman himself conceded. He knew the price he would have to pay to gather enough force to justify facing Hood, and that it would require some time. What he surely did not anticipate was that he would soon undergo the most inhuman assault upon a military man with an unsurpassed record in the entire history of the world. There is no precedent for such abuse and degradation as Grant would now heap upon him, although Grant himself was co-author of the situation for which he sought to condemn Thomas to eternal disgrace, and which Thomas, who must needs have been a military genius to surmount the difficulties, rose above, only to be further castigated as "slow." It comes

17. Van Horne, *op. cit.*, pp. 298-99.

as small surprise, in turning the pages of history relating to the American Civil War, that the war lasted four long and bloody years, what with such leadership. It is surprising that the North won the war at all. These are not mere words, as attested by the truth of Shiloh; the overcredit by Grant and Sherman to themselves for Chattanooga and their silence there regarding Thomas the real hero; the Atlanta campaign which saw that so useless waste of the Boys in Blue whose lives Thomas sought to preserve at Kenesaw Mountain; and the blood bath, that so needless spectacle of Cold Harbor, which Grant himself would have liked to recall. There must be some justice in the aggregate of American people for General Thomas, whose deeds shone like blazing suns before feeble candles. The full story for all Americans to read for themselves is here, there, and everywhere, if they would know more of the real truth of the Civil War. The faith that Thomas so hopefully expressed to his biographer, Thomas B. Van Horne, that "Time and history will do me justice," has not been fulfilled, but it is coming to be.

When Thomas was facing his troubles at Nashville, the people of the North were in a highly nervous and uncertain state. We have it from one of the best historians that people everywhere were asking, "Who shall revive the withered hopes that bloomed on the opening of Grant's campaign?" We are told that the most despondent were the people who possessed the best information. It is little wonder, then, that on July 2, 1864, the Congress adopted a resolution requesting the President to appoint a day for humiliation and prayer, following Grant's bloody battles against Lee. The resolution called upon the people "to meet at their usual places of worship that they might confess and repent of their manifold sins, implore the compassion and forgiveness of the Almighty, that, if consistent with His will the existing rebellion may be speedily suppressed, and implore Him, as the Supreme Ruler of the world, not to destroy us as a people." Pursuant to the resolution, the President designated the first Thursday in August "to be observed by the people of the United States as a day of national humiliation and prayer."[18]

A steadying thought regarding the terrible dilemma in which the North found itself relates to the result that might have occurred if Grant had removed the only consistently successful general of the war, and at a time when it so desperately needed successful generals. This Union was preserved by a none too wide margin, and the margin could have been, and probably was, George H. Thomas.

Gideon Welles, Secretary of the Navy under Presidents Lincoln and Johnson, has left a legacy of observations concerning General

18. James F. Rhodes, *History of the American Civil War, 1861-1865* (New York, 1923), p. 328.

Grant. "He is a man of low instincts, not of a nice sense of honor nor of proper self-respect, is wanting in truthfulness and sincerity, and is grossly, shamefully ignorant of the Constitution and of the structure of Government. . . . They [politicians] expect to use him, he intends to use them. They can intrigue, but he is, with low instincts, a man of cunning, and is destitute of affection out of the family circle. The War brought him again into the Army, but E. B. Washburne, his Representative in Congress, made it his study and business to indorse, extol, and advance Grant."[19] This would seem to well describe the Grant who badgered, humiliated, and would have destroyed the greatest soldier of the Civil War on the Union side.

In another instance, Welles told of Grant's ability for minimizing the achievements of others. At a meeting of Lincoln's Cabinet, Lincoln told of a dream he had before each of a number of great battles or important events, naming Fort Sumter, Bull Run, Antietam, Gettysburg, Stones River, Vicksburg, etc., and Grant interrupted to say that Stones River was no victory. The President looked at Grant curiously and inquiringly and said that they might differ on that point. Welles noted that this was the first occasion he had been given to notice Grant's jealous nature. Later there was jealousy manifested toward General Thomas and others who were non-satellites.[20]

Another observation concerned President Johnson's desire to remove General Sheridan, Grant's "Little Phil," from his command as governor of the Fifth Military District, comprising Louisiana and Texas, because of his disposition and difficulties with people. Grant opposed the removal, but Johnson said that General Thomas had superior qualifications and ability, and also calmer judgment. Welles was later convinced that Grant had secretly prompted Sheridan in his reprehensible conduct in New Orleans and Texas. Most military governors had secret telegrams or oral instructions from the general in chief, Grant, who was in collusion with Stanton. He accused Grant of duplicity and vulgar cunning, of deceiving the President and others, and Sheridan was encouraged to be insolent toward the President by his chief, Grant. Grant supported Johnson until the fall of 1866 when, flattered by attention, he developed aspirations for politics with little political intelligence or experience.[21]

Welles's diary records that "some men of both parties, although

19. John M. Schofield, *Forty-six Years in the Army* (New York, 1897), p. 295; Gideon Welles, *Diary of Gideon Welles* (Boston, 1911), Vol. III, p. 364.

20. Welles, *ibid.*, Vol. II, pp. 282-83.

21. George W. Cullum, *Biographical Register of Officers and Cadets of the U.S. Military Academy* (Boston, 1891), Vol. II, p. 356; Welles, *ibid.*, Vol. III, pp. 174-75.

aware that Grant was destitute of political intelligence and experience to qualify him, yet groomed him for the Presidency. Sensible men, aware of Grant's shortcomings, did not join these men. The Radicals felt that they could mold him to do their bidding, wishes and views, through his ignorance and lack of interest in political and civil matters, which made him more acceptable. During Grant's term as Secretary of War, while still ostensibly loyal to President Johnson, he was in daily communication with Johnson as a trusted officer of the Cabinet, while writing secretly to Sheridan and the other military governors under his control, seeking to counteract the measures of the Administration."[22] It comes as no surprise, these disclosures from Secretary Welles's diary, especially when considered in relation to Grant's unprecedentedly corrupt administration.

Here is another comment regarding this commander, who wrought virtual obscurity and near-disgrace and smote down the incomparable and indispensable General Thomas, who was incorruptible and invincible even though neither Grant nor the nation seemed to care. "He [Grant] cultivated rich men, and was happiest when in the company of men such as Jay Cooke who, for some select cigars, clutched choice lands for the Northern Pacific Railroad. Lest it be considered inappropriate, Grant was doing what was more the custom in his day than is the custom now, as bad as now sometimes appears to be. His acceptance of a fifty-thousand-dollar house in Philadelphia was over-matched by his friend, Sherman, who accepted one in Washington worth twice that amount." Thomas, the "slow" general, who never suffered defeat and was a target for Grant's ill will, was not a target for gifts of any kind. At the end of the war, when some citizens wanted to give him a reward for public services, he said this: "While fully apprehending the motives which induce these kind offers, I contend that I cannot accept them and be wholly independent. Whatever my services were, they were rendered to the country, and whatever reward for these services the government might offer me, I could accept freely without being under obligation to any person; but if I accept gifts from one or more individual citizens who owe me nothing more than respect and esteem, by doing so I place myself under obligations to them, which I could not cancel as a private citizen, and would not as a public officer; and to hold myself wholly independent, I make it a rule of my life to refuse all such offerings."[23] The word "incorruptible" in connection with Thomas's character almost seems like understatement.

---

22. Welles, *ibid.*, Vol. III, p. 175.

23. Vernon L. Parrington, *Beginnings of Critical Realism in America, 1860–1920* (New York, 1930); Van Horne, *op. cit.*, p. 423.

General Richard W. Johnson, one of Thomas's division commanders who knew both Grant and Sherman fairly well, had this to say, which affords some light on their relationship: "Each gave to the other the credit for the success which had fallen to him, and in this way 'honors were even,' and a warm personal friendship was maintained between them." Further, "While Grant was President, an attempt was made to get Sherman to antagonize some of his reconstruction ideas. 'No,' replied Sherman; 'Grant stood by me when I was crazy, and I stood by him when he was drunk, and now we stand by each other.' "[24] Nothing more is required to explain the relationship between Grant and Sherman, a type of combination that could have been developed at any time during the war between two or more generals with Congressional backing, as they had. If McClellan, for example, and Buell or Rosecrans, or any other combination of two or more generals having Congressional backing had agreed to work all for one and one for all, who knows but that any combination would have been better than Grant and Sherman from almost any conceivable standpoint?

General James H. Wilson reported that following the Battle of Franklin he wrote to General Rawlins commending Generals Thomas, Schofield, Stanley, and Cox for their conduct. He felt this was due them because of their discouragements and difficulties, in all of which they were successful in escaping disaster, although they were widely scattered a number of times. Furthermore, he thought that the entire campaign, including Spring Hill and Franklin, had been superbly managed in the face of Hood's greatly superior forces, and that Franklin offered no springboard for an offensive against Hood without the long-awaited reinforcements of General A. J. Smith.[25]

Nearly all authorities are agreed that Hood did not intend to march to the Ohio during the winter of 1864–1865, as General Grant so greatly feared, a fear that underlay his anxiety over Thomas's decision to gain strength before offering battle. Federal gunboats and ironclads were patrolling the Cumberland River from Carthage, Illinois, where it empties into the Ohio River, to near Nashville, Tennessee, and offered some insurance against such an invasion. The important assignment of Rear Admiral S. Phillips Lee was to prevent Hood from crossing the Cumberland.[26] Although those responsible for his

24. Richard W. Johnson, *A Soldier's Reminiscences* (Philadelphia, 1886), p. 308.

25. James H. Wilson, *Under the Old Flag* (New York, 1911), Vol. III, pp. 57, 59.

26. Fletcher Pratt, *The Civil War on Western Waters* (New York, 1956), p. 214.

containment held little fear of his performing such an undertaking, assurance was attempted to reduce the fears of the Washington authorities. It was impossible to reach the minds of those most concerned with such assurance. They could not seem to get it into their heads that Hood was a great distance from his base at Florence, Alabama. Another obstacle to Hood's advancement was his inability to maintain the railroads, although he had no problem on that score, nor would he, until he could first gain possession of them from General Thomas and his well-intrenched forces at Nashville.

Thomas's forces at Nashville had been increasing in strength since the Battle of Franklin, which was shortly before the barrage of dispatches began pouring in from a frightened if not frantic military hierarchy in Washington. It should be considered also that if Hood had undertaken such a foolhardy invasion, far from his base of supplies, in a country where the winters are more severe generally than in Tennessee, he would have been deserving of the consequences. These factors could not seem to penetrate the minds of Grant and Stanton, particularly Grant's, who acted somewhat like a caged lion. He was very likely remorseful at the thought of the consequences of disaster to both himself and Sherman if Thomas should be defeated. Then, no doubt, the nation would demand the discharge of both of them, particularly after its anxiety and distress over Grant's losses in the bloody battles before Richmond. The virus of distrust of Thomas spread to President Lincoln and General Halleck who, many hundreds of miles from the danger scene, presumed to know better than the well-tried Thomas on the scene, the one man who had never once let them down. Grant's entire correspondence disclosed a willingness, if not a settled purpose, to cause Thomas's removal and downfall, provided the authorities at Washington could be induced to take the responsibility for such radical action.[27]

General James Wilson, who worked perhaps more closely with General Thomas in this campaign than anyone else, and who knew the terrible ordeal to which he was subjected because of the problems of getting his army prepared, quite apart from the brutal treatment from Washington, reminds us that Thomas kept them informed of developments at all times.[28] "With the threat of removal hanging over him, Thomas went calmly ahead with his preparations." Those around him, however, described him as being much troubled in spirit when rain and ice covered the area, during which time he would sit by the window for an hour or more, "not speaking a word, gazing

---

27. Wilson, *op. cit.*, Vol. II, p. 267.
28. *Ibid.*

steadily out upon the forbidding prospect, as if he were trying to will the storm away."[29]

On December 1, 1864, the day after the Battle of Franklin, General Thomas informed General Halleck by telegraph: "After Schofield's fight of yesterday, feeling that the enemy far outnumbered him, both in infantry and cavalry, I determined to retire to the fortifications around Nashville, until General Wilson can get his cavalry equipped. He has now about one-fourth the number of the enemy, and consequently is no match for him. I have two ironclads here, with several gunboats, and commander Fitch assures me that Hood can neither cross the Cumberland nor blockade it. I therefore think it best to wait here until Wilson can equip all his cavalry. If Hood attacks me here, he will be more seriously damaged than he was yesterday; if he remains until Wilson gets equipped I can whip him and will move against him at once. I have Murfreesboro strongly held, and therefore feel easy in regard to its safety. Chattanooga, Bridgeport, Stevenson, and Elk River bridge also have garrisons."[30]

It is hard to imagine anything more convincing than this dispatch to Halleck and its nonacceptance can only mean that intermixed with a natural fright regarding Hood's movements was the stored-up animosity of Grant toward Thomas. It would have been little cause for wonderment if Thomas had expressed regret that he appealed to Washington to reverse his own promotion over Grant, which restored that man to his command of the Army of the Tennessee after Shiloh. Who can question that this was the worst mistake, for himself and for his country, that could have been made? Otherwise, Grant would almost certainly have been out of the war; Thomas would have retained command; and with his proved record for success the war would have ended without the blood bath to which Grant subjected the Army of the Potomac. Additionally, the March to the Sea would almost certainly not have taken place, with its accompanying postwar bitterness of the inhabitants whose descendants have never forgotten nor forgiven it. Further, Sherman and his distorted history, with Schofield's unwholesome influence on the glory of Thomas, would not have been possible. Finally, Grant's administration would hardly have become the most corrupt of all time, and General Thomas would be buried in the tomb now known as Grant's.

Washington's reaction produced an effect quite contrary to the contents and the purpose of Thomas's dispatch to Halleck. Secretary

29. Clarence E. Macartney, *Grant and His Generals* (New York, 1953), pp. 22, 23.

30. *Official Records, op. cit.,* Vol. XLV, Part 2, p. 3.

of War Stanton, surprisingly, it seems, after his endorsement of Thomas to succeed Buell and his opposition to Rosecrans, delivered himself on December 2 of this dispatch to General Grant: "The President feels solicitous about the disposition of General Thomas to lay in fortifications for an indefinite period 'until Wilson gets equipments.' This looks like the McClellan and Rosecrans strategy of do nothing and let the rebels raid the country. The President wishes you to consider the matter."

The response from Grant was prompt, as shown by his reply at one o'clock on the second, two and one-half hours later: "Immediately on receipt of Thomas' dispatch I sent him a dispatch, which no doubt you read as it passed through the office."[31]

Grant's dispatch is given herewith: "If Hood is permitted to remain quietly about Nashville, you will lose all the road back to Chattanooga, and possibly have to abandon the line of the Tennessee. Should he attack you it is all well, but if he does not you should attack him before he fortifies. Arm and put in the trenches your quartermaster employes, citizens, &c."[32]

This dispatch is revealing for its glaring oversight of Thomas's statement that his cavalry had to be equipped, since, if it was not, and he elected to fight Hood, he would be facing one of the greatest cavalry leaders developed by the war, Nathan B. Forrest. Forrest's cavalry all along outnumbered Wilson's cavalry, and to confront it on less than fairly even terms would be inviting virtual suicide. Another thing revealed in Grant's dispatch was the implied acknowledgment that Thomas was overmatched; this is indicated by his suggestion to arm civilian employes, the necessity for which lay directly at the door of Grant for leaving Thomas to fight a formidable army with inferior and inadequate troops. It is little wonder that Grant was worried, but he took it out on the man least deserving of it.

Grant by now must have felt encouraged to open up both barrels on Thomas, something he had not felt constrained to do at Chattanooga, when Thomas ignored his instructions. With Stanton apparently behind him, his almost every action, as revealed through these dispatches, indicated a determination to "get" Thomas. In just another thirty minutes, at one o'clock after his first dispatch to Thomas, he sent this one:

> With your citizen employes armed, you can move out of
> Nashville with all your army and force the enemy to retire or
> fight upon ground of your own choosing. After the repulse of

31. *Ibid.*, pp. 15-16.
32. *Ibid.*, p. 17.

Hood at Franklin, it looks to me that instead of falling back to Nashville, we should have taken the offensive against the enemy where he was. At this distance, however, I may err as to the best method of dealing with the enemy. You will now suffer incalculable injury upon your railroads, if Hood is not speedily disposed of. Put forth, therefore, every possible exertion to attain this end. Should you get him to retreating, give him no peace.[33]

There is little to complain of in this dispatch from Grant, other than that he was rejecting Thomas's dispatch of December 1 to Halleck outlining his general position. His suggestion to arm citizens sounds rather silly, since they could not become ready to fight, assuming that they agreed to take the oath of allegiance as soldiers, without some training. The history of untrained soldiery is a bad one, and no one should have known it better than Grant. Nevertheless, as Thomas tried to make him understand, it was horses with men on them that were most needed to offset Forrest's superiority.

At ten o'clock that night, December 2, Thomas replied lengthily to Grant as follows:

Your two telegrams of 11 A.M. and 1:30 P.M. to-day are received. At the time that Hood was whipped at Franklin, I had at this place but about 5,000 men of General Smith's command, which added to the force under General Schofield would not have given me more than 25,000 men; besides, General Schofield felt convinced that he could not hold the enemy at Franklin until the 5,000 could reach him. As General Wilson's cavalry force also numbered only about one-fourth that of Forrest's, I thought it best to draw the troops back to Nashville and wait the arrival of the remainder of General Smith's force, and also a force of about 5,000 commanded by Major General Steedman, which I had ordered up from Chattanooga. The division of General Smith arrived yesterday morning, and General Steedman's troops arrived last night. I now have infantry enough to assume the offensive, if I had more cavalry, and will take the field anyhow as the remainder of General McCook's division of cavalry reaches here, which I hope it will do in two or three days. We can neither get reinforcements or equipments at this great distance from the North very easily; and it must be remembered that my command was made up of the two weakest corps of General Sherman's army and all the dismounted cavalry except one brigade, and the task

---

33. *Ibid.*

of reorganizing and equipping has met with many delays, which have enabled Hood to take advantage of my crippled condition. I earnestly hope, however, that in a few more days I shall be able to give him a fight.[34]

There should be no doubt that Grant, of all people, was aware of the truth of what Thomas painstakingly explained to him in the foregoing dispatch. Grant knew it, but he must have been preparing to offer the alibi that it was Thomas's incapacity that prevented the success of the undertaking to defeat Hood, if it failed. He could then go before the country and say, in effect, "See, I have removed Thomas, the worthless commander responsible for the failure," the "Rock of Chickamauga," the hero of Mill Spring, of Murfreesboro, and the Atlanta campaign. This would be predicated on the hope that the country would then overlook Grant and Sherman, the real failures, for authoring the mess that they alone left for Thomas to solve.

The next dispatch was from Thomas to Halleck at ten o'clock the night of the second, promising to move against Hood when McCook's cavalry joined him, although his cavalry would still be not more than half of Hood's. Thomas complained that he had labored under many disadvantages, not least of which was the reorganizing, remounting, and equipping of a cavalry force sufficient to contend with Forrest. He reported that his signal officers and scouts reported that afternoon that Hood and his forces were moving to his right and taking position southwest of Nashville or below. Thomas observed that his position there would be the most advantageous Hood could take for him, as it would expose his line of communication more openly than in any other place. He added further reassurance that the Cumberland River was being patrolled as far as Carthage, Illinois.[35] After this, Thomas was assured by Stanton that he was authorized to "seize and impress horses and every other species of property needed for the military service in your command." In justice to the record, however, it should be reported that Thomas had already taken steps to procure animals before the authority from Stanton was received. On December 3, he informed Halleck as follows:

The enemy made no demonstration to-day, except to advance his pickets about 500 yards on the Nolensville, Franklin and Hillsborough pikes. I have a good intrenched line on the hills around Nashville, and hope to be able to report 10,000 cavalry mounted and equipped in less than a week, when I shall feel able to march against Hood. I gave the order for the impressment of horses

---

34. *Ibid.*, pp. 17-18.
35. *Ibid.*, p. 18.

last night, and received the authority of the Secretary of War this morning.[36]

On the third also, General Thomas reported to Rear Admiral Lee on the Cumberland River that he then had almost as much infantry as Hood, and hoped to have enough cavalry in a few days to assume the offensive. This basis for confidence was confirmed by the head of the telegraphic service in Washington and J. C. Van Duzer, a captain in the Quartermaster's Department at Nashville. Van Duzer reported that the Nashville defenses were strong, and that citizens and Negroes had been impressed to complete them.[37] This information showed that Thomas had not exaggerated his situation; also that he was keeping all concerned informed up to the minute. No one in the area where fighting would be done had any misgivings regarding the ability to cope with Hood; and Grant should have observed the minimum of decency toward Thomas by permitting him some latitude, as commander of an army, for the exercise of independent judgment. He was nothing if not observant of the proprieties with Sherman and his other generals, which alone proves his bad attitude toward Thomas.

It was observed that at the very time when Grant was interfering with the prerogatives of Thomas he was most solicitous in the same particular when it affected Schofield. This relates to Stanton's dispatch of December 5 to General Grant objecting to the appointment of General Stoneman as second in command of the Army of the Ohio. Grant was prompt in calling the matter to Stanton's attention, stating that the matter should be referred to Schofield, "and leave it discretionary then with him to employ Stoneman or relieve him from duty, as he deems best." Schofield's reaction was to agree with Grant, naturally. It was also observed that the reason for Grant's not invoking the rule for the benefit of Thomas would always remain a mystery, since nothing in the *Official Records* afforded any light on the matter. That observer thought that the trouble related to Halleck's preference for Thomas after Shiloh, added to the cold reception to Grant by Thomas at Chattanooga; but whatever the cause, it was noted that Grant did not give Thomas the considerate and kindly trust and confidence to which he was entitled, and that he accorded others.[38] That observer might have noted that there was no record to show that Grant was pulling any rugs from under Halleck, the man who replaced him by Thomas; but Grant was smart enough to know that with respect to Halleck, whom Lincoln appointed, he should toe the straight and narrow path.

---

36. *Ibid.*, p. 29.
37. *Ibid.*, p. 45.
38. *Ibid.*, p. 54; Wilson., *op. cit.*, Vol. II, pp. 73, 74.

Ignoring all of the factors that should have caused him at least to give surface indications of appreciating Thomas's position, which was fully made known to him, Grant would not be calmed down. Perhaps Halleck had something to do with it, perhaps not. At any rate, Halleck dispatched a telegram to Grant on December 5, stating: "The records show that there have been issued at Louisville, Lexington and Nashville since September 20, 22,000 cavalry horses. This number is exclusive of the cavalry horses previously issued and brought into the department by Grierson and others, and the commands of Burbridge and Garrard, and those sent to Sherman. If this number, without any campaign, is already reduced to 10,000 mounted men, as reported by General Wilson, it may be safely assumed that the cavalry of that army will never be mounted, for the destruction of horses in the last two months has there alone been equal to the remounts obtained from the entire West."[39]

General Wilson reported that in so far as Halleck's statement was apparently intended to apply to the Army of the Cumberland, including Wilson's cavalry, it was simply absurd and untrue. It overlooked in the main the equipping from that 22,000 the division of General Kilpatrick for the march with Sherman. Also sloughed over was the terrible campaign in which Wilson lost many animals keeping Forrest away from Schofield up to and including the Battle of Franklin. In brief, many horses were lost in battle, but Kilpatrick was hundreds of miles away with the strongest and best-mounted division of cavalry.[40]

Grant was not long in responding. On the fifth he asked Thomas, "Is there any danger of Forrest moving down the Cumberland to where he can cross it? It seems to me whilst you should be getting up your cavalry as rapidly as possible to look after Forrest, Hood should be attacked where he is. Time strengthens him, in all probability, as much as it does you." That very night, at ten o'clock, Thomas wired Halleck that on that day he had been along his entire line, and that Hood had not moved since the third. He informed Halleck that he hoped to attack on the seventh, provided he could perfect arrangements. This dispatch crossed the one Grant sent to him, which was answered at 8:00 P.M. on the sixth, since it was not received until a half-hour before. In this dispatch he told Grant that Wilson, having just then left him, had parties out pressing horses, and that he hoped to mount from 6,000 to 8,000 cavalry in the next three days. Thomas further stated that he felt it imprudent to attack Hood's 12,000 cavalry with less than 6,000. Forrest's cavalry was over-

---

39. *Official Records, ibid.*, p. 58.
40. Wilson, *op. cit.*, Vol. II, pp. 75-76.

estimated by Thomas and Wilson, neither of whom could know his strength; and it is also pertinent to recall that Schofield's reply to Thomas's inquiry showed that he also had overestimated the enemy cavalry.[41]

Upon receipt of Thomas's reply, Grant telegraphed at 8 P.M. on December 6, "Attack Hood at once, and wait no longer for a remount of your cavalry. There is great danger of delay resulting in a campaign back to the Ohio River." Thomas replied to Grant as follows: "Your telegram of 4 P.M. this day is just received. I will make the necessary dispositions and attack Hood at once, agreeably to your order, though I believe it will be hazardous with the small force of cavalry now at my service."[42]

At just what moment Thomas expected to thus attack against his own judgment is not clear. In the meantime, General Halleck issued another dispatch to Thomas on December 6, 1 P.M., stating that 22,000 cavalry horses were issued at Louisville, Lexington, and Nashville since September 20, necessitating Thomas's explanation to the effect that there had been great losses in action and from disease, and a large number of men were still without horses. The loss from disease was attributable by Thomas to glanders and distemper; but Thomas promised again to attack as soon as enough animals were accumulated. Wilson noted that help, at least in good will, and not carping criticism, was what Thomas and himself needed most. He used the pronoun "we" because he said that "it was my great honor and privilege to have been joined with Thomas, and under him, I was chiefly responsible for, and the chief object of, thoughtless bureaucratic criticism. Happily for me, as well as for the country, I had the Rock of Chickamauga at my back."[43] This certainly reflects greatly upon Grant, who was responsible for the entire nerve-wracking situation that ended with a question mark, wholly unjustified, against a man without an earned blemish. We see from dispatches that Thomas could not justifiably attack; that he imparted this knowledge to Grant and Halleck; but that nothing would convince them that they were wrong and Thomas was right.

Secretary Stanton's turn now came to stir up the muddied waters. On December 7, 10:20 A.M., he telegraphed Grant that "Thomas seems unwilling to attack because it is hazardous, as if all war was anything but hazardous. If he waits for Wilson to get ready, Gabriel will be blowing his last horn."[44] Grant's response indicated a promptness born of pent-up desire to get on with the job of taking Thomas apart

41. *Ibid.*, pp. 78-79; *Official Records, op. cit.*, Vol. XLV, Part 2, pp. 55, 70.
42. *Official Records, ibid.*, p. 70.
43. Wilson, *op. cit.*, Vol. II, p. 77; *Official Records, ibid.*, p. 71.

figuratively, but of encompassing his military demise in actuality. This dispatch to Stanton leaves little to complete the evidence of his injustice, while, of all things, recommending that Schofield be in charge of Thomas.

This is Grant's reply to Stanton: "You probably saw my order to Thomas to attack. If he does not do it promptly, I would recommend superseding him by Schofield, leaving Thomas subordinate. Steele is an admirable corps commander, and I would say order him to report to Canby until there is an opening to put him in command of a corps. I would have no objection [and] would like Steele appointed to command of Ninth Corps, and General Parke ordered to report to General Canby."[44]

Grant appeared to have the plan all ready, certainly one of the dirtiest, if not *the* dirtiest, cutthroat jobs ever performed on a man of even remotely equivalent ability; and Grant thereby earned, which he did not receive, the contempt of every American who believes in fair play. If Thomas had been lacking in any degree for command is one thing; but he was the man with the best record, who had saved his army more than once from defeat and lesser generals from disgrace because of incompetency, and was to be kicked out of the army and forever disgraced by a man like Grant. Shame on us! The nation needed Thomas far more than it ever needed Grant; and aside from his unmatched military record, Thomas stands forth in the light of history in a role given to few mortals, that as an exemplar of clean living and as a model for youth equaled by very few men in our entire history. After almost four years of war, in which the nation had suffered crushing, needless defeats because of haste and lack of preparation, the Government was permitting the bloodiest general in our history to ruin the man who refused to sacrifice his men needlessly. The wonder is that the President stood by and permitted this to happen, knowing as he did the greatness of Thomas. One fact emerged from this terrible ordeal, namely, further proof that Grant was incapable and that he was vindictive and unjust, as his entire record from the beginning proves him to have been.

If General Dwight D. Eisenhower, who commanded the largest military force ever assembled, as far as we know, on D-day, 1944, had been at Nashville in 1864, he also, unless a favorite, would have been in the same trouble as Thomas. General Eisenhower's campaign was not undertaken until every conceivable preparation had been made to insure success, as it should have been. Grant's record proves that he would have had none of it. He would have compelled General Eisenhower to get a move on, and, if he did not, the result would

44. *Official Records, ibid.,* p. 84.

have been dismissal. It is small wonder that the people of the North clamored for President Lincoln to remove Grant, what with a crepe on virtually every other door and still no promised victory over Lee. Lincoln said, "He fights!" He did, tragically, as long as the men held out; and if General Lee had been able to command half the force given to Grant he would have beaten him badly, which would have meant, of course, Southern independence. The Grant Legend, fostered and perpetuated by subordinates with favors to seek from Grant, invented Grant's greatness. One needs but to examine his biographers, particularly Adam Badeau, who compiled one of the least believable collections of distortion, twisted reasoning, and underrating of the achievements of generals not within Grant's circle, to know the truth of the Grant Legend.

Wilson gives Stanton and Halleck credit in this situation, that is, Grant's demand for Thomas's dismissal, ascribing Grant's failure to go through with it to these men. They did little for Thomas, and were the two who most encouraged Grant to believe he could get away with it. Although Wilson reminds us that they kept reinforcing him, or trying to do so, and strengthening him from every quarter, was not that the least they should have done, and was that not their responsibility?

The tenacious Grant, now determined to go through with it, wired Halleck at 4 P.M. on the eighth, asking him to direct General Dodge to send all available troops to General Thomas. He also reported to Halleck his opinion that it might be advisable to ask the states of Ohio, Indiana, and Illinois for 60,000 troops for thirty days. This suggestion would seem to be an admission that Thomas's problem was a shortage of men, and not a deficiency in generalship, which his dismissal would imply, although at this stage in the exchange of dispatches the problem was not so much men as horses. Grant then told Halleck, "If Thomas has not struck yet, he ought to be ordered to hand over his command to Schofield. There is no better man to repel an attack than Thomas, but I fear he is too cautious to ever take the initiative."[45] Ah, Schofield! One thing is crystal clear: Grant lacked the intestinal fortitude to dismiss Thomas without the concurrence of Halleck and Stanton.

General Halleck now came upon the stage, and although he did General Thomas some harm, through his dispatches to Grant, when the showdown came he stood up for him to the extent at least of not favoring his dismissal. Halleck had some regard for Thomas, of that there is no doubt. His response at 9 P.M. on the eighth was: "If you wish General Thomas relieved from [command] give the order.

---

45. Wilson, *op. cit.*, Vol. II, p. 81; *Official Records, ibid.*, p. 96.

No one here will, I think, interfere. The responsibility, however, will be yours, as no one here, so far as I am informed, wishes General Thomas' removal."[46]

Although Grant was now clothed with authority to remove Thomas, his rank of lieutenant general being a notch above his rank when in the presence of Thomas at Chattanooga, where, it was reported, his feelings told him that he was in the presence of a greatly superior man, which he was, he did not have the courage to go through with it. He was on his own, and wanted support that he had not yet received. He now hedged, as his next dispatch to Halleck shows: "Your dispatch of 9:00 P.M. just received. I want General Thomas reminded of the importance of immediate action. I sent him a dispatch this evening which will probably urge him on. I would not say relieve him until I hear further from him."[47] What brought this change in Grant? His previous dispatch stated that if Thomas had not yet struck he ought to be ordered to hand over his command, and Thomas had not yet struck. The truth is that Grant had fears. For Thomas? No, for Grant.

The next dispatch from Grant to Thomas was much more conciliatory, and something akin to what would normally pass between two commanders. Grant observed to Thomas that it appeared as if the enemy was trying to cross the Cumberland River and was scattered. He asked, "Why not attack at once? By all means avoid the contingency of a foot race to see which, you or Hood, can beat to the Ohio. . . . Now is one of the finest opportunities ever presented of destroying one of the three armies of the enemy. If destroyed, he never can replace it. Use the means at your command, and you can do this and cause a rejoicing that will resound from one end of the land to another."[48]

General Wilson reported on the same day, December 8, that although all was well, with reinforcements coming on to aid Thomas, and the enemy contained, at least to the point of not attempting the feared invasion to the Ohio, "measures of the gravest character were being matured at the War Department under the express direction of General Grant, due, most unhappily, to his misunderstanding of the facts and his persistent disregard of his own wise rule of non-interference in the plans and details of execution on the part of independent commanders and his inexplicable refusal to accord Thomas, incomparably the best of the lot, that freedom of judgment and action which he so generously extended to Meade, Sherman, Sheridan and

---

46. *Official Records, ibid.*
47. *Ibid.*
48. *Ibid.*, p. 97.

Schofield." This statement is interesting and important for its appraisal of Thomas as "incomparably the best of the lot," not a small compliment from one perhaps better qualified to evaluate these commanders than anyone else. Wilson also stated that Grant's part in the crisis "was perhaps the least creditable incident in his whole military career."[49]

General Grant was receiving the benefit of independent reports, as mentioned previously, from Captain Van Duzer of the Quartermaster's Department at Nashville to Major Eckert in Washington. The latest report to Eckert, on December 8 at 8 P.M., stated: "No change in position here since last report. Enemy still in force in front, as was found out by reconnaissance, and a large artillery force upon south bank of the Cumberland below, between here and the Shoals. One of our gunboats came to grief in exchange of iron at Bell's Ferry, Rebel General Lyon holds same bank below Harpeth, to Fort Donelson, but does not fight gunboats. Reinforcements now at Clarkesville; will reach here by railroad tomorrow night. Colonel Thompson's black brigade reached here yesterday, having come from Johnsonville, via Clarkesville. Deserters report Hood's headquarters seven miles out on Hillsborough pike; Forrest three miles on Granny White road, with main army on same road nearer town."[50]

Better assurance to Grant than the foregoing report was not possible, and it surely must have been brought to his attention. He chose to ignore it. He did not want the facts to change his mind in regard to Thomas. His stance of injustice, so long maintained, would not be abandoned in the face of his determination to get rid of him. No other conclusion is possible than that Grant meant to destroy Thomas, as his ignoring of this report, if nothing else, so definitely proves.

General Wilson again remarked upon the injustice by Grant, following the next dispatch, of December 9 at 11:00 A.M., by the statement, "Grant did himself the great wrong and Thomas the intolerable injustice disclosed in the following message to Halleck": "Dispatch of 8 P.M. last evening from Nashville shows the enemy scattered for more than seventy miles down the river, and no attack yet made by Thomas. Please telegraph orders, relieving him at once and placing Schofield in command. Thomas should be directed to turn all orders and dispatches received since the battle of Franklin to Schofield."[51] Schofield once more; what friendship!

This dispatch seemed to be the end of the road for Thomas, but not yet. In the first place, Grant seized upon the report from Van

49. Wilson, *op. cit.*, Vol. II, p. 84.
50. *Official Records, op. cit.*, Vol. XLV, Part 2, pp. 97-98.
51. *Ibid.;* Wilson, *op. cit.*, Vol. II, p. 5.

Duzer to Eckert, and from it drew a picture of the enemy in force, although scattered many miles along the river, raising the question of Thomas's failure to attack. It would appear that Grant's few years in military service before the war, and his long years of service out of it, also before the war, were revealing him as either not too capable or as wanting to finish Thomas off. The War Department next entered the crisis, for that it was, in a most significant way. Receiving Grant's order for the removal of Thomas, its implementation was begun by means of a General Order, but no one expedited its complete progress, and things began to happen.

The elements, sleet or freezing rain, Providence—call it what you will—intervened. Thomas, in reply to Halleck's dispatch of 10:30 A.M. on the ninth, in which Halleck again urged Thomas to attack and reminded him that Grant was very dissatisfied, wired this: "I regret that General Grant should feel dissatisfaction at my delay in attacking the enemy. I feel conscious that I have done everything in my power to prepare, and that the troops could not have been gotten ready before this, and if he should order me to be relieved I will submit without a murmur. A terrible storm of freezing rain has come on since daylight, which will render an attack impossible until it breaks."[52] For the first time, it seems, Thomas showed an awareness that he was really in danger of being removed; but that Schofield was to be his successor he apparently did not know until after the war, when Halleck imparted the news to him.

Earlier that day, December 9, Thomas also sent Grant a report on the situation, stating that he was about ready to attack on the tenth, the next morning, but that a "terrible storm of freezing rain had come on to-day, which will make it impossible for our men to fight to any advantage. I am therefore compelled to wait for the storm to break and make the attack immediately after." When Halleck asked Grant, also on the ninth, whether he still wanted Thomas removed from command and the orders telegraphed, he replied that although Thomas had promised to fight on the seventh, and had failed to give him a reason for not doing so, he was "unwilling to do injustice to an officer who has done as much good service as General Thomas has, however, and will, therefore, suspend the order relieving him until it is seen whether he will do anything."[53]

It must have become apparent to Grant that relieving Thomas might expose himself to some danger. At any rate, at 7:30 P.M. on the ninth, Grant sent him a dispatch stating: "I have as much confidence in your conducting a battle rightly as I have in any other officer;

52. *Official Records, ibid.,* p. 114.
53. *Ibid.,* p. 115.

but it has seemed to me you have been slow, and I have had no explanation of affairs to convince me otherwise. [Grant appears to have been downright stupid for this remark, since he and everyone concerned were given full details the entire time. He simply believed what he wanted to believe.] Receiving your dispatch at 2 P.M., from General Halleck, before I did the one to me, I telegraphed to suspend the order relieving you until we should hear further. I hope most sincerely that there will be no necessity of repeating the orders, and that the facts will show that you have been right all the time."[54]

The fact of the freezing rain, lasting four days at its worst, was confirmed by Van Duzer and Eckert in their dispatches, a circumstance that saved Thomas from removal by reason of their knowledge of his difficult situation, and enabled his force to utilize the additional time to complete preparations. "It is doubtful if in the life of any good and great man there was ever more timely or clear providential interference in his fortunes and in his favor than that pitiless 'terrible storm of freezing rain' reported to both Grant and Halleck by General Thomas." The suspension was too much to expect, apparently, and Grant was still in a bad frame of mind. He had no patience with Thomas, solely because "East is East, and West is West, and never the twain shall meet,"[55] and he would not or could not wait out the freezing weather.

On December 11, at 4 P.M., Grant resumed once more his drive on Thomas, although this was in the very heart of the freezing storm. "If you delay attack longer the mortifying spectacle will be witnessed of a rebel army moving for the Ohio River, and you will be forced to act, accepting such weather as you find. Let there be no further delay. Hood cannot stand even a drawn battle, so far from his supplies of ordnance stores. If he retreats and you follow, he must lose his material and much of his army. I am in hopes of receiving a dispatch from you to-day announcing that you have moved. Delay no longer for weather or reinforcements."[56] If it had not been sent, it would be difficult to believe that the commander of all Federal forces would order a campaign started on ice, when neither humans nor animals could stand up on it, much less fight on it. The wonder is that a man of such inferior qualifications became entrusted with such power.

Thomas replied at 10:30 P.M. that night. He said: "I will obey the order as promptly as possible, however much I may regret it, as the attack will have to be made under every disadvantage. The whole

54. *Ibid.*

55. Rudyard Kipling, "Ballad of East and West"; Wilson, *op. cit.*, pp. 88-89.

56. *Official Records, op. cit.*, Vol. XLV, Part 2, p. 143.

country is covered with a perfect sheet of ice and sleet, and it is with difficulty the troops are able to move about on level ground. It was my intention to attack Hood as soon as the ice melted, and would have done so yesterday had it not been for the storm." This appraisal from Thomas was fully supported in a dispatch from Van Duzer to Eckert at 9:30 P.M. on the eleventh, stating: "Frost still holds everybody, except wood-cutters, idle. No movement to report either on our part or that of the enemy for the past three days." Again, to show the continuance of bad weather, Van Duzer's report to Eckert at 8 P.M. on December 13 is revealing: "Reconnaissance to-day showed enemy's force all around; in greatest strength on right, where some artillery opened. Thaw has begun, and tomorrow we can move without skates." Even Schofield, the beneficiary if Thomas had been removed, in his dispatch of December 12, reported to Thomas: "I think the river should be guarded very carefully from here to Gallatin, and for a short distance above that point, though it seems hardly possible that Hood can attempt any move at this time."[57] There it is; the man who was scheduled to relieve Thomas would also have been unable to move, although under Grant's order he probably would have moved with disastrous results. Of course, from Grant's viewpoint, he would have disposed of Thomas, a consummation devoutly to be wished, good weather or bad, defeat or victory.

The next interesting development came in a dispatch on December 14 at 8:00 P.M. from Thomas to Halleck, in which he reported that the ice having melted away that day the enemy would be attacked on the fifteenth. He repeated his former statement: "Much as I regret the delay in attacking the enemy, it could not have been done before with any reasonable hope of success."

On December 13, Special Orders No. 149, authorized by General Grant, instructed as follows:

1. Maj. Gen. John A. Logan, U. S. Volunteers, will proceed immediately to Nashville, Tenn., reporting by telegraph to the lieutenant-general commanding his arrival at Louisville, Ky., and also his arrival at Nashville, Tenn.

By command of Lieutenant-General Grant:

T. S. Bowers,
Assistant Adjutant-General.[58]

Something apparently occurred between Schofield and Grant to have caused Grant to drop him, a West Pointer, in favor of Logan,

---

57. *Ibid.*, pp. 143, 145, 157, 171.
58. *Ibid.*, p. 171.

a non-West-Pointer and an Illinois politician, although reputedly a good commander. It will be recalled that some of General John M. Palmer's trouble stemmed from his not having been a West Pointer, which allegedly resulted in his removal from command of the Fourteenth Corps, as we have seen. It is interesting to speculate what influences were at work favoring Logan, and whether he also would have had similar difficulties if he had been given command of Thomas's army. This assumes that Logan was meant to replace Thomas, although the dispatch does not so state. It does not state either that Logan was to report to Thomas but to Grant himself; therefore it is hardly questionable that he was meant to replace Thomas.

It has been stated that General Logan was given to understand that he was to relieve Thomas, if, when he arrived at Nashville, Thomas had not begun to attack Hood. His instruction regarding Louisville apparently meant that he should check at that point, and if Thomas had attacked, he should return to Washington, as he actually did. On December 13, the same date, Grant is reported to have issued his second order, which Logan took with him to be delivered to Thomas, relieving the latter of his command. Even further, which indicates how disturbed Grant was, he made preparations to go in person to Nashville, as shown by his dispatch to Thomas at 11:30 P.M. on the fifteenth: "I was just on my way to Nashville, but receiving a dispatch from Van Duzer, detailing your splendid success of to-day, I shall go no further."[59]

Before Grant's cancellation of his proposed trip, however, he had had prepared a third order, following a conference with Lincoln, Stanton, and Halleck, at which Eckert was also present. Eckert was in attendance in connection with the disruption that day of the telegraph lines between Nashville and Washington, and following Grant's insistence upon their consent to Thomas's removal, Eckert was given the order for removal for transmission. Eckert could not relay the order for the reason that the telegraph lines were disrupted, and decided to defer any further attempts until he heard from his fellow worker at Nashville, Van Duzer. When the line was finally opened, Thomas's dispatch of December 15, 9:00 P.M., was received. It read: "I attacked the enemy's left this morning and drove it from the river, below the city, very nearly to the Franklin pike, a distance of about eight miles. Have captured General Chalmers' headquarters and train, and a second train of about 20 wagons, with between 800 and 1,000 prisoners and 16 pieces of artillery. The troops behaved splendidly,

59. *Ibid.*, p. 195.

all taking their share in assaulting and carrying the enemy's breast-works. I shall attack the enemy again tomorrow, if he stands to fight, and, if he retreats during the night, will pursue him, throwing a heavy cavalry force in his rear, to destroy his trains, if possible."[60]

When it was found impossible for Hood to be attacked on December 10, as hoped, Thomas that night called a meeting of his corps commanders at his headquarters to discuss affairs and to obtain their views. Thomas informed them of his dispatches from Grant and his replies, reminding them that his decision had been based upon his own judgment, and that he desired only to let them know what he had felt impelled to do. He implied that he would welcome their views as to his course of action, but assured them that they were in no wise bound by his action, and that he was responsible for the consequences. Wilson, who as junior corps commander spoke first, expressed hearty agreement with the action taken, declaring that if Hood had been attacked he could have repelled any attack made against him by using only baskets of brickbats. The reaction to such a defense, he maintained, would have made the attackers slip and dodge on the treacherous ice and recoil in confusion. Good old Tom Wood, next to speak, agreed with Wilson, and Smith and Steedman were equally in agreement that no attack could be made until the weather improved. Wilson reported that Schofield, on the testimony of all present, was silent, although he stated that he responded, "General Thomas, I will sustain you in your determination not to fight until you are fully ready."[61]

As the meeting disbanded, Thomas asked Wilson to remain for further discussion. When they were alone, Thomas said, "Wilson, the Washington authorities treat me as if I were a boy. They seem to think me incapable of planning a campaign or of fighting a battle, but if they will just let me alone till thawing weather begins and the ground is in condition for us to move at all I will show them what we can do. I am sure my plan of operations is correct, and that we shall lick the enemy, if he only stays to receive our attack." After some further discussion, Wilson related, "I went to camp that night with a higher opinion of Thomas and his character than I had ever had before." Wilson also stated: "He was an officer of unshakable resolution and of the highest character. His self-control was perfect, his bearing lofty and serene, and in all that he said and did he reminded me of the traditional Washington more than any man I had ever met. He was a patriot without flaw and a soldier without re-

60. *Ibid.*, p. 194; David H. Bates, *Lincoln in the Telegraph Office* (New York, 1907), pp. 310-15.

61. Schofield, *op. cit.*, p. 238; Wilson, *op. cit.*, Vol. II, pp. 101-2.

proach."[62] It is small wonder that Grant felt ill at ease in the presence of such a man; but it is ridiculous that Thomas should be subordinate to Grant.

General Schofield has been long suspected of treachery in connection with the Nashville campaign. His reported silence at General Thomas's meeting with his corps commanders on December 10, as aforesaid, gave color to the suspicion. Thomas's biographer, Van Horne, draws attention to an apparent coolness between them, a coolness that appears to run through the Schofield communications to Thomas during the campaign from Spring Hill to the end. This coolness is suggested by the terse, matter-of-fact, no-embellishment type of conveying ideas, which is not in evidence when people are on good terms with each other. There might have been reflected a warmth, so natural between former instructor and pupil, but there was not, and for a very good reason.

General Thomas's headquarters had been suspicious for some time after the campaign commenced that some Judas was telegraphing information to Washington, having for its purpose the undermining of Thomas. Naturally Thomas was solicitous regarding it and sought to locate the source. Calling upon General James B. Steedman, one of his corps commanders who also had his suspicions, for suggestions as to the leak, that hearty commander assigned Captain Marshall Davis to run it down. Davis went to the telegraph office and noted there a message from Schofield to Grant, stating: "Many officers here are of the opinion that General Thomas is certainly too slow in his movements." Returning promptly to General Thomas with the information, that noble man, who had been undergoing the torments of the damned from Grant's heartless and incessant barrage of dispatches to engage Hood, still clung to a vestige of disbelief that Schofield did it. After unmistakably recognizing Schofield's handwriting, he asked Steedman, "Why does he send such telegrams?" When Steedman reminded him that as second in command Schofield would succeed him if removed, the truth was brought home to Thomas in all of its bare, stark nakedness that Schofield had betrayed him.[63]

The undercutting of Thomas not only reflected upon Schofield, but more especially upon Grant, who permitted Schofield's dispatches to influence him in his attempt to disgrace Thomas. There appears to be in this incident some reason for Grant's shifting from Schofield to Logan, as has been stated. Perhaps Grant realized that, although he

---

62. Wilson, *ibid.*, p. 204.

63. Van Horne, *op. cit.*, p. 321; Cincinnati *Enquirer* reprint of article in Toledo *Northern Democrat* quoting General Steedman (Civil War clipping, "Robbing the Dead," in Library of Congress).

had been influenced by Thomas's subordinate, he should not be in the position of having rewarded him for it by putting him in Thomas's place. Schofield did all right, however, if not immediately, as shown by his becoming Secretary of War in 1868-1869; commander of the Department of the Missouri from March, 1869, to May, 1870; commander of the Division of the Pacific, Thomas's former command, although Thomas was then deceased; and continuing right on up the ladder with help from the hierarchy in which he was an influential member. Some interest is attracted to the fact that the material or evidence of Schofield's telegrams was missing from the War Department files when a search was made for them in 1879.[64] One would suppose that Grant might make some attempt at redress for the wrong done Thomas at Nashville; but if there was any change in his attitude it was not perceptible.

The following account of the Battle of Nashville is from General Thomas's report, since the plan and execution were his sole responsibility. He first prepared the plan, and after a meeting with his corps commanders discussed with them their respective participation in the battle. "No battle of the war was better planned, and none was so nearly carried out to the letter of the plan as the battle of Nashville. It has been said that this plan of Thomas's is the only one of the entire war that is now studied as a model in European military schools."[65] For this reason the plan, as given in Thomas's report, is included:

As soon as the state of the weather will admit of offensive operations, the troops will move against the enemy's position in the following order:

Maj. Gen. A. J. Smith, commanding Detachment of the Army of the Tennessee, after forming his troops on and near the Hardin pike, in front of his present position, will make a vigorous assault on the enemy's left.

Maj. General Wilson, commanding the Cavalry Corps, Military Division of the Mississippi, with three divisions, will move on and support General Smith's right, assisting, as far as possible, in carrying the left of the enemy's position, and be in readiness to throw his force upon the enemy the moment a favorable opportunity occurs. Major General Wilson will also send one division on the Charlotte pike to clear that road of the enemy and

64. The John N. Hough Papers (dated June 6, 1881, from Sanford Kellogg to Col. Alfred L. Hough, stating his belief that Schofield sought to replace Gen. Thomas at Nashville by damaging him).

65. *Photographic History of the Civil War* (New York, 1957), Vol. III, p. 264.

observe in the direction of Bell's Landing, to protect our right rear until the enemy's position is fairly turned, when it will rejoin the main force.

Brig. Gen. T. J. Wood, commanding the Fourth Corps, after leaving a strong skirmish line in his work from Laurens' Hill to his extreme right, will form the remainder of the Fourth Corps on Hillsborough pike, to support General Smith's left, and operate on the left and rear of the enemy's advanced position on the Montgomery Hill.

Major-General Schofield, commanding Twenty-third Army Corps, will replace Brigadier-General Kimball's division of the Fourth Corps, with his troops, and occupy the trenches from Fort Negley to Laurens' Hill with a strong skirmish line. He will move with the remainder of his force in front of the works and cooperate with General Wood, protecting the latter's left flank against an attack by the enemy.

Major-General Steedman, commanding District of the Etowah, will occupy the interior line in rear of his present position, stretching from the reservoir on the Cumberland River to Fort Negley, with a strong skirmish line, and mass the remainder of his force in its present position, to act according to the exigencies which may arise during these operations.

Brigadier-General Miller, with the troops forming the garrison of Nashville, will occupy the interior line from the battery on Hill 210 to the extreme right, including the inclosed work on the Hyde's Ferry road.

The quartermaster's troops, under command of Brigadier-General Donaldson, will, if necessary, be posted on the interior line from Fort Morton to the battery on Hill 210.

The troops occupying the interior line will be under the direction of Major-General Steedman, who is charged with the immediate defense of Nashville during the operations around the city.

Should the weather permit, the troops will be formed [in time] to commence operations at 6 A.M. on the 15th or as soon thereafter as practicable.

On the morning of the 15th of December, the weather being favorable, the army was formed and ready at an early hour to carry out the plan of battle promulgated in the special field order of the 14th. The formation of the troops was partially concealed from the enemy by the broken nature of the ground, as also by a dense fog, which only lifted toward noon. The enemy was apparently totally unaware of any intention on our part to attack his position, and more especially did he seem not to expect any movement against his left flank. To divert his attention still further from our real intentions, Major-General Steedman had, on the evening of the 14th, received orders to make a heavy demonstration with his command against the enemy's right, east of the Nolensville pike, which he accomplished with great success and some loss, succeeding, however, in attracting the enemy's attention to that part of his lines, and inducing him to draw reinforcements from toward his center and left. As soon as General Steedman had completed his movement, the commands of Generals Smith and Wilson moved out along the Hardin pike and commenced the grand movement of the day, by wheeling to the left and advancing against the enemy's position across the Hardin and Nolensville pikes. A division of cavalry [Johnson's] was sent at the same time to look after a battery of the enemy's on the Cumberland River at Bell's Landing, eight miles below Nashville. General Johnson did not get into position until late in the afternoon, when, in conjunction with the gunboats under Lieut. Commander LeRoy Fitch, the enemy's battery was engaged until after nightfall, and the place was found evacuated on the morning of the 16th. The remainder of General Wilson's command, Hatch's division leading and Knipe in reserve, moving on the right of General A. J. Smith's troops, first struck the enemy along Richland Creek, near Hardin's house, and drove him back rapidly, capturing a number of prisoners, wagons, &c., and continuing to advance, whilst slightly swinging to the left, came upon a redoubt containing four guns, which was splendidly carried by assault, at 1 P.M., by a portion of Hatch's division, dismounted, and the captured guns turned upon the enemy. A second redoubt, stronger than the first, was next assailed and carried by the same troops that captured the first position, taking 4 more guns and about 300 prisoners. The infantry, McArthur's division, of General A. J. Smith's command, on the left of the cavalry, participated in both of the assaults; and, indeed, the dismounted cavalry seemed to vie with the infantry who should first gain the works; as they reached the position nearly simultaneously, both lay claim to the artillery and prisoners captured.

Finding General Smith had not taken as much distance to the right as I expected he would have done, I directed General Schofield to move his command [the Twenty-third Corps] from the position in reserve to which it had been assigned over to the right of General Smith, enabling the cavalry thereby to operate more freely on the enemy's rear. This was rapidly accomplished

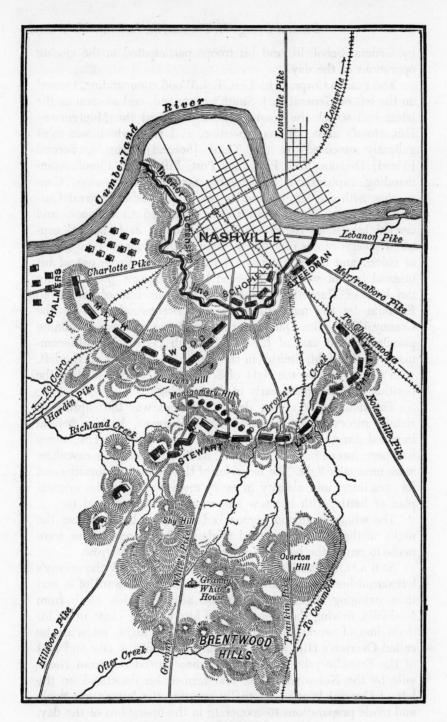

NASHVILLE, DECEMBER 15, 1864

by General Schofield, and his troops participated in the closing operations of the day.

The Fourth Corps, Brig. Gen. T. J. Wood commanding, formed on the left of General A. J. Smith's command, and as soon as the latter had struck the enemy's flank, assaulted the Montgomery Hill, Hood's most advanced position, at 1 P.M., which was most gallantly executed by the Third [Second] Brigade, Second [Third] Division, Col. P. Sidney Post, Fifty-ninth Illinois, commanding, capturing a considerable number of prisoners. Connecting with the left of Smith's troops [Brigadier-General Garrard's division], the Fourth Corps continued to advance, and carried by assault the enemy's entire line in its front and captured several pieces of artillery, about 500 prisoners, some stands of colors, and other material. The enemy was driven out of his original line of works and forced back to a new postion along the base of Harpeth Hills, still holding his line of retreat to Franklin—by the main pike, through Brentwood, and by the Granny White pike. Our line at nightfall was readjusted, running parallel to and east of the Hillsborough pike—Schofield's command on the right, Smith's in the center, and Wood's on the left, with the cavalry on the right of Schofield, Steedman holding the position he had gained early in the morning.

The total result of the day's operations was the capture of sixteen pieces of artillery and 1,200 prisoners, besides several hundred stand of small arms and about forty wagons. The enemy had been forced back at all points, with heavy loss; our casualties were unusually light. The behavior of the troops was unsurpassed for steadiness and alacrity in every movement, and the original plan of battle, with but few alterations, strictly adhered to.

The whole command bivouacked in line of battle during the night on the ground occupied at dark, whilst preparations were made to renew the battle at an early hour on the morrow.

At 6 A.M. on the 16th, Wood's corps pressed back the enemy's left skirmishers across the Franklin pike to the eastward of it, and then swinging slightly to the right, advanced due south from Nashville, driving the enemy before him until he came upon his main line of works, constructed during the night, on what he called Overton's Hill, about five miles south of the city and east of the Franklin pike. General Steedman moved out from Nashville by the Nolensville pike, and formed his command on the left of General Wood, effectually securing the latter's left flank, and made preparations to cooperate in the operations of the day. General A. J. Smith's command moved on the right of the Fourth

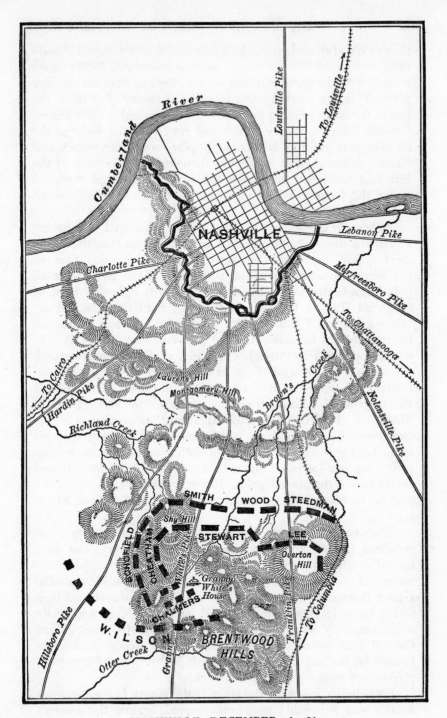

NASHVILLE, DECEMBER 16, 1864

Corps [Wood's], and establishing connection with General Wood's right, completed the new line of battle. General Schofield's troops remained in the position taken up by them at dark on the day previous, facing eastward and toward the enemy's left flank, the line of the corps running perpendicular to General Smith's troops. General Wilson's cavalry, which had rested for the night at the six-mile post on the Hillsborough pike, was dismounted and formed on the right of Schofield's command, and by noon of the 16th had succeeded in gaining the enemy's rear, and stretched across the Granny White pike, one of his two outlets toward Franklin.

As soon as the above dispositions were completed, and having visited the different commands, I gave directions that the movement against the enemy's left flank should be continued. Our entire line approached to within 600 yards of the enemy's at all points. His center was weak, as compared with either his right, at Overton's Hill, or his left, on the hills bordering the Granny White pike; still I had hopes of gaining his rear and cutting off his retreat from Franklin. About 3 P.M. Post's brigade of Wood's corps, supported by Streight's brigade, of the same command, was ordered by General Wood to assault Overton's Hill. This intention was communicated to General Steedman, who ordered the brigade of colored troops commanded by Colonel C. R. Thompson, Twelfth U. S. Colored Troops, to cooperate in the movement. The ground on which the two assaulting columns formed being open and exposed to the enemy's view, he, readily perceiving our intention, drew reinforcements from his left and center to the threatened point. This movement of troops on the part of the enemy was communicated along the line from left to right.

The assault was made, and received by the enemy with a tremendous fire of grape and canister and musketry; our men moved steadily onward up the hill until near the crest, when the reserve of the enemy rose and poured into the assaulting column a most destructive fire, causing the men first to waver and then to fall back, leaving their dead and wounded—black and white indiscriminately mingled—lying amid the abatis, the gallant Colonel Post among the wounded. General Wood readily reformed his command in the position it had previously occupied, preparatory to a renewal of the assault.

Immediately following the effort of the Fourth Corps, Generals Smith's and Schofield's commands moved against the enemy's works in their respective fronts, carrying all before them, irreparably breaking his line in a dozen places, and capturing all his artillery and thousands of prisoners, among the latter four general officers. Our loss was remarkably small, scarcely mentionable. All of the enemy that did escape were pursued over the tops of Brentwood and Harpeth Hills.

General Wilson's cavalry, dismounted, attacked the enemy simultaneously with Schofield and Smith, striking him in reverse, and gaining firm possession of the Granny White pike, cut off his retreat by that route.

Wood's and Steedman's troops, hearing the shouts of victory coming from the right, rushed impetuously forward, renewing the assault on Overton's Hill, and although meeting a very heavy fire, the onset was irresistible, artillery and innumerable prisoners falling into our hands. The enemy, hopelessly broken, fled in confusion through the Brentwood Pass, the Fourth Corps in a close pursuit, which was continued for several miles, when darkness closed the scene and the troops rested from their labors.

As the Fourth Corps pursued the enemy on Franklin pike, General Wilson hastily mounted Knipe's and Hatch's divisions of his command, and directed them to pursue along the Granny White pike and endeavor to reach Franklin in advance of the enemy. After proceeding about a mile they came upon the enemy's cavalry, under Chalmers, posted across the road and behind barricades. The position was charged by the Twelfth Tennessee Cavalry, Colonel Spalding commanding, and the enemy's lines broken, scattering him in all directions, and capturing quite a number of prisoners, among them Brig. Gen. E. W. Rucker.

During the two days' operations there were 4,462 prisoners captured including 287 officers of all grades from that of major-general, 53 pieces of artillery, and thousands of small arms. The enemy abandoned in the field all his dead and wounded.

Leaving directions for the collection of the captured property and for the care of the wounded left on the battlefield, the pursuit was continued at daylight on the 17th. The Fourth Corps pushed on toward Franklin by the direct pike, whilst the cavalry moved by the Granny White pike to its intersection with the Franklin pike, and then took the advance.

Johnson's division of cavalry was sent by General Wilson direct to Harpeth River, on the Hillsborough pike, with directions to cross and move rapidly toward Franklin. The main cavalry column, with Knipe's division in advance, came up with the enemy's rear-guard strongly posted at Hollow Tree Gap, four miles north of Franklin; the position was charged in front and in flank simultaneously, and handsomely carried, capturing 413 prisoners and 3 colors. The enemy then fell back rapidly to Franklin, and endeavored to defend the crossing of Harpeth River at that place; but Johnson's division coming up from below on the south side of the stream, forced him to retire from the river bank, and our cavalry took possession of the town, capturing the enemy's hospital, containing over 2,000 wounded, of whom about 200 were our own men.[66]

Thus ended General Thomas's report of the battle proper, although he was most conservative in giving due credit to himself. Perhaps he reasoned that all that was necessary was to give the straight facts without regard to who may have performed outstandingly.

Outside of Nashville is a monument, erected in 1926 by the Ladies' Battlefield Memorial Association, aided by contributions from patriotic citizens of the state of Tennessee and Davidson County. On the south side of the monument is the legend: "The Spirit of youth holds in check the fierce Battle of Nashville, December 16, 1864, sealing forever the bond of union by the blood of our heroic dead of the World War 1917-1918." On the north side of the monument are the following beautiful words, expressive of the heroism of both Northern and Southern participants and the resulting unified nation:

> Oh, valorous gray, in the grave of your fate,
> Oh, glorious blue, in the long dead years,
> You were sown in sorrow and harrowed in hate,
> But your harvest today is a nation's tears.
> For the message you left through the land has sped,
> From the lips of God to the heart of man:
> Let the past be past! Let the dead be dead—
> Now and forever American!

---

66. *Official Records, op. cit.*, Vol. XLV, Part 1, pp. 37-41.

CHAPTER XXIII

Grant Skeletonizes Thomas's Army

GENERAL THOMAS lost no time in giving pursuit to Hood's scattered and demoralized forces. His report stated that General Wilson pushed General Hood's rear guard slowly, under strong opposition, to about five miles south of Franklin. Here the enemy made a stand in some open fields north of West Harpeth River, apparently to await the pursuers. When Wilson arrived, he charged them with his bodyguard, the Fourth Cavalry, driving them off with the loss of their artillery. Darkness alone prevented pursuit and capture of the majority, who escaped. General Wood's Fourth Corps also pursued the cavalry to as far as the Harpeth River, over which the bridges were destroyed, and the infantry was unable to continue across. Soon a trestle bridge was erected, but night came on before it could be utilized. General Steedman also came up and camped near Wood on the banks of the Harpeth. Generals Schofield and Smith moved along the Granny White pike and camped that night at the intersection of the Franklin road.[1]

On December 18, General Wilson's cavalry continued after the enemy as far as Rutherford's Creek, about three miles from Columbia, and Wood's corps closed up behind Wilson's. The creek was impassable due to the high water, but a pontoon bridge, recently constructed at Nashville, had not been brought up due to the bad roads, and the pursuit was compelled to halt at that point. The next day it was still impossible to cross the stream in force, as the entire country was largely under water; however, Generals Smith and Schofield crossed the Harpeth River, Smith going to Spring Hill and Schofield to Franklin. The crossing of Rutherford's Creek was accomplished on the morning of December 20 by means of a floating bridge that had been built by General Hatch's men, after which his division moved on to Columbia; but at Duck River they learned that the enemy had crossed over with their pontoons and taken them with them. General

---

1. *Official Records of the War of the Rebellion* (Washington, 1880–1901). Vol. XLV, Part 1, p. 41.

Wood had crossed Rutherford's Creek during the day by means of an improvised foot bridge, enabling his infantry and a couple of batteries to head for Duck River.[2]

The pontoons arrived at noon on the twenty-first and were laid across Rutherford's Creek, after which Smith's troops crossed. The weather was now bitter cold, which handicapped the colored troops entrusted with construction of the bridge. The next important project was the construction of a bridge at Duck River, after which Wood was enabled to cross on the afternoon of December 22, and get in position on the Pulaski road, about two miles from Columbia. The water in the river fell so rapidly that frequent alterations were necessary and great delay resulted, but the lowered water disclosed artillery that had been thrown into the river during the enemy's hasty retreat. Despite the many serious delays, Thomas continued the pursuit of Hood's remnants with Wilson's cavalry and Wood's infantry, the infantry adhering to the road, and the cavalry operating on the flanks across the fields. Smith's and Schofield's corps followed leisurely for use as the occasion might demand.[3]

General Forrest had returned from an expedition with his cavalry and other detachments, and joined Hood at Columbia. Hood had formed a powerful rear guard of about 4,000 infantry under General Walthall, and united all of his cavalry under Forrest. Excepting this rear guard, Hood's army was disheartened and disorganized, virtually a rabble of half-armed and barefooted men who dropped their cause whenever the opportunity beckoned. The rear guard, however, was made of sterner stuff, and put up a brave fight to the very end.[4]

Wilson crossed Duck River on December 23 with his entire force, and advanced on the twenty-fourth, followed by Wood's corps. At Lynnville and Buford's Station they encountered the enemy and dislodged him after a short fight, their movement having been so rapid that the bridge over Richland Creek was saved from destruction by the enemy. On December 25, the Confederates deserted Pulaski and were followed toward Lamb's Ferry by way of a very bad road and through a desolate country. In the afternoon, Harrison's brigade encountered the well-intrenched enemy in a heavily wooded ravine surrounding the road, and awaited the cavalry before attacking. The enemy moved from his defenses at once and drove back Harrison's skirmishers, although the ground lost was soon recovered. As night ended the action the enemy had been ousted with the loss of some fifty prisoners. The cavalry, meanwhile, had moved so far in advance

2. *Ibid.*, pp. 41-42.
3. *Ibid.*, p. 42.
4. *Ibid.*

of the trains that both men and animals were in need of sustenance, and General Wood's men were close behind the cavalry. That night, December 25, Christmas, Wood and his cavalry camped about six miles from Pulaski on the Lamb's Ferry road.[5]

Next day, December 26, the pursuit was continued, and Wood reached Lexington, Alabama, about thirty miles from Pulaski, on the twenty-eighth. When it was learned that the Confederates had crossed the Tennessee River at Bainbridge, the chase was abandoned by order of General Thomas. The road from Pulaski to Bainbridge was littered with limbers, wagons, and other equipment that the enemy in his haste had abandoned. General Smith's command, meanwhile, reached Pulaski on the twenty-seventh, and Schofield was directed to remain at Columbia. On December 30, Thomas ordered the disposition of his several corps, but this was countermanded by Washington. Thomas had hoped to go into winter quarters, but Halleck told him that the army in Tennessee would not go into winter quarters. On December 31, Generals Schofield, Smith, and Wilson were directed to concentrate at Eastport, Mississippi, and Wood was ordered to Huntsville, preparatory to a campaign in Alabama and Tennessee.[6]

Beyond the mere words in Thomas's report of the campaign were naturally the incidents reflecting human emotion, which offer clues to the character of the participants. General Wilson recalled Thomas's sometimes repeated reference, when he was subjected to Grant's telegraphic assault, to Sherman's having taken with him on his unopposed march the choicest troops and equipment. Thomas also thought that Grant, with almost one hundred thousand seasoned veterans, a force that outnumbered Lee's army by a very wide margin, had some audacity to criticize him for not facing Hood in a period of but ten days, whereas he, Grant, had been getting nowhere with Lee for more than seven months. A further contrast lay in the fact that Hood at first outnumbered Thomas's hastily formed army.[7]

When the victory of Nashville was beyond doubt, Wilson related, and he was proceeding down the Granny White pike in pursuit of the enemy, he heard horses galloping behind him. Intuitively he thought it might be General Thomas, although it was too dark to recognize anyone. Reining his horse toward the side of the road, a heavy figure came abreast of him and called out, "Is that you, Wilson?" Recognizing the voice, he responded, "Yes, General Thomas!" This dignified man, probably giving way for the first time to the pent-

---

5. *Ibid.*, pp. 42, 43.

6. *Ibid.*, pp. 43, 44.

7. James H. Wilson, *Under the Old Flag* (New York, 1911), Vol. II, p. 105.

up emotion of Grant's cruelty and the ordeal of preparing and executing battle plans, shouted loudly, "Dang it to hell, Wilson, didn't I tell you we could lick 'em; didn't I tell you we could lick 'em?"[8]

If nothing else, Nashville was a clear vindication for General Thomas in his bitter exchange with the authorities in Washington, but it was far more than that. As we have seen, General Schofield was not given to complimenting General Thomas. In his *Forty-six Years in the Army,* he said that "the defeat and practical destruction of Hood's army in Tennessee was what paved the way to the speedy termination of the war, which the capture of Lee by Grant fully accomplished; and the result ought to have been essentially the same as to time if Sherman's march had never been made." In General John De Puyster's speech, January 5, 1875, before the New York Historical Society, he said that "Nashville showed genius, the pivot on which the war turned, wiped out an army, and made Appomattox possible. Had Hood been the victor the war would have begun all over again. A prominent officer said that 60,000 Confederates awaited Hood's operations prepared to take the field again if Hood won, which they gave up doing when Hood lost."[9] De Puyster also said: "The more one's mind reflects, the more, indeed, it will be convinced that, if this country ever produced a perfect character; if there be any such in our history, if the human mind could divest itself of prejudice or discern the true metal through the lacquer laid on more or less by Fortune; then our countrymen would recognize in Thomas the greatest and best man our institutions have developed. The writer said it and felt it while Thomas was living; he feels it, sees it, and must express it now while his remains, without a national monument, sleep beneath the soil his solid virtues and capacities preserved; yes, the genius of Thomas preserved."[10]

Thomas was not above self-criticism, either, as shown by the talk he gave before a scientific organization in Washington after the war. In explaining details of the Battle of Nashville with a decidedly impersonal touch, he showed no hesitancy in blaming himself for not sending a force to the rear of Hood's forces on the first day and cutting off all hope of retreat for him. When reminded that he was too critical of himself. Thomas refused to accept the defense offered and insisted that a general must assume some risks; this meant, of course,

8. *Ibid.,* p. 126.

9. John M. Schofield, *Forty-six Years in the Army* (New York, 1897), p. 348; Address on General Thomas by John Watts De Peyster, Jan. 5, 1875, before New York Historical Society (Library of Congress, Vol. No. 467, T-4, D-4).

10. De Peyster, *ibid.*

that if he had he would have captured Hood's entire army.[11] It is
too bad that for the benefit of history and himself he thus failed to
preserve his unmatched record, safe from the attacks of Grant, Sherman, and their supporters, although he all but destroyed Hood's army
and rendered it incapable of further organized action.

It is one thing to read Thomas's most complete report of the Nashville campaign; but in summary, and beyond the technicalities of
orders and movements, this is what was done on December 15 and 16:

On the morning of December 15, General Steedman opened with
a demonstration against Hood's right, following which General Wood
struck the Confederate center with sufficient force to encourage belief
that the main attack was coming there. After the demonstration by
Steedman, the Confederates could not know that it was not Schofield,
who, incidentally, had been making a circuitous march since before
dawn and was scheduled to attack the left-rear position that afternoon, which he did with complete success. General Wood attacked
the Confederate center, and General Smith followed with an attack
on Hood's left center, after Steedman's demonstration on the right.
Hood, by now fearful for his right flank, withdrew troops from his
left center before which Smith was exerting his strength; now into
the opening came Smith, who swept everything before him past the
fortifications and stormed along the line after taking considerable
Confederate artillery. That was pretty much the outline of events for
December 15 when darkness came, and from this stage they moved
a couple of miles to their next line of fortifications. Hood's men worked
during the night strengthening their positions, and were very much
exhausted before the commencement of fighting on the sixteenth; and
there would be enough of it to do. Overton's Hills was a circular summit on which Hood established a good line, but his left rested on
Shy's Hill, somewhat lower and not nearly so susceptible to defense.
Shy's Hill had been hard to come by, as during the night Wilson's
cavalry, which had performed heroically during the day, offered stout
resistance not only to its being strongly fortified, but to its being held
at all.[12]

On the early morning of the sixteenth, Thomas again concentrated
his heaviest attack against the Confederate left, this time with Wilson's cavalry, in combination with Generals Wood and Steedman
against Overton's Hill. Thomas was with General Wood to observe
the movement as it developed on the left. Wood himself was making
headway, but resistance had so stiffened that it became a question

---

11. *Ibid.*
12. Wilson, *op. cit.*, Vol. II, pp. 115, 116.

whether the drive there should be continued without making a demonstration elsewhere. Schofield's artillery had been enfilading the Confederate trenches, on the point or angle at which the line abruptly changed direction to form a right angle, since early dawn, and they decided to put a stop to it. Thomas noted their artillery moving rapidly in position on Shy's Hill in an attempt to counter Schofield's artillery, and ordered a reserve battery of his own to concentrate on stopping this new threat; the Union guns, being somewhat longer in range than the enemy's, it was not long before the latter were silenced. At about this time Wilson galloped to Thomas with the exciting news that his own dismounted men were in plain sight and moving under cover of artillery to the enemy's left and rear. Urging Thomas to order the infantry forward at once, no action was taken until, upon Wilson's emphasis, he raised his field glasses, took in the situation, and ordered Schofield to attack with his entire corps.[13] When Wilson returned to his command the damage to the enemy was already being felt, and he began at once a disorderly retreat. This was about 4 P.M.

Hood began his retreat on the Franklin pike, the only road open to him, after Wilson's dismounted troopers had captured his intrenchments before the oncoming infantry had reached them. In this operation the cavalry took fifteen guns, a total of some twenty-seven for the two days. Various accounts of what occurred during the remainder of the day are somewhat confusing, although it is well established that Hood used up his reserves to prolong his lines in confronting his opponent. After throwing in this last reserve he had nothing to hold back the advance of Smith, Steedman, and Wood. The Confederates between Schofield and Wilson were boxed in and entire brigades captured, including all of their artillery and equipment. That night, Thomas ordered Wilson and Wood to pursue Hood, which they did most convincingly; and the result was the most successful in our history. When Hood crossed the Tennessee River at Bainbridge, there were remaining in his army but nine thousand of the original fifty to fifty-five thousand with which he began the campaign. In addition, all of his guns had been captured or destroyed, his ammunition used up, and his supply trains lost.

Fletcher Pratt, the noted military writer, stated that when Thomas died, in 1870, it was too early for his own fame, and he was unable to take part in the great military debates that established for the commanders their desired place in the story of the war. He said further that Grant's was the controlling voice in most of these debates, and that the officers who were favorable to his views elaborated upon the slowness of Thomas until it became fixed in the public

---

13. *Ibid.*, p. 117.

mind.[14] This writer also stated that Thomas's genius consisted in reproducing on the largest scale whatever had turned out well on the small, just as did Frederick the Great.[15]

Many military experts regard Nashville as the decisive battle of the war, including Isaac R. Sherwood, who stated simply, "Nashville was the decisive battle of the war. Nashville ended the military career of Lieutenant General John Bell Hood, the most audacious and fighting general of the gray army—and immortalized General George H. Thomas, the most successful military strategist of the Union army; a general who never lost a battle."[16]

Another military writer, Stanley F. Horn, the well-known author of *The Army of Tennessee* and *The Decisive Battle of Nashville*, regards Nashville as the crowning battle, the one battle that, if it had gone the other way, would have made more of a difference by the result than any other battle of the war. All other battles in the West, Perryville, Murfreesboro, Chickamauga, Missionary Ridge, and Atlanta, and Fredericksburg, Chancellorsville, Gettysburg, The Wilderness, and Cold Harbor in the East, although bitterly fought, and accompanied by large numbers of killed and wounded, were not at all decisive. The war dragged on until after the climactic Battle of Nashville, following which no battle of major importance occurred during the remaining four months of the war. No further proof is necessary to demonstrate the finality of Nashville.[17]

The Federal objective of turning the Confederate position at Nashville and of destroying the Army of Tennessee, when accomplished finally, spelled the doom of the Confederacy and left unanswered only the question of time. Hood himself is authority for the statement that if he had won at Nashville, and had been able to replenish his supplies and satisfy recruitment requirements in Kentucky and Tennessee, he would have posed a threat to Cincinnati. If Sherman had then returned to confront him, or had in any way sought to obstruct him, he would surely have given him battle; and, if successful, either to reinforce General Lee's Army of Northern Virginia, or to attack General Grant's Army of the Potomac.[18] This plan does not appear absurd when it is recalled that General Sherman devoted a number of weary months seeking to catch Johnston and Hood on the way to Atlanta, but was not successful.

---

14. Fletcher Pratt, *Eleven Generals* (New York, 1956), p. 212.

15. *Ibid.*, p. 213.

16. Isaac R. Sherwood, *Memories of the War* (Toledo, 1923), p. 143.

17. Stanley F. Horn, *The Decisive Battle of Nashville* (Baton Rouge, 1957), pp. vi, vii; John B. Hood, *Advance and Retreat* (New Orleans, 1880), p. 267.

18. Horn, *ibid.*, p. viii; Hood, *ibid.*

One of the most debated points concerning Nashville relates to the number of men engaged on each side. Hood claimed something like twenty-three thousand effectives, or those in action, of a total present for duty of about thirty-six thousand; but he reported a total present of eighty thousand, which could mean that much of his army was scattered. It is ridiculous to believe, however, that with such a big potential, eighty thousand men, he had but twenty-three thousand on the firing line. The estimate of approximately fifty thousand in the battle appears most reasonable, and compares favorably with the fifty to fifty-five thousand commanded by Thomas at the battle.[19] According to reliable authorities, the forces were fairly even; and on this premise the greater credit is due Thomas for his success, since he faced a veteran army behind fortifications with a substantially inexperienced army.

Adam Badeau, Grant's biased and bumbling biographer, who appeared to hold a particular animosity for General Thomas, gave Thomas's strength at Nashville as fifty-five thousand, with twelve thousand additional comprising Wilson's cavalry. He gave the cavalry opposed to Wilson as seventeen hundred. In other words, Badeau gave Thomas a force of more than sixty-seven thousand, and accepted Hood's very inaccurate figure of twenty-three thousand. "Whatever may have been the intention of Badeau, his confused statements are quite as misleading as meditated deception could have made them." In the return from which Badeau quoted, the fifty-five thousand included those on garrison duty at Nashville, Murfreesboro, and Chattanooga.[20] Allowing for that figure, whatever it may have been, the remaining force of infantry and other services, added to Wilson's cavalry, probably aggregated between fifty and fifty-five thousand as aforesaid.

An interesting incident demonstrates the methodical care with which General Thomas did everything. As he was riding through Nashville to the battlefield, he suddenly beckoned Major Mills from the sidewalk. The major was a quartermaster in charge of fuel distribution. General Thomas asked him, "Have I drawn all my allowance of coal for this month?" Upon receiving a negative reply, he asked, "Will you please send fourteen bushels of coal to Mr. Harris, my neighbor? I was out of coal and borrowed this number of bushels from him the other day." Another incident shows his humanity. As

19. Thomas B. Van Horne, *The Life of Major General George H. Thomas* (New York, 1882), pp. 337-40; *Official Records, op. cit.,* Vol. XLV, Part 1, p. 663.

20. Van Horne, *ibid.,* p. 340; Adam Badeau, *Military History of U.S. Grant* (New York, 1881), Vol. III, p. 251.

he was riding over the battlefield, Thomas noted a number of dead colored troops commingled with the bodies of white troops slain in battle. Deeply impressed, he said, "This proves the manhood of the Negro." General De Peyster, years later, quoted Thomas as having said of the Negro that "it will take time for his regeneration, but he will come out purified by the terrible ordeal to which he has been subjected, and assume an honorable position in the ranks of humanity."[21]

The first official dispatch from Grant to Thomas concerning news of the Battle of Nashville advised, "I was just on my way to Nashville, but receiving a dispatch from Van Duzer, detailing your splendid success of to-day, I shall go no further. Push the enemy now and give him no rest until he is severely punished. . . ." The next word from Grant, at noon on December 18, informed him: "The armies operating against Richmond have fired two hundred guns in honor of your great victory. . . . In all your operations we hear nothing of Forrest. Great precautions should be taken to prevent him crossing the Cumberland or Tennessee Rivers below Eastport. After Hood is driven as far as it is possible to follow him, you want to re-occupy Decatur and all other abandoned points."[22]

General Halleck telegraphed on December 21:

> Permit me, General, to urge the vast importance of a hot pursuit of Hood's army. Every possible sacrifice should be made, and your men for a few days will submit to any hardships and privations to accomplish the great result. If you can capture or destroy Hood's army, General Sherman can entirely crush out the rebel military force in all the Southern States. . . .
>
> A most vigorous pursuit on your part is therefore of vital importance to General Sherman's plans. No sacrifice must be spared to obtain so important a result.[23]

General Thomas replied at noon the same day, with considerable emphasis.

> General Hood's army is being pursued as rapidly and as vigorously as it is possible for one army to pursue another. We cannot control the elements, and you must remember that to resist Hood's advance into Tennessee, I had to reorganize and almost thoroughly equip the force now under my command. I fought the battle of the fifteenth and sixteenth instants with the troops but

21. Van Horne, *op. cit.*. pp. 346-47.
22. *Official Records, op. cit.*, Vol. XLV, Part 2, pp. 195, 248.
23. *Ibid.*, p. 295.

partially equipped, and, notwithstanding the inclemency of the weather, and the partial equipment, have been enabled to drive the enemy beyond Duck River, crossing two streams with my troops, and driving the enemy from position to position without the aid of pontoons and with but little transportation to bring the supplies of provisions and ammunition. But pursuing an enemy through an exhausted country, over mud roads completely sogged with heavy rains, is no child's play and cannot be accomplished as quickly as thought of. I hope in urging me to push the enemy, the department remembers that General Sherman took with him the complete organization of the Military Division of the Mississippi, well equipped in every respect, leaving me only two corps partially stripped of their transportation to accommodate the force taken with him, to oppose the advance into Tennessee of that army which had resisted the army of the Military Division of the Mississippi on Atlanta, from the commencement of the campaign till its close, and which is now, in addition, aided by Forrest's cavalry. . . . But too much must not be expected of troops which have to be reorganized, especially when they have the task of destroying a force, in a winter's campaign, which was able to make an obstinate resistance to twice its numbers in spring and summer.[24]

The foregoing reply of Thomas to Halleck's ridiculous and wholly unnecessary prodding of the man who had just given the nation the war's greatest victory, despite handicaps, including the cruel goading by telegraph, was eminently to the point. No appraisal of Grant, Halleck, and Stanton in their attitude toward Thomas in the unhappy days before Nashville, and to some extent thereafter, would be complete if it did not consider Thomas's defense in the foregoing reply to Halleck. In fairness to Secretary Stanton, he wired Thomas on December 22, stating that he had seen the foregoing exchange between Halleck and him, and that the Department had the most unbounded confidence in his skill, vigor, and determination to utilize every means to pursue and destroy the enemy.[25] Grant, however, with that determination, tenacity, or whatever else it might be termed, never once let up on Thomas, as indicated by his use of every opportunity to yield honors to him grudgingly. As late as December 20, he wrote to Stanton, stating: "I think Thomas has won the major-generalcy, but I would wait a few days before giving it, to see the extent of damages done."[26] If there is any doubt about Grant's vindictiveness, that should

24. *Ibid.*, pp. 295-96.
25. *Ibid.*, p. 307.
26. *Ibid.*, p. 283.

dispel it. Nevertheless, although Stanton had previously shown impatience with Thomas, he now completely disclaimed any sympathy with Halleck's dispatch, and certainly dissociated himself from it.

General Grant wired Thomas on December 22 that his energy in pushing Hood was being congratulated by the public, but he did not inform him that Sherman was under orders to transport his army to Lee's front in Virginia. Since it was impossible to obtain enough transports, the suggestion by Sherman to move through the Carolinas was approved by Grant. About a month later, Grant wrote a letter to Sherman complaining of a lack of vigor on Thomas's part in pursuing Hood, and for his unwillingness to advance into Alabama. Grant commented also that Thomas indicated a sluggishness that satisfied him that Thomas "would never do to conduct one of your campaigns."[27] Grant should have completed the statement with the comment that of course he would need Thomas to fight Sherman's battles, as he always did when they were together. There can be no doubt that Grant hated Thomas with a perfect hatred, as evidenced by his constant faultfinding when there was no basis for it. This trait of Grant's is typical of the inferior toward the superior, and runs parallel with his temperament to continue attacking relentlessly, whether it be the enemy or Thomas. Secretary Stanton, for all his impatience before Nashville, was the only one of the three, the others being Grant and Halleck, who showed appreciation for Thomas's contribution. By contrast, the correspondence between Grant and Sherman sometimes took on the character of mutual-admiration exchanges.

Grant complained in his January 21 letter to Sherman that he had ordered Schofield to move northward, being "induced to do this because I did not believe Thomas could possibly be got off before spring." Further, he complained, "The command of the advance of the pursuit was left to subordinates, whilst Thomas followed far behind. When Hood had crossed the Tennessee, and those in pursuit had reached it, Thomas had not much more than half crossed the State, from which he returned to Nashville. . . ." This is nothing if not malicious, and Grant could not seem to make up his mind, as his letters in congratulation for the victory at Nashville and his criticisms concerning Thomas's not moving fast are contradictory on their face. He was congratulating Thomas for public consumption, since he had no other choice, but since Thomas never knew of this letter, he was stabbing him in the back, and, what is worse, perpetuating the myth of his own greatness while submerging the true greatness of Thomas.

General Dabney H. Maury, in discussing the Battle of Nashville,

---

27. William T. Sherman, *The Memoirs of General William T. Sherman*, (New York, 1891), Vol. II, p. 257; Van Horne, *op. cit.*, pp. 360-61, 372.

gave a Southern viewpoint of Thomas's conduct at Nashville and his pursuit of Hood afterward. He said, "I have never heard anybody who was in Hood's army justify the complaint that Thomas was slow. Thomas's letter in reply on that point shows the stuff of which he was made." He also said, "In calm review of these operations, it is but fair to say that in the whole course of the war, there was no finer illustration of generalship exhibited by any Federal commander than General Thomas's defense of Nashville."[28] How infinitely more accurate is this glowing tribute from a Confederate, a former enemy, than Grant's mean and contemptible slandering of Thomas! It has been said, "A general's opinion of another soldier, has no rightful place in history, unless sustained by facts. A great general's higher relations to history should not be endangered by his own utterance of unsupported statements—made from afar and in ignorance of facts—in regard to another great general, whose achievements have given him an unequivocal and brilliant fame. Grant and Thomas will both be accurately weighed when all partialities and prejudices are laid aside, and this will be done without reference to their opinions of each other. History has nicely adjusted balances, though their use is often long delayed."[29]

General Thomas recommended that the civil government of the state of Tennessee be reorganized, in a letter to Military Governor Andrew Johnson dated December 30, 1864.[30] The recommendation was acted upon shortly after its introduction in the Legislature in early 1865, and Tennessee became the first seceding state to return to the Union.

Thomas's appointment as major general in the United States Army was approved December 24, 1864, and Secretary Stanton told him that, for his skill, courage, and conduct in the brilliant military operations under his command, the President had directed that the appointment be made. The appointment was not without its irony, since Thomas knew that he should have received it for earlier successes. When he read the dispatch he sat silent as though forgetful of Stanton's warm words and the important promotion. He was human enough to remember, no doubt, the terrible ordeal from which he had just emerged, missing military oblivion by the narrowest of circumstances, a freezing rain. He also could have recalled the several times he had been ignored when promotions were given to others less deserving. When he did speak it was to say to the medical director of

28. Southern Historical Society Papers, speech of General Dabney H. Maury, June, 1876, Richmond, Va.

29. Van Horne, *op. cit.*, p. 368.

30. *Ibid.*, pp. 369-70.

his department, Surgeon George E. Cooper, "What do you think of that?" To the reply, "Thomas, it is better late than never," his answer was, "I suppose it is better late than never, but it is too late to be appreciated; I earned this at Chickamauga." After stating the truth, he became highly indignant at the mistreatment given him throughout, and gave expression to the most intense feeling. The remembrance that he had been doubted, mistrusted, denied promotions, subjected to humiliating subordination to inferiors in rank—all of these over-powered this great and good man, and he temporarily lost control of himself.[31]

Some time later, Thomas confided to a friend that there was one thing for which he was much gratified, namely, that he had never received a promotion "they dared to withhold. After Chickamauga they could not refuse a commission as brigadier general in the United States Army; and after Nashville, a major general's commission."[32]

The State of Tennessee General Assembly, on November 2, 1865, resolved: That the thanks of the General Assembly of the State of Tennessee, be presented to Major-General George H. Thomas, and the officers and soldiers under his command for his wise and spirited, and their brave and patriotic conduct in the Battle of Nashville, in defense of the capital of the State, in December, 1864, and that a gold medal be struck in commemoration of the great and decisive event and be presented to him.

Presentation of the gold medal was made by Governor William G. Brownlow, before the General Assembly, on December 15, 1865, one year from the opening of the Battle of Nashville. On this occasion the governor commended General Thomas and his command, also his magnificent army, for gallantry in the Battle of Nashville and the successful pursuit of Hood's army. Bronze copies of the medal were also struck and distributed to each corps commander who participated in the battle.[33]

Grant determined, as the record of his actions attests, to break up Thomas's command and take him out of the war. His slander, Thomas's "slowness," was his justification; and nothing, not even Nashville, with all prior successes, and the almost universal acclaim accorded him since Nashville, availed in changing Grant's mind. There can be no doubt that Grant sought Lee's destruction also, as was expected of

31. *Ibid.*, pp. 371-72; *Official Records, op. cit.*, Vol. XLV, Part 2, p. 318.
32. Van Horne, *ibid.*, p. 372.
33. *Ibid.*, pp. 373-74; letter from Gen. Thomas to Gen. James Wilson in the possession of Mr. Norm Flayderman, of Greenwich, Conn., dealer in antique firearms.

him; but he was not in so much of a hurry to get Lee as he was
to dispose of Thomas, if his haste to get Thomas into action before
Nashville is measured against his results before Lee. Yes, Grant had
determination, and little else; but with the troops available to lead
to the slaughter he could hold out longer than Lee, and he did. In
football, when the line cannot be breached by direct assault, some
other means is looked for, as, for example, taking to the air or skirt-
ing the ends. After the country could stomach Grant no longer, he
changed his tactics; but nothing compelled him to change his tactics
in regard to Thomas. Thomas must go! Perhaps Grant wanted none
of Thomas's superior ability to show up his own inferiority as he
had done at Chattanooga; and nothing in Grant's record speaks up
for him to affirm that he was the equal of Thomas in any way—
nothing, that is, but determination.

General Schofield, meanwhile, lent some strength to the existing
evidence of his undercutting of Thomas at Nashville by sending Grant
an "unofficial" letter, December 27, 1864, rquesting that he and his
army be transferred to the Army of the Potomac. In this "unofficial"
letter, Schofield stabbed Thomas in the back with this classic: "I am
aware that General Thomas contemplates a spring campaign into
Alabama or Mississippi, with the Tennessee River as a base, and believe he considers my command a necessary part of the operating
force. Without reference to the latter point, permit me to express the
opinion that such a campaign would not be an economical or advantageous use of so many troops."[34] Well, there is the Schofieldian brand,
which, in Thomas's last year, would sear his heart in more ruthless
fashion and confirm that Schofield's near dismissal from the Military
Academy (See Chapter XXIV) was a foreshadowing of the man.
How cleverly Schofield said "permit me to express the opinion," but
he had already expressed it, and after his statement to Grant that "[I]
believe he [Thomas] considers my command a necessary part of the
operating force." Here he was not sure, but he impliedly criticized
Thomas for having judgment not equal to his own.

If Grant had need of encouragement to make the life of Thomas
even more miserable, Schofield supplied it. Schofield's self-evaluated
superior judgment to that of Thomas erases any doubt that an unholy
alliance between himself and Grant did in fact exist. To see the situation otherwise would be to reflect a trust having no basis in fact whatever. Schofield's request was followed by his being ordered to the
East by Grant's directive to Halleck, January 7, 1865.[35] The break-up
of Thomas's army had now begun, and Grant was on the way to get-

---

34. Schofield, *op. cit.*, p. 253.
35. *Official Records, op. cit.*, Vol. XLV, Part 2, pp. 377, 529.

ting even with Thomas for stepping aside after Shiloh and permitting him, Grant, to be restored to command of the Army of the Tennessee. What ingratitude! Schofield, too, could easily forget that Thomas, and Stanley and Wilson, had saved him from disaster at Spring Hill, where his disobedience to orders, but for Hood's missed opportunity, would have taken him, and perhaps his entire Twenty-third Corps, out of the war.

General Halleck's instructions of January 19 to General Thomas requested his views concerning a move into Alabama against Selma and Montgomery, in order to cooperate with General Canby, who was moving in the same direction. Thomas replied to Halleck on January 24, stating that he thought it would be impossible to move from the Tennessee River upon Montgomery and Selma with a large force during the winter. This objection was based largely upon his knowledge that the roads required in transporting wagons and artillery were bad. Thomas also had in mind that Hood, despite his defeat, might offer trouble, particularly if he could increase his forces. If Thomas had moved into Alabama, Hood would have been free to join forces with Lee; besides, all objectives planned for Thomas's army were attained later by Wilson's cavalry.[36]

The opinion of General Thomas, that winter was an obstacle to a successful operation in northern Alabama and Mississippi, had support from Confederate commanders. General Hood wrote, on December 6, that "wagon transportation, at all times slow and limited, will become in the bad weather, which must soon set in, a matter of impossibility." General Forrest, that Confederate wizard of the saddle, who could ride with the best and without complaint, expressed his convictions regarding the country when he reported to his commander that it would require six weeks to restore his cavalry to required strength. Several commanders reported that the supplies for animal and human consumption in that country were so scarce that they could not long subsist on them. To add to the problem, a number of the streams to be traversed were impassable.[37]

When Halleck ordered Schofield's transfer to Grant's army, he was taking the first step toward ripping Thomas's army apart by sending segments to other commanders, as needed. He also ordered that no animals be sent to Thomas, ostensibly because they were needed by the other forces. That could be a legitimate military requirement; but the dirty remarks, the unjustified remarks, the remarks that had their origin in a heart filled with hatred, were wholly unnecessary. On the fifteenth, Grant communicated to Halleck: "I now

36. *Ibid.*, pp. 614, 627, 628; Van Horne, *op. cit.*, p. 380.
37. *Official Records, ibid.*, pp. 656, 756, 758, 759.

understand that Beauregard has gone west to gather up what he can save from Hood's army, to bring against Sherman. If this be the case, Selma and Montgomery can be easily reached. I do not believe, though, that General Thomas will ever get there from the north. He is too ponderous in his preparations and equipments to move through a country rapidly enough to live off of it."[38] Nowhere in any of Grant's correspondence is there even the suggestion of like criticism of any other officer; so let those who have been mistakenly led to believe that Grant was the cavalier, the soul of kindness, the great peacemaker to his former enemy, General Lee, reconcile his ceaseless disparagement of the greatest general in the army.

General Hood withdrew to Tupelo, Mississippi, with the remnants of his once splendid army. After his defeat at Nashville desertions multiplied, and, after the sending of some four thousand of his small force to Mobile, and the movement of General Forrest to Alabama and Mississippi, Hood advanced toward North Carolina with about fourteen thousand men. This alone was enough to justify Thomas's opposition to a movement southward, since only cavalry would be operating. Of course, it would be necessary to oppose Forrest, but nothing more, as all the major action would be to the northeastward.[39]

General Halleck informed General Thomas on January 29 that he believed General Grant would give him instructions to cooperate with General Canby when Canby was ready to take the field. On the thirty-first, however, General Grant sent this much different letter to Thomas:

> With this I send you a letter from General Sherman. At the time of writing it, General Sherman was not informed of the depletion of your command by my orders. It will be impossible for you at present to move south, as he contemplated, with the force of infantry indicated.
>
> General Sherman is advised before this of the changes made, and that for the winter you will be on the defensive. I think, however, an expedition from East Tennessee under General Stoneman might penetrate South Carolina well down towards Columbia, destroying the railroad and military resources of the country, thus visiting a portion of the State which will not be reached by Sherman's forces. . . . Three thousand cavalry would be a sufficient force to take. This probably can be raised in the old Department of the Ohio, without taking any now under General

---

38. Van Horne, *op. cit.*, p. 379.

39. *Ibid.*, pp. 380-81; Donn Piatt; *General George H. Thomas* (New York, 1887), p. 598.

Wilson. It would require, though, the reorganization of the regiments of Kentucky cavalry, which Stoneman had in his very successful raid into Southwestern Virginia.

It will be necessary, probably, for you to send, in addition to the force now in East Tennessee, a small division of infantry to enable General Gillem to hold the upper end of Holston Valley, and the mountain passes in rear of Stoneman. . . .[40]

Grant further degraded Thomas in this letter by first telling him that his command was being depleted "by my orders," and that he would have nothing to do with Stoneman other than to assist in his preparations. Then Thomas wired Halleck, on February 12, that he would need about one thousand horses to equip Stoneman, as his number of animals had been depleted by some eight thousand in satisfying General Smith's requirements. "Just what they counted upon or expected from Thomas, whom they had promoted to a major general of the regular army and who had fallen heir to the fragmentary command Sherman had left behind him, they never made clear. They sent Schofield with one army corps to the east, Smith with another to the northwestern corner of Alabama, and Wood to Huntsville. In other words they scattered their infantry around as well as the splendid body of cavalry I had got together with so much trouble."[41]

Wilson convinced Thomas that he could take care of Forrest with his seventeen thousand troopers, and that if permitted to do so he would take this force to central Alabama, defeat Forrest, and capture Tuscaloosa, Selma, Montgomery, and Columbus, in addition to destroying the last depots of manufacture and supply of the Confederacy. By March 1, the entire force under Wilson was increased to twenty-seven thousand, the majority of whom were equipped with the seven-shooter Spencer repeating rifle. Thomas obtained Grant's permission for Wilson to implement his plan, and he was clothed with independent authority to perform; in other words, Wilson was independent of both Sherman and Thomas.[42] He had with him the largest cavalry force ever seen on the North American continent up to that time; and its impressiveness may be inferred from the fact that one trooper would require the space of perhaps a yard, which, compounded for a 500-man regiment, would be almost one-third of a mile wide. A division would require about 5,000 yards' space, or almost three miles, and, although impressive beyond words, required appropriate terrain to permit full operating room.[43]

40. Van Horne *ibid.,* pp. 381-82.
41. Wilson, *op. cit.,* Vol. II, p. 180.
42. *Ibid.,* pp. 165, 180, 181; Piatt, *op. cit.,* pp. 595, 596.
43. Piatt, *ibid.,* pp. 595-99.

General Grant and his associates from far, far away were showing their customary impatience with Thomas, and proving themselves to be the most inconsiderate and impatient military hierarchy in our history. The time required to prepare for Wilson's operations had used up about nine weeks, from January 1 to March 1, in the dead of winter, when none of the other Union forces were actively engaged. It should be noted that, although Wilson had an unusually large force and did most important work, the campaign had little positive bearing on the outcome of the war.

On February 14, General Grant informed Thomas that General Canby was undertaking a movement against Mobile and central Alabama, with a force of about twenty thousand men in addition to General A. J. Smith's forces. Thomas was instructed to send Wilson with five thousand cavalry to demonstrate against Selma and Tuscaloosa. Thomas went to Eastport, Mississippi, to confer with Wilson before putting the order into effect. Wilson stated that a demonstration would have no value and would be military folly, when considered against the positive results to be gained by using his entire force to capture both Selma and Tuscaloosa, and, progressing to wherever circumstances might then dictate, sweep everything before them. This operation, it should be emphasized, was to be against that great cavalryman General Forrest, who was gathering all the forces he could muster to oppose such a force as Wilson might command.[44]

General Wilson, a young and resourceful Federal cavalryman, was most energetically occupied in preparing for Forrest, and was well informed as to his moves. He sent a capable staff officer under a flag of truce to Forrest to seek the transfer of prisoners and to obtain whatever information he could. Forrest was located at West Point, Mississippi, and straightforward regarding his plans. He, too, hoped to obtain information about Wilson and his command, and did not seem anxious to have a fight with him. When he learned that Wilson was a West Point man, with some knowledge of strategy and tactics, and had commanded a division of Sheridan's cavalry, Forrest commented that he did not have a military education and knew little of the arts of war, but he always made it his rule "to get there first with the most men." Forrest expressed with unmistakable conviction that in a cavalry fight he would "give more for fifteen minutes of the bulge on his enemy than for three days of tactics." Forrest also commented to the Federal officer, "Captain, tell your general that I have picked out a first-rate place for a cavalry battle, and if he'll come down here with any force he pleases to select, I'll meet him with the same number, and agree to win the fight." What Forrest meant was,

---

44. *Ibid.*, pp. 597-99.

in effect, that he with his ten thousand men could very well take care of the five thousand Grant planned for Wilson to "demonstrate" against him.[45]

General Thomas agreed with Wilson's observations that the entire force should be sent to take Selma and Tuscaloosa, and that in addition they should destroy the furnaces, foundries, factories, and depots, and break up the Confederacy's interior lines of supply and communication. Grant also concurred, and the expedition was to start as soon as weather permitted. Forrest, meanwhile, sent two brigades to Pickensville, Alabama, and another brigade to Columbus, Mississippi, to guard the Mobile and Ohio Railroad. Two other brigades were at West Point, Mississippi, and another one at Montevallo, Alabama, with a general watch being made of the roads of advance of Wilson's cavalry. Another detachment had been left at Corinth for defensive reasons, and two brigades were protecting the area around Mobile and observing the roads from the Lower Mississippi. To show that General Forrest, genius though he has been somewhat regarded, was human after all, as indicated by the wide dispersion of his forces, he was, in this situation, unable to bring to any given attack point the force necessary to insure success.[46]

On February 22 General Grant wrote that he understood the Confederates were ordered from Richmond to hold Mobile at all costs. He observed that Wilson's raid would cause a concentration of rebel forces and make his success easy, tending in the end to obtain everything desired without a long march into the interior by the infantry forces. Grant was not displaying occult powers in this last observation, since that precisely was what Thomas had reasoned early in the winter, and had been criticized for it. On the twenty-seventh, Grant directed Thomas to retain Stoneman between the Federal garrisons in East Tennessee and the enemy, now that he had been delayed in starting due to lack of horses. Grant now thought that "we may have to use a considerable force in that section [East Tennessee] the coming spring," and that preparations should be made for that possibility. Thomas promptly sent his Fourth Corps into that area, and Grant responded by stating that he approved of it, as also his sending of new troops to Chattanooga. All of this is indicative that Grant's plan to sidetrack Thomas was abandoned; circumstances had made that necessary, since the possibility arose that General Lee might loose the restrictions gathering about him and join Confederate forces in East Tennessee.[47]

45. *Ibid.*, pp. 598-99.
46. *Ibid.*, pp. 599-600.
47. Van Horne, *op. cit.*, pp. 385-86.

On March 1, Grant wired Thomas to start Wilson independently of Canby's forces, since Forrest was operating around Jackson, Mississippi. Grant thought that Wilson ought to start ahead of Canby, as Canby might not be able to cross at Vicksburg unless Wilson made a diversion in his favor. Any delay in obeying Grant's order for Wilson's advance was explained fully in General Wilson's report, in which he stated that heavy rains, swollen rivers, and impassable roads delayed him from March 4 until March 22. Eastern operations were also delayed during much of the period between December 20 and February 1, although he was ordered to advance to Richmond at all possible speed. Grant himself was not above being delayed by these conditions near Richmond, as he reported them to Sherman on March 16.[48]

General Thomas stated in his official report that about March 20 he heard of the possibility that Lee's army might move by way of Lynchburg, Virginia, from Richmond. He stated also that to guard against such possibility he had sent General Stoneman toward Lynchburg to destroy the railroad and material resources in that area and in western North Carolina. The Fourth Corps was ordered to East Tennessee from Huntsville, Alabama, to as far north as it could sustain itself, repairing the railroad as it proceeded and affording strong support for Stoneman's cavalry.[49]

In looking back, from the beginning of the Nashville campaign in November, 1864, the stamp of General Thomas's energy and ability was strongly in evidence in planning and conducting the campaign. It could be stated with truth that during that period he personally had done more to crush the rebellion than any other general or combination of generals. Despite all this, which the record sustains beyond contradiction, General Grant looked back and found nothing in Thomas's achievements to commend. He did find in this superlative record that Thomas was not equal, in other words he was unfit, to conduct an offensive movement. Thomas did, however, move his Fourth Corps into East Tennessee so quickly that even Grant stated his pleasure over it. Nothing can sustain General Grant in his charge that Thomas was sluggish, either then or at any other time; and the obvious falsity of the indictment is so transparent, that constant repetition is essential. General Grant stated the point so much that there is no escaping the conclusion that he was determined to ruin him in the eyes of his countrymen forever.

After crossing the Tennessee River on March 18, Wilson moved southward on the twenty-second, first driving General Forrest and his

---

48. *Ibid.*, pp. 387-88.
49. *Ibid.*, p. 388.

troops into the fortifications in front of Selma. At that point Wilson consolidated his forces, stormed the defenses, and compelled it to surrender on April 2. This was not easy, and was accomplished by a force of fifteen hundred men who advanced in the face of heavy artillery and musketry fire a distance of several hundred yards over deep and wide ditches and high parapets, in one of the most successful assaults of the war. Montgomery, the first capital of the Confederacy, fell to Wilson's forces on April 12.[50]

Moving toward Macon, Colonel Minty's Second Division was met by a flag of truce about fifteen miles from the city on March 20. The bearer, General Robertson, carried a message from General Cobb addressed to the commanding officer of the Union forces, General Wilson, who rushed into Macon. Wilson had already received news of Sherman's granting of a truce and had planned to stop before Macon's defenses; but before he could reach his troops in the advance of his column the city had surrendered.[51]

The problem presented by the general truce declared by Sherman affected Thomas also, or so it seemed. Thomas was in command of all forces in the Division of the Mississippi not under Sherman's control. The question at first was whether Sherman's order affected his area also; but the answer soon came in an announcement from Washington stating that the negotiations between Generals Johnston and Sherman had been annulled, and that offensive operations would be resumed at once. Thomas had asked Secretary Stanton whether Sherman's and Johnston's arrangement was the same as that between Grant and Lee, stating that he had offered the same terms to General Richard Taylor, Confederate commander in northern Georgia and a son of former President Zachary Taylor, and asked whether he was authorized to do so. General Halleck replied for Stanton that his offer was in order.[52]

Thomas's letter to General Wilson, dated April 17, enclosed a letter for General Taylor, outlining the surrender terms and stating that they were the same as General Lee accepted from General Grant, and that General Wilson was authorized to receive the surrender. "Rolls of all men and officers to be made in duplicate; one copy to be given to an officer to be designated by General Wilson, the other to be retained by such Confederate officer as you may designate. The officers to give their individual parole not to take up arms against the Government of the United States until properly exchanged, and each company, bat-

50. *Ibid.*, p. 392; *Official Records, op. cit.*, Vol. XLIX, Part 2, pp. 378-89, 383.

51. *Official Records, ibid.*, pp. 378, 379.

52. Van Horne, *op. cit.*, pp. 393-94; *Official Records, ibid.*, p. 376.

talion, or regimental commander to sign a like parole for the men under his command. The arms, artillery, and public property to be stacked and parked and turned over to the officer to be designated by General Wilson to receive them. This will not embrace side-arms of the officers nor their private horses or baggage. This done, each officer and man will be allowed to return to his home, not to be disturbed by the U. S. authorities so long as they preserve their parole and laws which were in force previous to January 1, 1861, where they may reside."[53]

General Wilson was not present to receive the letter with the terms of surrender, but terms were arranged between Taylor and Canby at Citronelle, about forty miles north of Mobile, Alabama. Other officers were given authority to receive the surrender of Confederate forces, including General Steedman. When General Thomas received word from Governor Brownlow and other sources that General Wofford was sincerely planning a raid on railroad communications between Chattanooga and Knoxville, he instructed Steedman to send a flag of truce to Wofford "and tell him that we are prepared, and if he makes the attempt I will so despoil Georgia that fifty years hence it will be a wilderness. But if they desire to have peace, I will accept his surrender upon the same terms as Lee surrendered to General Grant." The reference to Georgia's destruction was due to the fact that Wofford was stated to be fitting out his raiding party in northern Georgia.[54]

It is not surprising to learn that many Southerners, not satisfied that they were now back in the Union, against which they had fought for so long, were contemplating going elsewhere. For example, a number considered going to Mexico, and General Forrest is reported to have considered the matter himself.[55] It was inevitable that the pent-up bitterness of four years of war, not omitting all the emotional fervor that brought on the war, could not be shed like a blanket; and it is occasion for little wonder that the bitterness of the 1860's persists to this day in many Southern families and areas. The wonder of it all is that in times of great stress, as in two world wars, national differences were forgotten and the Southern soldier marched forth to war with as vigorous step and as much courage as did his ancestors in the Civil War. The wonder, the marvel of it all is that they were subdued at all. How they fought!

It would be remiss not to mention that the United States Senate

---

53. *Official Records, ibid.,* p. 379.

54. *Ibid.,* pp. 395-97.

55. Robert S. Henry, *"First With the Most" Forrest* (Indianapolis, 1944), p. 437.

and the House of Representatives adopted a resolution on March 3, 1865, stating "That the thanks of Congress are due and hereby tendered to Major General George H. Thomas, and the officers and soldiers under his command for their skill and dauntless courage by which the rebel army under General Hood was signally defeated and driven from the State of Tennessee."[56] This great soldier, who had no state on which he might have leaned, as did Grant, Sherman, and others, when recognition was nonexistent for him, was subsequently given other honors, including citizenship in the state of Tennessee.

On April 27, Secretary Stanton sent General Thomas a dispatch containing an excerpt from General Halleck's telegram advising that Confederate President Jefferson Davis had passed through Goldsborough, North Carolina, on his way south, and that he was moving rapidly. Halleck suggested that orders be transmitted to General Wilson, through General Thomas, that no orders from General Sherman be observed; also that General Canby and all other commanders, including those on the Mississippi, take measures to intercept General Davis. Stanton commented further that President Johnson disapproved of Sherman's proceedings, reminding Thomas that he had been so informed several days prior to disregard any such orders. Thomas replied that when he had been informed previously he immediately informed Generals Stoneman and Wilson accordingly. Thomas reported also that when he learned that Sherman had stopped Wilson from entering Macon, Georgia, he instructed Wilson that the action of Sherman in reaching the agreement with Johnston had been repudiated by the Government, and that he must not take orders from Sherman.[57] The effect of Stanton's order was to restore the authority withdrawn from Thomas by Grant, and to put a temporary crimp in Sherman's prerogatives.

President Davis had eluded Grant's forces and came into proximity to the forces of Sherman moving northward. Continuing to elude his pursuers, he was finally captured by General Wilson's cavalry on May 10, 1865, near Abbeville, Georgia, just a month and a day after Lee's surrender.[58]

---

56. Van Horne, *op. cit.*, p. 373.
57. *Official Records, op. cit.*, Vol. XLIX, Part 2, pp. 483-84.
58. Van Horne, *op. cit.*, p. 395.

CHAPTER XXIV

Reconstruction and Final Years

FOLLOWING the ending of hostilities the various military organizations were moved from one place to another as circumstances required. There were six major generals in the Regular Army, of whom General Thomas was youngest in seniority. This meant, when five military divisions were being planned, that Thomas, at the bottom of the list, would be the only one in the rank without proper command. He was naturally indignant, and lost no time in bringing the matter before a friend, General John F. Miller, commander of Nashville, who was on close terms with President Johnson. For the first time in his career he had someone to intercede for him, and he availed himself of it. Any man with red blood in his veins would not have done less. Presenting a map to General Miller, to illustrate to the President the area over which the several generals would command, and the respective commanders, Thomas said this:

I wish you to take the first train for Washington, and tell President Johnson that during the war I permitted the National authorities to do what they pleased with me; they put my juniors over me, and I served under them; the life of the Nation was then at stake, and it was not then proper to press questions of rank, but now that the war is over and the Nation saved, I demand a command suited to my rank, or I do not want any.

Not only did General Thomas present his own case; he also reminded the President that a number of recommendations for brevet rank should be approved as the Army of the Cumberland had not been accorded as liberal treatment as other armies.[1]

When General Miller talked with President Johnson regarding Thomas's right to consideration, the President remarked, "You know

---

1. Thomas B. Van Horne, *The Life of Major General George H. Thomas* (New York, 1882), pp. 395, 396.

my appreciation of General Thomas," whereupon he drew a line through the outer boundaries of Kentucky, Tennessee, Mississippi, Alabama and Georgia. He then said, "That is the military division for General Thomas," and followed the remark by indicating with his pencil that Nashville would be the headquarters. The five states were then designated as the Military Division of the Mississippi, and the arrangement made it necessary to assign General Sherman to the command of the Division of the Missouri.[2] Prior to this, President Lincoln had combined the Department of the Ohio with the Department of the Cumberland, embracing such parts of Alabama, Georgia, and Mississippi under control of Thomas's army.

Concerning General Thomas's dispatch to Secretary Stanton advising of the surrender of General Johnston, and suggesting that General Steedman be permitted to visit Mr. Stanton to convey his policy views for the surrendered states, Mr. Stanton expressed the hope that General Thomas himself might visit him instead. He stated further: "I would rather hear them from yourself, because I want to see and know personally so good and great a soldier that has served his country so well." When Thomas visited the Secretary, he complimented him for his eminent service during the war. He said, "I have always had great confidence in you," to which Thomas replied, "Mr. Stanton, I am sorry to hear you make this statement. I have not been treated as if you had confidence in me." Upon the Secretary's repeating the statement, Thomas replied, "I must accept your assertion but will say, nevertheless, that I have not been treated by the authorities as though they had confidence in me."[3] The surprising statement by Stanton, after he had teamed up with Grant and Halleck in making life miserable for Thomas, seems unbelievable. He had complained to Grant before Nashville that Thomas's alleged slowness "looks like the McClellan and Rosecrans strategy of do nothing, and let the enemy raid the country." Although Thomas may not have known of the exact phraseology used by the Secretary, he was well aware of his attitude at the time.

Stanton's double-talk, tragically enough, is of the type often resorted to by cheap politicians to curry favor and gain preferment. It becomes their stock in trade, without which political rewards might not be forthcoming. There are many evidences of Stanton's dislike for many people; but regardless of the general antipathy that seemed

2. *Ibid.*, p. 396; George W. Cullum, *Biographical Register of the Officers and Cadets at the U.S. Military Academy* (Boston, 1891), Vol. III, p. 135.
3. Van Horne, *op. cit.*, p. 396; *Official Records of the War of the Rebellion* (Washington, 1880–1901), Vol. XLIX, Part 2, pp. 514, 548.

to prevail against him, which he undoubtedly in large part encouraged or inspired, he apparently did entertain considerable respect and admiration for General Thomas. He was smart enough to know that in talking with Thomas he was talking with an honest man who would not use the first opportunity to undermine him. Perhaps Stanton realized that Thomas was one of the very few men in high place during the war whom he could respect and trust, which might have inspired him to tell Thomas that he always had had confidence in him. He must surely have realized that he, with others, Grant and Sherman in particular, had sadly abused this very great man; and when he saw the stature of him and compared it with the punishment administered to him so undeservedly, his conscience reacted normally and shamed him. He should have been ashamed. The pity is that Grant never reached that stage, although Halleck apparently did just before Thomas died.

On June 7, 1865, Thomas was given command of the newly organized Military Division of the Tennessee, comprising the Departments of Kentucky, Tennessee, Alabama, Georgia, Florida, and later, on June 22, the Department of Mississippi.[4] From this it may be deduced that General Thomas, although the war was over, was faring better than when he was under the complete domination of General Grant. All in all, General Thomas had a tremendous responsibility, since he was in command over much of the territory that formed the Confederacy, and the people were beaten, frustrated, belligerent, and ready for anything. Perhaps it is correct to state that the people under his jurisdiction ran the entire range of human emotions in their reaction to defeat. That Thomas was able to bring some order out of this chaos with a minimum of difficulty reflects his great humanity and administrative ability.

In a letter to Secretary Stanton on December 12, 1865, Thomas reported that after visiting a number of Southern cities—Vicksburg, Jackson, and Meridian, Mississippi, Mobile, Alabama, and others—the prevailing sentiment seemed to be for a restoration of the relations and functions of the states that prevailed before the war. General Thomas, and likewise Generals Grant and Schurz, had been sent on tours of inspection to learn the sentiment and intentions of the Southern people lately in revolt. Thomas was his usual candid self in making his report to President Johnson, as he was later, when called before the Congressional Committee on Reconstruction to testify regarding conditions in the former Confederate states.

During one period of questioning, Thomas spoke in favor of

---

4. *Official Records, ibid.,* pp. 964, 1022.

restoring the state of Tennessee to representation in Congress. When asked what he thought as to the possibility of another outbreak, he stated that, although he had heard rumors of organizations forming for various purposes, including involving the United States in a foreign war, he thought differently. He stated positively, "I do not think they will ever again attempt an outbreak on their own account, because they all admit they had a fair trial in the late rebellion, and got thoroughly worsted."

During December, 1865, General Thomas was confronted with an ecclesiastical problem. Bishop Wilmer, of the Protestant Episcopal Church in Alabama, admonished his flock to omit the prescribed prayer for the President of the United States. General Charles R. Woods, commander of the Department of Alabama, forbade the performing of such services until they would include the showing of proper allegiance to their Government, which would be evidenced by a resumption of the prayer for the President and those in civil authority, in addition to taking the amnesty oath prescribed by the President. General Thomas issued a General Order reviewing the case and stating the necessity for showing allegiance to the United States. He stated that the Bishop, "forgetting his mission to preach peace on earth and good will towards man, and being animated with the same spirit which through temptation beguiled the mother of men to the commission of the first sin, thereby entailing eternal toil and trouble on earth, issued, from behind the shield of his office, his manifesto . . . directing them to omit the usual and customary prayer for the President of the United States. . . . This man in his position of a teacher of religion, charity, and good fellowship with his brothers; whose paramount duty as such should have been characterized by frankness and freedom from all cunning, thus took advantage of the sanctity of his position to mislead the minds of those who naturally regarded him as a teacher in whom they could trust, and attempted to lead them back into the labyrinths of treason." This was a blistering attack on the bishop by Thomas, whose sensibilities were outraged by this conduct of a minister of the Gospel. The effect of Thomas's order was to deprive the bishop of the right to preach the Gospel, since it was evident that "he could not be trusted to officiate and confine his teachings to matters of religion alone. . . ."[5] From the tenor of this General Order it is abundantly evident that General Thomas was thoroughly aroused, and that he was extremely well qualified to express the situation in dynamic language.

The General Assembly of the State of Tennessee, upon learning

5. Van Horne, *op. cit.*, pp. 409, 410.

that General Thomas was assigned to the Military Division of the Tennessee, adopted the following Resolution on June 12, 1865:

WHEREAS, The pleasing intelligence has reached us that the distinguished soldier and commander, Major General George H. Thomas, has been assigned to this military division:

Resolved, by the General Assembly of the State of Tennessee, That we do most heartily congratulate our citizens upon the appointment of this model soldier, possessing as we do the most unbounded confidence in his ability and judgment, and believing that under his rule, early peace and quiet and Unionism will prevail in every section of our State.

Resolved, further, That we tender to the President and War Department our special thanks for their assignment of General Thomas over this military division, and, with his consent, we propose to adopt him as a Tennesseean, General Thomas having endeared himself to us, both by distinguished services and by many acts of noble and unostentatious kindness.[6]

General Thomas acknowledged the resolution adopting him as a citizen of the state of Tennessee, and expressed the hope that the patriotic efforts of its citizens might inspire public confidence and restore the state to peace and prosperity.

On August 25, 1866, the Tennessee General Assembly authorized the purchase of a painting of General Thomas for $1,000. This painting was done by Mr. George Dury of Nashville, Tennessee, and shows him at his full height. The painting hung in the state capitol for many years, but it was completely restored at the beginning of 1963. It will be stored in the Archives Building pending a decision by the Legislature as to which state building will display it.[7]

During the latter part of 1869, General Thomas was considerably annoyed by news that certain members of the General Assembly were in favor of selling the portrait of him that had been authorized by the more pro-Union Assembly of 1866. General Gates P. Thruston, residing at Nashville, a former officer under Thomas, offered to buy the painting on his own and a couple of friends' behalf, and have it removed from the State Library where it then hung. General Thomas and his brother Benjamin, the latter residing at Vicksburg, Mississippi, also attempted to purchase the painting, but without success. General Thomas, nevertheless, did not mince words in writing to a member of the legislature regarding the matter:

---

6. *Ibid.*, p. 414.

7. Tennessee Historical Commission, Nashville, Tenn., letter dated Jan. 8, 1963.

SAN FRANCISCO, CAL., Dec. 31, 1869.

HON. D. A. NUNN:

DEAR SIR,—I received your favor of the 20th, yesterday, and as I am sure of your friendly feeling toward me I take great pleasure in giving you my reasons for offering to refund to the present Legislature of Tennessee the cost of the portrait of myself, ordered to be painted by the Legislature of 1866, and remove it from the Library in the Capitol of your State. I will premise by stating that although I regretted at the time, the Legislature of 1866 had ordered, by joint resolution, a portrait of me, to be painted and placed in the State Library, yet being convinced it was done through motives of friendship and esteem, —the joint resolution having been passed without my knowledge, —I felt a natural delicacy in declining a compliment so unexpected, assured as I was of the sincerity of the act. From that day until the extraordinary proceedings had in the present Legislature, I had been led to believe that the act of the Legislature of 1866 had been generally approved throughout the State. On being informed of these recent proceedings, self-respect as well as a proper appreciation of the act of the Legislature of 1866 required that I should relieve the members of the present Legislature from the possibility of seeing a disagreeable picture every time they went into the State Library. The same reason impelled me to inform the Speaker that I shall return the medal as soon as I can get to New York, where I had it deposited last spring, before leaving the East to assume duty on this coast. Now let me assure you, that in taking the course I have, I disclaim any intention whatever to reject the compliment extended to me by the Legislature of 1866, but simply wish to return to the Legislature which repudiates their act, as far as in my power to do so, compensation for what they seem to consider a wrong perpetrated by a former Legislature on the people of that State in my behalf.[8]

When the foregoing letter was brought to the attention of the member who proposed selling the painting, he reacted as do all cowards by disclaiming any intention to sell it. He "explained" that he offered the proposal as a joke to call attention to certain falsely economic measures before the Legislature at that time. The fact that no condemnation of the proposal occurred was indication enough that the act was an insult and was so intended.

8. Van Horne, *op. cit.*, pp. 437-38.

The letter to Mr. Nunn of the Tennessee Legislature regarding his views of the attempt to sell the painting gives a splendid insight into the heart and soul of General Thomas. If there were nothing left by which to appraise him and his character but that one letter, it would tell enough. It would disclose that Thomas was a highly sensitive man; that he had tremendous pride; that he welcomed friendship, but wanted nothing to do with mere professions unsupported by solid sentiment; that he had great self-respect; that he was aware of his contribution to the Union victory, and that his acceptance of the painting in the first place did not exaggerate the importance of that contribution; and that he was extremely conscious of his capacity to offend those who had nothing to do with the insult to him.

General Garfield disclosed, during his famous speech before the Society of the Army of the Cumberland in 1870, following the death of General Thomas, that while on a visit to Washington in 1866, Thomas's friends persuaded him to appear before the House of Representatives. This was not accomplished without considerable persuasion; but when the representatives and guests stood to applaud him with enthusiastic indications of affection and reverence, following his being escorted to the Speaker's rostrum, his sensitiveness was indicated in another way. Speaker Colfax said that he noted, as he stood beside General Thomas, "that his hand trembled like an aspen leaf. He could bear the shock of battle, but he shrank before the storm of applause."[9]

One of the shortest and most informative dispatches to be found anywhere is that of General Thomas to his wife on December 15, the first day of the Battle of Nashville:

MRS. F. L. THOMAS,
NEW YORK HOTEL, NEW YORK.

We have whipped the enemy, taken many prisoners and considerable artillery.

GEO. H. THOMAS,
Major-General, U. S. Volunteers, Commanding[10]

In this dispatch to his wife, General Thomas displayed great dignity, reservation, and restraint, and a complete absence of vanity or gloating. The sentiment quite well matches the oft-repeated remark attributed to him, when commenting upon his feelings, "Colonel, I have taken a great deal of pains to educate myself not to feel."[11]

9. The Society of the Army of the Cumberland, *Yearbook 1870* (Cincinnati, 1871), p. 89.
10. *Official Records, op. cit.,* Vol. XLV, Part 2, p. 195.
11. Gamaliel Bradford, *Union Portraits* (Boston, 1916), p. 129.

General Thomas, as has been mentioned previously, wanted no baubles, no reward for having done his duty. Any token of affection or friendship, when it appeared to be based upon that and nothing else, he might accept, as for example the gold medal presented to him by the state of Tennessee on December 15, 1866 through Governor William G. Brownlow. In his words of presentation, Brownlow said, in part:

It is intended to express the high regard in which you are held by a loyal Tennessee legislature, as a military chieftain, a tried and devoted patriot, and a modest unassuming gentleman.

General, in no sense of flattery I must be permitted to say, that in the great struggle of four years, which recently convulsed the Nation, of all military commanders you are perhaps the only one that never lost a battle, and in the government of armies and departments never made a mistake.

The response by General Thomas, also in part, affords some light on the importance he attached to his obligations:

Some thirty years ago I received my diploma at the Military Academy, and soon after a commission in the Army.

On receiving that commission I took an oath to sustain the Constitution of the United States, and the Government, and to obey all officers of the Government placed over me. I have faithfully endeavored to keep that oath. I did not regard it so much as an oath, [but] as a solemn pledge on my part to return the Government some little service for the great benefit I had received in obtaining my education at the Academy.[12]

On August 6, the Department of the Tennessee was created and replaced the Military Division of the Tennessee, without diminishing the authority of General Thomas. It consisted of three districts and four subdistricts. The District of the Cumberland, under General Stoneman, comprised Kentucky and Tennessee, and the subdistricts of Kentucky and Tennessee were under Generals Jeff C. Davis and Clinton B. Fisk, respectively. The District of Mississippi was under General Tom Wood. The District of the Chattahoochee, under General Charles R. Woods, comprised Alabama and Georgia; and the subdistrict of Georgia was commanded by General Davis Tilson, while the subdistrict of Alabama was commanded by General Wagner Swayne.[13]

It is apparent that General Thomas was most solicitous toward

12. Van Horne, *op. cit.*, p. 416.
13. *Ibid.*, p. 418.

his late enemy, and realized that the best way to win the people back to their former allegiance was to treat them with kindness and humanity. Although this was always his concern, it was not always possible to have it that way, since many of the former Confederates were belligerent and rabble rousing. He would not abide the display of the Confederate flag, for example, when on the anniversary of Georgia's withdrawal from the Union the citizens of Rome, Georgia, boldly displayed their former flag. Mayor Charles H. Smith protested when General Thomas ordered the arrest of those responsible for the display of the Stars and Bars, contending that no disrespect to the United States flag, their flag, too, was intended. In bitterly scornful language, Thomas expressed himself to the mayor in no uncertain words, in part as follows:

> The sole cause of this, and similar offenses lies in the fact that certain citizens of Rome, and a portion of the people of the States lately in rebellion, do not and have not accepted the situation, and that is, that the late Civil War was a rebellion and history will so record it. Those engaged in it are and will be pronounced rebels; rebellion implies treason; and treason is a crime, and a heinous one too, and deserving of punishment; and that traitors have not been punished is owing to the magnanimity of the conquerors. With too many of the people of the South, the late Civil War is called a revolution, rebels are called "Confederates," loyalists to the whole country are called d——d Yankees and traitors, and over the whole great crime with its accursed record of slaughtered heroes, patriots murdered because of their true-hearted love of country, widowed wives and orphaned children, and prisoners of war slain amid such horrors as find no parallel in the history of the world, they are trying to throw the gloss of respectability, and are thrusting with contumely and derision from their society the men and women who would not join hands with them in the work of ruining their country. Everywhere in the States lately in rebellion, treason is respectable and loyalty odious. This, the people of the United States, who ended the Rebellion and saved the country, will not permit.[14]

This blast from General Thomas, regardless of its immediate purpose, does much to refute the completely unsupported allegation of General Fitzhugh Lee and certain Southern newspapers and individuals, and made only after the death of General Thomas, that he wavered in his decision to remain with the Union. Nothing in his lifetime supports such a claim; and in addition to solid evidence that

---

14. *Army and Navy Journal* (March 2, 1887).

refutes it, the foregoing letter to the mayor of Rome, Georgia, taken in consideration with the life of General Thomas throughout, stamps the charge as a baseless falsehood. General Thomas was no hypocrite, not in the least sense of the word; and he would not have been capable of wavering in his loyalty at one time, and later delivering such a denunciation of those who left the Union and would not accept the role of the conquered.

General Thomas's statement of the situation for those who would not acquiesce in the facts of the restored Union did little to reconcile the differences, or, in other words, to reduce friction. Their "cause," states rights, still persists in many minds in the former Confederate states; and at that time they were not inclined to become more cooperative after General Thomas had thus expressed his feelings. He had a responsibility to perform; and the citizens of the states in former revolt against the United States had the solemn duty to obey the laws, as in view of the agreement reached by their surrendering military commanders, Generals Lee, Johnston, and others, they should have done.

Shortly after the end of the war a secret organization known as the Ku Klux Klan had its origin in Pulaski, Tennessee. After about a year, during which a number of Dens were organized and recruited principally from former Confederate soldiers, a meeting of delegates was held in Nashville. This was in the spring of 1867. Little of their activities at the Nashville meeting is known for fact, other than that its members were determined to protect the rights of the whites, which it is believed underlay the original Den at Pulaski. The meeting resulted in the setting up of an organization under a single head, with a chain of command leading down to the lowliest member in the local Den.[15]

In its Revised and Amended Prescript, adopted afterward, the Klan recognized the relationship of its members to the United States Government, the Constitutional laws, and the Union of the States. Its objectives were to protect the weak and the innocent from indignities, wrongs, and outrages of the lawless, the violent, the brutal, and so on; to protect and defend the Constitution of the United States and all laws consistent therewith, and also to protect the people from any invasion from whatever source; and finally to aid and assist in executing all Constitutional laws, and to protect the people from unlawful seizure, and so on.[16]

General Nathan B. Forrest was reputed to have been an active

---

15. Robert S. Henry, *The Story of Reconstruction* (New York, 1938), p. 230.

16. *Ibid.*, pp. 230, 231.

member of the Klan and became the Grand Wizard, proving the dead earnestness of those active in bringing into being the organization. With their hooded regalia, and operating at the darkest hours of the night, they were something to throw fear into the newly created citizens or former slaves. Undoubtedly these efforts produced terror in the hearts of those inclined to reduce or limit the doctrine of white supremacy. There is some reason to believe, also, that their objectives were sometimes good, and that they had a deterrent effect in keeping in subjection the lawless and other unsavory elements. General Thomas was concerned lest the Klan be an active military organization whose real purpose was the controlling of elections in the formerly seceded states by intimidating colored voters from casting a ballot. He assembled all available data on the problem and forwarded it to Washington for a determination. He was attacked by the press for alleged misstatements regarding outrages committed. Local law-enforcement officers were unable to control the difficulties, because too many of them belonged to the Klan. One attempt to hold a city election in Nashville resulted in the sending of Federal troops to preserve order. The mayor of Nashville had also called extra policemen to "protect" his interests, as against those of Governor Brownlow who was in disfavor, but the outnumbered policemen were recalled by the mayor when he saw his chances were hopeless.

One of the pleasant occurrences after the war took place when Generals Hood and Thomas exchanged greetings in the Louisville Hotel in Louisville, Kentucky. According to the account of the incident, a Southern woman of distinguished social position and culture was requested by Hood to arrange a meeting for him with General Thomas. When she asked Thomas about it, he said, "Certainly, my dear madam. I shall be most happy to meet General Hood. Will he come to my room?" When Hood clattered into his room on crutches, Thomas threw his arm about him and helped him to a chair with a tenderness that was touching. Upon Hood's return to the woman, after spending an hour with Thomas, he said, with the trace of a tear, "Thomas is a grand man; he should have remained with us, where he would have been appreciated and loved."[17] This incident has led to speculation that Hood meant to convey that Thomas was dissatisfied, a suggestion that is ridiculous. Certainly Thomas had been treated shamefully by those in authority; but this did not change his loyalty in the slightest, as all evidence indicates.

On March 11, 1867, General Thomas was assigned to the command of the Third Military District, but requested an assignment elsewhere

---

17. Van Horne, *op. cit.*, p. 406; Donn Piatt, *General George H. Thomas* (Cincinnati, 1891), p. 51.

and was named to the Department of the Cumberland, comprising Kentucky, Tennessee, and West Virginia. Shortly thereafter, on August 17, 1867, he was ordered to command the Fifth Military District and the department consisting of the states of Louisiana and Texas, replacing General Sheridan, as stated elsewhere. This change in command was intended to replace Sheridan because of his difficulties in administering his responsibilities. The assignment of General Thomas, excepting his retention of the Department of the Cumberland, was changed because of his health at that time, and General Winfield S. Hancock, the great corps commander of the Army of the Potomac, was assigned to replace Sheridan.[18] General Thomas was emphatic in declaring that his physical condition was nothing serious. He described it as "a peculiar sensation which I had on my right side," which his physician ascribed to his liver, and regarding which he thought that unless blus mass was taken to restore a healthy action to that organ, he might eventually be attacked with some disease of the liver that would lead to disagreeable consequences. It is only conjectural, but highly possible, that General Thomas in this illness might have had a slight indication of his death, three years later.

President Johnson, on February 21, 1868, sent General Thomas's name to the Senate for confirmation as brevet lieutenant-general and brevet general in the army. The President was having trouble with General Grant, and of course his was one of the stormiest administrations in history, as shown by his near impeachment. Immediately upon hearing of the recommendation, General Thomas sent the following letter to Senator Ben Wade, President of the Senate:

> The morning papers of Louisville [February 22, 1868] announce officially that my name was yesterday sent to the Senate for confirmation as brevet lieutenant-general and brevet general.
>
> For the Battle of Nashville I was appointed a major-general in the United States Army. My services since the war do not merit so high a compliment, and it is now too late to be regarded as a compliment, if conferred for services during the war.
>
> I therefore earnestly request that the Senate will not confirm the nomination.[19]

General Thomas sent a similar request to President Johnson and explained his reasons. He probably knew that the President was having trouble with Grant, who, it was said, was in the throes of political activity, which culminated in his being elected to the White

---

18. Van Horne, *ibid.*, pp. 418, 419; Henry Coppee, *General Thomas* (New York, 1893), pp. 296-97.

19. Van Horne, *ibid.*, p. 420.

House. Here was a wonderful opportunity for General Thomas to retaliate in kind for the abuses, slights, degradation, standoffishness, or whatever else it might be termed; but, as this incident proves, Thomas was not an ordinary man in any sense of the word. When it was a matter of military differences, Thomas would stand toe to toe with Grant; but he was not a cheap ward-heeling politician, and wanted nothing to do with anything that smacked of it. He was a man from top to bottom and from here to there! When General Rosecrans was once asked, "Rosy, Thomas was an angel, was he not?" "Well," replied Rosecrans, "is not that going a little too far?" "Oh, but I mean as near to an angel as a mortal can be?" "Yes, I willingly agree to that."[20]

Although it is not generally known, just as his personal life is little known, General Thomas was requested by many friends to become a candidate for the Presidency in 1868. Among the number of solicitations he received and acknowledged was one from General Watts DePeyster. The letter is fairly self-explanatory:

I received your favor of the 9th inst. [April, 1867] some days ago, but have not had time to reply until to-day.

First, you must permit me to acknowledge my grateful sense of your kind appreciation of my services.

Second, I will here state, and hope you will report for me, whenever you hear my name mentioned in connection with the Presidency of the United States, that I never will consent to being brought before the people as a candidate for any office. I have too much regard for my own self-respect to voluntarily place myself in a position where my personal and private character can be assailed with impunity by newspapermen and scurrilous political pettifoggers and demagogues.[21]

A number of attempts were made by individuals and groups to give General Thomas presents, but with the exception of a beautiful jeweled badge of the Army of the Cumberland he declined all of them. One of the proffered gifts, a set of silver plate from the citizens of Nashville, was refused. His general attitude was that when anyone offered him anything that placed him under obligations he was duty bound to refuse it. Thus he maintained a cherished possession, his independence.

One of the matters to which General Thomas directed his interest

---

20. Address of John Watts De Peyster on General Thomas, before the New York Historical Society, Jan. 5, 1875.
21. *Ibid.*

during Reconstruction was the newly formed Society of the Army of the Cumberland. This organization, open to former members of that Army, elected General Thomas as its first president. The organization met in Cincinnati on February 6, 1868, and later participated in a joint meeting of the three organizations, the Army of the Cumberland, the Army of the Ohio, and the Army of the Tennessee, and the yet to be organized Army of Georgia association, held in Chicago on December 15 and 16, 1868.

The outstanding incident of this joint assemblage was the tremendous ovation given General Thomas during the oration of General Belknap. General Thomas had been designated to sit between Generals Grant and Sherman at the head of the great reunion. When Thomas was referred to as the individual who was "true to his trust wherever found, whether controlling the management of a complicated command, or, as when the fate of the Western army quivered in the balance, coolly stemming the tide of battle, he beat back the rebel host, crushed and conquered, stamping himself as the determined soldier . . . whose name . . . is told to the youth of the land as the synonym of purest patriotism, your own beloved commander, the Rock of Chickamauga," the burst of emotion that followed was unprecedented then or thereafter.[22] What a fitting moment for him to be thus vindicated by his own men before Generals Grant and Sherman, both of whom, if they had any humanity, must have felt some regret for the moment for their mistreatment of him.

It has been seen that General Thomas refused to be considered for the nomination to the Presidency, which meant, of course, that Grant had a much clearer field. How clear is purely a matter of conjecture; but with his and Sherman's smear on Thomas's alleged "slowness" brought out in the open as only a political campaign could do it, it is quite certain that the stature of Thomas would have been established then as superior to that of either of his detractors. Tennessee had already, in convention, taken a position by unanimous vote for Thomas before he stopped further effort in his behalf. Several of General Thomas's letters declining to be a candidate are on file in the Henry E. Huntington Library in San Marino, California, including those from the historian Henry M. Cist and John Tyler, Jr., son of former President Tyler. His reasons were varied, but he gave this explanation: "I will have nothing to do with politics. I am a soldier, and I know my duty; as a politician I would be lost. No, sir; not even if I were elected unanimously would I accept. I want to die

22. Van Horne, *op. cit.*, p. 429; *The Society, 1868*, p. 23; *The Army Reunion* (Chicago. 1869), pp. 13, 31, 32.

with a fair record, and this I will do if I keep out of the sea of politics and cling to my proper profession."[23] This statement, it should be noted, was not applicable to Grant. That is, with the worst administration in the nation's history, which almost any schoolboy knows to be the case, Grant is still remembered as the great warrior. The Grant Legend did its work so well that nothing seemed to hurt his military reputation.

After General Grant assumed the Presidency he named his friend Sherman to succeed himself with the rank of commander in chief, and appointed General Rawlins, his wartime chief of staff, as Secretary of War in place of General Schofield. This has the appearance of significance, since Grant must have learned by that time that he could not trust Schofield. It left a scramble for Sherman's vacated spot among Generals Meade, Sheridan, and Thomas, the answer as to who got it being a foregone conclusion. Sheridan was one of Grant's friends, his "Little Phil," who was not equal in ability to either Meade or Thomas, and of course friendship counted most with Grant. Grant's political support had given him an excellent education in the importance of knowing the right people and in placing friends in the right places. Sheridan was given the rank of lieutenant general and assigned to command the Military Division of the Missouri. Both Meade and Thomas were very disappointed, although Meade was given command of the Military Division of the Atlantic, and Thomas would get what was left. This was one of the many embarrassments that Thomas would suffer during the limited period of life left to him.

Colonel Alfred Hough, General Thomas's long-time aide, explained that General Thomas had requested an Eastern assignment in deference to his long service in the West, and perhaps also to the fact that during the entire war he took not one leave of absence. Since General Meade received the Eastern command, General Thomas was satisfied to remain in Louisville. Colonel Hough stated further that shortly after General's Grant's election he accompanied General Thomas on an evening call on him. They were late in arriving and found Grant alone. They spent an hour or more in the library in company with Mrs. Grant and her father. After some general conversation, General Grant said, "Thomas, there has got to be a change on the Pacific, and either you or Sheridan will have to go there; how would you like it?" When Thomas replied that he personally would have no objection, but that Mrs. Thomas would prefer remaining in the East with her friends, Mrs. Grant said, "Your having a

23. Henry E. Huntington Papers, San Marino, Calif.; Van Horne, *op. cit.*, pp. 422, 423; Richard W. Johnson, *Memoir of General George H. Thomas* (Philadelphia, 1881), p. 234.

wife is one reason why you should go there instead of Sheridan, as he ought to stay here where he can get one." Hough continued, "This was said laughingly, and caused a smile from the others, and immediately the conversation was changed by General Grant, not another word being spoken on the subject."[24] This narrative discloses, for all practical purposes, that Mrs. Grant, temporarily at least, assigned General Thomas to the Pacific Coast. It also makes clear that it was just another dirty deal to Thomas by Grant. Sheridan, his friend, much younger and single, would not have made nearly so much of a sacrifice as did Thomas, who lived hardly longer than a year afterward and needed the relaxation of being in the East after a lifetime of strenuous service to his country.

The conversation with Mrs. Grant did not end the Pacific assignment, however. General Halleck was at that time commander of the Military Division of the Pacific, but rumors persisted that he was to be relieved. Thomas believed that he would be sent there, although he said nothing about it. General Sherman informed Thomas, some time after Grant's inauguration, that Schofield was being assigned to the Pacific, whereupon Thomas asked where he was to be assigned. When Sherman told him he was to remain where he was, Thomas became indignant at the outrage, and told Sherman that if the assignment went through he would take the matter to the public. Sherman was concerned, naturally, and assured him that he would safeguard him against any indignity. Thomas was assigned to the Pacific Coast, all right; but after he had relieved Halleck the latter was assigned to Thomas's former post at Louisville and the command was made a division. This meant that they withheld the elevation until Thomas was out of the way and in virtual isolation, rather than give it to him. Sherman was Thomas's friend? It was natural that Thomas protested the appointment of Schofield, a younger man, to the Pacific to head a division, while he remained in charge of a department with lower rank. Schofield, of course, was to be elevated at his expense, and only his vigorous protest prevented it. It is understandable that Schofield would have little use for General Thomas, and that he would have an impact upon him until the last moment of his life.[25]

General Thomas assumed command of the Division of the Pacific on June 1, 1869, and soon afterward undertook a tour of inspection that took him from one end of his command to the other. His trip took in the interior military posts, extended through Nevada, Idaho, Oregon, and Washington Territory, and from thence to Portland. He there boarded a steamer for Alaska to inspect military posts,

24. Van Horne, *ibid.*, pp. 433-34.
25. *Ibid.*, p. 435.

including Baranov's outpost at Sitka, in addition to St. Paul's Island in the Bering Sea, from which point he returned to San Francisco on September 16. He made his report and recommended that military forces be retained in Alaska until the passing of laws to regulate the indiscriminate killing of fur-bearing animals. He reported also that gold prospectors had maintained friendly relations with the native Indians, but that if gold should be found in sufficient quantity there would be a rush to the area by adventurers with the attendant lawlessness usually accompanying such discoveries. General Thomas reported also that the natives were hard-working, civilized, and easygoing, but that the use of whiskey had demoralized them.[26]

A long-time friend, General Erasmus D. Keyes, who was Thomas's superior in the Florida War, met him just a few days before his death and was shocked at the tremendous change in his appearance. He noted that his countenance had undergone a marked change, and that in addition to the spark gone from his eyes, his lips were bordered by white lines.[27] He had made no complaints since his trip to the various posts and installations, but there was no doubt he was failing. It is small wonder that he was feeling under par, since he had completed a trip that would tax the energies of a much younger man. He had been considering a trip to California, where the climate might give him a lift, but nothing came of it.

Perhaps March 28, 1870, meant no more in the life of General Thomas, since taking over the command of the Military Division of the Pacific, than any other day as he began his duties. He reached his office as usual and held conversation with his aide, Colonel Hough. It would be ridiculous in the extreme to assume that the two did not discuss the recent article in the New York *Tribune* of March 12, 1870, under the heading "Secrets of History—The Battle of Nashville—Was Grant's Order a Blunder?" This article, signed "One Who Fought at Nashville," was inevitably the work of a coward who did not dare face the nation with his identity, because he knew that he was a liar, and that he was stabbing a great man in the back with cruel, cutting falsehoods. After some time, Colonel Hough left General Thomas to his work of drafting a reply to the newspaper attack, and did not return until early in the afternoon. When he arrived, at about 1:45, General Thomas was unconscious from a fatal attack of apoplexy. He rallied for a few minutes and the doctors at first thought he had

26. Johnson, *op. cit.*, pp. 238, 239; Van Horne, *ibid.*, pp. 436-37; *American Heritage* (April, 1959), p. 76; Thomas's Report to Sherman, Sept. 21, 1869, in National Archives.

27. Erasmus D. Keyes, *Fifty Years Observation of Men and Events* (New York, 1884), p. 167.

suffered a digestive attack, which had commenced at about 1:30, when he had left his desk and said, "I want air." He then fell to the floor.[28]

After about a half hour, General Thomas said that he felt no pain except at the right temple. The physicians confided that this was a bad sign, although the patient continued seemingly to get better and insisted on getting up; but after a few minutes he was compelled to lie down again. Mrs. Thomas arrived shortly afterward and sat by his side. They exchanged words and all except Mrs. Thomas and Colonel Hough left the room to await the action of the medication. He was heard to say that he felt no pain, but shortly afterward he had a convulsive action in the chest, which prompted him to attempt to rise, but he could not. The doctors were called from the adjoining room and at once pronounced his trouble apoplexy. He began to sink gradually soon thereafter and continued thus until his death at 7:25 P.M.[29]

Chaplain Van Horne, General Thomas's first biographer, reported that, shortly after the war, General Thomas related to him that he felt he would have an enemy when Sherman sent Schofield back to Nashville with his Twenty-third Corps. He also feared that an effort would be made to relieve him from command of the army. The unusual condition of affairs before and after Nashville strengthened his belief that Schofield was intriguing against him. Thomas told Van Horne further that Sherman had stated to him, Thomas, that he had given Schofield the choice of remaining on the March to the Sea or of going to Nashville. This all adds strength, if any were needed, in view of the intercepted telegram from Schofield to Grant, referred to in connection with the Nashville campaign, to Schofield's guilt, and Thomas certainly thought it did. Thomas did not then know that Grant had named Schofield as his successor until he reached San Francisco to succeed Halleck. That general, who was reputed to be somewhat indiscreet, gave a banquet in Thomas's honor, at which, in the course of conversation, he described to Thomas the circumstances of the order relieving him from command at Nashville and the naming of Schofield in his place. Thomas's reaction was immediate. He stated, "I knew it. I knew he was the man."[30]

When General Thomas said that he knew Schofield was the man, he gave expression to a belief that has been shared by almost everyone familiar with the details. Until recently it was not generally known that Schofield had a collaborator in the person of Major General

---

28. Van Horne, *op. cit.*, pp. 434, 442, 443.
29. *Ibid.*, p. 434.
30. *Ibid.*, p. 440.

Jacob D. Cox, the distinguished Civil War historian and former commander of a division in General Schofield's Twenty-third Corps. This comes as one of the most surprising occurrences in the entire field of research relating to this biography; in fact, it is extremely difficult to believe. It has been stated earlier in this work that General Cox had no particular warmth for General Thomas, but it was not believed at the time that his feelings would find expression in so reprehensible a deed as the writing of the New York *Tribune* letter, which many believe actually led to the death of General Thomas.

General David S. Stanley, able commander of the advance guard that held open the escape route that enabled General Schofield to withdraw from General Hood's encirclement at Spring Hill following Schofield's near-costly mistake through disobedience of orders, is authority for the accusation against Cox. According to Stanley's letter, dated December 10, 1889, and addressed to Colonel Hough, General Cox was motivated by revenge against General Thomas because of a reprimand Thomas gave him for encouraging his men to pull down a Union man's house that was occupied by helpless ladies. Stanley stated that Schofield did not tell him that Cox wrote the letter; but Schofield said he knew of the letter before its publication, and that ever since he deeply regretted it. Stanley stated also that he wanted to get everything well in hand to bring the facts into the open, and that Cox had thus far not answered his letter regarding the matter.[31] Since Schofield professed knowledge of the letter before it was published, it would be ridiculous to assume that he had nothing to do with it. Else why would he be aware that such a letter was written, and particularly before its publication? Someone wrote the letter, and the finger points unmistakably to Schofield's interest in it, because of the Nashville and Franklin discussion, which would affect no one so much as Schofield.

There was no doubt in the mind of Mrs. Thomas that General Schofield had wronged her husband greatly. In answer to a question, she stated that she was not prepared to say that General Thomas's death was attributable to the great wrong done him during and after the Nashville campaign. She said, "I will say that it preyed upon him and affected his health, which General Schofield's base attack on his military reputation added to, and which was the cause of the fatal attack on March 28, 1870." Continuing, Mrs. Thomas stated, "I have since felt that General Grant has not treated General Thomas since his death, with the same generosity General Thomas always, while living, [treated him], and from early in the war after the battle of Pittsburg Landing [Shiloh] when General Buell's army joined in

31. The John N. Hough Papers (copies in the author's possession).

the advance on Corinth and General Thomas was placed in command of a column in General Grant's place. He wrote me that General Grant did not like it."[32] This is fully explained in the chapter on Shiloh or Pittsburg Landing, with full details that General Thomas displayed one of the most magnanimous acts of kindness toward Grant by stepping down to permit Grant to step back up. General Grant proved his caliber thereafter by perpetrating numerous wrongs against General Thomas, as fully set forth herein.

Reverting to Colonel Hough's last meeting with General Thomas, just before his attack, he stated that General Thomas resolved to reply to the scurrilous newspaper attack on March 12, 1870. He quoted General Thomas as saying:

That criticism upon my plan is really funny reading. I am only astonished that the letter should have been published, for some of its statements are easily refuted, and others show an insubordination and intrigue that will astonish the public. The answer to it is a good and just one, and whoever wrote it has my thanks.* I am now satisfied that what I have suspected for some time is true, that is, that General Schofield intrigued for my removal, to enable him to get my command. I have long known that he asked to be sent back to me from Atlanta to Nashville, which always surprised me, as there was apparently at this time a much greater opportunity for gaining distinction with General Sherman than with me, and now I understand it. Now that he is piqued, that the order placing him in command is called a blunder, he is endeavoring to right himself before the public by attacking me, who have had nothing to do with this discussion; but it will fail, for plenty of my old officers will answer him, as I am assured by letters now. I say this, because the article was directly inspired by him. I am assured of this on the authority of a friend in St. Louis.

It is an outrageous article, and as a military criticism is ridiculous, and easily answered, as it is in this first reply to it; it will create much indignation among the officers who fought at Nashville, who will be astonished at some of the statements. At one statement, though, I am amazed, and it convinces me of Schofield's duplicity, and that is, that he, one of my subordinates should have applied, in his letter of December 26th, 1864 [Schofield's *Forty-six Years in the Army*, page 253, shows December 27, 1864], to General Grant, without my knowledge, to be trans-

*This refers to a reply by "Another Man," in the *Tribune* of March 19, 1870.

32. *Ibid.*

ferred with his command to the Atlantic; this is the first time I ever heard of this application. What will reflecting people say after hearing of this letter? If a subordinate officer can presume to ask that his commander be weakened to the extent to which this article states General Schofield did, is it not also reasonable to suppose that he had written letters previously to General Grant, so commenting on affairs at Nashville, as to suggest to him the propriety of substituting Schofield for me, and thereby have originated the causes for his present disagreeable situation? In the matter of winter quarters; suppose I had been permitted by General Grant to place my troops in winter quarters in accordance with my order, and after hearing of Sherman's successful march to the sea and intention to move in the direction of Richmond to join Grant, he does not see that I could have cooperated with Sherman by moving through the northern part of Georgia, Western North Carolina, and East Tennessee towards the same objective point, thus aiding somewhat towards the final triumph of our forces in Virginia. This, or whatever was necessary, would have been done by me, if my plans had not been upset by this letter of Schofield of December 26th, now for the first time known to me.[33]

What should not be overlooked in this recital by General Thomas is that Schofield's villainy at Nashville was made possible only because the commander in chief, General Grant, permitted it. He, the future President of the United States, in this incident showed his true character by granting Schofield's underhanded application to move his army to the Atlantic. This has been discussed previously, but the fact will not down that Grant's scruples were not what they should have been or he would have acquainted General Thomas of the disloyalty, not to say insubordination, of Schofield; on the contrary, what must we think of him for complying with the request? To suggest that Grant was anything but dishonest in this is to flaunt common sense. If any man in our history was more deserving of decent treatment than General Thomas, he does not come to mind; and by the same process of reasoning, if any man in our history was more wronged than was General Thomas by General Grant, that also does not come to mind. Not only is there no parallel for such treatment; there is nothing remotely resembling it. Surely Job, with his many afflictions and burdens, never suffered greater torment than Thomas. This nation should know the truth, at long last, of the great deeds of General Thomas and the underhanded performances of Grant and Schofield.

---

33. Van Horne, *op. cit.*, pp. 440-42.

Schofield's unsurpassed enmity toward General Thomas had its beginning on June 18, 1852, when Thomas was an instructor at West Point and Schofield was a cadet. Schofield, an upper classman, was assigned to instruct a group of candidates of the Class of 1856 for the entrance examination in mathematics. Since three of the four applicants who failed were from Schofield's group, inquiry was naturally directed to the cause; and after due investigation Schofield was adjudged responsible and dismissed from the Military Academy with the approval of the Secretary of War. Details concerning the inquiry are restricted, out of consideration to the families concerned, but enough is available to indicate that Schofield examined his charges in the functions of the reproductive and waste organs of the human anatomy.[34] The account given by Schofield, shown in part herewith, is considerably different from the information on file at West Point:

We had gone over the entire course upon which they were to be examined, and all were well prepared except two who seemed hopelessly deficient upon a few subjects which they had been unable to comprehend. . . . I took them to the blackboard and devoted fifteen or twenty minutes before the bugle-call. . . . While thus employed, several of my classmates came into the room and began talking to the other candidates. Though their presence annoyed me, it did not interfere with my work; so I kept on intently with the two young boys until the bugle sounded. I then went to my quarters without paying any attention to the interruption, or knowing anything of the character of what had occurred. But one of the candidates, perhaps by way of excuse for his failure, wrote to his parents some account of the "deviltry" in which my classmates had indulged that day. That report found its way to the War Department, and was soon followed by an order to the commandant of cadets to investigate. The facts were found fully to exonerate me from any participation in or countenance of the deviltry, except that I did not stop it; and showed that I had faithfully done my duty in teaching the candidates. . . . I was called upon to answer for my own conduct; and the names of the guilty classmates being unknown to the candidates, I was also held responsible for their conduct. I answered by showing, as I believed, my own innocence, except my neglect of duty in tolerating such a proceeding.[35]

---

34. Letter Sent File, 175, Report of Bradford R. Alden, with letter of Brewerton to Totten, July 8, 1852, in West Point Library.

35. John M. Schofield, *Forty-six Years in the Army* (New York, 1897), pp. 10-15.

From what is known of Schofield's mistreatment of General Thomas, there is no basis for confidence that his story of the incident is acceptable, as we shall see.

Schofield's explanation is distinctive for its freedom from resemblance to the details on file at the West Point Library, as stated, and for its failure to afford some inkling of the trouble. The court of inquiry undoubtedly developed a reason for its being convened, and that reason was surely known to the large number of cadets Schofield alleged were there. Therefore the reason was surely known to the accused who, if not guilty, might have been expected to express his disgust by labeling it something more serious than "deviltry." As opposed to such reticence, the incident was termed disgraceful by the authorities. His statement that he was so absorbed in the instructing of his charges that he did not know what occurred places an impossible burden upon the reader. Furthermore, it is difficult to believe that his classmates were so lacking in caution that they believed they would not be detected; therefore it is questionable whether the incident as he described it occurred at all. It is more acceptable that Schofield alone instructed the candidates, who would have been far more likely to keep the matter quiet than his classmates.

After about two weeks the court of inquiry was convened and Schofield was reinstated. He reported in his *Memoirs* that two of the thirteen-member court who voted against his reinstatement included General Thomas. He stated also that he did not learn of the vote of the court until two years before Thomas's death when, as Secretary of War, he had access to the files. In his own words, "time works legitimate revenge, and makes all things even,"[36] although unwittingly he wrote the index to his character. He sought revenge against a man who performed his whole duty always; and he did not give full play to "time" to make things even, as we have seen. If he did not know how Thomas had voted until after the war, the wonder is how he could have exceeded his display of enmity if he had known it before and after Nashville, when he was undermining Thomas by sending false and damaging information to Grant.

Schofield's statement that part of "time's revenge" was in the opportunity afforded him to avert Thomas's dismissal is sheer fiction, since the very opposite is true. He claimed credit for saving Thomas's army from disaster, but the records disclose no such thing; the records do disclose, as we have seen, that Schofield, not Thomas, was saved from disaster by General David S. Stanley and General James H. Wilson at Spring Hill, with help from Confederate lapses. In claiming that he saved Thomas from an inferior command, he could only have

---

36. *Ibid.*, p. 241.

had reference to the Pacific command;[37] but this is also fiction, since, as explained previously, Thomas himself, none other, protested the assignment of Schofield to that command to which he was entitled by right of seniority and by achievement on many battlefields. Thomas should have been given the command automatically, but Schofield had been given the command before Thomas demanded it as his due. If nothing else, these comments by Schofield reveal him as one, aside from his other undesirable characteristics, who was not over-zealous in dealing with the facts. They also cast more doubt on his version of his near-dismissal from West Point. To offset Schofield's conduct and statements, one need look no further than the life and record of General Thomas, which have no blemish of any kind against them. No better vindication of General Thomas is necessary than Schofield's own conduct and statements.

Following his death, the remains of General Thomas were embalmed at once and removed the next day to the Lick House, which the general had made his residence. No public demonstration was permitted by Mrs. Thomas, which was in keeping with the general's lifelong custom of avoiding display of any kind. After a short delay, his body was sent, in care of Colonel J. P. Willard, one of his aides, to Troy, New York, for burial.[38]

One of the first matters to which Mrs. Thomas directed her attention was to assign Colonel Hough to the task of separating all her husband's personal papers from his official papers. "This sad duty occupied me three days. Of course many of the papers were deeply interesting, but all of them only confirmed the strength and beauty of his character; not a paper was destroyed, and not one need ever be by Mrs. Thomas."[39]

Mrs. Thomas was compelled to remain in San Francisco until April 5, and did not arrive in Troy until the fourteenth. The general's body had left San Francisco on March 31 and reached New York on April 7, where it was placed in Saint Paul's Episcopal Church until burial, on April 8.[40]

General Sherman and other leading military leaders sought to have General Thomas's body interred at West Point, but Mrs. Thomas refused the request. In a dispatch to General Sherman, dated April 2, 1870, she stated:

I regret that I cannot yield to the desire of having the burial at West Point. As Troy will be my future home, I feel that I must

37. *Ibid.*
38. Van Horne, *op. cit.*, p. 443.
39. *Ibid.*, p. 444.
40. Troy *Daily Times,* April 7, 1870.

bury General Thomas in my family lot at the cemetery there. I will leave to you the arrangements for a military funeral at Troy. On the arrival of the remains there, they will be deposited temporarily in the receiving vault. Col. Willard knows my wishes. Private services have already been held here. Sincere thanks for your attention.

FRANCIS S. THOMAS[41]

There was deep mourning throughout the United States at the passing of so good and great a man as General Thomas. Of course, in a military funeral, as it was, the leading officers of the army were in attendance. The pallbearers were all major generals, namely, Meade, Rosecrans, Schofield, Hazen, Granger, Newton, McKay, and Hooker, and the body was interred in Oakwood Cemetery, as requested by Mrs. Thomas. Mrs. Thomas had erected on the grave a beautiful monument in the form of a sarcophagus, on which is mounted an American eagle grasping an accurate representation of the sword carried by General Thomas during the war.[42] On the front, in raised letters, is this inscription:

GEORGE H. THOMAS
Major-General U.S.A.

Born in Southampton County, Virginia,
July 31, 1816
Died, San Francisco, Cal.
March 28, 1870

An editorial in the Troy *Daily Times* of April 8, 1870, paid tribute to the man and soldier in a manner more in keeping with his true character than anything else discovered. This article, entitled *Thomas*, is as follows:

It is difficult to write upon any other topic than the one which is in all thoughts and upon all lips. We here in Troy are burying to-day a great soldier, a single-hearted patriot, a stainless gentleman, and the whole nation stands by this new grave with uncovered head. From one end of the Republic to the other people are talking to-day of what he was and what he did.

There have been many public men, both in civil and military life, over whose coffin their friends have felt it almost a necessity and sacred duty to pronounce elaborate eulogies. George H.

41. *Ibid.*, April 4, 1870.
42. *Ibid.*, April 4 and 8, 1870; Van Horne, *op. cit.*, pp. 448-49. (The representation of the sword has disappeared.)

Thomas was not of their number. He did the work which God gave him to do too well to need our feeble plaudits. The universal mourning of his countrymen is more eloquent than anything which the finest orator could say. In spite of that shy modesty which was sometimes mistaken for haughtiness, he was very near to their hearts, and they know what they have lost in losing him.

Many great and good men remain to serve the Republic, but not one greater or better than the illustrious soldier whom loving hands are even now laying to rest by the side of our majestic river. The fittest words to speak of him are those which Tacitus uses of Agricola: "Whatever we have loved and admired in him abides and will abide forever in the memory of his countrymen, and in the history of his country."

Perhaps it is fitting that General George H. Thomas was buried in Oakwood Cemetery, because there lies buried the body of Samuel Wilson, around whose name the initials "U. S.," the symbol of the United States, originated. Wilson was in the slaughterhouse business during the War of 1812, and supplied barrels of beef to the soldiers at near-by Greenbush, which he stamped "U. S." The soldiers from Troy caught the idea and began calling the beef "Uncle Sam's" beef, implying that it was furnished by Samuel Wilson. Other soldiers, thinking that the term applied to the letters "U. S." stood for United States, began applying it as we use it today.[43]

It would be appropriate to give the contents of the unfinished reply to the *Tribune* letter that General Thomas was preparing when stricken with his fatal attack:

The article in the Tribune was evidently brought out by the assertions in the Gazette correspondence that Grant would have committed a serious blunder had he relieved Thomas by Schofield, who as appears by the article, claims the battle of Franklin was fought under his immediate supervision, and was so eminently successful, that he consequently was as acceptable to the army as General Thomas. [That may or may not be.] It is hoped that the troops would have done their duty under any commander; but Wood and Stanley and many officers of rank, who participated in that battle, know the peculiar situation of affairs that rendered it necessary General Thomas should remain in Nashville to receive the reinforcements which were arriving daily, supervising and expediting their equipment [the cavalry sent back by General Sherman being all dismounted, the new regiments ar-

---

43. Brochure, Oakwood Cemetery, Troy, N. Y.

riving from the States needing equipage, etc., to enable them to take the field], and that Schofield happened to command the troops immediately opposing the advancing enemy, by virtue of his position as an army commander [he commanded the Army of the Ohio]. The criticisms on the plan of battle and point of attack [referring to Nashville], are too unimportant to notice. With regard to the mistake of not using 10,000 to great advantage, the original position of the 10,000 men [Schofield's Army of the Ohio, Twenty-third Corps, in reserve], being central, rendered them available for promptly reinforcing Steedman, should the enemy concentrate so heavily on him as to endanger his position, when he made his demonstration on the enemy's right, to draw attention from the real point of attack.

Steedman having reported early in the morning that he could not be driven from his position, this reserve was no longer needed where it then was, and was ordered to form in support of Smith, and support him in his advance on the enemy's left. Smith's advance leaving an interval between his right and the left of the cavalry, the 10,000 men were ordered to fill up the gap and became engaged toward the close of the day's operations. It is therefore left to candid minds to judge, whether the 10,000 men were advantageously posted originally and afterwards used to advantage, or not.

It is believed that no other officer of high rank in the army, except the writer of the Tribune article, will say that General Thomas was so fully convinced that the enemy had retreated at the close of the first day of the battle, that he gave no orders to continue operations the next day, but ordered a pursuit. The blunder of the pontoon train is admitted in so far, that the staff officer who wrote the order to the commander of the train, by mistake wrote Murfreesboro pike, instead of Nolensville pike, and the train had gone a mile or two on that pike before the mistake was discovered, but it was promptly rectified before it had gone four miles out of the way, and then joined the army, and got to the front perhaps as quickly as it could have done by the Franklin pike, as it marched across the country by a free and practicable road. It could not have reached Franklin, under any circumstances, in time to place a bridge for the crossing of the troops when the infantry reached that point. It was always supposed, too, that every officer of high rank, who fought in the battle of Nashville, knew that until Duck River was crossed, the enemy could be pursued with any prospect of success, only by the main road. Harpeth River, Rutherford Creek, and Duck River, were all then rendered impassible by high water, in consequence of the thaw, the day before the battle, and heavy rains during the battle. All bridges over those streams, for twenty or thirty miles on either side of the main road, had been destroyed. All practicable roads north of Duck River, emerged from the main road, and consequently troops following them would have been soon separated from the main column, and placed beyond supporting distance. The report of General Thomas explains the difficulties in laying a pontoon bridge across Rutherford Creek, and accounts for the delay at that stream, and also at Duck River. After Duck River was crossed at Columbia, the Waynesboro and Lawrenceburg roads might have been taken by a part of the force, which in all probability could not have reached thereby the flank of the enemy in time to have inflicted any serious damage, because Hood had by that time placed his main column south of Richland Creek, and within a day's march of the point on the Tennessee River, where his pontoon bridges had been in position for several weeks. The above sufficiently accounts for the statement in the Tribune article, that a corps frequently did not march more than its length in three days.

The infantry corps were at all events on the main road, where they could have been made available in case there was any necessity for using them, while the Fourth Corps closely following up the cavalry, enabled General Wilson to do exactly what "One who fought at Nashville" says might have been done if the infantry had been marched along the main road with three days' rations in haversacks.

Wilson's cavalry was constantly harassing the enemy's flanks, whenever the condition of the roads and streams would admit of his doing so; and it was this vigorous conduct of the cavalry which caused the enemy to retreat with such haste, as to get beyond the reach of the main column before all the infantry could cross Duck River.

The writer virtually admits that General Schofield believed there was no further necessity for pursuit after the enemy had crossed Richland Creek at Pulaski, as he says on the 26th of December he wrote to General Grant that Hood's army was then used up, that there was no further need of his troops in Tennessee, and asked to be ordered to the Army of the Potomac.

Here there is a little discrepancy between the Tribune article and the actual facts. The writer says after the escape of Hood, General Thomas published an order placing the troops in winter quarters, and commenced planning a campaign for the next spring and summer against Corinth, etc. By reference to General Thomas's report, it will be seen that the order was ignored on the 30th of December. Schofield says on the 26th. Perhaps General Schofield was not aware of the reasons for this objectionable order.

The report of General Sherman to the Committee on the Conduct of the War will explain it, as it will there be seen that General Thomas was expected to take care of Tennessee until Sherman reached the sea and gave further instructions. [Smith's corps was to go to Eastport, Miss.; Wood's corps to Huntsville and Athens; Schofield's corps to Dalton; Wilson's cavalry between Huntsville and Eastport, along the Tennessee River.]

If, when General Thomas was sent back to Nashville, his army had been sent with him, or the Fourteenth Corps and Fourth Corps, there would have been no cause for the present newspaper contest about the battle of Nashville. There is ample proof already published that Thomas had at his command when Hood commenced his movement against Sherman's communication only a small division of troops stationed along the two lines of communication between Nashville and Chattanooga to protect them against small raiding parties. When he reported the situation to General Sherman, and applied for reinforcements to meet the advance of Hood, the Fourth Corps and dismounted cavalry were first sent, and General Thomas was informed that he would get reinforcements by several new regiments then on their way to join Sherman's army. Afterwards Thomas was informed that A. J. Smith's command would be ordered to join him from Missouri.

Thomas then urged that additional reinforcements should be sent him, as most of the convalescing troops at Chattanooga belonged to different corps and different armies, and could not be relied upon from want of effective organization to more than defend that place. Schofield was then ordered to report to Thomas.

With the exception of the Fourth and Twenty-third corps, Croxton's, Hatch's and Capron's brigades of cavalry, all the troops sent by Sherman had to be equipped for field service, including transportation. To attend to the equipping of this force, as well as to be able to correspond with General Sherman, Thomas was compelled to remain in Nashville, whilst he placed Schofield in immediate charge of the troops engaged in watching the movement of Hood, and retarding his advance on Nashville. This necessity existing until the army fell back to Nashville, gave Schofield the opportunity to fight the battle of Franklin. This was a very brilliant battle, most disastrous to the enemy, and as the writer in the Tribune says, no doubt contributed materially to the crowning success at Nashville——

Colonel Kellogg has added: "A few blurred and disconnected lines follow, as the Angel of Death hovered near him, and then General Thomas fell to the floor of his office unconscious."[44]

44. Van Horne, *op. cit.*, pp. 450-55.

Epilogue

THE Hall of Fame for Great Americans, on the University Heights campus of New York University in New York City, enshrines eighty-nine Americans, but at this time Major General George H. Thomas, the one man whose heroics during the American Civil War were indispensable to our existence as "one nation, indivisible," is not represented. The Hall of Fame does enshrine General Thomas J. "Stonewall" Jackson and General Robert E. Lee, the two Confederate commanders whose abilities almost divided the Union.

There is a place of honor for both Jackson and Lee in the hearts of their countrymen who admire military ability and character. None can dispute their greatness, which their enshrinement recognizes. Since, however, these two Virginians who won no Union victories have been thus honored, the wonder is that General Thomas, another Virginian, who won honors on many battlefields for the Union cause, has not been similarly honored. Thomas gave everything to preserve the Union—family, state, friends, loyalty, and unmatched military genius that assured national unity. The inconsistency in enshrinement thus illustrated casts doubt upon the honor conferred, and affords further evidence of the relative oblivion to which General Thomas has been consigned. From what we know of them, Generals Jackson and Lee would be among the first to protest the unfairness in honoring themselves while General Thomas was not similarly honored. General Lee would not forget that it was General Thomas's victory at Nashville that insured his surrender at Appomattox, less than four months later.

In doing research for so fully documented a work, any prejudice toward either victor or vanquished has disappeared in the more than twelve years spent in its preparation. The author has found a kindred spirit with the departed hosts that wore the Gray, a spirit that rejects the labels "rebel" and "enemy" in a derogatory sense. These were Americans; and whether or not we agree with their cause, we cannot deny that they fought in the best tradition of the human race. We should never forget that the South is a part of America, and that within her borders is a spirit that all America could emulate. No more devoted people could ever have been assembled than the Southerners of 1861–1865; and the remarkable thing is that they were not beaten, but overwhelmed.

In the same spirit the author yields to no one in his admiration for Generals Jackson and Lee and in his pride for the contribution that they and their followers made to our American heritage of unsurpassed courage and devotion. Their deeds belong to all of us, if for no other reason than that they held on "when there was nothing in them, except the will which said to them, 'Hold on!'" This heritage of courage is something to be shared by all Americans; and it is an objective fervently to be hoped for, that all may now see, as did two of the Confederacy's most illustrious military leaders, Generals Edward P. Alexander and James Longstreet. It should not be forgotten also that Confederate Vice President Alexander H. Stephens showed rare courage before the war in seeking to prevent his state of Georgia from seceding.

Stephens begged his people to remain in the Union, although he promised to follow if they left. He said this: "The Government of the United States may not be perfect, but it is the best in the world." Again, "Shall the people of the South secede from the Union in consequence of the election of Mr. Lincoln to the Presidency of the United States? My countrymen, I tell you frankly, candidly, and earnestly, that I do not think they ought." Again, "You may select the wisest and best men for your legislators, and yet how many defects are apparent in your laws? And it is so in our government. But that this government of our fathers, with all its defects, comes nearer the objects of all good governments than any other on the face of the earth, is my settled conviction." It took courage for Stephens to say that.

In his book *Military Memoirs of a Confederate,* General Alexander, Longstreet's chief of artillery, offered one of the most interesting as well as surprising reflections on the "Lost Cause," although many years afterward:

The world has not stood still in the years since we took up arms for what we deemed our most invaluable right—that of self-government. We now enjoy the rare privilege of seeing what we fought for in the retrospect. It no longer seems so desirable. It would now prove only a curse. We have good cause to thank God for our escape from it, not alone for our sake, but for that of the whole country and even of the world.

Had our cause succeeded, divergent interests must soon have further separated the States into groups, and this continent would have been given over to divided nationalities, each weak and unable to command foreign credit. Since the days of Greece, Confederacies have only held together against foreign enemies, and in times of peace disintegrated. It is surely not necessary to contrast what would have been our prospects as citizens of such States with our condition now as citizens of the strongest, richest, and—strange for us to say who once called ourselves "conquered" and our cause "lost"—the freest nation on earth.

Another similar viewpoint, that of the great Confederate corps commander, General Longstreet, hero of many battlefields, is set forth in a letter to Union General Sickles.

> I believe it is now conceded that the advanced positions at the Peach Orchard [Gettysburg], taken by your corps and under your orders, saved that battle to the Union cause. It was the sorest and saddest reflection of my life for many years; but to-day I can say, with sincerest emotion, that it was and is the best that could have come to us all, North and South.

The Hall of Fame enshrines General Ulysses S. Grant, and the natural question is whether it was for this:

Grant's career was studded with blunders, as at Shiloh, where his and Sherman's neglect brought needless slaughter and near defeat; at Chattanooga, his order of November 7, 1863, if left unchallenged by General Thomas, would have brought defeat; at Missionary Ridge he gave the choice assignment to Sherman and his Army of the Tennessee, only to be saved by General Thomas and his low-regarded Army of the Cumberland; at Cold Harbor, a useless slaughter that he himself would have chosen to forget, thousands of the Boys in Blue fell within an hour; and his telegraphic assault on General Thomas at Nashville, threatening him with removal and naming his protégé Schofield, a proven insubordinate to Thomas, as Thomas's successor, finds no justification nor precedent.

The Hall of Fame enshrines General Sherman, a capable strategist in planning campaigns, but history has correctly failed to honor him with the name of victor in even one great battle. His responsibility for the unpardonable surprise at Shiloh was great, and although he devoted many years of his life and countless words in an attempt to bury his mistakes, he could not refute the record. Notable among his failures when in direct command was Tunnel Hill at the north end of Missionary Ridge, November 25, 1863, where Thomas rescued him and his army; and Kenesaw Mountain, to which General Thomas was **strongly opposed, which produced nothing but casualties, several** thousand of them. History credits him for his march from Atlanta to the sea, although he did relatively no fighting with the best troops available, including Thomas's famous Fourteenth Corps. History likewise gives little credit to Thomas for his great victory at Nashville, which made Sherman's march possible.

Nothing more is needed to illustrate the erosion of General Thomas's fame than the record of voting on his ten nominations to the Hall of Fame. That organization, founded in 1900, considers nominations which may be suggested by any citizen of the United States each five years. A simple majority is enough to elect, although not more than seven may be elected in any one election year. General Thomas received twenty-four votes in 1900; nineteen in 1905; eighteen in 1910; ten in 1915; nine in 1920; six in 1925; five in 1930; and none in 1940, 1945, and 1960.

The activities of the Hall of Fame are but as a particle of dust in the appalling neglect of General Thomas. He knew his decision from the beginning; and although we can feel pride that men like Alexander H. Stephens, Edward P. Alexander, and James Longstreet showed true courage in expressing their gratitude for a splendid nation, there is something to be said for Thomas, who had no regrets other than the mistreatment received from those enshrined in the Hall of Fame.

Bibliography

Abbott, J. S. C. *History of the Civil War in America*. 3 vols. New York, 1867.

Alden, John Richard. *The American Revolution, 1775–1783*. New York: Harper and Brothers, 1954.

Alexander, E. P. *Military Memoirs of a Confederate*. New York: Charles Scribner's Sons, 1908.

Anderson, Charles C. *Fighting by Southern Federals*. New York: Neale Publishing Co., 1912.

Angle, Paul M. *Lincoln's Speeches and Letters*. New York: E. P. Dutton and Co., 1957.

Badeau, Adam. *Military History of U. S. Grant*. 3 vols. New York: Appleton and Co., 1881.

Bates, David Homer. *Lincoln in the Telegraph Office*. New York The Century Co., 1907.

Battles and Leaders of the Civil War. 4 vols. New York, 1884.

Beatty, John. *Memoirs of a Volunteer*. (*The Citizen Soldier*. Cincinnati, 1879.) New York: W. W. Norton and Co., 1946.

Bickham, W. D. *Rosecrans' Campaign With the Fourteenth Army Corps*. Cincinnati: Moore, Wilstach, Keys and Co., 1863.

Biographical Sketches, Union Army. 8 vols. Madison, Wis.: Federal Publishing Co., 1908.

Bishop, Judson W. *The Story of a Regiment*. St. Louis, 1890.

Boynton, H. V. *Chattanooga and Chickamauga*. 1888. (Reprint of Boynton's wartime letters to the Cincinnati *Gazette*.)

_____. *The Chickamauga and Chattanooga National Military Park*. Cincinnati, 1895.

_____. *Sherman's Historical Raid: The Memoirs in the Light of the Record*. Cincinnati, 1895.

Bradford, Gamaliel. *Union Portraits*. Boston: Houghton Mifflin Co., 1916.

Brockett, Linus B. *Our Great Captains*. New York, 1865.

Buckeridge, J. O. *Lincoln's Choice*. Harrisburg: The Stackpole Co., 1956.

Campaign for Chattanooga, The. Chickamauga and Chattanooga National Park Commission, 1896.

Catton, Bruce. *This Hallowed Ground*. Garden City, N. Y.: Doubleday and Co., 1956.

————. *U. S. Grant and the American Military Tradition*. New York: Grosset and Dunlap, 1954.

Churchill, Winston. *A History of the English Speaking Peoples. The Great Democracies*. New York: Dodd, Mead and Co., 1958.

Cist, Henry M. *The Army of the Cumberland*. New York, 1882.

Cleaves, Freeman. *Rock of Chickamauga*. Norman: University of Oklahoma Press, 1949.

Coffin, Charles C. *The Drum Beat of the Nation*. New York: Harper and Brothers, 1887.

Coppee, Henry. *General Thomas*. New York: 1893.

Cox, Jacob D. *Atlanta*. New York: Charles Scribner's Sons, 1882.

————. *The March to the Sea*. New York: Charles Scribner's Sons, 1882.

————. *Military Reminiscences of the Civil War*. 2 vols. New York: Charles Scribner's Sons, 1900.

Cullum, George W. *Biographical Register of Officers and Cadets of the U.S. Military Academy*. 3 vols. Boston, 1891.

Dana, Charles A. *Recollections of the Civil War*, New York, 1913.

Day, L. W. *The Story of a Regiment. The One Hundred and First Ohio*. Cleveland: W. M. Bayne Printing Co., 1894.

Deaterick, J. B. *The Truth About Shiloh*. Memphis: S. C. Toof and Co., 1942.

Dedication of the Chickamauga and Chattanooga National Military Park. Washington, D.C.: Government Printing Office; 1896.

De Peyster, John Watts. *General George H. Thomas*, New York, 1875.

Drewry, William Sidney. *The Southampton Insurrection*. Washington, 1900.

Dumas, Alexander. *The Three Musketeers*.

Dyer, Frederick H. (ed.). *A Compendium of the War of the Rebellion*. New York: Thomas Yoseloff, 1959.

Eisenschiml, Otto, and Ralph Newman. *The American Iliad*. Indianapolis: Bobbs-Merrill Co., 1947.

Fiske, John. *The Mississippi Valley in the Civil War*. Boston, 1900.

Fitch, John. *Annals of the Army of the Cumberland*. Philadelphia: J. B. Lippincott and Co., 1864.

Fitch, Michael Hendrick. *The Chattanooga Campaign*. Wisconsin Historical Commission, 1911.

————. *Echoes of the Civil War*. New York: Renno and Co., 1905.

Force, M. F. *Campaigns of the Civil War—From Fort Henry to Corinth*. (A reprint.) New York: Noble Offset Printers, Inc., n.d.

Forman, Sidney. *The Educational Objectives of the United States Military Academy*. West Point, 1946.

Frantz, Mabel Goode. *Full Many a Name*. Jackson, Tenn.: McCowat-Mercer Press, Inc., 1961.

Freeman, Douglas Southall. *Lee's Lieutenants: A Study in Command*. New York: Charles Scribner's Sons, 1942.

————. *Robert E. Lee*. 4 vols. New York: Charles Scribner's Sons, 1935.

French, Samuel G. *Two Wars*. Nashville, 1901.

Geer, Walter. *Campaigns of the Civil War*. New York, 1926.

Gordon, John B. *Reminiscences of the Civil War*. New York: Charles Scribner's Sons, 1905.

Gracie, Archibald. *The Truth About Chickamauga*. Boston: Houghton Mifflin Co., 1911.

Grant, U. S. *Personal Memoirs*. Hartford, 1885.

Hart, H. Liddell. *Sherman: Soldier, Realist, American*. New York: Frederick A. Praeger, 1958.

Hay, Thomas R. *Hood's Tennessee Campaign*. New York: Walter Neale, 1925.

Heaps, Willard A. and Porter W. *The Singing Sixties*. Norman, Okla.: University of Oklahoma Press, 1960.

Hebert, Walter A. *"Fighting Joe" Hooker*. Indianapolis: Bobbs-Merrill Co., 1944.

Henry, Robert Selph. *"First With the Most" Forrest*. Indianapolis: Bobbs-Merrill Co., 1944.

————. *The Story of the Confederacy*. Indianapolis: Bobbs-Merrill Co., 1936.

————. *The Story of the Mexican War*. New York: Frederick Ungar Publishing Co., 1961.

————. *The Story of Reconstruction*. New York: Grosset and Dunlap, 1938.

Henry, W. S. *Campaign Sketches of the War With Mexico*. New York, 1847.

Hergesheimer, Joseph. *Sheridan*. Boston: Houghton Mifflin Co., 1931.

High, Edwin W. *History of the 68th Indiana Infantry*. 1902.

History of Our Country, The. 8 vols. Philadelphia: The History Co., 1899.

Hood, John B. *Advance and Retreat*. New Orleans, 1880.

Hopkins, Timothy. *The Kelloggs in the Old World and the New*. San Francisco, 1903.

Horn, Stanley F. *The Army of Tennessee*. Indianapolis: Bobbs-Merrill Co., 1941.

————. *The Decisive Battle of Nashville*. Baton Rouge: Louisiana State University Press, 1957.

Howard, Oliver Otis. *Autobiography*. 2 vols. New York, 1907.

Indiana at Chickamauga. Indianapolis: Sentinel Printing Co., 1900.

Jeans, William. *Parliamentary Reminiscences*. London: Chapman and Hall, Ltd., 1912.

Johnson, Richard W. *A Soldier's Reminiscences*. Philadelphia: J. B. Lippincott Co., 1886.

————. *Memoir of Major General George H. Thomas*. Philadelphia: J. B. Lippincott Co., 1881.

Johnson, Rossiter. *Fight for the Republic*. New York: G. P. Putnam's Sons, 1917.

Johnston, Joseph E. *A Narrative of Military Operations and Recollections*. New York, 1874.

Jones, John William. *Life and Letters of Robert E. Lee*. New York, 1906.

Kenly, John R. *Memoirs of a Maryland Volunteer*. Philadelphia, 1873.

Keyes, Erasmus D. *Fifty Years Observation of Men and Events*. New York, 1884.

King, Charles. *The True Ulysses S. Grant*. Philadelphia: J. B. Lippincott Co., 1914.

Kipling, Rudyard. *Ballad of East and West*. New York, 1885.

Lee, Fitzhugh. *General Lee*. 1894.

Lee, Robert E, Jr. *Recollections and Letters of General Lee*. New York, 1926.

Legend of the Operations of the Army of the Cumberland. Washington, D.C.: Government Printing Office, 1869.

Lewis, Lloyd. *Sherman: Fighting Prophet*. New York: Harcourt, Brace and Co., 1932.

Longstreet, James. *From Manassas to Appomattox*. 1896.

Lossing, Benson J. *A Pictorial History of the Civil War in the United States*. Elgin, Pa., 1885.

Macartney, Clarence E. *Grant and His Generals*. New York: McBride and Co., 1953.

Meade, George Gordon. *The Life and Letters of General George Gordon Meade*. 2 vols. New York: Charles Scribner's Sons, 1913.

McElroy, John. *General George H. Thomas*. Washington, D.C., 1896. (In the Library of Congress.)

Michigan at Chickamauga, Chattanooga and Missionary Ridge. Lansing, Mich: R. Smith Printing Co., 1899.

Miller, Marion Mills. *American Debate*. New York, 1900.

Milton, George F. *Conflict, The American Civil War*. 1941.

Nevins, Allan. *The War for the Union: The Improvised War, 1861–1862*. New York: Charles Scribner's Sons, 1959.

————.*The War for the Union: War Becomes Revolution, 1862–1863*. New York: Charles Scribner's Sons, 1960.

Nicolay, John G., and John Hay. *Abraham Lincoln: A History*. 10 vols. New York: The Century Co., 1909.

O'Connor, Richard. *Thomas, Rock of Chickamauga*. New York: Prentice-Hall, Inc., 1948.

Official Records of the War of the Rebellion. 129 vols. Washington, D.C., 1880–1901.

Palmer, John M. *Personal Recollections*. Cincinnati: Robert Clarke and Co., 1901.

Parrington, Vernon L. *The Beginnings of Critical Realism in America, 1860–1920*. New York: Harcourt, Brace and Co., 1930.

Patterson, Robert. *A Narrative of the Campaign in the Valley of the Shenandoah in 1861*. Philadelphia, 1865.

Peckham, Howard H. *The War for Independence: A Military History*. Chicago: University of Chicago Press, 1959.

Phister, Frederick. *Statistical Record, Campaigns of the Civil War*. New York: Jack Brussell, n.d.

Photographic History of the Civil War, The. 10 vols. New York: Thomas Yoseloff, 1957.

Piatt, Donn. *General George H. Thomas*. Cincinnati, 1891.

————. *Memories of the Men Who Saved the Union*. New York, 1887.

Porter, Horace. *Campaigning With Grant*. New York. 1897.

Pratt, Fletcher. *The Civil War on Western Waters*. New York: Henry Holt and Co., 1956.

————. *Eleven Generals: Studies in American Command*. New York: William Sloane Associates, 1949.

Reid, Whitelaw. *Ohio in the Civil War*. Columbus, Ohio, 1893.

Rhodes, James Ford. *History of the American Civil War, 1861–1865*. New York: The Macmillan Co., 1923.

Rochelle, J. H. *Life of Rear Admiral John Randolph Tucker*. Washington, D.C., 1903.

Rusling, James F. *Men and Things I Saw in Civil War Days*. New York, 1899.

Sandburg, Carl. *Abraham Lincoln: The War Years*. New York, 1939.

Schofield, John M. *Forty-six Years in the Army*. New York, 1897.

Seitz, Don C. *Braxton Bragg*. Columbia, S.C.: The State Co., 1924.

Shanks, W. F. G. *Personal Recollections of Distinguished Generals*. New York: Harper and Brothers, 1866.

Sheridan, Philip H. *Personal Memoirs*. 2 vols. New York, 1892.

Sherman, John. *Recollections of Forty Years in the U.S. Senate, House and Cabinet.* New York, 1895.

Sherman, William T. *The Memoirs of General William T. Sherman.* New York, 1891.

————. *The Sherman Letters.* Ed. R. S. Thorndike. New York: Charles Scribner's Sons, 1894.

Sherwood, Isaac R. *Memories of the War.* Toledo: The Chittenden Co., 1923.

Skinner, George W. *Pennsylvania at Chickamauga and Chattanooga.* 1897.

Smith, Justin H. *The War With Mexico.* 2 vols. New York, 1919.

Society of the Army of the Cumberland Yearbooks. Cincinnati: Robert Clarke and Co., 1868–1910. (Publication date one year after each meeting.)

Sorrel, G. Moxley. *Recollections of a Confederate Staff Officer.* New York, 1905.

Speed, Thomas. *Union Regiments of Kentucky.* New York, 1897.

Sprague, John T. *The Florida War.* New York, 1848.

Squires, W. H. T. *The Days of Yesteryear.* Portsmouth, Va.: Printcraft Press, Inc., 1928.

————. *The Land of Decision.* Portsmouth, Va.: Printcraft Press, Inc., 1931.

Steele, Matthew F. *American Campaigns.* Washington, D.C.: U.S. Infantry Association, 1931.

Stevenson, Alexander F. *The Battle of Stone's River.* Boston, 1884.

Stone, Henry. *Some Federal and Confederate Commanders.* Boston: Houghton Mifflin Co., 1895.

Swinton, William. *Campaigns of the Army of the Potomac.* New York: Charles Scribner's Sons, 1882.

————. *The Twelve Decisive Battles of the War.* New York: Dick and Fitzgerald, 1867.

Turchin, John B. *Chickamauga.* Chicago, 1888.

Vance, Wilson J. *Stone's River.* New York: Neale Publishing Co., 1914.

Van Horne, Thomas B. *History of the Army of the Cumberland.* 3 vols. Cincinnati: Robert Clarke and Co., 1875.

————. *The Life of Major General George H. Thomas.* New York: Charles Scribner's Sons, 1882.

Virginia. A Guide to the Old Dominion. New York: Oxford University Press, 1940–41. (Compiled by workers on the Writers' Project of the Works Progress Administration.)

Warner, Ezra J. *Generals in Gray.* Baton Rouge: Louisiana State University Press, 1959.

Welles, Gideon. *Diary of Gideon Wells.* 3 vols. Boston, 1911.

Werner, Edgar A. *Historical Sketch of the War of the Rebellion, 1861–1865.* 2 vols. New York, 1890.

Whitridge, Arnold. *No Compromise.* New York: Farrar, Straus and Cudahy, 1960.

Wilcox, Cadmus M. *History of the Mexican War.* Washington, D.C.: The Church News Publishing Co., 1892.

Wiley, Bell I. *The Life of Billy Yank.* Indianapolis: Bobbs-Merrill Co., 1952.

————.*The Life of Johnny Reb.* Indianapolis: Bobbs-Merrill Co., 1943.

Williams, T. Harry. *Lincoln and His Generals.* New York, 1952.

Wilson, James H. *Heroes of the Great Conflict: Life and Services of William F. Smith.* Wilmington, Del.: J. M. Rogers Press, 1904.

————. *Life of Charles A. Dana.* New York, 1907.

————. *Life of John A. Rawlins.* New York, 1916.

————. *Under the Old Flag.* 2 vols. New York: D. Appleton and Co., 1911.

Winston, Robert W. *Robert E. Lee.* New York: Grosset and Dunlap, 1934.

Wood, C. J. *Reminiscences of the War.* N.p., n.d.

Woods, Joseph T. *Steedman and His Men at Chickamauga.* Toledo, 1876.

Wooldridge, John. *History of Nashville.* Nashville, 1890.

Wyeth, John A. *Life of General Nathan Bedford Forrest.* New York, 1899.

————. *With Sabre and Scalpel.* New York, 1914.

MISCELLANEOUS

American Heritage, April, 1959.

Army and Navy Journal, March, 1887.

Buell Papers, The. (In custody of Rice University, Houston, Texas.)

Cincinnati *Enquirer.* (A reprint from an article in the Toledo *Northern Democrat* among Civil War clippings in Manuscript Room. Library of Congress.)

Downey, Fairfax. In *Ordnance* (bi-monthly), July–August, 1960.

Elson's History Series. (*The Civil War Through the Camera.* 16 parts. Springfield, Mass., 1912.)

Encyclopedia Americana. 30 vols. New York: Amercan Book–Stratford Press, Inc., 1954.

Encyclopaedia Britannica. 14th ed. Chicago, 1963.

Hammond's World Atlas. New York, 1953.

Hough Papers, The. (These deal with the life of General Thomas and are in the possession of the author.)

Huntington Papers, The. San Marino, Calif. (Copies of those dealing with General Thomas are in the author's possession.)

Military Order of the Loyal Legion of the United States. (The various commanderies of this order in the several states have published volumes dealing with the Civil War. Here have been cited:

————. District of Columbia Commandery. *Life and Services of Major General George H. Thomas.*

————. Illinois Commandery, 2 vols. Chicago, 1891, 1894.

————. Indiana Commandery. *Indiana War Papers. Indianapolis,* 1898.

————. Massachusetts Commandery, 2 vols. Boston, 1900.

————. New York Commandery, 2 vols. New York, 1891.

————. Ohio Commandery, 3 vols. Cincinnati, 1888, 1890.

————. Wisconsin Commandery, 1 vol. Milwaukee, 1891.)

National Archives and the Library of Congress. (Both sources of photographs of commanders and battle scenes, and letters referring to General Thomas.)

National Park Service. (This Service under the Department of the Interior has published several pamphlets on battles and memorial parks.)

North American Review. (In December, 1885, and January, 1886, issues are references to Sherman's attempt to suppress General James B. Fry. *See* Prologue.)

Oakwood Cemetery, Troy N.Y. (A brochure about this cemetery gives information on General Thomas and Samuel Wilson, also buried there, who is the supposed original of Uncle Sam and U.S.)

Porter Papers, The Fitz John. (In Library of Congress. Refers to his trial and dismissal from service for alleged negligence at Second Manassas.)

Southern Historical Society Papers. June, 1876. (Address on General Thomas by General Dabney H. Maury.)

Southampton County Minute Books and Tax Lists. (In Virginia State Library, Richmond, Va.)

Southampton County Census. (In National Archives, Washington, D.C.)

Stanard's Genealogical and Biographical Register. (Published by the *Virginia Magazine of History and Biography,* Richmond, Va.)

Troy (New York) *Times,* April 6, 1870.

Tyler Papers, The Mattie R. (In Southampton County, Virginia, Courthouse.)

U.S. Military Academy. *Official Register of West Point.*

_____. *West Point Assembly.* Sesquicentennial Edition, 1952.

_____. *West Point Atlas of American Wars.* Vol. I. 1689–1900. New York: Frederick Praeger, 1959.

Virginia Magazine of History and Biography; Vol. XL. (Oct. 1932), p. 331; Vol. LXIX (Jan. 1961), pp. 5–6.

William and Mary Quarterly, 1907–1908.

Index